BIBLICAL COMMENTARY

ON

THE PROPHECIES OF ISAIAH

BY

FRANZ DELITZSCH, D.D.,

Translated from the German,

BY

THE REV. JAMES MARTIN, B. A.

VOLUME II

This volume is a reproduction of
the third edition of Delitzsch's
work on Isaiah, in the translation
of the Rev. James Martin (1877).

CONTENTS

———◆———

PART V.

PART VI.

PART VII.

LXX. and Targum) rather than in the masculine, as Luther does, although the strong and mighty thing which the Lord holds in readiness is no doubt the Assyrian. He is simply the medium of punishment in the hand of the Lord, which is called *yâd* absolutely, because it is absolute in power,—as it were, the hand of all hands. This hand hurls Samaria to the ground (on the expression itself, compare ch. xxv. 12, xxvi. 5), so that they tread the proud crown to pieces with their feet (*têrâ-masnâh*, the more pathetic plural form, instead of the singular *têrâmēs*; Ges. § 47, Anm. 3, and Caspari on Obad. 13). The noun *sa'ar*, which is used elsewhere in the sense of shuddering, signifies here, like מְעָרָה, an awful tempest; and when connected with קֶטֶב, a tempest accompanied with a pestilential blast, spreading miasma. Such destructive power is held by the absolute hand. It is soon all over then with the splendid flower that has already begun to fade (צִיצַת נֹבֵל, like כְּלֵי הַקָּטָן in ch. xxii. 24). It happens to it as to a *bikkūrâh* (according to the Masora, written with *mappik* here, as distinguished from Hos. ix. 10, equivalent to *kᵉbhikkūrâthâh*; see Job xi. 9, "like an early fig of this valley;" according to others, it is simply euphonic). The gathering of figs takes place about August. Now, if any one sees a fig as early as June, he fixes his eyes upon it, and hardly touches it with his hand before he swallows it, and that without waiting to masticate it long. Like such a dainty bit will the luxuriant Samaria vanish. The fact that Shalmanassar, or his successor Sargon, did not conquer Samaria till after the lapse of three years (2 Kings xviii. 10), does not detract from the truth of the prophecy; it is enough that both the thirst of the conqueror and the utter destruction of Samaria answered to it.

The threat is now followed by a promise. This is essentially the same in character as ch. iv. 2–6. The place of the false glory thus overthrown is now filled by a glory that is divine and true. Vers. 5, 6. "*In that day will Jehovah of hosts be the adorning crown and the splendid diadem to the remnant of His people; and the spirit of justice to them that sit on the judgment-seat, and heroic strength to them that drive back war at the gate.*" "The remnant of His people" (שְׁאָר with a fixed *kametz*, as in ch. xxi. 17) is not Judah, as distinguished from Ephraim that had utterly perished; but Judah and the remaining portion of Ephraim, as distinguished from the portion which had perished. After the perishable thing in which they gloried had been swept away, the eternal person of Jehovah Himself would be the ornament and pride of His people. He, the Lord of the seven spirits (ch. xi. 2), would be to this remnant of His people the spirit of right and heroic strength. There would be an end to unjust judging and powerless submission. The judges are called "those who sit 'al-hammishpât" in the sense of "on the seat of judgment" (Ps. ix. 5, cxxii. 5); the warriors are called "those who press back milchâmâh shâʿrâh" (war at the gate), i.e. either war that has reached their own gate (ch. xxii. 7), or war which they drive back as far as the gate of the enemy (2 Sam. xi. 23; 1 Macc. v. 22). The promise in this last passage corresponds to Mic. v. 4, 5. The athnach in ver. 6 ought to stand at hammishpât; the second clause of the verse may be completed from the first, וְלִגְבוּרָה being equivalent to וּלְרוּחַ גְבוּרָה, and מְשִׁיבֵי to לִמְשִׁיבֵי. We might regard 2 Chron. xxx. as a fulfilment of what is predicted in ver. 6, if the feast of passover there described really fell in the age succeeding the fall of Samaria; for this feast of passover did furnish a representation and awaken a consciousness of that national unity which had been interrupted from the time of Rehoboam. But if we read the account in the Chronicles with unprejudiced minds, it is impossible to shut our eyes to the fact that this feast of passover took place in the second month of the first year of Hezekiah's reign, and therefore not after the depopulation of the northern kingdom by Shalmanassar, but after the previous and partial depopulation by Tiglath-pileser (see vol. i. p. 52). In fact, the fulfilment cannot be looked for at all in the space between the sixth and fourteenth years of Hezekiah, since the condition of Judah during that time does not answer at all to the promises given above. The prophet here foretells what might be hoped for, when Asshur had not only humbled Ephraim, but Judah also. The address consists of two connected halves, the promising beginnings of which point to one and the same future, and lay hold of one another.

With the words, "and they also," the prophet commences the second half of the address, and passes from Ephraim to Judah. Vers. 7, 8. "And they also reel with wine, and are

*giddy with meth ; priest and prophet reel with meth, are swal-
lowed up by wine : they are giddy with meth, reel when seeing
visions, stagger when pronouncing judgment. For all tables are
full of filthy vomit, without any more place.*" The Judæans are
not less overcome with wine than the Ephraimites, and especially the rulers of Judah. In wicked violation of the law of
God, which prohibited the priests from drinking strong drink
when performing priestly service, and that on pain of death
(Lev. x. 9, cf. Ezek. xliv. 21), they were intoxicated even in
the midst of their prophetic visions (הָרֹאֶה, literally " the thing
seeing," then the act of seeing ; equivalent to רְאִי, like חֹזֶה in
ver. 15 = חָזוּת; Olshausen, § 176, c), and when passing judicial
sentences. In the same way Micah also charges the prophets
and priests with being drunkards (Mic. iii. 1 sqq., cf. ii. 11).
Isaiah's indignation is manifested in the fact, that in the words
which he uses he imitates the staggering and stumbling of the
topers ; like the well-known passage, *Sta pes sta mi pes stas pes
ne labere mi pes.* Observe, for example, the threefold repetition
of *shâgu—tâghu, shâgu—tâghu, shâgu—pâqu.* The hereditary
priests and the four prophets represent the whole of the official
personages. The preterites imply that drunkenness had become
the fixed habit of the holders of these offices. The preposition
בְּ indicates the cause (" through," as in 2 Sam. xiii. 28 and
Esther i. 10), and *min* the effect proceeding from the cause (in
consequence of wine). In ver. 8 we can hear them vomit.
We have the same combination of the ק and צ in the verb
kotzen, Gothic *kozan.* All the tables of the carousal are full,
without there being any further room (cf. ch. v. 8) ; everything
swims with vomit. The prophet paints from nature, here without idealizing. He receives their conduct as it were in a mirror,
and then in the severest tones holds up this mirror before them,
adults though they were.

Vers. 9, 10. " *Whom then would he teach knowledge? And to
whom make preaching intelligible? To those weaned from the milk?
To those removed from the breast? For precept upon precept, precept upon precept, line upon line, line upon line, a little here, a little
there!*" They sneer at the prophet, that intolerable moralist.
They are of age, and free; and he does not need to bring knowledge to them (*da'ath* as in ch. xi. 9), or make them understand
the proclamation. They know of old to what he would lead.

Are they little children that have just been weaned (on the constructives, see ch. ix. 2, v. 11, xxx. 18 ; Ges. § 114, 1), and who must let themselves be tutored ? For the things he preaches are nothing but endless petty teazings. The short words (*tsâv*, as in Hos. v. 11), together with the diminutive עֵיר (equivalent to the Arabic *sugayyir*, mean, from *sagîr*, small), are intended to throw ridicule upon the smallness and vexatious character of the prophet's interminable and uninterrupted chidings, as ל (= עַל, אֶל ; comp. ל יָסַף, ch. xxvi. 15) implies that they are ; just as the philosophers in Acts xvii. 18 call Paul a σπερμολόγος, a collector of seeds, *i.e.* a dealer in trifles. And in the repetition of the short words we may hear the heavy babbling language of the drunken scoffers.

The prophet takes the *ki* (" for ") out of their mouths, and carries it on in his own way. It was quite right that their ungodliness should show itself in such a way as this, for it would meet with an appropriate punishment. Vers. 11–13. " *For through men stammering in speech, and through a strange tongue, will He speak to this people. He who said to them, There is rest, give rest to weary ones, and there is refreshing ! But they would not hear. Therefore the word of Jehovah becomes to them precept upon precept, precept upon precept, line upon line, line upon line, a little here, a little there, that they may go and stumble backwards, and be wrecked to pieces, and be snared and taken.*" Jehovah would speak to the scoffing people of stammering tongue a language of the same kind, since He would speak to them by a people that stammered in their estimation, *i.e.* who talked as barbarians (cf. βαρβαρίζειν and *balbutire ;* see ch. xxxiii. 19, compared with Deut. xxviii. 49). The Assyrian Semitic had the same sound in the ear of an Israelite, as Low Saxon (a provincial dialect) in the ear of an educated German ; in addition to which, it was plentifully mixed up with Iranian, and possibly also with Tatar elements. This people would practically interpret the will of Jehovah in its own *patois* to the despisers of the prophet. Jehovah had directed them, through His prophets, after the judgments which they had experienced with sufficient severity (ch. i. 5 sqq.), into the true way to rest and refreshing (Jer. vi. 16), and had exhorted them to give rest to the nation, which had suffered so much under Ahaz through the calamities of war (2 Chron. xxviii.), and not to drag it into another war by goading it on to rise against Assyria, or impose a new burden in addition to the tribute to Assyria by purchasing the help of Egypt. But they would not hearken (אָבוּא = אָבוּ, ch. xxx. 15, 16; Ges. § 23, 3, Anm. 3). Their policy was a very different one from being still, or believing and waiting. And therefore the word of Jehovah, which they regarded as an endless series of trivial commands, would be turned in their case into an endless series of painful sufferings. To those who thought themselves so free, and lived so free, it would become a stone on which they would go to pieces, a net in which they would be snared, a trap in which they would be caught (compare ch. viii. 14, 15).

The prophet now directly attacks the great men of Jerusalem, and holds up a Messianic prophecy before their eyes, which turns its dark side to them, as ch. vii. did to Ahaz. Vers. 14–17. " *Therefore hear the word of Jehovah, ye scornful lords, rulers of this people which is in Jerusalem! For ye say, We have made a covenant with death, and with Hades have we come to an agreement. The swelling scourge, when it cometh hither, will do us no harm; for we have made a lie our shelter, and in deceit have we hidden ourselves. Therefore thus saith the Lord Jehovah, Behold, I am He who hath laid in Zion a stone, a stone of trial, a precious corner-stone of well-founded founding; whoever believes will not have to move. And I make justice the line, and righteousness the level; and hail sweeps away the refuge of lies, and the hiding-place is washed away by waters.*" With *lâkhēn* (therefore) the announcement of punishment is once more suspended; and in ver. 16 it is resumed again, the exposition of the sin being inserted between, before the punishment is declared. Their sin is *lâtsōn*, and this free-thinking scorn rests upon a proud and insolent self-confidence, which imagines that there is no necessity to fear death and hell; and this self-confidence has for its secret reserve the alliance to be secretly entered into with Egypt against Assyria. What the prophet makes them say here, they do not indeed say exactly in this form; but this is the essential substance of the carnally devised thoughts and words of the rulers of the people of Jerusalem, as manifest to the Searcher of hearts. Jerusalem, the city of Jehovah, and such princes as these, who either proudly ignore Jehovah, or throw Him off as useless, what a

contrast! *Chōzeh,* and *châzūth* in ver. 18, signify an agreement, either as a decision or completion (from the radical
meaning of the verb *châzâh;* see vol. i. p. 71), or as a choice,
beneplacitum (like the Arabic *ray*), or as a record, *i.e.* the means
of selecting (like the talmudic *châzīth,* a countersign, a *ra'ăyâh,* a
proof or argument: Luzzatto). In *shōt shōtēph* ("the swelling
scourge," *chethib* שׁיט), the comparison of Asshur to a flood
(vers. 2, 8, 7), and the comparison of it to a whip or scourge, are
mixed together; and this is all the more allowable, because a
whip, when smacked, really does move in waving lines (compare Jer. viii. 6, where *shâtaph* is applied to the galoping of a
war-horse). The *chethib* עבר in ver. 15 (for which the *keri*
reads יַעֲבֹר, according to ver. 19) is to be read עָבַר (granting
that it shall have passed, or that it passes); and there is no
necessity for any emendation. The Egyptian alliance for
which they are suing, when designated according to its true
ethical nature, is *sheqer* (lie) and *kâzâbh* (falsehood); compare
2 Kings xvii. 4 (where we ought perhaps to read *sheqer* for
qesher, according to the LXX.), and more especially Ezek.
xvii. 15 sqq., from which it is obvious that the true prophets
regarded self-willed rebellion even against heathen rule as a
reprehensible breach of faith. The *lâkhēn* (therefore), which
is resumed in ver. 16, is apparently followed as strangely as
in ch. vii. 14, by a promise instead of a threat. But this
is only apparently the case. It is unquestionably a promise;
but as the last clause, " he that believeth will not flee," *i.e.* will
stand firm, clearly indicates, it is a promise for believers alone.
For those to whom the prophet is speaking here the promise is
a threat, a savour of death unto death. Just as on a former
occasion, when Ahaz refused to ask for a sign, the prophet
announced to him a sign of Jehovah's own selection; so here
Jehovah opposes to the false ground of confidence on which the
leaders relied, the foundation stone laid in Zion, which would
bear the believing in immoveable safety, but on which the
unbelieving would be broken to pieces (Matt. xxi. 44). This
stone is called *'ebhen bōchan,* a stone of proving, *i.e.* a proved
and self-proving stone. Then follow other epithets in a series
commencing anew with *pinnath* = *'ebhen pinnath* (compare Ps.
cxviii. 22): *angulus h. e. lapis angularis pretiositatis fundationis
fundatæ.* It is a corner-stone, valuable in itself (on *yiqrath,*

compare 1 Kings v. 31), and affording the strongest foundation
and inviolable security to all that is built upon it (*mûsâd* a
substantive in form like *mûsâr*, and *mûssâd* a *hophal* participle
in the form of those of the *verba contracta pe yod*). This stone
was not the Davidic sovereignty, but the true seed of David
which appeared in Jesus (Rom. ix. 33 ; 1 Pet. ii. 6, 7). The
figure of a stone is not opposed to the personal reference, since
the prophet in ch. viii. 14 speaks even of Jehovah Himself
under the figure of a stone. The majestically unique description renders it quite impossible that Hezekiah can be intended.
Micah, whose book forms the side piece of this cycle of prophecy, also predicted, under similar historical circumstances,
the birth of the Messiah in Bethlehem Ephratah (Mic. v. 1).
What Micah expresses in the words, " His goings forth are from
of old," is indicated here in the preterite *yissad* connected with
hin^eni (the construction is similar to that in Obad. 2, Ezek.
xxv. 7 ; compare ver. 2 above, and Jer. xlix. 15, xxiii. 19). It
denotes that which has been determined by Jehovah, and therefore is as good as accomplished. What is historically realized
has had an eternal existence, and indeed an ideal pre-existence
even in the heart of history itself (ch. xxii. 11, xxv. 1, xxxvii.
26). Ever since there had been a Davidic government at all,
this stone had lain in Zion. The Davidic monarchy not only
had in this its culminating point, but the ground of its continuance also. It was not only the Omega, but also the Alpha.
Whatever escaped from wrath, even under the Old Testament,
stood upon this stone. This (as the prophet predicts in
הַמַּאֲמִין לֹא יָחִישׁ : יָחִישׁ the *fut. kal*) would be the stronghold of
faith in the midst of the approaching Assyrian calamities (cf.
ch. vii. 9) ; and faith would be the condition of life (Hab.
ii. 4). But against unbelievers Jehovah would proceed according to His punitive justice. He would make this (justice and
righteousness, *mishpât* and *ts^edâqâh*) a norm, *i.e.* a line and
level. A different turn, however, is given to *qâv*, with a play
upon vers. 10, 11. What Jehovah is about to do is depicted
as a building which He is carrying out, and which He will carry
out, so far as the despisers are concerned, on no other plan than
that of strict retribution. His punitive justice comes like a
hailstorm and like a flood (cf. ver. 2, ch. x. 22). The hail
smites the refuge of lies of the great men of Jerusalem, and

clears it away (יָעָה, hence יָע, a shovel) ; and the flood buries
their hiding-place in the waters, and carries it away (the accentuation should be סֵתֶר *tifchah,* מַיִם *mercha*).

And the whip which Jehovah swings will not be satisfied
with one stroke, but will rain strokes. Vers. 18, 19. "*And
your covenant with death is struck out, and your agreement with
Hades will not stand ; the swelling scourge, when it comes, ye will
become a thing trodden down to it. As often as it passes it takes
you: for every morning it passes, by day and by night; and it is
nothing but shuddering to hear such preaching. For the bed is
too short to stretch in, and the covering too tight when a man
wraps himself in it.*" Although *bᵉrīth* is feminine, the predicate to it is placed before it in the masculine form (Ges. § 144).
The covenant is thought of as a document; for *khuppar* (for
which Hupfeld would read *thuphar ; Ps.* ii. 197) signifies here
obliterari (just as the *kal* is used in Gen. vi. 14 in the sense
of *oblinere ;* or in Prov. xxx. 20, the Targum, and the Syriac,
in the sense of *abstergere ;* and in the Talmud frequently in
the sense of wiping off = *qinnēăch,* or wiping out = *máchaq,*—
which meanings all go back, along with the meaning *negare,* to
the primary meaning, *tegere, obducere*). The covenant will be
"struck out," as you strike out a wrong word, by crossing it
over with ink and rendering it illegible. They fancy that they
have fortified themselves against death and Hades; but Jehovah
gives to both of these unlimited power over them. When the
swelling scourge shall come, they will become to it as *mirmâs,*
i.e. they will be overwhelmed by it, and their corpses become
like dirt of the streets (ch. x. 6, v. 5) ; וִהְיִיתֶם has the *mercha*
upon the *penult.,* according to the older editions and the smaller
Masora on Lev. viii. 26, the tone being drawn back on account
of the following לוֹ. The strokes of the scourge come incessantly, and every stroke sweeps them, *i.e.* many of them, away.
מִדֵּי (from דַּי, construct דֵּי, sufficiency, abundance) followed by
the infinitive, *quotiescunque irruet ; lâqach, auferre,* as in Jer.
xv. 15, and in the idiom *lâqach nephesh.* These scourgings
without end—what a painful lecture Jehovah is reading them !
This is the thought expressed in the concluding words : for
the meaning cannot be, that "even (*raq* as in Ps. xxxii. 6)
the report (of such a fate) is alarming," as Grotius and others
explain it ; or the report is nothing but alarming, as Gussetius

and others interpret it, since in that case שְׁמוּעָה שֵׁמַע (cf. ch.
xxiii. 5) would have been quite sufficient, instead of הָבִין שְׁמוּעָה.
There is no doubt that the expression points back to the scornful question addressed by the debauchees to the prophet in
ver. 9, "To whom will he make preaching intelligible?" *i.e.*
to whom will he preach the word of God in an intelligible
manner? (as if they did not possess *bīnâh* without this ; שְׁמוּעָה,
ἀκοή, as in ch. liii. 1.) As ver. 11 affirmed that Jehovah would
take up the word against them, the drunken stammerers, through
a stammering people ; so here the scourging without end is called
the *sh⁰mū'âh,* or sermon, which Jehovah preaches to them. At
the same time, the word *hâbhīn* is not causative here, as in ver.
9, viz. " to give to understand," but signifies simply " to understand," or have an inward perception. To receive into one's
comprehension such a sermon as that which was now being
delivered to them, was *raq-z⁰vá'âh,* nothing but shaking or
shuddering (*raq* as in Gen. vi. 5) ; זוּעַ (from which comes זְוָעָה,
or by transposition וְעָוָה) is applied to inward shaking as well
as to outward tossing to and fro. Jerome renders it " *tan-
tummodo sola vexatio intellectum dabit auditui,*" and Luther
follows him thus : " but the vexation teaches to take heed
to the word," as if the reading were תָּבִין. The alarming
character of the lecture is depicted in ver. 20, in a figure
which was probably proverbial. The situation into which
they are brought is like a bed too short for a man to stretch
himself in (*min* as in 2 Kings vi. 1), and like a covering
which, according to the measure of the man who covers
himself up in it (or perhaps still better in a temporal sense,
" when a man covers or wraps himself up in it," cf. ch.
xviii. 4), is too narrow or too tight. So would it be in their
case with the Egyptian treaty, in which they fancied that
there were rest and safety for them. They would have to
acknowledge its insufficiency. They had made themselves a
bed, and procured bed-clothes; but how mistaken they had
been in the measure, how miserably and ridiculously they had
miscalculated !

It would be with them as it was with the Philistines when
David turned their army into water at Baal-Perazim (2 Sam.
v. 20 ; 1 Chron. xiv. 11), or when on another occasion he drove
them before him from Gibeon to Gezer (1 Chron. xiv. 13

sqq.). Ver. 21. "*For Jehovah will rise up as in the mountain of Perazim, and be wroth as in the valley at Gibeon to work His work: astonishing is His work; and to act His act: strange is His act.*" The Targum wrongly supposes the first historical reminiscence to refer to the earthquake in the time of Uzziah, and the second to Joshua's victory over the Amorites. The allusion really is to the two shameful defeats which David inflicted upon the Philistines. There was a very good reason why victories over the Philistines especially should serve as similes. The same fate awaited the Philistines at the hands of the Assyrians, as predicted by the prophet in ch. xiv. 28 sqq. (cf. ch. xx.). And the strangeness and verity of Jehovah's work were just this, that it would fare no better with the magnates of Judah at the hand of Asshur, than it had with the Philistines at the hand of David on both those occasions. The very same thing would now happen to the people of the house of David as formerly to its foes. Jehovah would have to act in opposition to His gracious purpose. He would have to act towards His own people as He once acted towards their foes. This was the most paradoxical thing of all that they would have to experience.

But the possibility of repentance was still open to them, and at least a modification of what had been threatened was attainable. Ver. 22. "*And now drive ye not mockeries, lest your fetters be strengthened; for I have heard from the Lord, Jehovah of hosts, a judgment of destruction, and an irrevocable one, upon the whole earth.*" It is assumed that they are already in fetters, namely, the fetters of Asshur (Nah. i. 13). Out of these fetters they wanted to escape by a breach of faith, and with the help of Egypt without Jehovah, and consequently they mocked at the warnings of the prophet. He therefore appeals to them at any rate to stop their mocking, lest they should fall out of the bondage in which they now were, into one that would bind them still more closely, and lest the judgment should become even more severe than it would otherwise be. For it was coming without fail. It might be modified, and with thorough repentance they might even escape; but that it would come, and that upon the whole earth, had been revealed to the prophet by Jehovah of hosts. This was the *sh⁰mū'ăh* which the prophet had heard from Jehovah, and which he gave them to

hear and understand, though hitherto he had only been scoffed
at by their wine-bibbing tongues.

The address of the prophet is here apparently closed. But
an essential ingredient is still wanting to the second half, to
make it correspond to the first. There is still wanting the
fringe of promise coinciding with vers. 5, 6. The prophet has
not only to alarm the scoffers, that if possible he may pluck
some of them out of the fire through fear (Judg. v. 23); he
has also to comfort believers, who yield themselves as disciples
to him and to the word of God (ch. viii. 16). He does this
here in a very peculiar manner. He has several times assumed
the tone of the *mashal,* more especially in ch. xxvi. ; but here
the consolation is dressed up in a longer parabolical address,
which sets forth in figures drawn from husbandry the disciplinary and saving wisdom of God. Isaiah here proves himself
a master of the *mashal.* In the usual tone of a mashal song,
he first of all claims the attention of his audience as a teacher
of wisdom. Ver. 23. " *Lend me your ear, and hear my voice;
attend, and hear my address !* " Attention is all the more need-
ful, that the prophet leaves his hearers to interpret and apply
the parable themselves. The work of a husbandman is very
manifold, as he tills, sows, and plants his field. Vers. 24–26.
" *Does the ploughman plough continually to sow ? to furrow and
to harrow his land ? Is it not so : when he levels the surface
thereof, he scatters black poppy seed, and strews cummin, and puts
in wheat in rows, and barley in the appointed piece, and spelt on
its border ? And He has instructed him how to act rightly :
his God teaches it him.*" The ploughing (*chârash*) which
opens the soil, *i.e.* turns it up in furrows, and the harrowing
(*siddēd*) which breaks the clods, take place to prepare for the
sowing, and therefore not interminably, but only so long as is
necessary to prepare the soil to receive the seed. When the
seed-furrows have been drawn in the levelled surface of the
ground (*shivvâh*), then the sowing and planting begin ; and
this also takes place in various ways, according to the different
kinds of fruit. *Qetsach* is the black poppy (*nigella sativa,*
Arab. *habbe soda,* so called from its black seeds), belonging
to the ranunculaceæ. *Kammōn* was the cummin (*cuminum
cyminum*) with larger aromatic seeds, Ar. *kammûn,* neither of
them our common carraway (*Kümmel, carum*). The wheat he

sows carefully in rows (*sōrâh, ordo; ad ordinem*, as it is translated by Jerome), *i.e.* he does not scatter it about carelessly, like
the other two, but lays the grains carefully in the furrows,
because otherwise when they sprang up they would get massed
together, and choke one another. *Nismân*, like *sōrâh*, is an *acc.
loci :* the barley is sown in a piece of the field specially marked
off for it, or specially furnished with signs (*sīmânīm*); and
kussemeth, the spelt (ζειά, also mentioned by Homer, *Od.* iv.
604, between wheat and barley), along the edge of it, so that
spelt forms the rim of the barley field. It is by a divine
instinct that the husbandman acts in this manner; for God,
who established agriculture at the creation (*i.e.* Jehovah, not
Osiris), has also given men understanding. This is the meaning of *v'yiss'rō lammishpât : and* (as we may see from all this)
He (his God: the subject is given afterwards in the second
clause) *has led him* (Prov. xxxi. 1) *to the right* (this is the
rendering adopted by Kimchi, whilst other commentators have
been misled by Jer. xxx. 11, and last of all Malbim Luzzatto,
" *Cosi Dio con giustizia corregge ;*" he would have done better,
however, to say, *con moderazione*).

Again, the labour of the husbandman is just as manifold
after the reaping has been done. Vers. 27-29. " *For the black
poppy is not threshed with a threshing sledge, nor is a cart wheel
rolled over cummin; but black poppy is knocked out with a stick,
and cummin with a staff. Is bread corn crushed ? No ; he does not
go on threshing it for ever, and drive the wheel of his cart and his
horses over it : he does not crush it. This also, it goeth forth from
Jehovah of hosts : He gives wonderful intelligence, high understanding.*" *Ki* (for) introduces another proof that the husbandman is instructed by God, from what he still further does.
He does not use the threshing machine (*chârūts*, syn. *mōrag*,
Ar. *naureg, nôreg*), or the threshing cart ('*ăgâláh :* see Winer's
Real-Wörterbuch, art. *Dreschen*), which would entirely destroy
the more tender kinds of fruit, but knocks them out with a
staff (*baculo excutit :* see at ch. xxvii. 12). The sentence *lechem
yūdâq* is to be accentuated as an interrogative : Is bread corn
crushed ? Oh no, he does not crush it. This would be the case
if he were to cause the wheel (*i.e.* the wheels, *gilgal*, constr. to
galgal) of the threshing cart with the horses harnessed in front
to rattle over it with all their might (*hâmam,* to set in noisy

violent motion). *Lechem,* like the Greek *sitos,* is corn from
which bread is made (ch. xxx. 23 ; Ps. civ. 14). אָדוֹשׁ is metaplastic (as if from אָדַשׁ) for דּוֹשׁ (see Ewald, § 312, *b*). Instead
of וּפָרָשָׁיו, the pointing ought to be וּפָרָשָׁיו (from פָּרָשׁ with *kametz*
before the tone = Arab. *fărăs,* as distinguished from פָּרָשׁ with
a fixed *kametz,* equivalent to *farras,* a rider) : "his horses," here
the threshing horses, which were preferred to asses and oxen.
Even in this treatment of the fruit when reaped, there is an
evidence of the *wonderful intelligence* (הִפְלָא, as written הִפְלִיא)
and *exalted understanding* (on תּוּשִׁיָּה, from יָשָׁה, see at Job xxvi.
3) imparted by God.　The expression is one of such grandeur,
that we perceive at once that the prophet has in his mind the
wisdom of God in a higher sphere.　The wise, divinely inspired
course adopted by the husbandman in the treatment of the field
and fruit, is a type of the wise course adopted by the divine
Teacher Himself in the treatment of His nation.　Israel is
Jehovah's field.　The punishments and chastisements of Jehovah are the ploughshare and harrow, with which He forcibly
breaks up, turns over, and furrows this field.　But this does
not last for ever.　When the field has been thus loosened,
smoothed, and rendered fertile once more, the painful process
of ploughing is followed by a beneficent sowing and planting
in a multiform and wisely ordered fulness of grace.　Again,
Israel is Jehovah's child of the threshing-floor (see ch. xxi. 10).
He threshes it ; but He does not thresh it only : He also knocks ;
and when He threshes, He does not continue threshing for ever,
i.e. as Caspari has well explained it, "He does not punish all
the members of the nation with the same severity ; and those
whom He punishes with greater severity than others He does
not punish incessantly, but as soon as His end is attained,
and the husks of sin are separated from those that have been
punished, the punishment ceases, and only the worst in the
nation, who are nothing but husks, and the husks on the
nation itself, are swept away by the punishments" (compare
ch. i. 25, xxix. 20, 21).　This is the solemn lesson and
affectionate consolation hidden behind the veil of the parable.
Jehovah punishes, but it is in order that He may be able to
bless.　He sifts, but He does not destroy.　He does not thresh
His own people, but He knocks them ; and even when He
threshes, they may console themselves in the face of the

approaching period of judgment, that they are never crushed
or injured.

The prophecy here passes from the fall of Samaria, the
crown of flowers (ch. xxviii. 1–4), to its formal parallel. Jerusalem takes its place by the side of Samaria, the crown of
flowers, under the emblem of a hearth of God. '*Arī'ēl* might,
indeed, mean a lion of God. It occurs in this sense as the
name of certain Moabitish heroes (2 Sam. xxiii. 20; 1 Chron.
xi. 22), and Isaiah himself used the shorter form אֲרְאֵל for the
heroes of Judah (ch. xxxiii. 7). But as אֲרִיאֵל (God's hearth, interchanged with הַרְאֵל, God's height) is the name given in Ezek.
xliii. 15, 16, to the altar of burnt-offering in the new temple,
and as Isaiah could not say anything more characteristic of
Jerusalem, than that Jehovah had a fire and hearth there (ch.
xxxi. 9) ; and, moreover, as Jerusalem the city and community
within the city would have been compared to a lioness rather
than a lion, we take אֲרִיאֵל in the sense of *ara Dei* (from אָרָה,
to burn). The prophet commences in his own peculiar way
with a grand summary introduction, which passes in a few
gigantic strides over the whole course from threatening to
promise. Ver. 1. " *Woe to Ariel, to Ariel, the castle where
David pitched his tent! Add year to year, let the feasts revolve :
then I distress Ariel, and there is groaning and moaning; and so
she proves herself to me as Ariel.*" By the fact that David
fixed his headquarters in Jerusalem, and then brought the
sacred ark thither, Jerusalem became a hearth of God. Within
a single year, after only one more round of feasts (to be interpreted according to ch. xxxii. 10, and probably spoken at the
passover), Jehovah would make Jerusalem a besieged city, full
of sighs (*vahătsīqōthī, perf. cons.,* with the tone upon the ultimate) ; but " she becomes to me like an Ariel," *i.e.,* being
qualified through me, she will prove herself a hearth of God,
by consuming the foes like a furnace, or by their meeting with
their destruction at Jerusalem, like wood piled up on the altar
and then consumed in flame. The prophecy has thus passed
over the whole ground in a few majestic words. It now starts

from the very beginning again, and first of all expands the
hoi. Vers. 3 and 4. "*And I encamp in a circle round about thee,
and surround thee with watch-posts, and erect tortoises against
thee. And when brought down thou wilt speak from out of the
ground, and thy speaking will sound low out of the dust; and thy
voice cometh up like that of a demon from the ground, and thy
speaking will whisper out of the dust.*" It would have to go so
far with Ariel first of all, that it would be besieged by a hostile
force, and would lie upon the ground in the greatest extremity,
and then would whisper with a ghostlike softness, like a dying
man, or like a spirit without flesh and bones. *Kaddūr* signifies
sphœra, orbis, as in ch. xxii. 18 and in the Talmud (from
kâdar = kâthar; cf. *kudur* in the name *Nabu-kudur-ussur,*
Nebo protect the crown, κίδαριν), and is used here poetically
for סָבִיב. Jerome renders it *quasi sphœram* (from *dūr, orbis*).
מֻצָּב (from יָצַב, נָצַב) might signify "firmly planted" (Luzzatto,
immobilmente; compare *shūth,* ch. xxii. 7); but according to
the parallel it signifies a military post, like מַצָּב, נְצִיב. *Mᵉtsu-
rōth* (from *mâtsōr,* Deut. xx. 20) are instruments of siege, the
nature of which can only be determined conjecturally. On
'ōbh, see ch. viii. 19;[1] there is no necessity to take it as standing
for *ba'al 'ōbh.*

Thus far does the unfolding of the *hoi* reach. Now follows
an unfolding of the words of promise, which stand at the end
of ver. 1 : "And it proves itself to me as Ariel." Vers. 5–8.
"*And the multitude of thy foes will become like finely powdered
dust, and the multitude of the tyrants like chaff flying away ; and
it will take place suddenly, very suddenly. From Jehovah of
hosts there comes a visitation with crash of thunder and earthquake and great noise, whirlwind and tempest, and the blazing up
of devouring fire. And the multitude of all the nations that
gather together against Ariel, and all those who storm and distress
Ariel and her stronghold, will be like a vision of the night in a*

---

[1] The *'akkūbh* mentioned there is equivalent to *anbūb,* Arab. a knot on a
reed stalk, then that part of such a reed which comes between two knots,
then the reed stalk itself ; root נב, to rise up, swell, or become convex
without and concave within (Fl.). It is possible that it would be better to
trace *'ōbh* back to this radical and primary meaning of what is hollow (and
therefore has a dull sound), whether used in the sense of a leather-bag, or
applied to a spirit of incantation, and the possessor of such a spirit.

dream. And it is just as a hungry man dreams, and behold he eats; and when he wakes up his soul is empty: and just as a thirsty man dreams, and behold he drinks; and when he wakes up, behold, he is faint, and his soul is parched with thirst: so will it be to the multitude of the nations which gather together against the mountain of Zion." The hostile army, described four times as *hámōn*, a groaning multitude, is utterly annihilated through the terrible co-operation of the forces of nature which are let loose upon them (ch. xxx. 30, cf. ch. xvii. 13). "*There comes a visitation:*" *tippáqēd* might refer to Jerusalem in the sense of "it will be visited" in mercy, viz. by Jehovah acting thus upon its enemies. But it is better to take it in a neuter sense: "punishment is inflicted." The simile of the dream is applied in two different ways: (1.) Ver. 7. They will dissolve into nothing, as if they had only the same apparent existence as a vision in a dream. (2.) Ver. 8. Their plan for taking Jerusalem will be put to shame, and as utterly brought to nought as the eating or drinking of a dreamer, which turns out to be a delusion as soon as he awakes. Just as the prophet emphatically combines two substantives from the same verbal root in ver. 1, and two adverbs from the same verb in ver. 5; so does he place צָבָא and צָבָה together in ver. 7, the former with עַל relating to the crowding of an army for the purpose of a siege, the latter with an objective suffix (compare Ps. liii. 6) to the attack made by a crowded army. The *mᵉtsōdáh* of Ariel (*i.e.* the watch-tower, *specula*, from *tsūd*, to spy [1]) is the mountain of Zion mentioned afterwards in ver. 8. כַּאֲשֶׁר, as if; comp. Zech. x. 6, Job x. 19. וְהִנֵּה אוֹכֵל without הוּא; the personal pronoun is frequently omitted, not only in the leading participial clause, as in this instance (compare ch. xxvi. 3, xl. 19; Ps. xxii. 29; Job xxv. 2; and Köhler on Zech. ix. 12), but also with a minor participial clause, as in Ps. vii. 10, lv. 20, and Hab. ii. 10. The hungering and thirsting of the waking man are attributed to his *nephesh* (soul: cf. ch. xxxii. 6, v. 14; Prov. vi. 30), just because the soul is the cause of the physical life, and without it the action of the senses would be followed by no sensation or experience whatever. The hungry stomach is simply the object of feeling,

---

[1] In Arabic, also, *masâd* signifies a lofty hill or mountain-top, from a secondary form of *tsud*; and *massara*, to lay the foundations of a fortified city (ʿîr mâtsōr, Ps. xxxi. 22), from *tsūr*.

and everything sensitive in the bodily organism is merely the medium of sensation or feeling; that which really *feels* is the soul. The soul no sooner passes out of the dreaming state into a waking condition, than it feels that its desires are as unsatisfied as ever. Just like such a dream will the army of the enemy, and that victory of which it is so certain before the battle is fought, fade away into nothing.

This enigma of the future the prophet holds out before the eyes of his contemporaries. The prophet received it by revelation of Jehovah; and without the illumination of Jehovah it could not possibly be understood. The deep degradation of Ariel, the wonderful deliverance, the sudden elevation from the abyss to this lofty height,—all this was a matter of faith. But this faith was just what the nation wanted, and therefore the understanding depending upon it was wanting also. The *shᵉmuʻâh* was there, but the *bînâh* was absent; and all הבין שמועה was wrecked on the obtuseness of the mass. The prophet, therefore, who had received the unhappy calling to harden his people, could not help exclaiming (ver. 9*a*), " *Stop, and stare; blind yourselves, and grow blind!*" הִתְמַהְמְהוּ, to show one's self delaying (from מָהָה, according to Luzzatto the reflective of תְּמַהְמַהּ, an emphatic form which is never met with), is connected with the synonymous verb תָּמַהּ, to be stiff with astonishment; but to שָׁעַע, to be plastered up, *i.e.* incapable of seeing (cf. ch. vi. 10), there is attached the *hithpalpel* of the same verb, signifying "to place one's self in such circumstances," *se oblinere* (differently, however, in Ps. cxix. 16, 47, compare ch. xi. 8, *se permulcere*). They could not understand the word of God, but they were confused, and their eyes were, so to speak, festered up : therefore this self-induced condition would become to them a God-appointed punishment. The imperatives are judicial words of command.

This growth of the self-hardening into a judicial sentence of obduracy, is proclaimed still more fully by the prophet. Vers. 9*b*–12. " *They are drunken, and not with wine; they reel, and not with meth. For Jehovah hath poured upon you a spirit of deep sleep, and bound up your eyes; the prophets and your heads, the seers, He has veiled. And the revelation of all this will be to you like words of a sealed writing, which they give to him who understands writing, saying, Pray, read this; but he*

*says, I cannot, it is sealed. And they give the writing to one
who does not understand writing, saying, Pray, read this ; but
he says, I do not understand writing.*" They were drunken
and stupid ; not, however, merely because they gave themselves
up to sensual intoxication (יַיִן, dependent upon שָׁכְרוּ, *ebrii vino*),
but because Jehovah had given them up to spiritual confusion
and self-destruction. All the punishments of God are inflicted
through the medium of His no less world-destroying than
world-sustaining Spirit, which, although not willing what is
evil, does make the evil called into existence by the creature
the means of punishing evil. *Tardēmâh* is used here to signify
the powerless, passive state of utter spiritual insensibility. This
judgment had fallen upon the nation in all its members, even
upon the eyes and heads of the nation, *i.e.* the prophets. Even
they whose duty it was to see to the good of the nation, and
lead it, were blind leaders of the blind ; their eyes were fast
shut (עָצַם, the intensive form of the *kal*, ch. xxxiii. 15 ; *Aram.*
עֲצַם ; *Talmud* also עְמֵץ : to shut the eyes, or press them close),
and over their heads a cover was drawn, as over sleepers in the
night. Since the time of Koppe and Eichhorn it has become
a usual thing to regard אֶת־הַנְּבִיאִים and הַחֹזִים as a gloss, and
indeed as a false one (compare ch. ix. 13, 14) ; but the reason
assigned—namely, that Isaiah's polemics are directed not against
the prophets, but against the stupid staring people—is utterly
groundless (compare ch. xxviii. 7, and the polemics of his contemporary Micah, *e.g.* ch. iii. 5-8). Moreover, the author of a
gloss would have been more likely to interpret רָאשֵׁיכֶם by הַשָּׂרִים
or הַפֹּחֲנִים (compare Job ix. 24). And vers. 11 and 12 are also
opposed to this assumption of a gloss. For by those who understood what was written (*sēpher*), it is evident that the prophets
and rulers of the nation are intended ; and by those who did
not understand it, the great mass of the people. To both of
them, " the vision of all," *i.e.* of all and everything that God
had shown to His true prophets, was by the judgment of God
completely sealed. Some of them might have an outward
knowledge ; but the inward understanding of the revelation
was sealed to them. Some had not even this, but stared at the
word of the prophet, just as a man who cannot read stares at
what is written. The *chethib* has הַסֵּפֶר ; the *keri* סֵפֶר, though
without any ground, since the article is merely generic. In-

stead of קְרָא נָא־זֶה, we should write קְרָא־נָא זֶה in both cases, as certain codices and old editions do.

This stupefaction was the self-inflicted punishment of the dead works with which the people mocked God and deceived themselves. Vers. 13, 14. " *The Lord hath spoken : Because this people approaches me with its mouth, and honours me with its lips, and keeps its heart far from me, and its reverence of me has become a commandment learned from men : therefore, behold, I will proceed wondrously with this people, wondrously and marvellously strange ; and the wisdom of its wise men is lost, and the understanding of its intelligent men becomes invisible.*" Ever since the time of Asaph (Ps. l., cf. lxxviii. 36, 37), the lamentation and condemnation of hypocritical ceremonial worship, without living faith or any striving after holiness, had been a leading theme of prophecy. Even in Isaiah's introductory address (ch. i.) this complaint was uttered quite in the tone of that of Asaph. In the time of Hezekiah it was peculiarly called for, just as it was afterwards in that of Josiah (as the book of Jeremiah shows). The people had been obliged to consent to the abolition of the public worship of idols, but their worship of Jehovah was hypocrisy. Sometimes it was conscious hypocrisy, arising from the fear of man and favour of man ; sometimes unconscious, inasmuch as without any inward conversion, but simply with work-righteousness, the people contented themselves with, and even prided themselves upon, an outward fulfilment of the law (Mic. vi. 6–8, iii. 11). Instead of נִגַּשׁ (LXX., Vulg., Syr., Matt. xv. 8, Mark vii. 6), we also meet with the reading נָגַשׂ, " because this people harasses itself as with tributary service ;" but the antithesis to *richaq* (LXX. πόῤῥω ἀπέχει) favours the former reading *niggash, accedit;* and *b^e phiv* (with its mouth) must be connected with this, though in opposition to the accents. This self-alienation and self-blinding, Jehovah would punish with a wondrously paradoxical judgment, namely, the judgment of a hardening, which would so completely empty and confuse, that even the appearance of wisdom and unity, which the leaders of Israel still had, would completely disappear. יוֹסִיף (as in ch. xxxviii. 5) is not the third person *fut. hiphil* here (so that it could be rendered, according to ch. xxviii. 16, " Behold, I am he who ;" or more strictly still, " Behold me, who ;" which, however, would give a prominence

to the subject that would be out of place here), but the *part. kal*
for יוֹסֵף. That the language really allowed of such a lengthening of the primary form *qaṭǐl* into *qaṭîl*, and especially in the
case of יוֹסִיף, is evident from Eccles. i. 18 (see at Ps. xvi. 5).
In הַפְלֵא וָפֶלֶא, פֶּלֶא (cf. Lam. i. 9) alternates with the gerundive
(see at ch. xxii. 17): the fifth example in this one address of
the emphatic juxtaposition of words having a similar sound and
the same derivation (*vid.* vers. 1, 5, 7, 9).

Their hypocrisy, which was about to be so wonderfully
punished according to the universal law (Ps. xviii. 26, 27),
manifested itself in their self-willed and secret behaviour, which
would not inquire for Jehovah, nor suffer itself to be chastened
by His word. Vers. 15, 16. " *Woe unto them that hide plans
deep from Jehovah, and their doing occurs in a dark place, and
they say, Who saw us then, and who knew about us? Oh for your
perversity! It is to be regarded as potters' clay; that a work
could say to its maker, He has not made me; and an image to its
sculptor, He does not understand it!*" Just as Ahaz had carefully
kept his appeal to Asshur for help secret from the prophet; so
did they try, as far as possible, to hide from the prophet the
plan for an alliance with Egypt. לַסְתִּיר is a syncopated *hiphil*
for לְהַסְתִּיר, as in ch. i. 12, iii. 8, xxiii. 11. הֶעֱמִיק adds the
adverbial notion, according to our mode of expression (comp.
Joel ii. 20, and the opposite thought in Joel ii. 26; Ges. §
142). To hide from Jehovah is equivalent to hiding from
the prophet of Jehovah, that they might not have to listen to
reproof from the word of Jehovah. We may see from ch.
viii. 12 how suspiciously they watched the prophet in such circumstances as these. But Jehovah saw them in their secrecy,
and the prophet saw through the whole in the light of Jehovah.
הַפְכְּכֶם is an exclamation, like תִּפְלַצְתְּךָ in Jer. xlix. 16. They
are perverse, or ('*im*) " is it not so?" They think they can
dispense with Jehovah, and yet they are His creatures; they
attribute cleverness to themselves, and practically disown Jehovah, as if the pot should say to the potter who has turned it,
He does not understand it.

But the prophet's God, whose omniscience, creative glory,
and perfect wisdom they so basely mistook and ignored, would
very shortly turn the present state of the world upside down, and
make Himself a congregation out of the poor and wretched,

whilst He would entirely destroy this proud ungodly nation.
Vers. 17–21. " *Is it not yet a very little, and Lebanon is turned
into a fruitful field, and the fruitful field esteemed as a forest?
And in that day the deaf hear scripture words, and the eyes of the
blind will see out of obscurity and out of darkness. And the joy
of the humble increases in Jehovah, and the poor among men will
rejoice in the Holy One of Israel. For tyrants are gone, and it is
over with scoffers; and all who think evil are rooted out, who condemn a man for a word, and lay snares for him that is free-spoken
in the gate, and overthrow the righteous through shameful lies.*"
The circumstances themselves, as well as the sentence passed,
will experience a change, in complete contrast with the present
state of things. This is what is affirmed in ver. 17; probably
a proverb transposed into a more literary style. What is now
forest becomes ennobled into garden ground; and what is
garden ground becomes in general estimation a forest (לְכַרְמֶל,
לְיַעַר, although we should rather expect לְ, just as in ch. xxxii.
15). These emblems are explained in vers. 18 sqq. The
people that are now blind and deaf, so far as the word of
Jehovah is concerned, are changed into a people with open
ears and seeing eyes. Scripture words, like those which the
prophet now holds before the people so unsuccessfully, are
heard by those who have been deaf. The unfettered sight of
those who have been blind pierces through the hitherto sur-
rounding darkness. The heirs of the new future thus transformed are the 'ănâvîm (" meek") and the 'ebhyōnîm (" poor").
אָדָם (the antithesis of אֲנָשִׁים, e.g. ver. 13) heightens the representation of lowliness; the combination is a superlative one,
as in צְעִירֵי הַצֹּאן, Jer. xlix. 20, and עֲנִיֵּי הַצֹּאן in Zech. xi. 7 (cf.
פְּרִיץ חַיּוֹת in ch. xxxv. 9): needy men who present a glaring
contrast to, and stand out from, the general body of men.
Such men will obtain ever increasing joy in Jehovah (*yâsaph*
as in ch. xxxvii. 31). Such a people of God would take the
place of the oppressors (cf. ch. xxviii. 12) and scoffers (cf.
ch. xxviii. 14, 22), and those who thought evil (*shâqad, invigi-
lare, sedulo agere*), *i.e.* the wretched planners, who made a חֹטֵא
of every one who did not enter into their plans (*i.e.* who called
him a *chōtē*; cf. Deut. xxiv. 4, Eccles. v. 5), and went to
law with the man who openly opposed them in the gate
(Amos v. 10; *y'qōshūn*, possibly the *perf. kal*, cf. Jer. l. 24;

according to the syntax, however, it is the *fut. kal* of *qūsh* = *yâqōsh:* see at ch. xxvi. 16; Ges. § 44, Anm. 4), and thrust away the righteous, *i.e.* forced him away from his just rights (ch. x. 2), by *tōhū, i.e.* accusations and pretences of the utmost worthlessness; for these would all have been swept away. This is the true explanation of the last clause, as given in the Targum, and not "into the desert and desolation," as Knobel and Luzzatto suppose; for with Isaiah *tōhū* is the synonym for all such words as signify nothingness, groundlessness, and fraud. The prophet no doubt had in his mind, at the time that he uttered these words, the conduct of the people towards himself and his fellow-prophets, and such as were like-minded with them. The charge brought against him of being a conspirator, or a traitor to his country, was a *tōhū* of this kind. All these conspirators and persecutors Jehovah would clear entirely away.

Everything that was incorrigible would be given up to destruction; and therefore the people of God, when it came out of the judgment, would have nothing of the same kind to look for again. Vers. 22–24. "*Therefore thus saith Jehovah of the house of Jacob, He who redeemed Abraham: Jacob shall not henceforth be ashamed, nor shall his face turn pale any more. For when he, when his children see the work of my hands in the midst of him, they will sanctify my name, and sanctify the Holy One of Jacob, and shudder before the God of Israel. And those who were of an erring spirit discern understanding, and murmurers accept instruction.*" With אֶל (for which Luzzatto, following Lowth, reads אֵל, "the God of the house of Jacob") the theme is introduced to which the following utterance refers. The end of Israel will correspond to the holy root of its origin. Just as Abraham was separated from the human race that was sunk in heathenism, to become the ancestor of a nation of Jehovah, so would a remnant be separated from the great mass of Israel that was sunk in apostasy from Jehovah; and this remnant would be the foundation of a holy community well pleasing to God. And this would never be confounded or become pale with shame again (on *bōsh*, see at ch. i. 29; *châvar* is a poetical Aramaism); for both sins and sinners that called forth the punishments of God, which had put them to shame, would have been swept away (cf. Zeph. iii. 11). In the presence of this decisive work of punishment (*ma'ăseh* as in ch. xxviii. 21, x. 12, v. 12, 19), which Jehovah would perform in the heart of Israel, Israel itself would undergo a thorough change. יְלָדָיו is in apposition to the subject in בִּרְאֹתוֹ, "when he, namely his children" (comp. Job xxix. 3); and the expression "his children" is intentionally chosen instead of "his sons" (*bânîm*), to indicate that there would be a new generation, which would become, in the face of the judicial self-manifestation of Jehovah, a holy church, sanctifying Him, the Holy One of Israel. *Yaqdīshū* is continued in *v^ehiqdīshū*: the prophet intentionally repeats this most significant word, and *he'ĕrīts* is the parallel word to it, as in ch. viii. 12, 13. The new church would indeed not be a sinless one, or thoroughly perfect; but, according to ver. 24, the previous self-hardening in error would have been exchanged for a willing and living appropriation of right understanding, and the former murmuring resistance to the admonitions of Jehovah would have given place to a joyful and receptive thirst for instruction. There is the same interchange of *Jacob* and *Israel* here which we so frequently meet with in ch. xl. sqq. And, in fact, throughout this undisputedly genuine prophecy of Isaiah, we can detect the language of ch. xl.-lxvi. Through the whole of the first part, indeed, we may trace the gradual development of the thoughts and forms which predominate there.

THE THIRD WOE: THE MOMENTOUS RESULT OF THE ALLIANCE WITH EGYPT.—CHAP. XXX.

The plan which, according to ch. xxix. 15, was already projected and prepared in the deepest secrecy, is now much further advanced. The negotiations by means of ambassadors have already been commenced; but the prophet condemns what he can no longer prevent. Vers. 1-5. "*Woe to the stubborn children, saith Jehovah, to drive plans, and not by my impulse, and to plait alliance, and not according to my Spirit, to heap sin upon sin: that go away to travel down to Egypt, without having asked my mouth, to fly to Pharaoh's shelter, and to conceal themselves under the shadow of Egypt. And Pharaoh's shelter becomes a shame to them, and the concealment under the shadow of Egypt a disgrace. For Judah's princes have appeared*

*in Zoan, and his ambassadors arrive in Hanes. They will all
have to be ashamed of a people useless to them, that brings no
help and no use, but shame, and also reproach.*" *Sōrᵉrīm* is followed by infinitives with *Lamed* (cf. ch. v. 22, iii. 8): who are
bent upon it in their obstinacy. *Massēkhâh* designates the
alliance as a plait (*massēkheth*). According to Cappellus and
others, it designates it as formed with a libation (σπονδή, from
σπένδεσθαι) ; but the former is certainly the more correct view,
inasmuch as *massēkhâh* (from *nâsakh, fundere*) signifies a cast,
and hence it is more natural here to take *nâsakh* as equivalent to
sâkhakh, plectere (Jerome: *ordiremini telam*). The context leaves
no doubt as to the meaning of the adverbial expressions וְלֹא־מִנִּי
and וְלֹא־רוּחִי, viz. without its having proceeded from me, and
without my Spirit being there. "Sin upon sin :" inasmuch as
they carry out further and further to perfect realization the
thought which was already a sinful one in itself. The prophet
now follows for himself the ambassadors, who are already on
the road to the country of the Nile valley. He sees them
arrive in Zoan, and watches them as they proceed thence into
Hanes. He foresees and foretells what a disgraceful opening
of their eyes will attend the reward of this untheocratical beginning. On *lâ'ōz b'*, see at ch. x. 31: *'ōz* is the infinitive
constr. of *'ūz* ; *mâ'ōz*, on the contrary, is a derivative of
'âzaz, to be strong. The suffixes of שָׂרָיו (his princes) and
מַלְאָכָיו (his ambassadors) are supposed by Hitzig, Ewald, and
Knobel, who take a different view of what is said, to refer to
the princes and ambassadors of Pharaoh. But this is by no
means warranted on the ground that the prophet cannot so
immediately transfer to Zoan and Hanes the ambassadors of
Judah, who were still on their journey according to ver. 2.
The prophet's vision overleaps the existing stage of the desire
for this alliance ; he sees the great men of his nation already
suing for the favour of Egypt, first of all in Zoan, and then
still further in Hanes, and at once foretells the shameful termination of this self-desecration of the people of Jehovah.
The LXX. give for חִנָּם יַגִּעוּ, μάτην κοπιάσουσιν, i.e. חִנָּם יִיגָעוּ,
and Knobel approves this reading ; but it is a misunderstanding, which only happens to have fallen out a little better this
time than the rendering ὡς Δαυίδ given for כַּדּוּר in ch. xxix. 3.
If *chinnâm* had been the original reading, it would hardly have

entered any one's mind to change it into *chânēs*. The latter
was the name of a city on an island of the Nile in Central
Egypt, the later Heracleopolis (Eg. *Hnēs; Ehnēs*), the *Anysis*
of Herodotus (ii. 137). On *Zoan*, see at ch. xix. 11. At that
time the Tanitic dynasty was reigning, the dynasty preceding
the Ethiopian. Tanis and Anysis were the two capitals. הִבְאִישׁ
(= הֹבִישׁ, a metaplastic *hiphil* of יָבֵשׁ = בּוֹשׁ, a different word
from יָבֵשׁ) is incorrectly pointed for הִבְאִישׁ, like רֵאישָׁנָה (*keri*)
for רִאישׁנָה in Josh. xxi. 10. הִבְאִישׁ signifies elsewhere, "to
make stinking" (to calumniate, Prov. xiii. 5), or "to come into
ill odour" (1 Sam. xxvii. 12); here, however, it means to be
put to shame (בָּאַשׁ = בּוֹשׁ).

The prophet's address is hardly commenced, however, when
a heading is introduced of the very same kind as we have
already met with several times in the cycle of prophecies
against the heathen nations. Gesenius, Hitzig, Umbreit, and
Knobel, rid themselves of it by pronouncing it a gloss founded
upon a misunderstanding. But nothing is more genuine in the
whole book of Isaiah than the words *massâ' bahămōth negebh*.
The heading is emblematical, like the four headings in ch. xxi.,
xxii. And the *massâ'* embraces vers. 6, 7. Then follows the
command to write it on a table by itself. The heading is an
integral part of the smaller whole. Isaiah breaks off his
address to communicate an oracle relating to the Egyptian
treaty, which Jehovah has specially commanded him to hand
down to posterity. The same interruption would take place if
we expunged the heading; for in any case it was vers. 6, 7
that he was to write upon a table. This is not an address to
the people, but the preliminary text, the application of which
is determined afterwards. The prophet communicates in the
form of a citation what has been revealed to him by God, and
then states what God has commanded him to do with it. We
therefore enclose vers. 6, 7 in inverted commas as a quotation,
and render the short passage, which is written in the tone of
ch. xxi., as follows: Vers. 6, 7. "*Oracle concerning the water-
oxen of the south: Through a land of distress and confinement,
whence the lioness and lion, adders and flying dragons; they carry
their possessions on the shoulders of asses' foals, and their treasures on the humps of camels, to a nation that profits nothing.
And Egypt, worthlessly and hollowly will they help; therefore*

I call this Egypt, Great-mouth that sits still." The "water-ox of the south" is the Nile-horse; and this is the emblem of Egypt, the land of the south (in Daniel and Zechariah Babylonia is "the land of the north"). *Bahămōth* is the construct of *bᵉhēmōth* (Job xl.), which is a Hebraized form of an Egyptian word, *p-ehe-mau* (though the word itself has not yet been met with), *i.e.* the ox of the water, or possibly *p-ehe-mau-t* (with the feminine article at the close, though in *hesmut*, another name for a female animal, *mut = t. mau* signifies "the mother:" see at Job xl. 15). The animal referred to is the hippopotamus, which is called *bomarino* in Italian, Arab. the Nile-horse or water-pig. The emblem of Egypt in other passages of the Old Testament is *tannin*, the water-snake, or *leviathan*, the crocodile. In Ps. lxviii. 31 this is called *chayyath qâneh*, "the beast of the reed," though Hengstenberg supposes that the Nile-horse is intended there. This cannot be maintained, however; but in the passage before us this emblem is chosen, just because the fat, swine-like, fleshy colossus, whose belly nearly touches the ground as it walks, is a fitting image of Egypt, a land so boastful and so eager to make itself thick and broad, and yet so slow to exert itself in the interest of others, and so unwilling to move from the spot. This is also implied in the name *rahabh-hēm-shâbheth*. *Rahab* is a name applied to Egypt in other passages also (ch. li. 9; Ps. lxxxvii. 4, lxxxix. 11), and that in the senses attested by the LXX. at Job xxvi. 12 (cf. ix. 13), viz. κῆτος, a sea-monster, *monstrum marinum.* Here the name has the meaning common in other passages, viz. violence, domineering pride, boasting (ἀλαζονεία, as one translator renders it). הֵם is a term of comparison, as in Gen. xiv. 2, 3, etc.; the plural refers to the people called *rahabh.* Hence the meaning is either, "The bragging people, they are sit-still;" or, "Boast-house, they are idlers." To this deceitful land the ambassadors of Judah were going with rich resources (*chăyâlīm, opes*) on the shoulder of asses' foals, and on the hump (*dabbesheth*, from *dâbhash*, according to Luzzatto related to *gâbhash*, to be hilly) of camels, without shrinking from the difficulties and dangers of the road through the desert, where lions and snakes spring out now here and now there (מֵהֶם, neuter, as in Zeph. ii. 7, comp. ch. xxxviii. 16; see also Deut. viii. 15, Num. xxi. 6). Through this very desert, through which God had led their fathers when

He redeemed them out of the bondage of Egypt, they were now marching to purchase the friendship of Egypt, though really, whatever might be the pretext which they offered, it was only to deceive themselves; for the vainglorious land would never keep the promises that it made.

So runs the divine oracle to which the following command refers. Ver. 8. "*Now go, write it on a table with them, and note it in a book, and let it stand there for future days, for ever, to eternity.*" The suffixes of *kothbâh* (write it) and *chuqqâh* (note it) refer in a neuter sense to vers. 6, 7 ; and the expression "go" is simply a general summons to proceed to the matter (cf. ch. xxii. 15). *Sēpher* could be used interchangeably with *lūăch*, because a single leaf, the contents of which were concluded, was called *sēpher* (Ex. xvii. 14). Isaiah was to write the oracle upon a table, a separate leaf of durable material ; and that "with them," *i.e.* so that his countrymen might have it before their eyes (compare ch. viii. 1, Hab. ii. 2). It was to be a memorial for posterity. The reading לְעֵד (Sept., Targ., Syr.) for לָעַד is appropriate, though quite unnecessary. The three indications of time form a climax: for futurity, for the most remote future, for the future without end.

It was necessary that the worthlessness of the help of Egypt should be placed in this way before the eyes of the people. Vers. 9–11. "*For it is a refractory people, lying children, children who do not like to hear the instruction of Jehovah, who say to the seers, See not ; and to the prophets, Prophesy not unto us right things ! Speak flatteries to us ! Get out of the way, turn aside from the path, remove from our face the Holy One of Israel.*" On the expression ʻam *mᵉrī* (a people of stubbornness), see at ch. iii. 8. The vowel-pointing of בַּחֲשִׁים follows the same rule as that of הֶחָכָם. The prophet traces back their words to an unvarnished expression of their true meaning, just as he does in ch. xxviii. 15. They forbid the prophets of Jehovah to prophesy, more especially *nᵉkhōchōth*, straight or true things (things not agreeable to their own wishes), but would rather hear *chălâqōth*, *i.e.* smooth, insinuating, and flattering things, and even *mahăthallōth* (from *hâthal*, Talm. *tal, ludere*), *i.e.* illusions or deceits. Their desire was to be entertained and lauded, not repelled and instructed. The prophets are to adopt another course (מִנִּי only occurs here, and that twice, instead of the more usual מִנִּי‎ = מִן‎, after the form אֱלֵי‎, עֲלֵי‎), and not trouble them any more with the Holy One of Israel, whom they (at least Isaiah, who is most fond of calling Jehovah by this name) have always in their mouths.

Thus do they fall out with Jehovah and the bearers of His word. Vers. 12–14. "*Therefore thus saith the Holy One of Israel, Because ye dislike this word, and put your trust in force and shufflings, and rely upon this; therefore will this iniquity be to you like a falling breach, bent forwards in a high-towering wall, which falls to ruin suddenly, very suddenly. And He smites it to pieces, as a potter's vessel falls to pieces, when they smash it without sparing, and of which, when it lies smashed to pieces there, you cannot find a sherd to fetch fire with from the hearth, or to take water with out of a cistern.*" The "word" towards which they cherished *mĕʻōs* (read *mŏʼoskhem*), was the word of Jehovah through His prophet, which was directed against their untheocratic policy of reckoning upon Egypt. *Nâlōz*, bent out or twisted, is the term used to denote this very policy, which was ever resorting to bypaths and secret ways; whilst *ʻōsheq* denotes the squeezing out of the money required to carry on the war of freedom, and to purchase the help of Egypt (compare 2 Kings xv. 20). The guilt of Judah is compared to the broken and overhanging part of a high wall (*nibhʻeh*, bent forwards; compare בַּעְבֻּעַ‎, a term applied to a diseased swelling). Just as such a broken piece brings down the whole of the injured wall along with it, so would the sinful conduct of Judah immediately ruin the whole of its existing constitution. Israel, which would not recognise itself as the image of Jehovah, even when there was yet time (ch. xxix. 16), would be like a vessel smashed into the smallest fragments. It is the captivity which is here figuratively threatened by the prophet; for the smashing had regard to Israel as a state. The subject to וּשְׁבָרָהּ‎ in ver. 14 is Jehovah, who would make use of the hostile power of man to destroy the wall, and break up the kingdom of Judah into such a diaspora of broken *sherds*. The reading is not וְשִׁבְּרָהּ‎ (LXX., Targum), but וּשְׁבָרָהּ‎, *et franget eam*. *Kâthōth* is an infinitive statement of the mode; the participle *kâthūth*, which is adopted by the Targum, Kimchi, Norzi, and others, is less suitable. It was necessary to proceed with לֹא יַחְמֹל‎ (without his sparing), simply because the infinitive absolute cannot be con-

nected with לֹא (Ewald, § 350, a). לַחְשׂוֹף (to be written thus
with *dagesh* both here and Hag. ii. 16) passes from the primary
meaning *nudare* to that of scooping up, as עָרָה does to that of
pouring out.

Into such small sherds, a heap thus scattered hither and
thither, would the kingdom of Judah be broken up, in consequence of its ungodly thirst for self-liberation. Vers. 15–17.
"*For thus saith the Lord Jehovah, the Holy One of Israel,
Through turning and rest ye would be helped; your strength would
show itself in quietness and confidence; but ye would not. And
ye said, No, but we will fly upon horses; therefore ye shall flee:
and, We will ride upon racehorses; therefore your pursuers will
race. A thousand, ye will flee from the threatening of one, from
the threatening of five, until ye are reduced to a remnant, like
a pine upon the top of the mountain, and like a banner upon the
hill.*" The conditions upon which their salvation depended,
and by complying with which they would attain to it, were
shūbhâh, turning from their self-chosen way, and *nachath*, rest
from self-confident work of their own (from *nūăch*, like *rachath*,
ventilabrum, from *rūăch*, and *shachath*, *fovea*, from *shūăch*).
Their strength (*i.e.* what they would be able to do in opposition
to the imperial power) would show itself (*hâyâh*, arise, come to
the light, as in ch. xxix. 2) in *hashqēt*, laying aside their busy
care and stormy eagerness, and *bitchâh*, trust, which cleaves to
Jehovah and, renouncing all self-help, leaves Him to act alone.
This was the leading and fundamental principle of the prophet's
politics even in the time of Ahaz (ch. vii. 4). But from the
very first they would not act upon it; nor would they now that
the alliance with Egypt had become an irreversible fact. To
fly upon horses, and ride away upon racehorses (*kal*, like κέλης,
celer[1]), had been and still was their proud and carnal ambition,
which Jehovah would answer by fulfilling upon them the
curses of the *thorah* (Lev. xxvi. 8, 36; Deut. xxviii. 25, xxxii.
30). One, or at the most five, of the enemy would be able
with their snorting to put to flight a whole thousand of the
men of Judah. The verb *nūs* (ver. 16), which rhymes with *sūs*,
is used first of all in its primary sense of " flying" (related to

[1] We regard the Sanscrit *kal*, to drive or hunt, the Greek κέλλ(όκέλλ)ειν,
and the Semitic *qal*, as all having the same root: cf. Curtius, *Grundzüge der
griech. Etymol.* i. 116.

nūts, cf. Ex. xiv. 27), and then in its more usual sense of
" fleeing." (Luzzatto, after Abulwalîd : *vogliamo far sui cavalli
gloriosa comparsa,* from *nūs,* or rather *nâsas,* hence *nânōs,* from
which comes *nēs, excellere.*) יָקֵלּוּ, the fut. *niphal,* signifies to be
light, *i.e.* swift ; whereas יֵקַל, the fut. *kal,* had become a common
expression for light in the sense of despised or lightly esteemed.
The horses and chariots are Judah's own (ch. ii. 7 ; Mic. v. 9),
though possibly with the additional allusion to the Egyptian
cavalry, of world-wide renown, which they had called to their
help. In ver. 17*a* the subject of the first clause is also that
of the second, and consequently we have not וּמִפְּנֵי (compare
the asyndeta in ch. xvii. 6). The insertion of *r͏ᵉbhâbhâh* (ten
thousand) after *chămisshâh* (five), which Lowth, Gesenius, and
others propose, is quite unnecessary. The play upon the words
symbolizes the divine law of retribution (*talio*), which would
be carried out with regard to them. The nation, which had
hitherto resembled a thick forest, would become like a lofty pine
(*tōren,* according to the talmudic *tūrnīthâ', Pinus pinea*), standing solitary upon the top of a mountain, and like a flagstaff
planted upon a hill—a miserable remnant in the broad land so
fearfully devastated by war. For עַד אִם followed by a preterite
(equivalent to the *fut. exactum*), compare ch. vi. 11 and Gen.
xxiv. 19.

The prophet now proceeds with וְלָכֵן, to which we cannot
give any other meaning than *et propterea,* which it has everywhere else. The thought of the prophet is the perpetually
recurring one, that Israel would have to be reduced to a small
remnant before Jehovah would cease from His wrath. Ver.
18. " *And therefore will Jehovah wait till He inclines towards
you, and therefore will He withdraw Himself on high till He has
mercy upon you; for Jehovah is a God of right, salvation to those
who wait for Him.*" In other places *lâkhēn* (therefore) deduces
the punishment from the sin ; here it infers, from the nature
of the punishment, the long continuance of the divine wrath.
Chikkâh, to wait, connected as it is here with *Lamed,* has at least
the idea, if not the actual signification, of *delay* (as in 2 Kings
ix. 3 ; compare Job xxxii. 4). This helps to determine the
sense of *yârūm,* which does not mean, He will show Himself
exalted as a judge, that through judgment He may render it
possible to have mercy upon you (which is too far-fetched a

meaning); but, He will raise Himself up, so as to be far away (cf. Num. xvi. 45, "Get you up from among this congregation;" and Ps. x. 5, *mârōm* = "far above," as far as heaven, out of his sight), that thus (after having for a long time withdrawn His gracious presence; cf. Hos. v. 6) He may bestow His mercy upon you. A dark prospect, but only alarming to unbelievers. The salvation at the remotest end of the future belongs to believers even now. This is affirmed in the word *'ashrē* (blessed), which recals Ps. ii. 12. The prophet uses *châkhâh* in a very significant double sense here, just as he did *nūs* a short time before. Jehovah is waiting for the time when He can show His favour once more, and blessed are they who meet His waiting with their own waiting.

None but such are heirs of the grace that follows the judgment—a people, newly pardoned in response to its cry for help, conducted by faithful teachers in the right way, and renouncing idolatry with disgust. Vers. 19–22. "*For a people continues dwelling in Zion, in Jerusalem; thou shalt not weep for ever: He will prove Himself gracious to thee at the sound of thy cry for help; as soon as He hears, He answers thee. And the Lord giveth you bread in penury, and water for your need; and thy teachers will not hide themselves any more, and thine eyes come to see thy teachers. And thine ears will hear words behind thee, saying, 'This is the way, walk ye in it!' whether ye turn to the right hand or to the left. And ye defile the covering of thy graven images of silver, and the clothing of thy molten images of gold; thou wilt scatter them like a filthy thing: 'Get out!' thou sayest to it.*" We do not render ver. 19*a*, "For O people that dwelleth in Zion, in Jerusalem!" For although the personal pronoun may be omitted after *Vav* in an apostrophizing connection (Prov. viii. 5; Joel ii. 23), we should certainly expect to find אַתָּה here. The accent very properly marks these words as forming an independent clause. The apparent tautology in the expression, "in Zion, in Jerusalem," is emphatic and explanatory. The fate of Zion-Jerusalem will not be the same as that of the imperial city (ch. xiii. 20, xxv. 2); for it is the city of Jehovah, which, according to His promise, cannot become an eternally deserted ruin. After this promising declaration, the prophet turns and addresses the people of the future in the people of his own time: *bâkhō* strengthens the verbal

notion with the mark of duration; *chānōn* with the mark of
certainty and fulness. יְחָנְךָ, with an advanced ŏ, as in Gen.
xliii. 29, for יְחָנְךָ. כְּ is the shortest expression used to denote
simultaneous occurrence; answering and hearing would coincide (*shom'âh, nomen actionis,* as in ch. xlvii. 9, lv. 2; Ges. § 45,
1*b*; *'ânâkh,* the pausal form here, as in Jer. xxiii. 37). From
this lowest stage of response to the penitential cry for help, the
promise rises higher and higher. The next stage is that in
which Jerusalem is brought into all the distress consequent
upon a siege, as threatened by the prophet in ch. xxix. 3, 4;
the besieged would not be allowed by God to die of starvation,
but He would send them the necessary support. The same expression, but very little altered, viz. "to give to eat *lechem lachatz
ūmayim lachatz,*" signifies to put any one upon the low rations
of a siege or of imprisonment, in 1 Kings xxii. 27 and 2 Chron.
xviii. 26; but here it is a promise, with the threat kept in the
background. צָר and לַחַץ are connected with the absolute nouns
לֶחֶם and מַיִם, not as adverbial, but as appositional definitions (like
יֵין תַּרְעֵלָה, " wine which is giddiness," in Ps. lx. 5; and מַיִם בִּרְכַּיִם,
" water which is knees," *i.e.* which has the measure of the knees,
where *birkayim* is also in apposition, and not the accusative of
measurement): literally, bread which is necessity, and water
which is affliction; that is to say, nourishment of which there is
extreme need, the very opposite of bread and water in abundance.
Umbreit and Drechsler understand this spiritually. But the
promise rises as it goes on. There is already an advance, in
the fact that the faithful and well-meaning teachers (*mōrīm*)
no longer keep themselves hidden because of the hard-hearted-
ness and hatred of the people, as they have done ever since
the time of Ahaz (נִכְנַף, a denom. : to withdraw into כָּנָף,
πτέρυξ, the utmost end, the most secret corner; though *kânaph*
in itself signifies to cover or conceal). Israel, when penitent,
would once more be able to rejoice in the sight of those whom
it longed to have back again. מוֹרֶיךָ is a plural, according to
the context (on the singular of the previous predicate, see Ges.
§ 147). As the shepherds of the flock, they would follow the
people with friendly words of admonition, whilst the people
would have their ears open to receive their instruction. תַּאֲמִינוּ
is here equivalent to תֵּימִינוּ, תַּיְמִינוּ. The abominations of idolatry (which continued even in the first years of Hezekiah's

reign: ch. xxxi. 7; Mic. i. 5, v. 11–13, vi. 16) would now be
regaided as abominations, and put away.   Even gold and
silver, with which the images that were either carved or cast
in inferior metal were overlaid, would be made unclean (see
2 Kings xxiii. 8 sqq.); that is to say, no use would be made of
them.   *Dâvâh* is a shorter expression for *kᵉlī dâvâh*, the cloth
worn by a woman at the monthly period.   On *zârâh*, to dispense—to which *dâvâh* would be inappropriate if understood
of the woman herself, as it is by Luzzatto—compare 2 Kings
xxiii. 6.   With זָהָבֶךָ, the plural used in the general address
passes over into the individualizing singular; לֹו is to be taken
as a neuter pointing back to the plunder of idols.

The promise, after setting forth this act of penitence, rises
higher and higher; it would not stop at bread in time of need.
Vers. 23–25. "*And He gives rain to thy seed, with which thou
sowest the land; and bread of the produce of the land, and it is
full of sap and fat: in that day your flocks will feed in roomy
pastures.   And the oxen and the young asses, which work the
land, salted mash will they eat, which is winnowed with the
winnowing shovel and winnowing fork!   And upon every high
mountain, and every hill that rises high, there are springs, brooks
in the day of the great massacre, when the towers fall.*"   The
blessing which the prophet depicts is the reverse of the day of
judgment, and stands in the foreground when the judgment is
past.   The expression "in that day" fixes, as it were, the evening of the day of judgment, which is followed by the depicted
morning of blessing.   But the great mass of the Jewish nation
would be first of all murdered in war; the towers must fall,
i.e. (though without any figure, and merely as an exemplifying
expression) all the bulwarks of self-confidence, self-help, and
pride (ch. ii. 15; Mic. v. 9, 10).   In the place of the self-
induced calamities of war, there would now come the God-
given rich blessings of peace; and in the place of the proud
towers, there would come fruitful heights abounding with
water.   The field would be cultivated again, and produce
luxuriant crops of nutritious corn; so that not only the labour
of man, but that of the animals also, would receive a rich reward.   "Rain to thy seed:" this is the early rain commencing
about the middle of October.   אֲשֶׁר is an accusative, זָרַע being
construed with a double accusative, as in Deut. xxii. 9.   מִקְנֶיךָ

might be the singular, so far as the form is concerned (see
i. 30, v. 12, xxii. 11) ; but, according to Ex. xvii. 3, it must
be taken as a plural, like מוֹרִיד. The *ălāphīm* are the oxen
used in ploughing and threshing; the *'ăyārīm*, the asses used
for carrying manure, soil, the sheaves, or the grain. *Bᵉlīl
châmīts* is a mash (composed of oats, barley, and vetches, or
things of that kind) made more savoury with salt and sour
vegetables;[1] that is to say, a *farrago* (from *bâlal*, to mix; *Job*,
vol. ii. p. 362). According to Wetzstein, it is ripe barley (un-
threshed during the harvest and threshing time, and the grain
itself for the rest of the year) mixed with salt or salt vegetables. In any case, *bᵉlīl* is to be understood as referring to
the grain; this is evident from the relative clause, " which has
been winnowed" (= *mᵉzōreh*, Ewald, § 169, *d*), or perhaps more
correctly, "which he (one) winnows" (*part. kal*), the participle standing for the third person, with the subject contained
within itself (Ewald, § 200), *i.e.* not what was generally given
from economy, viz. barley, etc., mixed with chopped straw (*tibn*),
but pure grain (*habb mahd*, as they say at the present day).
Rachath is a winnowing shovel, which is still used, according to
Wetzstein, in *Merj*, *Gedur*, and *Hauran*; *mizreh*, on the other
hand, is the winnowing fork with six prongs. Dainty food,
such as was only given occasionally to the cattle, as something
especially strengthening, would then be their regular food, and
would be prepared in the most careful manner. " Who cannot
see," exclaims Vitringa, " that this is to be taken spiritually ? "
He appeals to what Paul says in 1 Cor. ix. 9, viz. that God
does not trouble Himself about oxen. But Paul did not mean
this in the same sense as Aristotle, who maintained that the
minima were entirely excluded from the providence of God.
What the Scriptures say concerning cattle, they do not say for
the sake of the cattle, but for the sake of men; though it does
not follow that the cattle are to be understood figuratively, as
representing men. And this is the case here. What the prophet paints in this idyllic style, in colours furnished by the
existing customs,[2] is not indeed intended to be understood in
the letter; and yet it is to be taken literally. In the age of

---

[1] Such as *Salsola kali, Salsola tragus, Salsola soda*, and other plants of
the family of the chenopodiaceæ.

[2] Asses particularly, even those of a guest, are generally very much

glory, even on this side of eternity, a gigantic stride will be taken forward towards the glorification of universal nature, and towards the end of all those sighs which are so discernible now, more especially among domestic animals. The prophecy is therefore to be interpreted according to Rom. viii. 19 sqq.; from which we may clearly see that God does trouble Himself about the sighing of an ox or ass that is overburdened with severe toil, and sometimes left to starve.

The promise now rises higher and higher, and passes from earth to heaven. Ver. 26. "*And the light of the moon will be as the light of the sun, and the light of the sun will be multiplied sevenfold, like the light of seven days, in the day that Jehovah bindeth the hurt of His people, and healeth the crushing of His stroke.*" Modern commentators from Lowth downwards for the most part pronounce כְּאוֹר שִׁבְעַת הַיָּמִים a gloss; and there is one external evidence in favour of this, which is wanting in the case of the other supposed glosses in Isaiah, namely, that the words are omitted by the LXX. (though not by the Targum, the Syriac, or Jerome). Even Luther (although he notices these words in his exposition and sermons) merely renders them, *der Sonnen schein wird siebenmal heller sein denn jtzt* (the sunlight will be seven times as bright as it is now). But the internal evidence does not favour their spuriousness even in the case before us; for the fact that the regularity of the verse, as consisting of four members, is thereby disturbed, is no evidence at all, since the verse could be arranged in a pentastic quite as well as in a tetrastic form. We therefore decide in this instance also in favour of the conclusion that the prophet composed the gloss himself. But we cannot maintain, with Umbreit, that the addition was necessary, in order to guard against the idea that there would be seven suns shining in the sky; for the prophet does not predict a multiplication of the sun by seven, but simply the multiplication of its light. The seven days are the length of an ordinary week. Drechsler gives it correctly: " The radiated light, which is sufficient to produce the daylight for a whole week according to the existing order of things, will then be concentrated into a single day." Luther renders it in

neglected. The host throws them a little grass, and then hangs up the fodder-sack full of chopped straw ; and it is a sign of extraordinary hospitality if corn is given to the asses as well as to the horses.—WETZSTEIN.

this way, *als wenn sieben tag ynn eynander geschlossen weren* (as if seven days were enclosed in one another). This also is not meant figuratively, any more than Paul means it figuratively, when he says, that with the manifestation of the " glory" of the children of God, the " corruption" of universal nature will come to an end. Nevertheless, it is not of the new heaven that the prophet is speaking, but of the glorification of nature, which is promised by both the Old Testament prophecy and by that of the New at the closing period of the world's history, and which will be the closing typical self-annunciation of that eternal glory in which everything will be swallowed up. The brightest, sunniest days then alternate, as the prophet foretells, with the most brilliant moonlight nights. No other miracles will be needed for this than that wonder-working power of God, which even now produces those changes of weather, the laws of which no researches of natural science have enabled us to calculate, and which will then give the greatest brilliancy and most unchangeable duration to what is now comparatively rare,—namely, a perfectly unclouded sky, with sun or moon shining in all its brilliancy, yet without any scorching from the one, or injurious effects from the other. Heaven and earth will then put on their sabbath dress; for it will be the Sabbath of the world's history, the seventh day in the world's week. The light of the seven days of the world's week will be all concentrated in the seventh. For the beginning of creation was light, and its close will be light as well. The darkness all comes between, simply that it may be overcome. At last will come a *bōqer* (morning), after which it will no more be said, "And evening was, and morning was." The prophet is speaking of the last type of this morning. What he predicts here precedes what he predicted in ch. xxiv. 23, just as the date of its composition precedes that of ch. xxiv.–xxvii.; for there the imperial city was Babylon, whereas here the glory of the latter day is still placed immediately after the fall of Assyria.

Vers. 27, 28. " *Behold, the name of Jehovah cometh from far, burning His wrath, and quantity of smoke: His lips are full of wrathful foam, and His tongue like devouring fire. And His breath is like an overflowing brook, which reaches half-way to the neck, to sift nations in the sieve of nothingness; and a misleading*

bridle comes to the cheeks of the nations." Two figures are here
melted together,—namely, that of a storm coming up from the
farthest horizon, which turns the sky into a sea of fire, and
kindles whatever it strikes, so that there rises up a heavy
burden, or thick mass of smoke (*kōbhed massâ'âh*, like *mas'ēth* in
Judg. xx. 40, cf. 38; on this attributive combination, burning
His wrath (Ewald, § 288, *c*) and a quantity, etc., see ch. xiii.
9); and that of a man burning with wrath, whose lips foam,
whose tongue moves to and fro like a flame, and whose breath
is a snorting that threatens destruction, which when it issues
from Jehovah swells into a stream, which so far covers a
man that only his neck appears as the visible half. We had
the same figure in ch. viii. 8, where Asshur, as it came upon
Judah, was compared to such an almost overwhelming and
drowning flood. Here, again, it refers to Judah, which the
wrath of Jehovah had almost though not entirely destroyed.
For the ultimate object of the advancing name of Jehovah
(*shēm*, name, relating to His judicial coming) is to sift nations,
etc.: *lahănâphâh* for *l'hânīph* (like *lahăzâdâh* in Dan. v. 20),
to make it more like *nâphâh* in sound. The *sieve of nothingness*
is a sieve in which everything, that does not remain in it as
good corn, is given up to annihilation; שָׁוְא is want of being,
i.e. of life from God, and denotes the fate that properly belongs
to such worthlessness. In the case of *v'resen* (and a bridle,
etc.) we must either supply in thought לָשִׂים (שָׂם), or, what is
better, take it as a substantive clause: " a misleading bridle" (or
a bridle of misleading, as Böttcher renders it, *math'eh* being
the form *mashqeh*) holds the cheeks of the nations. The nations
are regarded as wild horses, which could not be tamed, but
which were now so firmly bound and controlled by the wrath
of God, that they were driven down into the abyss.

This is the issue of the judgment which begins at the house
of God, then turns against the instrument employed, namely
the heathen, and becomes to the Israel that survives a counterpart of the deliverance from Egypt. Ver. 29. " *Your song
will then sound as in the night, when the feast is celebrated; and
ye will have joy of heart like those who march with the playing
of flutes, to go up to the mountain of Jehovah, to the Rock of
Israel.*" In the word *châg* (feast), which is generally used with
special reference to the feast of tabernacles, there is here an

unmistakeable allusion to the passover, as we may see from the introduction of "the night," which evidently means the night before the passover (*lēl shimmurīm*, Ex. xii. 42), which was so far a festal night, that it preceded and introduced the feast of unleavened bread. The prophet has taken his figure from the first passover-night in Egypt, when Israel was rejoicing in the deliverance which it was just about to receive, whilst the destroying angel was passing through the land. Such would be the song which they would be able to sing, when Jehovah poured out His judgment upon His people's enemies outside. The church is shut up in its chamber (ch. xxvi. 20), and its joy resembles the heartfelt joy of those who go on pilgrimage on one of the three great feasts, or in the procession that carries up the first-fruits to Jerusalem (*Biccurim*, iii. 3), going up with the sound of flutes to the mountain of Jehovah, to appear before Him, the Rock of Israel.

Israel is marching in such a joyful way to a sacred and glorious height, whilst outside Jehovah is sweeping the world-power entirely away, and that without any help from Israel. Vers. 30–33. "*And Jehovah causes His majestic voice to be heard, and causes the lowering of His arm to be seen, with the snorting of wrath and the blazing of devouring fire, the bursting of a cloud, and pouring of rain and hailstones. For Asshur will be terrified at the voice of Jehovah, when He smites with the staff. And it will come to pass, every stroke of the rod of destiny, which Jehovah causes to fall upon Asshur, is dealt amidst the noise of drums and the playing of guitars; and in battles of swinging arm He fights it. For a place for the sacrifice of abominations has long been made ready, even for the king is it prepared; deep, broad has He made it: its funeral-pile has fire and wood in abundance; the breath of Jehovah like a stream of brimstone sets it on fire.*" The imposing crash (on *hōd*, see Job xxxix. 20) of the cry which Jehovah causes to be heard is thunder (see Ps. xxix.); for the catastrophe occurs with a discharge of all the destructive forces of a storm (see ch. xxix. 6). *Nephets* is the "breaking up" or "bursting," viz. of a cloud. It is through such wrath-announcing phenomena of nature that Jehovah manifests the otherwise invisible letting down of His arm to smite (*nachath* may possibly not be the derivative of *nūăch*, " a settling down," but of *nâchath*, " the coming down,"

as in Ps. xxxviii. 3 ; just as *shebheth* in 2 Sam. xxiii. 7 is not
derived from *shūbh*, but from *shābhath*, to go to ruin). Ver. 31,
commencing with *ki* (for), explains the terrible nature of what
occurs, from the object at which it is directed : Asshur is
alarmed at the voice of Jehovah, and thoroughly goes to pieces.
We must not render this, as the Targum does, "which smites
with the rod," *i.e.* which bears itself so haughtily, so tyrannically (after ch. **x.** 24). The smiter here is Jehovah (**LXX.,**
Vulg., Luther) ; and *basshēbhet yakkeh* is either an attributive
clause, or, better still, a circumstantial determining clause, *eo
virga percutiente.* According to the accents, *vᵉhāyāh* in ver. 32
is introductory : " And it will come to pass, every stroke of the
punishing rod falls (supply יִהְיֶה) with an accompaniment of
drums and guitars" (the *Beth* is used to denote instrumental
accompaniment, as in ver. 29, ch. xxiv. 9, Ps. xlix. 5, etc.),—
namely, on the part of the people of Jerusalem, who have
only to look on and rejoice in the approaching deliverance.
Mūsâdâh with *mattēh* is a verbal substantive used as a genitive,
" an appointment according to decree" (comp. *yâsad* in Hab.
i. 12, and *yâʿad* in Mic. vi. 9). The fact that drums and
guitars are heard along with every stroke, is explained in
ver. 32*b* : " Jehovah fights against Asshur with battles of
swinging," *i.e.* not with darts or any other kind of weapon, but
by swinging His arm incessantly, to smite Asshur without its
being able to defend itself (cf. ch. xix. 16). Instead of בָּהּ,
which points back to *Asshur*, not to *matteh*, the *keri* has בָּם,
which is not so harsh, since it is immediately preceded by עָלָיו.
This cutting down of the Assyrians is accounted for in
ver. 33, (*ki*, for), from the fact that it had long ago been
decreed that they should be burned as dead bodies. '*Ethmūl* in
contrast with *mâchâr* is the past : it has not happened to-day,
but yesterday, *i.e.*, as the predestination of God is referred to,
" long ago." *Tophteh* is the primary form of *tōpheth* (from
tūph, not in the sense of the Neo-Persian *tâften*, Zend. *tap*, to
kindle or burn, from which comes *tafedra*, melting ; but in the
Semitic sense of vomiting or abhorring : see at Job xvii. 6),
the name of the abominable place where the sacrifices were
offered to Moloch in the valley of Hinnom: a Tophet-like place.
The word is variously treated as both a masculine and feminine,
possibly because the place of abominable sacrifices is described

first as *bâmâh* in Jer. vii. 31. In the clause גַּם־הוּא לַמֶּלֶךְ הוּכָן, the *gam*, which stands at the head, may be connected with *lammelekh*, " also for the king is it prepared" (see at Job ii. 10); but in all probability *lammelekh* is a play upon *lammolekh* (*e.g.* Lev. xviii. 2), " even this has been prepared for the Melekh," viz. the king of Asshur. Because he was to be burned there, together with his army, Jehovah had made this Tophet-like place very deep, so that it might have a far-reaching background, and very broad, so that in this respect also there might be room for many sacrifices. And their *m^edûrâh*, *i.e.* their pile of wood (as in Ezek. xxiv. 9, cf. 5, from *dûr*, Talm. *dayyēr*, to lay round, to arrange, pile), has abundance of fire and wood (a *hendiadys*, like " cloud and smoke" in ch. iv. 5). Abundance of fire: for the breath of Jehovah, pouring upon the funeral pile like a stream of brimstone, sets it on fire. בְּעַר בְּ, not to burn up, but to set on fire. בָּהּ points back to *tophteh*, like the suffix of *m^edurâthâh*.[1]

THE FOURTH WOE.—THE FALSE HELP; THE DESPISED ONE PITIED; AND THE NEW ERA.—CHAP. XXXI.–XXXII. 1-8.

There is nothing to surprise us in the fact, that the prophet returns again and again to the alliance with Egypt. After his warning had failed to prevent it, he wrestled with it in spirit, set before himself afresh the curse which would be its certain fruit, brought out and unfolded the consolation of believers that lay hidden in the curse, and did not rest till the cursed fruit, that had become a real thing, had been swallowed up by the promise, which was equally real. The situation of this fourth woe is just the same as that of the previous one. The alliance with Egypt is still in progress. Vers. 1–3. " *Woe to*

---

[1] So far as the form of the text is concerned, *kōl* has the disjunctive *yethib* before *pashta*, which occurs eleven times according to the Masora. Nevertheless the word is logically connected in the closest manner with what follows (comp. '*ēth tōrath* in ch. v. 24). The *âh* of *mûsâdâh* is *rafatum pro mappicato*, according to the Masora; in which case the suffix would refer to Asshur. In the place of נֵס הוּא we also meet with גֵּס הִיא, with this *chethib* and *keri* reversed; but the former, according to which הוּכָן is equivalent to הוּכָנָה, has many examples to support it in the Masora. הוּכָן has *kametz* in correct MSS. in half pause; whereas Kimchi (*Michlol*, 117*b*) regards it as a participle.

them that go down to Egypt for help, and rely upon horses, and put their trust in chariots, that there are many of them; and in horsemen, that there is a powerful multitude of them; and do not look up to the Holy One of Israel, and do not inquire for Jehovah! And yet He also is wise; thus then He brings evil, and sets not His words aside; and rises up against the house of miscreants, and against the help of evil-doers. And Egypt is man, and not God; and its horses flesh, and not spirit. And when Jehovah stretches out His hand, the helper stumbles, and he that is helped falls, and they all perish together." The expression " them that go down" (*hayyōrᵉdīm*) does not imply that the going down was taking place just then for the first time. It is the participle of qualification, just as God is called הַבֹּרֵא. לְעֶזְרָה with *Lamed* of the object, as in ch. xx. 6. The horses, chariots, and horsemen here, are those of Egypt, which Diodorus calls ἱππάσιμος, on account of its soil being so suitable for cavalry (see Lepsius in Herzog's *Cyclopædia*). The participle is combined in the finite verb. Instead of וְעַל־סוּסִים, we also find the reading preferred by Norzi, of עַל without *Vav*, as in ch. v. 11 (cf. 23). The perfects, לֹא שָׁעוּ and לֹא דָרָשׁוּ, are used without any definite time, to denote that which was always wanting in them. The circumstantial clause, " whilst He is assuredly also wise," *i.e.* will bear comparison with their wisdom and that of Egypt, is a touching μείωσις. It was not necessary to think very highly of Jehovah, in order to perceive the reprehensible and destructive character of their apostasy from Him. The fut. consec. וַיָּבֵא is used to indicate the inevitable consequence of their despising Him who is also wise. He will not set aside His threatening words, but carry them out. The house of miscreants is Judah (ch. i. 4) ; and the help (*abstr. pro concr.*, just as Jehovah is frequently called " my help," *'ezrāthī*, by the Psalmist) of evil-doers is Egypt, whose help has been sought by Judah. The latter is "man" (*'ādām*), and its horses "flesh" (*bāsār*) ; whereas Jehovah is God (*El*) and spirit (*rūăch ; see Psychol.* p. 85). Hofmann expounds it correctly : " As *rūăch* has life in itself, it is opposed to the *bāsār*, which is only rendered living through the *rūăch ;* and so *El* is opposed to the corporeal *'ādām*, who needs the spirit in order to live at all." Thus have they preferred the help of the impotent and conditioned, to the help of the almighty and all-conditioning One.

Jehovah, who is God and spirit, only requires to stretch out His hand (an anthropomorphism, by the side of which we find the rule for interpreting it); and the helpers, and those who are helped (*i.e.* according to the terms of the treaty, though not in reality), that is to say, both the source of the help and the object of help, are all cast into one heap together.

And things of this kind would occur. Ver. 4. "*For thus hath Jehovah spoken to me, As the lion growls, and the young lion over its prey, against which a whole crowd of shepherds is called together; he is not alarmed at their cry, and does not surrender at their noise; so will Jehovah of hosts descend to the campaign against the mountain of Zion, and against their hill.*" There is no other passage in the book of Isaiah which sounds so Homeric as this (*vid. Il.* xviii. 161, 162, xii. 299 sqq.). It has been misunderstood by Knobel, Umbreit, Drechsler, and others, who suppose לִצְבֹּא עַל to refer to Jehovah's purpose to fight for Jerusalem: Jehovah, who would no more allow His city to be taken from Him, than a lion would give up a lamb that it had taken as its prey. But how could Jerusalem be compared to a lamb which a lion holds in its claws as *tereph?* (ch. v. 29.) We may see, even from ch. xxix. 7, what construction is meant to be put upon צָבָא עַל. Those sinners and their protectors would first of all perish; for like a fierce indomitable lion would Jehovah advance against Jerusalem, and take it as His prey, without suffering Himself to be thwarted by the Judæans and Egyptians, who set themselves in opposition to His army (the Assyrians). The mountain of Zion was the citadel and temple; the hill of Zion the city of Jerusalem (ch. x. 32). They would both be given up to the judgment of Jehovah, without any possibility of escape. The commentators have been misled by the fact, that a simile of a promising character follows immediately afterwards, without anything to connect the one with the other. But this abrupt μετάβασις was intended as a surprise, and was a true picture of the actual fulfilment of the prophecy; for in the moment of the greatest distress, when the actual existence of Jerusalem was in question (cf. ch. x. 33, 34), the fate of Ariel took suddenly and miraculously a totally different turn (ch. xxix. 2). In this sense, a pleasant picture is placed side by side with the terrible one (compare Mic. v. 6, 7).

Jehovah suddenly arrests the work of punishment, and the love which the wrath enfolds within itself begins to appear. Ver. 5. "*Like fluttering birds, so will Jehovah of Hosts screen Jerusalem; screening and delivering, sparing and setting free.*" The prophet uses the plural, " like fluttering birds," with an object—namely, not so much to represent Jehovah Himself, as the tender care and, as it were, *maternal* love, into which His leonine fierceness would be changed. This is indicated by the fact, that he attaches the feminine ʿ*áphōth* to the common gender *tsippŏrīm*. The word *pâsōăch* recals to mind the deliverance from Egypt (as in ch. xxx. 29) in a very significant manner. The sparing of the Israelites by the destroyer passing over their doors, from which the passover derived its name, would be repeated once more. We may see from this, that in and along with Assyria, Jehovah Himself, whose instrument of punishment Assyria was, would take the field against Jerusalem (ch. xxix. 2, 3); but His attitude towards Jerusalem is suddenly changed into one resembling the action of birds, as they soar round and above their threatened nests. On the inf. abs. *kal* (*gânōn*) after the *hiphil*, see Ewald, § 312, *b*; and on the continuance of the inf. abs. in the finite verb, § 350, *a*. This generally takes place through the future, but here through the preterite, as in Jer. xxiii. 14, Gen. xxvi. 13, and 1 Sam. ii. 26 (if indeed *vᵉgâdēl* is the third pers. preterite there).

On the ground of this half terrible, half comforting picture of the future, the call to repentance is now addressed to the people of the prophet's own time. Ver. 6. "*Then turn, O sons of Israel, to Him from whom men have so deeply departed.*" Strictly speaking, " to Him with regard to whom (אֲשֶׁר) ye are deeply fallen away" (*heʿĕmīq*, as in Hos. ix. 9, and *sârâh*, that which is alienated, alienation, as in ch. i. 5); the transition to the third person is like the reverse in ch. i. 29. This call to repentance the prophet strengthens by two powerful motives drawn from the future.

The first is, that idolatry would one day be recognised in all its abomination, and put away. Ver. 7. "*For in that day they will abhor every one their silver idols and their gold idols, which your hands have made you for a sin,*" *i.e.* to commit sin and repent, with the preponderance of the latter idea, as in Hos. viii. 11*b* (compare 1 Kings xiii. 34). חֵטְא, a second accusative

to עָשָׂה, indicating the result.   The prospect is the same as that
held out in ch. xxx. 22, xxvii. 9, xvii. 8, ii. 20.

The second motive is, that Israel will not be rescued by
men, but by Jehovah alone; so that even He from whom they
have now so deeply fallen will prove Himself the only true
ground of confidence.   Vers. 8, 9.   "*And Asshur falls by a
sword not of a man, and a sword not of a man will devour him;
and he flees before a sword, and his young men become tributary.
And his rock, for fear will it pass away, and his princes be
frightened away by the flags: the saying of Jehovah, who has His
fire in Zion, and His furnace in Jerusalem.*"   The LXX, and
Jerome render this falsely φεύξεται οὐκ (לֹא) ἀπὸ προσώπου
μαχαίρας.   לֹו is an ethical dative, and the prophet intentionally
writes "before a sword" without any article, to suggest the
idea of the unbounded, infinite, awful (cf. ch. xxviii. 2, *b°yâd;
Psalter*, vol. i. p. 15).   A sword is drawn without any human
intervention, and before this Asshur falls, or at least so many of
the Assyrians as are unable to save themselves by flight.   The
power of Asshur is for ever broken; even its young men will
henceforth become tributary, or perform feudal service.   By
"his rock" most commentators understand the rock upon which
the fugitive would gladly have taken refuge, but did not dare
(Rosenmüller, Gesenius, Knobel, etc.); others, again, the military force of Asshur, as its supposed invincible refuge (Saad.,
etc.); others, the apparently indestructible might of Asshur
generally (Vulgate, Rashi, Hitzig).   But the presence of "his
princes" in the parallel clause makes it most natural to refer
"his rock" to the king; and this reference is established with
certainty by what ch. xxxii. 2 affirms of the king and princes of
Judah.   Luther also renders it thus: *und jr Fels wird fur furcht
wegzihen* (and their rock will withdraw for fear).   Sennacherib
really did hurry back to Assyria after the catastrophe in a
most rapid flight.   *Minnēs* are the standards of Asshur, which
the commanders of the army fly away from in terror, without
attempting to rally those that were scattered.   Thus speaks
Jehovah, and this is what He decrees who has His *'ūr* and
tannūr in Jerusalem.   We cannot suppose that the allusion
here is to the fire and hearth of the sacrifices; for *tannūr* does
not mean a hearth, but a furnace (from *nūr*, to burn).   The
reference is to the light of the divine presence, which was out-

wardly a devouring fire for the enemies of Jerusalem, an unapproachable red-hot furnace (*ignis et caminus qui devorat pecca-
tores et ligna, fœnum stipulamque consumit :* Jerome).

For Judah, sifted, delivered, and purified, there now begins
a new era. Righteous government, as a blessing for the people,
is the first beneficent fruit. Ch. xxxii. 1, 2. "*Behold, the king
will reign according to righteousness ; and the princes, according
to right will they command. And every one will be like a shelter
from the wind, and a covert from the storm; like water-brooks in
a dry place, like the shadow of a gigantic rock in a languishing
land.*" The kingdom of Asshur is for ever destroyed ; but the
kingdom of Judah rises out of the state of confusion into
which it has fallen through its God-forgetting policy and disregard of justice. King and princes now rule according to the
standards that have been divinely appointed and revealed. The
Lamed in *ŭl°sârîm* (and the princes) is that of reference (*quod
attinet ad*, as in Ps. xvi. 3 and Eccles. ix. 4), the exponent
of the usual *casus abs.* (Ges. § 146, 2) ; and the two other
Lameds are equivalent to κατά, *secundum* (as in Jer. xxx. 11).
The figures in ver. 2 are the same as in ch. xxv. 4. The rock
of Asshur (*i.e.* Sennacherib) has departed, and the princes of
Asshur have deserted their standards, merely to save themselves. The king and princes of Judah are now the defence
of their nation, and overshadow it like colossal walls of rock.
This is the first fruit of the blessing.

The second is an opened understanding, following upon
the ban of hardening. Vers. 3, 4. "*And the eyes of the
seeing no more are closed, and the ears of the hearing attend.
And the heart of the hurried understands to know, and the
tongue of stammerers speaks clear things with readiness.*" It
is not physical miracles that are predicted here, but a spiritual change. The present judgment of hardening will be
repealed : this is what ver. 3 affirms. The spiritual defects,
from which many suffer who do not belong to the worst, will
be healed : this is the statement in ver. 4. The form תִּשְׁעֶינָה
is not the future of שָׁעָה here, as in ch. xxxi. 1, xxii. 4,
xvii. 7, 8 (in the sense of, they will no longer stare about
restlessly and without aim), but of שָׁעָה = עָשַׁע, a metaplastic
future of the latter, in the sense of, to be smeared over or
closed (see ch. xxix. 9, vi. 10 ; cf. *tach* in ch. xliv. 18).

On *qâshabh* (the *kal* of which is only met with here), see at ch. xxi. 7. The times succeeding the hardening, of which Isaiah is speaking here, are "the last times," as ch. vi. clearly shows; though it does not therefore follow that the king mentioned in ver. 1 (as in ch. xi. 1 sqq.) is the Messiah Himself. In ver. 1 the prophet merely affirms, that Israel as a national commonwealth will then be governed in a manner well pleasing to God; here he predicts that Israel as a national congregation will be delivered from the judgment of not seeing with seeing eyes, and not hearing with hearing ears, and that it will be delivered from defects of weakness also. The *nimhârim* are those that fall headlong, the precipitate, hurrying, or rash; and the עִלְּגִים, stammerers, are not scoffers (ch. xxviii. 7 sqq., xxix. 20), as Knobel and Drechsler maintain, but such as are unable to think and speak with distinctness and certainty, more especially concerning the exalted things of God. The former would now have the gifts of discernment (*yâbhîn*), to perceive things in their true nature, and to distinguish under all circumstances that which is truly profitable (*lâda'ath*); the latter would be able to express themselves suitably, with refinement, clearness, and worthiness. *Tsachôth* (old ed. *tsâchôth*) signifies that which is light, transparent; not merely intelligible, but refined and elegant. תְּמַהֵר gives the adverbial idea to *l'dabbēr* (Ewald, § 285, *a*).

A third fruit of the blessing is the naming and treating of every one according to his true character. Vers. 5-8. "*The fool will no more be called a nobleman, nor the crafty a gentleman. For a fool speaks follies, and his heart does godless things, to practise tricks and to speak error against Jehovah, to leave the soul of hungry men empty, and to withhold the drink of thirsty ones. And the craft of a crafty man is evil, who devises stratagems to destroy suffering ones by lying words, even when the needy exhibits his right. But a noble man devises noble things, and to noble things he adheres.*" Nobility of birth and wealth will give place to nobility of character, so that the former will not exist or not be recognised without the latter. *Nâdîbh* is properly one who is noble in character, and then, dropping the ethical meaning, one who is noble by rank. The meaning of the word *generosus* follows the same course in the opposite direction. *Shôa'* is the man who is raised to eminence by the possession of property; the gentle-

man, as in Job xxxiv. 19. The prophet explains for himself in
what sense he uses the words *nâbhâl* and *kīlai*. We see from his
explanation that *kīlai* neither signifies the covetous, from *kūl*
(Saad.), nor the spendthrift, from *killâh* (Hitzig). Jerome
gives the correct rendering, viz. *fraudulentus;* and Rashi and
Kimchi very properly regard it as a contraction of *n^ekhīlai*. It
is an adjective form derived from בְּיל = נְבִיל, like נָשִׂיא = שִׂיא (Job
xx. 6). The form בְּלַי in ver. 1 is used interchangeably with
this, merely for the sake of the resemblance in sound to כֵּלָיו
(*machinatoris machinæ pravæ*). In ver. 6, commencing with *ki*
(for), the fact that the *nâbhâl* (fool) and *kīlai* (crafty man) will
lose their titles of honour, is explained on the simple ground
that such men are utterly unworthy of them. *Nâbhâl* is a scoffer
at religion, who thinks himself an enlightened man, and yet at
the same time has the basest heart, and is a worthless egotist.
The infinitives with *Lamed* show in what the immorality (*'âven*)
consists, with which his heart is so actively employed. In ver.
6, *ūbh^edabbēr* (" and if he speak") is equivalent to, " even in the
event of a needy man saying what is right and well founded:"
Vâv = et in the sense of *etiam* (cf. 2 Sam. i. 23; Ps. xxxi. 12;
Hos. viii. 6; Eccles. v. 6); according to Knobel, it is equivalent
to *et quidem*, as in Eccles. viii. 2, Amos iii. 11, iv. 10; whereas
Ewald regards it as *Vav conj.* (§ 283, *d*), "and by going to law
with the needy," but אֶת־אֶבְיֹן would be the construction in this
case (*vid.* 2 Kings xxv. 6). According to ver. 8, not only does
the noble man devise what is noble, but as such (הוּא) he adheres
to it. We might also adopt this explanation, " It is not upon
gold or upon chance that he rises;" but according to the Arabic
equivalents, *qūm* signifies *persistere* here.

AGAINST THE WOMEN OF JERUSALEM.—CHAP. XXXII. 9-20.

APPENDIX TO THE FOURTH WOE.

This short address, although rounded off well, is something
more than a fragment complete in itself, like the short para-
bolic piece in ch. xxviii. 23–29, which commences in a similar
manner. It is the last part of the fourth woe, just as that was
the last part of the first. It is a side piece to the threatening
prophecy of the time of Uzziah-Jotham (ch. iii. 16 sqq.), and
chastises the frivolous self-security of the women of Jerusalem,

just as the former chastises their vain and luxurious love of finery. The prophet has now uttered many a woe upon Jerusalem, which is bringing itself to the verge of destruction; but notwithstanding the fact that women are by nature more delicate, and more easily affected and alarmed, than men, he has made no impression upon the women of Jerusalem, to whom he now foretells a terrible undeceiving of their carnal ease, whilst he holds out before them the ease secured by God, which can only be realized on the ruins of the former. The first part of the address proclaims the annihilation of their false ease. Vers. 9–14. " *Ye contented women, rise up, hear my voice; ye confident daughters, hearken to my speech! Days to the year: then will ye tremble, confident ones! for it is all over with the vintage, the fruit harvest comes to nought. Tremble, contented ones! Quake, ye confident ones! Strip, make yourselves bare, and gird your loins with sackcloth! They smite upon their breasts for the pleasant fields, for the fruitful vine. On the land of my people there come up weeds, briers; yea, upon all joyous houses of the rejoicing city. For the palace is made solitary; the crowd of the city is left desolate; the ofel and watch-tower serve as caves for ever, for the delight of wild asses, for the tending of flocks.*" The summons is the same as in Gen. iv. 23 and Jer. ix. 19 (comp. ch. xxviii. 23); the attributes the same as in Amos vi. 1 (cf. ch. iv. 1, where Isaiah apostrophizes the women of Samaria). שַׁאֲנַנּוֹת, lively, of good cheer; and בֹּטְחוֹת, trusting, namely to nothing. They are to rise up (*qōmnāh*), because the word of God must be heard standing (Judg. iii. 20). The definition of the time " days for a year" (*yāmīm 'al-shānāh*) appears to indicate the length of time that the desolation would last, as the word *tirgaznāh* is without any *Vav apod.* (cf. ch. lxv. 24, Job i. 16–18); but ch. xxix. 1 shows us differently, and the *Vav* is omitted, just as it is, for example, in Dan. iv. 28. *Shānāh* is the current year. In an undefined number of days, at the most a year from the present time (which is sometimes the meaning of *yāmīm*), the trembling would begin, and there would be neither grapes nor fruit to gather. Hence the spring harvest of corn is supposed to be over when the devastation begins. יָמִים is an *acc. temporis;* it stands here (as in ch. xxvii. 6, for example; *vid.* Ewald, § 293, 1) to indicate the starting point, not the period of duration. The *milel*-forms חֲגֹרָה, עֹרָה, פְּשֹׁטָה,

are explained by Ewald, Drechsler, and Luzzatto, as *plur. fem.*
imper. with the *Nun* of the termination *nâh* dropped,—an elision
that is certainly never heard of. Others regard it as *inf.* with
He femin. (Credner, *Joel*, p. 141) ; but קְטֹלָה for the infinitive
קְטְלָה is unexampled ; and equally unexampled would be the
inf. with *He* indicating the summons, as suggested by Böttcher,
"to the shaking!" "to the stripping!" They are *sing. masc.*
imper., such as occur elsewhere apart from the pause, *e.g.* מְלוּכָה
(for which the *keri* has מָלְכָה) in Judg. ix. 8 ; and the singular
in the place of the plural is the strongest form of command.
The masculine instead of the feminine appears already in חִרְדוּ,
which is used in the place of חֲרַדְנָה. The prophet then proceeds in the singular number, comprehending the women as a
mass, and using the most massive expression. The *He* introduced into the summons required that the feminine forms, רְגְזִי,
etc., should be given up. עֹרָה, from עָרָר, to be naked, to strip
one's self. חֲגֹרָה absolute, as in Joel i. 13 (cf. ch. iii. 24), signifies to gird one's self with sackcloth (*saq*). We meet with the
same remarkable *enall. generis* in ver. 12. Men have no breasts
(*shâdaim*), and yet the masculine *sōphᵉdīm* is employed, inasmuch as the prophet had the whole nation in his mind, throughout which there would be such a *plangere ubera* on account of
the utter destruction of the hopeful harvest of corn and wine.
Shâdaim (breasts) and שְׁדֵי (construct to *sâdōth*) have the same
common ring as *ubera* and *ubertas frugum.* In ver. 13 *ta'āleh*
points back to *qōts shâmīr*, which is condensed into one neuter
idea. The *ki* in ver. 13*b* has the sense of the Latin *imo*
(Ewald, § 330, *b*). The genitive connection of קִרְיָה עַלִּיזָה with
בָּתֵּי מָשׂוֹשׂ (joy-houses of the jubilant city) is the same as in ch.
xxviii. 1. The whole is grammatically strange, just as in the
Psalms the language becomes all the more complicated, dis-
jointed, and difficult, the greater the wrath and indignation of
the poet. Hence the short shrill sentences in ver. 14 : palace
given up (cf. ch. xiii. 22) ; city bustle forsaken (*i.e.* the city
generally so full of bustle, ch. xxii. 2). The use of בְּעַד is the
same as in Prov. vi. 26, Job ii. 4. *'Ofel, i.e.* the south-eastern
fortified slope of the temple mountain, and the *bachan* (*i.e.* the
watch-tower, possibly the flock-tower which is mentioned in
Mic. iv. 8 along with *'ofel*), would be *pro speluncis, i.e.* would
be considered and serve as such. And in the very place where

the women of Jerusalem had once led their life of gaiety, wild
asses would now have their delight, and flocks their pasture (on
the wild asses, *p⁴rā'īm*, that fine animal of the woodless steppe,
see at Job xxiv. 5, xxxix. 5–8). Thus would Jerusalem, with its
strongest, proudest places, be laid in ruins, and that in a single
year, or even less than a year.

The state would then continue long, very long, until at last
the destruction of the false rest would be followed by the realization of the true. Vers. 15–19. " *Until the Spirit is poured
out over us from on high, and the wilderness becomes a fruitful
field, and the fruitful field is counted as the forest. And justice
makes its abode in the desert, and righteousness settles down upon
the fruit-field. And the effect of righteousness will be peace, and
the reward of righteousness rest and security for ever. And my
people dwells in a place of peace, and in trustworthy, safe dwell-
ings, and in cheerful resting-places. And it hails with the overthrow of the forest, and into lowliness must the city be brought
low.*" There is a limit, therefore, to the " for ever "of ver. 14.
The punishment would last till the Spirit, which Israel had not
then dwelling in the midst of it (see Hag. ii. 5), and whose
fulness was like a closed vessel to Israel, should be emptied out
over Israel from the height of heaven (compare the *piel* עָרָה,
Gen. xxiv. 20), *i.e.* should be poured out in all its fulness.
When that was done, a great change would take place, the
spiritual nature of which is figuratively represented in the same
proverbial manner as in ch. xxix. 17. At the same time, a
different turn is given to the second half in the passage before
us. The meaning is, not that what was now valued as a fruit-
bearing garden would be brought down from its false eminence,
and be only regarded as forest; but that the whole would be so
glorious, that what was now valued as a fruit-garden, would be
thrown into the shade by something far more glorious still, in
comparison with which it would have the appearance of a forest,
in which everything grew wild. The whole land, the uncultivated pasture-land as well as the planted fruitful fields of corn
and fruit, would then become the tent and seat of justice and
righteousness. " Justice and righteousness" (*mishpât* and
ts⁴dâqâh) are throughout Isaiah the stamp of the last and
perfect time. As these advance towards self-completion, the
produce and *result* of these will be peace (*ma'ăseh* and *'ăbhōdâh*

are used to denote the fruit or self-reward of work and pains-taking toil ; compare פְּעֻלָּה). But two things must take place before this calm, trustworthy, happy peace, of which the existing carnal security is only a caricature, can possibly be realized. In the *first* place, it must *hail*, and *the wood must fall*, being beaten down with hail. We already know, from ch. x. 34, that " the wood" was an emblem of Assyria ; and in ch. xxx. 30, 31, we find " the hail" mentioned as one of the forces of nature that would prove destructive to Assyria. And *secondly*, " *the city*" (הָעִיר, a play upon the word, and a counterpart to הַיַּעַר) must first of all *be brought low into lowliness* (*i.e.* be deeply humiliated). Rosenmüller and others suppose the imperial city to be intended, according to parallels taken from ch xxiv.–xxvii. ; but in this cycle of prophecies, in which the imperial city is never mentioned at all, " the city" must be Jerusalem, whose course from the false peace to the true lay through a humiliating punishment (ch. xxix. 2–4, xxx. 19 sqq., xxxi. 4 sqq.).

In the face of this double judgment, the prophet congratu-lates those who will live to see the times after the judgment. Ver. 20. " *Blessed are ye that sow by all waters, and let the foot of the oxen and asses rove in freedom.*" Those who lived to see these times would be far and wide the lords of a quiet and fruitful land, cleared of its foes, and of all disturbers of peace. They would sow wherever they pleased, by all the waters that fertilized the soil, and therefore in a soil of the most productive kind, and one that required little if any trouble to cultivate. And inasmuch as everything would be in the most copious abundance, they would no longer need to watch with anxiety lest their oxen and asses should stray into the corn-fields, but would be able to let them wander wherever they pleased. There cannot be the slightest doubt that this is the correct explanation of the verse, according to ch. xxx. 23–25 (compare also ch. vii. 21 sqq.).

This concludes the four woes, from which the fifth, that immediately follows, is distinguished by the fact, that in the former the Assyrian troubles are still in the future, whereas the fifth places us in the very midst of them. The prophet commenced (ch. xxviii. 1–4) with the destruction of Samaria ; he then threatened Judah and Jerusalem also. But it is uncommonly difficult to combine the different features of the threat into a complete picture. Sifting even to a small remnant is a leading thought, which runs through the threat. And we also read throughout the whole, that Asshur will meet with its own destruction in front of that very Jerusalem which it is seeking to destroy. But the prophet also knows, on the one hand, that Jerusalem is besieged by the Assyrians, and will not be rescued till the besieged city has been brought to the last extremity (ch. xxix. 1 sqq., xxxi. 4 sqq.); and, on the other hand, that this will reach even to the falling of the towers (ch. xxx. 25), the overthrow of the wall of the state (ch. xxx. 13, 14), the devastation of the land, and the destruction of Jerusalem itself (ch. xxxii. 12 sqq.); and for both of these he fixes the limit of a year (ch. xxix. 1, xxxii. 10). This double threat may be explained in the following manner. The judgments which Israel has still to endure, and the period of glory that will follow them, lie before the mental eye of the prophet like a long deep diorama. While threatening the existing generation, he penetrates more or less deeply into the judgments which lie in perspective before him. He threatens at one time merely a siege that will continue till it is brought to the utmost extremity; at another time utter destruction. But the imperial power intended, by which this double calamity is to be brought upon Judah, must be Assyria; since the prophet knew of no other in the earliest years of Hezekiah, when these threatening addresses were uttered. And this gives rise to another difficulty. Not only was the worst prediction—namely, that of the destruction of Jerusalem—not fulfilled; but even the milder prophecy—namely, that of a siege, which would bring them to the deepest distress—was not accomplished. There never was any actual siege of Jerusalem by the Assyrians. The explanation of this is, that, according to Jer. xviii. 7, 8, and 9, 10, neither the threatenings of punishment nor the promises of blessing uttered by the prophets were so unconditional, that they were certain to be fulfilled and that with absolute necessity, at such and such a time, or upon such and such a generation. The threatened punishment might be repealed or modified, if repentance ensued on the part of the persons threatened (Jonah iii. 4; 1 Kings xxi. 29; 2 Kings xxii. 15–20; 2 Chron. xii. 5–8). The words of the prophecy did not on that account fall to the ground. If they produced repentance, they answered the very purpose for which they were intended; but if the circumstances which called for punishment should return, their force returned as well in all its fulness. If the judgment was one irrevocably determined, it was merely delayed by this, to be discharged upon the generation which should be ripest for it. And we have also an express historical testimony, which shows that this is the way in which the non-fulfilment of what Isaiah threatened as about to take place within a year is to be accounted for. Not only Isaiah, but also his contemporary Micah, threatened, that along with the judgment upon Samaria, the same judgment would also burst upon Jerusalem. Zion would be ploughed as a field, Jerusalem would be laid in ruins, and the temple mountain would be turned into a wooded height (Mic. iii. 12). This prophecy belongs to the first year of Hezekiah's reign, for it was then that the book of Micah was composed. But we read in Jer. xxvi. 18, 19, that, in their alarm at this prophecy, Hezekiah and all Judah repented, and that Jehovah withdrew His threat in consequence. Thus, in the very first year of Hezekiah, a change for the better took place in Judah; and this was necessarily followed by the withdrawal of Isaiah's threatenings, just as those threatenings had co-operated in the production of this conversion (see Caspari, *Micha*, p. 160 sqq.). Not one of the three threats (Isa. xxix. 1–4, xxxii. 9–14; Mic. iii. 12), which form an ascending climax, was fulfilled. Previous threatenings so far recovered their original force, when the insincerity of the conversion became apparent, that the Assyrians did unquestionably march through Judah, devastating everything as they went along. But because of Hezekiah's self-humiliation and faith, the threat was turned from that time forward into a promise. In direct opposition to his former threatening, Isaiah now promised that Jerusalem would not be besieged by the Assyrians (ch. xxxvii. 33–35), but that, before the siege was actually established, Assyria would fall under the walls of Jerusalem.

THE FIFTH WOE.—WOE CONCERNING ASSHUR ; DELIVERANCE
AND GLORY OF JERUSALEM.—CHAP. XXXIII.

We are now in the fourteenth year of Hezekiah's reign.
The threatenings of the first years, which the repentance of
the people had delayed, are now so far in force again, and so
far actually realized, that the Assyrians are already in Judah,
and have not only devastated the land, but are threatening
Jerusalem. The element of promise now gains the upper
hand, the prophet places himself between Asshur and his own
nation with the weapons of prophecy and prayer, and the woe
turns from the latter to the former. Ver. 1. " *Woe, devastator,
and thyself not devastated ; and thou spoiler, and still not spoiled !
Hast thou done with devastating ? thou shalt be devastated. Hast
thou attained to rob ? men rob thee.*" Asshur is described as not
devastated and not spoiled (which could not be expressed by a
participle as with us, since *bâgad* is construed with *Beth*, and
not with the accusative of the person), because it had not yet
been visited by any such misfortune as that which had fallen
upon other lands and nations. But it would be repaid with
like for like as soon as (בְּ indicating simultaneousness, as in ch.
xxx. 19 and xviii. 5, for example) its devastating and spoiling
had reached the point determined by Jehovah. Instead of בְּךָ,
we find in some codd. and editions the reading בֹן, which is
equally admissible. In כַּהֲתִימְךָ (from תָּמַם) the radical syllable
is lengthened, instead of having *dagesh*. כַּנְּלוֹתְךָ is equivalent to
כְּהַנְלוֹתְךָ, a *hiphil* syncopated for the sake of rhythm (as in ch.
iii. 8, Deut. i. 33, and many other passages), written here with
dagesh dirimens, from the verb *nâlâh*, which is attested also
by Job xv. 29. The coincidence in meaning with the verb

نال (fut. *i* and *u*), to acquire or attain (see *Job*, vol. i. 296, ii.
165), has been admitted by the earliest of the national grammarians, Ben-Koreish, Chayug, etc. The conjecture כְּכַלּוֹתְךָ
(in addition to which Cappellus proposed כְּנִלְאוֹתְךָ) is quite
unnecessary. The play upon the sound sets forth the punishment of the hitherto unpunished one as the infallible echo of
its sin.

In ver. 2 the prophet's word of command is changed into a

believing prayer: *"Jehovah, be gracious to us; we wait for
Thee: be their arm with every morning, yea, our salvation in
time of need!"* *"Their arm,"* i.e. the power which shelters and
defends them, viz. Thy people and my own. *"Yea,"* 'aph, is
emphatic. Israel's arm every morning, because the danger is
renewed every day; Israel's salvation, i.e. complete deliverance (ch. xxv. 9), because the culminating point of the trouble
is still in prospect.

While the prophet is praying thus, he already sees the
answer. Vers. 3, 4. *"At the sound of a noise peoples pass away;
at Thy rising nations are scattered. And your booty is swept
away as a swarm of locusts sweeps away; as beetles run, they run
upon it."* The indeterminate hâmōn, which produces for that
very reason the impression of something mysterious and terrible,
is at once explained. The noise comes from Jehovah, who is
raising Himself judicially above Assyria, and thunders as a judge.
Then the hostile army runs away (נָפֹצוּ=נָפְצוּ, from the *niphal*
נָפַץ, 1 Sam. xiii. 11, from פֹוץ=פָּצָץ, from פּוּץ); and your booty
(the address returns to Assyria) is swept away, just as when a
swarm of locusts settles on a field, it soon eats it utterly away.
Jerome, Cappellus, and others follow the Septuagint rendering,
ὃν τρόπον ἐάν τις συναγάγῃ ἀκρίδας. The figure is quite as
appropriate, but the article in *hechâsīl* makes the other view the
more natural one; and ver. 4b places this beyond all doubt.
Shâqaq, from which the participle *shōqēq* and the substantive
masshâq are derived, is used here, as in Joel ii. 9, to signify a
busy running hither and thither (*discursitare*). The syntactic
use of *shōqēq* is the same as that of לְרָא (they call) in ch. xxi.
11, and *sōpheᵈīm* (they smite) in ch. xxxii. 12. The inhabitants of Jerusalem swarm in the enemy's camp like beetles;
they are all in motion, and carry off what they can.

The prophet sees this as he prays, and now feasts himself
on the consequences of this victory of Jehovah, prophesying in
vers. 5, 6: *"Jehovah is exalted; for, dwelling on high, He has
filled Zion with justice and righteousness. And there will be
security of thy times, riches of salvation, of wisdom, and knowledge. Fear of Jehovah is then the treasure of Judah."* *Exalted*:
for though highly exalted in Himself, He has performed an act
of justice and righteousness, with the sight and remembrance
of which Zion is filled as with an overflowing rich supply of

instruction and praise. A new time has dawned for the people of Judah. The prophet addresses them in ver. 6 ; for there is nothing to warrant us in regarding the words as addressed to Hezekiah. To the times succeeding this great achievement there would belong *'ĕmūnâh*, *i.e.* durability (Ex. xvii. 12),—a uniform and therefore trustworthy state of things (compare ch. xxxix. 8, " peace and truth"). Secondly, there would also belong to them חֹסֶן, a rich store of salvation, wisdom, and knowledge (compare the verb in ch. xxiii. 18). We regard these three ideas as all connected with *chōsen*. The prophet makes a certain advance towards the unfolding of the seven gifts in ch. xi. 2, which are implied in " salvation ;" but he hurries at once to the lowest of them, which forms the ground-work of all the rest, when he says, thirdly, that the fear of Jehovah will be the people's treasure. The construct form, *chokhmath*, instead of *chokhmâh*, is a favourite one, which Isaiah employs, even apart from the genitive relation of the words, for the purpose of securing a closer connection, as ch. xxxv. 2, li. 21 (compare *pârash* in Ezek. xxvi. 10), clearly show. In the case before us, it has the further advantage of consonance in the closing sound.

The prophet has thus run through the whole train of thought with a few rapid strides, in accordance with the custom which we have already frequently noticed ; and now he commences afresh, mourning over the present miserable condition of things, in psalm-like elegiac tones, and weeping with his weeping people. Vers. 7–9. " *Behold, their heroes weep without ; the messengers of peace weep bitterly. Desolate are roads, disappeared are travellers ; he has broken covenant, insulted cities, despised men. The land mourns, languishes ; Lebanon stands ashamed, parched ; the meadow of Sharon has become like a steppe, and Bashan and Carmel shake their leaves.*" אֶרְאֶלָּם is probably chosen with some allusion to *'Ariel*, the name of Jerusalem in ch. xxix. ; but it has a totally different meaning. We have rendered it " heroes," because אֶרְאֵל is here synonymous with אֲרִיאֵל in the *Nibelung*-like piece contained in 2 Sam. xxiii. 20 and 1 Chron. xi. 22. This *'ărī'ēl*, which is here contracted into *'er'el* (compare the biblical name *'Ar'ēlī* and the post-biblical name of the angels, *'Er'ellīm*), is compounded of *'ărī* (a lion) and *'El* (God), and therefore signifies " the lion of

God," but in this sense, that *El* (God) gives to the idea of leonine courage merely the additional force of extraordinary or wonderful; and as a composite word, it contents itself with a singular, with a collective sense according to circumstances, without forming any plural at all. The *dagesh* is to be explained from the fact that the word (which tradition has erroneously regarded as a compound of אֲרְאֵה לָהֶם) is pointed in accordance with the form כַּרְמֶל (כַּרְמִלּוֹ). The heroes intended by the prophet were the messengers sent to Sennacherib to treat with him for peace. They carried to him the amount of silver and gold which he had demanded as the condition of peace (2 Kings xviii. 14). But Sennacherib broke the treaty, by demanding nothing less than the surrender of Jerusalem itself. Then the heroes of Jerusalem cried aloud, when they arrived at Jerusalem, and had to convey this message of disgrace and alarm to the king and nation; and bitterly weeping over such a breach of faith, such deception and disgrace, the embassy, which had been sent off, to the deep self-humiliation of Judah and themselves, returned to Jerusalem. Moreover, Sennacherib continued to storm the fortified places, in violation of his agreement (on *mâ'as 'ârîm*, see 2 Kings xviii. 13). The land was more and more laid waste, the fields were trodden down; and the autumnal aspect of Lebanon, with its faded foliage, and of Bashan and Carmel, with their falling leaves, looked like shame and grief at the calamities of the land. It was in the autumn, therefore, that the prophet uttered these complaints; and the definition of the time given in his prophecy (ch. xxxii. 10) coincides with this. קָמֵל is the pausal form for קָמֵל, just as in other places an *ê* with the tone, which has sprung from *i*, easily passes into *a* in pause; the sharpening of the syllable being preferred to the lengthening of it, not only when the syllable which precedes the tone syllable is an open one, but sometimes even when it is closed (*e.g.* Judg. vi. 19, וַיַּגֵּשׁ). Instead of בָּעֲרֵבָה we should read בָּעֲרָבָה (without the article), as certain codd. and early editions do.[1] Isaiah having mourned in the tone of the Psalms, now comforts himself with the words of a

---

[1] We find the same in Zech. xiv. 10, and בְּעַרְבִים in ch. xliv. 4, whereas we invariably have בַּעֲרָבָה (see *Michlol*, 45*b*), just as we always find בָּאֲבָנִים, and on the other hand כַּאֲבָנִים.

psalm. Like David in Ps. xii. 6, he hears Jehovah speak.
The measure of Asshur's iniquity is full; the hour of Judah's
redemption is come; Jehovah has looked on long enough, as
though sitting still (ch. xviii. 4). Ver. 10. *" Now will I arise,
saith Jehovah, now exalt myself, now lift up myself."* Three
times does the prophet repeat the word *'attâh* (now), which is
so significant a word with all the prophets, but more especially
with Hosea and Isaiah, and which always fixes the boundary-
line and turning-point between love and wrath, wrath and love.
אֲרוֹמֵם (in half pause for אֲרוֹמֵם) is contracted from אֶתְרוֹמֵם (Ges.
§ 54, 2, *b*). Jehovah would rise up from His throne, and show
Himself in all His greatness to the enemies of Israel.

After the prophet has heard this from Jehovah, he knows
how it will fare with them. He therefore cries out to them
in triumph (ver. 11), *" Ye are pregnant with hay, ye bring
forth stubble! Your snorting is the fire that will devour you."*
Their vain purpose to destroy Jerusalem comes to nothing;
their burning wrath against Jerusalem becomes the fire of
wrath, which consumes them (for *chăshash* and *qash*, see at
ch. v. 24).

The prophet announces this to them, and now tells openly
what has been exhibited to him in his mental mirror as the purpose of God. Ver. 12. *"And nations become as lime burnings,
thorns cut off, which are kindled with fire."* The first simile sets
forth the totality of the destruction: they will be so completely burned up, that nothing but ashes will be left, like the
lump of lime left at the burning of lime. The second contains
a figurative description of its suddenness: they have vanished
suddenly, like dead brushwood, which is cut down in consequence, and quickly crackles up and is consumed (ch. v.
24, cf. ix. 17): *kâsach* is the Targum word for *zâmar*, ampu-
tare, whereas in Arabic it has the same meaning as *sâchâh,
verrere.*

But the prophet, while addressing Asshur, does not overlook
those sinners of his own nation who are deserving of punishment. The judgment upon Asshur is an alarming lesson, not
only for the heathen, but for Israel also; for there is no respect
of persons with Jehovah. Vers. 13, 14. *" Hear, ye distant
ones, what I have accomplished; and perceive, ye near ones, my
omnipotence! The sinners in Zion are afraid; trembling seizes*

the hypocrites : who of us can abide with devouring fire? who of us abide with everlasting burnings?" Even for the sinners in Jerusalem also there is no abiding in the presence of the Almighty and Just One, who has judged Asshur (the act of judgment is regarded by the prophet as having just occurred); they must either repent, or they cannot remain in His presence. Jehovah, so far as His wrath is concerned, is " a consuming fire" (Deut. iv. 24, ix. 3); and the fiery force of His anger is " everlasting burnings" (*mōkᵉdē ʿōlâm*), inasmuch as it consists of flames that are never extinguished, never burn themselves out. And this God had His fire and His furnace in Jerusalem (ch. xxxi. 9), and had just shown what His fire could do, when once it burst forth. Therefore do the sinners inquire in their alarm, whilst confessing to one another (*lânū;* cf. Amos ix. 1) that none of them can endure it, " Who can dwell with devouring fire?" etc. (*gūr* with the *acc. loci*, as in Ps. v. 5).

The prophet answers their question. Vers. 15, 16. " *He that walketh in righteousness, and speaketh uprightness ; he that despiseth gain of oppressions, whose hand keepeth from grasping bribes ; he that stoppeth his ear from hearing murderous counsel, and shutteth his eyes from looking at evil ; he will dwell upon high places ; rocky fastnesses are his castle ; his bread is abundant, his waters inexhaustible.*" Isaiah's variation of Ps. xv. and xxiv. 3–6 (as Jer. xvii. 5–8 contains Jeremiah's variation of Ps. i.). *Tsᵉdâqōth* is the accusative of the object, so also is *mēshârīm:* he who walks in all the relations of life in the full measure of righteousness, *i.e.* who practises it continually, and whose words are in perfect agreement with his inward feelings and outward condition. The third quality is, that he not only does not seek without for any gain which injures the interests of his neighbour, but that he inwardly abhors it. The fourth is, that he diligently closes his hands, his ears, and his eyes, against all danger of moral pollution. Bribery, which others force into his hand, he throws away (cf. Neh. v. 13); against murderous suggestions, or such as stimulate revenge, hatred, and violence, he stops his ear; and from sinful sights he closes his eyes firmly, and that without even winking. Such a man has no need to fear the wrath of God. Living according to the will of God, he lives in the love of God; and in that he is

shut in as it were upon the inaccessible heights and in the impregnable walls of a castle upon a rock. He suffers neither
hunger nor thirst; but his bread is constantly handed to him
(*nittân, partic.*), namely, by the love of God; and his waters
never fail, for God, the living One, makes them flow. This is
the picture of a man who has no need to be alarmed at the
judgment of God upon Asshur.

Over this picture the prophet forgets the sinners in Zion,
and greets with words of promise the thriving church of the
future. Ver. 17. " *Thine eyes will see the king in his beauty,
will see a land that is very far off.*" The king of Judah,
hitherto so deeply humbled, and, as Micah instances by way of
example, " smitten upon the cheeks," is then glorified by the
victory of his God; and the nation, constituted as described in
vers. 15, 16, will see him in his God-given beauty, and see the
land of promise, cleared of enemies as far as the eye can reach
and the foot carry, restored to Israel without reserve, and
under the dominion of this sovereign enjoying all the blessedness of peace.

The tribulation has passed away like a dream. Vers. 18, 19.
" *Thy heart meditates upon the shuddering. Where is the valuer?
where the weigher? where he who counted the towers? The rough
people thou seest no more, the people of deep inaudible lip, of
stammering unintelligible tongue.*" The dreadful past is so
thoroughly forced out of mind by the glorious present, that
they are obliged to turn back their thoughts (*hâgâh, meditari,*
as Jerome renders it) to remember it at all. The *sōphēr* who
had the management of the raising of the tribute, the *shōqēl*
who tested the weight of the gold and silver, the *sōphēr 'eth
hammigdâlīm* who drew up the plan of the city to be besieged
or stormed, are all vanished. The rough people (עַם נוֹעָז, the
niphal of עָז, from יָעַז), that had shown itself so insolent, so
shameless, and so insatiable in its demands, has become invisible.
This attribute is a perfectly appropriate one; and the explanation given by Rashi, Vitringa, Ewald, and Fürst, who take it
in the sense of *lōʿēz* in Ps. cxiv. 1, is both forced and groundless. The expressions *ʿimkē* and *nilʿag* refer to the obscure and
barbarous sound of their language; *misshᵉmōăʿ* to the unintelli-
gibility of their speech; and אֵין בִּינָה to the obscurity of their
meaning. Even if the Assyrians spoke a Semitic language,

they were of so totally different a nationality, and their manners were so entirely different, that their language must have sounded even more foreign to an Israelite than Dutch to a German.

And how will Jerusalem look when Asshur has been dashed to pieces on the strong fortress? The prophet passes over here into the tone of Ps. xlviii. (vers. 13, 14.) Ps. xlvi. and xlviii. probably belong to the time of Jehoshaphat; but they are equally applicable to the deliverance of Jerusalem in the time of Hezekiah. Ver. 20. " *Look upon Zion, the castle of our festal meeting. Thine eyes will see Jerusalem, a pleasant place, a tent that does not wander about, whose pegs are never drawn, and none of whose cords are ever broken.*" Jerusalem stands there unconquered and inviolable, the fortress where the congregation of the whole land celebrates its feasts, a place full of good-cheer (ch. xxxii. 18), in which everything is now arranged for a continuance. Jerusalem has come out of tribulation stronger than ever,—not a nomadic wandering tent (*tsa'an*, a nomad word, to wander, *lit.* to pack up = *ta'an* in Gen. xlv. 17), but one set up for a permanent dwelling.

It is also a great Lord who dwells therein, a faithful and almighty defender. Vers. 21, 22. " *No, there dwells for us a glorious One, Jehovah; a place of streams, canals of wide extent, into which no fleet of rowing vessels ventures, and which no strong man of war shall cross. For Jehovah is our Judge; Jehovah is our war-Prince; Jehovah is our King; He will bring us salvation.*" Following upon the negative clauses in ver. 20*b*, the next verse commences with *kī 'im (imo)*. Glorious ('*addīr*) is Jehovah, who has overthrown Lebanon, *i.e.* Assyria (ch. x. 34). He dwells in Jerusalem for the good of His people,— a place of streams, *i.e.* one resembling a place of streams, from the fact that He dwells therein. Luzzatto is right in maintaining, that בּוֹ and יַעַבְרֶנּוּ point back to מְקוֹם, and therefore that *mᵉkōm* is neither equivalent to *loco* (*tachath*, instead of), which would be quite possible indeed, as 1 Kings xxi. 19, if not Hos. ii. 1, clearly proves (cf. ch. xxii. 38), nor used in the sense of substitution or compensation. The meaning is, that, by virtue of Jehovah's dwelling there, Jerusalem had become a place, or equivalent to a place, of broad streams, like those which in other instances defended the cities they surrounded (*e.g.* Babylon, the " twisted snake," ch. xxvii. 1), and of broad canals, which kept off the enemy, like moats around a fortification. The word יְאֹרִים was an Egyptian word, that had become naturalized in Hebrew; nevertheless it is a very natural supposition, that the prophet was thinking of the *No* of Egypt, which was surrounded by waters, probably Nile-canals (see Winer, *R.W.* Nah. iii. 8). The adjective in which *yâdaim* brings out with greater force the idea of breadth, as in ch. xxii. 18 (" on both sides"), belongs to both the nouns, which are placed side by side, ἀσυνδέτως (because permutative). The presence of Jehovah was to Jerusalem what the broadest streams and canals were to other cities; and into these streams and canals, which Jerusalem had around it spiritually in Jehovah Himself, no rowing vessels ventured (הָלַךְ בְּ, *ingredi*). Luzzatto renders the word " ships of roving," *i.e.* pirate ships; but this is improbable, as *shût*, when used as a nautical word, signifies to row. Even a majestic *tsî, i.e. trieris magna*, could not cross it: a colossal vessel of this size would be wrecked in these mighty and dangerous waters. The figure is the same as that in ch. xxvi. 1. In the consciousness of this inaccessible and impenetrable defence, the people of Jerusalem gloried in their God, who watched as a *shôphêt* over Israel's rights and honour, who held as *m^echoqêq* the commander's rod, and ruled as *melekh* in the midst of Israel; so that for every future danger it was already provided with the most certain help.

Now indeed it was apparently very different from this. It was not Assyria, but Jerusalem, that was like a ship about to be wrecked; but when that which had just been predicted should be fulfilled, Jerusalem, at present so powerless and sinful, would be entirely changed. Vers. 23, 24. " *Thy ropes hang loose; they do not hold fast the support of thy mast; they do not hold the flag extended: then is booty of plunder divided in abundance; even lame men share the prey. And not an inhabitant will say, I am weak: the people settled there have their sins forgiven.*" Nearly every commentator (even Luzzatto) has taken ver. 23 as addressed to Assyria, which, like a proud vessel of war, would cross the encircling river by which Jerusalem was surrounded. But Drechsler has very properly given up this view. The address itself, with the suffix *ayikh* (see at ch. i. 26), points to Jerusalem; and the reference to this gives the most appropriate sense, whilst the contrast between the *now* and *then* closes the prophecy in the most glorious manner. Jerusalem is now a badly appointed ship, dashed about by the storm, the sport of the waves. Its rigging hangs loose (Jerome, *laxati sunt*); it does not hold the *kēn tornâm* fast, *i.e.* the support of their mast, or cross beam with a hole in it, into which the mast is slipped (the *mesodme* of Homer, *Od.* xv. 289), which is sure to go to ruin along with the falling mast, if the ropes do not assist its bearing power (*malum sustinentes thecœ succurrant*, as Vitruvius says). And so the ropes of the ship Jerusalem do not keep the *nēs* spread out, *i.e.* the ἐπίσημον of the ship, whether we understand by it a flag or a sail, with a device worked upon it (see Winer, *R.W. s. v. Schiffe*). And this is the case with Jerusalem now; but then (*'âz*) it will be entirely different. Asshur is wrecked, and Jerusalem enriches itself, without employing any weapons, from the wealth of the Assyrian camp. It was with a prediction of this spoiling of Asshur that the prophet commenced in ver. 1; so that the address finishes as it began. But the closing words of the prophet are, that the people of Jerusalem are now strong in God, and are נְשֻׂא עָוֹן (as in Ps. xxxii. 1), lifted up, taken away from their guilt. A people humbled by punishment, penitent, and therefore pardoned, would then dwell in Jerusalem. The strength of Israel, and all its salvation, rest upon the forgiveness of its sins.

PART VI.

FINALE OF THE JUDGMENT UPON ALL THE WORLD (MORE ESPECIALLY UPON EDOM), AND REDEMPTION OF THE PEOPLE OF JEHOVAH.

CHAP. XXXIV. XXXV.

THESE two chapters stand in precisely the same relation to ch. xxviii.–xxxiii. as ch. xxiv.–xxvii. to ch. xiii.–xxiii. In both instances the special prophecies connected with the history of the prophet's own times are followed by a comprehensive *finale* of an apocalyptic character. We feel that we are carried entirely away from the stage of history. There is no longer that foreshortening, by which the prophet's perspective was characterized before the fall of Assyria. The tangible shapes of the historical present, by which we have been hitherto surrounded, are now spiritualized into something perfectly ideal. We are transported directly into the midst of the last things; and the eschatological vision is less restricted, has greater mystical depth, belongs more to another sphere, and has altogether more of a New Testament character. The totally different impression which is thus made by ch. xxxiv. xxxv., as compared with ch. xxviii.–xxxiii., must not cause any misgivings as to the authenticity of this closing prophecy. The relation in which Jeremiah and Zephaniah stand to ch. xxxiv. and xxxv., is quite sufficient to drive all doubts away. (Read Caspari's article, " Jeremiah a Witness to the Genuineness of Isa. xxxiv., and therefore also to the Genuineness of Isa. xl.–lxvi., xiii.–xiv. 23, and xxi. 1–10," in the *Lutherische Zeitschrift*, 1843, 2 ; and Nägelsbach's *Jeremia und Babylon*, pp. 107–113, on the relation of Jer. l. li. more especially to Isa. xxxiv. xxxv.) There are many passages in Jeremiah (viz. ch. xxv. 31, 33, 34, xlvi. 10, l. 27, 39, li. 40) which cannot be explained in any other way than on the supposition that Jeremiah had the prophecy of Isaiah in ch. xxxiv. before him. We cannot escape from the conclusion, that just as we find Jeremiah introducing earlier prophecies generally into his cycle of prophecies against the nations, and, in the addresses already mentioned, borrowing from Amos and Nahum, and placing side by side with a passage from Amos (compare Jer. xxv. 30 with Amos i. 2) one of a similar character, and agreeing with Isa. xxxiv., so he also had Isa. xxxiv. and xxxv. before him, and reproduced it in the same sense as he did other and earlier models. It is equally certain that Zeph. i. 7, 8, and ii. 14, stand in a dependent relation to Isa. xxxiv. 6, 11 ; just as Zeph. ii. 15 was taken from Isa. xlvii. 8, and Zeph. i. 7 *fin.* and iii. 11 from Isa. xiii. 3; whilst Zeph. ii. 14 also points back to Isa. xiii. 21, 22. We might, indeed, reverse the relation, and make Jeremiah and Zephaniah into the originals in the case of the passages mentioned; but this is opposed to the generally reproductive and secondary character of both these prophets, and also to the evident features of the passages in question. We might also

follow Movers, De Wette, and Hitzig, who get rid of the testimony of Isaiah by assuming that the passages resting upon
Isa. xxxiv., and other disputed prophecies of Isaiah, are interpolated; but this is opposed to the moral character of all
biblical prophecy, and, moreover, it could only apply to Jeremiah, not to Zephaniah.   We must in this case " bring reason
into captivity to obedience" to the external evidence; though
internal evidence also is not wanting to set a seal upon these
external proofs.   Just as ch. xxiv.–xxvii. are full of the clearest
marks of Isaiah's authorship, so is it also with ch. xxxiv. xxxv.
It is not difficult to understand the marked contrast which we
find between these two closing prophecies and the historical
prophecies of the Assyrian age.   These two closing prophecies
were appended to ch. xiii.–xxiii. and xxviii.–xxxiii. at the time
when Isaiah revised the complete collection.   They belong to
the latest revelations received by the prophet, to the last steps
by which he reached that ideal height at which he soars in
ch. xl.–lxvi., and from which he never descends again to the
stage of passing history, which lay so far beneath.   After
the fall of Assyria, and when darkness began to gather on the
horizon again, Isaiah broke completely away from his own
times.   " The end of all things" became more and more his
own true home.   The obscure foreground of his prophecies is no
longer *Asshur*, which he has done with now so far as prophecy
is concerned, but *Babel* (Babylon).   And the bright centre of
his prophecies is not the fall of Asshur (for this was already
prophetically a thing of the past, which had not been followed
by complete salvation), but deliverance from Babylon.   And
the bright noon-day background of his prophecies is no longer
the realized idea of the kingdom of prophecy,—realized, that
is to say, in the one person of the Messiah, whose form had
lost the sharp outlines of ch. vii.–xii. even in the prophecies
of Hezekiah's time,—but the *parousia* of Jehovah, which *all
flesh* would see.   It was the revelation of the mystery of the
incarnation of God, for which all this was intended to prepare
the way.   And there was no other way in which that could be
done, than by completing the perfect portrait of the Messiah
in the light of the ultimate future, so that both the factors in
the prophecy might be assimilated.   The spirit of Isaiah, more
than that of any other prophet, was the laboratory of this great

process in the history of revelation. The prophetic cycles in ch. xxiv.–xxvii. and xxxiv. xxxv. stand in the relation of preludes to it. In ch. xl.–lxvi. the process of assimilation is fully at work, and there is consequently no book of the Old Testament which has gone so thoroughly into New Testament depths, as this second part of the collection of Isaiah's prophecies, which commences with a prediction of the parousia of Jehovah, and ends with the creation of the new heaven and new earth. Ch. xxxiv. and xxxv. are, as it were, the first preparatory chords. Edom here is what Moab was in ch. xxiv.–xxvii. By the side of Babylon, the empire of the world, whose policy of conquest led to its enslaving Israel, it represents the world in its hostility to Israel as the people of Jehovah. For Edom was Israel's brother-nation, and hated Israel as the chosen people. In this its unbrotherly, hereditary hatred, it represented the sum-total of all the enemies and persecutors of the church of Jehovah. The special side-piece to ch. xxxiv. is ch. lxiii. 1–6.

What the prophet here foretells relates to all nations, and to every individual within them, in their relation to the congregation of Jehovah. He therefore commences with the appeal in vers. 1–3: " *Come near, ye peoples, to hear; and ye nations, attend. Let the earth hear, and that which fills it, the world, and everything that springs from it. For the indignation of Jehovah will fall upon all nations, and burning wrath upon all their host; He has laid the ban upon them, delivered them to the slaughter. And their slain are cast away, and their corpses— their stench will arise, and mountains melt with their blood.*" The summons does not invite them to look upon the completion of the judgment, but to hear the prophecy of the future judgment; and it is issued to everything on the earth, because it would all have to endure the judgment upon the nations (see at ch. v. 25, xiii. 10). The expression *qetseph layehōvâh* implies that Jehovah was ready to execute His wrath (compare *yōm layehōvâh* in ver. 8 and ch. ii. 12). The nations that are hostile to Jehovah are slaughtered, the bodies remain unburied, and the streams of blood loosen the firm masses of the mountains, so that they melt away. On the stench of the corpses, compare Ezek. xxxix. 11. Even if *châsam*, in this instance, does not mean "to take away the breath with the stench," there is no doubt that Ezekiel had this prophecy of Isaiah in his mind, when prophesying of the destruction of Gog and Magog (Ezek. xxxix.).

The judgment foretold by Isaiah also belongs to the last things ; for it takes place in connection with the simultaneous destruction of the present heaven and the present earth. Ver. 4. *" And all the host of the heavens moulder away, and the heavens are rolled up like a scroll, and all their host withers as a leaf withers away from the vine, and like withered leaves from the fig-tree."* *Nâmaq,* to be dissolved into powdered mother (ch. iii. 24, v. 24) ; *nâgōl* (for *nâgal,* like *nâzōl* in ch. lxiii. 19, lxiv. 2, and *nârōts* in Eccles. xii. 6), to be rolled up,—a term applied to the cylindrical book-scroll. The heaven, that is to say, the present system of the universe, breaks up into atoms, and is rolled up like a book that has been read through ; and the stars fall down as a withered leaf falls from a vine, when it is moved by even the lightest breeze, or like the withered leaves shaken from the fig-tree. The expressions are so strong, that they cannot be understood in any other sense than as relating to the end of the world (ch. lxv. 17, lxvi. 22 ; compare Matt. xxiv. 29). It is not sufficient to say that " the stars appear to fall to the earth," though even Vitringa gives this explanation.

When we look, however, at the following *kī* (for), it undoubtedly appears strange that the prophet should foretell the passing away of the heavens, simply because Jehovah judges Edom. But Edom stands here as the representative of all powers that are hostile to the church of God as such, and therefore expresses an idea of the deepest and widest cosmical signification (as ch. xxiv. 21 clearly shows). And it is not only a doctrine of Isaiah himself, but a biblical doctrine universally, that God will destroy the present world as soon as the measure of the sin which culminates in unbelief, and in the persecution of the congregation of the faithful, shall be really full.

If we bear this in mind, we shall not be surprised that the prophet gives the following reason for the passing away of the present heavens. Vers. 5–7. *" For my sword has become intoxicated in the heaven ; behold, it comes down upon Edom, and upon the people of my ban to judgment. The sword of Jehovah fills itself with blood, is fattened with fat, with blood*

*of lambs and he-goats, with kidney-fat of rams; for Jehovah has
a sacrifice in Bozrah, and a great slaughter in the land of Edom.
And buffaloes fall with them, and bullocks together with bulls;
and their land becomes intoxicated with blood, and their dust
fattened with fat.*" Just as in ch. lxiii. Jehovah is represented
as a treader of the wine-press, and the nations as the grapes;
so here He is represented as offering sacrifice, and the nations
as the animals offered (*zebhach*: cf. Zeph. i. 7; Jer. xlvi. 10;
Ezek. xxxix. 17 sqq.: all three passages founded upon this).
Jehovah does not appear here in person as judge, as He does
there, but His sword appears; just as in Gen. iii. 24, the
" sword which turned every way" is mentioned as an independent power standing by the side of the cherub.   The sword
is His executioner, which has no sooner drunk deeply of wrath
in heaven, i.e. in the immediate sphere of the Deity (*rivv͏ᵉthâh*,
an intensive form of the *kal*, like *pittēăch*, ch. xlviii. 8; Ewald,
§ 120, *d*), than it comes down in wild intoxication upon
Edom, the people of the ban of Jehovah, *i.e.* the people upon
whom He has laid the ban, and there, as His instrument of
punishment, fills itself with blood, and fattens itself with fat.
הִדֻּשָּׁנָה is the *hothpaal* = הִתְדַּשְּׁנָה, with the ת of the preformative
syllable assimilated (compare הוּבְּאוּ in ch. i. 16, and אֲדַמֶּה in ch.
xiv. 14).   The penultimate has the tone, the *nâh* being treated
as in the plural forms of the future.   The dropping of the
dagesh in the שׁ is connected with this.   The reading מֵחֲלֶב, in
ver. 6, is an error that has been handed down in modern copies
(in opposition to both codices and ancient editions); for חֵלֶב
(primary form, *chilb*) is the only form met with in the Old
Testament.   The lambs, he-goats, and rams, represent the
Edomitish nation, which is compared to these smaller sacrificial
animals.   *Edom* and *Bozrah* are also placed side by side in ch.
lxiii. 1.   The latter was one of the chief cities of the Edomites
(Gen. xxxvi. 33; Amos i. 12; Jer. xlix. 13, 22),—not the
Bozrah in Auranitis (*Haurân*), however, which is well known
in church history, but Bozrah in the mountains of Edom,
upon the same site as the village of *Buzaire* (*i.e.* Minor
Bozrah), which is still surrounded by its ruins.   In contrast with the three names of the smaller animals in ver. 6,
the three names of oxen in ver. 7 represent the lords of Edom.
They also will fall, smitten by the sword (*yâr͏ᵉdû*: cf. Jer. l. 27,

li. 40; also Jer. xlviii. 15). The feast of the sword is so abundant, that even the earth and the dust of the land of Edom are satiated with blood and fat.

Thus does Jehovah avenge His church upon Edom. Vers. 8–10. " *For Jehovah hath a day of vengeance, a year of recompense, to contend for Zion. And the brooks of Edom are turned into pitch, and its dust into brimstone, and its land becomes burning pitch. Day and night it is not quenched; the smoke of Edom goes up for ever: it lies waste from generation to generation; no one passes through it for ever and ever.*" The one expression, " to contend for Zion," is like a flash of lightning, throwing light upon the obscurity of prophecy, both backwards and forwards. A day and a year of judgment upon Edom (compare ch. lxi. 2, lxiii. 4) would do justice to Zion against its accusers and persecutors (*rîbh, vindicare,* as in ch. li. 22). The everlasting punishment which would fall upon it is depicted in figures and colours, suggested by the proximity of Edom to the Dead Sea, and the volcanic character of this mountainous country. The unquenchable fire (for which compare ch. lxvi. 24), and the eternally ascending smoke (cf. Rev. xix. 3), prove that the end of all things is referred to. The prophet meant primarily, no doubt, that the punishment announced would fall upon the land of Edom, and within its geographical boundaries; but this particular punishment represented the punishment of all nations, and all men who were Edomitish in their feelings and conduct towards the congregation of Jehovah.

The land of Edom, in this geographical and also emblematical sense, would become a wilderness; the kingdom of Edom would be for ever destroyed. Vers. 11, 12. " *And pelican and hedgehog take possession of it, and eared-owl and raven dwell there; and he stretches over it the measure of Tohu and the level of Bohu. Its nobles—there is no longer a monarchy which they elected; and all its princes come to nought.*" The description of the ruin, which commences in ver. 11*a* with a list of animals that frequent marshy and solitary regions, is similar to the one in ch. xiii. 20–22, xiv. 23 (compare Zeph. ii. 14, which is founded upon this). Isaiah's was the original of all such pictures of ruin which we meet with in the later prophets. The *qippōd* is the hedgehog, although we find it here in the company of birds (from *qâphad,*

to draw one's self together, to roll up; see ch. xiv. 23). קָאָת is
written here with a double *kametz*, as well as in Zeph. ii. 14,
according to *codd.* and Kimchi, *W.B.* (Targ. *qâth*, elsewhere
qâq; Saad. and Abulwalid, *qûq*: see at Ps. cii. 7). According to well-established tradition, it is the long-necked pelican,
which lives upon fish (the name is derived either from קוֹא, to
vomit, or, as the construct is קָאַת, from a word קָאָה, formed in
imitation of the animal's cry). *Yanshûph* is rendered by the
Targum *qîppôphîn* (Syr. *kafûfo*), *i.e.* eared-owls, which are frequently mentioned in the Talmud as birds of ill omen (Rashi, or
Berachoth 57*b*, *chouette*). As the parallel to *qâv*, we have אַבְנֵי
(*stones*) here instead of מִשְׁקֶלֶת, the *level*, in ch. xxviii. 17. It is
used in the same sense, however,—namely, to signify the weight
used in the plumb or level, which is suspended by a line. The
level and the measure are commonly employed for the purpose
of building up; but here Jehovah is represented as using these
for the purpose of pulling down (a figure met with even before
the time of Isaiah: *vid.* Amos vii. 7–9, cf. 2 Kings xxi. 13,
Lam. ii. 8), inasmuch as He carries out this negative reverse of
building with the same rigorous exactness as that with which
a builder carries out his well-considered plan, and throws
Edom back into a state of desolation and desert, resembling
the disordered and shapeless chaos of creation (compare Jer.
iv. 23, where *tōhū vábhōhū* represents, as it does here, the state
into which a land is reduced by fire). תֹהוּ has no *dagesh lene;*
and this is one of the three passages in which the opening
mute is without a *dagesh*, although the word not only follows,
but is closely connected with, one which has a soft consonant as
its final letter (the others are Ps. lxviii. 18 and Ezek. xxiii. 42).
Thus the primeval kingdom with its early monarchy, which so
long preceded that of Israel, is brought to an end (Gen. xxxvi.
31). חֹרֶיהָ stands at the head as a kind of protasis. Edom was
an elective monarchy; the hereditary nobility electing the new
king. But this would be done no more. The electoral princes
of Edom would come to nothing. Not a trace would be left
of all that had built up the glory of Edom.

The allusion to the monarchy and the lofty electoral dignity
leads the prophet on to the palaces and castles of the land.
Starting with these, he carries out the picture of the ruins in
vers. 13–15. " *And the palaces of Edom break out into thorns,*

*nettles and thistles in its castles; and it becomes the abode of
wild dogs, pasture for ostriches. And martens meet with jackals,
and a wood-devil runs upon its fellow; yea, Lîlîth dwells there,
and finds rest for itself. There the arrow-snake makes its nest,
and breeds and lays eggs, and broods in the shadow there; yea,
there vultures gather together one to another."* The feminine
suffixes refer to Edom, as they did in the previous instance, as
בַּת־אֱדוֹם or אֶרֶץ אֱדוֹם. On the *tannîm, tsiyyîm,* and *'iyyîm,* see at
ch. xiii. 21, 22. It is doubtful whether *châtsîr* here corresponds to the Arabic word for an enclosure (= חָצֵר), as Gesenius,
Hitzig, and others suppose, as elsewhere to the Arabic for
green, a green field, or garden vegetable. We take it in
the latter sense, viz. a *grassy place,* such as was frequented
by ostriches, which live upon plants and fruits. The word
tsiyyim (steppe animals) we have rendered " martens," as the
context requires a particular species of animals to be named.
This is the interpretation given by Rashi (*in loc.*) and Kimchi
in Jer. l. 39 to the Targum word *tamván.* We do not render
'iyyîm " wild cats " (*chattûlîn*), but "*jackals,*" after the Arabic.
קָרָא with עַל we take in the sense of קָרָה (as in Ex. v. 3). *Lîlîth*
(Syr. and Zab. *lelitho*), lit. the creature of the night, was a
female demon (*shêdâh*) of the popular mythology; according to
the legends, it was a malicious fairy that was especially hurtful
to children, like some of the fairies of our own fairy tales.
There is life in Edom still; but what a caricature of that
which once was there! In the very spot where the princes of
Edom used to proclaim the new king, satyrs now invite one
another to dance (ch. xiii. 21); and where kings and princes
once slept in their palaces and country houses, the *lîlîth,* which
is most at home in horrible places, finds, as though after a
prolonged search, the most convenient and most comfortable resting-place. Demons and serpents are not very far distant from
one another. The prophet therefore proceeds in ver. 15 to the
arrow-snake, or springing-snake (Arabic *qiffâze,* from *qâphaz,*
related to *qâphats,* Song of Sol. ii. 8, to prepare for springing,
or to spring; a different word from *qippôd,* which has the same
root). This builds its nest in the ruins; there it breeds (*millêt,*
to let its eggs slide out) and lays eggs (*bâqa',* to split, *i.e.* to
bring forth); and then it broods in the shade (*dâgar* is the
Targum word in Job xxxix. 14 for *chimmêm* (*ithpael* in Lam.

i. 20 for חֲמַרְמַר), and is also used in the rabbinical writings for
fovere, as Jerome renders it here). The literal sense of the
word is probably to keep the eggs together (Targum, Jer. xvii.
11, מְכַבֵּשׁ בֵּעִין, LXX. συνήγαγεν), since דָּגַר (syn. חַמַּר) signifies
"to collect." Rashi has therefore explained it in both passages
as meaning *glousser,* to cluck, the noise by which a fowl calls
its brood together. The *dayyáh* is the vulture. These fowls
and most gregarious birds of prey also collect together there.

Whenever any one compared the prophecy with the fulfilment, they would be found to coincide. Vers. 16, 17. " *Search
in the book of Jehovah, and read ! Not one of the creatures
fails, not one misses the other: for my mouth—it has commanded
it ; and His breath—it has brought them together. And He
has cast the lot for them, and His hand has assigned it (this land)
to them by measure : they will possess it for ever ; to generation
and generation they will dwell therein."* The phrase כָּתַב עַל is
used for entering in a book, inasmuch as what is written there
is placed *upon* the page ; and דָּרַשׁ מֵעַל for searching in a book,
inasmuch as a person leans *over* the book when searching in it,
and gets the object of his search *out of* it. The prophet applied
the title " The Book of Jehovah" to his collection of the prophecies with which Jehovah had inspired him, and which He
had commanded him to write down. Whoever lived to see the
time when the judgment should come upon Edom, would have
only to look inquiringly into this holy scripture ; and if he compared what was predicted there with what had been actually
realized, he would find the most exact agreement between them.
The creatures named, which loved to frequent the marshes and
solitary places, and ruins, would all really make their homes in
what had once been Edom. But the *satyrs* and the *lilith,*
which were only the offspring of the popular belief—what of
them ? They, too, would be there ; for in the sense intended
by the prophet they were actual devils, which he merely calls
by well-known popular names to produce a spectral impression.
Edom would really become a rendezvous for all the animals
mentioned, as well as for such unearthly spirits as those which
he refers to here. The prophet, or rather Jehovah, whose
temporary organ he was, still further confirms this by saying,
" My mouth hath commanded it, and His breath has brought
them (all these creatures) together." As the first creating

word proceeded from the mouth of Jehovah, so also does the word of prophecy, which resembles such a word; and the breath of the mouth of Jehovah, *i.e.* His Spirit, is the power which accomplishes the fiat of prophecy, as it did that of creation, and moulds all creatures and their history according to the will and counsel of God (Ps. xxxiii. 6). In the second part of ver. 16*b* the prophet is speaking of Jehovah; whereas in the first Jehovah speaks through him,—a variation which vanishes indeed if we read פִּיו (Olshausen on Job ix. 20), or, what would be better, פִּיהוּ, but which may be sustained by a hundred cases of a similar kind. There is a shadow, as it were, of this change in the לָהֶם, which alternates with לָהֶן in connection with the animals named. The suffix of *chillᵉqattáh* (without *mappik*, as in 1 Sam. i. 6) refers to the land of Edom. Edom is, as it were, given up by a divine lot, and measured off with a divine measure, to be for ever the horrible abode of beasts and demons such as those described. A prelude of the fulfilment of this swept over the mountainous land of Edom immediately after the destruction of Jerusalem (see Köhler on Mal. i. 2–5); and it has never risen to its previous state of cultivation again. It swarms with snakes, and the desolate mountain heights and barren table-lands are only inhabited by wild crows and eagles, and great flocks of birds. But the ultimate fulfilment, to which the appeal in ver. 16 refers, is still in the future, and will eventually fall upon the abodes of those who spiritually belong to that circle of hostility to Jehovah (Jesus) and His church, of which ancient Edom was merely the centre fixed by the prophet.

Edom falls, never to rise again. Its land is turned into a horrible wilderness. But, on the other hand, the wilderness through which the redeemed Israel returns, is changed into a flowery field. Ch. xxxv. 1, 2. " *Gladness fills the desert and the heath; and the steppe rejoices, and flowers like the crocus. It flowers abundantly, and rejoices; yea, rejoicing and singing: the glory of Lebanon is given to it, the splendour of Carmel and the plain of Sharon; they will see the glory of Jehovah, the splendour of our God.*" יְשֻׂשׂוּם מִדְבָּר (to be accentuated with *tiphchah munach*, not with *mercha tiphchah*) has been correctly explained by Aben-Ezra. The orignal *Nun* has been assimilated to the following *Mem*, just as *pidyōn* in Num. iii. 49 is after-

wards written *pidyōm* (Ewald, § 91, *b*). The explanation given
by Rashi, Gesenius, and others (*lætabuntur his*), is untenable, if only because *sūs* (*sīs*) cannot be construed with the
accusative of the object (see at ch. viii. 6) ; and to get rid of
the form by correction, as Olshausen proposes, is all the more
objectionable, because " the old full plural in *ūn* is very
frequently met with before *Mem*" (Böttcher), in which case it
may have been pronounced as it is written here.[1] According
to the Targum on Song of Sol. ii. 1 (also Saad., Abulw.),
the *chăbhatstseleth* is the narcissus; whilst the Targum on the
passage before us leaves it indefinite—*sicut lilia.* The name (a
derivative of *bâtsal*) points to a bulbous plant, probably the
crocus and primrose, which were classed together.[2] The sandy
steppe would become like a lovely variegated plain covered with
meadow flowers.[3] On *gīlath*, see at ch. xxxiii. 6 (cf. ch. lxv. 18) :
the infin. noun takes the place of an inf. abs., which expresses
the abstract verbal idea, though in a more rigid manner ; *'aph*
(like *gam* in Gen. xxxi. 15, xlvi. 4) is an exponent of the
increased emphasis already implied in the gerunds that come
after. So joyful and so gloriously adorned will the barren
desert, which has been hitherto so mournful, become, on account of the great things that are in store for it. Lebanon,
Carmel, and Sharon have, as it were, shared their splendour
with the desert, that all might be clothed alike in festal dress,
when the glory of Jehovah, which surpasses everything else in

[1] Böttcher calls *ûm* the oldest primitive form of the plural ; but it is
only a strengthening of *ûn* ; cf. *tannīm = tannīn, Hanameel = Hananeel*,
and such Sept. forms as Gesem, Madiam, etc. (see Hitzig on Jer. xxxii. 7).
Wetzstein told me of a Bedouin tribe, in whose dialect the third pers.
præt. regularly ended in *m*, *e.g. akalum* (they have eaten).

[2] The crocus and the primrose (חַמְצָלִיתָא in Syriac) may really be easily
confounded, but not the narcissus and primrose, which have nothing in
common except that they are bulbous plants, like most of the flowers of
the East, which shoot up rapidly in the spring, as soon as the winter rains
are over. But there are other colchicaceæ beside our *colchicum autumnale*,
which flowers before the leaves appear and is therefore called *filius ante
patrem* (*e.g.* the eastern *colchicum variegatum*).

[3] Layard, in his *Nineveh and Babylon*, describes in several places the
enchantingly beautiful and spring-like variation of colours which occurs
in the Mesopotamian " desert ; " though what the prophet had in his mind
was not the real *midbâr*, or desert of pasture land, but, as the words *tsiyâh*
and *'ărâbhâh* show, the utterly barren sandy desert.

its splendour, should appear; that glory which they would not
only be privileged to behold, but of which they would be
honoured to be the actual scene.

The prophet now exclaims to the afflicted church, in language of unmixed consolation, that Jehovah is coming. Vers.
3, 4. "*Strengthen ye the weak hands, and make the trembling
knees strong! Say to those of a terrified heart, Be strong!
Fear ye not! Behold, your God will come for vengeance, for a
divine retribution: He will come, and bring you salvation.*"
Those who have become weak in faith, hopeless and despairing,
are to cheer up; and the stronger are to tell such of their
brethren as are perplexed and timid, to be comforted now: for
Jehovah is coming *nâqâm* (*i.e.* as vengeance), and *g^{e}mûl 'Elōhīm*
(*i.e.* as retribution, such as God the highly exalted and Almighty
Judge inflicts; the expression is similar to that in ch. xxx. 27,
xiii. 9, cf. xl. 10, but a bolder one; the words in apposition
stand as abbreviations of final clauses). The infliction of
punishment is the immediate object of His coming, but the
ultimate object is the salvation of His people (וְיִשְׁעֲכֶם a contracted future form, which is generally confined to the aorist).
Vers. 5–7. "*Then the eyes of the blind will be opened, and the
ears of the deaf unstopped. Then will the lame man leap as the
stag, and the tongue of the dumb man shout; for waters break
out in the desert, and brooks in the steppe. And the mirage
becomes a fish-pond, and the thirsty ground gushing water-springs;
in the place of jackals, where it lies, there springs up grass with
reeds and rushes.*" The bodily defects mentioned here there is
no reason for regarding as figurative representations of spiritual
defects. The healing of bodily defects, however, is merely
the outer side of what is actually effected by the coming of
Jehovah (for the other side, comp. ch. xxxii. 3, 4). And so,
also, the change of the desert into a field abounding with water
is not a mere poetical ornament; for in the last times, the era
of redemption, nature itself will really share in the *doxa* which
proceeds from the manifested God to His redeemed. *Shârâbh*
(Arab. *sarâb*) is essentially the same thing as that which we
call in the western languages the *mirage*, or *Fata morgana*; not
indeed every variety of this phenomenon of the refraction of
light, through strata of air of varying density lying one above
another, but more especially that appearance of water, which is

produced as if by magic in the dry, sandy desert [1] (literally
perhaps the " desert shine," just as we speak of the " Alpine
glow;" see ch. xlix. 10). The antithesis to this is *'ăgam* (Chald.
'agmă', Syr. *egmo*, Ar. *ag'am*), a fish-pond (as in ch. xli. 18,
different from *'âgâm* in ch. xix. 10). In the arid sandy desert,
where the jackal once had her lair and suckled her young (this
is, according to Lam. iv. 3, the true explanation of the permutative *ribhtsâh*, for which *ribhtsâm* would be in some respects
more suitable), grass springs up even into reeds and rushes; so
that, as ch. xliii. 20 affirms, the wild beasts of the desert praise
Jehovah.

In the midst of such miracles, by which all nature is
glorified, the people of Jehovah are redeemed, and led home to
Zion. Vers. 8–10. " *And a highway rises there, and a road,
and it will be called the Holy Road; no unclean man will pass
along it, as it is appointed for them : whoever walks the road,
even simple ones do not go astray. There will be no lion there,
and the most ravenous beast of prey will not approach it, will not
be met with there ; and redeemed ones walk. And the ransomed
of Jehovah will return, and come to Zion with shouting, and everlasting joy upon their head : they lay hold of gladness and joy,
and sorrow and sighing flee away.*" Not only unclean persons
from among the heathen, but even unclean persons belonging
to Israel itself, will never pass along that holy road ; none but
the church purified and sanctified through sufferings, and those
connected with it. הוּא לָמוֹ, to them, and to them alone, does
this road belong, which Jehovah has made and secured, and
which so readily strikes the eye, that even an idiot could not
miss it ; whilst it lies so high, that no beast of prey, however
powerful (*p^e rîts chayyōth*, a superlative verbal noun : Ewald,
§ 313, *c*), could possibly leap up to it : not one is ever encoun-
tered by the pilgrim there. The pilgrims are those whom
Jehovah has redeemed and delivered, or set free from captivity
and affliction (גָּאַל, גֹּל, related to חֵל, *solvere ;* פָּדָה, פֹּר, *scindere,
abscindere*). Everlasting joy soars above their head ; they lay
fast hold of delight and joy (compare on ch. xiii. 8), so that it
never departs from them. On the other hand, sorrow and
sighing flee away. The whole of ver. 10 is like a mosaic from
ch. li. 11, lxi. 7, li. 3 ; and what is affirmed of the holy road,

---

[1] See G. Rawlinson, *Monarchies,* i. p. 38.

is also affirmed in ch. lii. 1 of the holy city (compare ch. lxii. 12, lxiii. 4). A prelude of the fulfilment is seen in what Ezra speaks of with gratitude to God in Ezra viii. 31. We have intentionally avoided crowding together the parallel passages from ch. xl.–lxvi. The whole chapter is, in every part, both in thought and language, a prelude of that book of consolation for the exiles in their captivity. Not only in its spiritual New Testament thoughts, but also in its ethereal language, soaring high as it does in majestic softness and light, the prophecy has now reached the highest point of its development.

PART VII.

FULFILMENTS OF PROPHECY; AND PROPHECIES BELONGING TO THE FOURTEENTH YEAR OF HEZEKIAH'S REIGN, AND THE TIMES IMMEDIATELY FOLLOWING.

CHAP. XXXVI.–XXXIX.

To the first six books of Isaiah's prophecies there is now appended a seventh. The six form three syzygies. In the "Book of Hardening," ch. i.–vi. (apart from ch. i., which belonged to the times of Uzziah and Jotham), we saw Israel's day of grace brought to an end. In the " Book of Immanuel," ch. vii.–xii. (from the time of Ahaz), we saw the judgment of hardening and destruction in its first stage of accomplishment; but Immanuel was a pledge that, even if the great mass should perish, neither the whole of Israel nor the house of David would be destroyed. The separate judgments through which the way was to be prepared for the kingdom of Immanuel, are announced in the " Book concerning the Nations," ch. xiii.–xxiii. (from the times of Ahaz and Hezekiah); and the general judgment in which they would issue, and after which a new Israel would triumph, is foretold in the " Book of the great Catastrophe," ch. xxiv.–xxvii. (after the fifteenth year of Hezekiah). These two syzygies form the first great orbit of the collection. A second opens with the " Book of Woes, or of the Precious Corner-stone," ch. xxviii.–xxxiii. (xxviii.–xxxii., from the first years of Hezekiah, and xxxiii. from the fourteenth year), by the side of which is placed the " Book of the Judgment upon Edom, and of the Restoration of Israel," ch. xxxiv. xxxv. (after Hezekiah's fifteenth year). The former shows how Ephraim succumbs to the power of Asshur, and Judah's trust in Egypt is put to shame ; the latter, how the world, with its hostility to the church, eventually succumbs to the vengeance of Jehovah, whereas the church itself is redeemed and glorified. Then follows, in ch. xxxvi.–xxxix., a " Book of Histories," which returns from the ideal distances of ch. xxxiv. xxxv. to the historical realities of ch. xxxiii., and begins by stating that " at the conduit of the upper pool in the highway of the fuller's field," where Ahaz had formerly preferred the help of Asshur to that of Jehovah, there stood an embassy from the king of Asshur with a detachment of his army (ch. xxxvi. 2), scornfully demanding the surrender of Jerusalem.

Just as we have found throughout a well-considered succession and dovetailing of the several parts, so here we can see reciprocal bearings, which are both designed and expressive ; and it is *à priori* a probable thing that Isaiah, who wrote the historical introduction to the Judæo-Assyrian drama in the second book, is the author of the concluding act of the same drama, which is here the subject of Book vii. The fact that the murder of Sennacherib is related in ch. xxxvii. 37, 38, in accordance with the prophecy in ch. xxxvii. 7, does not render this impossible, since, according to credible tradition, Isaiah outlived Hezekiah (see vol. i. 34). The assertion made by Hitzig and others—that the speciality of the prophecy, and the miraculous character of the events recorded in ch. xxxvi.–xxxix., preclude the possibility of Isaiah's authorship, inasmuch as, " according to a well-known critical rule," such special prophecies as these are always *vaticinia ex eventu*, and accounts of miracles are always more recent than their historical germ—rests upon a foregone conclusion which was completed before any investigation took place, and which we have good ground for rejecting, although we are well acquainted with the valuable service that has been rendered by this philosopher's stone. The statement that accounts of miracles as such are never contemporaneous with the events themselves, is altogether at variance with experience; and if the advance from the general to the particular were to be blotted out of Isaiah's prophecy in relation to Asshur, this would be not only unhistorical, but unpsychological also.

The question whether Isaiah is the author of ch. xxxvi.–xxxix. or not, is bound up with the question whether the original place of these histories is in the book of Isaiah or the book of Kings, where the whole passage is repeated with the exception of Hezekiah's psalm of thanksgiving (2 Kings xviii. 13–xx. 19). We shall find that the text of the book of Kings is in several places the purer and more authentic of the two (though not so much so as a biassed prejudice would assume), from which it apparently follows that this section is not in its original position in the book of Isaiah, but has been taken from some other place and inserted there. But this conclusion is a deceptive one. In the relation in which Jer. lii. and 2 Kings xxiv. 18–xxv. stand to one another, we have a proof that the text of a passage may be more faithfully preserved in a secondary place than in its original one. For in this particular instance it is equally certain that the section relating to king Zedekiah and the Chaldean catastrophe was written by the author of the book of Kings, whose style was formed on that of Deuteronomy, and also, that in the book of Jeremiah it is an appendix taken by an unknown hand from the book of the Kings. But it is also an acknowledged fact, that the text of Jer. lii. is incomparably the purer of the two, and also that there are many other instances in which the passage in the book of Kings is corrupt—that is to say, in the form in which it lies before us now—whereas the Alexandrian translator had it in his possession in a partially better form. Consequently, the fact that Isa. xxxvi.–xxxix. is in some respects less pure than 2 Kings xviii. 13–xx. 19, cannot be any argument in itself against the originality of this section in the book of Isaiah.

It is indeed altogether inconceivable, that the author of the book of Kings should have written it; for, on the one hand, the liberality of the prophetic addresses communicated point to a written source (see vol. i. 16) ; and, on the other hand, it is wanting in that Deuteronomic stamp, by which the hand of this author is so easily recognised. Nor can it have been copied by him out of the annals of Hezekiah (*dibhrē hayyâmîm*), as is commonly supposed, since it is written in prophetic and not in annalistic style. Whoever has once made himself

acquainted with these two different kinds of historical composition, the fundamentally different characteristics of which we
have pointed out in the Introduction (vol. i. p. 2 sqq.), can
never by any possibility confound them again. And this
passage is written in a style so peculiarly prophetical, that, like
the magnificent historical accounts of Elijah, for example,
which commence so abruptly in 2 Kings xvii. 1, it must have
been taken from some special and prophetical source, which
had nothing to do with other prophetico-historical portions of
the book of Kings. And the following facts are sufficient to
raise the probability, that this source was no other than the
book of Isaiah itself, into an absolute certainty. In the *first*
place, the author of the book of Kings had the book of Isaiah
amongst the different sources, of which his apparatus was composed; this is evident from 2 Kings xvi. 5, a passage which
was written with Isa. vii. 1 in view. And *secondly*, we have
express, though indirect, testimony to the effect that this section, which treats of the most important epoch in Hezekiah's
reign, is in its original place in the book of Isaiah. The
author of the book of Chronicles says, in 2 Chron. xxxii. 32 :
" Now the rest of the acts of Hezekiah, and the gracious
occurrences of his life, behold, they are written in the vision
(*châzōn*) of Isaiah the son of Amoz, and in the book of the
kings of Judah and Israel." This notice clearly proves that a
certain historical account of Hezekiah had either been taken
out of the collection of Isaiah's prophecies, which is headed
châzōn (vision), and inserted in the " book of the kings of
Judah and Israel," or else had been so inserted along with the
whole collection. The book of the Kings was the principal
source employed by the chronicler, which he calls " the *midrash*
of the book of the Kings" in 2 Chron. xxiv. 27. Into this
Midrash, or else into the still earlier work upon which it was a
commentary, the section in question was copied from the book
of Isaiah ; and it follows from this, that the writer of the history of the kings made use of our book of Isaiah for one portion
of the history of Hezekiah's reign, and made extracts from it.
The chronicler himself did not care to repeat the whole section,
which he knew to be already contained in the canonical book
of Kings (to say nothing of the book of Isaiah). At the same
time, his own historical account of Hezekiah in 2 Chron. xxvii

clearly shows that he was acquainted with it, and also that the historical materials, which the annals supplied to him through the medium of the Midrash, were totally different both in substance and form from those contained in the section in question. These two testimonies are further strengthened by the fact, that Isaiah is well known to us as a historian through another passage in the Chronicles, namely, as the author of a complete history of Uzziah's reign (see vol. i. 38); also by the fact, that the prophetico-historical style of ch. xxxvi.-xxxix., with their fine, noble, pictorial prose, which is comparable to the grandest historical composition to be met with in Hebrew, is worthy of Isaiah, and bears every mark of Isaiah's pen; thirdly, by the fact, that there are other instances in which Isaiah has interwoven historical accounts with his prophecies (ch. vii. viii. and xx.), and that in so doing he sometimes speaks of himself in the first person (ch. vi. 1, viii. 1-4), and sometimes in the third (ch. vii. 3 sqq., and xx.), just as in ch. xxxvi.-xxxix.; and fourthly, by the fact that, as we have already observed, ch. vii. 3 and xxxvi. 2 bear the clearest marks of having had one and the same author; and, as we shall also show, the order in which the four accounts in ch. xxxvi.-xxxix. are arranged, corresponds to the general plan of the whole collection of prophecies,— ch. xxxvi. and xxxvii. looking back to the prophecies of the Assyrian era, and ch. xxxviii. and xxxix. looking forwards to those of the Babylonian era, which is the prophet's ideal present from ch. xl. onwards.

A. FIRST ASSYRIAN ATTEMPT TO COMPEL THE SURRENDER OF JERUSALEM.—CHAP. XXXVI.-XXXVII. 7.

Marcus v. Niebuhr, in his *History of Asshur and Babel* (p. 164), says, " Why should not Hezekiah have revolted from Asshur as soon as he ascended the throne? He had a motive for doing this, which other kings had not,—namely, that as he held his kingdom in fief from his God, obedience to a temporal monarch was in his case sin." But this assumption, which is founded upon the same idea as that in which the question was put to Jesus concerning the tribute money, is not at all in accordance with Isaiah's view, as we may see from ch. xxviii.-xxxii.; and Hezekiah's revolt cannot have occurred

even in the sixth year of his reign (see vol. i. 51). For Shalmanassar, or rather Sargon, made war upon Egypt and Ethiopia
after the destruction of Samaria (ch. xx.; cf. Oppert, *Les
Inscriptions des Sargonides*, pp. 22, 27), without attempting
anything against Hezekiah. It was not till the time of Sargon,
who overthrew the reigning house of Assyria, that the actual
preparations for the revolt were commenced, by the formation
of an alliance between the kingdom of Judah on the one hand,
and Egypt, and probably Philistia, on the other, the object of
which was the rupture of the Assyrian yoke.[1] The campaign
of Sennacherib the son of Sargon, into which we are transported in the following history, was the third of his expeditions,
the one to which Sennacherib himself refers in the inscription
upon the prism : " *dans ma 3ᵉ campagne je marchai vers la
Syrie.*" The position which we find Sennacherib taking up
between Philistia and Jerusalem, to the south-west of the latter,
is a very characteristic one in relation to both the occasion and
the ultimate object of the campaign. Ch. xxxvi. 1.[2] " *And it
came to pass in the* (K. *and in the*) *fourteenth year of king Hizkiyahu, Sancherib king of Asshur came up against all the fortified cities of Judah, and took them.* (K. adds : *Then Hizkiyah
king of Judah sent to the king of Asshur to Lachish, saying, I
have sinned, withdraw from me again; what thou imposest upon
me I will raise. And the king of Asshur imposed upon Hizkiyah
king of Judah three hundred talents of silver, and thirty talents
of gold. And Hizkiyah gave up all the silver that was in the
house of Jehovah, and in the treasures of the king's house. At
the same time Hizkiyah mutilated the doors of the temple of
Jehovah, and the pillars which Hizkiyah king of Judah had
plated with gold, and gave it to the king of Asshur*)." This long
addition, which is distinguished at once by the introduction of
חזקיה in the place of חזקיהו, is probably only an annalistic
interpolation, though one of great importance in relation
to Isa. xxxiii. 7. What follows in Isaiah does not dovetail

---

[1] The name *Amgarron* upon the earthenware prism of Sennacherib
does not mean *Migron* (Oppert), but *Ekron* (Rawlinson).

[2] We shall show the variations in the text of 2 Kings xviii. 13 sqq., as
far as we possibly can, in our translation. K. signifies the book of Kings.
But the task of pronouncing an infallible sentence upon them all we shall
leave to those who know everything.

well into this addition, and therefore does not presuppose its existence. Ver. 2. " *Then the king of Asshur sent Rabshakeh* (K.: *Tartan, and Rabsaris, and Rabshakeh) from Lachish towards Jerusalem to king Hizkiyahu with a great army, and he advanced* (K.: *to king H. with a great army to Jerusalem; and they went up and came to Jerusalem, and went up, and came and advanced) to the conduit of the upper pool by the road of the fuller's field.*" Whereas in K. the repeated ויעלו ויבאו (and went up and came) forms a " dittography," the names *Tartan* and *Rab-saris* have apparently dropped out of the text of Isaiah, as ch. xxxvii. 6 and 24 presuppose a plurality of messengers. The three names are not names of persons, but official titles, viz. the commander-in-chief (*Tartan*, which really occurs in an Assyrian list of offices; see Rawlinson, *Monarchies*, ii. 412), the chief eunuch (see the plate in Rawlinson, ii. 118), and the chief cup-bearer (רַבְשָׁקֵה with *tzere* = רַבְשָׁקָא). The situation of *Lachish* is marked by the present ruins of *Umm Lakis*, to the south-west of *Bet-Gibrin* (Eleutheropolis) in the Shephelah. The messengers come from the south-west with the *ultima ratio* of a strong detachment (חֵיל a connecting form, from חַיִל, like גיא גדולה, Zech. xiv. 4; Ewald, § 287, *a*); they therefore halt on the western side of Jerusalem (on the locality, see at ch. vii. 3, xxii. 8–11; compare Keil on Kings).

Hezekiah's confidential ministers go there also. Ver. 3 (K. " *And they called to the king), and there went out to him* (K. *to them) Eliakim son of Hilkiyahu, the house-minister, and Shebna the chancellor, and Joah son of Asaph, the recorder.*" On the office of the house-minister, or major-domo, which was now filled by Eliakim instead of Shebna (שבנא, K. twice שבנה), see ch. xxii. 15 sqq.; and on that of *sōphēr* and *mazkīr*, see vol. i. pp. 7, 8. Rabshakeh's message follows in vers. 4–10: " *And Rabshakeh said to them, Say now to Hizkiyahu, Thus saith the great king, the king of Asshur, What sort of confidence is this that thou hast got? I say* (K. *thou sayest, i.e.* thou talkest), *vain talk is counsel and strength for war: now, then, in whom dost thou trust, that thou hast rebelled against me?* (K. *Now) Behold, thou trustest* (K. לָךְ) *in this broken reed-staff there, in Egypt, on which one leans, and it runs into his hand and pierces it; so does Pharaoh king of Egypt to all who trust in him. But if thou sayest to me* (K. *ye say), We trust in Jehovah our God;*

is it not He whose high places and altars Hizkiyahu has removed,
and has said to Judah and Jerusalem, Ye shall worship before
the altar (K. adds, *in Jerusalem*)? *And now take a wager with*
my lord (K. *with*) *the king of Asshur; I will deliver thee two*
thousand horses, if thou art able for thy part to give horsemen
upon them. And how couldst thou repel the advance of a single
satrap among the least of the servants of my lord?! Thou
puttest thy trust then in Egypt for chariots and riders! And
(omitted in K.) *now have I come up without Jehovah against*
this land to destroy it (K. *against this place, to destroy it*)?
Jehovah said to me, Go up to (K. *against*) *this land, and destroy*
it." The chronicler has a portion of this address of Rabshakeh
in 2 Chron. xxxii. 10–12. And just as the prophetic words in
the book of Kings have a Deuteronomic sound, and those in
the Chronicles the ring of a chronicle, so do Rabshakeh's words,
and those which follow, sound like the words of Isaiah himself.
"The great king" is the standing royal title appended to the
names of Sargon and Sennacherib upon the Assyrian monuments (compare ch. x. 8). Hezekiah is not thought worthy of
the title of king, either here or afterwards. The reading
אָמַרְתָּ in ver. 5 (thou speakest vain talk) is not the preferable
one, because in that case we should expect דִּבַּרְתָּ, or rather
(according to the usual style) אַךְ דִּבַּרְתָּ. The meaning is, that
he must look upon Hezekiah's resolution, and his strength
(עֵצָה וּגְבוּרָה connected as in ch. xi. 2) for going to war, as mere
boasting ("lip-words," as in Prov. xiv. 23), and must therefore
assume that there was something in the background of which
he was well aware. And this must be Egypt, which would
not only be of no real help to its ally, but would rather do him
harm by leaving him in the lurch. The figure of a reed-staff
has been borrowed by Ezekiel in ch. xxix. 6, 7. It was a
very appropriate one for Egypt, with its abundance of reeds
and rushes (ch. xix. 6), and it has Isaiah's peculiar ring (for
the expression itself, compare ch. xlii. 3; and for the fact
itself, ch. xxx. 5, and other passages). רָצוּץ does not mean
fragile (Luzz. *quella fragil canna*), but broken, namely, in
consequence of the loss of the throne by the native royal
family, from whom it had been wrested by the Ethiopians
(ch. xviii.), and the defeats sustained at the hands of Sargon
(ch. xx.). The construction *cui quis innititur et intrat* is para-

tactic for *cui si quis*. In ver. 7 the reading תֹּאמְרוּן commends
itself, from the fact that the sentence is not continued with
הֲסִירֹתָ; but as Hezekiah is addressed throughout, and it is to
him that the reply is to be made, the original reading was probably תֹּאמַר. The fact that Hezekiah had restricted the worship of Jehovah to Jerusalem, by removing the other places
of worship (2 Kings xviii. 4), is brought against him in a
thoroughly heathen, and yet at the same time (considering
the inclination to worship other gods which still existed in the
nation) a very crafty manner. In vers. 8, 9, he throws in his
teeth, with most imposing scorn, his own weakness as compared with Asshur, which was chiefly dreaded on account of
its strength in cavalry and war-chariots. הִתְעָרֶב נָא does not
refer to the performance and counter-performance which
follow, in the sense of "connect thyself" (Luzz. *associati*), but
is used in a similar sense to the Homeric μιγῆναι, though with
the idea of vying with one another, not of engaging in war
(the synonym in the Talmud is *himrâh*, to bet, *e.g. b. Sabbath*
31*a*): a bet and a pledge are kindred notions (Heb. עֵרָבוֹן, cf.
Lat. *vadari*). On *pechâh* (for *pachâh*), which also occurs as an
Assyrian title in Ezek. xxiii. 6, 23, see vol. i. p. 267, note 3.
פַּחַת אַחַד, two constructives, the first of which is to be explained
according to Ewald, § 286, *a* (compare above, ver. 2, חֵיל כָּבֵד),
form the logical *regens* of the following *servorum domini mei
minimorum;* and *hĕshȋbh pᵉnē* does not mean here to refuse a
petitioner, but to repel an antagonist (ch. xxviii. 6). The
fut. consec. וַתִּבְטַח deduces a consequence : Hezekiah could not
do anything by himself, and therefore he trusted in Egypt,
from which he expected chariots and horsemen. In ver. 10,
the prophetic idea, that Asshur was the instrument employed
by Jehovah (ch. x. 5, etc.), is put into the mouth of the
Assyrian himself. This is very conceivable, but the colouring
of Isaiah is undeniable. The concluding words, in which the
Assyrian boasts of having Jehovah on his side, affect the
messengers of Hezekiah in the keenest manner, especially
because of the people present. Ver. 11. "*Then said Eliakim
(K. the son of Hilkiyahu), and Shebna, and Joah, to Rabshakeh,
Pray, speak to thy servants in Aramœan, for we understand it;
and do not speak to (K. with) us in Jewish, in the ears of the
people that are on the wall.*" They spoke Yᵉhŭdȋth, *i.e.* the

colloquial language of the kingdom of Judah. The kingdom
of Israel was no longer in existence, and the language of the
Israelitish nation, as a whole, might therefore already be called
Judæan (Jewish), as in Neh. xiii. 24, more especially as there
may have been a far greater dialectical difference between the
popular speech of the northern and southern kingdoms, than we
can gather from the biblical books that were written in the one
or the other. Aramæan (*'ărâmīth*), however, appears to have
been even then, as it was at a later period (Ezra iv. 7), the
language of intercourse between the empire of Eastern Asia and
the people to the west of the Tigris (compare Alex. Polyhistor
in Euseb. *chron. arm.* i. 43, where Sennacherib is said to have
erected a monument with a Chaldean inscription); and consequently educated Judæans not only understood it, but were able
to speak it, more especially those who were in the service of the
state. Assyrian, on the contrary, was unintelligible to Judæans
(ch. xxviii. 11, xxxiii. 19), although this applied comparatively
less to the true Assyrian dialect, which was Semitic, and can
be interpreted for the most part from the Hebrew (see Oppert's
" Outlines of an Assyrian Grammar" in the *Journal Asiatique*,
1859), than to the motley language of the Assyrian army,
which was a compound of Arian and Turanian elements. The
name Sennacherib (*Sanchĕŗībh* = סַן־אֲחִי־יְרִב, LXX. *Sennachē-
reim, i.e.* " Sin, the moon-god, had multiplied the brethren")
is Semitic; on the other hand, the name Tartan, which cannot
be interpreted either from the Semitic or the Arian, is an
example of the element referred to, which was so utterly
strange to a Judæan ear.

The harsh reply is given in ver. 12. " *Then Rabshakeh
said* (K. *to them*), *Has my lord sent me to* (K. הַעַל) *thy lord and
to thee, not rather to* (both texts, עַל) *the men who sit upon the
wall, to eat their dung, and to drink their urine together with
you?*"—namely, because their rulers were exposing them to a
siege which would involve the most dreadful state of famine.

After Rabshakeh had refused the request of Hezekiah's
representatives in this contemptuous manner, he turned in
defiance of them to the people themselves. Vers. 13–20.
" *Then Rabshakeh went near, and cried with a loud voice in
the Jewish language* (K. *and spake*), *and said, Hear the words*
(K. *the word*) *of the great king, the king of Asshur. Thus saith*

the king, Let not Hizkiyahu practise deception upon you (יַשִּׁא,
K. יַשִּׁיא); *for he cannot deliver you* (K. *out of his hand*). *And
let not Hizkiyahu feed you with hope in Jehovah, saying, Jehovah
will deliver, yea, deliver us:* (K. *and*) *this city will not be delivered
into the hand of the king of Asshur. Hearken not to Hizkiyahu;
for thus saith the king* (*hammelekh,* K. *melekh*) *of Asshur, Enter
into a connection of mutual good wishes with me, and come out to
me: and enjoy every one his vine, and every one his fig-tree, and
drink every one the water of his cistern; till I come and take you
away into a land like your land, a land of corn and wine, a land
of bread-corn and vineyards* (K. *a land full of fine olive-trees and
honey, and live and do not die, and hearken not to Hizkiyahu*);
that Hizkiyahu do not befool you (K. *for he befools you*), *saying,
Jehovah will deliver us! Have the gods of the nations delivered*
(K. *really delivered*) *every one his land out of the hand of the
king of Asshur? Where are the gods of Ḥamath and Arpad?
where the gods of Sepharvayim* (K. adds, *Henaʿ and ʿIvah*)? *and
how much less* (וְכִי, K. כִּי) *have they delivered that Samaria out
of my hand? Who were they among all the gods of these* (K. *of
the*) *lands, who delivered their land out of my hand? how much
less will Jehovah deliver Jerusalem out of my hand!?*" The
chronicler also has this continuation of Rabshakeh's address
in part (2 Chron. xxxii. 13–15), but he has fused into one the
Assyrian self-praise uttered by Rabshakeh on his first and
second mission. The encouragement of the people, by referring
to the help of Jehovah (2 Chron. xxxii. 6–8), is placed by him
before this first account is given by Isaiah, and forms a conclusion to the preparations for the contest with Asshur as there
described. Rabshakeh now draws nearer to the wall, and
harangues the people. הִשִּׁיא is construed here with a dative (to
excite treacherous hopes); whereas in 2 Chron. xxxii. 15 it is
written with an accusative. The reading מִידוֹ is altered from
מִידִי in ver. 20, which is inserted still more frequently by the
chronicler. The reading אֶת־הָעִיר with נִתַּן is incorrect; it
would require יֻתַּן (Ges. § 143, 1a). To make a *bᵉrâkháh* with
a person was equivalent to entering into a relation of blessing,
i.e. into a state of mind in which each wished all prosperity to
the other. This was probably a common phrase, though we
only meet with it here. יָצָא, when applied to the besieged, is
equivalent to surrendering (*e.g.* 1 Sam. xi. 3). If they did

that, they should remain in quiet possession and enjoyment,
until the Assyrian fetched them away (after the Egyptian campaign was over), and transported them to a land which he
describes to them in the most enticing terms, in order to soften
down the inevitable transportation. It is a question whether
the expansion of this picture in the book of Kings is original
or not; since הֵנַע וְעֻּזֶּה in ver. 19 appears to be also tacked on
here from Isa. xxxvii. 13 (see at this passage). On *Hamath*
and *Arpad* (to the north of Haleb in northern Syria, and a
different place from *Arvad* = *Arad*), see ch. x. 9. *Sᵉpharvayim*
(a dual form, the house of the *Sᵉpharvīm*, 2 Kings xvii. 31)
is the Sipphara of Ptol. v. 18, 7, the southernmost city of
Mesopotamia, on the left bank of the Euphrates; Pliny's *Hip-
parenum* on the *Narraga*, *i.e.* the canal, *nᵉhar malkâ'*, the key
to the irrigating or inundating works of Babylon, which were
completed afterwards by Nebuchadnezzar (Plin. *h. n.* vi. 30);
probably the same place as the sun-city, *Sippara*, in which
Xisuthros concealed the sacred books before the great flood
(see K. Müller's *Fragmenta Historicorum Gr.* ii. 501–2). פֶּן
in ver. 18 has a warning meaning (as if it followed הִשָּׁמְרוּ לכם);
and both וְכִי and כִּי in vers. 19, 20, introduce an exclamatory
clause when following a negative interrogatory sentence: "and
that they should have saved," or "that Jehovah should save,"
equivalent to "how much less have they saved, or will He
save" (Ewald, § 354, *c*; comp. אַף־כִּי, 2 Chron. xxxii. 15). Rabshakeh's words in vers. 18–20 are the same as those in Isa. x.
8–11. The manner in which he defies the gods of the heathen,
of Samaria, and last of all of Jerusalem, corresponds to the prophecy there. It is the prophet himself who acts as historian
here, and describes the fulfilment of the prophecy, though
without therefore doing violence to his character as a prophet.

The effect of Rabshakeh's words. Vers. 21, 22. "*But they
held their peace* (K. *and they, the people, held their peace*), *and
answered him not a word; for it was the king's commandment,
saying, Ye shall not answer him. Then came Eliakim son of
Hilkiyahu* (K. *Hilkiyah*), *the house-minister, and Shebna the
chancellor, and Joah son of Asaph, the recorder, to Hizkiyahu,
with torn clothes, and told him the words of Rabshakeh.*" It is
only a superficial observation that could commend the reading
in Kings, "They, the people, held their peace," which Hitzig

and Knobel prefer, but which Luzzatto very properly rejects.
As the Assyrians wished to speak to the king himself (2 Kings
xviii. 18), who sent the three to them as his representatives,
the command to hear, and to make no reply, can only have
applied to them (and they had already made the matter worse by
the one remark which they had made concerning the language);
and the reading וַיַּחֲרִישׁוּ in the text of Isaiah is the correct one.
The three were silent, because the king had imposed the duty
of silence upon them; and regarding themselves as dismissed,
inasmuch as Rabshakeh had turned away from them to the
people, they hastened to the king, rending their clothes, in
despair and grief at the disgrace they had experienced.

The king and the deputation apply to Isaiah. Ch. xxxvii.
1–4. " *And it came to pass, when king Hizkiyahu had heard,*
he rent his clothes, and wrapped himself in mourning linen, and
went into the house of Jehovah. And sent Eliakim the house-
minister, and Shebna (K. omits אֶת) *the chancellor, and the eldest*
of the priests, wrapped in mourning linen, to Isaiah son of Amoz,
the prophet (K. has what is inadmissible : *the prophet son of*
Amoz). And they said to him, Thus saith Hizkiyahu, A day
of affliction, and punishment, and blasphemy is this day ; for
children are come to the matrix, and there is no strength to bring
them forth. Perhaps Jehovah thy God will hear the words
(K. *all the words) of Rabshakeh, with which the king of Asshur*
his lord has sent him to revile the living God ; and Jehovah thy
God will punish for the words which He hath heard, and thou
wilt make intercession for the remnant that still exists." The
distinguished embassy is a proof of the distinction of the
prophet himself (Knobel). The character of the deputation
accorded with its object, which was to obtain a consolatory
word for the king and people. In the form of the instructions
we recognise again the flowing style of Isaiah. תּוֹכֵחָה, as a
synonym of מוּסָר, נָקָם, is used as in Hos. v. 9 ; נָאֲצָה (from the
kal נָאַץ) according to ch. i. 4, v. 24, lii. 5, like נֶאָצָה (from the
piel נִאֵץ), Neh. ix. 18, 26 (reviling, *i.e.* reviling of God, or
blasphemy). The figure of there not being sufficient strength
to bring forth the child, is the same as in ch. lxvi. 9. מַשְׁבֵּר
(from שָׁבַר, syn. פֶּרֶץ, Gen. xxxviii. 29) does not signify the
actual birth (Luzzatto, *punto di dover nascere*), nor the deliver-
ing-stool (Targum), like *mashbēr shel-chayyáh*, the delivering-

stool of the midwife (*Kelim* xxiii. 4) ; but as the subject is the children, and not the mother, the matrix or mouth of the womb, as in Hos. xiii. 13, " He (Ephraim) is an unwise child ; when it is time does he not stop in the children's passage" (*mashbēr bânīm*), *i.e.* the point which a child must pass, not only with its head, but also with its shoulders and its whole body, for which the force of the pains is often not sufficient ? The existing condition of the state resembled such unpromising birth-pains, which threatened both the mother and the fruit of the womb with death, because the matrix would not open to give birth to the child. לֵדָה like הֵעָה in ch. xi. 9. The timid inquiry, which hardly dared to hope, commences with *'ūlai.* The following future is continued in perfects, the force of which is determined by it : " and He (namely Jehovah, the Targum and Syriac) will punish for the words," or, as we point it, " there will punish for the words which He hath heard, Jehovah thy God (*hōkhīăch*, referring to a judicial decision, as in a general sense in ch. ii. 4 and xi. 4) ; and thou wilt lift up prayer" (*i.e.* begin to offer it, ch. xiv. 4). " He will hear," namely as judge and deliverer ; " He hath heard," namely as the omnipresent One. The expression, " to revile the living God" (*l͏ᵉchârēph 'Elōhīm chai*), sounds like a comparison of Rabshakeh to Goliath (1 Sam. xvii. 26, 36). The " existing remnant" was Jerusalem, which was not yet in the enemy's hand (compare ch. i. 8, 9). The deliverance of the remnant is a key-note of Isaiah's prophecies. But the prophecy would not be fulfilled, until the grace which fulfilled it had been met by repentance and faith. Hence Hezekiah's weak faith sues for the intercession of the prophet, whose personal relation to God is here set forth as a closer one than that of the king and priests.

Isaiah's reply. Vers. 5–7. " *And the servants of king Hizkiyahu came to Isaiah. And Isaiah said to them* (אֲלֵיהֶם, K. לְהֶם), *Speak thus to your lord, Thus saith Jehovah, Be not afraid of the words which thou hast heard, with which the servants of the king of Asshur have blasphemed me ! Behold, I will bring a spirit upon him, and he will hear a hearsay, and return to his land; and I cut him down with the sword in his own land.*" Luzzatto, without any necessity, takes וַיֹּאמְרוּ in ver. 3 in the modal sense of what they were to do (*e dovevano dirgli*) :

they were to say this to him, but he anticipated them at once with the instructions given here. The fact, so far as the style is concerned, is rather this, that ver. 5, while pointing back, gives the ground for ver. 6 : " and when they had come to him (saying this), he said to them." נְעָרִי we render "servants" (*Knappen*[1]) after Esth. ii. 2, vi. 3, 5 ; it is a more contemptuous expression than עֲבָדֶי. The *rŭăch* mentioned here as sent by God is a superior force of a spiritual kind, which influences both thought and conduct, as in such other connections as ch. xix. 14, xxviii. 6, xxix. 10 (*Psychol.* p. 295, Anm.).

The external occasion which determined the return of Sennacherib, as described in ch. xxxvii. 36, 37, was the fearful mortality that had taken place in his army. The *sh^emŭ'ăh* (rumour, hearsay), however, was not the tidings of this catastrophe, but, as the continuation of the account in vers. 8, 9, clearly shows, the report of the advance of Tirhakah, which compelled Sennacherib to leave Palestine in consequence of this catastrophe. The prediction of his death is sufficiently special to be regarded by modern commentators, who will admit nothing but the most misty figures as prophecies, as a *vaticinium post eventum*. At the same time, the prediction of the event which would drive the Assyrian out of the land is intentionally couched in these general terms. The faith of the king, and of the inquirers generally, still needed to be tested and exercised. The time had not yet come for him to be rewarded by a clearer and fuller announcement of the judgment.

B. SECOND ATTEMPT OF THE ASSYRIANS TO FORCE THE SURRENDER OF JERUSALEM. ITS MIRACULOUS DELIVERANCE.—CHAP. XXXVII. 8 SQQ.

Rabshakeh, who is mentioned alone in both texts as the leading person engaged, returns to Sennacherib, who is induced to make a second attempt to obtain possession of Jerusalem, as a position of great strength and decisive importance. Vers. 8, 9. " *Rabshakeh thereupon returned, and found the king of*

---

[1] *Knappe* is the same word as " *Knave ;*" but we have no word in use now which is an exact equivalent, and *knave* has entirely lost its original sense of *servant.*—Tr.

*Asshur warring against Libnah : for he had heard that he had
withdrawn from Lachish. And he heard say concerning Tirhakah
king of Ethiopia,* (K. *Behold), he has come out to make war with
thee ; and heard, and sent* (K. *and repeated, and sent) messengers to Hizkiyahu, saying."* Tirhakah was cursorily referred to
in ch. xviii. The twenty-fifth dynasty of Manetho contained
three Ethiopian rulers : *Sabakon, Sebichōs* (סוֹא = כְּוָא, although,
so far as we know, the Egyptian names begin with *Sh*), and
Tarakos (Tarkos), Egypt. *Taharka,* or Heb. with the tone upon
the penultimate, *Tirháqáh.* The only one mentioned by Herodotus is Sabakon, to whom he attributes a reign of fifty years
(ii. 139), *i.e.* as much as the whole three amount to, when
taken in a round sum. If Sebichos is the biblical *So',* to whom
the lists attribute from twelve to fourteen years, it is perfectly
conceivable that Tirhakah may have been reigning in the
fourteenth year of Hezekiah. But if this took place, as
Manetho affirms, 366 years before the conquest of Egypt by
Alexander, *i.e.* from 696 onwards (and the *Apis-stele,* No. 2037,
as deciphered by Vic. de Rougé, *Revue archéol.* 1863, confirms
it), it would be more easily reconcilable with the Assyrian
chronology, which represents Sennacherib as reigning from
702–680 (Oppert and Rawlinson), than with the current biblical
chronology, according to which Hezekiah's fourteenth year is
certainly not much later than the year 714.[1] It is worthy of
remark also, that Tirhakah is not described as Pharaoh here,
but as the king of Ethiopia (*melekh Kûsh;* see at ver. 36).
Libnah, according to the Onom. a place *in regione Eleuthero-
politana,* is probably the same as *Tell es-Safieh* ("hill of the
pure " = of the white), to the north-west of *Bet Gibrin,* called
Alba Specula (*Blanche Garde*) in the middle ages. The expression וַיִּשְׁמַע ("and he heard"), which occurs twice in the
text, points back to what is past, and also prepares the way for
what follows : "having heard this, he sent," etc. At the same
time it appears to have been altered from וַיָּשָׁב.

The message. Vers. 10–13. " *Thus shall ye say to Hizkiyahu
king of Judah, saying, Let not thy God in whom thou trustest
deceive thee, saying, Jerusalem will not be given into the hand of
the king of Asshur. Behold, thou hast surely heard what* (K.

[1] On the still prevailing uncertainty with regard to the synchronism,
see Keil on Kings ; and Duncker, *Geschichte des Alterthums.* pp. 713–4.

that which) *the kings of Asshur have done to all lands, to lay the ban upon them; and thou, thou shouldst be delivered?! Have the gods of the nations, which my fathers destroyed, delivered them: Gozan, and Haran, and Rezeph, and the Bᵉnē-ʿEden, which are in Telassar? Where is* (K. *where is he*) *the king of Hamath, and the king of Arpad, and the king of ʿIr-Sepharvaim, Henaʿ, and ʿIvah?"* Although אֶרֶץ is feminine, אוֹתָם (K. אֹתָם), like לְהַחֲרִימָם, points back to the lands (in accordance with the want of any thoroughly developed distinction of the genders in Hebrew); likewise אֲשֶׁר *quas pessumdederunt.* There is historical importance in the fact, that here Sennacherib attributes to his fathers (Sargon and the previous kings of the Derketade dynasty which he had overthrown) what Rabshakeh on the occasion of the first mission had imputed to Sennacherib himself. On Gozan, see vol. i. p. 51. It is no doubt identical with the *Zuzan* of the Arabian geographers, which is described as a district of outer Armenia, situated on the *Chabur, e.g.* in the *Merasid.* "The *Chabur* is the *Chabur* of *el-Hasaniye,* a district of *Mosul,* to the east of the Tigris; it comes down from the mountains of the land of *Zuzan,* flows through a broad and thickly populated country in the north of *Mosul,* which is called outer Armenia, and empties itself into the Tigris." Ptolemy, on the other hand (v. 18, 14), is acquainted with a Mesopotamian *Gauzanitis;* and, looking upon northern Mesopotamia as the border land of Armenia, he says, κατέχει δὲ τῆς χώρας τὰ μὲν πρὸς τῇ Ἀρμενίᾳ ἡ Ἀνθεμουσία (not far from Edessa) ὑφ' ἣν ἡ Χαλκῖτις, ὑπὸ δὲ ταύτην ἡ Γαυζανῖτις, possibly the district of *Gulzan,* in which *Nisibin,* the ancient *Nisibis,* still stands.[1] For *Hârân* (Syr. *Horon;* Joseph. *Charran* of Mesopotamia), the present Harrân, not far from *Charmelik,* see *Genesis,* p. 327. The *Harran* in the *Guta* of Damascus (on the southern arm of the *Harus*), which Beke has recently identified with it, is not connected with it in any way. *Retseph* is the *Rhesapha* of Ptol. v. 18, 6, below Thapsacus, the present *Rusafa* in the Euphrates-valley of *ez-Zor,* between the Euphrates and Tadmur (Palmyra; see Robinson, *Pal.*). *Telassar,* with which the Targum (ii. iii.) and Syr. confound the Ellasar of Gen. xiv. 1, *i.e.* Artemita (Artamita), is not the *Thelseæ* of the *Itin. Antonini* and of the *Notitia*

[1] See Oppert, *Expédition,* i. 60.

dignitatum,—in which case the *Bᵉnē-'Eden* might be the tribe of *Bêt Genn* (Bettegene) on the southern slope of Lebanon (*i.e.* the 'Eden of Cœlesyria, Amos i. 5; the *Paradeisos* of Ptol. v. 15, 20; *Paradisus,* Plin. v. 19),—but the *Thelser* of the *Tab. Peuting.,* on the eastern side of the Tigris; and *Bᵉnē 'Eden* is the tribe of the *'Eden* mentioned by Ezekiel (xxvii. 23) after Haran and Ctesiphon. Consequently the enumeration of the warlike deeds describes a curve, which passes in a north-westerly direction through Hamath and Arpad, and then returns in Sepharvaim to the border of southern Mesopotamia and Babylonia. *'Ir-Sᵉpharvaim* is like 'Ir-Nâchâsh, 'Ir-Shemesh, etc. The legends connect the name with the sacred books. The form of the name is inexplicable; but the name itself probably signifies the double shore (after the Aramæan), as the city, which was the southernmost of the leading places of Mesopotamia, was situated on the Euphrates. The words הֵנַע וְעִוָּה, if not taken as proper names, would signify, "he has taken away, and overthrown;" but in that case we should expect הֵנִיעַ וְעִוָּה or הֲנִיעֹתִי וְעִוִּיתִי. They are really the names of cities which it is no longer possible to trace. *Henaᶜ* is hardly the well-known *Avatho* on the Euphrates, as Gesenius, v. Niebuhr, and others suppose; and *'Ivah,* the seat of the *Avvīm* (2 Kings xvii. 31), agrees still less, so far as the sound of the word is concerned, with "the province of *Hebeh* (? *Hebeb:* Ritter, *Erdk.* xi 707), situated between *Anah* and the *Chabur* on the Euphrates," with which v. Niebuhr combines it.[1]

This intimidating message, which declared the God of Israel to be utterly powerless, was conveyed by the messengers of Sennacherib in the form of a letter. Vers. 14, 15. "*And Hizkiyahu took the letter out of the hand of the messengers, and read it* (K. *read them*), *and went up to the house of Jehovah; and Hizkiyahu spread it before Jehovah.*" *Sᵉphârīm* (the sheets) is equivalent to *the letter* (not a letter *in duplo*), like *literæ* (cf. *grammata*). וַיִּקְרָאֵהוּ (changed by K. into ם־) is construed according to the singular idea. Thenius regards this spreading out of the letter as a *naiveté;* and Gesenius even goes so far as to speak of the praying machines of the Buddhists. But it was simply prayer without words—an act of prayer, which afterwards passed into vocal prayer. Vers. 16–20. "*And Hizkiyahu prayed to* (K. *before*)

[1] For other combinations of equal value, see Oppert, *Expédition,* i. 220.

Jehovah, saying (K. *and said*), *Jehovah of hosts* (K. omits *ts͏ᵉbhâ-*
'ōth), *God of Israel, enthroned upon the cherubim, Thou, yea Thou*
alone, art God of all the kingdoms of the earth; Thou, Thou hast
made the heavens and the earth.   Incline Thine ear, Jehovah, and
hear (וּשֲׁמָע, various reading in both texts וּשֲׁמַע)! *Open Thine*
eyes (K. with *Yod* of the plural), *Jehovah, and see; and hear the*
(K. *all the*) *words of Sennacherib, which he hath sent* (K. *with*
which he hath sent him, i.e. Rabshakeh) *to despise the living*
God!   Truly, O Jehovah, the kings of Asshur have laid waste
all lands, and their land (K. *the nations and their land*), *and have*
put (*vᵉnâthōn,* K. *vᵉnâthᵉnū*) *their gods into the fire: for they were*
not gods, only the work of men's hands, wood and stone; therefore
they have destroyed them.   And now, Jehovah our God, help us
(K. adds *pray*) *out of his hand, and all the kingdoms of the earth*
may know that Thou Jehovah (K. *Jehovah Elohim*) *art it alone.*"
On כְּרֻבִים (no doubt the same word as γρυπές, though not
fabulous beings like these, but a symbolical representation of
heavenly beings), see my *Genesis*, p. 626; and on *yōshēbh hak-*
kᵉrubhīm (enthroned on the cherubim), see at Ps. xviii. 11 and
lxxx. 2.   הוּא in אַתָּה־הוּא is an emphatic repetition, that is to say
a strengthening, of the subject, like ch. xliii. 25, li. 12, 2 Sam.
vii. 28, Jer. xlix. 12, Ps. xliv. 5, Neh. ix. 6, 7, Ezra v. 11:
tu ille (not *tu es ille*, Ges. § 121, 2) = *tu, nullus alius.*   Such
passages as ch. xli. 4, where הוּא is the predicate, do not
belong here.   עֵינֶךָ is not a singular (like עֵינִי in Ps. xxxii. 8,
where the LXX. have עֵינַי); but a defective plural, as we should
expect after *páqach.*   On the other hand, the reading *shᵉlâchō*
("hath sent him"), which cannot refer to *dᵉbhârīm* (the words),
but only to the person bringing the written message, is to be
rejected.   Moreover, Knobel cannot help giving up his preference for the reading *vᵉnâthōn* (compare Gen. xli. 43; Ges.
§ 131, 4*a*); just as, on the other hand, we cannot help regarding
the reading אֶת־כָּל־הָאֲרָצוֹת וְאֶת־אַרְצָם as a mistake, when compared
with the reading of the book of Kings.   Abravanel explains
the passage thus: "The Assyrians have devastated the lands,
and *their* own land" (cf. ch. xiv. 20), of which we may find
examples in the list of victories given above; compare also
Beth-Arbel in Hos. x. 14, if this is *Irbil* on the Tigris, from
which Alexander's second battle in Persia, which was really
fought at Gaugamela, derived its name.   But how does this

tally with the fact that they threw the gods of these lands—that
is to say, of their own land also (for אֱלֹהֵיהֶם could not possibly
refer to הארצות, to the exclusion of ארצם)—into the fire? If we
read *haggōyīm* (the nations), we get rid both of the reference
to their own land, which is certainly purposeless here, and also
of the otherwise inevitable conclusion that they burned the
gods of their own country. The reading הארצות appears to
have arisen from the fact, that after the verb החריב the lands
appeared to follow more naturally as the object, than the tribes
themselves (compare, however, ch. lx. 12). The train of
thought is the following: The Assyrians have certainly destroyed nations and their gods, because these gods were nothing
but the works of men: do Thou then help us, O Jehovah,
that the world may see that Thou alone art it, viz. God
('*Elōhīm*, as K. adds, although, according to the accents,
Jehovah Elohim are connected together, as in the books of
Samuel and Chronicles, and very frequently in the mouth of
David: see *Symbolæ in Psalmos*, pp. 15, 16).

The prophet's reply. Vers. 21, 22a. "*And Isaiah the son of
Amoz sent to Hizkiyahu, saying, Thus saith Jehovah the God
of Israel, That which thou hast prayed to me concerning Sennacherib the king of Asshur* (K. adds, *I have heard*): *this is the
utterance which Jehovah utters concerning him.*" He sent, *i.e.*
sent a message, viz. by one of his disciples (*limmūdīm*, ch. viii.
16). According to the text of Isaiah, אֲשֶׁר would commence the
protasis to זֶה הַדָּבָר (as for that which—this is the utterance);
or, as the *Vav* of the apodosis is wanting, it might introduce
relative clauses to what precedes ("I, to whom:" Ges. § 123, 1,
Anm. 1). But both of these are very doubtful. We cannot
dispense with שָׁמַעְתִּי (I have heard), which is given by both
the LXX. and Syr. in the text of Isaiah, as well as that of
Kings.

The prophecy of Isaiah which follows here, is in all respects
one of the most magnificent that we meet with. It proceeds
with strophe-like strides on the *cothurnus* of the Deborah style:
Vers. 22b, 23. "*The virgin daughter of Zion despiseth thee,
laugheth thee to scorn; the daughter of Jerusalem shaketh her head
after thee. Whom hast thou reviled and blasphemed, and over
whom hast thou spoken loftily, that thou hast lifted up thine eyes
on high? Against the Holy One of Israel.*" The predicate is

written at the head, in ver. 22*b*, in the masculine, *i.e.* without any precise definition; since בָּזָה is a verb ל"ה, and neither the participle nor the third pers. fem. of בּוּ. Zion is called a virgin, with reference to the shame with which it was threatened though without success (ch. xxiii. 12); *b*ᵉ*thūlath bath* are subordinate appositions, instead of co-ordinate. With a contented and heightened self-consciousness, she shakes her head behind him as he retreats with shame, saying by her attitude, as she moves her head backwards and forwards, that it must come to this, and could not be otherwise (Jer. xviii. 16; Lam. ii. 15, 16). The question in ver. 23 reaches as far as עֵינֶיךָ, although, according to the accents, ver. 23 is an affirmative clause: "and thou turnest thine eyes on high against the Holy One of Israel" (Hitzig, Ewald, Drechsler, and Keil). The question is put for the purpose of saying to Asshur, that He at whom they scoff is the God of Israel, whose pure holiness breaks out into a consuming fire against all by whom it is dishonoured. The *fut. cons.* וַתִּשָּׂא is essentially the same as in ch. li. 12, 13, and מָרוֹם is the same as in ch. xl. 26.

Second turn, ver. 24. "*By thy servants* (K. *thy messengers*) *hast thou reviled the Lord, in that thou sayest, With the multitude* (K. *chethib* ברכב) *of my chariots have I climbed the height of the mountains, the inner side of Lebanon; and I shall fell the lofty growth of its cedars, the choice* (mibhchar, K. *mibhchōr*) *of its cypresses: and I shall penetrate* (K. *and will penetrate*) *to the height* (K. *the halting-place*) *of its uttermost border, the grove of its orchard.*" The other text appears, for the most part, the preferable one here. Whether *mal'ăkhekhá* (thy messengers, according to ch. ix. 14) or *'ăbhâdekhá* (thy servants, viz. Rabshakeh, Tartan, and Rabsaris) is to be preferred, may be left undecided; also whether ברכב רכבי is an error or a superlative expression, "with chariots of my chariots," *i.e.* my countless chariots; also, thirdly, whether Isaiah wrote *mibhchōr*. He uses *mistōr* in ch. iv. 6 for a special reason; but such obscure forms befit in other instances the book of Kings, with its colouring of northern Palestine; and we also meet with *mibhchōr* in 2 Kings iii. 19, in the strongly Aramaic first series of histories of Elisha. On the other hand, מְלוֹן קִצֹּה is certainly the original reading, in contrast with מְרוֹם קִצּוֹ. It is important, as bearing upon the interpretation of the passage, that both texts have

וָאֶכְרֹת, not וָאֶכְרַת, and that the other text confirms this pointing, inasmuch as it has וְאָבוֹאָה instead of וְאָבוֹא. The Lebanon here, if not purely emblematical (as in Jer. xxii. 6 = the royal city Jerusalem; Ezek. xvii. 3 = Judah-Jerusalem), has at any rate a synecdochical meaning (cf. xiv. 8), signifying the land of Lebanon, *i.e.* the land of Israel, into which he had forced a way, and all the fortresses and great men of which he would destroy. He would not rest till Jerusalem, the most renowned height of the land of Lebanon, was lying at his feet. Thenius is quite right in regarding the "resting-place of the utmost border" and "the pleasure-garden wood" as containing allusions to the holy city and its royal citadel (compare the allegory in ch. v. vol. i. pp. 164–5).

Third turn, ver. 25. "*I, I have digged and drunk* (K. *foreign*) *waters, and will make dry with the sole of my feet all the Nile-arms* (יְאֹרֵי, K. יְאוֹרֵי) *of Matsor.*" If we take עָלִיתִי in ver. 24 as a perfect of certainty, ver. 25*a* would refer to the overcoming of the difficulties connected with the barren sandy steppe on the way to Egypt (viz. *et-Tih*); but the perfects stand out against the following futures, as statements of what was actually past. Thus, in places where there were no waters at all, and it might have been supposed that his army would inevitably perish, there he had dug them (*qūr*, from which *māqōr* is derived, *fodere;* not *scaturire*, as Luzzatto supposes), and had drunk up these waters, which had been called up, as if by magic, upon foreign soil; and in places where there were waters, as in Egypt (*mâtsōr* is used in Isaiah and Micah for *mitsrayim*, with a play upon the appellative meaning of the word: an enclosing fence, a fortifying girdle: see Ps. xxxi. 22), the Nile-arms and canals of which appeared to bar all farther progress, it was an easy thing for him to set at nought all these opposing hindrances. The Nile, with its many arms, was nothing but a puddle to him, which he trampled out with his feet.

And yet what he was able to do was not the result of his own power, but of the counsel of God, which he subserved. Fourth turn, vers. 26, 27. "*Hast thou not heard?* *I have done it long ago, from* (K. *l'min, since*) *the days of ancient time have I formed it, and now brought it to pass* (הֲבֵיאתִיהָ, K. הֲבֵאתִיהָ): *that thou shouldst lay waste fortified cities into desolate stone heaps; and their inhabitants, powerless, were terrified, and were*

put to shame (וֹבֵשׁ, K. וַיֵּבֹשׁ): *became herb of the field and green
of the turf, herb of the house-tops, and a corn-field* (וּשְׁדֵמָה, K.
and blighted corn) *before the blades."* *L'mĕrâchōq* (from afar) is
not to be connected with the preceding words, but according to
the parallel with those which follow. The historical reality, in
this instance the Assyrian judgment upon the nations, had had
from all eternity an ideal reality in God (see at ch. xxii. 11).
The words are addressed to the Assyrian; and as his instrumentality formed the essential part of the divine purpose, וּתְהִי
does not mean " there should," but " thou shouldest," ἔμελλες
ἐξηρεμῶσαι (cf. ch. xliv. 14, 15, and Hab. i. 17). K. has
לַהְשׁוֹת instead of לְהַשְׁאוֹת (though not as *chethib*, in which case
it would have to be pointed לְהַשִּׁאוֹת), a singularly syncopated
hiphil (for לְשַׁאוֹת). The point of comparison in the four figures
is the facility with which they can be crushed. The nations in
the presence of the Assyrian became, as it were, weak, delicate
grasses, with roots only rooted in the surface, or like a corn-
field with the stalk not yet formed (*shᵉdēmâh*, ch. xvi. 8),
which could easily be rooted up, and did not need to be cut
down with the sickle. This idea is expressed still more
strikingly in Kings, " like corn blighted (*shᵉdēphâh*, compare
shiddâphōn, corn-blight) before the shooting up of the stalk;"
the Assyrian being regarded as a parching east wind, which
destroys the seed before the stalk is formed.

Asshur is Jehovah's chosen instrument while thus casting
down the nations, which are " short-handed against him," *i.e.*
incapable of resisting him. But Jehovah afterwards places this
lion under firm restraint; and before it has reached the goal set
before it, He leads it back into its own land, as if with a ring
through its nostril. Fifth turn, vers. 28, 29. " *And thy sitting
down, and thy going out, and thy entering in, I know; and thy
heating thyself against me. On account of thy heating thyself
against me, and because thy self-confidence has risen up into mine
ears, I put my ring into thy nose, and my muzzle into thy lips,
and lead thee back by the way by which thou hast come.*" Sitting
down and rising up (Ps. cxxxix. 2), going out and coming in
(Ps. cxxi. 8), denote every kind of human activity. All
the thoughts and actions, the purposes and undertakings of
Sennacherib, more especially with regard to the people of
Jehovah, were under divine control. יָדַע is followed by the

infinitive, which is then continued in the finite verb, just as in ch. xxx. 12. שַׁאֲנַנְךָ (another reading, שַׁאֲנָךְ) is used as a substantive, and denotes the Assyrians' complacent and scornful self-confidence (Ps. cxxiii. 4), and has nothing to do with שָׁאוֹן (Targum, Abulw., Rashi, Kimchi, Rosenmüller, Luzzatto). The figure of the leading away with a nose-ring (*chachî* with a latent *dagesh*, חֲח to prick, hence *chŏăch*, Arab. *chôch*, *chôcha*, a narrow slit, literally means a cut or aperture) is repeated in Ezek. xxxviii. 4. Like a wild beast that had been subdued by force, the Assyrian would have to return home, without having achieved his purpose with Judah (or with Egypt).

The prophet now turns to Hezekiah. Ver. 30. "*And let this be a sign to thee, Men eat this year what is self-sown; and in the second year what springs from the roots* (*shâchĭs*, K. *sâchĭsh*); *and in the third year they sow and reap and plant vineyards, and eat* (*chethib* אָכוֹל) *their fruit.*" According to Thenius, *hasshânâh* (this year) signifies the first year after Sennacherib's invasion, *hasshânâh hasshēnĭth* (the second year) the current year in which the words were uttered by Hezekiah, *hasshânâh hasshᵉlĭshĭth* (the third year) the year that was coming in which the land would be cleared of the enemy. But understood in this way, the whole would have been no sign, but simply a prophecy that the condition of things during the two years was to come to an end in the third. It would only be a "sign" if the second year was also still in the future. By *hasshânâh*, therefore, we are to understand what the expression itself requires (cf. ch. xxix. 1, xxxii. 10), namely the current year, in which the people had been hindered from cultivating their fields by the Assyrian who was then in the land, and therefore had been thrown back upon the *sâphĭăch*, *i.e.* the after growth (αὐτόματα, LXX., the self-sown), or crop which had sprung up from the fallen grains of the previous harvest (from *sâphach*, *adjicere*, see at Hab. ii. 15; or, according to others, *effundere*, see vol. i. 165). It was autumn at the time when Isaiah gave this sign (ch. xxxiii. 9), and the current civil year was reckoned from one autumnal equinox to the other, as, for example, in Ex. xxiii. 16, where the feast of tabernacles or harvest festival is said to fall at the close of the year; so that if the fourteenth year of Hezekiah was the year 714, the current year would extend from Tishri 714 to Tishri 713. But if in the next year also,

713–712, there was no sowing and reaping, but the people were to eat *shâchîs*, *i.e.* that which grew of itself (αὐτοφυές, Aq., Theod.), and that very sparingly, not from the grains shed at the previous harvest, but from the roots of the wheat, we need not assume that this year, 713–712, happened to be a sabbatical year, in which the law required all agricultural pursuits to be suspended.[1] It is very improbable in itself that the prophet should have included a circumstance connected with the calendar in his " sign ;" and, moreover, according to the existing chronological data, the year 715 had been a sabbatical year (see Hitzig). It is rather presupposed, either that the land would be too thoroughly devastated and desolate for the fields to be cultivated and sown (Keil) ; or, as we can hardly imagine such an impossibility as this, if we picture to ourselves the existing situation and the kind of agriculture common in Palestine, that the Assyrian would carry out his expedition to Egypt in this particular year (713–12), and returning through Judah, would again prevent the sowing of the corn (Hitzig, Knobel). But in the third year, that is to say the year 712–11, freedom and peace would prevail again, and there would be nothing more to hinder the cultivation of the fields or vineyards. If this should be the course of events during the three years, it would be a sign to king Hezekiah that the fate of the Assyrian would be no other than that predicted. The year 712–11 would be the peremptory limit appointed him, and the year of deliverance.

Seventh turn, vers. 31, 32. " *And that which is escaped of the house of Judah, that which remains will again take root downward, and bear fruit upward. For from Jerusalem will a remnant go forth, and a fugitive from Mount Zion ; the zeal of Jehovah of hosts* (K. *chethib* omits *ts͏ͤbhâ'ōth*) *will carry this out.*" The agricultural prospect of the third year shapes itself here into a figurative representation of the fate of Judah. Isaiah's watchword, " a remnant shall return," is now fulfilled ; Jerusalem has been spared, and becomes the source of national rejuvenation. You hear the echo of ch. v. 24, ix. 6, and also of ch. xxvii. 6. The word *ts͏ͤbhâ'ōth* is wanting in Kings, here as well as in ver. 17 ; in fact, this

---

[1] There certainly is no necessity for a sabbatical year followed by a year of jubilee, to enable us to explain the " sign," as Hofmann supposes.

divine name is, as a rule, very rare in the book of Kings, where it only occurs in the first series of accounts of Elijah (1 Kings xviii. 15, xix. 10, 14; cf. 2 Kings iii. 14).

The prophecy concerning the protection of Jerusalem becomes more definite in the last turn than it ever has been before. Vers. 33–35. *" Therefore thus saith Jehovah concerning the king of Asshur, He will not enter into this city, nor shoot off an arrow there; nor do they assault it with a shield, nor cast up earthworks against it. By the way by which he came* (K. *will come*) *will he return; and he will not enter into this city, saith Jehovah. And I shield this city* (עַ, K. אֶל), *to help it, for mine own sake, and for the sake of David my servant."* According to Hitzig, this conclusion belongs to the later reporter, on account of its "suspiciously definite character." Knobel, on the other hand, sees no reason for disputing the authorship of Isaiah, inasmuch as in all probability the pestilence had already set in (ch. xxxiii. 24), and threatened to cripple the Assyrian army very considerably, so that the prophet began to hope that Sennacherib might now be unable to stand against the powerful Ethiopian king. To us, however, the words "Thus saith Jehovah" are something more than a flower of speech; and we hear the language of a man exalted above the standard of the natural man, and one who has been taken, as Amos says (iii. 7), by God, the moulder of history into "His secret." Here also we see the prophecy at its height, towards which it has been ascending from ch. vi. 13 and x. 33, 34 onwards, through the midst of obstacles accumulated by the moral condition of the nation, but with the same goal invariably in view. The Assyrian will not storm Jerusalem; there will not even be preparations for a siege. The verb *qiddēm* is construed with a double accusative, as in Ps. xxi. 4; *sōlᵉlâh* refers to the earthworks thrown up for besieging purposes, as in Jer. xxxii. 24. The reading יָבֹא instead of בָּא has arisen in consequence of the eye having wandered to the following יבא. The promise in ver 35a sounds like ch. xxxi. 5. The reading אֶל for עַל is incorrect. One motive assigned ("for my servant David's sake") is the same as in 1 Kings xv. 4, etc.; and the other ("for mine own sake") the same as in ch. xliii. 25, xlviii. 11 (compare, however, ch. lv. 3 also). On the one hand, it is in accordance with the honour and faithfulness of Jehovah, that Jerusalem is delivered; and, on the other hand, it is the worth of David, or, what is the same thing, the love of Jehovah turned towards him, of which Jerusalem reaps the advantage.

To this culminating prophecy there is now appended an account of the catastrophe itself. Vers. 36–38. "*Then* (K. *And it came to pass that night, that) the angel of Jehovah went forth and smote (vayyakkeh, K. vayyakh) in the camp of Asshur a hundred and eighty-five thousand; and when men rose up in the morning, behold, they were all lifeless corpses. Then Sennacherib king of Asshur decamped, and went forth and returned, and settled down in Nineveh. And it came to pass, as he was worshipping in the temple of Nisroch, his god, Adrammelech and Sharezer his sons (K. chethib omits 'his sons') smote him with the sword; and when they escaped to the land of Ararat, Esarhaddon ascended the throne in his stead.*" The first pair of histories closes here with a short account of the result of the Assyrian drama, in which Isaiah's prophecies were most gloriously fulfilled: not only the prophecies immediately preceding, but all the prophecies of the Assyrian era since the time of Ahaz, which pointed to the destruction of the Assyrian forces (*e.g.* x. 33–4), and to the flight and death of the king of Assyria (ch. xxxi. 9, xxx. 33). If we look still further forward to the second pair of histories (ch. xxxviii. xxxix.), we see from ch. xxxviii. 6 that it is only by anticipation that the account of these closing events is finished here; for the third history carries us back to the period before the final catastrophe. We may account in some measure for the haste and brevity of this closing historical fragment, from the prophet's evident wish to finish up the history of the Assyrian complications, and the prophecy bearing upon it. But if we look back, there is a gap between ch. xxxvii. 36 and the event narrated here. For, according to ver. 30, there was to be an entire year of trouble between the prophecy and the fulfilment, during which the cultivation of the land would be suspended. What took place during that year? There can be no doubt that Sennacherib was engaged with Egypt; for (1) when he made his second attempt to get Jerusalem into his power, he had received intelligence of the advance of Tirhakah, and therefore had withdrawn the centre of his army from Lachish, and encamped before Libnah (ch. xxxvii. 8, 9); (2) according to Josephus

(*Ant.* **x.** 1, 4), there was a passage of Berosus, which has been lost, in which he stated that Sennacherib "made an expedition against all Asia and Egypt;" (3) Herodotus relates (ii. 141) that, after Anysis the blind, who lost his throne for fifty years in consequence of an invasion of Egypt by the Ethiopians under Sabakoa, but who recovered it again, Sethon the priest of Hephæstus ascended the throne. The priestly caste was so oppressed by him, that when Sanacharibos, the king of the Arabians and Assyrians, led a great army against Egypt, they refused to perform their priestly functions. But the priest-king went into the temple to pray, and his God promised to help him. He experienced the fulfilment of this prophecy before Pelusium, where the invasion was to take place, and where he awaited the foe with such as continued true to him. "Immediately after the arrival of Sanacharibos, an army of field-mice swarmed throughout the camp of the foe, and devoured their quivers, bows, and shield-straps, so that when morning came on they had to flee without arms, and lost many men in consequence. This is the origin of the stone of Sethon in the temple of Hephæstus (at Memphis), which is standing there still, with a mouse in one hand, and with this inscription: Whosoever looks at me, let him fear the gods!" This Σέθως (possibly the *Zet* whose name occurs in the lists at the close of the twenty-third dynasty, and therefore in the wrong place) is to be regarded as one of the Saitic princes of the twenty-sixth dynasty, who seem to have ruled in Lower Egypt contemporaneously with the Ethiopians[1] (as, in fact, is stated in a passage of the Armenian Eusebius, *Æthiopas et Saitas regnasse aiunt eodem tempore*), until they succeeded at length in ridding themselves of the hateful supremacy. Herodotus evidently depended in this instance upon the hearsay of Lower Egypt, which transferred the central point of the Assyrian history to their own native princely house. The question,

---

[1] A seal of Pharaoh *Sabakon* has been found among the ruins of the palace of Kuyunjik. The colossal image of *Tarakos* is found among the bas-reliefs of Medinet-Habu. He is holding firmly a number of Asiatic prisoners by the hair of their head, and threatening them with a club. There are several other stately monuments in imitation of the Egyptian style in the ruins of Nepata, the northern capital of the Meroitic state, which belong to him (Lepsius, *Denkmäler*, p. 10 of the programme).

whether the disarming of the Assyrian army in front of Pelusium
merely rested upon a legendary interpretation of the mouse in
Sethon's hand,[1] which may possibly have been originally intended as a symbol of destruction; or whether it was really
founded upon an actual occurrence which was exaggerated in
the legend,[2] may be left undecided. But it is a real insult to
Isaiah, when Thenius and G. Rawlinson place the scene of ver.
36 at Pelusium, and thus give the preference to Herodotus.
Has not Isaiah up to this point constantly prophesied that the
power of Asshur was to be broken in the holy mountain land of
Jehovah (ch. xiv. 25), that the Lebanon forest of the Assyrian
army would break to pieces before Jerusalem (ch. x. 32–34),
and that there the Assyrian camp would become the booty of
the inhabitants of the city, and that without a conflict? And
is not the catastrophe that would befal Assyria described in
ch. xviii. as an act of Jehovah, which would determine the
Ethiopians to do homage to God who was enthroned upon
Zion? We need neither cite 2 Chron. xxxii. 21 nor Ps. lxxvi.
(LXX. ᾠδὴ πρὸς τὸν Ἀσσύριον), according to which the weapons of Asshur break to pieces upon Jerusalem; Isaiah's prophecies are quite sufficient to prove, that to force this Pelusiac
disaster[3] into ver. 36 is a most thoughtless concession to
Herodotus. The final catastrophe occurred before Jerusalem,
and the account in Herodotus gives us no certain information
even as to the issue of the Egyptian campaign, which took
place in the intervening year. Such a gap as the one which
occurs before ver. 36 is not without analogy in the historical
writings of the Bible; see, for example, Num. xx. 1, where
an abrupt leap is made over the thirty-seven years of the
wanderings in the desert. The abruptness is not affected
by the addition of the clause in the book of Kings, "It came
to pass that night." For, in the face of the "sign" mentioned in ver. 30, this cannot mean "in that very night" (viz.
the night following the answer given by Isaiah); but (un-

[1] This Sethos monument has not yet been discovered (Brugsch, *Reise-
berichte*, p. 79). The temple of Phta was on the south side of Memphis;
the site is marked by the ruins at Mitrahenni.

[2] The inhabitants of Troas worshipped *mice*, " because they gnawed the
strings of the enemies' bows" (see Wesseling on *Il.* i. 39).

[3] G. Rawlinson, *Monarchies*, ii. 445.

less it is a careless interpolation) it must refer to vers. 33, 34, and mean *illa nocte*, viz. the night in which the Assyrian had encamped before Jerusalem. The account before us reads just like that of the slaying of the first-born in Egypt (Ex. xii. 12, xi. 4). The plague of Egypt is marked as a pestilence by the use of the word *nâgaph* in connection with *hikkâh* in Ex. xii. 23, 13 (compare Amos iv. 10, where it seems to be alluded to under the name דֶּבֶר); and in the case before us also we cannot think of anything else than a divine judgment of this kind, which even to the present day defies all attempts at an ætiological solution, and which is described in 2 Sam. xxiv. as effected through the medium of angels, just as it is here. Moreover, the concise brevity of the narrative leaves it quite open to assume, as Hensler and others do, that the ravages of the pestilence in the Assyrian army, which carried off thousands in the night (Ps. xci. 6), even to the number of 185,000, may have continued for a considerable time.[1] The main thing is the fact that the prophecy in ch. xxxi. 8 was actually fulfilled. According to Josephus (*Ant.* x. 1, 5), when Sennacherib returned from his unsuccessful Egyptian expedition, he found the detachment of his army, which he had left behind in Palestine, in front of Jerusalem, where a pestilential disease sent by God was making great havoc among the soldiers, and that on the very first night of the siege. The three verses, "he broke up, and went away, and returned home," depict the hurried character of the retreat, like "*abiit excessit evasit erupit*" (Cic. ii. *Catil. init.*). The form of the sentence in ver. 38 places Sennacherib's act of worship and the murderous act of his sons side by side, as though they had occurred simultaneously. The connection would be somewhat different if the reading had been וַיִּכְּהוּ (cf. Ewald, § 341, *a*). *Nisroch* apparently signifies the eagle-like, or hawk-like (from *nisr, nesher*), possibly like '*Arioch* from '*ărī*. The LXX. transcribe it νασαραχ, A ασαραχ, א ασαρακ (K ἐσθραχ, where B has μεσεραχ), and explorers of the monuments imagined at one time that they had discovered this god as

---

[1] The pestilence in Mailand in 1629 carried off, according to Tadino, 160,000 men; that in Vienna, in 1679, 122,849; that in Moscow, at the end of the last century, according to Martens, 670,000; but this was during the whole time that the ravages of the pestilence lasted.

Asarak;[1] but they have more recently retracted this, although there really is a hawk-headed figure among the images of the Assyrian deities or genii.[2] The name has nothing to do with that of the supreme Assyrian deity, *Asur, Asshur.* A better derivation of *Nisroch* would be from סְרַךְ, שָׂרַךְ, שָׂרַג; and this is confirmed by Oppert, who has discovered among the inscriptions in the harem of Khorsabad a prayer of Sargon to Nisroch, who appears there, like the Hymen of Greece, as the patron of marriage, and therefore as a " uniter."[3] The name '*Adram-melekh* (a god in 2 Kings xvii. 31) signifies, as we now know, "*gloriosus* ('*addir*) *est rex;*" and *Sharetser* (for which we should expect to find *Saretser*), *dominator tuebitur.* The Armenian form of the latter name (in Moses Choren. i. 23), *San-asar* (by the side of *Adramel,* who is also called *Arcamozan*), probably yields the original sense of "*Lunus* (the moon-god *Sin*) *tuebitur.*" Polyhistorus (in Euseb. *chron. arm.* p. 19), on the authority of Berosus, mentions only the former, *Ardumuzan,* as the murderer, and gives eighteen years as the length of Sennacherib's reign. The murder did not take place immediately after his return, as Josephus says (*Ant.* x. 1, 5; cf. Tobit i. 21–25, Vulg.); and the expression used by Isaiah, he " dwelt (settled down) in Nineveh," suggests the idea of a considerable interval. This interval embraced the suppression of the rebellion in Babylon, where Sennacherib made his son *Asordan* king, and the campaign in Cilicia (both from Polyhistorus),[4] and also, according to the monuments, wars both by sea and land with Susiana, which supported the Babylonian thirst for independence. The *Asordan* of Polyhistorus is *Esar-haddon* (also written without the *makkeph, Esarhaddon*), which is generally supposed to be the Assyrian form of אִשּׁוּר-אַחִידֻן, *Assur fratrem dedit.* It is so difficult to make the chronology tally here, that Oppert, on Isa. xxxvi. 1, proposes to alter the fourteenth year into the twenty-ninth, and Rawlinson would alter it into the twenty-seventh.[5] They both of them assign to king

---

[1] *Journal of the Royal Asiatic Society*, xii. 2, pp. 426–7.

[2] Rawlinson, *Monarchies*, ii. 265.

[3] *Expédition Scientifique en Mesopotamie*, t. ii. p. 339.

[4] *Vid.* Richter, *Berosi quæ supersunt* (1825), p. 62; Müller, *Fragmenta Hist. Gr.* ii. 504.

[5] *Sargonides*, p. 10, and *Monarchies*, ii. 434.

Sargon a reign of seventeen (eighteen) years, and to Senna-cherib (in opposition to Polyhistorus) a reign of twenty-three (twenty-four) years; and they both agree in giving 680 as the year of Sennacherib's death. This brings us down below the first decade of Manasseh's reign, and would require a different author from Isaiah for vers. 37, 38. But the accounts given by Polyhistorus, Abydenus, and the astronomical canon, however we may reconcile them among themselves, do not extend the reign of Sennacherib beyond 693.[1] It is true that even then Isaiah would have been at least about ninety years old. But the tradition which represents him as dying a martyr's death in the reign of Manasseh, does really assign him a most unusual old age. Nevertheless, vers. 37, 38 may possibly have been added by a later hand. The two parricides fled to the "land of Ararat," *i.e.* to Central Armenia. The Armenian history describes them as the founders of the tribes of the Sassunians and Arzerunians. From the princely house of the latter, among whom the name of Sennacherib was a very common one, sprang Leo the Armenian, whom Genesios describes as of Assyrio-Armenian blood. If this were the case, there would be no less than ten Byzantine emperors who were descendants of Sennacherib, and consequently it would not be till a very late period that the prophecy of Nahum was fulfilled.[2]

C. HEZEKIAH'S ILLNESS. ISAIAH ASSURES HIM OF HIS RECOVERY.—CHAP. XXXVIII.

There is nothing to surprise us in the fact that we are carried back to the time when Jerusalem was still threatened by the Assyrian, since the closing verses of ch. xxxvii. merely

[1] See Duncker, *Gesch. des Alterthums.* i. pp. 708-9.

[2] Duncker, on the contrary (p. 709), speaks of the parricides as falling very shortly afterwards by their brother's hand, and overlooks the Armenian tradition (cf. Rawlinson, *Monarchies*, ii. 465), which transfers the flight of the two, who were to have been sacrificed, as is reported by their own father, to the year of the world 4494, *i.e.* B.C. 705 (see the historical survey of Prince Hubbof in the *Miscellaneous Translations*, vol. ii. 1834). The Armenian historian Thomas (at the end of the ninth century) expressly states that he himself had sprung from the Arzerunians, and therefore from Sennacherib; and for this reason his historical work is chiefly devoted to Assyrian affairs (see Aucher on Euseb. *chron.* i. p. xv).

contain an anticipatory announcement, introduced for the purpose of completing the picture of the last Assyrian troubles,
by adding the fulfilment of Isaiah's prediction of their termination. It is within this period, and indeed in the year of
the Assyrian invasion (ch. xxxvi. 1), since Hezekiah reigned
twenty-nine years, and fifteen of these are promised here, that
the event described by Isaiah falls,—an event not merely of
private interest, but one of importance in connection with the
history of the nation also.—Vers. 1–3. " *In those days Hizkiyahu
became dangerously ill. And Isaiah son of Amoz, the prophet,
came to him, and said to him, Thus saith Jehovah, Set thine
house in order : for thou wilt die, and not recover. Then Hizkiyahu turned* (K. om.) *his face to the wall, and prayed to Jehovah,
and said* (K. *saying*), *O Jehovah, remember this, I pray, that I
have walked before thee in truth, and with the whole heart, and
have done what was good in Thine eyes ! And Hizkiyahu wept
with loud weeping.*" " Give command to thy house " (לְ, cf. אֶל,
2 Sam. xvii. 23) is equivalent to, " Make known thy last will to
thy family" (compare the rabbinical *tsavvâ'âh*, the last will
and testament) ; for though *tsivvâh* is generally construed with
the accusative of the person, it is also construed with *Lamed*
(*e.g.* Ex. i. 22 ; cf. אֶל, Ex. xvi. 34). חָיָה in such a connection
as this signifies to revive or recover. The announcement of
his death is unconditional and absolute. As Vitringa observes,
" the condition was not expressed, because God would draw
it from him as a voluntary act." The sick man turned his
face towards the wall (הֵסֵב פָּנָיו, hence the usual fut. cons. וַיַּסֵּב,
as in 1 Kings xxi. 4, 8, 14), to retire into himself and to God.
The supplicatory אָנָּה (here, as in Ps. cxvi. 4, 16, and in all six
times, with ה) always has the principal tone upon the last
syllable before יהוה = אֲדֹנָי (Neh. i. 11). The *metheg* has sometimes passed into a conjunctive accent (*e.g.* Gen. l. 17, Ex.
xxxii. 31). אֵת אֲשֶׁר does not signify that which, but this, that,
as in Deut. ix. 7, 2 Kings viii. 12, etc. " In truth," *i.e.* without
wavering or hypocrisy. בְּלֵב שָׁלֵם, with a complete or whole
heart, as in 1 Kings viii. 61, etc. He wept aloud, because it was
a dreadful thing to him to have to die without an heir to the
throne, in the full strength of his manhood (in the thirty-ninth
year of his age), and with the nation in so unsettled a state.

 The prospect is now mercifully changed. Vers. 4–6. " *And*

it came to pass (K. *Isaiah was not yet out of the inner city; keri*
חָצֵר, *the forecourt, and) the word of Jehovah came to Isaiah* (K.
to him) as follows: Go (K. *turn again) and say to Hizkiyahu*
(K. adds, *to the prince of my people), Thus saith Jehovah, the
God of David thine ancestor, I have heard thy prayer, seen thy
tears; behold, I* (K. *will cure thee, on the third day thou
shalt go up to the house of Jehovah) add* (K. *and I add) to thy
days fifteen years. And I will deliver thee and this city out
of the hand of the king of Asshur, and will defend this city*
(K. *for mine own sake and for David my servant's sake)."* In
the place of הָעִיר (the city) the *keri* and the earlier translators
have חָצֵר. The city of David is not called the "inner city"
anywhere else; in fact, Zion, with the temple hill, formed the
upper city, so that apparently it is the inner space of the city
of David that is here referred to, and Isaiah had not yet passed
through the middle gate to return to the lower city, where he
dwelt (vol. i. pp. 70, 390). The text of Kings is the more
authentic throughout; except that נְגִיד עַמִּי, "the prince of my
people," is an annalistic adorning which is hardly original.
הָלוֹךְ in Isaiah is an inf. abs. used in an imperative sense; שׁוּב,
on the other hand, which we find in the other text, is imperative. On *yōsiph,* see at ch. xxix. 14.

The text of Isaiah is not only curtailed here in a very
forced manner, but it has got into confusion; for vers. 21 and
22 are removed entirely from their proper place, although even
the Septuagint has them at the close of Hezekiah's psalm.
They have been omitted from their place at the close of ver. 6
through an oversight, and then added in the margin, where
they now stand (probably with a sign, to indicate that they were
supplied). We therefore insert them here, where they properly
belong. Vers. 21, 22. " *Then Isaiah said they were to bring*
(K. *take) a fig-cake; and they plaistered* (K. *brought and covered)
the boil, and he recovered. And Hizkiyahu said* (K. *to Isaiah),
What sign is there that* (K. *Jehovah will heal me, so that I go
up) I shall go up into the house of Jehovah?"* As *sh͏ͤchīn* never
signifies a plague-spot, but an abscess (indicated by heightened
temperature), more especially that of leprosy (cf. Ex. ix. 9,
Lev. xiii. 18), there is no satisfactory ground, as some suppose,
for connecting Hezekiah's illness (taken along with ch. xxxiii.
24) with the pestilence which broke out in the Assyrian army.

The use of the figs does not help us to decide whether we are
to assume that it was a boil (*bubon*) or a carbuncle (*charbon*).
Figs were a well-known *emolliens* or *maturans*, and were used
to accelerate the rising of the swelling and the subsequent discharge. Isaiah did not show any special medical skill by order-
ing a softened cake of pressed figs to be laid upon the boil, nor
did he expect it to act as a specific, and effect a cure : it was
merely intended to promote what had already been declared to
be the will of God. וַיִּמְרְחוּ עַל is probably more original than
the simpler but less definite וַיָּשִׂימוּ עַל. Hitzig is wrong in rendering וַיְחִי, "that it (the boil) may get well;" and Knobel in
rendering it, "that he may recover." It is merely the anticipation of the result so common in the historical writings of
Scripture (see at ch. vii. 1 and xx. 1), after which the historian
goes back a step or two.

The pledge desired. Vers. 7, 8. "(K. *Then Isaiah said*) *and*
(K. om.) *let this be the sign to thee on the part of Jehovah, that*
(אֲשֶׁר, K. כִּי) *Jehovah will perform this* (K. *the*) *word which He has
spoken; Behold, I make the shadow retrace the steps, which it has
gone down upon the sun-dial of Ahaz through the sun, ten steps
backward. And the sun went back ten steps upon the dial, which
it had gone down*" (K. "*Shall the shadow go forward* [הָלַךְ, read
הָלֹךְ *according to Job* xl. 2, *or* [הֲיֵלֵךְ] *ten steps, or shall it go back
ten steps? Then Yechizkiyahu said, It is easy for the shadow
to go down ten steps; no, but the shadow shall go back ten steps.
Then Isaiah the prophet cried to Jehovah, and turned back the
shadow by the steps that it had gone down upon the sun-dial of
Ahaz, ten steps backward*"). "*Steps of Ahaz*" was the name
given to a sun-dial erected by him. As *ma'ălâh* may signify
either one of a flight of steps or a degree (syn. *madrigâh*), we
might suppose the reference to be to a dial-plate with a
gnomon; but, in the first place, the expression points to an
actual succession of steps, that is to say, to an obelisk upon a
square or circular elevation ascended by steps, which threw the
shadow of its highest point at noon upon the highest steps, and
in the morning and evening upon the lowest, either on the
one side or the other, so that the obelisk itself served as a
gnomon. It is in this sense that the Targum on 2 Kings ix. 13
renders *gerem hamma'ălōth* by *d*rag shă'ayyă*, step (flight of
steps) of the sun-dial; and the obelisk of Augustus, on the

Field of Mars at Rome, was one of this kind, which served as
a sun-dial. The going forward, going down, or declining of
the shadow, and its going back, were regulated by the meridian
line, and under certain circumstances the same might be said
of a vertical dial, *i.e.* of a sun-dial with a vertical dial-plate ;
but it applies more strictly to a step-dial, *i.e.* to a sun-dial in
which the degrees that measure definite periods of time are
really *gradus.* The step-dial of Ahaz may have consisted of
twenty steps or more, which measured the time of day by half-
hours, or even quarters. If the sign was given an hour before
sunset, the shadow, by going back ten steps of half-an-hour
each, would return to the point at which it stood at twelve
o'clock. But how was this effected? Certainly not by giving
an opposite direction to the revolution of the earth upon its axis,
which would have been followed by the most terrible convul-
sions over the entire globe ; and in all probability not even by
an apparently retrograde motion of the sun (in which case the
miracle would be optical rather than cosmical) ; but as the
intention was to give a sign that should serve as a pledge, and
therefore had no need whatever to be supernatural (vol. i. 214),
it may have been simply through a phenomenon of refraction,
since all that was required was that the shadow which was
down at the bottom in the afternoon should be carried upwards
by a sudden and unexpected refraction.   *Hammaʿălōth* (the
steps) in ver. 8 does not stand in a genitive relation to *tsēl*
(the shadow), as the accents would make it appear, but is an
accusative of measure, equivalent to בְּמַעֲלוֹת in the sum of the
steps (2 Kings xx. 11). To this accusative of measure there
is appended the relative clause : *quos* (*gradus*) *descendit* (יָרְדָה ;
צֵל being used as a feminine) *in scala Ahasi per solem, i.e.*
through the onward motion of the sun. When it is stated that
" the sun returned," this does not mean the sun in the heaven,
but the sun upon the sun-dial, upon which the illumined surface moved upwards as the shadow retreated ; for when the
shadow moved back, the sun moved back as well. The event
is intended to be represented as a miracle ; and a miracle it
really was. The force of will proved itself to be a power
superior to all natural law ; the phenomenon followed upon the
prophet's prayer as an extraordinary result of divine power, not
effected through his astronomical learning, but simply through

that faith which can move mountains, because it can set in
motion the omnipotence of God.

As a documentary proof of this third account, a psalm of
Hezekiah is added in the text of Isaiah, in which he celebrates
his miraculous rescue from the brink of death. The author
of the book of Kings has omitted it; but the genuineness is
undoubted. The heading runs thus in ver. 9 : " *Writing of
Hizkiyahu king of Judah, when he was sick, and recovered from
his sickness.*" The song which follows might be headed
Mikhtam, since it has the characteristics of this description of
psalm (see at Ps. xvi. 1). We cannot infer from *bachălōthō*
(when he was sick) that it was composed by Hezekiah during
his illness (see at Ps. li. 1); *vayyechi* (and he recovered) stamps
it as a song of thanksgiving, composed by him after his recovery.
In common with the two Ezrahitish psalms, Ps. lxxxviii. and
lxxxix., it has not only a considerable number of echoes of the
book of Job, but also a lofty sweep, which is rather forced
than lyrically direct, and appears to aim at copying the best
models.

Strophe 1 consists indisputably of seven lines :

Vers. 10–12. " *I said, In quiet of my days shall I depart
into the gates of Hades :
I am mulcted of the rest of my years.
I said, I shall not see Jah, Jah, in the land of the living :
I shall behold man no more, with the inhabitants of the regions
of the dead.
My home is broken up, and is carried off from me like a
shepherd's tent :
I rolled up my life like a weaver ; He would have cut me loose
from the roll :
From day to night Thou makest an end of me.*"

" In quiet of my days" is equivalent to, in the midst of the
quiet course of a healthy life, and is spoken without reference
to the Assyrian troubles, which still continued. דְּמִי, from דָּמָה,
to be quiet, lit. to be even, for the radical form דם has the
primary idea of a flat covering, of something stroked smooth,
of that which is level and equal, so that it could easily branch
out into the different ideas of *æquabilitas,* equality of measure,
æquitas, equanimity, *æquitas,* equality, and also of destruction

= *complanatio*, levelling. On the cohortative, in the sense of that which is to be, see Ewald, § 228, *a*; אֵלְכָה, according to its verbal idea, has the same meaning as in Ps. xxxix. 14 and 2 Chron. xxi. 20; and the construction with בְ (= אלכה וְאָבוֹאָה) is *constructio prægnans* (Luzzatto). The *pual* פֻּקַּדְתִּי does not mean, "I am made to want" (Rashi, Knobel, and others), which, as the passive of the causative, would rather be הֻפְקַדְתִּי, like הֻנְחַלְתִּי, I am made to inherit (Job vii. 3); but, I am visited with punishment as to the remnant, mulcted of the remainder, deprived, as a punishment, of the rest of my years. The clause, "Jah in the land of the living," *i.e.* the God of salvation, who reveals Himself in the land of the living, is followed by the corresponding clause, עִם־יוֹשְׁבֵי חָדֶל, "I dwelling with the in-habitants of the region of the dead;" for whilst חֶלֶד signifies temporal life (from *châlad*, to glide imperceptibly away, Job xi. 17), חָדֵל signifies the end of this life, the negation of all conscious activity of being, the region of the dead. The body is called a dwelling (*dōr*, Arab. *dâr*), as the home of a man who possesses the capacity to distinguish himself from everything belonging to him (*Psychol.* p. 227). It is compared to a nomadic tent. רֹעִי (a different word from that in Zech. xi. 17, where it is the *chirek compaginis*) is not a genitive (= רֹעֶה, Ewald, § 151, *b*), but an adjective in *i*, like רֹעֶה אֱוִילִי in Zech. xi. 15. With *niglâh* (in connection with נִפַּע, as in Job iv. 21), which does not mean to be laid bare (Luzz.), nor to be wrapt up (Ewald), but to be obliged to depart, compare the New Testament ἐκδημεῖν ἐκ τοῦ σώματος (2 Cor. v. 8). The ἀπ. γεγρ. קִפַּד might mean to cut off, or shorten (related to *qâphach*); it is safer, however, and more appropriate, to take it in the sense of rolling up, as in the name of the badger (ch. xiv. 23, xxxiv. 11), since otherwise what Hezekiah says of him-self and of God would be tautological. I rolled or wound up my life, as the weaver rolls up the finished piece of cloth : *i.e.* I was sure of my death, namely, because God was about to give me up to death; He was about to cut me off from the thrum (the future is here significantly interchanged with the perfect). *Dallâh* is the thrum, *licium*, the threads of the warp upon a loom, which becomes shorter and shorter the further the weft proceeds, until at length the piece is finished, and the weaver cuts through the short threads, and so sets it free (בִּצֵּעַ,

cf. Job vi. 9, xxvii. 8). The strophe closes with the deep
lamentation which the sufferer poured out at that time : ne
could not help feeling that God would put an end to him
(*shâlam*, syn. *kâlâh, tâmam, gâmar*) from day to night, *i.e.* in
the shortest time possible (compare Job iv. 20).

In *strophe* 2 the retrospective glance is continued. His
sufferings increased to such an extent, that there was nothing
left in his power but a whining moan—a languid look for
help.

> Vers. 13, 14. " *I waited patiently till the morning ; like the
> lion,*
> *So He broke in pieces all my bones :*
> *From day to night Thou makest it all over with me.*
> *Like a swallow, a crane, so I chirped ;*
> *I cooed like the dove :*
> *Mine eyes pined for the height.*
> *O Lord, men assault me !   Be bail for me.*"

The meaning of *shivvithi* may be seen from Ps. cxxxi. 2, in
accordance with which an Arabic translator has rendered the
passage, " I smoothed, *i.e.* quieted (*sâweitu*) my soul, notwithstanding the sickness, all night, until the morning." But the
morning brought no improvement ; the violence of the pain,
crushing him like a lion, forced from him again and again the
mournful cry, that he must die before the day had passed, and
should not live to see another. The Masora here has a remark,
which is of importance, as bearing upon Ps. xxii. 17, viz. that
כַּאֲרִי occurs twice, and בתרי לישני with two different meanings.
The meaning of כְּסוּס עָגוּר is determined by Jer. viii. 7, from
which it is evident that עָגוּר is not an attribute of סוּס here, in
the sense of " chirping mournfully," or " making a circle in
its flight," but is the name of a particular bird, namely the
crane. For although the Targum and Syriac both seem to
render סוּס in that passage (*keri* סִיס, which is the *chethib* here,
according to the reading of Orientals) by כּוּרְכְיָא (a crane, Arab.
Kurki), and עָגוּר by סְנוּנִיתָא (the ordinary name of the swallow,
which Haji Gaon explains by the Arabic *chuttaf*), yet the
relation is really the reverse : *sûs* (*sîs*) is the swallow, and ʿ*âgûr*
the crane. Hence Rashi, on *b. Kiddusin* 44*a* (" then cried
Res Lakis like a crane"), gives ʿ*âgûr*, Fr. *grue*, as the rendering

of ברוכיא ; whereas Parchon (*s.v.* 'ágūr) confounds the crane with the hoarsely croaking stork (*ciconia alba*). The verb 'ătsaphtsēph answers very well not only to the *flebile murmur* of the swallow (into which the penitential Progne was changed, according to the Grecian myth), but also to the shrill shriek of the crane, which is caused by the extraordinary elongation of the windpipe, and is onomatopoetically expressed in its name 'ágūr.[1] *Tsiphtsēph*, like τρίζειν, is applied to every kind of shrill, penetrating, inarticulate sound. The ordinary meaning of *dallū*, to hang long and loose, has here passed over into that of pining (syn. *kâlâh*). The name of God in ver. 14*b* is *Adonai*, not *Jehovah*, being one of the 134 וַדָּאִין, *i.e.* words which are really written *Adonai*, and not merely to be read so.[2] It is impossible to take עָשְׁקָה־לִּי as an imperative. The pointing, according to which we are to read 'ashqa, admits this (compare *shâmrâh* in Ps. lxxxvi. 2, cxix. 167 ; and on the other hand, *zochrālli*, in Neh. v. 19, etc.) ;[3] but the usage of the language does not yield any appropriate meaning for such an imperative. It is either the third person, used in a neuter sense, " it is sorrowful with me ;" or, what Luzzatto very properly considers still more probable, on account of the antithesis of 'ashqâh and 'árbēni, a substantive ('ashqah for 'osheq), " there is pressure upon me" (compare רְזִי־לִי, ch. xxiv. 16), *i.e.* it presses me like an unmerciful creditor ; and to this there is appended the petition, Guarantee me, *i.e.* be bail for me, answer for me (see at Job xvii. 3).

In *strophe* 3 he now describes how Jehovah promised him help, how this promise put new life into him, and how it was fulfilled, and turned his sufferings into salvation.

Vers. 15–17. " *What shall I say, that He promised me, and*
      He hath carried it out :
I should walk quietly all my years, on the trouble of my soul ?!

---

[1] The call of the parent cranes, according to Naumann (*Vögel Deutschlands*, ix. 364), is a rattling *kruh* (*gruh*), which is uncommonly violent when close, and has a trumpet-like sound, which makes it audible at a very great distance. With the younger cranes it has a somewhat higher tone, which often passes, so to speak, into a falsetto.

[2] *Vid.* Bär, *Psalterium*, p. 133.

[3] *Vid.* Bär, *Thorath Emeth*, pp. 22, 23.

' *O Lord, by such things men revive, and the life of my spirit*
    is always therein:
And so wilt Thou restore me, and make me to live!'
Behold, bitterness became salvation to me, bitterness;
And Thou, Thou hast delivered my soul in love out of the pit
    of destruction
For Thou hast cast all my sins behind Thy back."

The question, "What shall I say?" is to be understood as in
2 Sam. vii. 20, viz. What shall I say, to thank Him for having
promised me, and carried out His promise? The *Vav* in וַיֹּאמֶר
introduces the statement of his reason (Ges. § 155, 1, c). On
הִדְדָה (= הִתְדַּדָּה), from דָּדָה (= דְּאָא), see at Ps. xlii. 5. The
future here, in ver. 15b, gives the purpose of God concerning
him. He was to walk (referring to the walk of life, not the
walk to the temple) gently (without any disturbance) all his
years upon the trouble of his soul, *i.e.* all the years that followed upon it, the years that were added to his life. This is
the true explanation of עַל, as in ch. xxxviii. 5, xxxii. 10, Lev.
xv. 25; not "in spite of" (Ewald), or "with," as in Ps. xxxi.
24, Jer. vi. 14, where it forms an adverb. A better rendering
than this would be "for," or "on account of," *i.e.* in humble
salutary remembrance of the way in which God by His free
grace averted the danger of death. What follows in ver. 16
can only be regarded in connection with the petition in ver. 16b,
as Hezekiah's reply to the promise of God, which had been
communicated to him by the prophet. Consequently the
neuters עֲלֵיהֶם and בָּהֶן (cf. ch. lxiv. 4, Job xxii. 21, Ezek. xxxiii.
18, 19) refer to the gracious words and gracious acts of God.
These are the true support of life (עַל as in Deut. viii. 3) for
every man, and in these does the life of his spirit consist, *i.e.*
his inmost and highest source of life, and that " on all sides "
(לְכֹל, which it would be more correct to point לַכֹּל, as in 1 Chron.
vii. 5; cf. *bakkōl*, in every respect, 2 Sam. xxiii. 5). With this
explanation, the conjecture of Ewald and Knobel, that the
reading should be רוּחוֹ, falls to the ground. From the general
truth of which he had made a personal application, that the
word of God is the source of all life, he drew this conclusion,
which he here repeats with a retrospective glance, " So wilt
Thou then make me whole (see the *kal* in Job xxxix. 4), and

keep me alive" (for וְתְחַיֵּנִי; with the hope passing over into a
prayer). The praise for the fulfilment of the promise commences with the word *hinnēh* (behold). His severe illness had
been sent in anticipation of a happy deliverance (on the radical
signification of *mar*, which is here doubled, to give it a superlative force, see *Job*, vol. i. 279). The Lord meant it for good;
the suffering was indeed a chastisement, but it was a chastisement of love. Casting all his sins behind Him, as men do
with things which they do not wish to know, or have no desire to
be reminded of (compare *e.g.* Neh. ix. 26), He "loved him out,"
i.e. drew him lovingly out, of the pit of destruction (*châshaq*,
love as a firm inward bond; *b'lī*, which is generally used as a
particle, stands here in its primary substantive signification,
from *bâlâh*, to consume).

In *strophe* 4 he rejoices in the preservation of his life as
the highest good, and promises to praise God for it as long as
he lives.

> Vers. 18-20. "*For Hades does not praise Thee; death does
>   not sing praises to Thee:*
> *They that sink into the grave do not hope for Thy truth.*
> *The living, the living, he praises Thee, as I do to-day;*
> *The father to the children makes known Thy truth.*
> *Jehovah is ready to give me salvation;*
> *Therefore will we play my stringed instruments all the days
>   of my life*
> *In the house of Jehovah.*"

We have here that comfortless idea of the future state,
which is so common in the Psalms (*vid.* Ps. vi. 6, xxx. 10,
lxxxviii. 12, 13, cf. cxv. 17), and also in the book of Ecclesiastes (Eccles. ix. 4, 5, 10). The foundation of this idea, notwithstanding the mythological dress, is an actual truth (*vid.
Psychol.* p. 409), which the personal faith of the hero of Job
endeavours to surmount (*Comment.* pp. 150–153, and elsewhere),
but the decisive removal of which was only to be effected by
the progressive history of salvation. The verse is introduced
with "for" (*kī*), inasmuch as the gracious act of God is accounted
for on the ground that He wished to be still further glorified
by His servant whom He delivered. לֹא, in ver. 18*a*, is written
only once instead of twice, as in ch. xxiii. 4. They "sink

into the grave," *i.e.* are not thought of as dying, but as already
dead. "Truth" ('*ĕmeth*) is the sincerity of God, with which
He keeps His promises. Ver. 19*b* reminds us that Manasseh,
who was twelve years old when he succeeded his father, was
not yet born (cf. ch. xxxix. 7). The יְהוָֹה לְהוֹשִׁיעֵנִי, μέλλει σώζειν
με, is the same as in ch. xxxvii. 26. The change in the number
in ver. 20*b* may be explained from the fact that the writer
thought of himself as the choral leader of his family ; *ay* is a
suffix, not a substantive termination (Ewald, § 164, p. 427).
The impression follows us to the end, that we have cultivated
rather than original poetry here. Hezekiah's love to the older
sacred literature is well known. He restored the liturgical
psalmody (2 Chron. xxix. 30). He caused a further collection
of proverbs to be made, as a supplement to the older book of
Proverbs (Prov. xxv. 1). The "men of Hezekiah" resembled
the Pisistratian Society, of which Onomacritos was the head.

On vers. 21, 22, see the notes at the close of vers. 4-6,
where these two verses belong.

D. THREATENING OF THE BABYLONIAN CAPTIVITY OCCA-
SIONED BY HEZEKIAH.—CHAP. XXXIX.

From this point onwards the text of the book of Kings (2
Kings xx. 12–19, cf. 2 Chron. xxxii. 24–31) runs parallel to
the text before us. Babylonian ambassadors have an interview
with the convalescent king of Judah. Ver. 1. "*At that time
Merodach Bal'adan* (K. *Berodach Bal'adan*), *son of Bal'adan
king of Babel, sent writings and a present to Hizkiyahu, and
heard* (K. *for he had heard*) *that he* (K. *Hizkiyahu*) *had been sick,
and was restored again.*" The two texts here share the original
text between them. Instead of the unnatural וַיִּשְׁמַע (which
would link the cause on to the effect, as in 2 Sam. xiv. 5), we
should read כִּי שָׁמַע, whereas וַיֶּחֱזַק in our text appears to be the
genuine word out of which חִזְקִיָּהוּ in the other text has sprung,
although it is not indispensable, as חָלָה has a pluperfect sense.
In a similar manner the name of the king of Babylon is given
here correctly as מְרֹאדַךְ (Nissel, מְרֹדַךְ without א, as in Jer. l. 2),
whilst the book of Kings has בְּראֹדַךְ (according to the Masora
with א), probably occasioned by the other name Bal'ădân, which
begins with *Beth*. It cannot be maintained that the words

ben Bal'ădân are a mistake; at the same time, Bal'ădân (Jos. *Baladas*) evidently cannot be a name by itself if $M^e r\breve{o}' d\lrcorner kh$ *Bal'ădân* signifies "*Merodach* (the Babylonian *Bel* or Jupiter[1]) *filium dedit.*"[2] In the Canon Ptol. *Mardokempados* is preceded by a *Jugæus;* and the inscriptions, according to G. Rawlinson, *Mon.* ii. 395, indicate Merodach-Baladan as the "son of *Yakin.*" They relate that the latter acknowledged Tiglath-pileser as his feudal lord; that, after reigning twelve years as a vassal, he rose in rebellion against Sargon in league with the Susanians and the Aramæan tribes above Babylonia, and lost everything except his life; that he afterwards rebelled against Sennacherib in conjunction with a Chaldean prince named *Susub,* just after Sennacherib had returned from his first[3] Judæan campaign to Nineveh; and that having been utterly defeated, he took refuge in an island of the Persian Gulf. He does not make his appearance any more; but *Susub* escaped from his place of concealment, and being supported by the Susanians and certain Aramæan tribes, fought a long and bloody battle with Sennacherib on the Lower Tigris. This battle he lost, and *Nebo-som-iskun,* a son of Merodach Baladan, fell into the hands of the conqueror. In the midst of these details, as given by the inscriptions, the statement of the *Can. Ptol.* may still be maintained, according to which the twelve years of *Mardokempados* (a contraction, as Ewald supposes, of *Mardokempalados*) commence with the year 721. From this point onwards the biblical and extra-biblical accounts dovetail together; whereas in Polyhistor (Eus. *chron. arm.*) the following Babylonian rulers are mentioned: "a brother of Sennacherib, *Acises,* who reigned hardly a month; *Marodach Baladan,* six months; *Elibus* into the third year; *Asordan,* Sennacherib's son, who was made king after the defeat of Elibus." Now, as the *Can. Ptolem.* also gives a *Belibos* with a three years' reign, the identity of *Mardokempados* and *Marodach Baladan* is indisputable. The *Can. Ptol.* seems only to take into account his legitimate reign as a vassal, and Polyhistor (from Berosus) only his last act of rebellion. At the same time, this is very far from removing all the difficulties that lie in the way of a reconciliation, more

---

[1] Rawlinson, *Monarchies,* i. 169.
[2] Oppert, *Expédition,* ii. 355.
[3] The inscriptions mention two campaigns.

especially the chronological difficulties. Rawlinson, who places
the commencement of the (second) Judæan campaign in the
year 698, and therefore transfers it to the end of the twenty-
ninth year of Hezekiah's reign instead of the middle, sets
himself in opposition not only to ch. xxxvi. 1, but also to
ch. xxxviii. 5 and 2 Kings xviii. 2. According to the biblical
accounts, as compared with the *Can. Ptol.*, the embassy must
have been sent by Merodach Baladan during the period of his
reign as vassal, which commenced in the year 721. Apparently
it had only the harmless object of congratulating the king upon
his recovery (and also, according to 2 Chron. xxxii. 31, of
making some inquiry, in the interests of Chaldean astrology,
into the *mōphēth* connected with the sun-dial); but it certainly had also the secret political object of making common
cause with Hezekiah to throw off the Assyrian yoke. All that
can be maintained with certainty beside this is, that the embassy
cannot have been sent before the fourteenth year of Hezekiah's
reign; for as he reigned twenty-nine years, his illness must
have occurred, according to ch. xxxviii. 5, in the fourteenth
year itself, *i.e.* the seventh year of Mardokempados. Such
questions as whether the embassy came before or after the
Assyrian catastrophe, which was still in the future at the time
referred to in ch. xxxviii. 4–6, or whether it came before or
after the payment of the compensation money to Sennacherib
(2 Kings xviii. 14–16), are open to dispute. In all probability
it took place immediately before the Assyrian campaign,[1] as
Hezekiah was still able to show off the abundance of his riches
to the Babylonian ambassadors.

Ver. 2. "*And Hezekiah rejoiced* (K. *heard,* which is quite
inappropriate) *concerning them, and showed them* (K. *all*) *his
storehouse: the silver, and the gold, and the spices, and the fine oil*
(*hasshâmen,* K. *shemen*), *and all his arsenal, and all that was in
his treasures: there was nothing that Hezekiah had not shown
them, in his house or in all his kingdom.*" Although there were

---

[1] A reviewer in the *Theol. L. Bl.* 1857, p. 12, inquires: "How could
the prophet have known that all that Hezekiah showed to the Babylonian
ambassador would one day be brought to Babylon, when in a very short
time these treasures would all have been given by Hezekiah to the king of
Assyria?" Answer: The prophecy is so expressed in ch. xxxix. 6, 7, that
this intervening occurrence does not prejudice its truth at all.

spices kept in נכת בֵּית, נכת is not equivalent to נְכֹאת (from נָכָא, to break to pieces, to pulverize), which is applied to gum-dragon and other drugs, but is the *niphal* נָכֹת from כּוּת (*piel*, Arab. *kayyata*, to cram full, related to כּוּס (כִּים), נָכָס (נֵכֶס), and possibly also to כָּתַם, *katama* (Hitzig, Knobel, Fürst), and consequently it does not mean "the house of his spices," as Aquila, Symmachus, and the Vulgate render it, but his "treasurehouse or storehouse" (Targ., Syr., Saad.). It differs, however, from *bêth kēlīm*, the wood house of Lebanon (ch. xxii. 8). He was able to show them all that was worth seeing "in his whole kingdom," inasmuch as it was all concentrated in Jerusalem, the capital.

The consequences of this coqueting with the children of the stranger, and this vain display, are pointed out in vers. 3–8: "*Then came Isaiah the prophet to king Hizkiyahu, and said to him, What have these men said, and whence come they to thee? Hizkiyahu said, They came to me from a far country* (K. omits *to me*), *out of Babel. He said further, What have they seen in thy house? Hizkiyahu said, All that is in my house have they seen: there was nothing in my treasures that I had not shown them. Then Isaiah said to Hizkiyahu, Hear the word of Jehovah of hosts* (K. omits *tsᵉbhâʿōth*); *Behold, days come, that all that is in thy house, and all that thy fathers have laid up unto this day, will be carried away to Babel* (בָּבֶל, K. בָּבֶלָה): *nothing will be left behind, saith Jehovah. And of thy children that proceed from thee, whom thou shalt beget, will they take* (K. chethib, '*will he take*') ; *and they will be courtiers in the palace of the king of Babel. Then said Hizkiyahu to Isaiah, Good is the word of Jehovah which thou hast spoken. And he said further, Yea* (כִּי, K. הֲלוֹא אִם), *there shall be peace and stedfastness in my days.*" Hezekiah's two candid answers in vers. 3 and 4 are an involuntary condemnation of his own conduct, which was sinful in two respects. This self-satisfied display of worthless earthly possessions would bring its own punishment in their loss ; and this obsequious suing for admiration and favour on the part of strangers, would be followed by plundering and enslaving on the part of those very same strangers whose envy he had excited. The prophet here foretells the Babylonian captivity ; but, in accordance with the occasion here given, not as the destiny of the whole nation, but as that of the house of David.

Even political sharp-sightedness might have foreseen, that some such disastrous consequences would follow Hezekiah's imprudent course; but this absolute certainty, that Babylon, which was then struggling hard for independence, would really be the heiress to the Assyrian government of the world, and that it was not from Assyria, which was actually threatening Judah with destruction for its rebellion, but from Babylon, that this destruction would really come, was impossible without the spirit of prophecy. We may infer from ver. 7 (cf. ch. xxxviii. 19, and for the fulfilment, Dan. i. 3) that Hezekiah had no son as yet, at least none with a claim to the throne; and this is confirmed by 2 Kings xxi. 1. So far as the concluding words are concerned, we should quite misunderstand them, if we saw nothing in them but common egotism. כִּי (for) is explanatory here, and therefore confirmatory. הֲלוֹא אִם, however, does not mean "yea, if only," as Ewald supposes (§ 324, b), but is also explanatory, though in an interrogative form, "Is it not good (i.e. still gracious and kind), if," etc.? He submits with humility to the word of Jehovah, in penitential acknowledgment of his vain, shortsighted, untheocratic conduct, and feels that he is mercifully spared by God, inasmuch as the divine blessings of peace and stability (אֱמֶת a self-attesting state of things, without any of those changes which disappoint our confident expectations) would continue. "Although he desired the prosperity of future ages, it would not have been right for him to think it nothing that God had given him a token of His clemency, by delaying His judgment" (Calvin).

Over the kingdom of Judah there was now hanging the very same fate of captivity and exile, which had put an end to the kingdom of Israel eight years before. When the author of the book of Kings prefaces the four accounts of Isaiah in 2 Kings xviii. 13–20, with the recapitulation in 2 Kings xviii. 9–12 (cf. ch. xvii. 5, 6), his evident meaning is, that the end of the kingdom of Israel, and the beginning of the end of the kingdom of Judah, had their meeting-point in Hezekiah's time. As Israel fell under the power of the Assyrian empire, which foundered upon Judah, though only through a miraculous manifestation of the grace of God (see Hos. i. 7); so did Judah fall a victim to the Babylonian empire. The four accounts are so arranged, that the first two, together with the epilogue in Isa. xxxvii. 36 sqq., which contains the account of the fulfilment, bring the Assyrian period of judgment to a close; and the last two, with the eventful sketch in ch. xxxix. 6, 7, open the way for the great bulk of the prophecies which now follow in ch. xl.–lxvi., relating to the Babylonian period of judgment. This Janus-headed arrangement of the contents of ch. xxxvi.–xxxix. is a proof that this historical section formed an original part of the " vision of Isaiah." At any rate, it leads to the conclusion that, whoever arranged the four accounts in their present order, had ch. xl.–lxvi. before him at the time. We believe, however, that we may, or rather, considering the prophetico-historical style of ch. xxxvi.–xxxix., that we must, draw the still further conclusion, that Isaiah himself, when he revised the collection of his prophecies at the end of Hezekiah's reign, or possibly not till the beginning of Manasseh's, bridged over the division between the two halves of the collection by the historical trilogy in the seventh book.

SECOND HALF OF THE COLLECTION.

CHAP. XL.–LXVI.

THE first half consisted of seven parts; the second consists of
three. The trilogical arrangement of this cycle of prophecies
has hardly been disputed by any one, since Rückert pointed it
out in his *Translation of the Hebrew Prophets* (1831). And it
is equally certain that each part consists of 3×3 addresses.
The division of the chapters furnishes an unintentional proof
of this, though the true commencement is not always indicated. The *first* part embraces the following nine addresses:
ch. xl.; xli.; xlii. 1–xliii. 13; xliii. 14–xliv. 5; xliv. 6–23;
xliv. 24–xlv.; xlvi.; xlvii.; xlviii. The *second* part includes
the following nine: ch. xlix.; l.; li.; lii. 1–12; lii. 13–liii.;
liv.; lv.; lvi. 1–8; lvi. 9–lvii. The *third* part the following
nine: ch. lviii.; lix.; lx.; lxi.; lxii.; lxiii. 1–6; lxiii. 7–lxiv.;
lxv.; lxvi. It is only in the middle of the first part that the
division is at all questionable. In the other two it is hardly
possible to err. The theme of the whole is the comforting
announcement of the approaching deliverance, and its attendant
summons to repentance. For the deliverance itself was for the
Israel, which remained true to the confession of Jehovah in
the midst of affliction and while redemption was delayed, and
not for the rebellious, who denied Jehovah in word and deed,
and thus placed themselves on the level of the heathen.
" *There is no peace, saith Jehovah, for the wicked:*" with these
words does the first part of the twenty-seven addresses close in
ch. xlviii. 22. The second closes in ch. lvii. 21 in a more
excited and fuller tone : " *There is no peace, saith my God, for
the wicked.*" And at the close of the third part (ch. lxvi. 24)
the prophet drops this form of refrain, and declares the miserable end of the wicked in deeply pathetic though horrifying
terms : " *Their worm shall not die, and their fire shall not be*

quenched, and they shall be an abhorrence to all flesh;" just as, at
the close of the fifth book of the Psalms, the shorter form of
b'râkhâh (blessing) is dropt, and an entire psalm, the Hallelujah
(Ps. cl.), takes its place.

The three parts, which are thus marked off by the prophet
himself, are only variations of the one theme common to them
all. At the same time, each has its own leading thought, and
its own special key-note, which is struck in the very first words.
In each of the three parts, also, a different antithesis stands
in the foreground: viz. in the *first* part, ch. xl.-xlviii., the contrast between Jehovah and the idols, and between Israel and
the heathen; in the *second* part, ch. xlix.-lvii., the contrast
between the present suffering of the Servant of Jehovah and
His future glory; in the *third* part, ch. lviii.-lxvi., the contrast observable in the heart of Israel itself, between the hypocrites, the depraved, the rebellious, on the one side, and the
faithful, the mourning, the persecuted, on the other. The first
part sets forth the deliverance from Bàbylon, in which the
prophecy of Jehovah is fulfilled, to the shame and overthrow of
the idols and their worshippers; the second part, the way of
the Servant of Jehovah through deep humiliation to exaltation
and glory, which is at the same time the exaltation of Israel to
the height of its world-wide calling; the third part, the indispensable conditions of participation in the future redemption
and glory. There is some truth in Hahn's opinion, that the
distinctive characteristics of the three separate parts are exhibited in the three clauses of ch. xl. 2: *"that her distress is
ended, that her debt is paid, that she has received* (according to
his explanation, *' will receive'*) *double for all her sins."* For
the central point of the first part is really the termination of
the Babylonian distress; that of the second, the expiation of
guilt by the self-sacrifice of the Servant of Jehovah; and that
of the third, the assurance that the sufferings will be followed
by "a far more exceeding weight of glory." The promise
rises higher and higher in the circular movements of the 3×9
addresses, until at length it reaches its zenith in ch. lxv. and
lxvi., and links time and eternity together.

So far as the language is concerned, there is nothing more
finished or more elevated in the whole of the Old Testament
than this trilogy of addresses by Isaiah. In ch. i.-xxxix. of

the collection, the prophet's language is generally more compressed, chiselled (*lapidarisch*), plastic, although even there his style passes through all varieties of colour. But here in ch. xl.–lxvi., where he no longer has his foot upon the soil of his own time, but is transported into the far distant future, as into his own home, even the language retains an ideal and, so to speak, ethereal character. It has grown into a broad, pellucid, shining stream, which floats us over as it were into the world beyond, upon majestic yet gentle and translucent waves. There are only two passages in which it becomes more harsh, turbid, and ponderous, viz. ch. liii. and lvi. 9–lvii. 11*a*. In the former it is the emotion of sorrow which throws its shadow upon it; in the latter, the emotion of wrath. And in every other instance in which it changes, we may detect at once the influence of the object and of the emotion. In ch. lxiii. 7 the prophet strikes the note of the liturgical *t'phillâh;* in ch. lxiii. 19*b*–lxiv. 4 it is sadness which chokes the stream of words; in ch. lxiv. 5 you hear, as in Jer. iii. 25, the key-note of the liturgical *vidduy,* or confessional prayer.

And when we turn to the contents of his trilogy, it is more incomparable still. It commences with a prophecy, which gave to John the Baptist the great theme of his preaching. It closes with the prediction of the creation of a new heaven and new earth, beyond which even the last page of the New Testament Apocalypse cannot go. And in the centre (ch. lii. 13–liii.) the sufferings and exaltation of Christ are proclaimed as clearly, as if the prophet had stood beneath the cross itself, and had seen the Risen Saviour. He is transported to the very commencement of the New Testament times, and begins just like the New Testament evangelists. He afterwards describes the death and resurrection of Christ as completed events, with all the clearness of a Pauline discourse. And lastly, he clings to the heavenly world beyond, like John in the Apocalypse. Yet the Old Testament limits are not disturbed; but within those limits, evangelist, apostle, and apocalyptist are all condensed into one. Throughout the whole of these addresses we never meet with a strictly Messianic prophecy; and yet they have more christological depth than all the Messianic prophecies taken together. The bright picture of the coming King, which is met with in the earlier Messianic prophecies, undergoes a metamorphosis here, out of which it issues enriched by many essential elements, viz. those of the two *status*, the *mors vicaria*, and the *munus triplex*. The dark typical background of suffering, which the mournful Davidic psalms give to the figure of the Messiah, becomes here for the first time an object of direct prediction. The place of the Son of David, who is only a King, is now taken by the Servant of Jehovah, who is *Prophet* and *Priest* by virtue of His self-sacrifice, and *King* as well; the Saviour of Israel and of the Gentiles, persecuted even to death by His own nation, but exalted by God to be both Priest and King. So rich and profound a legacy did Isaiah leave to the church of the captivity, and to the church of the future also, yea, even to the New Jerusalem upon the new earth. Hengstenberg has very properly compared these prophecies of Isaiah to the Deuteronomic "last words" of Moses in the steppes of Moab, and to the last words of the Lord Jesus, within the circle of His own disciples, as reported by John. It is a thoroughly esoteric book, left to the church for future interpretation. To none of the Old Testament prophets who followed him was the ability given perfectly to open the book. Nothing but the coming of the Servant of Jehovah in the person of Jesus Christ could break all the seven seals. But was Isaiah really the author of this book of consolation? Modern criticism visits all who dare to assert this with the double ban of want of science and want of conscience. It regards Isaiah's authorship as being quite as impossible as any miracle in the sphere of nature, of history, or of the spirit. No prophecies find any favour in its eyes, but such as can be naturally explained. It knows exactly how far a prophet can see, and where he must stand, in order to see so far. But we are not tempted at all to purchase such omniscience at the price of the supernatural. We believe in the supernatural reality of prophecy, simply because history furnishes indisputable proofs of it, and because a supernatural interposition on the part of God in both the inner and outer life of man takes place even at the present day, and can be readily put to the test. But this interposition varies greatly both in degree and kind; and even in the far-sight of the prophets there were the greatest diversities, according to the measure of their charisma. It is quite possible, therefore, that Isaiah may have foreseen the calamities of the Babylonian age and the deliverance that followed " by an excellent spirit," as the son of Sirach says (Ecclus. xlviii. 24), and may have lived and moved in these "last things," even at a time when the Assyrian empire was still standing. But we do not regard all that is possible as being therefore real. We can examine quite impartially whether this really was the case, and without our ultimate decision being under the constraint of any unalterable foregone conclusion, like that of the critics referred to. All that we have said in praise of ch. xl.–lxvi. would retain its fullest force, even if the author of the whole should prove to be a prophet of the captivity, and not Isaiah.

We have already given a cursory glance at the general and particular grounds upon which we maintain the probability, or rather the certainty, that Isaiah was the author of ch. xl.–lxvi. (*vid.* vol. i. pp. 57–62); and we have explained them more fully in the concluding remarks to Drechsler's *Commentary* (vol. iii. pp. 361–416), to which we would refer any readers who wish to obtain a complete insight into the *pro* and *con* of this critical question. All false supports of Isaiah's authorship have there been willingly given up; for the words of Job to his friends (xiii. 7, 8) are quite as applicable to a biblical theologian of the present day.

We have admitted, that throughout the whole of the twenty-seven prophecies, the author of ch. xl.–lxvi. has the captivity as his fixed standpoint, or at any rate as a standpoint that is only so far a fluctuating one, as the eventual deliverance approaches nearer and nearer, and that without ever betraying the difference between the real present and this ideal one; so that as the prophetic vision of the future has its roots in every other instance in the soil of the prophet's own time, and springs out of that soil, to all appearance he is an exile himself. But notwithstanding this, the following arguments may be adduced in support of Isaiah's authorship. In the first place, the deliverance foretold in these prophecies, with all its attendant circumstances, is referred to as something beyond the reach of human foresight, and known to Jehovah alone, and as something the occurrence of which would prove Him to be the God of Gods. Jehovah, the God of the prophecy, knew the name of Cyrus even before he knew it himself; and He demonstrated His Godhead to all the world, inasmuch as He caused the name and work of the deliverer of Israel to be foretold (ch. xlv. 4–7). *Secondly*, although these prophecies rest throughout upon the soil of the captivity, and do not start with the historical basis of Hezekiah's time, as we should expect them to do, with Isaiah as their author; yet the discrepancy between this phenomenon and the general character of prophecy elsewhere, loses its full force as an argument against Isaiah's authorship, if we do not separate ch. xl.–lxvi. from ch. i.–xxxix. and take it as an independent work, as is generally done. The whole of the first half of the collection is a staircase, leading up to these addresses to the exiles, and bears the same relation to them, as a whole, as the Assyrian pedestal in ch. xiv. 24–27 to the Babylonian *massâ'* in ch. xiii.–xiv. 26 (see vol. i. 317). This relation between the two—namely, that Assyrian prophecies lay the foundation for Babylonian—runs through the whole of the first half. It is so arranged, that the prophecies of the Assyrian times throughout have intermediate layers, which reach beyond those times; and whilst the former constitute the groundwork, the latter form the gable. This is the relation in which ch. xxiv.–xxvii. stand to ch. xiii.–xxiii., and ch. xxxiv. xxxv. to ch. xxviii.–xxxiii. And within the cycle of prophecies against the nations, three Babylonian prophecies — viz. ch. xiii.–xiv. 23, xxi. 1–10, and xxiii.—form the commencement, middle, and end. The Assyrian prophecies lie within a circle, the circumference and diameter of which consist of prophecies that have a longer span. And are all these prophecies, that are inserted with such evident skill and design, to be taken away from our prophet? The oracle concerning Babel, in ch. xiii.–xiv. 23, has all the ring of a prophecy of Isaiah's, as we have already seen; and in the epilogue, in ch. xiv. 24–27, it has Isaiah's signature. The second oracle concerning Babel, in ch. xxi. 1–10, is not only connected with three passages of Isaiah's that are acknowledged as genuine, so as to form a tetralogy; but in style and spirit it is most intimately bound up with them. The cycle of prophecies of the final catastrophe (ch. xxiv.–xxvii.) commences so thoroughly in Isaiah's style, that nearly every word and every turn in the first three verses bears Isaiah's stamp; and in ch. xxvii. 12, 13, it dies away, just like the book of Immanuel, ch. xi. 11 sqq. And the genuineness of ch. xxxiv. and xxxv. has never yet been disputed on any valid grounds. Knobel, indeed, maintains that the historical background of this passage establishes its spuriousness ; but it is impossible to detect any background of contemporaneous history. Edom in this instance represents the world, as opposed to the people of God, just as Moab does in ch. xxv. Consider, moreover, that these disputed prophecies form a series which constitutes in every respect a prelude to ch. xl.-lxvi. Have we not in ch. xiv. 1, 2, the substance of ch. xl.-lxvi., as it were, *in nuce* ? Is not the trilogy " Babel," in ch. xlvi.-xlviii., like an expansion of the vision in ch. xxi. 1–10 ? Is not the prophecy concerning Edom in ch. xxxiv. the side-piece to ch. lxiii. 1–6 ? And do we not hear in ch. xxxv. the direct prelude to the melody, which is continued in ch. xl.-lxvi. ? And to this we may add still further the fact, that prominent marks of Isaiah are common alike to the disputed prophecies, and to those whose genuineness is acknowledged. The name of God, which is so characteristic of Isaiah, and which we meet with on every hand in acknowledged prophecies in ch. i.-xxxix., viz. " the Holy One of Israel," runs also through ch. xl.-lxvi. (vol. i. 193). And so again do the confirmatory words, " Thus saith Jehovah," and the interchange of the national names Jacob and Israel (compare, for example, ch. xl. 27 with ch. xxix. 23).[1] The rhetorical figure called *epanaphora*, which may be illustrated by an Arabic proverb,[2]—

" Enjoy the scent of the yellow roses of Negd ;
   For when the evening is gone, it is over with the yellow roses,"—

is very rare apart from the book of Isaiah (Gen. vi. 9, xxxv. 12 ; Lev. xxv. 41 ; Job xi. 7) ; whereas in the book of Isaiah itself it runs like a favourite oratorical turn from beginning to end (*vid.* ch. i. 7, iv. 3, vi. 11, xiii. 10, xiv. 25, xv. 8, xxx. 20, xxxiv. 9, xl. 19, xlii. 15, 19, xlviii. 21, li. 13, liii. 6, 7, liv. 4, 13, l. 4, lviii. 2, lix. 8,—a collection of examples which could probably be still further increased). But there are still deeper lines of connection than these. How strikingly, for example,

---

[1] The remark which we made at vol. i. p. 117, to the effect that Isaiah prefers Israel, is therefore to be qualified, inasmuch as in ch. xl.-lxvi. Jacob takes precedence of Israel.

[2] See Mehren, *Rhetorik der Araber*, p. 161 sqq.

does ch. xxviii. 5 ring in harmony with ch. lxii. 3, and ch.
xxix. 23 (cf. v. 7) with ch. lx. 21 ! And does not the leading
thought which is expressed in ch. xxii. 11, xxxvii. 26 (cf. ch.
xxv. 1), viz. that whatever is realized in history has had its
pre-existence as an idea in God, run with a multiplied echo
through ch. xl.–lxvi. ? And does not the second half repeat,
in ch. lxv. 25, in splendidly elaborate paintings, and to some
extent in the very same words (which is not unlike Isaiah),
what we have already found in ch. xi. 6 sqq., xxx. 26, and
other passages, concerning the future glorification of the earthly
and heavenly creation ? Yea, we may venture to maintain
(and no one has ever attempted to refute it), that the second
half of the book of Isaiah (ch. xl.–lxvi), so far as its theme, its
standpoint, its style, and its ideas are concerned, is in a state
of continuous formation throughout the whole of the first (ch.
i.–xxxix.). On the frontier of the two halves, the prediction in
ch. xxxix. 5, 7 stands like a sign-post, with the inscription, " To
Babylon." There, viz. in Babylon, is henceforth Isaiah's spiritual home ; there he preaches to the church of the captivity
the way of salvation, and the consolation of redemption, but to
the rebellious the terrors of judgment.

That this is the case, is confirmed by the reciprocal relation
in which ch. xl.–lxvi. stand to all the other literature of the
Old Testament with which we are acquainted. In ch. xl.–lxvi.
we find reminiscences from the book of Job (compare ch. xl.
23 with Job xii. 24 ; xliv. 25 with Job xii. 17, 20 ; xliv. 24 with
Job ix. 8 ; xl. 14 with Job xxi. 22 ; lix. 4 with Job xv. 35 and
Ps. vii. 15). And the first half points back to Job in just the
same manner. The poetical words גֵּוַע, הִתְגַּבֵּר, צֶאֱצָאִים, are only
met with in the book of Isaiah and the book of Job. Once at
least, namely ch. lix. 7, we are reminded of *mishlē* (Prov. i. 16) ;
whilst in the first half we frequently met with imitations of
the *mâshâl* of Solomon. The two halves stand in exactly the
same relation to the book of Micah ; compare ch. lviii. 1 with
Mic. iii. 8, like ii. 2–4 with Mic. iv. 1–4, and xxvi. 21 with
Mic. i. 3. And the same relation to Nahum runs through the
two ; compare Nah. iii. 4, 5 with ch. xlvii., ii. 1 with lii. 7*a*, 1*b*,
and ii. 11 with xxiv. 1, iii. 13 with xix. 16. We leave the
question open, on which side the priority lies. But when we
find in Zephaniah and Jeremiah points of contact not only with

ch. xl.–lxvi., but also with ch. xiii.–xiv. 23, xxi. 1–10, xxxiv.–
xxxv., which preclude the possibility of accident, it is more than
improbable that these two prophets should have been imitated
by the author of ch. xl.–lxvi., since it is in them above all
others that we meet with the peculiar disposition to blend the
words and thoughts of their predecessors with their own. Not
only does Zephaniah establish points of contact with Isa. xiii.
and xxxiv. in by no means an accidental manner, but compare
ch. ii. 15 with Isa. xlvii. 8, 10, and ch. iii. 10 with Isa. lxvi.
20. The former passage betrays its derivative character by
the fact that עַלִּיז is a word that belongs exclusively to Isaiah ;
whilst the latter is not only a compendium of Isa. lxvi. 20,
but also points back to Isa. xviii. 1, 7, in the expression
מֵעֵבֶר לְנַהֲרֵי־כוּשׁ. In Jeremiah, the indication of dependence upon
Isaiah comes out most strongly in the prophecy against Babylon
in Jer. l. li. ; in fact, it is so strong, that Movers, Hitzig,
and De Wette regard the anonymous author of ch. xl.–lxvi.
as the interpolator of this prophecy. But it also contains echoes
of Isa. xiii., xiv., xxi., and xxxiv., and is throughout a Mosaic
of earlier prophecies. The passage in Jer. x. 1–16 concerning the nothingness of the gods of the nations, sounds also
most strikingly like Isaiah's ; compare more especially Isa. xliv.
12–15, xli. 7, xlvi. 7, though the attempt has also been made
to render this intelligible by the interpolation hypothesis. It
is not only in vers. 6–8 and 10, which are admitted to be
Jeremiah's, that we meet with the peculiar characteristics of
Jeremiah ; but even in passages that are rejected we find such
expressions of his as פְּקֻדָּה, תַּעְתֻּעִים, נִבְעַר, אַתָּה for אוֹתָם, יָפֶה, a
penal visitation, such as we never meet with in Isaiah ɪɪ. And
the whole of the consolatory words in Jer. xxx. 10, 11, and
again in xlvi. 27, 28, which sound so much like the deutero-
Isaiah, are set down as having been inserted in the book of
Jeremiah by Isaiah ɪɪ. But Caspari has shown that this is impossible, because the concluding words of the promise, "I will
correct thee in measure, and will not leave thee altogether
unpunished," would have no meaning at all if uttered at the
close of the captivity ; and also, because such elements as are
evidently Jeremiah's, and in which it coincides with prophecies
of Jeremiah that are acknowledged to be genuine, far outweigh
those of the deutero-Isaiah. And yet in this passage, when

Israel is addressed as "my servant," we hear the tone of the deutero-Isaiah. Jeremiah fuses in this instance, as in many other passages, the tones of Isaiah with his own. There are also many other passages which coincide with passages of the second part of Isaiah, both in substance and expression, though not so conclusively as those already quoted, and in which we have to decide between regarding Jeremiah as an imitator, or Isaiah II. as an interpolator. But if we compare Jer. vi. 15 with Isa. lvi. 11, and Isa. xlviii. 6 with Jer. xxxiii. 3, where Jeremiah, according to his usual custom, gives a different turn to the original passages by a slight change in the letters, we shall find involuntary reminiscences of Isaiah in Jeremiah, in such parallels as Jer. iii. 16, Isa. lxv. 17; Jer. iv. 13, Isa. lxvi. 15; Jer. xi. 19, Isa. liii.; and shall hear the ring of Isa. li. 17–23 in Jeremiah's *qīnōth*, and that of Isa. lvi. 9–lvii. 11a in the earlier reproachful addresses of Jeremiah, and not *vice versa*.

In conclusion, let us picture to ourselves the gradual development of Isaiah's view of the *captivity*, that penal judgment already threatened in the law. (1.) In the *Uzziah-Jotham* age the prophet refers to the captivity, in the most general terms that can be conceived, in ch. vi. 12, though he mentions it casually by its own name even in ch. v. 13. (2.) In the time of *Ahaz* we already see him far advanced beyond this first sketchy reference to the captivity. In ch. xi. 11 sqq. he predicts a second deliverance, resembling the Egyptian exodus. Asshur stands at the head of the countries of the *diaspora*, as the imperial power by which the judgment of captivity is carried out. (3.) In the early years of *Hezekiah*, ch. xxii. 18 appears to indicate the carrying away of Judah by Asshur. But when the northern kingdom had succumbed to the judgment of the Assyrian banishment, and Judah had been mercifully spared this judgment, the eyes of Isaiah were directed to Babylon as the imperial power destined to execute the same judgment upon Judah. We may see this from ch. xxxix. 5–7. Micah also speaks of Babylon as the future place of punishment and deliverance (Mic. iv. 10). The prophecies of the overthrow of Babylon in ch. xiii. 14, 21, are therefore quite in the spirit of the prophecies of Hezekiah's time. And ch. xl.–lxvi. merely develop on all sides what was already contained in germ in ch. xiv 1, 2, xxi. 10. It is well known that in the time of

Hezekiah Babylon attempted to break loose from Assyria; and so also the revolt of the Medes from Asshur, and the union of their villages and districts under one monarch named *Deyoces*, occurred in the time of Hezekiah.[1] It is quite characteristic of Isaiah that he never names the Persians, who were at that time still subject to the Medes. He mentions *Madai* in ch. xiii. 17 and xxi. 2, and *Kōresh* (*Kurus*), the founder of the Persian monarchy; but not that one of the two leading Iranian tribes, which gained its liberty through him in the time of Astyages, and afterwards rose to the possession of the imperial sway.

But how is it possible that Isaiah should have mentioned Cyrus by name centuries before this time (210 years, according to Josephus, *Ant.* xi. 1, 2)? Windischmann answers this question in his *Zoroastrische Studien*, p. 137. "No one," he says, "who believes in a living, personal, omniscient God, and in the possibility of His revealing future events, will ever deny that He possesses the power to foretell the name of a future monarch." And Albrecht Weber, the Indologian, finds in this answer "an evidence of self-hardening against the scientific conscience," and pronounces such hardening nothing less than "devilish."

It is not possible to come to any understanding concerning this point, which is the real nerve of the prevailing settled conclusion as to ch. xl.–lxvi. We therefore hasten on to our exposition. *And in relation to this, if we only allow that the prophet really was a prophet, it is of no essential consequence to what age he belonged.* For in this one point we quite agree with the opponents of its genuineness, namely, that the standpoint of the prophet is the second half of the captivity. If the author is Isaiah, as we feel constrained to assume for reasons that we have already stated here and elsewhere, he is entirely carried away from his own times, and leads a pneumatic life among the exiles. There is, in fact, no more "Johannic" book in the whole of the Old Testament than this book of consolation. It is like the product of an Old Testament gift of tongues. The fleshly body of speech has been changed into a glorified body; and we hear, as it were, spiritual voices from the world beyond, or world of glory.

[1] Spiegel (*Eran*, p. 313 sqq.) places the revolt of the Medes in the year 714, and Deyoces in the year 708.

PART I.

FIRST PROPHECY.—Chap. xl.

WORDS OF COMFORT, AND THE GOD OF COMFORT.

In this first address the prophet vindicates his call to be the preacher of the comfort of the approaching deliverance, and explains this comfort on the ground that Jehovah, who called him to this comforting proclamation, was the incomparably exalted Creator and Ruler of the world. The first part of this address (vers. 1–11) may be regarded as the prologue to the whole twenty-seven. The theme of the prophetic promise, and the irresistible certainty of its fulfilment, are here declared. Turning to the people of the captivity, whom Jehovah has neither forgotten nor rejected, the prophet commences thus in ver. 1: *"Comfort ye, comfort ye my people, saith your God."* This is the divine command to the prophets. *Nachămū* (*piel*, literally, to cause to breathe again) is repeated, because of its urgency (*anadiplosis*, as in ch. xli. 27, xliii. 11, xxv., etc.). The word יֹאמַר, which does not mean "will say" here (Hofmann, Stier), but "saith" (LXX., Jerome),—as, for example, in 1 Sam. xxiv. 14,—affirms that the command is a continuous one. The expression *"saith your God"* is peculiar to Isaiah, and common to both parts of the collection (ch. i. 11, 18, xxxiii. 10, xl. 1, 25, xli. 21, lxvi. 9). The future in all these passages is expressive of that which is taking place or still continuing. And it is the same here. The divine command has not been issued once only, or merely to one prophet, but is being continually addressed to many prophets. "Comfort ye, comfort ye my people," is the continual charge of the God of the exiles, who has not ceased to be their God even in the midst of wrath, to His messengers and heralds the prophets.

The summons is now repeated with still greater emphasis, the substance of the consoling proclamation being also given Ver. 2. *"Speak ye to the heart of Jerusalem, and cry unto her, that her affliction is ended, that her debt is paid, that she has received from the hand of Jehovah double for all her sins."* The holy city is thought of here in connection with the population belonging to it. דַּבֵּר עַל־לֵב (to speak to the heart) is an expression applied in Gen. xxxiv. 3 and Judg. xix. 3 to words adapted to win the heart; in Gen. l. 21, to the words used by Joseph to inspire his brethren with confidence; whilst here it is used in precisely the same sense as in Hos. ii. 16, and possibly not without a reminiscence of this earlier prophecy. קָרָא אֶל (to call to a person) is applied to a prophetic announcement made to a person, as in Jer. vii. 27, Zech. i. 4. The announcement to be made to Jerusalem is then introduced with כִּי, ὅτι, which serves as the introduction to either an indirect or a direct address (Ges. § 155, 1, *e*). (1.) Her affliction has become full, and therefore has come to an end. צָבָא, military service, then feudal service, and hardship generally (Job vii. 1); here it applies to the captivity or exile—that unsheltered bivouac, as it were, of the people who had been transported into a foreign land, and were living there in bondage, restlessness, and insecurity. (2.) Her iniquity is atoned for, and the justice of God is satisfied: *nirtsâh*, which generally denotes a satisfactory reception, is used here in the sense of meeting with a satisfactory payment, like רָצָה עָוֹן in Lev. xxvi. 41, 43, to pay off the debt of sin by enduring the punishment of sin. (3.) The third clause repeats the substance of the previous ones with greater emphasis and in a fuller tone: Jerusalem has already suffered fully for her sins. In direct opposition to לָקְחָה, which cannot, when connected with two actual perfects as it is here, be taken as a perfect used to indicate the certainty of some future occurrence, Gesenius, Hitzig, Ewald, Umbreit, Stier, and Hahn suppose *kiphlayim* to refer to the double favour that Jerusalem was about to receive (like *mishneh* in ch. lxi. 7, and possibly borrowed from Isaiah in Zech. ix. 12), instead of to the double punishment which Jerusalem had endured (like *mishneh* in Jer. xvi. 18). It is not to be taken, however, in a judicial sense; in which case God would appear over-rigid, and therefore unjust. Jerusalem had not suffered more than its sins had deserved; but the compassion of God regarded what His justice had been obliged to inflict upon Jerusalem as superabundant. This compassion also expresses itself in the words " for all" (*b'khol, c. Beth pretii*): there is nothing left for further punishment. The turning-point from wrath to love has arrived. The wrath has gone forth in double measure. With what intensity, therefore, will the love break forth, which has been so long restrained!

There is a *sethume* in the text at this point. The first two verses form a small *parashah* by themselves, the prologue of the prologue. After the substance of the consolation has been given on its negative side, the question arises, What positive salvation is to be expected? This question is answered for the prophet, inasmuch as, in the ecstatic stillness of his mind as turned to God, he hears a marvellous voice. Ver. 3. "*Hark, a crier! In the wilderness prepare ye a way for Jehovah, make smooth in the desert a road for our God.*" This is not to be rendered "a voice cries" (Ges., Umbreit, etc.); but the two words are in the construct state, and form an interjectional clause, as in ch. xiii. 4, lii. 8, lxvi. 6: Voice of one crying! Who the crier is remains concealed; his person vanishes in the splendour of his calling, and falls into the background behind the substance of his cry. The cry sounds like the long-drawn trumpet-blast of a herald (cf. ch. xvi. 1). The crier is like the outrider of a king, who takes care that the way by which the king is to go shall be put into good condition. The king is Jehovah; and it is all the more necessary to prepare the way for Him in a becoming manner, that this way leads through the pathless desert. *Bammidbâr* is to be connected with *pannû*, according to the accents on account of the parallel (*zakeph katan* has a stronger disjunctive force here than *zakeph gadol*, as in Deut. xxvi. 14, xxviii. 8, 2 Kings i. 6), though without any consequent collision with the New Testament description of the fulfilment itself. And so also the Targum and Jewish expositors take קוֹל קוֹרֵא בַמִּדְבָּר together, like the LXX., and after this the Gospels. We may, or rather apparently we must, imagine the crier as advancing into the desert, and summoning the people to come and make a road through it. But why does the way of Jehovah lie through the desert, and whither does it lead? It was through the desert that He went to redeem Israel out of Egyptian bondage, and to reveal Himself to Israel from Sinai (Deut. xxxiii. 2; Judg. v. 4; Ps. lxviii. 8); and in Ps. lxviii. 4 (5) God the Redeemer of His people is called *hârōkhēbh bâʿărâbhōth*. Just as His people looked for Him then, when they were between Egypt and Canaan; so was He to be looked

for by His people again, now that they were in the "desert of
the sea" (ch. xxi. 1), and separated by *Arabia deserta* from
their fatherland.   If He were coming at the head of His
people, He Himself would clear the hindrances out of His way;
but He was coming through the desert to Israel, and therefore
Israel itself was to take care that nothing should impede the
rapidity or detract from the favour of the Coming One.   The
description answers to the reality; but, as we shall frequently
find as we go further on, the literal meaning spiritualizes itself
in an allegorical way.

The summons proceeds in a commanding tone.   Ver. 4.
"*Let every valley be exalted, and every mountain and hill made
low; and let the rugged be made a plain, and the ledges of rocks
a valley.*"   וְהָיָה, which takes its tone from the two jussive verbs,
is also itself equivalent to וִיהִי.   Instead of גֶּיא (from גַּיְא), the
pointing in Zech. xiv. 4, we have here (according to Kimchi)
the vowel-pointing גַּיְא; at the same time, the editions of Brescia,
Pesaro, Venice 1678, have גֵּיא (with *tzere*), and this is also the
reading of a codex of Luzzatto without Masoretic notes.   The
command, according to its spiritual interpretation, points to the
encouragement of those that are cast down, the humiliation of
the self-righteous and self-secure, the changing of dishonesty
into simplicity, and of unapproachable haughtiness into submission (for '*âqōbh*, hilly, rugged,[1] compare Jer. xvii. 9 together
with Hab. ii. 4).   In general, the meaning is that Israel is to
take care, that the God who is coming to deliver it shall find it
in such an inward and outward state as befits His exaltation
and His purpose.

The cry of the crier proceeds thus in ver. 5: "*And the
glory of Jehovah will be revealed, and all flesh seeth together: for
the mouth of Jehovah hath spoken it.*"   The *pret. cons.* וְנִגְלָה is
here *apodosis imper.*   When the way is prepared for Jehovah
the Coming One, the glory of the God of salvation will unveil
itself (on the name *Jehovah*, which is applied to God, the absolute I, as living and revealing Himself in history, more especially in the history of salvation, see vol. i. p. 67).   His *parousia*
is the revelation of His glory (1 Pet. iv. 13).   This revelation
is made for the good of Israel, but not secretly or exclusively;

---

[1] In this ethical sense Essex applied the word to Queen Elizabeth.   See
Hefele, *Ximenes*, p. 90 (ed. 2).

for all the human race, called here designedly "all flesh" (*kol
bâsâr*), will come to see it (compare Luke iii. 6, "the salvation
of God"). Man, because he is flesh, cannot see God without
dying (Ex. xxxiii. 20) ; but the future will fill up this gulf of
separation. The object to the verb "see" is not what follows,
as Rosenmüller supposes, viz. "that the mouth of Jehovah hath
spoken," for the word of promise which is here fulfilled is not
one addressed to all flesh ; nor does it mean, "see that Jehovah
hath spoken with His own mouth," *i.e.* after having become
man, as Stier maintains, for the verb required in this case would
be מְדֻבָּר, not דִּבֶּר. The clause, "for the mouth of Jehovah hath
spoken it," is rather Isaiah's usual confirmation of the foregoing prophecy (see vol. i. p. 425). Here the crier uses it to
establish the certainty of what he foretells, provided that Israel
will do what he summons it to perform.

The prophet now hears a second voice, and then a third,
entering into conversation with it. Vers. 6–8. "*Hark, one
speaking, Cry! And he answers, What shall I cry? All flesh
is grass, and all its beauty as the flower of the field. Grass
is withered, flower faded : for the breath of Jehovah has blown
upon it. Surely grass is the people ; grass withereth, flower
fadeth: yet the word of our God will stand for ever.*" A second
voice celebrates the divine word of promise in the face of the
approaching fulfilment, and appoints a preacher of its eternal
duration. The verb is not וָאֹמַר (*et dixi*, LXX., Vulg.), but
וְאָמַר ; so that the person asking the question is not the prophet
himself, but an ideal person, whom he has before him in visionary objectiveness. The appointed theme of his proclamation
is the perishable nature of all flesh (ver. 5 πᾶσα σάρξ, here
πᾶσα ἡ σάρξ), and, on the other hand, the imperishable nature
of the word of God. Men living in the flesh are universally
impotent, perishing, limited ; God, on the contrary (ch. xxxi. 3),
is the omnipotent, eternal, all-determining ; and like Himself, so
is His word, which, regarded as the vehicle and utterance of His
willing and thinking, is not something separate from Himself,
and therefore is the same as He. *Chasdō* is the charm or grace-
fulness of the outward appearance (LXX. ; 1 Pet. i. 24, δόξα :
see Schott on the passage, Jas. i. 11, εὐπρέπεια). The comparison instituted with grass and flower recals ch. xxxvii. 27
and Job viii. 12, and still more Ps. xc. 5, 6, and Job xiv. 2.

Ver. 7a describes what happens to the grass and flower. The preterites, like the Greek *aoristus gnomicus* (cf. ch. xxvi. 10), express a fact of experience sustained by innumerable examples: *exaruit gramen, emarcuit flos;*[1] consequently the כִּי which follows is not hypothetical (granting that), but explanatory of the reason, viz. "because *rūăch Jehovah* hath blown upon it," *i.e.* the "breath" of God the Creator, which pervades the creation, generating life, sustaining life, and destroying life, and whose most characteristic elementary manifestation is the wind. Every breath of wind is a drawing of the breath of the whole life of nature, the active indwelling principle of whose existence is the *rūăch* of God. A fresh verse ought to commence now with אָכֵן. The clause אָכֵן חָצִיר הָעָם is genuine, and thoroughly in Isaiah's style, notwithstanding the LXX., which Gesenius and Hitzig follow. אכן is not equivalent to a comparative כֵּן (Ewald, § 105, *a*), but is assuring, as in ch. xlv. 15, xlix. 4, liii. 4; and *hâ‘âm* (the people) refers to men generally, as in ch. xlii. 5. The order of thought is in the form of a *triolet*. The explanation of the striking simile commences with '*âkhēn* (surely); and then in the repetition of the words, "grass withereth, flower fadeth," the men are intended, who resemble the grass and the flower. Surely grass is the human race; such grass withereth and such flower fadeth, but the word of our God (Jehovah, the God of His people and of sacred history) *yâqūm l°ōlâm*, *i.e.* it rises up without withering or fading, and endures for ever, fulfilling and verifying itself through all times. This general truth refers, in the present instance, to the word of promise uttered by the voice in the desert. If the word of God generally has an eternal duration, more especially is this the case with the word of the *parousia* of God the Redeemer, the word in which all the words of God are yea and amen. The imperishable nature of this word, however, has for its dark foil the perishable nature of all flesh, and all the beauty thereof. The oppressors of Israel are mortal, and their *chesed* with which they impose and bribe is perishable; but the word of God, with which Israel can console itself, pre-

---

[1] נֵבֵל has *munach* here and in ver. 8 attached to the penultimate in all correct texts (hence *milel*, on account of the monosyllable which follows), and *metheg* on the *tzere* to sustain the lengthening.

serves the field, and ensures it a glorious end to its history.
Thus the seal, which the first crier set upon the promise of
Jehovah's speedy coming, is inviolable ; and the comfort which
the prophets of God are to bring to His people, who have now
been suffering so long, is infallibly sure.

The prophet accordingly now takes, as his standpoint, the
time when Jehovah will already have come. Ver. 9. " *Upon
a high mountain get thee up, O evangelistess Zion ; lift up thy
voice with strength, evangelistess Jerusalem : lift up, be not
afraid ; say to the cities of Judah, Behold your God.*" Knobel
and others follow the LXX. and Targum, and regard *Zion*
and *Jerusalem* as accusatives of the object, viz. " preacher of salvation (*i.e.* a chorus of preachers) to Zion-Jerusalem ;" but
such parallels as ch. lii. 7 and lxii. 11 are misleading here.
The words are in apposition (A. S. Th. εὐαγγελιζομένη Σιών).
Zion-Jerusalem herself is called an evangelistess : the personification as a female renders this probable at the outset, and it
is placed beyond all doubt by the fact, that it is the cities of
Judah (the daughters of Zion-Jerusalem) that are to be evan-
gelized. The prophet's standpoint here is in the very midst
of the *parousia*. When Jerusalem shall have her God in the
midst of her once more, after He has broken up His home
there for so long a time ; she is then, as the restored mother-
community, to ascend a high mountain, and raising her voice
with fearless strength, to bring to her daughters the joyful
news of the appearance of their God. The verb *bissēr* signifies
literally to smooth, to unfold, then to make glad, more especially with joyful news.[1] It lies at the root of the New Testament εὐαγγελίζειν (evangelize), and is a favourite word of the

---

[1] The verb *bissēr* signifies primarily to stroke, rub, shave, or scratch
the surface of anything ; then to stroke off or rub off the surface, or anything which covers it ; then, suggested by the idea of " rubbing smooth "
(*glatt*), " to smooth a person " (*jemanden glätten ;* compare the English, *to
gladden* a person), *i.e. vultum ejus diducere,* to make him friendly and
cheerful, or " to look smoothly upon a person," *i.e.* to show him a friendly
face ; and also as an intransitive, " *to be glad,*" to be friendly and cheerful ;
and lastly, in a general sense, *aliquid attingere, tractare, attrectare,* to
grasp or handle a thing (from which comes *bâsâr,* the flesh, as something
tangible or material). In harmony with the Hebrew *bissēr* (Jer. xx. 15),
they say in Arabic *basarahu* (or intensive, *bassarahu*) *bi-maulûdin,* he has
gladdened him with the news of the birth of a son.

author of ch. xl.–lxvi., that Old Testament evangelist, though it is no disproof of Isaiah's authorship (cf. Nahum ii. 1). Hitherto Jerusalem has been in despair, bowed down under the weight of the punishment of her sins, and standing in need of consolation. But now that she has Jehovah with her again, she is to lift up her voice with the most joyful confidence, without further anxiety, and to become, according to her true vocation, the messenger of good tidings to all Judæa.

In ver. 10 the prophet goes back from the standpoint of the fulfilment to that of the prophecy. "*Behold the Lord, Jehovah, as a mighty one will He come, His arm ruling for Him; behold, His reward is with Him, and His retribution before Him.*" We must not render the first clause "with strong," *i.e.* with strength, as the LXX. and Targum do. The *Beth* is *Beth essentiæ* (cf. ch. xxvi. 4; Ges. § 154, 3, *a*). He will come in the essence, strength, and energy of a strong one; and this is still further defined by the participial, circumstantial clause, "His arm ruling for Him" (*brachio suo ipsi dominante*). It is His arm that rules for Him, *i.e.* that either brings into subjection to Him, or else overthrows whatever opposes Him. Nevertheless, ver. 10*b* does not present Him merely in one aspect, namely as coming to judge and punish, but in both aspects, viz. that of the law and that of the gospel, as a righteous rewarder; hence the double name of God, *Adonai Jehovah* (compare ch. iii. 15, xxviii. 16 xxx. 15, all in the first part), which is used even in the Pentateuch, and most frequently by Amos and Ezekiel, and which forms, as it were, an anagram. פְּעֻלָּה is already met with in Lev. xix. 13 as a synonym of שָׂכָר, passing from the general idea of *work* to that of something earned and forfeited. Jehovah brings with Him the penal reward of the enemies of His people, and also the gracious reward of the faithful of His people, whom He will compensate for their previous sufferings with far exceeding joys (see ch. lxii. 11).

The prophet dwells upon this, the redeeming side not the judicial, as he proceeds to place the image of the good shepherd by the side of that of the Lord Jehovah. Ver. 11. "*He will feed His flock like a shepherd, take the lambs in His arm, and carry them in His bosom, and gently lead those that are giving suck.*" The flock is His people, now dispersed in a foreign

land. The love with which He tends this flock is shown, by
way of example, in His conduct towards the טְלָאִים (= טְלָיִים from
טָלֶה = טְלִי), the young lambs that have not long been born,
and the עָלוֹת‎, those giving suck, *lactantes* (Vulg. *fetæ*), not
those that are sucking, *sugentes* (from עוּל *med. Vav*, to nourish,
cf. vol. i. p. 138). Such as cannot keep pace with the flock he
takes in his arms, and carries in the bosom of his dress; and
the mothers he does not overdrive, but יְנַהֵל (see at Ps. xxiii. 2),
lets them go gently along, because they require care (Gen.
xxxiii. 13). With this loving picture the prologue in vers. 1–11
is brought to a close. It stands at the head of the whole, like
a divine inauguration of the prophet, and like the quintessence
of what he is commanded to proclaim. Nevertheless it is also
an integral part of the first address. For the questions which
follow cannot possibly be the commencement of the prophecy,
though it is not very clear how far they form a continuation.

The connection is the following: The prophet shows both
didactically and parænetically what kind of God it is whose
appearance to redeem His people has been prophetically announced in vers. 1–11. He is the incomparably exalted One.
This incomparable exaltation makes the ignorance of the worshippers of idols the more apparent, but it serves to comfort
Israel. And Israel needs such consolation in its present banishment, in which it is so hard for it to comprehend the ways of
God.

In order to bring His people to the full consciousness of the
exaltation of Jehovah, the prophet asks in ver. 12, " *Who hath
measured the waters with the hollow of his hand, and regulated
the heavens with a span, and taken up the dust of the earth in a
third measure, and weighed the mountains with a steelyard, and
hills with balances?* " Jehovah, and He alone, has given to all
these their proper quantities, their determinate form, and their
proportionate place in the universe. How very little can a man
hold in the hollow of his hand (*shŏ῾al*)![1] how very small is the
space which a man's span will cover! how little is contained in

---

[1] The root שָׁל سل has the primary meaning of easily moving or being
easily moved; then of being loose or slack, of hanging down, or sinking,
—a meaning which we meet with in שָׁעֲל and שָׁאַל. Accordingly, *shŏ῾al*
signifies the palm (*i.e.* the depression made by the hand), and *she῾ōl* not
literally a hollowing or cavity, but a depression or low ground.

the third of an ephah (*shâlîsh*; see at Ps. lxxx. 6)! and how trifling in either bulk or measure is the quantity you can weigh in scales, whether it be a *peles*, *i.e.* a steelyard (*statera*), or *mō'z^enayim*, a tradesman's balance (*bilances*), consisting of two scales.[1] But what Jehovah measures with the hollow of His hand, and with His span, is nothing less than the waters beneath and the heavens above. He carries a scoop, in which there is room for all the dust of which the earth consists, and a scale on which He has weighed the great colossal mountains.

A second question follows in vers. 13, 14. " *Who regulated the Spirit of Jehovah, and (who) instructed Him as His counsellor? With whom took He counsel, and who would have explained to Him and instructed Him concerning the path of right, and taught Him knowledge, and made known to Him a prudent course?*" The first question called to mind the omnipotence of Jehovah; this recalls His omniscience, which has all fulness in itself, and therefore precludes all instruction from without. " The Spirit of Jehovah " is the Spirit which moved upon the waters at the creation, and by which chaos was reduced to order. "Who," inquires this prophet,—" who furnished this Spirit with the standard, according to which all this was to be done?" תִּכֵּן as in ver. 12, to bring into conformity with rule, and so to fit for regulated working. Instead of *mercha tifchah athnach*, which suggests the Targum rendering, " *quis direxit spiritum? Jehova*" (*vid.* Prov. xvi. 2), it would be more correct to adopt the accentuation *tifchah munach athnach* (cf. Ex. xxi. 24, xxiii. 9), and there are certain codices in which we find this (see Dachselt). In ver. 13*b* we might follow the Septuagint translation, καὶ τίς αὐτοῦ σύμβουλος ἐγένετο, ὃς σύμβιβᾷ (Rom. xi. 34; 1 Cor. ii. 16, συμβιβάσει) αὐτόν, but in this case we miss the verb הָיָה. The rendering we have given above is not so harsh, and the accentuation is indifferent here, since *silluk* is never written without *tifchah* if only a single word precedes it. In ver. 14 the reciprocal נוֹעַץ is connected with אֶת = אִם. The *futt. cons.* retain their literal meaning: with whom did He

---

[1] According to the meaning, to level or equalize, which is one meaning of *pillēs*, the noun *peles* is applied not only to a level used to secure equilibrium, which is called *mishqeleth* in ch. xxviii. 17, but also to a steelyard used for weighing, the beam of which consists of a lever with unequal arms, which flies up directly the weight is removed.

consult, so that he supplied Him with understanding in consequence (*hēbhīn*, generally to understand, here in a causative
sense). The verbs of instruction are sometimes construed with
בְּ of the lesson taught, sometimes with a double accusative.
In reply to the questions in vers. 13, 14, which are essentially
one, Israel must acknowledge that its God is the possessor of
absolute might, and also of absolute wisdom.

From His exaltation as Creator, the prophet now proceeds
to His exaltation as Governor of the world. Ver. 15. "*Behold,
nations like a little drop on a bucket, and like a grain of sand in
a balance, are they esteemed; behold, islands like an atom of dust
that rises in the air.*" Upon Jehovah, the King of the world,
does the burden rest of ruling over the whole human race,
which is split up into different nations; but the great masses of
people over whom Jehovah rules are no more burden to Him
than a drop hanging upon a bucket is a burden to the man who
carries it (*min* is used in the same sense as in Song of Sol.
iv. 1, vi. 5), no more than the weight in a balance is perceptibly
increased or diminished by a grain of sand that happens to lie
upon it (*shachaq*, from *shâchaq*, to grind to powder). The
islands, those fragments of firm ground in the midst of the
ocean (אִי = *ivy*, from אָוָה, to betake one's self to a place, and
remain there), upon which the heathen world was dispersed
(Gen. x.), are to Him who carries the universe like the small
particle of dust (דַּק from דָּקַק, to crush or pulverize), which is
lifted up, viz. by the slightest breath of wind (יִטּוֹל metaplastic
fut. niph. of *tūl* = *nâtal*, ch. lxiii. 9). The rendering of
Knobel, "dust which is thrown," would require עָפָר (ch. xli. 2);
and neither that of Gesenius, viz. "He takes up islands like a
particle of dust," nor that of Hitzig, "He carries islands," etc.,
is admissible, for טוּל = נָטַל signifies *tollere*, not *portare*; and the
former, viz. *insulas tollit*, furnishes no answer to the question,
"How so, and to what end?"

By the side of this vanishing diminutiveness on the part of
man as contrasted with Jehovah, everything by which man
could express his adoration of the exalted One comes incomparably short of His exaltation. Ver. 16. "*And Lebanon is
not a sufficiency of burning, nor its game a sufficiency of burnt-
offerings;*" *i.e.* there is not enough wood to sustain the fire, nor a
sufficient supply of sacrificial animals to be slaughtered, and to

ascend in fire.   דַי (constr. דֵי) signifies that which suffices (and
then that which is plentiful) ; it differs therefore from τὸ δέον,
what is requisite.[1]

From the obverse of the thought in ver. 15 the prophet
returns to the thought itself, and dwells upon it still further.
Ver. 17. " *All the nations are as nothing before Him; they are
regarded by Him as belonging to nullity and emptiness.*" 'Ephes
is the end at which a thing ceases, and in an absolute sense
that at which all being ceases, hence non-existence or nullity.
Tōhŭ (from tâhâh, related to shâ'âh; vid. Job, vol. ii. p. 296), a
horrible desolation, like the chaos of creation, where there is
nothing definite, and therefore as good as nothing at all (see
p. 25); min is hardly comparative in the sense of "more
nothing than nothing itself" (like Job. xi. 17, where "brighter"
is to be supplied, or Mic. vii. 4, where "sharper" is similarly
required), but is used in the same partitive sense as in ch. xli. 24
(cf. xliv. 11 and Ps. lxii. 10).

The conclusion drawn from ver. 17, that Jehovah is therefore the matchless Being, shapes itself into a question, which is
addressed not to idolaters, but to such of the Israelites as needed
to be armed against the seductive power of idolatry, to which
the majority of mankind had yielded.   Ver. 19. " *And to
whom can ye liken God, and what kind of image can ye place
beside Him !*"   The וְ before וְאֶל is conclusive, as in ch.
xxviii. 26, and the futures are *modi potent.* : with what can ye
bring into comparison (אֵל as in ch. xiv. 10) *El*, *i.e.* God, the
one Being who is absolutely the Mighty? and what kind of
d^emūth (*i.e.* divine, like Himself) can ye place by His side?

Least of all can an idol bear comparison with Him.   Ver.
19. " *The idol, when the smith has cast it, the melter plates it
with gold, and melteth silver chains for it.*" The object (happesel,
the idol), which is here placed first as the theme in the accusative (lit. the image hewn out), denotes in this instance an idol
generally.   חָרָשׁ is as comprehensive as *faber*.   רִקַּע בַּזָּהָב signifies
here to cover over with a רִקַּע זָהָב (laminâ auri), the verb being
used in a denominative sense, and not in its primary meaning.

<hr/>

[1] The derivation of דַי is still more obscure than that of δεῖ, which signifies, according to Benfey (*Wurzelwörterbuch*, ii. 205), " there needs ;"
according to Sonne, " it binds, *scil.* ἡ ἀνάγκη."

As we must assume, according to ver. 20, that the prophet intends to carry us into the midst of the process of manufacturing the idol, the paratactic expression is to be pointed as above, viz. "after the (a) smith has cast it (compare Arab. *nasik*, a piece of cast metal), the (a) melter (goldsmith) covers it with gold plate;" and *tsōrēph*, which is palindromically repeated, according to Isaiah's custom (p. 134), is not the third pers. *poel* (on the *poel* of strong stems, see at Job ix. 15 and Ps. cix. 10), but a participle, equivalent to צוֹרֵף הוּא (as in ch. xxix. 8, which see; and also, according to the accents, ch. xxxiii. 5), "and he melteth chains of silver," viz. to fasten the image.

This is the origin of a metal idol. The wooden idol is described in ver. 20: "*The man who is impoverished in oblations, he chooseth a block of wood that will not rot; he seeketh for himself a skilful smith, to prepare an idol that will not shake.*" He who has fallen into such poverty that he can only offer to his God a poor oblation (*t'rūmâh*, accusative, according to Ewald, § 284, *c*), has an idol cut for himself out of a block of wood. That *sâkhan* (Arab. *sakana* or *sakuna*) [1] is an ancient word, is evident from Deut. viii. 9. The verb *yimmōt*, like *yittōl* in ver. 15, is a *fut. niphal*, to be made to shake. A wooden image, which is planed at the bottom, and made heavier below than above, to prevent its falling over with every shock, is to be a god! The thing carries its own satire, even when described with the greatest seriousness.

Having thus depicted in a few strokes the infatuation of idolatry, the prophet addresses the following question to such of the Israelites as are looking at it with longing eyes, even if they have not already been deluded by it. Ver. 21. "*Do ye not know? Do ye not hear? Is it not proclaimed to you from the beginning? Have ye not obtained an insight into the foundations of the earth?*" We have here four questions chiastically

---

[1] Both forms occur in this sense, according to the evidence of original sources, with the common imperative *yaskunu*, the infinitive *sukûne* passed over by Freytag, the verbal substantive *maskane*, and the adjective *miskin* or *meskin*, primarily to be forced to inactivity through weakness, destitution, or outward influences, not to be able to move and exert one's self; or, more particularly, not to be able to defend one's self (as it were to be obliged to sit still or keep still). Hence more especially *opibus et facultatibus carens*, being in distress, destitute, poor.

arranged. The absolute being of God, which is above all created things, is something which may be either inferred *per ratiocinationem,* or learned *per traditionem.* When Israel failed to acknowledge the absolute distinctness and unequalled supremacy of Jehovah its God, it hardened itself against the knowledge which it might acquire even in a natural way (cf. Ps. xix. and Rom. i. 20), and shut its ears against the teaching of revelation and tradition, which had come down from the very beginning of its history. The first two questions are construed with futures, the other two with perfects; the former refer to what is possible, the latter to what is an actual fact. Have you—this is the meaning of the four questions—have you obtained no knowledge of the foundations of the earth, namely, as to the way in which they were laid?

The prophet now proceeds to describe the God whom both His works and word proclaim. The participles which follow are predicates of the subject, which filled the consciousness of the prophet as well as that of every believer. Ver. 22. "*He who is enthroned above the vault of the earth, and its inhabitants resemble grasshoppers; who has spread out the heavens like gauze, and stretched them out like a tent-roof to dwell in.*" He, the manifested and yet unknown, is He who has for His throne the circle of the heavens (*chūg shâmayim,* Job xxii. 14), which arches over the earth, and to whom from His inaccessible height men appear as diminutive as grasshoppers (Num. xiii. 33); He who has spread out the blue sky like a thin transparent garment (*dōq,* a thin fabric, like *daq,* fine dust, in ver. 15), and stretched it out above the earth like a tent for dwelling in ('*ōhel*[1] *lâshebheth*). The participle brings to view the actions and circumstances of all times. In the present instance, where it is continued in the historical sense, it is to be resolved into the perfect; in other cases, the preservation of the world is evidently thought of as a *creatio continua* (see *Psychol.* p. 111).

---

[1] The noun '*ōhel* is derived from the root אל, from which come اول, *coaluit, cohæsit,* to thicken within or gain consistency (hence, regarded on another side, to lose in outward extent or outward bulk, to shrink; to go back to its original or essential condition; to issue in something as the final result; or generally, to draw back or return from a distance), and آل, to attach one's self or accustom one's self to a person or thing, equiva-

This is followed by a series of predicates of God the Ruler
of the universe. Vers. 23, 24. "*He who giveth up rulers to
annihilation; maketh judges of the earth like a desolation. They
are hardly planted, hardly sown, their stem has hardly taken
root in the earth, and He only blows upon them, and they dry up,
and the storm carries them away like stubble.*" There is nothing
so high and inaccessible in the world, that He cannot bring it
to nothing, even in the midst of its most self-confident and
threatening exaltation. *Rōzᵉnīm* are solemn persons, σεμνοί,
possessors of the greatest distinction and influence (vol. i. p. 207);
shōphᵉṭīm, those who combine in themselves the highest judicial
and administrative power. The former He gives up to annihilation; the latter He brings into a condition resembling the
negative state of the *tōhū* out of which the world was produced,
and to which it can be reduced again. We are reminded here
of such descriptions as Job xii. 17, 24 (p. 135). The suddenness of the catastrophe is depicted in ver. 24. אַף בַּל (which
only occurs here), when followed by וְגַם in the apodosis (cf.
2 Kings xx. 4), signifies that even this has not yet taken place
when the other also occurs: hence *vixdum plantati sunt*, etc.
The *niphal* נִטַּע and the *pual* זֹרָע denote the hopeful commencement; the *poel* שֹׁרֵשׁ the hopeful continuation. A layer
or seed excites the hope of blossom and fruit, more especially
when it has taken root; but nothing more is needed than a
breath of Jehovah, and it is all over with it (the verb *nâshaph*
is used in this verse, where plants with stems are referred to;
a verb with a softer labial, *nâshabh*, was employed above in
connection with grass and flowers). A single withering breath
lays them at rest; and by the power of Jehovah there rises a
stormy wind, which carries them away like light dry stubble
(נָשָׂא; compare, on the other hand, the verb used in ver. 15, viz.
tūl = nâtal, to lift up, to keep in the air).

lent to *alifa* and *anisa;* to take up one's abode in a place, or absolutely, to
commence housekeeping by marrying, like the Italian *accasarsi*, Turkish
ewlenmek (from *ew*, a house); or, when applied to a place itself, to be
habitable, inhabited, and cultivated (= pass. *uhila*, more especially in the
participle *âhil*, = ´*âmir* = *ma´mûr*). Hence *ahl*, one who belongs to a person
or place, with its numerous applications, and also אֹהֶל, a tent (primarily a
dwelling generally, Engl. *abode*), which stands at the end of this etymo-
logical series.

The thought of ver. 18 now recurs like a refrain, a conclusion being appended to the premises by means of ו, as was the case there. Ver. 25. "*And to whom will ye compare me, to whom I can be equal? saith the Holy One.*" Not *haqqâdōsh*, because a poetical or oratorical style omits the article wherever it can be dispensed with. The Holy One asks this, and can ask it, because as such He is also exalted above the whole world (Job xv. 15, xxv. 5).

After the questions in vers. 18 and 25, which close syllogistically, a third start is made, to demonstrate the incomparable nature of Jehovah. Ver. 26. "*Lift up your eyes on high, and see: who hath created these things? It is He who bringeth out their host by number, calleth them all by names, because of the greatness of (His) might, and as being strong in power: there is not one that is missing.*" Jehovah spoke in ver. 25; now the prophet speaks again. We have here the same interchange which occurs in every prophetic book from Deuteronomy downwards, and in which the divine fulness of the prophets is displayed. The answer does not begin with הַמּוֹצִיא, in the sense of " He who brings them out has created them;" but the participle is the predicate to the subject of which the prophet's soul is full: Jehovah, it is He who brings out the army of stars upon the plane of heaven, as a general leads out his army upon the field of battle, and that *b᷎emispâr*, by number, counting the innumerable stars, those children of light in armour of light, which meet the eye as it looks up by night. The finite verb יִקְרָא denotes that which takes place every night. He calls them all by name (comp. the derivative passage, Ps. cxlvii. 4): this He does on account of the greatness and fulness of His might (*'ōnīm, vires, virtus*), and as strong in power, *i.e.* because He is so. This explanation is simpler than Ewald's (§ 293, *c*), viz. " because of the power (τὸ κρατερὸν) of the Strong One." The call addressed to the stars that are to rise is the call of the Almighty, and therefore not one of all the innumerable host remains behind. אִישׁ individualizes; נֶעְדָּר (participle), as in ch. xxxiv. 16, suggests the idea of a sheep that is missed from the flock through staying behind. The second part of the address closes here, having demonstrated the folly of idolatry from the infinite superiority of God; and from this the third part deduces consolation for Israel in the midst of its despair.

Such of the Israelites as require first of all to be brought to a consciousness of the folly of idolatry are not called Israel at all, because they place themselves on a par with the *gōyīm*. But now the prophet addresses those of little faith, who nevertheless desire salvation; those who are cast down, but not in utter despair. Ver. 27. " *Why sayest thou, O Jacob, and speakest, O Israel, My way is hidden from Jehovah, and my right is overlooked by my God?* " The name *Jacob* stands here at the head, as in ch. xxix. 22, as being the more exquisite name, and the one which more immediately recalled their patriarchal ancestor. They fancied that Jehovah had completely turned away from them in wrath and weariness. " My way" refers to their thorny way of life; " my right" (*mishpâtī*) to their good right, in opposition to their oppressors. Of all this He appeared to take no notice at all. He seemed to have no thought of vindicating it judicially (on the double *min*, away from him, see Ges. § 154, 3, *c*).

The groundlessness of such despondency is set before them in a double question. Ver. 28. " *Is it not known to thee, or hast thou not heard, an eternal God is Jehovah, Creator of the ends of the earth: He fainteth not, neither becomes weary; His understanding is unsearchable.*" Those who are so desponding ought to know, if not from their own experience, at least from information that had been handed down, that Jehovah, who created the earth from one end to the other, so that even Babylonia was not beyond the range of His vision or the domain of His power, was an eternal God, *i.e.* a God eternally the same and never varying, who still possessed and manifested the power which He had displayed in the creation. Israel had already passed through a long history, and Jehovah had presided over this, and ruled within it; and He had not so lost His power in consequence, as to have now left His people to themselves. He does not grow faint, as a man would do, who neglected to take the repeated nourishment requisite to sustain the energy of his vital power; nor does He become weary, like a man who has exhausted his capacity for work by over-exertion. And if He had not redeemed His people till then, His people were to know that His course was pure *tᵉbhūnâh* or understanding, which was in the possession of infallible criteria for determining the right point of time at which to interpose with His aid.

Jehovah is so far from becoming faint, that it is He who gives strength to the fainting. Ver. 29. " *Giving power to the faint, and to the incapable He giveth strength in abundance.*" לְאֵין אוֹנִים is equivalent to לַאֲשֶׁר אֵין אוֹנִים; אֵין is used exactly like a privative to form a negative adjective (*e.g.* Ps. lxxxviii. 5; Prov. xxv. 3).

Faith is all that is needed to ensure a participation in the strength (עָצְמָה after the form חָכְמָה), which He so richly bestows and so powerfully enhances. Vers. 30, 31. "*And youths grow faint and weary, and young men suffer a fall. But they who wait for Jehovah gain fresh strength; lift up their wings like eagles; run, and are not weary; go forward, and do not faint.*" Even youths, even young men in the early bloom of their morning of life (*bachūrīm*, youths, from בָּחַר, related to בָּכַר, בְּנֵי), succumb to the effects of the loss of sustenance or over-exertion (both futures are defective, the first letter being dropped), and any outward obstacle is sufficient to cause them to fall (נִכְשֵׁל with *inf. abs. kal,* which retains what has been stated for contemplation, according to Ges. § 131, 3, Anm. 2). In ver. 30*a* the verb stands first, ver. 30 being like a concessive clause in relation to ver. 31. " Even though this may happen, it is different with those who wait for Jehovah," *i.e.* those who believe in Him; for the Old Testament applies to faith a number of synonyms denoting trust, hope, and longing, and thus describes it according to its inmost nature, as *fiducia* and as hope, directed to the manifestation and completion of that which is hoped for. The *Vav cop.* introduces the antithesis, as in ver. 8. הֶחֱלִיף, to cause one to pursue, or new to take the place of the old (Lat. *recentare*). The expression יַעֲלוּ וגו' is supposed by early translators, after the Sept., Targ. Jer., and Saad., to refer to the moulting of the eagle and the growth of the new feathers, which we meet with in Ps. ciii. 5 (cf. Mic. i. 16) as a figurative representation of the renewal of youth through grace. But Hitzig correctly observes that הֶעֱלָה is never met with as the causative of the *kal* used in ch. v. 6, and moreover that it would require נוֹצָה instead of אֵבֶר. The proper rendering therefore is, " they cause their wings to rise, or lift their wings high, like the eagles" ('*ēbher* as in Ps. lv. 7). Their course of life, which has Jehovah for its object, is as it were possessed of wings. They draw from Him strength upon strength (see Ps. lxxxiv. 8); running does not tire them, nor do they become faint from going ever further and further.

The first address, consisting of three parts (vers. 1–11, 12–26, 27–31), is here brought to a close.

SECOND PROPHECY.—Chap. XLI.

THE GOD OF THE WORLD'S HISTORY, AND OF PROPHECY.

Jehovah comes forward here, and speaking in the tone in which He already began to speak in ch. xl. 25, invites the idolatrous nations to contend with Him, declares the raising up of the conqueror from the east to be His work, and adduces this as the sign that He has been the Author and Guider of the world's history from the beginning. But what if the question should be asked on the part of the nations, With what right does He do this? The acts of the conqueror prove themselves to be a work of the God who is exalted above the idols, from the fact that they bring destruction to the idolatrous nations, and to the people of Jehovah the long-desired redemption. It is in this that the conclusiveness of the illustration lies. The argument, however, presupposes that Cyrus has already entered upon his victorious course. It is evident at the outset that future events, or events still unfulfilled, would have no force as present proofs. And the words also clearly imply, that the work which Jehovah attributes to Himself, in opposition to the gods of the nations, is already in progress.

Ver. 1. Summons to the contest: "*Be silent to me, ye islands; and let the nations procure fresh strength: let them come near, then speak; we will enter into contest together.*" The words are addressed to the whole of the heathen world, and first of all to the inhabitants of the western islands and coasts. This was the expression commonly employed in the Old Testament to designate the continent of Europe, the solid ground of which is so deeply cut, and so broken up, by seas and lakes, that it looks as if it were about to resolve itself into nothing but islands and peninsulas. הַחֲרִישׁ אֵל is a pregnant expression for turning in silence towards a person; just as in Job xiii. 13 it is used with *min*, in the sense of forsaking a person in silence. That they may have no excuse if they are defeated, they are to put on fresh strength; just as in ch. xl. 31 believers are spoken of as drawing fresh strength out of Jehovah's fulness. They are to draw near, then speak, *i.e.* to reply after hearing the evidence, for Jehovah desires to go through all the forms of a legal process with them in *pro et contra.* The *mishpât* is thought of here in a local sense, as a forum or tribunal. But if Jehovah is one party to the cause, who is the judge to pronounce the decision? The answer to this question is the same as at ch. v. 3. "The nations," says Rosenmüller, "are called to judgment, not to the tribunal of God, but to that of reason." The deciding authority is reason, which cannot fail to recognise the facts, and the consequences to be deduced from them.

The parties invited are now to be thought of as present, and Jehovah commences in ver. 2: " *Who hath raised up the man from the rising of the sun, whom justice meets at his foot, He giveth up nations before him, and kings He subdues, giveth men like the dust to his sword, and like driven stubble to his bow?* " The sentence governed by "who" (*mî*) ends at *l^ragclô* (at his foot); at the same time, all that follows is spoken with the echo of the interrogative accent. The person raised up is Cyrus, who is afterwards mentioned by name. The coming one (if, that is to say, we adhere to the belief in Isaiah's authorship of these addresses) first approaches gradually within the horizon of the prophet's ideal present; and it is only little by little that the prophet becomes more intimately acquainted with a phenomenon which belongs to so distant a future, and has been brought so close to his own eyes. Jehovah has raised up the new great hero "from the east" (*mimmizrâch*), and, according to ver. 25, "from the north" also. Both of these were fulfilled; for Cyrus was a Persian belonging to the clan of Achæmenes (*Hakhâmanis*), which stood at the head of the tribe, or of the Pasargadæ. He was the son of Cambyses; and even if the Median princess Mandane were not his mother, yet, according to nearly all the ancient accounts, he was connected with the royal house of Media; at any rate, after Astyages was dethroned, he became head and chief of the Medes as well as of the Persians (hence the name of "Mule" which was given to him by the oracle, and that given by Jerome, " *agitator bigæ*"). Now Media was to the north of Babylonia, and Persia

to the east; so that his victorious march, in which, even before
the conquest of Babylon, he subjugated all the lands from
the heights of Hinduku to the shores of the Ægean Sea, had
for its starting-point both the east and north.[1] The clause
צֶדֶק יִקְרָאֵהוּ לְרַגְלוֹ is an attributive clause, and as such a virtual
object: "him whom (supply אֶת־אֲשֶׁר) justice comes to meet (קָרָא
= קָרָה, Ges. § 75, vi.) on his track" (cf. Gen. xxx. 30; Job
xviii. 11; Hab. iii. 5). The idea of *tsedeq* is determined by what
follows: Jehovah gives up nations before him, and causes
kings to be trodden down (causative of *rádáh*). Accordingly,
tsedeq is either to be understood here in an attributive sense, as
denoting the justice exercised by a person (viz. the justice executed successfully by Cyrus, as the instrument of Jehovah, by
the force of arms); or objectively of the justice awarded to a
person (to which the idea of "meeting" is more appropriate),
viz. the favourable result, the victory which procures justice
for the just cause of the combatant. Rosenmüller, Knobel,
and others, are wrong in maintaining that *tsedeq* (*tseˈdáqáh*) in
ch. xl.–lxvi. signifies primarily justice, and then prosperity and
salvation as its reward. The word means straightness, justice,
righteousness, and nothing more (from *tsádaq*, to be hard, firm,
extended, straight, *e.g. rumh-un-tsadq*, a hard, firm, and straight
lance); but it has a double aspect, because justice consists,
according to circumstances, of either wrath or favour, and
therefore has sometimes the idea of the strict execution of
justice, as in this instance, sometimes of a manifestation of
justice in fidelity to promises, as in ver. 10. יִתֵּן is repeated
here in ver. 2 (just like וַיְלַמְּדֵהוּ in ch. xl. 14) with the same
subject, but in a different sense. To make sword and bow the
subject, in the sense of "his sword gives (*sc.* ' the foe '),"
is a doubtful thing in itself; and as *cherebh* and *qesheth* are
feminines, it is by no means advisable. Moreover, in other
instances, the comparative כ leaves it to the reader to carry
out the figure indicated according to his own fancy. And
this is the case here: He (Jehovah) makes his sword as if
there were dust, his bow as if there were hunted stubble
(Böttcher), *i.e.* pounding the enemy like dust, and hunting
it like flying stubble. Our text has כֶּעָפָר, but in certain
codices we find כְּעָפָר with *tzere;* and this reading, which is

[1] See Pahle's *Geschichte des Oriental. Alterthums.* (1864), p. 170 sqq.

contrary to rule, has in its favour the express testimony of
Moses the punctuator.[1]

The conqueror is now still further described in futures,
which might be defined by הֵעִיר, and so express a simultaneous
past (synchronistic imperfects), but which it is safer to take as
standing traits in the picture drawn of the conqueror referred
to. Ver. 3. " *He pursueth them, and marcheth in peace by a
course which he never trod with his feet.*" He marches victoriously further and further, " *shâlōm,*" *i.e.* " in safety" (or, as an
adjective, safely; Job xxi. 9), without any one being able to
do him harm, by a course (accus. Ges. § 138, 1) which he has
not been accustomed to tread with his feet (*ingredi*).

The great fact of the present time, which not one of the
gods of the heathen can boast of having brought to pass, is now
explained. Jehovah is its author. Ver. 4. " *Who hath wrought
and executed it? He who calleth the generations of men from
the beginning, I Jehovah am first, and with the last am I* HE."
The synonyms פָּעַל and עָשָׂה are distinguished from each other in
the same way as " to work" (or bring about) and " to realize"
(or carry out). Hence the meaning is, Who is the author to
whom both the origin and progress of such an occurrence are
to be referred? It is He who " from the beginning," *i.e.* ever
since there has been a human history, has called into existence
the generations of men through His authoritative command.
And this is no other than Jehovah, who can declare of Himself, in contrast with the heathen and their gods, who are of
yesterday, and to-morrow will not be: I am Jehovah, the very
first, whose being precedes all history; and with the men of the
latest generations yet to come " I am it."   הוּא is not introduced
here to strengthen the subject, *ego ille* (" I and no other," as in
ch. xxxvii. 16, which see); but, as in ch. xliii. 10, 13, xlvi. 4,
xlviii. 12, it is a predicate of the substantive clause, *ego sum is*
(*ille*), viz. '*Elōhīm ;* or even as in Ps. cii. 28 (cf. Job iii. 19 and
Heb. xiii. 8), *ego sum idem* (Hitzig). They are both included,
without any distinction in the assertion. He is this, viz. God
throughout all ages, and is through all ages HE, *i.e.* the Being
who is ever the same in this His deity. It is the full meaning
of the name Jehovah which is unfolded here; for God is called

---

[1] In his דרכי הנקוד (rules of pointing), with which the *Masora finalis*
is surrounded.

Jehovah as the absolute I, the absolutely free Being, pervading all history, and yet above all history, as He who is Lord of His own absolute being, in revealing which He is purely self-determined; in a word, as the unconditionally free and unchangeably eternal personality.

In the following verse we have not a description of the impression made upon the heathen by the argument of Jehovah, but the argument itself is continued. Ver. 5. "*Islands have seen it, and shuddered; the ends of the earth trembled; they have approached, and drawn near.*" We have here a description of the effects which the victorious course of Cyrus had begun to produce in the heathen world. The perfects denote the past, and the futures a simultaneous past; so that we have not to compare ver. 5a with Hab. iii. 10 so much as with Ps. lxxvii. 17. The play upon the words רָאוּ ... וַיִּירָאוּ pairs together both seeing and fearing. The Cumæans, when consulting the oracle, commenced thus: ἡμεῖς δὲ δειμαίνοντες τὴν Περσέων δύναμιν. The perfect with the aorist following in ver. 5b places the following picture upon the stage: They have approached and drawn near (from all directions) to meet the threatening danger; and how? Vers. 6, 7. "*One helped his companion, and he said to his brother, Only firm! The caster put firmness into the melter, the hammer-smoother into the anvil-smiter, saying of the soldering, It is good; and made him firm with nails, that he should not shake.*" *Him*, viz. the idol. Everything is in confusion, from the terror that prevails; and the gods from which they expect deliverance are not made till now, the workmen stimulating one another to work. The *chârâsh*, who casts the image, encourages the *tsōrēph*, whose task it is to provide it with the plating of gold and silver chains (ch. xl. 19), to work more bravely; and the man who smooths with the hammer (*pattish, instrumentalis*) does the same to the man who smites the anvil (הוֹלֶם with *seghol*, whereas in other cases, *e.g.* Ezek. xxii. 25, the tone generally gives way without any change in the vowel-pointing). The latter finds the soldering all right, by which the gold plates of the covering are fastened together, so as to give to the golden idol a massive appearance. He is the last into whose hands it comes; and nothing more is wanting, than that he should forge upon the anvil the nails with which it is fastened, to prevent it from falling. To such foolish, fruitless proceedings have the nations resorted when threatened with subjugation by Cyrus.

The proof adduced by Jehovah of His own deity closes here. But instead of our hearing whether the nations, with which He has entered upon the contest, have any reply to make, the address turns to Israel, upon which deliverance dawns from that very quarter, from which the others are threatened with destruction. Vers. 8–10. "*And thou, Israel my servant, Jacob whom I have chosen, seed of Abraham my friend, thou whom I have laid hold of from the ends of the earth, and called from the corners thereof, and said to thee, Thou art my servant, I have chosen and not despised thee; fear thou not, for I am with thee; be not afraid, for I am thy God: I have chosen thee, I also help thee, I also hold thee with the right hand of my righteousness.*" The ‍ before וְאַתָּה connects together antitheses, which show themselves at once to be antitheses. Whereas the nations, which put their trust in idols that they themselves had made, were thrown into alarm, and yielded before the world-wide commotions that had originated with the eastern conqueror, Israel, the nation of Jehovah, might take comfort to itself. Every word here breathes the deepest affection. The address moves on in soft undulating lines. The repetition of the suffix ךָ, with which אֲשֶׁר forms a relative of the second person, for which we have no equivalent in our language (Ges. § 123, Anm. 1), gives to the address a pressing, clinging, and, as it were, loving key-note. The reason, which precedes the comforting assurance in ver. 10, recals the intimate relation in which Jehovah had placed Himself towards Israel, and Israel towards Himself. The leading thought, "servant of Jehovah," which is characteristic of ch. xl.–xlvi., and lies at the root of the whole spirit of these addresses, more especially of their Christology, we first meet with here, and that in a popular sense. It has both an objective and a subjective side. On the one hand, Israel is the servant of Jehovah by virtue of a divine act; and this act, viz. its election and call, was an act of pure grace, and was not to be traced, as the expression "I have chosen and not despised thee" indicates, to any superior excellence or merit on the part of Israel. On the contrary, Israel was so obscure that Jehovah might have despised it; nevertheless He had anticipated it in free un-merited love with this stamp of the *character indelibilis* of a servant of Jehovah. On the other hand, Israel was the servant of Jehovah, inasmuch as it acted out what Jehovah had made it, partly in reverential worship of this God, and partly in active obedience. עֶבֶד אַתָּה, *i.e.* "serving Jehovah," includes both liturgical service (also עֶבֶד absolutely, ch. xix. 23) and the service of works. The divine act of choosing and calling is dated from Abraham. From a Palestinian point of view, Ur of Chaldæa, within the old kingdom of Nimrod, and Haran in northern Mesopotamia, seemed like the ends and corners of the earth (*ätsīlīm*, remote places, from '*ātsal*, to put aside or apart). Israel and the land of Israel were so inseparably connected, that whenever the origin of Israel was spoken of, the point of view could only be taken in Palestine. To the far distant land of the Tigris and Euphrates had Jehovah gone to fetch Abraham, "the friend of God" (Jas. ii. 23), who is called in the East even to the present day, *chalil ollah*, the friend of God. This calling of Abraham was the furthest *terminus a quo* of the existence of Israel as the covenant nation; for the leading of Abraham was providentially appointed with reference to the rise of Israel as a nation. The latter was pre-existent in him by virtue of the counsel of God. And when Jehovah adopted Abraham as His servant, and called him "my servant" (Gen. xxvi. 24), Israel, the nation that was coming into existence in Abraham, received both the essence and name of a "servant of Jehovah." Inasmuch then as, on looking back to its past history, it could not fail to perceive that it was so thoroughly a creation of divine power and grace, it ought not to be fearful, and look about with timidity and anxiety; for He who had presented Himself at the very beginning as its God, was still always near. The question arises, in connection with the word אֲמַצְתִּיךָ, whether it means to strengthen (ch. xxxv. 3; Ps. lxxxix. 22), or to lay firm hold of, to attach firmly to one's self, to choose. We decide in favour of the latter meaning, which is established by ch. xliv. 14, cf. Ps. lxxx. 16, 18. The other perfects affirm what Jehovah has ever done, and still continues to do. In the expression "by the right hand of my righteousness," the justice or righteousness is regarded pre-eminently on its brighter side, the side turned towards Israel; but it is also regarded on its fiery side, or the side turned towards the enemies of Israel. It is the righteousness which aids the oppressed congregation against its oppressors. The repeated אַף heaps one synonym upon another, expressive of the divine love; for וְ simply connects, גַּם appends, אַף heaps up (*cumulat*). Language is too contracted to hold all the fulness of the divine love; and for this reason the latter could not find words enough to express all that it desired.

With the exclamation *hēn* (behold) the eyes of Israel are now directed to the saving interposition of Jehovah in the immediate future. Vers. 11–13. "*Behold, all they that were incensed against thee must be ashamed and confounded; the men of thy conflict become as nothing, and perish. Thou wilt seek them, and not find them, the men of thy feuds; the men of thy warfare become as nothing, and nonentity. For I, Jehovah thy God, lay hold of thy right hand, He who saith to thee, Fear not; I will help thee.*" The comprehensive expression *omnes inflammati in te* (niphal, as in ch. xlv. 24) stands at the head; and then, in order that every kind may be included, the enemies are called by a different name every time. The three substantives bear much the same relation to one another as *lis, rixa, bellum* (*milchâmâh*, lit. throng = war-tumult, like the epic κλόνος), hence *adversarii, inimici, hostes*. The suffixes have the force of objective genitives. We have founded our translation upon the reading מַצֻּתֶיךָ. The three names of the enemies are placed emphatically at the close of the sentences, and these are long drawn out, whilst the indignation gives vent to itself; whereas in ver. 13 there follows nothing but short sentences, in which the persecuted church is encouraged and affectionately embraced. Two clauses, which are made to rhyme with *ēm*, announce the utter destruction of their foes; then the inflective rhyme *ekha* is repeated five times; and the sixth time it passes over into *ikha*.

The consolatory words, "Fear not," are now repeated, for the purpose of once more adding the promise that Israel will not succumb to its foes, but will acquire power over its enemies. Vers. 14–16. "*Fear not, thou worm Jacob, and handful Israel: I will help thee, saith Jehovah; and thy Redeemer is the Holy One of Israel. Behold, I have made thee a threshing roller, a sharp new one, with double edges: thou wilt thresh mountains, and pound them; and hills thou wilt make like chaff. Thou wilt winnow them, and wind carries them away, and tempest scatters them: and thou wilt rejoice in Jehovah, and glory in the Holy One of Israel."* Israel, which is now helplessly oppressed, is called "worm of Jacob" (*gen. appos.*) in compassion, *i.e.* Jacob that is like a worm, probably with some allusion to Ps. xxii. 7; for the image of the Messiah enriches itself in these discourses, inasmuch as Israel itself is looked upon in a Messianic light, so that the second David does not stand by the side of Israel, but appears as Israel's heart, or true and inmost essence. The people are then addressed as the " people of Israel," with some allusion to the phrase מְתֵי מִסְפָּר (*i.e.* few men, easily numbered) in Gen. xxxiv. 30, Deut. iv. 27 (LXX. ὀλιγοστὸς Ἰσραήλ; Luther, *Ir armer hauffe Israel*, ye poor crowd of Israel). They no longer formed the compact mass of a nation; the band of the commonwealth was broken: they were melted down into a few individuals, scattered about hither and thither. But it would not continue so. "I help thee" (perfect of certainty) is Jehovah's solemn declaration; and the Redeemer (*redemtor*, Lev. xxv. 48, 49) of His now enslaved people is the Holy One of Israel, with His love, which perpetually triumphs over wrath. Not only will He set it free, but He will also endow it with might over its oppressors; *samtīkh* is a perfect of assurance (Ges. § 126, 4); *mōrag* (roller) signifies a threshing-sledge (Arab. *naureg, nôreg*), which has here the term חָרוּץ (ch. xxviii. 27) as a secondary name along with חָדָשׁ, and is described as furnished on the under part of the two arms of the sledge not only with sharp knives, but with two-edged knives (פִּיפִיּוֹת a reduplication, like סַאסְּאָה in ch. xxvii. 8, whereas מֵימֵי is a double plural). Just like such a threshing machine would Israel thresh and grind to powder from that time forth both mountains and hills. This is evidently a figurative expression for proud and mighty foes, just as wind and tempest denote the irresistible force of Jehovah's aid. The might of the enemy would be broken down to the very last remnant, whereas Israel would be able to rejoice and glory in its God.

At the present time, indeed, the state of His people was a helpless one, but its cry for help was not in vain. Vers. 17–20. *" The poor and needy, who seek for water and there is none, their tongue faints for thirst. I Jehovah will hear them, I the God of Israel will not forsake them. I open streams upon hills of the*

*field, and springs in the midst of valleys; I make the desert
into a pond, and dry land into fountains of water. I give in
the desert cedars, acacias, and myrtles, and oleasters; I set in the
steppe cypresses, plane-trees, and sherbin-trees together, that they
may see, and know, and lay to heart and understand all together,
that the hand of Jehovah hath accomplished this, and the Holy
One of Israel hath created it."* Kimchi, Hitzig, and others
refer these promises to the returning exiles; but there is also a
description, without any restriction to the return home, of the
miraculous change which would take place in the now comfortless and helpless condition of the exiles. The *sh⁽e⁾phâyîm, i.e.*
bare, woodless hills rising up from the plain, Jer. xii. 12, the
b⁽e⁾qâ'ôth, or deep valleys, by the sides of which there rise precipitous mountains, and the *'erets tsiyyâh,* the land of burning
heat or drought (cf. Ps. lxiii. 2), depict the homeless condition
of Israel, as it wandered over bald heights and through waterless plains about a land with parched and gaping soil. For
the characteristics of the object, which is placed before אֲעֶנֵם,
we may therefore compare such passages as ch. xliv. 3, lv. 1.
נָשַׁתָּה is either a pausal form for נָשְׁתָה, and therefore the *niphal*
of שָׁתַת (to set, become shallow, dry up), or a pausal form for
נִשְׁתָה, and therefore the *kal* of נָשַׁת with *dagesh affectuosum,* like
נִתְּצוּ in Ezek. xxvii. 19 (Olshausen, § 83, *b*). The form נָשְׁתָה in
Jer. li. 30 may just as well be derived from שָׁתַת (Ges. § 67,
Anm. 11) as from נָשַׁת, whereas נִשְּׁתוּ may certainly be taken as
the *niphal* of שָׁתַת after the form נִחַר, נִמֹּל (Ges. § 67, Anm. 5),
though it would be safer to refer it to a *kal* נָשַׁת, which seems
to be also favoured by יִנַּתְשׁוּ in Jer. xviii. 14 as a transposition
of יִנָּשְׁתוּ. The root נש, of which נָשַׁת would be a further expansion, really exhibits the meaning to dry up or thirst, in the
Arabic *nassa;* whereas the verbs נוּשׁ, אָנַשׁ, נָסַס (ch. x. 18), נָשָׁה,
Syr. *nas', nos',* Arab. *nâsa, nasnasa,* with the primary meaning
to slacken, lose their hold, and נָשָׁא, נָשָׁה, נָסַע, to deceive, de-
range, and advance, form separate families. Just when they
are thus on the point of pining away, they receive an answer
to their prayer: their God opens streams, *i.e.* causes streams to
break forth on the hills of the field, and springs in the midst
of the valleys. The desert is transformed into a lake, and the
steppe of burning sand into fountains of water. What was
predicted in ch. xxxv. 6, 7 is echoed again here,—a figurative

representation of the manifold fulness of refreshing, consolation, and marvellous help which was to burst all at once upon
those who were apparently forsaken of God What is depicted in vers. 19, 20, is the effect of these. It is not merely a
scanty vegetation that springs up, but a corresponding manifold fulness of stately, fragrant, and shady trees ; so that the
steppe, where neither foot nor eye could find a resting-place,
is changed, as by a stroke of magic, into a large, dense, well-
watered forest, and shines with sevenfold glory,—an image of
the many-sided manifestations of divine grace which are experienced by those who are comforted now. Isaiah is especially fond of such figures as these (*vid.* ch. v. 7, vi. 13,
xxvii. 6, xxxvii. 31). There are seven (4 + 3) trees named;
seven indicating the divine character of this manifold development (*Psychol.* p. 188). '*Erez* is the generic name for the
cedar ; *shittâh,* the acacia, the Egyptian *spina (ἄκανθα),* Copt.
shont ; hădas, the myrtle ; '*ēts shemen,* the wild olive, as distinguished from *zayith (ἡ ἀγριέλαιος,* opposed to ἡ ἐλαία in
Rom. xi. 17) ; *b°rōsh,* the cypress, at any rate more especially
this ; *tidhâr* we have rendered the " plane-tree," after Saad. ;
and *t°asshūr* the " sherbin" (a kind of cedar), after Saad. and
Syr. The crowded synonyms indicating sensual and spiritual
perception in ver. 20*a* (יָשִׂימוּ, *sc.* לְבָּם, ver. 22) are meant to
express as strongly as possible the irresistible character of the
impression. They will be quite unable to regard all this as
accidental or self-produced, or as anything but the production
of the power and grace of their God.

There follows now the second stage in the suit. Vers. 21–23.
" *Bring hither your cause, saith Jehovah ; bring forward your
proofs, saith the king of Jacob. Let them bring forward, and
make known to us what will happen : make known the beginning,
what it is, and we will fix our heart upon it, and take knowledge
of its issue ; or let us hear what is to come. Make known what is
coming later, and we will acknowledge that ye are gods : yea, do
good, and do evil, and we will measure ourselves, and see together.*"
In the first stage Jehovah appealed, in support of His deity, to
the fact that it was He who had called the oppressor of the
nations upon the arena of history. In this second stage He
appeals to the fact that He only knows or can predict the
future. There the challenge was addressed to the worshippers

of idols, here to the idols themselves; but in both cases both of these are ranged on the one side, and Jehovah with His people upon the other. It is with purpose that Jehovah is called the "King of Jacob," as being the tutelar God of Israel, in contrast to the tutelar deities of the heathen. The challenge to the latter to establish their deity is first of all addressed to them directly in ver. 21, and then indirectly in ver. 22*a*, where Jehovah connects Himself with His people as the opposing party; but in ver. 22*b* He returns again to a direct address. עֲצֻמוֹת are evidences (lit. *robora*, cf. ὀχυρώματα, 2 Cor. x. 4, from עָצַם, to be strong or stringent; *mishn.* נִתְעַצֵּם, to contend with one another *pro et contra*); here it signifies proofs that they can foresee the future. Jehovah for His part has displayed this knowledge, inasmuch as, at the very time when He threatened destruction to the heathen at the hands of Cyrus, He consoled His people with the announcement of their deliverance (vers. 8–20). It is therefore the turn of the idol deities now: "Let them bring forward and announce to us the things that will come to pass." The general idea of what is in the future stands at the head. Then within this the choice is given them of proving their foreknowledge of what is afterwards to happen, by announcing either רִאשֹׁנוֹת, or even בָּאוֹת. These two ideas, therefore, are generic terms within the range of the things that are to happen. Consequently הראשנות cannot mean "earlier predictions," *prius prædicta*, as Hitzig, Knobel, and others suppose. This explanation is precluded in the present instance by the logic of the context. Both ideas lie upon the one line of the future; the one being more immediate, the other more remote, or as the expression alternating with הבאות implies הָאֹתִיּוֹת לְאָחוֹר, *ventura in posterum* ("in later times," compare ch. xlii. 23, "at a later period;" from the participle אֹתֶה, radical form אֹתִי, *vid.* Ges. § 75, Anm. 5, probably to distinguish it from אֹתוֹת). This is the explanation adopted by Stier and Hahn, the latter of whom has correctly expounded the word, as denoting "the events about to happen first in the immediate future, which it is not so difficult to prognosticate from signs that are discernible in the present." The choice is given them, either to foretell "*things at the beginning*" (*haggîdu* in our editions is erroneously pointed with *kadma* instead of *geresh*), *i.e.* that which will take place first or next, "*what they be*" (*quæ et qualia sint*), so that now, when the *achărīth*, "the latter end" (*i.e.* the issue of that which is held out to view), as prognosticated from the standpoint of the present, really occurs, the prophetic utterance concerning it may be verified; or "things to come," *i.e.* things further off, in later times (in the remote future), the prediction of which is incomparably more difficult, because without any point of contact in the present. They are to choose which they like (אוֹ from אָוָה, like *vel* from *velle*): "ye do good, and do evil," *i.e.* (according to the proverbial use of the phrase; cf. Zeph. i. 12 and Jer. x. 5) only express yourselves in some way; come forward, and do either the one or the other. The meaning is, not that they are to stir themselves and predict either good or evil, but they are to show some sign of life, no matter what. "*And we will measure ourselves* (*i.e.* look one another in the face, testing and measuring), *and see together*," viz. what the result of the contest will be. הִשְׁתָּעָה like הִתְרָאָה in 2 Kings xiv. 8, 11, with a cohortative *âh*, which is rarely met with in connection with verbs ה"ל, and the tone upon the penultimate, the *âh* being attached without tone to the voluntative נִשְׁתַּע in ver. 5 (Ewald, § 228, *c*). For the *chethib* וְנִרְאָה, the *keri* has the voluntative וְנֵרֶא.

Jehovah has thus placed Himself in opposition to the heathen and their gods, as the God of history and prophecy. It now remains to be seen whether the idols will speak, to prove their deity. By no means; not only are they silent, but they cannot speak. Therefore Jehovah breaks out into words of wrath and contempt. Ver. 24. "*Behold, ye are of nothing, and your doing of nought: an abomination whoever chooseth you.*" The two מִן are partitive, as in ch. xl. 17; and מֵאֶפַע is not an error of the pen for מֵאֶפֶס, as Gesenius and others suppose, but אֶפַע from אָפַע=פָּה (from which comes פֶּה), פֶּעָה, ch. xlii. 14 (from which comes אֶפְעֶה, ch. lix. 5), to breathe, stands as a synonym to רוּחַ, הֶבֶל, אֶן. The attributive clause יִבְחַר בָּכֶם (supply הוּא אֲשֶׁר) is a virtual subject (Ewald, § 333, *b*): ye and your doings are equally *nil;* and whoever chooses you for protectors, and makes you the objects of his worship, is morally the most degraded of beings.

The more conclusively and incontrovertibly, therefore, does Jehovah keep the field as the moulder of history and foreteller of the future, and therefore as God above all gods. Ver. 25.

"*I have raised up from the north, and he came: from the rising of the sun one who invokes my name; and he treads upon satraps as mud, and like a potter kneadeth clay.*" The object of the verb *hâʿīrōthī* (I have wakened up) is he who came when wakened up by Jehovah from the north and east, *i.e.* from Media and Persia (וַיֵּאָת = וַיַּאַת for וַיַּאַת, with evasion of the auxiliary *pathach*, Ges. § 76, 2, *c*), and, as the second clause affirms, who invokes or *will invoke* the name of Jehovah (at any rate, *qui invocabit* is the real meaning of *qui invocat*). For although the Zarathustrian religion, which Cyrus followed, was nearest to the Jehovah religion of all the systems of heathenism, it was a heathen religion after all. The doctrine of a great God (*baga vazarka*), the Creator of heaven and earth, and at the same time of a great number of Bagas and Yazatas, behind whose working and worship the great God was thrown into the shade, is (apart from the dualism condemned in ch. xlv. 7) the substance of the sacred writings of the Magi in our possession, as confirmed by the inscriptions of the Achemenides.[1] But the awakened of Jehovah would, as is here predicted, " call with the name, or by means of the name, of Jehovah," which may mean either call upon this name (Zeph. iii. 9; Jer. x. 25), or call out the name (compare Ex. xxxiii. 19, xxxiv. 5, with Ex. xxxv. 30) in the manner in which he does make use of it in the edict setting the exiles free (Ezra i. 2). The verb יָבֹא which follows (cf. ver. 2) designates him still further as a conqueror of nations; the verb construed with an accusative is used here, as is very frequently the case, in the sense of hostile attack. The word *Sâgân*, which is met with first in Ezekiel— apart, that is to say, from the passage before us—may have owed its meaning in the Hebrew vocabulary to its similarity in sound to *sōkhēn* (ch. xxii. 15); at any rate, it is no doubt a Persian word, which became naturalized in the Hebrew (ζωγάνης in Athenæus, and Neo-Pers. *sichne*, a governor: see Ges. *Thes.*), though this comparison is by no means so certain[2] as

---

[1] Windischmann, *Zoroastrische Studien*, pp. 134, 135.

[2] Spiegel has the following remarks upon the subject : There is but very little probability in the etymologies which can be suggested for the word *sâgân* through the help of the old Persian. The new Persian *shihne* cannot be traced beyond Neo-Persian, and even there it is somewhat suspicious on account of the ז which it contains, and which is not Persian. The only

that σατράπης is the same as the *Ksatrapâvan* of the inscriptions, *i.e.* protector of the kingdom.[1] Without at all overlooking the fact that this word *s^egânîm*, so far as it can really be supposed to be a Persian word, favours the later composition of this portion of the book of Isaiah, we cannot admit that it has any decisive weight, inasmuch as the Persian word *pardēs* occurs even in the Song of Solomon. And the indications which might be found in the word *s^egânîm* unfavourable to Isaiah's authorship are abundantly counterbalanced by what immediately follows.

As ver. 25 points back to the first charge against the heathen and their gods (vers. 2–7), so vers. 26–28 point back to the second. Not only did Jehovah manifest Himself as the Universal Ruler in the waking up of Cyrus, but as the Omniscient Ruler also. Vers. 26–28. *" Who hath made it known from the beginning, we will acknowledge it, and from former time, we will say He is in the right?! Yea, there was none that made known; yea, none that caused to hear; yea, none that heard your words. As the first I said to Zion, Behold, behold, there it is : and I bestow evangelists upon Jerusalem. And I looked, and there was no man; and of these there was no one answering whom I could ask, and who would give me an answer."* If any one of the heathen deities had foretold this appearance of Cyrus so long before as at the very commencement of that course of history

real Persian word to which I could think of tracing it is *shahr*, a city (old Bactrian *khshathra*, or *shoithra*, a place of abode); or it might possibly have sprung from *shoithraka*, a supposititious word, in the sense of governor of a district, but with the *r* changed into *n* (a change which only occurs in Huzvaresh) and the ﬡ into ﬡ. There are also difficulties in the comparison of the old Bactrian *çanh*, to say or express solemnly. An adjective *çanhâna* (expressing, commanding), formed from this verb, would be pronounced *çahâna* or even *çâna* in old Persian; and from this *Sâgân* would have to be obtained, so that we should still want the *n* to take the place of the *Gimel*. At the same time, there is a still harsher form of the root *çanh* in the Gatha dialect, namely *çak* (not the same as the Sanskrit *çak*, to be strong, as Haug supposes), from which the Neo-Persian *sachan, sachun*, a word, is derived; so that it appears to have been also current in old Persian. Accordingly, the form *çakâna* may also have been used in the place of *çanhâna*, and this might suit in some degree for *sâgân*.

[1] See H. Rawlinson, *Asiatic Journal*, xi. 1, p. 116 ss.; and Spiegel, *Keil-inschriften*, p. 194.

which had thus reached its goal, Jehovah with His people,
being thus taught by experience, would admit and acknowledge their divinity. מֵרֹאשׁ is used in the same sense as in
ch. xlviii. 16 : and also in ch. xli. 4 and xl. 21, where it refers,
according to the context in each case, to the beginning of the
particular line of history. צַדִּיק signifies either " he is right," i.e.
in the right (compare the Arabic *siddik*, genuine), or in a neuter
sense, " it is right" (= true), i.e. the claim to divine honours is
really founded upon divine performances. But there was not
one who had proclaimed it, or who gave a single sound of himself; no one had heard anything of the kind from them. אַף
receives a retrospective character from the connection; and
bearing this in mind, the participles may be also resolved into
imperfects. The repeated אַף, passing beyond what is set down
as possible, declares the reality of the very opposite. What
Jehovah thus proves the idols to want, He can lay claim to for
Himself. In ver. 27 we need not assume that there is any
hyperbaton, as Louis de Dieu, Rosenmüller, and others have
done : " I first will give to Zion and Jerusalem one bringing
glad tidings : behold, behold them." After what has gone
before in ver. 26 we may easily supply אָמַרְתִּי, " I said," in ver.
27a (compare ch. viii. 19, xiv. 16, xxvii. 2), not אֹמַר, for the
whole comparison drawn by Jehovah between Himself and the
idols is retrospective, and looks back from the fulfilment in
progress to the prophecies relating to it. The only reply that
we can look for to the question in ver. 26 is not, " I on the
contrary *do* it," but " I *did* it." At the same time, the rendering is a correct one : " Behold, behold *them*" (*illa;* for the
neuter use of the masculine, compare ch. xlviii. 3, xxxviii. 16,
xlv. 8). " As the first," Jehovah replies (*i.e.* without any one
anticipating me), " have I spoken to Zion : behold, behold, there
it is," pointing with the finger of prophecy to the coming salvation, which is here regarded as present; " and I gave to
Jerusalem messengers of joy;" *i.e.* long ago, before what is
now approaching could be known by any one, I foretold to my
church, through the medium of prophets, the glad tidings of
the deliverance from Babylon. If the author of ch. xl.-lxvi.
were a prophet of the captivity, his reference here would be
to such prophecies as Isa. xi. 11 (where Shinar is mentioned
as a land of dispersion), and more especially still Mic. iv. 10,

" There in Babylon wilt thou be delivered, there will Jehovah
redeem thee out of the hand of thine enemies;" but if Isaiah
were the author, he is looking back from the ideal standpoint
of the time of the captivity, and of Cyrus more especially, to
his own prophecies before the captivity (such as ch. xiii. 1–xiv.
23, and xxi. 1–10), just as Ezekiel, when prophesying of Gog
and Magog, looks back in ch. xxxviii. 17 from the ideal standpoint of this remote future, more especially to his own prophecies in relation to it.   In that case the *m^ebhassēr*, or evangelist,
more especially referred to is the prophet himself (Grotius
and Stier), namely, as being the foreteller of those prophets to
whom the commission in ch. xl. 1, " Comfort ye, comfort ye,"
is addressed, and who are greeted in ch. lii. 7, 8 as the bearers
of the joyful news of the existing fulfilment of the deliverance
that has appeared, and therefore as the *m^ebhassēr* or evangelist
of the future מבשׂרים.   In any case, it follows from vers.
26, 27 that the overthrow of Babylon and the redemption of
Israel had long before been proclaimed by Jehovah through
His prophets ; and if our exposition is correct so far, the
futures in ver. 28 are to be taken as imperfects : And I looked
round (וָאֵרֶא, a voluntative in the hypothetical protasis, Ges.
§ 128, 2), and there was no one (who announced anything of
the kind) ; and of these (the idols) there was no adviser (with
regard to the future, Num. xxiv. 14), and none whom I could
ask, and who answered me (the questioner).   Consequently,
just as the raising up of Cyrus proclaimed the sole omnipotence
of Jehovah, so did the fact that the deliverance of Zion-
Jerusalem, for which the raising up of Cyrus prepared the
way, had been predicted by Him long before, proclaim His
sole omniscience.

This closing declaration of Jehovah terminates with similar
words of wrath and contempt to those with which the judicial
process ended in ver. 24.   Ver. 29. " *See them all, vanity ;
nothingness are their productions, wind and desolation their
molten images.*"   מַעֲשֵׂיהֶם are not the works of the idols, but, as
the parallel shows, the productions (plural, as in Ezek. vi. 6, Jer.
i. 16) of the idolaters,—in other words, the idols themselves,—
a parallel expression to נִסְכֵּיהֶם (from נֶסֶךְ, as in ch. xlviii. 5 =
massēkhâh, ch. xlii. 17).   אֶן אֶפֶס is an emotional asyndeton
(Ges. § 155, 1, *a*).   The address is thus rounded off by return-

ing to the idolaters, with whom it first started. The first part, vers. 1–24, contains the judicial pleadings; the second part, vers. 25 sqq., recapitulates the evidence and the verdict.

THIRD PROPHECY.—Chap. xlii. 1–xliii. 13.

THE MEDIATOR OF ISRAEL AND SAVIOUR OF THE GENTILES.

The *hēn* (behold) in ch. xli. 29 is now followed by a second *hēn*. With the former, Jehovah pronounced sentence upon the idolaters and their idols; with the latter, He introduces His "servant." In ch. xli. 8 this epithet was applied to the nation, which had been chosen as the servant and for the service of Jehovah. But the servant of Jehovah who is presented to us here is distinct from Israel, and has so strong an individuality and such marked personal features, that the expression cannot possibly be merely a personified collective. Nor can the prophet himself be intended; for what is here affirmed of this servant of Jehovah goes infinitely beyond anything to which a prophet was ever called, or of which a man was ever capable. It must therefore be the future Christ; and this is the view taken in the Targum, where the translation of our prophecy commences thus: "*Hâ' 'abhdî Mᵉshîchâ'.*" Still there must be a connection between the national sense, in which the expression "servant of Jehovah" was used in ch. xli. 8, and the personal sense in which it is used here. The coming Saviour is not depicted as the Son of David, as in ch. vii.–xii., and elsewhere, but appears as the embodied idea of Israel, *i.e.* as its truth and reality embodied in one person. The idea of "the servant of Jehovah" assumed, to speak figuratively, the form of a pyramid. The base was Israel as a whole; the central section was that Israel, which was not merely Israel according to the flesh, but according to the spirit also; the apex is the person of the Mediator of salvation springing out of Israel. And the last of the three is regarded (1) as the centre of the circle of the promised kingdom—the *second David;* (2) the centre of the circle of the people of salvation—the *second Israel;* (3) the centre of the circle of the human race—the *second Adam.* Throughout the whole of these prophecies in ch. xl.–lxvi. the knowledge of salvation is still in its second stage, and about to pass into the third. Israel's true nature as a servant of God, which had its roots in the election and calling of Jehovah, and manifested itself in conduct and action in harmony with this calling, is all concentrated in Him, the One, as its ripest fruit. The gracious purposes of God towards the whole human race, which were manifested even in the election of Israel, are brought by Him to their full completion. Whilst judgments are inflicted upon the heathen by the oppressor of the nations, and display the nothingness of idolatry, the servant of Jehovah brings to them in a peaceful way the greatest of all blessings. Ver. 1. *" Behold my servant, whom I uphold; mine elect, whom my soul loveth: I have laid my Spirit upon Him; He will bring out right to the Gentiles."* We must not render the first clause " by whom I hold." *Tâmakh b'* means to lay firm hold of and keep upright (*sustinere*). רָצְתָה נַפְשִׁי (supply בּוֹ or אֹתוֹ, Job xxxiii. 26) is an attributive clause. The amplified subject extends as far as *naphshī;* then follows the predicate : I have endowed Him with my Spirit, and by virtue of this Spirit He will carry out *mishpât, i.e.* absolute and therefore divine right, beyond the circle in which He Himself is to be found, even far away to the Gentiles. *Mishpât* is the term employed here to denote true religion regarded on its practical side, as the rule and authority for life in all its relations, *i.e.* religion as the law of life, νομός.

The prophet then proceeds to describe how the servant of Jehovah will manifest Himself in the world outside Israel by the promulgation of this right. Ver. 2. *" He will not cry, nor lift up, nor cause to be heard in the street, His voice."* " His voice" is the object of "lift up," as well as " cause to be heard." With our existing division of the verse, it must at least be supplied in thought. Although he is certain of His divine call, and brings to the nations the highest and best, His manner of appearing is nevertheless quiet, gentle, and humble; the very opposite of those lying teachers, who endeavoured to exalt themselves by noisy demonstrations. He does not seek His own, and therefore denies Himself; He brings what commends itself, and therefore requires no forced trumpeting.

With this unassuming appearance there is associated a tender pastoral care. Ver. 3. *" A bruised reed He does not break, and a glimmering wick He does not put out: according to truth He brings out right."* " Bruised :" *râtsūts* signifies here,

as in ch. xxxvi. 6, what is cracked, and therefore half-broken
already.   *Glimmering*: *kēheh* (a form indicative of defects,
like עִוֵּר), that which is burning feebly, and very nearly extinguished.   Tertullian understands by the "bruised reed"
(*arundinem contusam*) the faith of Israel, and by the "glimmering wick" (*linum ardens*) the momentary zeal of the
Gentiles.   But the words hardly admit of this distinction; the
reference is rather a general one, to those whose inner and outer
life is only hanging by a slender thread.   In the statement
that in such a case as this He does not completely break or ex-
tinguish, there is more implied than is really expressed.   Not
only will He not destroy the life that is dying out, but He will
actually save it; His course is not to destroy, but to save.   If
we explain the words that follow as meaning, "He will carry
out right to truth," *i.e.* to its fullest efficacy and permanence
(LXX. εἰς ἀλήθειαν; instead of which we find εἰς νῖκος, "unto
victory," in Matt. xii. 20,[1] as if the reading were לָנֶצַח, as in
Hab. i. 4), the connection between the first and last clauses of
ver. 3 is a very loose one.   It becomes much closer if we take
the לְ as indicating the standard, as in ch. xi. 3 and xxxii. 1,
and adopt the rendering "according to truth" (Hitzig and
Knobel).   It is on its subjective and practical side that truth
is referred to here, viz. as denoting such a knowledge, and
acknowledgment of the true facts in the complicated affairs of
men, as will promote both equity and kindness.

The figures in ver. 3*a* now lead to the thought that the
servant of God will never be extinguished or become broken
Himself.   Ver. 4.   "*He will not become faint or broken, till He
establish right upon earth, and the islands wait for His instruction.*"   As יִכְהֶה (become faint) points back to כהה פִּשְׁתָּה (the
faint or glimmering wick), so יָרוּץ must point back to קָנֶה רָצוּץ
(the bruised or broken reed); it cannot therefore be derived
from רוּץ (to run) in the sense of "He will not be rash or impe-
tuous, but execute His calling with wise moderation," as Hengstenberg supposes, but as in Eccles. xii. 6, from רָצַץ = יָרֹץ (Ges.
§ 67, Anm. 9), in the neuter sense of *infringetur* (will break).
His zeal will not be extinguished, nor will anything break His
strength, till He shall have secured for right a firm standing on
the earth (יָשִׂים is a *fut. ex.* so far as the meaning is concerned,

---

[1] "*Ad victoriam enim κρίσιν perducit qui ad veritatem perducit.*"—ANGER.

like יִבְצַע in ch. x. 12). The question arises now, whether what
follows is also governed by עַד, in the sense of " and until the
islands shall have believed his instruction," as Hitzig supposes;
or whether it is an independent sentence, as rendered by the
LXX. and in Matt. xii. 21. We prefer the latter, both
because of ch. li. 5, and also because, although יַחֵל לִדְבַר ה' may
certainly mean to exercise a believing confidence in the word
of God (Ps. cxix. 74, 81), יַחֵל לְתוֹרָתוֹ can only mean " to wait
with longing for a person's instruction" (Job xxix. 23), and
especially in this case, where no thought is more naturally suggested, than that the messenger to the Gentile world will be
welcomed by a consciousness of need already existing in the
heathen world itself. There is a *gratia præparans* at work in
the Gentile world, as these prophecies all presuppose, in perfect
harmony with the Gospel of John, with which they have so
much affinity; and it is an actual fact, that the cry for redemption runs through the whole human race, *i.e.* an earnest longing,
the ultimate object of which, however unconsciously, is the servant of Jehovah and his instruction from Zion (ch. ii. 3),—in
other words, the gospel.

The words of Jehovah are now addressed to His servant
himself. He has not only an exalted vocation, answering to
the infinite exaltation of Him from whom he has received his
call; but by virtue of the infinite might of the caller, he may
be well assured that he will never be wanting in power to
execute his calling. Vers. 5-7. " *Thus saith God, Jehovah,
who created the heavens, and stretched them out; who spread the
earth, and its productions; who gave the spirit of life to the people
upon it, and the breath of life to them that walk upon it: I,
Jehovah, I have called thee in righteousness, and grasped thy
hand; and I keep thee, and make thee the covenant of the people,
the light of the Gentiles, to open blind eyes, to bring out prisoners
out of the prison, them that sit in darkness out of the prison-
house.*" The perfect *'âmar* is to be explained on the ground
that the words of God, as compared with the prophecy which
announces them, are always the earlier of the two. הָאֵל (the
absolutely Mighty) is an anticipatory apposition to Jehovah
(Ges. § 113**). The attributive participles we have resolved
into perfects, because the three first at least declare facts of
creation, which have occurred once for all. נוֹטֵיהֶם is not to be

regarded as a plural, after ch. liv. 5 and Job xxxv. 10; but as
בּוֹרֵא precedes it, we may take it as a singular with an original
quiescent *Yod*, after ch. v. 12, xxii. 11, xxvi. 12 (cf. vol. i. p. 108).
On רְקַע (construct of רָקַע), see ch. xl. 19.   The ו of וְצֶאֱצָאֶיהָ (a
word found both in Job and Isaiah, used here in its most direct
sense, to signify the vegetable world) must be taken in accordance with the sense, as the *Vav* of appurtenance; since רְקַע
may be affirmed of the globe itself, but not of the vegetable
productions upon it (cf. Gen. iv. 20; Judg. vi. 5; 2 Chron.
ii. 3).   *N*e*shâmâh* and *rŭăch* are epithets applied to the divine
principle of life in all created corporeal beings, or, what is the
same thing, in all beings with living souls.   At the same time,
*n*e*shâmâh* is an epithet restricted to the self-conscious spirit of
man, which gives him his personality (*Psychol.* p. 76, etc.);
whereas *rŭăch* is applied not only to the human spirit, but to
the spirit of the beast as well.   Accordingly, עָם signifies the
human race, as in ch. xl. 7.   What is it, then, that Jehovah,
the Author of all being and all life, the Creator of the heaven
and the earth, says to His servant here?   " I Jehovah have
called thee ' in righteousness' " (*b*e*tsedeq*: cf. ch. xlv. 13, where
Jehovah also says of Cyrus, " I have raised him up in righteousness").   צֶדֶק, derived from צָדַק, to be rigid, straight, denotes
the observance of a fixed rule.   The righteousness of God is
the stringency with which He acts, in accordance with the will
of His holiness.   This will of holiness is, so far as the human
race is concerned, and apart from the counsels of salvation, a
will of wrath; but from the standpoint of these counsels it is
a will of love, which is only changed into a will of wrath
towards those who despise the grace thus offered to them.
Accordingly, *tsedeq* denotes the action of God in accordance
with His purposes of love and the plan of salvation.   It signifies just the same as what we should call in New Testament
phraseology the *holy love* of God, which, because it is a *holy*
love, has wrath against its despisers as its obverse side, but
which acts towards men not according to the law of works,
but according to the law of grace.   The word has this evangelical sense here, where Jehovah says of the Mediator of His
counsels of love, that He has called Him in strict adherence to
the will of His love, which will show mercy as right, but at
the same time will manifest a right of double severity towards

those who scornfully repel the offered mercy. That He had been called in righteousness, is attested to the servant of Jehovah by the fact that Jehovah has taken Him by the hand (וָאֶחְזֵק contracted after the manner of a future of sequence), and guards Him, and appoints Him לִבְרִית עָם לְאוֹר גּוֹיִם. These words are a decisive proof that the idea of the expression "servant of Jehovah" has been elevated in ch. xlii. 1 sqq., as compared with ch. xli. 8, from the national base to the personal apex. Adherence to the national sense necessarily compels a resort to artifices which carry their own condemnation, such as that ברית עם signifies the "covenant nation," as Hitzig supposes, or "the mediating nation," as Ewald maintains, whereas either of these would require עַם ברית; or "national covenant" (Knobel), in support of which we are referred, though quite inconclusively, to Dan. xi. 28, where בְּרִית קֹדֶשׁ does not mean the covenant of the patriots among themselves, but the covenant religion, with its distinctive sign, circumcision; or even that עם is collective, and equivalent to עַמִּים (Rosenmüller), whereas עם and גוים, when standing side by side, as they do here, can only mean Israel and the Gentiles; and so far as the passage before us is concerned, this is put beyond all doubt by ch. xlix. 8 (cf. ver. 6). An unprejudiced commentator must admit that the "servant of Jehovah" is pointed out here, as He in whom and through whom Jehovah concludes a new covenant with His people, in the place of the old covenant that was broken,—namely, the covenant promised in ch. liv. 10, lxi. 8, Jer. xxxi. 31–34, Ezek. xvi. 60 sqq. The mediator of this covenant with Israel cannot be Israel itself, not even the true Israel, as distinguished from the mass (where do we read anything of this kind?); on the contrary, the remnant left after the sweeping away of the mass is the object of this covenant.[1] Nor can the expression refer to the prophets as a body, or, in fact, have any collective meaning at all: the form of the

[1] This is equally applicable to V. F. Oehler (*Der Knecht Jehova's im Deuterojesaia*, 2 Theile, 1865), who takes the "servant of Jehovah" as far as ch. lii. 14 in a national sense, and supposes "the transition from the 'servant' as a collective noun, to the 'servant' as an individual," to be effected there; whereas two younger theologians, E. Schmutz (*Le Serviteur de Jéhova*, 1858) and Ferd. Philippi (*Die bibl. Lehre vom Knechte Gottes*, 1864), admit that the individualizing commences as early as ch. xlii. 1.

word, which is so strongly personal, is in itself opposed to this. It cannot, in fact, denote any other than that Prophet who is more than a prophet, namely, Malachi's "Messenger of the covenant" (ch. iii. 1). Amongst those who suppose that the "servant of Jehovah" is either Israel, regarded in the light of its prophetic calling, or the prophets as a body, Umbreit at any rate is obliged to admit that this collective body is looked at here in the ideal unity of one single Messianic personality; and he adds, that "in the holy countenance of this prophet, which shines forth as the ideal of future realization, we discern exactly the loved features of Him to whom all prophecy points, and who saw Himself therein." This is very beautiful; but why this roundabout course? Let us bear in mind, that the servant of Jehovah appears here not only as one who is the medium of a covenant to the nation, and of light to the Gentiles, but as being himself the people's covenant and heathen's light, inasmuch as in his own person he is the band of a new fellowship between Israel and Jehovah, and becomes in his own person the light which illumines the dark heathen world. This is surely more than could be affirmed of any prophet, even of Isaiah or Jeremiah. Hence the "servant of Jehovah" must be that one Person who was the goal and culminating point to which, from the very first, the history of Israel was ever pressing on; that One who throws into the shade not only all that prophets did before, but all that had been ever done by Israel's priests or kings; that One who arose out of Israel, for Israel and the whole human race, and who stood in the same relation not only to the wider circle of the whole nation, but also to the inner circle of the best and noblest within it, as the heart to the body which it animates, or the head to the body over which it rules. All that Cyrus did, was simply to throw the idolatrous nations into a state of alarm, and set the exiles free. But the Servant of Jehovah opens blind eyes; and therefore the deliverance which He brings is not only redemption from bodily captivity, but from spiritual bondage also. He leads His people (cf. ch. xlix. 8, 9), and the Gentiles also, out of night into light; He is the Redeemer of all that need redemption and desire salvation.

Jehovah pledges His name and honour that this work of the Servant of Jehovah will be carried into effect. Ver. 8. "*I*

*am Jehovah; that is my name, and my glory I give not to another,
nor my renown to idols.*" That is His name, which affirms how
truly He stands alone in His nature, and recals to mind the
manifestations of His life, His power, and His grace from the
very earliest times (cf. Ex. iii. 15). He to whom this name
belongs cannot permit the honour due to Him to be permanently transferred to sham gods. He has therefore made preparations for putting an end to idolatry. Cyrus does this
provisionally by the tempestuous force of arms ; and the Servant of Jehovah completes it by the spiritual force of His
simple word, and of His gentle, unselfish love.

First the overthrow of idolatry, then the restoration of
Israel and conversion of the Gentiles : this is the double work
of Jehovah's zeal which is already in progress. Ver. 9. "*The
first, behold, is come to pass, and new things am I proclaiming;
before it springs up, I let you hear it.*" The "first" is the rise
of Cyrus, and the agitation of the nations which it occasioned,
—events which not only formed the starting-point of the prophecy in these addresses, whether the captivity was the prophet's historical or ideal standpoint, but which had no less
force in themselves, as the connection between the first and
second halves of the verse before us imply, as events both
foreknown and distinctly foretold by Jehovah. The "new
things" which Jehovah now foretells before their visible development (ch. xliii. 19), are the restoration of Israel, for which
the defeat of their oppressors prepares the way, and the conversion of the heathen, to which an impulse is given by the
fact that God thus glorifies Himself in His people.

The prediction of these "new things," which now follows,
looks away from all human mediation. They are manifestly
the work of Jehovah Himself, and consist primarily in the
subjugation of His enemies, who are holding His people in
captivity. Vers. 10–13. "*Sing ye to Jehovah a new song,
His praise from the end of the earth, ye navigators of the sea,
and its fulness ; ye islands, and their inhabitants. Let the
desert and the cities thereof strike up, the villages that Kedar
doth inhabit; the inhabitants of the rock-city may rejoice, shout
from the summits of the mountains. Let them give glory to
Jehovah, and proclaim His praise in the islands. Jehovah, like
a hero will He go forth, kindle jealousy like a man of war; He*

*will break forth into a war-cry, a yelling war-cry, prove Himself
a hero upon His enemies.*" The "new things" furnish the
impulse and materials of "a new song," such as had never
been heard in the heathen world before. This whole group of
verses is like a variation of ch. xxiv. 14, 15. The standing-
place, whence the summons is uttered, is apparently *Ezion-
geber*, at the head of the Elanitic Gulf, that seaport town
from which in the time of the kings the news of the nations
reached the Holy Land through the extensive commerce of
Israel. From this point the eye stretches to the utmost circle
of the earth, and then returns from the point where it meets
with those who "go down to the sea," *i.e.* who navigate the
ocean which lies lower than the solid ground. These are to
sing, and everything that lives and moves in the sea is to join
in the sailors' song. The islands and coast lands, that are
washed by the sea, are likewise to sing together with their
inhabitants. After the summons has drawn these into the net
of the song of praise, it moves into the heart of the land. The
desert and its cities are to lift up (viz. "their voice"), the
villages which Kedar inhabits. The reference to *Sela'*, the
rock-city of Edomitish Nabatæa, which is also mentioned in
ch. xvi. 1 (the *Wadi Musa*, which is still celebrated for its
splendid ruins), shows by way of example what cities are intended. Their inhabitants are to ascend the steep mountains
by which the city is surrounded, and to raise a joyful cry
(*yitsvâchū*, to cry out with a loud noise; cf. ch. xxiv. 11).
Along with the inhabitants of cities, the stationary Arabs, who
are still called *Hadariye* in distinction from *Wabariye*, the
Arabs of the tents, are also summoned; *hadar* (*châtsēr*) is a
fixed abode, in contrast to *bedû*, the steppe, where the tents are
pitched for a short time, now in one place and now in another.
In ver. 12 the summons becomes more general. The subject
is the heathen universally and in every place; they are to give
Jehovah the glory (Ps. lxvi. 2), and declare His praise upon
the islands, *i.e.* to the remotest ends of the whole world of
nations. In ver. 13 there follows the reason for this summons,
and the theme of the new song in honour of the God of Israel,
viz. His victory over His enemies, the enemies of His people.
The description is anthropomorphically dazzling and bold, such
as the self-assurance and vividness of the Israelitish idea of

God permitted, without any danger of misunderstanding. Jehovah goes out into the conflict like a hero; and like a "man of war," *i.e.* like one who has already fought many battles, and is therefore ready for war, and well versed in warfare, He stirs up jealousy (see at ch. ix. 6). His jealousy has slumbered as it were for a long time, as if smouldering under the ashes; but now He stirs it up, *i.e.* makes it burn up into a bright flame. Going forward to the attack, יָרִיעַ, "He breaks out into a cry," אַף־יַצְרִיחַ, "yea, a yelling cry" (*kal* Zeph. i. 14, to cry with a yell; *hiphil*, to utter a yelling cry). In the words, "He will show Himself as a hero upon His enemies," we see Him already engaged in the battle itself, in which He proves Himself to possess the strength and boldness of a hero (*hithgabbar* only occurs again in the book of Job). The overthrow which heathenism here suffers at the hand of Jehovah is, according to our prophet's view, the final and decisive one. The redemption of Israel, which is thus about to appear, is redemption from the punishment of captivity, and at the same time from all the troubles that arise from sin. The period following the captivity and the New Testament times here flow into one.

The period of punishment has now lasted sufficiently long; it is time for Jehovah to bring forth the salvation of His people. Ver. 14. "*I have been silent eternally long, was still, restrained myself; like a travailing woman, I now breathe again, snort and snuff together.*" The standpoint of these prophecies has the larger half of the captivity behind it. It has already lasted a long time, though only for several decades; but in the estimation of Jehovah, with His love to His people, this time of long-suffering towards their oppressors is already an "eternity" (see ch. lvii. 11, lviii. 12, lxi. 4, lxiii. 18, 19, lxiv. 4, cf. vers. 10, 11). He has kept silence, has still forcibly restrained Himself, just as Joseph is said to have done to prevent himself from breaking out into tears (Gen. xliii. 31). Love impelled Him to redeem His people; but justice was still obliged to proceed with punishment.

Three real futures now take the place of imperfects regulated by הֶחֱשֵׁיתִי. They are not to be understood as denoting the violent breathing and snorting of a hero, burning with rage and thirsting for battle (Knobel); nor is אֶשֹּׁם to be derived from שָׁמֵם, as Hitzig supposes, through a mistaken comparison

of Ezek. xxxvi. 3, though the latter does not mean to lay
waste, but to be waste (see Hitzig on Ezek. xxxvi. 3). The
true derivation is from נָשַׁם, related to נָשַׁב, נָפַשׁ, נָשַׁף. To the
figure of a hero there is now added that of a travailing woman;
פָּעָה is short breathing (with the glottis closed); נָשַׁם the snorting of violent inspiration and expiration; שָׁאַף the earnest
longing for deliverance pressing upon the burden in the womb;
and יַחַד expresses the combination of all these several strainings
of the breath, which are associated with the so-called labour-
pains. Some great thing, with which Jehovah has, as it were,
long been pregnant, is now about to be born.

The delivery takes place, and the whole world of nature
undergoes a metamorphosis, which is subservient to the great
work of the future. Ver. 15. "*I make waste mountains and
hills, and all their herbage I dry up, and change streams into
islands, and lakes I dry up.*" Here is another example of
Isaiah's favourite palindromy, as Nitzsch calls this return to a
word that has been used before, or linking on the close of a
period to its commencement (see p. 134). Jehovah's panting in
labour is His almighty fiery breath, which turns mountains and
hills into heaps of ruins, scorches up the vegetation, condenses
streams into islands, and dries up the lakes; that is to say,
turns the strange land, in which Israel has been held captive,
into a desert, and at the same time removes all the hindrances
to His people's return, thus changing the present condition of
the world into one of the very opposite kind, which displays
His righteousness in wrath and love.

The great thing which is brought to pass by means of this
catastrophe is the redemption of His people. Ver. 16. "*And
I lead the blind by a way that they know not; by steps that they
know not, I make them walk: I turn dark space before them into
light, and rugged places into a plain. These are the things that
I carry out, and do not leave.*" The "blind" are those who
have been deprived of sight by their sin, and the consequent
punishment. The unknown ways in which Jehovah leads
them, are the ways of deliverance, which are known to Him
alone, but which have now been made manifest in the fulness
of time. The "dark space" (*machshâk*) is their existing state
of hopeless misery; the "rugged places" (*ma'ăqasshĭm*) the
hindrances that met them, and dangers that threatened them

on all sides in the foreign land. The mercy of Jehovah adopts the blind, lights up the darkness, and clears every obstacle away. *" These are the things"* (*hadd*ᵉ*bhârim*) : this refers to the particulars already sketched out of the double manifestation of Jehovah in judgment and in mercy. The perfects of the attributive clause are perfects of certainty.

In connection with this, the following verse declares what effect this double manifestation will produce among the heathen. Ver. 17. *" They fall back, are put deeply to shame, that trust in molten images, that say to the molten image, Thou art our God."* *Bōsheth* takes the place of an inf. intens.; cf. Hab. iii. 9. Jehovah's glorious acts of judgment and salvation unmask the false gods, to the utter confusion of their worshippers. And whilst in this way the false religions fall, the redemption of Israel becomes at the same time the redemption of the heathen. The first half of this third prophecy is here brought to a close.

The thought which connects the second half with the first is to be found in the expression in ver. 16, "I will bring the blind by a way." It is the blind whom Jehovah will lead into the light of liberty, the blind who bring upon themselves not only His compassion, but also His displeasure ; for it is their own fault that they do not see. And to them is addressed the summons, to free themselves from the ban which is resting upon them. Ver. 18. *" Ye deaf, hear ; and ye blind, look up, that ye may see."* הַחֵרְשִׁים and הָעִוְרִים (this is the proper pointing, according to the codd. and the Masora[1]) are vocatives. The relation in which הִבִּיט and רָאָה stand to one another is that of design and accomplishment (ch. lxiii. 15, Job xxxv. 5, 2 Kings iii. 14, etc.) ; and they are used interchangeably with פָּקַח עֵינָיו and רָאָה (*e.g.* 2 Kings xix. 16), which also stand in the same relation of design and result.

The next verse states who these self-willed deaf and blind are, and how necessary this arousing was. Ver. 19. *" Who is blind, but my servant ? and deaf, as my messenger whom I send ? who blind as the confidant of God, and blind as the servant of Jehovah ?"* The first double question implies that Jehovah's servant and messenger is blind and deaf in a singular and un-

---

[1] The Masora observes expressly כל סמיין רפוין ופתחין, *omnes cæci raphati et pathachati;* but our editions have both here and in 2 Sam. v. 6, 8, העורים.

paralleled way. The words are repeated, the questioner dwelling upon the one predicate *'ivvēr*, "blind," in which everything is affirmed, and, according to Isaiah's favourite custom, returning palindromically to the opening expression "servant of Jehovah" (cf. ch. xl. 19, xlii. 15, and many other passages). מְשֻׁלָּם does not mean "the perfect one," as Vitringa renders it, nor "the paid, *i.e.* purchased one," as Rosenmüller supposes, but one allied in peace and friendship, the confidant of God. It is the passive of the Arabic *muslim*, one who trusts in God (compare the *hophal* in Job v. 23). It is impossible to read the expression, "My messenger whom I send," without thinking of ch. xlii. 1 sqq., where the "servant of Jehovah" is represented as a messenger to the heathen. (Jerome is wrong in following the Jewish commentators, and adopting the rendering, *ad quem nuntios meos misi*.) With this similarity both of name and calling, there must be a connection between the "servant" mentioned here, and the "servant" referred to there. Now the "servant of Jehovah" is always Israel. But since Israel might be regarded either according to the character of the overwhelming majority of its members (the mass), who had forgotten their calling, or according to the character of those living members who had remained true to their calling, and constituted the kernel, or as concentrated in that one Person who is the essence of ▸Israel in the fullest truth and highest potency, statements of the most opposite kind could be made with respect to this one homonymous subject. In ch. xli. 8 sqq. the "servant of Jehovah" is caressed and comforted, inasmuch as there the true Israel, which deserved and needed consolation, is addressed, without regard to the mass who had forgotten their calling. In ch. xlii. 1 sqq. that One person is referred to, who is, as it were, the centre of this inner circle of Israel, and the head upon the body of Israel. And in the passage before us, the idea is carried from this its highest point back again to its lowest basis; and the servant of Jehovah is blamed and reproved for the harsh contrast between its actual conduct and its divine calling, between the reality and the idea. As we proceed, we shall meet again with the "servant of Jehovah" in the same *systole* and *diastole*. The expression covers two concentric circles, and their one centre. The inner circle of the "Israel according to the Spirit" forms

the connecting link between Israel in its widest sense, and
Israel in a personal sense.   Here indeed Israel is severely
blamed as incapable, and unworthy of fulfilling its sacred
calling ; but the expression " whom I send " nevertheless
affirms that it will fulfil it,—namely, in the *person* of the servant of Jehovah, and in all those members of the " servant of
Jehovah" in a national sense, who long for deliverance from
the ban and bonds of the present state of punishment (see ch.
xxix. 18).   For it is really the mission of Israel to be the
medium of salvation and blessing to the nations ; and this is
fulfilled by the servant of Jehovah, who proceeds from Israel,
and takes his place at the head of Israel.   And as the history
of the fulfilment shows, when the foundation for the accomplishment of this mission had been laid by the servant of
Jehovah in person, it was carried on by the servant of Jehovah
in a national sense ; for the Lord became " a covenant of the
people" through His own preaching and that of His apostles.
But " a light of the Gentiles" He became purely and simply
through the apostles, who represented the true and believing
Israel.

The reproof, which affects Israel *a potiori*, now proceeds
still further, as follows.   Vers. 20–22. " *Thou hast seen much,
and yet keepest not ; opening the ears, he yet doth not hear.
Jehovah was pleased for His righteousness' sake : He gave a
thorah great and glorious.   And yet it is a people robbed and
plundered ; fastened in holes all of them, and they are hidden in
prison-houses : they have become booty, without deliverers ; a
spoil, without any one saying, Give it up again !*"   In ver. 20
" thou" and " he" alternate, like " they" and " ye" in ch. i.
29, and " I" and " he" in ch. xiv. 30. רָאִיתָ, which points back
to the past, is to be preserved.   The reading of the *keri* is רָאוֹת
(inf. abs. like שָׁתוֹת, ch. xxii. 13, and עָרוֹת, Hab. iii. 13), which
makes the two half-verses uniform.   Israel has had many and
great things to see, but without keeping the admonitions they
contained ; opening its ears, namely to the earnestness of the
preaching, it hears, and yet does not hear, *i.e.* it only hears
outwardly, but without taking it into itself.   Ver. 21 shows us
to what ver. 20 chiefly refers. חָפֵץ is followed here by the
future instead of by *Lamed* with an infinitive, just as in ch. liii.
10 it is followed by the perfect (Ges. § 142, 3, *b*).   Jehovah

was pleased for His righteousness' sake (which is mentioned here, not as that which recompenses for works of the law, but as that which bestows mercy according to His purpose, His promise, and the plan of salvation) to make *thorâh, i.e.* the direction, instruction, revelation which He gave to His people, great and glorious. The reference is primarily and chiefly to the Sinaitic law, and the verbs relate not to the solemnity of the promulgation, but to the riches and exalted character of the contents. But what a glaring contrast did the existing condition of Israel present to these manifestations and purposes of mercy on the part of its God! The intervening thought expressed by Hosea (Hos. viii. 12*b*), viz. that this condition was the punishment of unfaithfulness, may easily be supplied. The inf. abs. הָפֵחַ is introduced to give life to the picture, as in ch. xxii. 13. Hahn renders it, "They pant (*hiphil* of *pûăch*) in the holes all of them," but *kullâm* (all of them) must be the accusative of the object; so that the true meaning is, "They have fastened (*hiphil* of *pâchach*) all of them," etc. (Ges. § 131, 4, *b*). Schegg adopts the rendering, "All his youths fall into traps," which is wrong in two respects; for *bachūrīm* is the plural of *chūr* (ch. xi. 8), and it is parallel to the double plural בָּתֵּי כְלָאִים, houses of custodies. The whole nation in all its members is, as it were, put into bonds, and confined in prisons of all kinds (an allegorizing picture of the homelessness and servitude of exile), without any one thinking of demanding it back (הָשֵׁב = הָשֵׁב, as in Ezek. xxi. 35; a pausal form here: *vid.* Ges. § 29, 4 Anm.).

When they ceased to be deaf to this crying contradiction, they would recognise with penitence that it was but the merited punishment of God. Vers. 23–25. "*Who among you will give ear to this, attend, and hear afar off? Who has given up Jacob to plundering, and Israel to the spoilers? Is it not Jehovah, against whom we have sinned? and they would not walk in His ways, and hearkened not to His law. Then He poured upon it in burning heat His wrath, and the strength of the fury of war: and this set it in flames round about, and it did not come to be recognised; it set it on fire, and it did not lay it to heart.*" The question in ver. 23 has not the force of a negative sentence, "No one does this," but of a wish, "O that one would" (as in 2 Sam. xxiii. 15, xv. 4; Ges. § 136, 1). If they had but an

inward ear for the contradiction which the state of Israel presented to its true calling, and the earlier manifestations of
divine mercy, and would but give up their previous deafness
for the time to come: this must lead to the knowledge and
confession expressed in ver. 24. The names Jacob and Israel
here follow one another in the same order as in ch. xxix. 23,
xl. 27 (compare ch. xli. 8, where this would have been imprac-
ticable). זוּ belongs to לוֹ in the sense of *cui*. The punctuation does not acknowledge this relative use of זוּ (on which, see
at ch. xliii. 21), and therefore puts the *athnach* in the wrong
place (see Rashi). In the words " we have sinned" the prophet identifies himself with the exiles, in whose sin he knew and
felt that he was really involved (cf. ch. vi. 5). The objective
affirmation which follows applies to the former generations, who
had sinned on till the measure became full. הָלוֹךְ takes the
place of the object to אָבוּ (see ch. i. 17); the more usual expression would be לָלֶכֶת; the inverted order of the words makes
the assertion all the more energetic. In ver. 25 the genitive
relation חֲמַת אַפּוֹ is avoided, probably in favour of the similar
ring of חֵמָה and מִלְחָמָה. חֵמָה is either the accusative of the
object, and אַפּוֹ a subordinate statement of what constituted the
burning heat (cf. Ewald, § 287, *k*), or else an accusative, of more
precise definition = בְּחֵמָה in ch. lxvi. 15 (Ges. § 118, 3). The
outpouring is also connected by *zeugma* with the " violence of
war." The *milchâmâh* then becomes the subject. The war-
fury raged without result. Israel was not brought to reflection.

The tone of the address is now suddenly changed. The
sudden leap from reproach to consolation was very significant.
It gave them to understand, that no meritorious work of their
own would come in between what Israel was and what it was
to be, but that it was God's free grace which came to meet it.
Ch. xliii. 1, 2. " *But now thus saith Jehovah thy Creator, O
Jacob, and thy Former, O Israel! Fear not, for I have redeemed
thee; I have called thee by name, thou art mine. When thou goest
through the water, I am with thee; and through rivers, they shall
not drown thee: when thou goest into fire, thou shalt not be
burned; and the flame shall not set thee on fire.*" The punishment has now lasted quite long enough; and, as וְעַתָּה affirms,
the love which has hitherto retreated behind the wrath returns
to its own prerogatives again. He who created and formed

Israel, by giving Abraham the son of the promise, and caused the seventy of Jacob's family to grow up into a nation in Egypt, He also will shelter and preserve it. He bids it be of good cheer; for their early history is a pledge of this. The perfects after כִּי in ver. 1b stand out against the promising futures in ver. 2, as retrospective glances: the expression " I have redeemed thee" pointing back to Israel's redemption out of Egypt; "I have called thee by thy name" (lit. I have called with thy name, i.e. called it out), to its call to be the peculiar people of Jehovah, who therefore speaks of it in ch. xlviii. 12 as " My called." This help of the God of Israel will also continue to arm it against the destructive power of the most hostile elements, and rescue it from the midst of the greatest dangers, from which there is apparently no escape (cf. Ps. lxvi. 12; Dan. iii. 17, 27; and Ges. § 103, 2).

Just as in ver. 1b, kī (for), with all that follows, assigns the reason for the encouraging " Fear not;" so here a second kī introduces the reason for the promise which ensures them against the dangers arising from either water or fire. Vers. 3, 4. "For I Jehovah am thy God; (I) the Holy One of Israel, thy Saviour: I give up Egypt as a ransom for thee, Ethiopia and Seba in thy stead. Because thou art dear in my eyes, highly esteemed, and I loved thee; I give up men in thy stead, and peoples for thy life." Both " Jehovah" and " the Holy One of Israel" are in apposition to " I" ('ănī), the force of which is continued in the second clause. The preterite năthattī (I have given), as the words " I will give" in ver. 4b clearly show, states a fact which as yet is only completed so far as the purpose is concerned. " A ransom:" kōpher (λύτρον) is literally the covering (see vol. i. 397 and ii. 11),—the person making the payment, or the person for whom he makes it, being covered by the payment. סְבָא is the land of Meroë, which is enclosed between the White and Blue Nile, the present Dâr Sennâr, district of Sennâr (Sen-ârti, i.e. island of Senâ), or the ancient Meroitic priestly state settled about this enclosed land, probably included in the Mudrâya (Egypt) of the Achæmenidian arrow-headed inscriptions; though it is uncertain whether the Kusiya (Heb. Kūshīm) mentioned there are the predatory tribe of archers called Κοσσαῖοι (Strabo, xi. 13, 6), whose name has been preserved in the present Chuzistan, the eastern Ethiopians

of the Greeks (as Lassen and Rawlinson suppose), or the
African Ethiopians of the Bible, as Oppert imagines. The
fact that Egypt was only conquered by Cambyses, and not by
Cyrus, who merely planned it (Herod. i. 153), and to whom it
is only attributed by a legend (Xen. *Cyr.* viii. 6, 20, λέγεται
καταστρέψασθαι Αἴγυπτον), does no violence to the truth of
the promise. It is quite enough that Egypt and the neighbouring kingdoms were subjugated by the new imperial power
of Persia, and that through that empire the Jewish people
recovered their long-lost liberty. The free love of God was
the reason for His treating Israel according to the principle
laid down in Prov. xi. 8, xxi. 18. מֵאֲשֶׁר does not signify *ex quo
tempore* here, but is equivalent to מִפְּנֵי אֲשֶׁר in Ex. xix. 18, Jer.
xliv. 23 ; for if it indicated the *terminus a quo*, it would be
followed by a more distinct statement of the fact of their
election. The personal pronoun " and I" (*va'ănî*) is introduced in consequence of the change of persons. In the place
of וְנָתַתִּי (*perf. cons.*), וְאֶתֵּן commended itself, as the former had
already been used in a somewhat different function. All that
composed the chosen nation are here designated as " man"
(*ádâm*), because there was nothing in them but what was
derived from Adam. תַּחַת has here a strictly substitutionary
meaning throughout.

The encouraging " Fear not " is here resumed, for the purpose of assigning a still further reason. Vers. 5-7. "*Fear not;
for I am with thee : I bring thy seed from the east, and from the
west will I gather them ; I will say to the north, Give up ; and
to the south, Keep not back : bring my sons from far, and my
daughters from the end of the earth ; everything that is called
by my name, and I have created for my glory, that I have
formed, yea finished !*" The fact that Jehovah is with Israel
will show itself in this, that He effects its complete restoration
from all quarters of the heaven (compare the lands of the
diaspora in all directions already mentioned by Isaiah in
ch. xi. 11, 12). Jehovah's command is issued to north and
south to give up their unrighteous possession, not to keep
it back, and to restore His sons and daughters (compare the
similar change in the gender in ch. xi. 12), which evidently
implies the help and escort of the exiles on the part of
the heathen (ch. xiv. 2). The four quarters and four winds

are of the feminine gender. In ver. 7 the object is more precisely defined from the standpoint of sacred history. The
three synonyms bring out the might, the freeness, and the
riches of grace, with which Jehovah called Israel into existence,
to glorify Himself in it, and that He might be glorified by it.
They form a climax, for בָּרָא signifies to produce as a new
thing; יָצַר, to shape what has been produced; and עָשָׂה, to
make it perfect or complete, hence *creavi, formavi, perfeci.*

We come now to the third turn in the second half of this
prophecy. It is linked on to the commencement of the first
turn (" Hear, ye deaf, and look, ye blind, that ye may see"),
the summons being now addressed to some one to bring forth
the Israel, which has eyes and ears without seeing or hearing;
whilst, on the other hand, the nations are all to come together,
and this time not for the purpose of convincing them, but of
convincing Israel. Vers. 8–10. *" Bring out a blind people, and
it has eyes ; and deaf people, and yet furnished with ears ! All
ye heathen, gather yourselves together, and let peoples assemble !
Who among you can proclaim such a thing? And let them cause
former things to be heard, appoint their witnesses, and be justified. Let these hear, and say, True ! Ye are my witnesses, saith
Jehovah, and my servant whom I have chosen ; that ye may know
and believe me, and see that it is I: before me was no God
formed, and there will be none after me."* " Bring out " does
not refer here to bringing out of captivity, as in Ezek. xx. 34,
41, xxxiv. 13, since the names by which Israel is called are
hardly applicable to this, but rather to bringing to the place
appointed for judicial proceedings. The verb is in the imperative. The heathen are also to gather together *en masse ;* נִקְבְּצוּ
is also an imperative here, as in Joel iv. 11 = הִקָּבְצוּ (cf. נִלְוּוּ,
Jer. l. 5; Ewald, § 226, *c*). In ver. 9*b* we have the commencement of the evidence adduced by Jehovah in support of His
own divine right: Who among the gods of the nations can proclaim this ? *i.e.* anything like my present announcement of the
restoration of Israel ? To prove that they can, let them cause
" former things " to be heard, *i.e.* any former events which they
had foretold, and which had really taken place ; and let them
appoint witnesses of such earlier prophecies, and so prove themselves to be gods, that is to say, by the fact that these witnesses
have publicly heard their declaration and confirm the truth

thereof. The subject to וְיִשְׁמְעוּ וגו' (they may hear, etc.) is the witnesses, not as now informing themselves for the first time, but as making a public declaration. The explanation, " that men may hear," changes the subject without any necessity. But whereas the gods are dumb and lifeless, and therefore cannot call any witnesses for themselves, and not one of all the assembled multitude can come forward as their legitimate witness, or as one able to vindicate them, Jehovah can call His people as witnesses, since they have had proofs in abundance that He possesses infallible knowledge of the future. It is generally assumed that " and my servant" introduces a second subject: " Ye, and (especially) my servant whom I have chosen." In this case, " my servant" would denote that portion of the nation which was so, not merely like the mass of the people according to its divine calling, but also by its own fidelity to that calling; that is to say, the kernel of the nation, which was in the midst of the mass, but had not the manners of the mass. At the same time, the sentence which follows is much more favourable to the unity of the subject; and why should not " my servant" be a second predicate? The expression " *ye*" points to the people, who were capable of seeing and hearing, and yet both blind and deaf, and who had been brought out to the forum, according to ver. 8. *Ye*, says Jehovah, are *my* witnesses, and ye are my servant whom I have chosen; I can appeal to what I have enabled you to experience and to perceive, and to the relation in which I have in mercy caused you to stand to myself, that ye may thereby be brought to consider the great difference that there is between what ye have in your God and that which the heathen (here present with you) have in their idols. " I am He," *i.e.* God exclusively, and God for ever. His being has no beginning and no end; so that any being apart from His, which could have gone before or could follow after, so as to be regarded as divine (in other words, the deity of the artificial and temporal images which are called gods by the heathen), is a contradiction in itself.

The address now closes by holding up once more the object and warrant of faith. Vers. 11–13. "*I, I am Jehovah; and beside me there is no Saviour. I, I have proclaimed and brought salvation, and given to perceive, and there was no other god among you: and ye are my witnesses, saith Jehovah, and I*

*am God. Even from the day onwards I am so ; and there is
no deliverer out of my hand : I act, and who can turn it back ?"*
The proper name " *Jehovah* " is used here (ver. 13) as a name
indicating essence : " I and no other am the absolutely existing
and living One," *i.e.* He who proves His existence by His
acts, and indeed by His saving acts. מוֹשִׁיעַ and Jehovah are
kindred epithets here ; just as in the New Testament the
name Jehovah sets, as it were, but only to rise again in the
name Jesus, in which it is historically fulfilled.   Jehovah's
previous self-manifestation in history furnished a pledge of
the coming redemption.   The two synonyms הִגַּדְתִּי and הִשְׁמַעְתִּי
have הוֹשַׁעְתִּי in the midst.   He proclaimed salvation, brought
salvation, and in the new afflictions was still ever preaching
salvation, without there having been any *zâr, i.e.* any strange
or other god in Israel (Deut. xxxii. 16 ; see above, ch. xvii.
10), who proved his existence in any such way, or, in fact,
gave any sign of existence at all.   This they must themselves confess ; and therefore (*Vav* in sense equivalent to
ergo, as in ch. xl. 18, 25) He, and He alone, is *El,* the absolutely mighty One, *i.e.* God.   And from this time forth He
is so, *i.e.* He, and He only, displays divine nature and divine
life.   There is no reason for taking מִיּוֹם in the sense of
מִהְיוֹת יוֹם, " from the period when the day, *i.e.* time, existed "
(as the LXX., Jerome, Stier, etc., render it).   Both the *gam*
(also) and the future *'eph'al* (I will work) require the meaning
supported by Ezek. xlviii. 35, " from the day onwards," *i.e.*
from this time forth (syn. לְפְנֵי-יוֹם, ch. xlviii. 7).   The concluding words give them to understand, that the predicted salvation is coming in the way of judgment.   Jehovah will go
forward with His work ; and if He who is the same yesterday
and to-day sets this before Him, who can turn it back, so that
it shall remain unaccomplished ?   The prophecy dies away,
like the *massâ' Bâbhel* with its epilogue in ch. xiv. 27.   In the
first half (ch. xlii. 1–17) Jehovah introduced His servant, the
medium of salvation, and proclaimed the approaching work of
salvation, at which all the world had reason to rejoice.   The
second half (ch. xlii. 18–xliii. 13) began with reproaching, and
sought to bring Israel through this predicted salvation to reflect upon itself, and also upon its God, the One God, to whom
there was no equal.

FOURTH PROPHECY.—CHAP. XLIII. 14–XLIV. 5.

AVENGING AND DELIVERANCE ; AND OUTPOURING OF THE SPIRIT.

In close connection with the foregoing prophecy, the present one commences with the dissolution of the Chaldean empire. Vers. 14, 15. "*Thus saith Jehovah, your Redeemer, the Holy One of Israel, For your sake I have sent to Babel, and will hurl them all down as fugitives, and the Chaldeans into the ships of their rejoicing. I, Jehovah, am your Holy One; (I) Israel's Creator, your King.*" Hitzig reads בָּאֲנִיּוֹת, and adopts the rendering, " and drowned the shouting of the Chaldeans in groaning." Ewald also corrects ver. 14*a* thus : " And plunge their guitars into groanings, and the rejoicing of the Chaldeans into sighs." We cannot see any good taste in this un-Hebraic bombast. Nor is there any more reason for altering בְּרִיחִים (LXX. φεύγοντας) into בְּרִיחִים (Jerome, *vectes*), as Umbreit proposes : " and make all their bolts[1] fall down, and the Chaldeans, who rejoice in ships" (*băŏniyōth*). None of these alterations effect any improvement. For your sakes, says Jehovah, *i.e.* for the purpose of releasing you, I have sent to Babylon (*sc.* the agents of my judgments, ch. xiii. 3), and will throw them all down (viz. the πάμμικτος ὄχλος of this market of the world; see ch. xiii. 14, xlvii. 15) as fugitives (*bărīchīm* with a fixed *kametz*, equivalent to *barrīchīm*), *i.e.* into a hurried flight; and the Chaldeans, who have been settled there from a hoary antiquity, even they shall be driven into the ships of their rejoicing (*bŏŏniyōth*, as in Prov. xxxi. 14), *i.e.* the ships which were previously the object of their jubilant pride and their jubilant rejoicing. וְהוֹרַדְתִּי stands in the *perf. consec.*, as indicating the object of all the means already set in motion. The ships of pleasure are not air-balloons, as Hitzig affirms. Herodotus (i. 194) describes the freight ships discharging in Babylon ; and we know from other sources that the Chaldeans not only navigated the Euphrates, but the Persian Gulf as well, and employed vessels built by Phœnicians for warlike purposes

---

[1] This would require כָּל־בְּרִיחֶיהָ.

also.[1] הוֹרִיד itself might indeed signify "to hurl to the ground" (Ps. lvi. 8, lix. 12); but the allusion to ships shows that הוֹרִיד בְּ are to be connected (cf. ch. lxiii. 14), and that a general driving down both by land and water to the southern coast is intended. By thus sweeping away both foreigners and natives out of Babylon into the sea, Jehovah proves what He is in Himself, according to ver. 15, and also in His relation to Israel; we must supply a repetition of אֲנִי here (ver. 15*b*), as in ver. 3*a*. The congregation which addresses Him as the Holy One, the people who suffer Him to reign over them as their King, cannot remain permanently despised and enslaved.

There now follows a second field of the picture of redemption; and the expression "for your sake" is expounded in vers. 16–21: "*Thus saith Jehovah, who giveth a road through the sea, and a path through tumultuous waters; who bringeth out chariot and horse, army and hero; they lie down together, they never rise: they have flickered away, extinguished like a wick. Remember not things of olden time, nor meditate upon those of earlier times! Behold, I work out a new thing: will ye not live to see it? Yea, I make a road through the desert, and streams through solitudes. The beast of the field will praise me, wild dogs and ostriches: for I give water in the desert, streams in solitude, to give drink to my people, my chosen. The people that I formed for myself, they shall show forth my praise.*" What Jehovah really says commences in ver. 18. Then in between He is described as Redeemer out of Egypt; for the redemption out of Egypt was a type and pledge of the deliverance to be looked for out of Babylon. The participles must not be rendered *qui dedit, eduxit;* but from the mighty act of Jehovah in olden time general attributes are deduced: He who makes a road in the sea, as He once showed. The sea with the tumultuous waters is the Red Sea (Neh. ix. 11); '*izzūz*, which rhymes with *vāsūs*, is a concrete, as in Ps. xxiv. 8, the army with the heroes at its head. The expression "bringeth out," etc., is not followed by "and suddenly destroys them," but we are transported at once into the very midst of the scenes of destruction. יִשְׁכְּבוּ shows them to us entering upon the sleep of death, in which they lie without hope (ch. xxvi. 14). The close (*kappishtâh khâbhû*) is iambic, as in Judg. v. 27. The

[1] See G. Rawlinson, *Monarchies,* i. 128, ii. 448.

admonition in ver. 18 does not commend utter forgetfulness and disregard (see ch. xlvi. 9); but that henceforth they are to look forwards rather than backward. The new thing which Jehovah is in the process of working out eclipses the old, and deserves a more undivided and prolonged attention. Of this new thing it is affirmed, "even now it sprouts up;" whereas in ch. xlii. 9, even in the domain of the future, a distinction was drawn between "the former things" and "new things," and it could be affirmed of the latter that they were not yet sprouting up. In the passage before us the entire work of God in the new time is called *chădáshâh* (new), and is placed in contrast with the *ri'shōnōth*, or occurrences of the olden time; so that as the first part of this new thing had already taken place (ch. xlii. 9), and there was only the last part still to come, it might very well be affirmed of the latter, that it was even now sprouting up (not already, which עתה may indeed also mean, but as in ch. xlviii. 7). In connection with this, הֲלוֹא תֵדָעוּהָ (a verbal form with the suffix, as in Jer. xiii. 17, with *kametz* in the syllable before the tone, as in ch. vi. 9, xlvii. 11, in pause) does not mean, "Will ye then not regard it," as Ewald, Umbreit, and others render it; but, "shall ye not, *i.e.* assuredly ye will, experience it." The substance of the *chădáshâh* (the new thing) is unfolded in ver. 19*b*. It enfolds a rich fulness of wonders: אַף affirming that, among other things, Jehovah will do this one very especially. He transforms the pathless, waterless desert, that His chosen one, the people of God, may be able to go through in safety, and without fainting. And the benefits of this miracle of divine grace reach the animal world as well, so that their joyful cries are an unconscious praise of Jehovah. (On the names of the animals, see vol. i. 305; and Köhler on Mal. i. 3.) In this we can recognise the prophet, who, as we have several times observed since ch. xi. (compare especially ch. xxx. 23, 24, xxxv. 7), has not only a sympathizing heart for the woes of the human race, but also an open ear for the sighs of all creation. He knows that when the sufferings of the people of God shall be brought to an end, the sufferings of creation will also terminate; for humanity is the heart of the universe, and the people of God (understanding by this the people of God according to the Spirit) are the heart of humanity. In ver. 21 the promise is brought to a general

close : the people that (*zu* personal and relative, as in ch. xlii.
24[1]) I have formed for myself will have richly to relate how I
glorified myself in them.

It would be the praise of God, however, and not the merits
of their own works, that they would have to relate ; for there
was nothing at all that could give them any claim to reward.
There were not even acts of ceremonial worship, but only the
guilt of grievous sins. Vers. 22–24. "*And thou hast not called
upon me, O Jacob, that thou shouldst have wearied thyself for
me, O Israel !   Thou hast not brought me sheep of thy burnt-
offerings, and thou hast not honoured me with thy slain-offerings.
I have not burdened thee with meat-offerings, and have not
troubled thee about incense.   Thou hast bought me no spice-cane
for silver, nor hast thou refreshed me with fat of thy slain-
offerings.   No ; thou hast wearied me with thy sins, troubled me
with thine iniquities.*"   We cannot agree with Stier, that these
words refer to the whole of the previous worship of Israel,
which is treated here as having no existence, because of its
heartlessness and false-holiness.   And we must also not forget,
that all these prophecies rested on either the historical or the
ideal soil of the captivity.   The charge commences with the
worship of prayer (with calling upon Jehovah, as in Ps. xiv. 4,
xviii. 7), to which the people were restricted when in exile, since
the law did not allow them to offer sacrifice outside the holy
land.   The personal pronoun אֹתִי, in the place of the suffix, is
written first of all for the sake of emphasis, as if the meaning
were, " Israel could exert itself to call upon other gods, but
not upon Jehovah."   The following *kī* is equivalent to *ut* (Hos.
i. 6), or '*ad-kī* in 2 Sam. xxiii. 10, *adeo ut laborasses me colendo*
(so as to have wearied thyself in worshipping me).   They are
also charged with having offered no sacrifices, inasmuch as in a
foreign land this duty necessarily lapsed of itself, together with

---

[1] The pointing connects עַם־זוּ with *makkeph*, so that the rendering
would be, "The people there I have formed for myself ;" but according
to our view, עַם should be accented with *yethib*, and *zu* with *munach*.   In
just the same way, *zu* is connected with the previous noun as a demonstrative, by means of *makkeph*, in Ex. xv. 13, 16, Ps. ix. 16, lxii. 12, cxlii. 4,
cxliii. 8, and by means of a subsidiary accent in Ps. x. 2, xii. 8.   The idea
which underlies ch. xlii. 24 appears to be, " This is the retribution that
we have met with from him."   But in none of these can we be bound by
the punctuation.

the self-denial that it involved. The spelling הֲבִיאֵת (as in
Num. xiv. 31) appears to have been intended for the pronunciation הֲבִיאֹת (compare the pronunciation in 2 Kings xix. 25,
which comes between the two). The *'ōlōth* (burnt-offerings)
stand first, as the expression of adoration, and are connected
with *sēh*, which points to the daily morning and evening sacrifice (the *tāmīd*). Then follow the *z*e*bhāchīm* (slain-offerings),
the expression of the establishment of fellowship with Jehovah
(וּבְזָחֶיךָ is equivalent to וּבְזִבְחֶיךָ, like חֵמָה = בְּחֵמָה, ch. xliii. 25).
The " fat" (*chēlebh*) in ver. 24 refers to the portions of fat
that were placed upon the altar in connection with this kind
of sacrifice. After the *z*e*bhāchīm* comes the *minchāh*, the expression of desire for the blessing of Jehovah, a portion of
which, the so-called remembrance portion ('*azkārāh*), was placed
upon the altar along with the whole of the incense. And
lastly, the *qāneh* (spice-cane), *i.e.* some one of the *Amoma*,[1]
points to the holy anointing oil (Ex. xxx. 23), or if it refer to
spices generally, to the sacred incense, though *qāneh* is not
mentioned as one of the ingredients in Ex. xxx. 34. The
nation, which Jehovah was now redeeming out of pure un-
mingled grace, had not been burdened with costly tasks of this
description (see Jer. vi. 20); on the contrary, it was Jehovah
only who was burdened and troubled. He denies that there
was any " causing to serve" (הֶעֱבִיד, lit. to make a person a
servant, to impose servile labour upon him) endured by Israel,
but affirms this rather of Himself. The sins of Israel pressed
upon Him, as a burden does upon a servant. His love took
upon itself the burden of Israel's guilt, which derived its gravitating force from His own holy righteous wrath; but it was
a severe task to bear this heavy burden, and expunge it,—a
thoroughly divine task, the significance of which was first
brought out in its own true light by the cross on Golgotha.
When God creates, He expresses His *fiat*, and what He wills
comes to pass. But He does not blot out sin without balancing

[1] The *qāneh* is generally supposed to be the *Calamus*; but the calamus
forms no stalk, to say nothing of a cane or hollow stalk. It must be some
kind of aromatic plant, with a stalk like a cane, either the *Cardamum*,
Ingber, or *Curcuma*; at any rate, it belonged to the species *Amomum*.
The aroma of this was communicated to the anointing oil, the latter being
infused, and the resinous parts of the former being thereby dissolved.

His love with His justice; and this equalization is not effected without conflict and victory.

Nevertheless, the sustaining power of divine love is greater than the gravitating force of divine wrath. Ver. 25. " *I, I alone, blot out thy transgressions for my own sake, and do not remember thy sins.*" Jehovah Himself here announces the *sola gratia* and *sola fides*. We have adopted the rendering " I alone," because the threefold repetition of the subject, " I, I, He is blotting out thy transgressions," is intended to affirm that this blotting out of sin is so far from being in any way merited by Israel, that it is a sovereign act of His absolute freedom; and the expression " for my own sake," that it has its foundation only in God, namely, in His absolute free grace, that movement of His love by which wrath is subdued. For the debt stands written in God's own book. Justice has entered it, and love alone blots it out (*mâchâh*, ἐξαλείφει, as in ch. xliv. 22, Ps. li. 3, 11, cix. 14); but, as we know from the actual fulfilment, not without paying with blood, and giving the quittance with blood.

Jehovah now calls upon Israel, if this be not the case, to remind Him of any merit upon which it can rely. Ver. 26. " *Call to my remembrance; we will strive with one another: tell now, that thou mayst appear just.*" Justification is an *actus forensis* (see ch. i. 18). Justice accuses, and grace acquits. Or has Israel any actual merits, so that Justice would be obliged to pronounce it just? The object to *hazkīrēnī* and *sappēr*, which never have the closed sense of pleading, as Böttcher supposes, is the supposed meritorious works of Israel.

But Israel has no such works; on the contrary, its history has been a string of sins from the very first. Ver. 27. " *Thy first forefather sinned, and thy mediators have fallen away from me.*" By the first forefather, Hitzig, Umbreit, and Knobel understand Adam; but Adam was the forefather of the human race, not of Israel; and the debt of Adam was the debt of mankind, and not of Israel. The reference is to Abraham, as the first of the three from whom the origin and election of Israel were dated; Abraham, whom Israel from the very first had called with pride " our father" (Matt. iii. 9). Even the history of Abraham was stained with sin, and did not shine in the light of meritorious works, but in that of grace, and of faith laying hold of grace. The *m^elītsīm*, interpreters, and mediators generally (2 Chron. xxxii. 31; Job xxxiii. 23), are the prophets and priests, who stood between Jehovah and Israel, and were the medium of intercourse between the two, both in word and deed. They also had for the most part become unfaithful to God, by resorting to ungodly soothsaying and false worship. Hence the sin of Israel was as old as its very earliest origin; and apostasy had spread even among those who ought to have been the best and most godly, because of the office they sustained.

Consequently the all-holy One was obliged to do what had taken place. Ver. 28. " *Then I profaned holy princes, and gave up Jacob to the curse, and Israel to blasphemies.*" וָאֲחַלֵּל might be an imperfect, like וָאֹכַל, " I ate," in ch. xliv. 19, and וָאַבִּיט, " I looked," in ch. lxiii. 5; but וָאֶתְּנָה by the side of it shows that the pointing sprang out of the future interpretation contained in the Targum; so that as the latter is to be rejected, we must substitute וָאֶתְּנָה, וָאֲחַלֵּל (Ges. § 49, 2). The " holy princes" (*sârē qōdesh*) are the hierarchs, as in 1 Chron. xxiv. 5, the supreme spiritual rulers as distinguished from the temporal rulers. The profanation referred to was the fact that they were ruthlessly hurried off into a strange land, where their official labours were necessarily suspended. This was the fate of the leaders of the worship; and the whole nation, which bore the honourable names of Jacob and Israel, was given up to the ban (*chērem*) and the blasphemies (*giddūphīm*) of the nations of the world.

The prophet cannot bear to dwell any longer upon this dark picture of their state of punishment; the light of the promise breaks through again, and in this third field of the fourth prophecy in all the more intensive form. Ch. xliv. 1–4. " *And now hear, O Jacob my servant, and Israel whom I have chosen. Thus saith Jehovah, thy Creator, and thy Former from the womb, who cometh to thy help; Fear not, my servant Jacob; and Jeshurun, whom I have chosen! For I will pour out water upon thirsty ones, and brooks upon the dry ground; will pour out my Spirit upon thy seed, and my blessing upon thine after-growth; and they shoot up among the grass, as willows by flowing waters.*" In contrast with the *chērem, i.e.* the setting apart for destruction, there is here presented the promise of the pouring out of

the Spirit and of blessing; and in contrast with the *gidduphim*,
the promise of general eagerness to come and honour Israel
and its God (ver. 5). The epithets by which Jehovah designates Himself, and those applied to Israel in vers. 1, 2, make
the claim to love all the more urgent and emphatic. The
accent which connects וְיֹצֶרְךָ מִבֶּטֶן, so as to make יָעְזְרֶךָ by itself
an attributive clause like בְּחַרְתִּי בוֹ, is confirmed by ver. 24
and ch. xlix. 5 : Israel as a nation and all the individuals
within it are, as the chosen servant of Jehovah (ch. xlix. 1),
the direct formation of Jehovah Himself from the remotest
point of their history. In ver. 26, *Jeshurun* is used interchangeably with Jacob. This word occurs in three other
passages (viz. Deut. xxxii. 15, xxxiii. 5, 26), and is always
written with *kibbutz*, just as it is here. The rendering Ἰσραελ-
ίσκος in *Gr. Ven.* is founded upon the supposition that the
word is equivalent to יִשְׂרָאֵלֻן,—a strange contraction, which is
inadmissible, if only on account of the substitution of שׂ for שׁ.
The שׂ points back to יָשַׁר, to be straight or even ; hence *A. S.*
Th. εὐθύς (elsewhere εὐθύτατος), Jerome *rectissimus* (though in
Deut. xxxii. 15 he renders it, after the LXX., *dilectus*). It is
an offshoot of יָשֻׁר=יָשָׁר (Ps. xxv. 21), like זְבֻלֻן, יִדְתֻן from זְבֻל,
יָדֻת ; and *ûn* (= *ôn*) does not stamp it as a diminutive (for
אִישׁוֹן, which Kamphausen adduces in opposition to Hengstenberg and Volck, does not stand in the same relation to אִישׁ as
mannikin to man, but rather as the image of a man to a man
himself ; compare the Arabic *insân*). We must not render it
therefore as an affectionate diminutive, as Gesenius does, the
more especially as Jehovah, though speaking in loving terms,
does not adopt the language of a lover. The relation of
Jeshurun to יָשֻׁר is rather the same as that of שְׁלֹמֹה to שָׁלוֹם, so
that the real meaning is " gentleman," or one of gentlemanly
or honourable mind, though this need not appear in the translation, since the very nature of a proper name would obliterate
it. In ver. 3, the blessings to be expected are assigned as the
reason for the exhortation to be of good cheer. In ver. 3*a*
water is promised in the midst of drought, and in ver. 3*b* the
Spirit and blessing of God, just as in Joel the promise of rain
is first of all placed in contrast with drought; and this is followed by the promise of the far surpassing antitype, namely,
the outpouring of the Spirit. There is nothing at variance with

this in the fact that we have not the form צְמֵאָה in the place of
צָמֵא (according to the analogy of עֲיֵפָה אֶרֶץ, צִיָּה, נִלְאָה, Ps. lxviii.
10). By צָמֵא we understand the inhabitants of the land who
are thirsting for rain, and by *yabbâshâh* the parched land itself.
Further on, however, an express distinction is made between the
abundance of water in the land and the prosperous growth of
the nation planted by the side of water-brooks (Ps. i. 3). We
must not regard 3a, therefore, as a figure, and 3b as the explanation, or turn 3a into a simile introduced in the form of a
protasis, although unquestionably water and mountain streams
are made the symbol, or rather the anagogical type, of spiritual
blessings coming down from above in the form of heavenly
gifts, by a gradual ascent from מַיִם and נוֹזְלִים (from נָזַל, to trickle
downwards, Song of Sol. iv. 15, Jer. xviii. 14) to רוּחַ ה׳ and
בִּרְכַּת ה׳ (בִּרְכַּת). When these natural and spiritual waters flow
down upon the people, once more restored to their home, they
spring up among (בְּבֵין only met with here, LXX. and Targum
כְּבֵין) the grass, like willows by water-brooks. The willows [1]

---

[1] "The *garab*," says Wetzstein, "was only met with by me in one locality,
or, at any rate, I only noticed it once, namely in the *Wady So'êb*, near to
a ford of the river which is called the *Hôd* ford, from the *chirbet el-Hôd*, a
miserable ruin not far off. It is half an hour to the west of *Nimrin* (*Nim-
rim*, ch. xv. 6), or, speaking more exactly, half an hour above (*i.e.* to the
east of) *Zafât Nimrîn*, an antique road on the northern bank of the river,
hewn in a precipitous wall of rock, like the ladder of Tyre. I travelled
through the valley in June 1860, and find the following entry in my diary:
'At length the ravine opened up into a broader valley, so that we could
get down to the clear, copious, and rapid stream, and were able to cross
it. Being exhausted by the heat, we lay down near the ford among the
oleanders, which the mass of flowers covered with a rosy glow. The reed
grows here to an unusual height, as in the *Wady Yarmûk*, and willows
(*zafzaf*) and *garab* are mingled together, and form many-branched trees
of three or four fathoms in height. The vegetation, which is fresh and
luxuriant by the water-side, is scorched up with the heat in the valley
within as little as ten paces from the banks of the stream. The farthest
off is the '*osar* plant, with its thick, juicy, dark green stalks and leaves, and
its apple-like fruit, which is of the same colour, and therefore not yet ripe.
The *garab* tree has already done flowering. The leaves of this tree stand
quite close around the stem, as in the case of the *Sindiana* (the Syrian oak),
and, like the leaves of the latter, are fringed with little thorns; but, like
the willow, it is a water plant, and our companions *Abdallah* and *Nasrallah*
assured us that it was only met with near flowing water and in hot low-
lands. Its bunches of flowers are at the points of the slender branches, and

are the nation, which has hitherto resembled withered plants in a barren soil, but is now restored to all the bloom of youth through the Spirit and blessing of God. The grass stands for the land, which resembles a green luxuriant plain; and the water-brooks represent the abundant supply of living waters, which promote the prosperity of the land and its inhabitants.

When Jehovah has thus acknowledged His people once more, the heathen, to whose *gidduphīm* (blasphemies) Israel has hitherto been given up, will count it the greatest honour to belong to Jehovah and His people. Ver. 5. " *One will say, I belong to Jehovah; and a second will solemnly name the name of Jacob; and a third will inscribe himself to Jehovah, and name the name of Israel with honour.*" The threefold *zeh* refers to the heathen, as in Ps. lxxxvii. 4, 5. One will declare himself

assume an umbelliferous form. This is the עֲרָב of the Bible.' Consequently the *garab* or (as *nom. unitatis*) the *garaba* cannot be regarded as a species of willow; and Winer's assumption (*Real- Wörterbuch, s.v. Weiden*), that the weeping willow is intended at any rate in Ps. cxxxvii. 2, is an error. In Arabic the weeping willow is always called *shafshaf mustachi* (the drooping tree). At the same time, we may render עֲרָבִים ' willows,' since the *garab* loves running water as well as the willow, and apparently they seek one another's society; it is quite enough that the difference should be clearly pointed out in the commentary. The reason why the *garab* did not find its way into my herbarium was the following. On my arrival in Salt, I received the first intelligence of the commencement of the slaughter of the Christians on Antilibanus, and heard the report, which was then commonly believed, that a command had been sent from Constantinople to exterminate Christianity from Syria. This alarming report compelled me to inquire into the actual state of affairs; therefore, leaving my luggage and some of my companions behind, I set off with all speed to Jerusalem, where I hoped to obtain reliable information, accompanied by Herr Dörgen, my kavas, and two natives, viz. *Abdallah* the smith, from Salt, and *Nasrallah* the smith, from *Ain Genna*. For a ride like this, which did not form part of the original plan of my journey, everything but weapons, even a herbarium, would have been in the way. Still there are small caravans going every week between Salt and Jerusalem, and they must always cross the *Hôd* ford, so that it would be easy to get a twig of the *garab*. So far as I remember, the remains of the blossom were of a dirty white colour." (Compare vol. i. 328, where we have taken *nachal hâ'ărâbhīm*, according to the meaning of the words, as a synonym of *Wady Sufsaf*, or, more correctly, *Safsâf*. From the description given above, the *garab* is a kind of *viburnum* with indented leaves. This tree, which is of moderate height, is found by the side of streams along with the willow. According to Sprengel (*Gesch. der Botanik*, i. 25), the *safsâf* is the *salix subserrata* of Wildenow).

to belong to Jehovah ; another will call with the name of Jacob,
i.e. (according to the analogy of the phrase קְרָא בְשֵׁם הֹ) make
it the medium and object of solemn exclamation ; a third will
write with his hand (יָדוֹ, an acc. of more precise definition,
like חֵמָה in ch. xlii. 25, and זבחיך in ch. xliii. 23), " To Jehovah,"
thereby attesting that he desires to belong to Jehovah, and
Jehovah alone. This is the explanation given by Gesenius,
Hahn, and others; whereas Hitzig and Knobel follow the LXX.
in the rendering, " he will write upon his hand ' lay῾hŏvâh,' *i.e.*
mark the name of Jehovah upon it." But apart from the fact
that *kâthabh*, with an accusative of the writing materials, would
be unprecedented (the construction required would be עַל־יָדוֹ),
this view is overthrown by the fact that tattooing was prohibited
by the Israelitish law (Lev. xix. 28 ; compare the mark of the
beast in Rev. xiii. 16). קרא בשם is interchanged with כִּנָּה בשם,
to surname, or entitle (the Syriac and Arabic are the same ;
compare the Arabic *kunye*, the name given to a man as the
father of such and such a person, *e.g.* *Abu-Muhammed*, rhetorically called metonymy). The name *Israel* becomes a name or
title of honour among the heathen. This concludes the fourth
prophecy, which opens out into three distinct fields. With
וְעַתָּה in ch. xliv. 1 it began to approach the close, just as the
third did in ch. xliii. 1,—a well-rounded whole, which leaves
nothing wanting.

FIFTH PROPHECY.—Chap. xliv. 6-23.

THE RIDICULOUS GODS OF THE NATIONS ; AND THE GOD OF
ISRAEL, WHO MAKES HIS PEOPLE TO REJOICE.

A new pledge of redemption is given, and a fresh exhortation to trust in Jehovah ; the wretchedness of the idols and
their worshippers being pointed out, in contrast with Jehovah,
the only speaking and acting God. Ver. 6. " *Thus saith
Jehovah the King of Israel, and its Redeemer, Jehovah of hosts ;
I am first, and I last ; and beside me there is no God.*" The
fact that His deity, which rules over not only the natural
world, but history as well, is thus without equal and above
all time, is now proved by Him from the fact that He alone
manifests Himself as God, and that by the utterance of pro-

phecy. Ver. 7. "*And who preaches as I do? Let him make it
known, and show it to me; since I founded the people of ancient
time! And future things, and what is approaching, let them
only make known.*" Jehovah shows Himself as the God of
prophecy since the time that He founded עַם־עוֹלָם (יִקְרָא refers
to the continued preaching of prophecy). *'Am 'ōlâm* is the
epithet applied in Ezek. xxvi. 20 to the people of the dead,
who are sleeping the long sleep of the grave; and here it does
not refer to Israel, which could neither be called an "eternal"
nation, nor a people of the olden time, and which would have
been more directly named; but according to ch. xl. 7 and xlii. 5,
where *'am* signifies the human race, and Job xxii. 15 sqq., where
'ōlâm is the time of the old world before the flood, it signifies
humanity as existing from the very earliest times. The prophecies of Jehovah reach back even to the history of paradise.
The parenthetical clause, "Let him speak it out, and tell it me,"
is like the apodosis of a hypothetical protasis : "if any one
thinks that he can stand by my side." The challenge points to
earlier prophecies; with וְאֹתִיּוֹת it takes a turn to what is future,
אֹתִיּוֹת itself denoting what is absolutely future, according to
ch. xli. 23, and אֲשֶׁר תָּבֹאנָה what is about to be realized immediately; *lâmō* is an ethical dative.

Of course, none of the heathen gods could in any way answer
to the challenge. So much the more confident might Israel be,
seeing that it had quite another God. Ver. 8. "*Despair ye not,
neither tremble : have not I told thee long ago, and made known,
and ye are my witnesses : is there a God beside me? And nowhere
a rock; I know of none.*" The Jewish lexicographers derive תִּרְהוּ
(with the first syllable closed) from רָהָה (רה); whereas modern
lexicographers prefer some of them to read תִּרְהוּ, *tîrᵉhū*, from
יָרַה (Ges., Knobel), and others תִּירָאוּ (Ewald). But the possibility of there being a verb רָהָה, to tremble or fear, cannot for
a moment be doubted when we think of such words as יָרֵא, יָרַע,

compare also راٰ (applied to water moving to and fro). It was

not of the heathen deities that they were directed not to be
afraid, as in Jer. x. 5, but rather the great catastrophe coming
upon the nations, of which Cyrus was the instrument. In the
midst of this, when one nation after another would be overthrown, and its tutelar gods would prove to be worthless, Israel

would have nothing to fear, since its God, who was no dumb idol, had foretold all this, and that indeed long ago (מֵאָז, cf. מֵרֹאשׁ, ch. xli. 26), as they themselves must bear witness.   Prophecies before the captivity had foretold the conquest of Babylon by Medes and Elamites, and the deliverance of Israel from the Babylonian bondage; and even these prophecies themselves were like a spirit's voice from the far distant past, consoling the people of the captivity beforehand, and serving to support their faith.   On the ground of such well-known self-manifestations, Jehovah could well ask, "Is there a God beside me?" —a virtual denial in the form of an interrogation, to which the categorical denial, "There is no rock (i.e. no ground of trust, ch. xxvi. 4, xvii. 10), I know of none (beside me)," is attached.

The heathen gods are so far from being a ground of trust, that all who trust in them must discover with alarm how they have deceived themselves. Vers. 9–11. " *The makers of idols, they are all desolation, and their bosom-children worthless; and those who bear witness for them see nothing and know nothing, that they may be put to shame.   Who hath formed the god, and cast the idol to no profit?   Behold, all its followers will be put to shame; and the workmen are men: let them all assemble together, draw near, be alarmed, be all put to shame together.*"   The *chămūdīm* (favourites) of the makers of idols are the false gods, for whose favour they sue with such earnestness.   If we retain the word הֵמָּה, which is pointed as critically suspicious, and therefore is not accentuated, the explanation might possibly be, " Their witnesses (i.e. witnesses against themselves) are they (the idols) : they see not, and are without consciousness, that they (those who trust in them) may be put to shame."   In any case, the subject to *yēbhōshū* (shall be put to shame) is the worshippers of idols.   If we erase הֵמָּה, עֵדֵיהֶם will be those who come forward as witnesses for the idols.   This makes the words easier and less ambiguous.   At the same time, the Septuagint retains the word (καὶ μάρτυρες αὐτῶν εἰσίν).   As " not seeing" here signifies to be blind, so " not knowing " is also to be understood as a self-contained expression, meaning to be irrational, just as in ch. xlv. 20, lvi. 10 (in ch. i. 3, on the other hand, we have taken it in a different sense).   לְמַעַן implies that the will of the sinner in his sin has also destruction for its object; and this is not something added to the sin, but growing out of it.   The

question in ver. 10 summons the maker of idols for the purpose of announcing his fate, and in לְבִלְתִּי הוֹעִיל (to no profit) this
announcement is already contained. Ver. 11 is simply a development of this expression, " to no profit." יֵצֶר, like נֶטַע in
ver. 14, is contrary to the rhythmical law *milra* which prevails
elsewhere. חֲבֵרָיו (its followers) are not the fellow-workmen of
the maker of idols (inasmuch as in that case the maker himself
would be left without any share in the threat), but the associates
(*i.e.* followers) of the idols (Hos. iv. 17; 1 Cor. x. 20). It is a
pernicious work that they have thus had done for them. And
what of the makers themselves ? They are numbered among
the men. So that they who ought to know that they are
made by God, become makers of gods themselves. What an
absurdity ! Let them crowd together, the whole guild of god-
makers, and draw near to speak to the works they have made.
All their eyes will soon be opened with amazement and alarm.

The prophet now conducts us into the workshops. Vers.
12, 13. " *The iron-smith has a chisel, and works with red-hot
coals, and shapes it with hammers, and works it with his powerful
arm. He gets hungry thereby, and his strength fails; if he
drink no water, he becomes exhausted. The carpenter draws the
line, marks it with the pencil, carries it out with planes, and
makes a drawing of it with the compass, and carries it out like
the figure of a man, like the beauty of a man, which may dwell
in the house.*" The two words *chârash barzel* are connected
together in the sense of *faber ferrarius*, as we may see from
the expression *chârash 'ētsīm* (the carpenter, *faber lignarius*),
which follows in ver. 13. *Chârash* is the construct of *chârâsh*
(= *charrâsh*), as in Ex. xxviii. 11. The second *kametz* of this
form of noun does indeed admit of contraction, but only to the
extent of a full short vowel ; consequently the construct of the
plural is not חָרְשֵׁי, but חָרָשֵׁי (ch. xlv. 16, etc.). Hence ver. 12
describes how the smith constructs an idol of iron, ver. 13 how
the carpenter makes one of wood. But the first clause, חָרַשׁ בַּרְזֶל
מַעֲצָד, is enigmatical. In any case, מַעֲצָד is a smith's tool of some
kind (from עָצַד, related to חָצַד). And consequently Gesenius,
Umbreit, and others, adopt the rendering, " the smith an axe,
that does he work, . . . ;" but the further account of the origin
of an idol says nothing at all about this axe, which the smith
supplies to the carpenter, that he may hew out an idol with it.

Hitzig renders it, " The smith, a hatchet does he work, and forms it (viz. into an idol) ;" but what a roundabout way ! first to make a hatchet and then make it into an idol, which would look very slim when made. Knobel translates it, " As for the cutting-smith, he works it ;" but this guild of cutting-smiths certainly belongs to Utopia. The best way to render the sentence intelligible, would be to supply לוֹ : " The smith has (uses) the *maʻătsâd*." But in all probability a word has dropped out; and the Septuagint rendering, ὅτι ὤξυνεν τέκτων σίδηρον σκεπάρνῳ εἰργάσατο, κ.τ.λ., shows that the original reading of the text was חדד חרש ברזל מעצד, and that חדד got lost on account of its proximity to יחד. The meaning therefore is, " The smith has sharpened, or sharpens (*chiddēd*, syn. *shinnēn*) the *maʻătsâd*," possibly the chisel, to cut the iron upon the anvil; and works with red-hot coals, making the iron red-hot by blowing the fire. The piece of iron which he cuts off is the future idol, and this he shapes with hammers (יִצְּרֵהוּ, the future of יָצַר). And what of the carpenter ? He stretches the line upon the block of wood, to measure the length and breadth of the idol; he marks it. upon the wood with red-stone (*sered, rubrica*, used by carpenters), and works it with planes (*maqtsuʻōth*, a feminine form of מַקְצוֹעַ, from קָצַע, to cut off, pare off, plane ; compare the Arabic *miktaʻ*), and with the compasses (*mᵉchūgâh*, the tool used, *lâchūg*, *i.e.* for making a circle) he draws the outline of it, that is to say, in order that the different parts of the body may be in right proportion ; and he constructs it in such a manner that it acquires the shape of a man, the beautiful appearance of a man, to be set up like a human inmate in either a temple or private house. The *piel* תֵּאֵר (תִּאַר), from which comes yᵉtăărēhū, is varied here (according to Isaiah's custom ; cf. ch. xxix. 7, xxvi. 5) with the *poel* תֹּאֵר, which is to be understood as denoting the more exact configuration. The preterites indicate the work for which both smith and carpenter have made their preparations ; the futures, the work in which they are engaged.

The prophet now traces the origin of the idols still further back. Their existence or non-existence ultimately depends upon whether it rains or not. Vers. 14–17. " *One prepares to cut down cedars, and takes holm and oak-tree, and chooses for himself among the trees of the forest. He has planted a fig, and the rain draws it up. And it serves the man for firing: he takes thereof, and warms himself; he also heats, and bakes bread; he also works it into a god, and prostrates himself; makes an idol of it, and falls down before it. The half of it he has burned in the fire: over the half of it he eats flesh, roasts a roast, and is satisfied; he also warms himself, and says, Hurrah, 1 am getting warm, I feel the heat. And the rest of it he makes into a god, into his idol, and says, Save me, for thou art my god."* The subject of the sentence is not the carpenter of the previous verse, but " any one." אֲרָזִים apparently stands first, as indicating the species; and in the Talmud and Midrash the trees named are really described as מיני ארזים. But *tirzâh* (from *târaz*, to be hard or firm) does not appear to be a coniferous tree; and the connection with *'allōn*, the oak, is favourable to the rendering ἀγριοβάλανος (LXX., A. Th.), *ilex* (Vulg.). On *'immēts*, to choose, see ch. xli. 10. אֹרֶן (with *Nun minusculum*), plur. אֲרוֹנִים (*b. Ros-ha Sana* 23*a*) or אֲרָנִים (*Para* iii. 8), is explained by the Talmud as עָרִי, sing. עָרָא, *i.e.* according to Aruch and Rashi, *laurier*, the berries of which are called *baies.* We have rendered it *" fig,"* according to the LXX. and Jerome, since it will not do to follow the seductive guidance of the similarity in sound to *ornus* (which is hardly equivalent to ὀρεινός).[1] The description is genealogical, and therefore moves retrogressively, from the felling to the planting. וְהָיָה in ver. 15*a* refers to the felled and planted tree, and primarily to the ash. מֵהֶם (of such as these) is neuter, as in ch. xxx. 6; at the same time, the prophet had the עֵצִים (the wood, both as produce and material) in his mind. The repeated אַף lays emphasis upon the fact, that such different things are done with the very same wood. It is used for warming, and for the preparation of food, as well as for making a god. On the verbs of adoration, *hishtachăvâh* (root *shach*, to sink, to settle down) and *sâgad*, which is only applied to idolatrous worship, and from which *mes'gid*, a mosque, is derived, see Holemann's *Bibelstudien*, i. 3. לָמוֹ may no doubt be taken as a plural (= לָהֶם, as in ch. xxx. 5), " such things (*talia*) does he worship," as Stier supposes; but it is probably pathetic, and equivalent to

---

[1] The ἀπία of Theophrastus is probably *quercus ilex*, which is still called ἀριά; the *laurus nobilis* is now called βαϊνά, from the branches which serve instead of palm-branches.

לֹ, as in ch. liii. 8 (compare Ps. xi. 7; Ewald, § 247, *a*). According to the double application of the wood mentioned in ver. 15, a distinction is drawn in vers. 16, 17 between the one half of the wood and the other. The repeated *chetsyō* (the half of it) in ver. 16 refers to the first half, which furnishes not only fuel for burning, but shavings and coals for roasting and baking as well. And as a fire made for cooking warms quite as much as one made expressly for the purpose, the prophet dwells upon this benefit which the wood of the idol does confer. On the tone upon the last syllable of *chammōthī*, see at Job xix. 17; and on the use of the word רָאָה as a comprehensive term, embracing every kind of sensation and perception, see my *Psychologie*, p. 234. Diagoras of Melos, a pupil of Democritus, once threw a wooden standing figure of Hercules into the fire, and said jocularly, " Come now, Hercules, perform thy thirteenth labour, and help me to cook the turnips."

So irrational is idolatry; but yet, through self-hardening, they have fallen under the judgment of hardness of heart (ch. vi. 9, 10, xix. 3, xxix. 10), and have been given up to a reprobate mind (Rom. i. 28). Vers. 18, 19. " *They perceive not, and do not understand: for their eyes are smeared over, so that they do not see; their hearts, so that they do not understand. And men take it not to heart, no perception and no understanding, that men should say, The half of it I have burned in the fire, and also baked bread upon the coals thereof; roasted flesh, and eaten: and ought I to make the rest of it an abomination, to fall down before the produce of a tree?*" Instead of טָח, Lev. xiv. 42, the third person is written טַח (from *tâchach*, Ges. § 72, Anm. 8) in a circumstantial sense: their eyes are, as it were, smeared over with plaster. The expression הֵשִׁיב אֶל־לֵב or עַל־לֵב (ch. xlvi. 8), literally to carry back into the heart, which we find as well as שִׂים עַל־לֵב, to take to heart (ch. xlii. 25), answers exactly to the idea of reflection, here with reference to the immense contrast between a piece of wood and the Divine Being. The second and third לֹא in ver. 19 introduce substantive clauses, just as verbal clauses are introduced by וְאֵין. לֵאמֹר is used in the same manner as in ch. ix. 8: "perception and insight showing themselves in their saying." On *būl*, see Job xl. 20; the meaning " block " cannot be established: the talmudic *būl*, a lump or piece, which Ewald adduces, is the Greek βῶλος.

This exposure of the infatuation of idolatry closes with an epiphonem in the form of a gnome (cf. ch. xxvi. 7, 10). Ver. 20. "*He who striveth after ashes, a befooled heart has led him astray, and he does not deliver his soul, and does not think, Is there not a lie in my right hand?*" We have here a complete and self-contained sentence, which must not be broken up in the manner proposed by Knobel, "He hunts after ashes; his heart is deceived," etc. He who makes ashes, *i.e.* things easily scattered, perishable, and worthless, the object of his effort and striving (compare *rūăch* in Hos. xii. 2), has been led astray from the path of truth and salvation by a heart overpowered by delusion; he is so certain, that he does not think of saving his soul, and it never occurs to him to say, "Is there not a lie in my right hand?" All that belongs to idolatry is *sheqer*—a fabrication and a lie. רָעָה means primarily to pasture or tend, hence to be concerned about, to strive after. הוּתַל is an attributive, from *tâlal* = *hâthal*, *ludere*, *ludificare* (see at ch. xxx. 10).

The second half of the prophecy commences with ver. 21. It opens with an admonition. Ver. 21. "*Remember this, Jacob and Israel; for thou art my servant: I have formed thee; thou art servant to me, O Israel: thou art not forgotten by me.*" The thing to which the former were blind, — namely, that idolatry is a lie,—Jacob was to have firmly impressed upon its mind. The words "and Israel," which are attached, are a contraction for "and remember this, O Israel" (compare the vocatives after *Vâv* in Prov. viii. 5 and Joel ii. 23). In the reason assigned, the tone rests upon *my* in the expression "my servant," and for this reason "servant to me" is used interchangeably with it. Israel is the servant of Jehovah, and as such it was formed by Jehovah; and therefore reverence was due to Him, and Him alone. The words which follow are rendered by the LXX., Targum, Jerome, and Luther as though they read לֹא תִנָּשֵׁנִי, though Hitzig regards the same rendering as admissible even with the reading תִנָּשֵׁנִי, inasmuch as the *niphal* נָשָׁה has the middle sense of ἐπιλανθάνεσθαι, *oblivisci*. But it cannot be shown that *nizkar* is ever used in the analogous sense of μιμνήσκεσθαι, *recordari*. The *niphal*, which was no doubt originally reflective, is always used in Hebrew to indicate simply the passive endurance of something which originated with the subject of the action referred to, so that *nisshâh* could only signify "to forget one's self." We must indeed admit the possibility of the meaning "to forget one's self" having passed into the meaning "to be forgetful," and this into the meaning "to forget." The Aramæan אִתְנְשִׁי also signifies to be forgotten and (with an accent following) to forget, and the connection with an objective suffix has a support in וַיִּלְחָמוּנִי in Ps. cix. 3. But the latter is really equivalent to וילחמו אתּי, so that it may be adduced with equal propriety in support of the other rendering, according to which תִּנָּשֵׁנִי is equivalent to תנשה לי (Ges., Umbr., Ewald, Stier). There are many examples of this brachyological use of the suffix (Ges. § 121, 4), so that this rendering is certainly the safer of the two. It also suits the context quite as well as the former, "Oh, forget me not;" the assurance "thou wilt not be forgotten by me" (compare ch. xlix. 15 and the lamentation of Israel in ch. xl. 27) being immediately followed by an announcement of the act of love, by which the declaration is most gloriously confirmed.—Ver. 22. "*I have blotted out thy transgressions as a mist, and thy sins as clouds: return to me; for I have redeemed thee.*" We have adopted the rendering "mist" merely because we have no synonym to "cloud;" we have not translated it "thick cloud," because the idea of darkness, thickness, or opacity, which is the one immediately suggested by the word, had become almost entirely lost (see ch. xxv. 5). Moreover, עָב קַל is evidently intended here (see ch. xix. 1), inasmuch as the point of comparison is not the dark, heavy multitude of sins, but the facility and rapidity with which they are expunged. Whether we connect with מָחִיתִי the idea of a stain, as in Ps. li. 3, 11, or that of a debt entered in a ledger, as in Col. ii. 14, and as we explained it in ch. xliii. 25 (cf. *mâchâh*, Ex. xxxii. 32, 33), in any case sin is regarded as something standing between God and man, and impeding or disturbing the intercourse between them. This Jehovah clears away, just as when His wind sweeps away the clouds, and restores the blue sky again (Job xxvi. 13). Thus does God's free grace now interpose at the very time when Israel thinks He has forgotten it, blotting out Israel's sin, and proving this by redeeming it from a state of punishment. What an evangelical sound the preaching of the Old Testament evangelist has in this passage also! Forgiveness and redemption are not offered on condition of conversion, but the mercy of God comes to Israel in direct contrast to what its works deserve, and Israel is merely called upon to reciprocate this by conversion and renewed obedience. The perfects denote that which has essentially taken place. Jehovah has blotted out Israel's sin, inasmuch as He does not impute it any more, and thus has redeemed Israel. All that yet remains is the outward manifestation of this redemption, which is already accomplished in the counsel of God.

There is already good ground, therefore, for exuberant rejoicing; and the reply of the church to these words of divine consolation is as follows : Ver. 23. " *Exult, O heavens; for Jehovah hath accomplished it : shout, ye depths of the earth; break out, ye mountains, into exulting; thou forest, and all the wood therein : for Jehovah hath redeemed Jacob, and He showeth Himself glorious upon Israel.*" All creation is to rejoice in the fact that Jehovah has completed what He purposed, that He has redeemed His people, and henceforth will show Himself glorious in them. The heavens on high are to exult; also the depths of the earth, *i.e.* not Hades, which would be opposed to the prevailing view of the Old Testament (Ps. lxvi., cf. lxxxviii. 13), but the interior of the earth, with its caves, its pits, and its deep abysses (see Ps. cxxxix. 15) ; and the mountains and woods which rise up from the earth towards heaven— all are to unite in the exultation of the redeemed : for the redemption that is being accomplished in man will extend its effects in all directions, even to the utmost limits of the natural world.

This exulting finale is a safe boundary-stone of this fifth prophecy. It opened with "Thus saith the Lord," and the sixth opens with the same.

SIXTH PROPHECY.—Chap. xliv. 24–xlv.

CYRUS, THE ANOINTED OF JEHOVAH, AND DELIVERER OF ISRAEL.

The promise takes a new turn here, acquiring greater and greater speciality. It is introduced as the word of Jehovah, who first gave existence to Israel, and has not let it go to ruin.

Vers. 24-28. " *Thus saith Jehovah, thy Redeemer, and He that formed thee from the womb, I Jehovah am He that accomplisheth all; who stretched out the heavens alone, spread out the earth by Himself; who bringeth to nought the signs of the prophets of lies, and exposeth the soothsayers as raging mad; who turneth back the wise men, and maketh their science folly; who realizeth the word of His servant, and accomplisheth the prediction of His messengers; who saith to Jerusalem, She shall be inhabited! and to the cities of Judah, They shall be built, and their ruins I raise up again! who saith to the whirlpool, Dry up; and I dry its streams! who saith to Koresh, My shepherd and he will perform all my will; and will say to Jerusalem, She shall be built, and the temple founded!*" The prophecy which commences with ver. 24a is carried on through this group of verses in a series of participial predicates to אָנֹכִי (I). Jehovah is *'ōseh kōl*, accomplishing all (*perficiens omnia*), so that there is nothing that is not traceable to His might and wisdom as the first cause. It was He who alone, without the co-operation of any other being, stretched out the heavens, who made the earth into a wide plain by Himself, *i.e.* so that it proceeded from Himself alone: מֵאִתִּי, as in Josh. xi. 20 (compare מִנִּי, ch. xxx. 1; and *mimmennī* in Hos. viii. 4), *chethib* מִי אִתִּי, "who was with me," or "who is it beside me?" The Targum follows the *keri*; the Septuagint the *chethib*, attaching it to the following words, τίς ἕτερος διασκεδάσει. Ver. 25 passes on from Him whom creation proves to be God, to Him who is proving Himself to be so in history also, and that with obvious reference to the Chaldean soothsayers and wise men (ch. xlvii. 9, 10), who held out to proud Babylon the most splendid and hopeful prognostics. " *Who brings to nought (mēphēr, opp. mēqīm) the signs,*" *i.e.* the marvellous proofs of their divine mission which the false prophets adduced by means of fraud and witchcraft. The LXX. render *baddīm*, ἐγγαστριμύθων, Targ. *bīdīn* (in other passages = *'ōb*, Lev. xx. 27; *'ōbōth*, Lev. xix. 31; hence = πύθων, πύθωνες). At ch. xvi. 6 and Job xi. 3 we have derived it as a common noun from בְּרָה = בָּטָא, to speak at random; but it is possible that בְּרָה may originally have signified to produce or bring forth, without any reference to βαττολογεῖν, then to invent, to fabricate, so that *baddīm* as a personal name (as in Jer. l. 36) would be synonymous with

baddâ'îm, mendaces. On *qōsᵉmîm,* see ch. iii. 2 (vol. i. 131); on
yᵉhōlēl, Job xii. 17, where it occurs in connection with a similar
predicative description of God according to His works. In
ver. 26 a contrast is drawn between the heathen soothsayers
and wise men, and the servant and messengers of Jehovah,
whose word, whose *'ētsâh, i.e.* determination or disclosure concerning the future (cf. *yâ'ats,* ch. xli. 28), he realizes and perfectly fulfils. By "his servant" we are to understand Israel
itself, according to ch. xlii. 19, but only relatively, namely, as
the bearer of the prophetic word, and therefore as the kernel
of Israel regarded from the standpoint of the prophetic mission
which it performed; and consequently "his messengers" are
the prophets of Jehovah who were called out of Israel. The
singular "his servant" is expanded in "his messenger" into
the plurality embraced in the one idea. This is far more
probable than that the author of these prophetic words, who
only speaks of himself in a roundabout manner even in ch. xl.
6, should here refer directly to himself (according to ch. xx. 3).
In ver. 26b the predicates become special prophecies, and hence
their outward limits are also defined. As we have תּוּשֵׁב and
not תּוּשְׁבִי, we must adopt the rendering *habitetur* and *œdificentur,*
with which the continuation of the latter *et vastata ejus erigam*
agrees. In ver. 27 the prophecy moves back from the restoration of Jerusalem and the cities of Judah to the conquest of
Babylon. The expression calls to mind the drying up of the
Red Sea (ch. li. 10, xliii. 16); but here it relates to something
future, according to ch. xlii. 15, l. 2,—namely, to the drying up
of the Euphrates, which Cyrus turned into the enlarged basin
of Sepharvaim, so that the water sank to the depth of a single
foot, and men could "go through on foot" (Herod. i. 191).
But in the complex view of the prophet, the possibility of the
conqueror's crossing involved the possibility of the exiles' departing from the prison of the imperial city, which was surrounded
by a natural and artificial line of waters (ch. xi. 15). צוּלָה
(from צול = צָלַל, to whiz or whirl) refers to the Euphrates,
just as *mᵉtsūlâh* in Job xli. 23, Zech. x. 11, does to the Nile;
נְתָרֹתֶיהָ is used in the same sense as the Homeric Ὠκεάνοιο
ῥέεθρα. In ver. 28 the special character of the promise reaches
its highest shoot. The deliverer of Israel is mentioned by
name: "That saith to Koresh, My shepherd (*i.e.* a ποιμὴν

λαῶν appointed by me), and he who performs all my will"
(*chēphets*, θέλημα, not in the generalized sense of πρᾶγμα), and
that inasmuch as he (Cyrus) saith to (or of) Jerusalem, It shall
be built (*tibbâneh*, not the second pers. *tibbânī*), and the foundation of the temple laid (*hēkhâl* a masculine elsewhere, here a
feminine). This is the passage which is said by Josephus to
have induced Cyrus to send back the Jews to their native land:
" Accordingly, when Cyrus read this, and admired the divine
power, an earnest desire and ambition seized upon him to fulfil
what was so written" (Jos. *Ant.* xi. 2). According to Ctesias
and others, the name of Cyrus signifies the sun. But all that
can really be affirmed is, that it sounds like the name of the
sun. For in Neo-Pers. the sun is called *chår*, in Zendic *hvarĕ*
(*karĕ*), and from this proper names are formed, such as *chårs'îd*
(Sunshine, also the Sun) ; but Cyrus is called *Kuru* or *Khuru*
upon the monuments, and this cannot possibly be connected
with our *chur*, which would be *uwara* in Old Persian (Rawlinson, Lassen, Spiegel), and *Kōresh* is simply the name of *Kuru*
(Κῦρ-ος) Hebraized after the manner of a segholate. There is
a marble-block, for example, in the Murghab valley, not far
from the mausoleum of Cyrus, which contained the golden
coffin with the body of the king (see Strabo, xv. 3, 7) ; and on
this we find an inscription that we also meet with elsewhere,
viz. *adam. k'ur'us. khsâya | thiya. hakhâmanisiya, i.e.* I am Kuru
the, king of the Achæmenides.[1] This name is identical with
the name of the river *Kur* (Κῦρος; see i. 393, note) ; and what
Strabo says is worthy of notice,—namely, that "there is also a
river called Cyrus, which flows through the so-called cave of
Persis near Pasargadæ, and whence the king took his name,
changing it from Agradates into Cyrus" (Strab. xv. 3, 6). It
is possible also that there may be some connection between the
name and the Indian princely title of *Kuru*.

The first strophe of the first half of this sixth prophecy

---

[1] See the engraving of this tomb of Cyrus, which is now called the
" Tomb of Solomon's mother," in Vaux's *Nineveh and Persepolis* (p. 345).
On the identity of *Murghâb* and *Pasargadæ*, see Spiegel, *Keil-inschriften*,
pp. 71, 72 ; and with regard to the discovery of inscriptions that may still
be expected around the tomb of Cyrus, the *Journal of the Asiatic Society*,
x. 46, note 4 (also compare Spiegel's *Geschichte der Entzifferung der Keil-
schrift, im " Ausland,"* 1865, p. 413).

(ch. xliv. 24 sqq.), the subject of which is Cyrus, the predicted
restorer of Jerusalem, of the cities of Judah, and of the
temple, is now followed by a second strophe (ch. xlv. 1–8),
having for its subject Cyrus, the man through whose irresistible career of conquest the heathen would be brought to
recognise the power of Jehovah, so that heavenly blessings
would come down upon the earth.   The naming of the great
shepherd of the nations, and the address to him, are continued
in ch. xlv. 1–3 : " *Thus saith Jehovah to His anointed, to Koresh,*
whom I have taken by his right hand to subdue nations before
him ; and the loins of kings I ungird, to open before him doors
and gates, that they may not continue shut.   I shall go before
thee, and level what is heaped up : gates of brass shall I break
in pieces, and bolts of iron shall I smite to the ground.   And I
shall give thee treasures of darkness, and jewels of hidden places,
that thou mayest know that I Jehovah am He who called out
thy name, (even) *the God of Israel.*"   The words addressed to
Cyrus by Jehovah commence in ver. 2, but promises applying
to him force themselves into the introduction, being evoked by
the mention of his name.   He is the only king of the Gentiles
whom Jehovah ever calls *mᵉshīchī* (my anointed ; LXX. τῷ
χριστῷ μου).   The fundamental principle of the politics of
the empire of the world was all-absorbing selfishness.   But the
politics of Cyrus were pervaded by purer motives, and this
brought him eternal honour.   The very same thing which the
spirit of Darius, the father of Xerxes, is represented as saying
of him in the *Persæ* of Æschylus (v. 735), Θεὸς γὰρ οὐκ
ἤχθησεν, ὡς εὔφρων ἔφυ (for he was not hateful to God, because he was well-disposed), is here said by the Spirit of revelation, which by no means regards the virtues of the heathen
as *splendida vitia.*   Jehovah has taken him by his right hand,
to accomplish great things through him while supporting him
thus.   (On the inf. *rad* for *rōd*, from *rādad,* to tread down,
see Ges. § 67, Anm. 3.)   The dual *dᵉlâthaim* has also a plural
force : " double doors " (*fores*) in great number, viz. those of
palaces.   After the two infinitives, the verb passes into the
finite tense : " loins of kings I ungird " (*discingo ; pittēăch,*
which refers primarily to the loosening of a fastened garment,
is equivalent to depriving of strength).   The gates—namely,
those of the cities which he storms—will not be shut, *sc.* in

perpetuity, that is to say, they will have to open to him.
Jerome refers here to the account given of the elder Cyrus
in Xenophon's *Cyropædia*. A general picture may no doubt
be obtained from this of his success in war; but particular
statements need support from other quarters, since it is only a
historical romance. Instead of אוֹשֵׁר (אוֹשֵׁר?) in ver. 2, the *keri*
has אֲיַשֵּׁר; just as in Ps. v. 9 it has הַיְשַׁר instead of הוֹשֵׁר. A
hiphil הוֹשִׁיר cannot really be shown to have existed, and the
abbreviated future form אוֹשֵׁר would be altogether without
ground or object here. הֲדוּרִים (*tumida;* like נְעִימִים, *amœna*,
and others) is meant to refer to the difficulties piled up in the
conqueror's way. The "*gates of brass*" (*nᵉdhūshāh*, brazen,
poetical for *nᵉchōsheth*, brass, as in the derivative passage, Ps.
cvii. 16) and "*bolts of iron*" remind one more especially of
Babylon with its hundred "brazen gates," the very posts and
lintels of which were also of brass (Herod. i. 179); and the
treasures laid up in deep darkness and *jewels* preserved in
hiding-places, of the riches of Babylon (Jer. l. 37, li. 13), and
especially of those of the Lydian Sardes, "the richest city of
Asia after Babylon" (*Cyrop.* vii. 2, 11), which Cyrus conquered first. On the treasures which Cyrus acquired through
his conquests, and to which allusion is made in the *Persæ* of
Æschylus, v. 327 ("O Persian, land and harbour of many
riches thou"), see Plin. *h. n.* xxxiii. 2. Brerewood estimates
the quantity of gold and silver mentioned there as captured by
him at no less than £126,224,000 sterling. And all this success is given to him by Jehovah, that he may know that it is
Jehovah the God of Israel who has called out with his name,
i.e. called out his name, or called him to be what he is, and as
what he shows himself to be.

A second and third object are introduced by a second and
third לְמַעַן. Vers. 4–7. "*For the sake of my servant Jacob, and
Israel my chosen, I called thee hither by name, surnamed thee
when thou knewest me not. I Jehovah, and there is none else,
beside me no God: I equipped thee when thou knewest me not;
that they may know from the rising of the sun, and its going
down, that there is none without me: I Jehovah, and there is
none else, former of the light, and creator of the darkness;
founder of peace, and creator of evil: I Jehovah am He who
worketh all this.*" The וָאֶקְרָא which follows the second reason

assigned like an apodosis, is construed doubly : "I called to thee, calling thee by name." The parallel אֲכַנְּךָ refers to such titles of honour as "my shepherd" and "my anointed," which had been given to him by Jehovah. This calling, distinguishing, and girding, *i.e.* this equipment of Cyrus, took place at a time when Cyrus knew nothing as yet of Jehovah, and by this very fact Jehovah made known His sole Deity. The meaning is, not that it occurred while he was still worshipping false gods, but, as the *refrain*-like repetition of the words "though thou hast not known me" affirms with strong emphasis, before he had been brought into existence, or could know anything of Jehovah. The passage is to be explained in the same way as Jer. i. 5, "Before I formed thee in the womb, I knew thee" (see *Psychol.* pp. 36, 37, 39) ; and what the God of prophecy here claims for Himself, must not be questioned by false criticism, or weakened down by false apologetics (*i.e.* by giving up the proper name *Cyrus* as a gloss in ch. xliv. 28 and xlv. 1 ; or generalizing it into a king's name, such as Pharaoh, Abimelech, or Agag). The third and last object of this predicted and realized success of the oppressor of nations and deliverer of Israel is the acknowledgment of Jehovah, spreading over the heathen world from the rising and setting of the sun, *i.e.* in every direction. The *ah* of וּמִמַּעֲרָבָה is not a feminine termination (LXX., Targ., Jer.), but a feminine suffix with *He raphato pro mappic* (Kimchi) ; compare ch. xxiii. 17, 18, xxxiv. 17 (but not נְצָה in ch. xviii. 5, or מוּסָדָה in ch. xxx. 32).

Shemesh (the sun) is a feminine here, as in Gen. xv. 17, Nah. iii. 17, Mal. iii. 20, and always in Arabic ; for the west is invariably called מַעֲרָב (Arab. *magrib*). In ver. 7 we are led by the context to understand by darkness and evil the penal judgments, through which light and peace, or salvation, break forth for the people of God and the nations generally. But as the prophecy concerning Cyrus closes with this self-assertion of Jehovah, it is unquestionably a natural supposition that there is also a contrast implied to the dualistic system of Zarathustra, which divided the one nature of the Deity into two opposing powers (see Windischmann, *Zoroastrische Studien*, p. 135). The declaration is so bold, that Marcion appealed to this passage as a proof that the God of the Old Testament was

a different being from the God of the New, and not the God
of goodness only. The Valentinians and other gnostics also
regarded the words "There is no God beside me" in Isaiah,
as deceptive words of the Demiurgus. The early church met
them with Tertullian's reply, "*de his creator profitetur malis
quæ congruunt judici,*" and also made use of this self-attestation
of the God of revelation as a weapon with which to attack
Manicheeism. The meaning of the words is not exhausted by
those who content themselves with the assertion, that by the
evil (or *darkness*) we are not to understand the evil of guilt
(*malum culpæ*), but the evil of punishment (*malum pœnæ*).
Undoubtedly, evil as an act is not the direct working of God,
but the spontaneous work of a creature endowed with freedom.
At the same time, evil, as well as good, has in this sense its
origin in God,—that He combines within Himself the first
principles of love and wrath, the possibility of evil, the self-
punishment of evil, and therefore the consciousness of guilt as
well as the evil of punishment in the broadest sense. When
the apostle celebrates the glory of free grace in Rom. ix. 11
sqq., he stands on that giddy height, to which few are able
to follow him without falling headlong into the false conclu-
sions of a *decretum absolutum,* and the denial of all creaturely
freedom.

In the prospect of this ultimate and saving purpose of the
mission of Cyrus, viz. the redemption of Israel and the conversion of the heathen, heaven and earth are now summoned to
bring forth and pour down spiritual blessings in heavenly gifts,
according to the will and in the power of Jehovah, who has in
view a new spiritual creation. Ver. 8. "*Cause to trickle down,
ye heavens above, and let the blue sky rain down righteousness;
let the earth open, and let salvation blossom, and righteousness;
let them sprout together: I Jehovah have created it.*" What the
heavens are to cause to trickle down, follows as the object to
יַזִּלוּ. And what is to flower when the earth opens (*pâthach* as
in Ps. cvi. 17; compare *aprilis* and the Neo-Greek *anoixis,*
spring), is salvation and righteousness. But *tzedek* (righteousness) is immediately afterwards the object of a new verb; so
that יֵשַׁע וּצְדָקָה, which are thought of as combined, as the word
יַחַד (together) shows, are uncoupled in the actual expression.
Knobel expresses a different opinion, and assumes that יֵשַׁע is

regarded as a collective noun, and therefore construed with a plural, like אִמְרָה in Ps. cxix. 103, and חֶמְדָּה in Hag. ii. 7. But the use of *yachad* (together) favours the other interpretation. The suffix of בְּרָאתִיו points to this fulness of righteousness and salvation. It is a creation of Jehovah Himself. Heaven and earth, when co-operating to effect this, are endowed with their capacity through Him from whom cometh every good and perfect gift, and obey now, as at the first, His creative fiat. This "*rorate cœli desuper et nubes pluant justum,*" as the Vulgate renders it, is justly regarded as an old advent cry.

The promise is now continued in a third strophe (ch. xlv. 9–13), and increases more and more in the distinctness of its terms; but just as in ch. xxix. 15-21, it opens with a reproof of that pusillanimity (ch. xl. 27; cf. ch. li. 13, xlix. 24, lviii. 3), which goes so far to complain of the ways of Jehovah. Vers. 9, 10. "*Woe to him that quarrelleth with his Maker—a pot among the pots of earthenware? Can the clay indeed say to him that shapeth it, What makest thou? and thy work, He hath no hands? Woe to him that saith to his father, What begettest thou? and to the woman, What bringest thou forth?*" The comparison drawn between a man as the work of God and the clay-work of a potter suggested itself all the more naturally, inasmuch as the same word *yōtsēr* was applied to God as Creator, and also to a potter (*figulus*). The word *cheres* signifies either a sherd, or fragment of earthenware (ch. xxx. 14), or an earthenware vessel (Jer. xix. 1; Prov. xxvi. 23). In the passage before us, where the point of comparison is not the fragmentary condition, but the earthen character of the material (*'adâmâh*), the latter is intended: the man, who complains of God, is nothing but a vessel of clay, and, more than that, a perishable vessel among many others of the very same kind.[1] The questions which follow are meant to show the folly of this complaining. Can it possibly occur to the clay to raise a complaint against him who has it in hand, that he has formed it in such and such a manner, or for such and such a purpose (compare Rom. ix. 20, "Why hast thou made me thus")? To the words "or thy work" we must supply *num dicet* (shall it

---

[1] The Septuagint reads *shin* for *sin* in both instances, and introduces here the very unsuitable thought already contained in ch. xxviii. 24, "Shall the ploughman plough the land the whole day?"

say); *pōʻal* is a manufacture, as in ch. i. 31. The question is addressed to the maker, as those in ch. vii. 25 are to the husbandman: Can the thing made by thee, O man, possibly say in a contemptuous tone, "He has no hands?"—a supposition the ridiculous absurdity of which condemns it at once; and yet it is a very suitable analogy to the conduct of the man who complains of God. In ver. 10 a woe is denounced upon those who resemble a man who should say to his own father, What children dost thou beget? or to a wife, What dost thou bring forth? (*tᵉchīlīn* an emphatic, and for the most part pausal, *fut. parag.*, as in Ruth ii. 8, iii. 18.) This would be the rudest and most revolting attack upon an inviolably tender and private relation; and yet Israel does this when it makes the hidden providential government of its God the object of expostulation.

After this double woe, which is expressed in general terms, but the application of which is easily made, the words of Jehovah are directly addressed to the presumptuous criticizers. Ver. 11. "*Thus saith Jehovah, the Holy One of Israel, and its Maker, Ask me what is to come; let my sons and the work of my hands be committed to me!*" The names by which He calls Himself express His absolute blamelessness, and His absolute right of supremacy over Israel. שְׁאָלוּנִי is an imperative, like שְׁמָעֵנִי in Gen. xxiii. 8; the third person would be written שְׁאָלֻנִי. The meaning is: If ye would have any information or satisfaction concerning the future ("things to come," ch. xli. 23, xliv. 7), about which ye can neither know nor determine anything of yourselves, inquire of me. צִוָּה with an accusative of the person, and עַל of the thing, signifies to commit anything to the care of another (1 Chron. xxii. 12). The fault-finders in Israel were to leave the people of whom Jehovah was the Maker (a retrospective allusion to vers. 10 and 9), in the hands of Him who has created everything, and on whom everything depends. Ver. 12. "*I, I have made the earth, and created men upon it; I, my hands have stretched out the heavens, and all their host have I called forth.*" אֲנִי יָדַי, according to Ges. § 121, 3, is equivalent to my hands, and mine alone,— a similar arrangement of words to those in Gen. xxiv. 27, 2 Chron. xxviii. 10, Eccles. ii. 15. Hitzig is wrong in his rendering, "all their host do I command." That of Ewald is the correct one, "did I appoint;" for *tsivvāh*, followed by an accusative of the person. means to give a definite order or command to any one, the command in this case being the order to come into actual existence (= *esse jussi*, cf. Ps. xxxiii. 9).

He who created all things, and called all things into existence, had also raised up this Cyrus, whose victorious career had increased the anxieties and fears of the exiles, instead of leading them to lift up their heads, because their redemption was drawing nigh. Ver. 13. "*I, I have raised him up in righteousness, and all his ways shall I make smooth: He will build my city, and release my banished ones, not for price nor for reward, saith Jehovah of hosts.*" All the anxieties of the exiles are calmed by the words "in righteousness," which trace back the revolutions that Cyrus was causing to the righteousness of Jehovah, *i.e.* to His interposition, which was determined by love alone, and tended directly to the salvation of His people, and in reality to that of all nations. And they are fully quieted by the promise, which is now expressed in the clearest and most unequivocal words, that Cyrus would build up Jerusalem again, and set the captivity free (*gâlûth*, as in ch. xx. 4), and that without redemption with money (ch. lii. 3),—a clear proof that Jehovah had not only raised up Cyrus himself, but had put his spirit within him, *i.e.* had stirred up within him the resolution to do this (see the conclusion to the books of Chronicles, and the introduction to that of Ezra). This closes the first half of our sixth prophecy.

The second half is uttered in the prospect, that the judgment which Cyrus brings upon the nations will prepare the way for the overthrow of heathenism, and the universal acknowledgment of the God of Israel. The heathen submit, as the first strophe or group of verses (ch. xlv. 14–17) affirms, to the congregation and its God; the idolatrous are converted, whilst Israel is for ever redeemed. With the prospect of the release of the exiles, there is associated in the prophet's perspective the prospect of an expansion of the restored church, through the entrance of "the fulness of the Gentiles." Ver. 14. "*Thus saith Jehovah, The productions of Egypt, and gain of Ethiopia, and the Sabœans, men of tall stature, will come over to thee, and belong to thee: they will come after thee; in chains they will come over, and cast themselves down to thee; they pray to thee, Surely God is in thee, and there is none else; no Deity at all.*" Assuming that יַעֲבֹרוּ has the same meaning in both cases, the prophet's meaning appears to be, that the Egyptians, Ethiopians, and Meroites (see ch. xliii. 3), who had been enslaved by the imperial power of Persia, would enter the miraculously emancipated congregation of Israel (Ewald). But if they were thought of as in a state of subjugation to the imperial power of Asia, how could the promise be at the same time held out that their riches would pass over into the possession of the church? And yet, on the other hand, the chains in which they come over cannot be regarded, at least in this connection, where such emphasis is laid upon the voluntary character of the surrender, as placed upon them by Israel itself (as in ch. lx. 11 and Ps. cxlix. 8). We must therefore suppose that they put chains upon themselves voluntarily, and of their own accord, and thus offer themselves spontaneously to the church, to be henceforth its subjects and slaves. Egypt, Ethiopia, and Saba are the nations that we meet with in other passages, where the *hæreditas gentium* is promised to the church, and generally in connection with Tyre (*vid.* Ps. lxviii. 32, lxxii. 10; compare ch. xviii. 7, xix. 16 sqq., xxiii. 18). Whilst the labour of Egypt (*i.e.* the productions of its labour) and the trade of Ethiopia (*i.e.* the riches acquired by trade) are mentioned; in the case of Saba the prophecy looks at the tall and handsome tribe itself, a tribe which Agatharchides describes as having σώματα ἀξιολογώτερα. These would place themselves at the service of the church with their invincible strength. The voluntary character of the surrender is pointed out, not only in the expression " they will come over," but also in the confession with which this is accompanied. In other cases the words *hithpallēl 'el* are only used of prayer to God and idols; but here it is to the church that prayer is offered. In the prophet's view, Jehovah and His church are inseparably one (compare 1 Cor. xii. 12, where " Christ" stands for the church as one body, consisting of both head and members; also the use of the word " worship" in Rev. iii. 9, which has all the ring of a passage taken from Isaiah). אַךְ is used here in its primary affirmative sense, as in Ps. lviii. 12. There can be no doubt that Paul had this passage of Isaiah in his mind when writing 1 Cor. xiv. 24, 25, ἀπαγγέλλων ὅτι ὁ Θεὸς ὄντως ἐν ὑμῖν ἐστί, or, according to a better arrangement of the words, ὅτι

ὄντως (= אַף) ὁ Θεὸς ἐν ὑμῖν ἐστίν. 'Ephes does not signify
præter (as a synonym of בִּלְעָדַי, זוּלָתִי) either here or anywhere
else, but is a substantive used with a verbal force, which stands
in the same relation to אַיִן as " there is not at all (absolutely
not)" to " there is not;" compare ch. v. 8, xlv. 6, xlvi. 9, also
Deut. xxxii. 36 (derivative passage, 2 Kings xiv. 26), and
Amos vi. 10, 2 Sam. ix. 3; *vid.* ch. xlvii. 8.

What follows in ver. 15 is not a continuation of the words
of the Gentiles, but a response of the church to their confession. The nations that have been idolatrous till now, bend
in humble spontaneous worship before the church and its God;
and at the sight of this, the church, from whose soul the prophet
is speaking, bursts out into an exclamation of reverential amazement. Ver. 15. "*Verily Thou art a mysterious God, Thou God
of Israel, Thou Saviour.*" Literally, a God who hides Himself
(*mistattēr*: the resemblance to μυστηρ-ιώδης is quite an accidental one; the *ē* is retained in the participle even in pause).
The meaning is, a God who guides with marvellous strangeness the history of the nations of the earth, and by secret ways,
which human eyes can never discern, conducts all to a glorious
issue. The exclamation in Rom. xi. 33, " O the depth of the
riches," etc., is a similar one.

The way in which this God who hides Himself is ultimately
revealed as the God of salvation, is then pointed out in vers.
16, 17 : "*They are put to shame, and also confounded, all of
them ; they go away into confusion together, the forgers of idols.
Israel is redeemed by Jehovah with everlasting redemption: ye
are not put to shame nor confounded to everlasting eternities.*"
The perfects are expressive of the ideal past. Jehovah shows
Himself as a Saviour by the fact, that whereas the makers
of idols perish, Israel is redeemed an everlasting redemption
(acc. obj. as in ch. xiv. 6, xxii. 17; Ges. § 138, 1, Anm. 1),
i.e. so that its redemption is one that lasts for æons (αἰωνία
λύτρωσις, Heb. ix. 12) :—observe that *tᵉshū'áh* does not literally
signify redemption or rescue, but transfer into a state of wide
expanse, *i.e.* of freedom and happiness. The plural 'ōlāmīm
(eternities=αἰϜῶνες, æva) belongs, according to Knobel, to the
later period of the language ; but it is met with as early as in
old Asaphite psalms (Ps. lxxvii. 6). When the further promise
is added, Ye shall not be put to shame, etc., this clearly shows,

what is also certain on other grounds,—namely, that the redemption is not thought of merely as an outward and bodily
one, but also as inward and spiritual, and indeed (in accordance
with the prophetic blending of the end of the captivity with
the end of all things) as a final one. Israel will never bring
upon itself again such a penal judgment as that of the captivity by falling away from God; that is to say, its state of sin
will end with its state of punishment, even עַד־עוֹלְמֵי עַד, *i.e.*,
since עַד has no plural, εἰς αἰῶνας τῶν αἰώνων.

The second and last strophe of this prophecy commences
with ver. 18. By the fulfilment of the promise thus openly
proclaimed, those of the heathen who have been saved from
the judgment will recognise Jehovah as the only God; and the
irresistible will of Jehovah, that all mankind should worship
Him, be carried out. The promise cannot remain unfulfilled.
Vers. 18, 19. " *For thus saith Jehovah, the creator of the*
heavens (He is the Deity), the former of the earth, and its finisher;
He has established it (He has not created it a desert, He has
formed it to be inhabited): I am Jehovah, and there is none
else. I have not spoken in secret, in a place of the land of
darkness; I did not say to the seed of Jacob, Into the desert
seek ye me! I Jehovah am speaking righteousness, proclaiming
upright things." The *athnach* properly divides ver. 18 in half.
Ver. 18*a* describes the speaker, and what He says commences
in ver. 18*b*. The first parenthesis affirms that Jehovah is God
in the fullest and most exclusive sense; the second that He has
created the earth for man's sake, not " as a desert" (*tōhū* : the
LXX., Targum, and Jerome render this with less accuracy,
non in vanum), *i.e.* not to be and continue to be a desert, but to
be inhabited. Even in Gen. i. 2, *chaos* is not described as of
God's creation, because (whatever may be men's opinions concerning it in other respects) the creative activity of God merely
made use of this as a starting-point, and because, although it
did not come into existence without God, it was at any rate not
desired by God for its own sake. The words of Jehovah commence, then, with the assertion that Jehovah is the absolute
One; and from this two thoughts branch off: (1.) The first is,
that the prophecy which emanates from Him is an affair of
light, no black art, but essentially different from heathen soothsaying. By " a dark place of the earth" we are to understand,

according to Ps. cxxxix. 15, the interior of the earth, and
according to Job x. 21, Hades; the intention being to point
out the contrast between the prophecies of Jehovah and the
heathen cave-oracles and spirit-voices of the necromancists,
which seemed to rise up from the interior of the earth (see ch.
lxv. 4, viii. 19, xxix. 4).   (2.) The second thought is, that the
very same love of Jehovah, which has already been displayed
in the creation, attests itself in His relation to Israel, which He
has not directed to Himself "into the desert" (*tōhū*), just as
He did not create the earth a *tōhū*.   Meier and Knobel suppose
that *baqshūnī*, which is written here, according to a well-supported
reading, with *Koph raphatum* (whereas in other cases the *dagesh*
is generally retained, particularly in the imperative of *biqqēsh*),
refers to seeking for disclosures as to the future; but the word
דִּרְשׁוּנִי would be used for this, as in ch. viii. 19.   He has not said,
"Seek ye me (as in Zeph. ii. 3) into the desert," *i.e.* without
the prospect of meeting with any return for your pains.   On
the contrary, He has attached promises to the seeking of Himself, which cannot remain unfulfilled, for He is "one speaking
righteousness, declaring things that are right;" *i.e.* when He
promises, He follows out the rule of His purpose and of His
plan of salvation, and the impulse of sincere desire for their
good, and love which is ever true to itself.   The present word
of prophecy points to the fulfilment of these promises.

The salvation of Israel, foretold and realized by Jehovah,
becomes at the same time the salvation of the heathen world.
Vers. 20, 21. "*Assemble yourselves and come; draw near together,
ye escaped of the heathen!   Irrational are they who burden
themselves with the wood of their idol, and pray to a god that
bringeth no salvation.   Make known, and cause to draw near;
yea, let them take counsel together: Who has made such things
known from the olden time, proclaimed it long ago? have not I,
Jehovah? and there is no Deity beside me; a God just, and bringing salvation: there is not without me!*"   The fulness of the
Gentiles, which enters into the kingdom of God, is a remnant of
the whole mass of the heathen: for salvation comes through judgment; and it is in the midst of great calamities that the work
of that heathen mission is accomplished, which is represented in
these prophecies on the one hand as the mission of Cyrus, and
on the other hand as the mission of Jehovah and His servant.

Hence this summons to listen to the self-assertion of the God of revelation, is addressed to the escaped of the heathen, who are not therefore the converted, but those who are susceptible of salvation, and therefore spared. By "the heathen" (*haggōyim*) Knobel understands the allies and auxiliaries of the Babylonians, whom Cyrus put to flight (according to the *Cyropædia*) before his Lydian campaign. But this is only an example of that exaggerated desire to turn everything into history, which not only prevented his seeing the poetry of the form, but obscured the fact that prophecy is both human and divine. For the future was foreshortened to the telescopic glance of the prophet, so that he could not see it in all its length and breadth. He saw in one mass what history after-wards unrolled; and then behind the present he could just see as it were the summit of the end, although a long eventful way still lay between the two. Accordingly, our prophet here takes his stand not at the close of any particular victory of Cyrus, but at the close of all his victories; and, in his view, these terminate the whole series of catastrophes, which are outlived by a remnant of the heathen, who are converted to Jehovah, and thus complete the final glory of the restored people of God. Throughout the whole of these prophecies we see immediately behind the historical foreground this eschato-logical background lifting up its head. The heathen who have been preserved will assemble together; and from the fact that Jehovah proves Himself the sole foreteller of the events that are now unfolding themselves, they will be brought to the conviction that He is the only God. The *hithpael hithnaggēsh* does not occur anywhere else. On the absolute ידע לא, see at ch. xliv. 9 (cf. i. 3). To the verb *haggīshū* we must supply, as in ch. xli. 22, according to the same expression in ver. 21, עַצְמֹתֵיכֶם (your proofs). "*This*" refers to the fall of Babylon and redemption of Israel—salvation breaking through judg-ment. On *mē'âz*, from the olden time, compare ch. xliv. 8. God is "a just God and a Saviour," as a being who acts most stringently according to the demands of His holiness, and wherever His wrath is not wickedly provoked, sets in motion His loving will, which is ever concerned to secure the salvation of men.

It is in accordance with this holy loving will that the cry is published in ver. 22 : "*Turn unto me, and be ye saved, all ye ends of the earth; for I am God, and none else.*" The first imperative is hortatory, the second promising (cf. ch. xxxvi. 16 and viii. 9) : Jehovah desires both, viz. the conversion of all men to Himself ; and through this their salvation, and this His gracious will, which extends to all mankind, will not rest till its object has been fully accomplished. Ver. 23. "*By myself have I sworn, a word has gone out of a mouth of right-eousness, and will not return, That to me every knee shall bend, every tongue swear.*" Swearing by Himself (see Gen. xxii. 16), God pledges what He swears with His own life (compare Rom. xiv. 11, "as I live"). Parallel to בִּי נִשְׁבַּעְתִּי is the clause יָצָא מִפִּי צְדָקָה דָּבָר וְלֹא יָשׁוּב. Here Rosenmüller connects צדקה דבר together as if with a hyphen, in the sense of a truth-word (Jerome, *justitiæ verbum*). But this is grammatically impossible, since it would require דְּבַר צדקה ; moreover, it is opposed both to the accents, and to the *dagesh* in the *Daleth*. Hitzig's rendering is a better one : "Truth (LXX. δικαιο-σύνη), a word that does not return,"—the latter being taken as an explanatory permutative ; but in that case we should require לֹא for וְלֹא, and *tseḍâqâh* is not used in the sense of truth anywhere else (compare *tsaddîq*, however, in ch. xli. 26). On the other hand, צדקה might be equivalent to בצדקה ("in righteousness ;" cf. ch. xlii. 25, חֵמָה = בְּחֵמָה), if it were not incomparably more natural to connect together מפי צדקה as a genitive construction ; though not in the sense in which מפי הגבורה is used in post-biblical writings,—namely, as equivalent to "out of the mouth of God" (see Buxtorf, *Lex. Chald. Col.* 385), —but rather in this way, that the mouth of God is described attributively as regulated in its words by His holy will (as "speaking righteousness," ver. 19b). A word has gone forth from this mouth of righteousness ; and after it has once gone forth, it does not return without accomplishing its object (ch. lv. 11). What follows is not so much a promising prediction (that every knee will bend to me), as a definitive declaration of will (that it shall or must bend to me). According to ch. xix. 18, xliv. 5, "to me" is to be regarded as carried forward, and so to be supplied after "shall swear" (the Septuagint rendering, ὀμεῖται . . . τὸν Θεόν, is false ; that of Paul in Rom. xiv. 11, ἐξομολογήσεται τῷ Θεῷ, is correct ; and in this case, as in others also, the *Cod. Al.* of the Sept. has been corrected from the New Testament quotations).

This bending of the knee, this confession as an oath of homage, will be no forced one. Ver. 24. " *Only in Jehovah, do men say of me, is fulness of righteousness and strength ; they come to Him, and all that were incensed against Him are put to shame.*" The parenthetical insertion of אָמַר לִי (?, with reference to, as in ch. xli. 7, xliv. 26, 28) is the same as in Ps. cxix. 57. אַךְ has a restrictive sense here, which springs out of the affirmative (cf. Ps. xxxix. 7, lxxiii. 1), just as, in the case of *raq,* the affirmative grows out of the primary restrictive sense. The " righteousness" is abounding (superabundant) righteousness (Rom. v. 15 sqq.). עֹז is the strength of sanctification, and of the conquest of the world. The subject to יָבוֹא (which is not to be changed, according to the Masora, into the more natural יָבֹאוּ, as it is by the LXX., Syr., and Vulg.) is, whoever has seen what man has in Jehovah, and made confession of this ; such a man does not rest till he has altogether come over to Jehovah, whereas all His enemies are put to shame. They separate themselves irretrievably from the men who serve Him, the restoration of whom is His direct will, and the goal of the history of salvation. Ver. 25. " *In Jehovah all the seed of Israel shall become righteous, and shall glory.*" Ruetschi has very properly observed on this verse, that the reference is to the Israel of God out of all the human race, *i.e.* the church of the believers in Israel expanded by the addition of the heathen ; which church is now righteous, *i.e.* reconciled and renewed by Jehovah, and glories in Him, because by grace it is what it is.

This brings the sixth prophecy to a close. Its five strophes commence with "Thus saith the Lord;" at the same time, the fifth strophe has two "woes" (*hoi*) before this, as the ground upon which it rests.

SEVENTH PROPHECY.—CHAP. XLVI.

FALL OF THE GODS OF BABEL.

There follows now a trilogy of prophecies referring to Babylon. After the prophet has shown what Israel has to expect of Cyrus, he turns to what awaits Babylon at the hands of Cyrus. Vers. 1, 2. "*Bel sinketh down, Nebo stoopeth; its images come to the beast of burden and draught cattle : your litters are laden, a burden for the panting. They stooped, sank down all at once, and could not get rid of the burden; and their own self went into captivity.*" The reference to Babylon comes out at once in the names of the gods. *Bēl* was the Jupiter of the Babylonians and, as *Bel-Merodach*, the tutelar deity of Babylon; *Nebo* was Mercury, the tutelar deity of the later Chaldean royal family, as the many kings' names in which it appears clearly show (*e.g. Nabonassar, Nabo-polassar*, etc.). The pyramidal heap of ruins on the right bank of the Euphrates, which is now called *Birs Nimrud*, is the ruin of the temple of Bel, of which Herodotus gives a description in i. 181–183, and probably also of the tower mentioned in Gen. xi., which was dedicated to Bel, if not to *El* = Saturn. Herodotus describes two golden statues of Bel which were found there (cf. Diodorus, ii. 9, 5), but the way in which Nebo was represented is still unknown. The judgment of Jehovah falls upon these gods through Cyrus. Bel suddenly falls headlong, and Nebo stoops till he also falls. Their images come to (fall to the lot of) the *chayyâh, i.e.* the camels, dromedaries, and elephants; and *bᵉhēmâh, i.e.* horses, oxen, and asses. Your נְשֻׂאֹת, *gestamina*, the prophet exclaims to the Babylonians, *i.e.* the images hitherto carried by you in solemn procession (ch. xlv. 20; Amos v. 26; Jer. x. 5), are now packed up, a burden for that which is wearied out, *i.e.* for cattle that has become weary with carrying them. In ver. 1, as the two participial clauses show, the prophet still takes his stand in the midst of the catastrophe; but in ver. 2 it undoubtedly lies behind him as a completed act. In ver. 2*a* he continues, as in ver. 1, to enter into the delusion of the heathen, and distinguish between the *numina* and *simulacra*. The gods of Babylon have all stooped at once, have sunken down, and have been unable to save their images which were packed upon the cattle, out of the hands of the conquerors. In ver. 2*b* he destroys this delusion : they are going into captivity (Hos. x. 5; Jer. xlviii. 7, xlix. 3), even " their ownself" (*naphshâm*), since the self or personality of the beingless beings consists of nothing more than the wood and metal of which their images are composed.

From this approaching reduction of the gods of Babylon to their original nothingness, several admonitions are now derived. The first admonition is addressed to all Israel. Vers. 3–5. " *Hearken unto me, O house of Jacob, and all the remnant of the house of Israel: ye, lifted up from the womb; ye, carried from the mother's lap! And till old age it is I, and to grey hair I shall bear you on my shoulder: I have done it, and I shall carry; and I put upon my shoulder, and deliver. To whom can ye compare me, and liken, and place side by side, that we should be equal?*" The house of Jacob is Judah here, as in Obad. 18 (see Caspari on the passage), Nah. ii. 3, and the house of Israel the same as the house of Joseph in Obadiah; whereas in Amos iii. 13, vi. 8, vii. 2, Jacob stands for Israel, in distinction from Judah. The Assyrian exile was earlier than the Babylonian, and had already naturalized the greater part of the exiles in a heathen land, and robbed them of their natural character, so that there was only a remnant left by whom there was any hope that the prophet's message would be received. What the exiles of both houses were to hear was the question in ver. 5, which called upon them to consider the incomparable nature of their God, as deduced from what Jehovah could say of Himself in relation to all Israel, and what He does say from הָעֲמֻסִים onwards. Babylon carried its idols, but all in vain: they were carried forth, without being able to save themselves; but Jehovah carried His people, and saved them. The expressions, "from the womb, and from the mother's lap," point back to the time when the nation which had been in process of formation from the time of Abraham onwards came out of Egypt, and was born, as it were, into the light of the world. From this time forward it had lain upon Jehovah like a willingly adopted burden, and He had carried it as a nurse carries a suckling (Num. xi. 12), and an eagle its young (Deut. xxxii. 11). In ver. 4 the attributes of the people are carried on in direct (not relative) self-assertions on the part of Jehovah. The *senectus* and *canities* are obviously those of the people,— not, however, as though it was already in a state of dotage (as Hitzig maintains, appealing erroneously to ch. xlvii. 6), but as denoting the future and latest periods of its history. Even till then Jehovah is He, *i.e.* the Absolute, and always the same (see ch. xli. 4). As He has acted in the past, so will He act

at all times—supporting and saving His people. Hence He
could properly ask, Whom could you place by the side of me,
so that we should be equal? (*Vav consec.* as in ch. xl. 25.)

The negative answer to this question is the direct result of
what precedes, but a still further proof is given in vers. 6, 7.
"*They who pour gold out of the bag, and weigh silver with the
balance, hire a goldsmith to make it into a god, that they may fall
down, yea, throw themselves down.   They lift it up, carry it
away upon their shoulder, and set it down in its place : there it
stands ; from its place it does not move : men also cry to it, but it
does not answer ; it saves no one out of distress.*"   There is no
necessity for assuming that הַזָּלִים is used in the place of the
finite verb, as Hitzig imagines, or as equivalent to הֵם זָלִים, as
Rosenmüller and Gesenius suppose ; but up to יִשְׁקְרוּ the whole
is subject, and therefore יִשְׁקְלוּ is the point at which the change
into the finite verb occurs (Ges. § 131, 2).   The point in *haz-
zâlîm* is not the extravagant expenditure, as Ewald thinks, but
the mean origin of the god, which commences with the pouring
out of gold from a purse (*zūl* = *zâlal*, to shake, to pour out).
Qâneh is the lever of the scales (κανών).   The metal weighed
out is given to a goldsmith, who plates the idol with the gold,
and makes the ornaments for it of silver.   When it is finished,
they lift it up, or shoulder it (יִשָּׂאֻהוּ, with a distinctive Great
Telisha), carry it home, and set it down in the place which it
is to have *under it* (תַּחְתָּיו).   There it stands firm, immoveable,
and also deaf and dumb, hearing no one, answering no one,
and helping no one.   The subject to יִצְעַק is any צֹעֵק.   The first
admonition closes here.   The gods who are carried fall without
being able to save themselves, whereas Israel's God carries and
saves His people ; He, the Incomparable, more especially in
contrast with the lifeless puppets of idols.

The second admonition is addressed to those who would
imitate the heathen.   Vers. 8–11.   "*Remember this, and become
firm ; take it to heart, ye rebellious ones !   Remember the beginning from the olden time, that I am God, and none else :
Deity, and absolutely none like me ; proclaiming the issue from
the beginning, and from ancient times what has not yet taken
place, saying, My counsel shall stand, and all my good pleasure
I carry out : calling a bird of prey from the east, the man of
my counsel from a distant land : not only have I spoken, I also*

bring it; I have purposed it, I also execute it." The object to which "this" points back is the nothingness of idols and idolatry. The persons addressed are the פּשְׁעִים (those apostatizing), but, as הִתְאֹשָׁשׁוּ shows, whether it mean ἀνδρίζεσθε or κραταιοῦσθε (1 Cor. xvi. 13), such as have not yet actually carried out their rebellion or apostasy, but waver between Jehovahism and heathenism, and are inclined to the latter. הִתְאֹשָׁשׁוּ is hardly a denom. *hithpalel* of אִישׁ in the sense of "man yourselves," since אִישׁ, whether it signifies a husband or a social being, or like אֱנוֹשׁ, a frail or mortal being, is at any rate equivalent to אֱנָשׁ, and therefore never shows the modification *u*. אָשֵׁשׁ (אָשָׁה) signifies to be firm, strong, compact; in the *piel* (rabb.), to be well-grounded; *nithpael*, to be fortified, established; here *hithpoel*, "show yourselves firm" (Targ., Jer.: *fundamini ne rursum subitus idololatriæ vos turbo subvertat*). That they may strengthen themselves in faith and fidelity, they are referred to the history of their nation; רִאשׁנוֹת are not prophecies given at an earlier time,—a meaning which the *priora* only acquire in such a connection as ch. xliii. 9, —but former occurrences. They are to pass before their minds the earlier history, and indeed "from the olden time." "*Remember:*" *zikhrū* is connected with the accusative of the object of remembrance, and כִּי points to its result. An earnest and thoughtful study of history would show them that Jehovah alone was *El*, the absolutely Mighty One, and *'Elōhīm*, the Being who united in Himself all divine majesty by which reverence was evoked. The participles in vers. 10, 11 are attached to the "I" of כָּמוֹנִי. It is Jehovah, the Incomparable, who has now, as at other times from the very commencement of the new turn in history, predicted the issue to which it would lead, and *miqqedem, i.e.* long before, predicted things that have not yet occurred, and which therefore lie outside the sphere of human combination,—another passage like ch. xli. 26, xlv. 21, etc., in which what is predicted in these prophecies lays claim to the character of a prediction of long standing, and not of one merely uttered a few years before. The רִאשִׁית, in which the רִאשׁנוֹת are already in progress (ch. xlii. 9), is to be regarded as the prophet's ideal present; for Jehovah not only foretells before the appearance of Cyrus what is to be expected of him, but declares that His determination must be realized, that He will bring to pass everything upon which His will is set, and summons the man upon the stage of history as the instrument of its accomplishment, so that He knew Cyrus before he himself had either consciousness or being (ch. xlv. 4, 5). The east is Persis (ch. xli. 2); and the distant land, the northern part of Media (as in ch. xiii. 5). Cyrus is called an eagle, or, strictly speaking, a bird of prey ('ayit[1]), just as in Jer. xlix. 22 and Ezek. xvii. 3 Nebuchadnezzar is called a *nesher*. According to *Cyrop.* vii. 1, 4, the campaign of Cyrus was ἀετὸς χρυσοῦς ἐπὶ δόρατος μακροῦ ἀνατεταμένος. Instead of אִישׁ עֲצָתוֹ, the *keri* reads more clearly, though quite unnecessarily, אִישׁ עֲצָתִי (see *e.g.* ch. xliv. 26). The correlate אַף (ver. 11*b*), which is only attached to the second verb the second time, affirms that Jehovah does not only the one, but the other also. His word is made by Him into a deed, His idea into a reality. יָצַר is a word used particularly by Isaiah, to denote the ideal preformation of the future in the mind of God (cf. ch. xxii. 11, xxxvii. 26). The feminine suffixes refer in a neuter sense to the theme of the prophecy—the overthrow of idolatrous Babel, upon which Cyrus comes down like an eagle, in the strength of Jehovah. So far we have the *nota bene* for those who are inclined to apostasy. They are to lay to heart the nothingness of the heathen gods, and, on the other hand, the self-manifestation of Jehovah from the olden time, that is to say, of the One God who is now foretelling and carrying out the destruction of the imperial city through the eagle from the east.

A third admonition is addressed to the *forts esprits* in vers. 12, 13. "*Hearken to me, ye strong-hearted, that are far from righteousness ! I have brought my righteousness near; it is not far off, and my salvation tarrieth not : and I give salvation in Zion, my glory to Israel.*" All that is called in Hellenic and Hellenistic νοῦς, λόγος συνείδησις, θυμός, is comprehended in καρδία; and everything by which *bâsâr* and *nephesh* are affected comes into the light of consciousness in the heart (*Psychol.* p. 251).

---

[1] The resemblance to ἀετός (αἰετός) is merely accidental. This name for the eagle is traceable, like *avis*, to a root *vâ*, to move with the swiftness of the wind. This was shown by Passow, compare Kuhn's *Zeitschrift*, i. 29, where we also find at 10, 126 another but less probable derivation from a root *i*, to go (compare *eva*, a course).

According to this biblico-psychological idea, אַבִּירֵי לֵב may signify either the courageous (Ps. lxxvi. 6), or, as in this instance, the strong-minded ; but as a synonym of חִזְקֵי לֵב (Ezek. ii. 4) and קְשֵׁי לֵב (Ezek. iii. 7), viz. in the sense of those who resist the impressions of the work and grace of God in their consciousness of mental superiority to anything of the kind, and not in the sense of those who have great mental endowments. These are " far from righteousness" (ts^edâqâh), that is to say, they have despaired of the true, loving fidelity of Jehovah, and have no wish for any further knowledge of it. Therefore they shall hear, and possibly not without impression, that this loving fidelity is about to manifest itself, and salvation is about to be realized. Jehovah has given salvation in Zion, that is to say, is giving it even now, so that it will become once more the centre of the renovated nation, and impart its glory to this, so that it may shine in the splendour bestowed upon it by its God. We have here the side of light and love, turned towards us by the two-faced ts^edâqâh, as a parallel word to th^eshu'âh, or salvation. With this admonition to the indifferent and careless, to whom the salvation of which they have given up all hope is proclaimed as at the door, this prophecy is brought to a close. In three distinct stages, commencing with " hearken," " remember," " hearken," it has unfolded the spiritual influences which the fact declared in vers. 1, 2 ought to have upon Israel, and resembles a pastoral sermon in its tone.

EIGHTH PROPHECY.—Chap. xlvii.

FALL OF BABEL, THE CAPITAL OF THE EMPIRE OF THE WORLD.

From the gods of Babylon the proclamation of judgment passes on to Babylon itself. Vers. 1–4. " *Come down, and sit in the dust, O virgin daughter Babel ; sit on the ground without a throne, O Chaldœans-daughter !   For men no longer call thee delicate and voluptuous. Take the mill, and grind meal: throw back thy veil, lift up the train, uncover the thigh, wade through streams. Let thy nakedness be uncovered, even let thy shame be seen ; I shall take vengeance, and not spare men. Our Redeemer, Jehovah of hosts is His name, Holy One of Israel.*" This is the first strophe in the prophecy. As ver. 36 clearly shows, what

precedes is a penal sentence from Jehovah. Both בַּת in relation to בְּתוּלַת (ch. xxiii. 12, xxxvii. 22), and בָּבֶל and כַּשְׂדִּים in
relation to בַּת, are appositional genitives ; Babel and Chaldeans
(כַּשְׂדִּים as in ch. xlviii. 20) are regarded as a woman, and that
as one not yet dishonoured. The unconquered oppressor is
threatened with degradation from her proud eminence into
shameful humiliation ; sitting on the ground is used in the same
sense as in ch. iii. 26. Hitherto men have called her, with
envious admiration, *rakkâh va'ânuggâh* (from Deut. xxviii. 56),
mollis et delicata, as having carefully kept everything disagree-
able at a distance, and revelled in nothing but luxury (compare
'*ōneg*, ch. xiii. 22). Debauchery with its attendant rioting
(ch. xiv. 11, xxv. 5), and the Mylitta worship with its licensed
prostitution (Herod. i. 199), were current there ; but now all
this was at an end. תּוֹסִיפִי, according to the Masora, has only
one *pashta* both here and in ver. 5, and so has the tone upon
the last syllable, and accordingly *metheg* in the *antepenult*.
Isaiah's artistic style may be readily perceived both in the three
clauses of ver. 1 that are comparable to a long trumpet-blast
(compare ch. xl. 9 and xvi. 1), and also in the short, rugged, in-
voluntarily excited clauses that follow (compare vol. i. 427). The
mistress becomes the maid, and has to perform the low, menial
service of those who, as Homer says in *Od.* vii. 104, ἀλετρεύουσι
μύλης ἔπι μήλοπα καρπόν (grind at the mill the quince-coloured
fruit ; compare at Job xxxi. 10). She has to leave her palace
as a prisoner of war, and, laying aside all feminine modesty,
to wade through the rivers upon which she borders. *Chespī* has
ĕ instead of ĭ, and, as in other cases where a sibilant precedes,
the mute *p* instead of *f* (compare '*ispī*, Jer. x. 17). Both the
prosopopeia and the parallel, " thy shame shall be seen," require
that the expression " thy nakedness shall be uncovered" should
not be understood literally. The shame of Babel is her shameful conduct, which is not to be exhibited in its true colours,
inasmuch as a stronger one is coming upon it to rob it of its
might and honour. This stronger one, apart from the instrument employed, is Jehovah: *vindictam sumam, non parcam
homini.* Stier gives a different rendering here, namely, " I will
run upon no man, *i.e.* so as to make him give way;" Hahn,
" I will not meet with a man," so destitute of population will
Babylon be ; and Ruetschi, " I will not step in as a man."

Gesenius and Rosenmüller are nearer to the mark when they suggest *non pangam* (*paciscar*) *cum homine;* but this would require at any rate אֶת־אָדָם, even if the verb פֶּנַע really had the meaning to strike a treaty.   It means rather to strike against a person, to assault any one, then to meet or come in an opposite direction, and that not only in a hostile sense, but, as in this instance, and also in ch. lxiv. 4, in a friendly sense as well. Hence, "I shall not receive any man, or pardon any man" (Hitzig, Ewald, etc.).   According to an old method of writing the passage, there is a pause here.   But ver. 4 is still connected with what goes before.   As Jehovah is speaking in ver. 5, but Israel in ver. 4, and as ver. 4 is unsuitable to form the basis of the words of Jehovah, it must be regarded as the antiphone to vers. 1–3 (cf. ch. xlv. 15).   Our Redeemer, exclaims the church in joyfully exalted self-consciousness, He is Jehovah of hosts, the Holy One of Israel !   The one name affirms that He possesses the all-conquering might ; the other that He possesses the will to carry on the work of redemption,—a will influenced and constrained by both love and wrath.

In the second strophe the penal sentence of Jehovah is continued.   Vers. 5–7. " *Sit silent, and creep into the darkness, O Chaldeans-daughter! for men no longer call thee lady of kingdoms.   I was wroth with my people; I polluted mine inheritance, and gave them into thy hand: thou hast shown them no mercy; upon old men thou laidst thy yoke very heavily.   And thou saidst, I shall be lady for ever; so that thou didst not take these things to heart: thou didst not consider the latter end thereof.*"   Babylon shall sit down in silent, brooding sorrow, and take herself away into darkness, just as those who have fallen into disgrace shrink from the eyes of men.   She is looked upon as an empress (ch. xiii. 9 ; the king of Babylon called himself the king of kings, Ezek. xxvi. 7), who has been reduced to the condition of a slave, and durst not show herself for shame.   This would happen to her, because at the time when Jehovah made use of her as His instrument for punishing His people, she went beyond the bounds of her authority, showing no pity, and ill-treating even defenceless old men. According to Koppe, Gesenius, and Hitzig, Israel is here called *zâqēn,* as a decayed nation awakening sympathy; but according to the Scripture, the people of God is always young, and never

decays; on the contrary, its *ziqnâh*, *i.e.* the latest period of its
history (ch. xlvi. 4), is to be like its youth.   The words are to
be understood literally, like Lam. iv. 16, v. 12: even upon old
men, Babylon had placed the heavy yoke of prisoners and
slaves.   But in spite of this inhumanity, it flattered itself that
it would last for ever.   Hitzig adopts the reading עַד גְּבֶרֶת, and
renders it, "To all future times shall I continue, mistress to all
eternity."   This may possibly be correct, but it is by no means
necessary, inasmuch as it can be shown from 1 Sam. xx. 41,
and Job xiv. 6, that עַד is used as equivalent to עַד אֲשֶׁר, in the
sense of "till the time that;" and *gᵉbhereth*, as the feminine
of *gâbhēr = gebher*, may be the absolute quite as well as the
construct.   The meaning therefore is, that the confidence of
Babylon in the eternal continuance of its power was such, that
"these things," *i.e.* such punishments as those which were
now about to fall upon it according to the prophecy, had never
come into its mind; such, indeed, that it had not called to
remembrance as even possible "the latter end of it," *i.e.* the
inevitably evil termination of its tyranny and presumption.

A third strophe of this proclamation of punishment is
opened here with וְעַתָּה, on the ground of the conduct censured.
Vers. 8–11. "*And now hear this, thou voluptuous one, she who
sitteth so securely, who sayeth in her heart, I am it, and none
else: I shall not sit a widow, nor experience bereavement of
children.   And these two will come upon thee suddenly in one
day: bereavement of children and widowhood; they come upon
thee in fullest measure, in spite of the multitude of thy sorceries,
in spite of the great abundance of thy witchcrafts.   Thou trustedst
in thy wickedness, saidst, No one seeth me.   Thy wisdom and thy
knowledge, they led thee astray; so that thou saidst in thy heart,
I am it, and none else.   And misfortune cometh upon thee, which
thou dost not understand how to charm away: and destruction
will fall upon thee, which thou canst not atone for; there will come
suddenly upon thee ruin which thou suspectest not.*"   In the sur-
names given to Babylon here, a new reason is assigned for the
judgment,—namely, extravagance, security, and self-exaltation.
עֲדִין is an intensive form of עֵדֶן (LXX. τρυφερά).   The *i* of
אַפְסִי is regarded by Hahn as the same as we meet with in
אַתְּי = אַתְּ; but this is impossible here with the first person.
Rosenmüller, Ewald, Gesenius, and others, take it as *chirek*

compaginis, and equivalent to אֵין עוֹד, which would only occur in this particular formula. Hitzig supposes it to be the suffix of the word, which is meant as a preposition in the sense of *et præter me ultra (nemo)*; but this *nemo* would be omitted, which is improbable. The more probable explanation is, that אֶפֶס signifies absolute non-existence, and when used as an adverb, " exclusively, nothing but," *e.g.* אֶפֶס קָצֵהוּ, nothing, the utmost extremity thereof, *i.e.* only the utmost extremity of it (Num. xxiii. 13; cf. xxii. 35). But it is mostly used with a verbal force, like אֵין (אַיִן), (*utique*) *non est* (see ch. xlv. 14); hence אַפְסִי, like אֵינִי, (*utique*) *non sum*. The form in which the presumption of Babylon expresses itself, viz. " I (am it), and I am absolutely nothing further," sounds like self-deification, by the side of similar self-assertion on the part of Jehovah (ch. xlv. 5, 6, xviii. 22 ; cf. vers. xxi. 14 and ch. xlvi. 9). Nineveh speaks in just the same way in Zeph. ii. 15 (on the secondary character of this passage, see p. 67); compare Martial : " *Terrarum Dea gentiumque Roma cui par est nihil et nihil secundum.*" Babylon also says still further (like the Babylon of the last days in Rev. xviii. 7) : " I shall not sit as a widow (viz. mourning thus in solitude, Lam. i. 1, iii. 28 ; and secluded from the world, Gen. xxxviii. 11), nor experience the loss of children" (*orbitatem*). She would become a widow, if she should lose the different nations, and " the kings of the earth who committed fornication with her" (Rev. xviii. 9); for her relation to her own king cannot possibly be thought of, inasmuch as the relation in which a nation stands to its temporal king is never thought of as marriage, like that of Jehovah to Israel. She would also be a mother bereaved of her children, if war and captivity robbed her of her population. But both of these would happen to her suddenly in one day, so that she would succumb to the weight of the double sorrow. Both of them would come upon her *kᵉthummâm (secundum integritatem eorum)*, *i.e.* so that she would come to learn what the loss of men and the loss of children signified in all its extent and in all its depth, and that in spite of (בְּ, with, equivalent to "notwithstanding," as in ch. v. 25; not " through = on account of," since this tone is adopted for the first time in ver. 10) the multitude of its incantations, and the very great mass (*'ŏtsmâh*, an inf. noun, as in ch. xxx. 19, lv. 2, used here, not as in ch. xl. 29, in an intensive sense, but,

like *'átsūm,* as a parallel word to *rabh* in a numerical sense)
of its witchcrafts (*chebher,* binding by means of incantations,
κατάδεσμος). Babylonia was the birth-place of astrology, from
which sprang the twelve-fold division of the day, the horoscope
and sun-dial (Herod. ii. 109); but it was also the home of magic,
which pretended to bind the course of events, and even the
power of the gods, and to direct them in whatever way it pleased
(Diodorus, ii. 29). Thus had Babylon trusted in her wickedness (ch. xiii. 11), viz. in the tyranny and cunning by which
she hoped to ensure perpetual duration, with the notion that
she was exalted above the reach of any earthly calamity. She
thought, "None seeth me" (*non est videns me*), thus suppressing
the voice of conscience, and practically denying the omnipotence and omnipresence of God. רֹאָנִי (with a verbal suffix,
videns me, whereas רֹאִי in Gen. xvi. 3 signifies *videns mei =
meus*), also written רֹאֵנִי, is a pausal form in half pause for רֹאֵנִי
(ch. xxix. 15). *Tzere* passes in pause both into *pathach* (*e.g.*
ch. xlii. 22), and also, apart from such *hithpael* forms as ch.
xli. 16, into *kametz,* as in קִימָנוּ (Job xxii. 20, which see). By
the "wisdom and knowledge" of Babylon, which had turned
her aside from the right way, we are to understand her policy,
strategy, and more especially her magical arts, *i.e.* the mysteries
of the Chaldeans, their ἐπιχώριοι φιλόσοφοι (Strabo, xxi. 1, 6).
On *hōváh* (used here and in Ezek. vii. 26, written *havváh* elsewhere), according to its primary meaning, "yawning," χαῖνον,
then a yawning depth, χάσμα, utter destruction, see at Job
xxxvii. 6. שֹׁאָה signifies primarily a desert, or desolate place,
here destruction; and hence the derivative meaning, waste
noise, a dull groan. The perfect consec. of the first clause
precedes its predicate רָעָה in the radical form בָא (Ges, § 147, *a*).
With the parallelism of כַּפְּרָהּ, it is not probable that שַׁחְרָהּ,
which rhymes with it, is a substantive, in the sense of "from
which thou wilt experience no morning dawn" (*i.e.* after the
night of calamity), as Umbreit supposes. The suffix also causes
some difficulty (hence the Vulgate rendering, *ortum ejus,* sc.
mali); and instead of תֵּדְעִי, we should expect תִּרְאִי. In any
case, *shachráh* is a verb, and Hitzig renders it, "which thou
wilt not know how to unblacken;" but this privative use of
shichēr as a word of colour would be without example. It
would be better to translate it, "which thou wilt not know how

to spy out" (as in ch. xxvi. 9), but better still, " which thou wilt
not know how to conjure away" (*shichēr* = سَحَّر, as it were
incantitare, and here *incantando averruncare*). The last relative
clause affirms what *shachrâh* would state, if understood according to ch. xxvi. 9 : destruction which thou wilt not know, *i.e.*
which will come suddenly and unexpectedly.

Then follows the concluding strophe, which, like the first,
announces to the imperial city in a triumphantly sarcastic tone
its inevitable fate ; whereas the intermediate strophes refer
rather to the sins by which this fate has been brought upon it.
Vers. 12–15. " *Come near, then, with thine enchantments, and*
with the multitude of thy witchcrafts, wherein thou hast laboured
from thy youth : perhaps thou canst profit, perhaps thou wilt
inspire terror.   Thou art wearied through the multitude of thy
consultations ; let the dissectors of the heavens come near, then, and
save thee, the star-gazers, they who with every new moon bring
things to light that will come upon thee.   Behold, they have become
like stubble : fire has consumed them : there is not a red-hot coal
to warm themselves, a hearth-fire to sit before.   So is it with thy
people, for whom thou hast laboured : thy partners in trade from
thy youth, they wander away every one in his own direction ; no
one who brings salvation to thee."   Hitzig and others adopt the
simple rendering, " Persevere, then, with thine enchantments."
It is indeed true, that in Lev. xiii. 5 עָמַד בְּ signifies " to remain
standing by anything," *i.e.* to persevere with it, just as in
Ezek. xiii. 5 it signifies to keep one's standing in anything ; in
2 Kings xxiii. 3, to enter upon anything ; and in Eccles. viii. 3,
to engage in anything ; but there is no reason for taking it here
in any other sense than in ver. 13.   Babylon is to draw near
with all the processes of the black art, wherein (בַּאֲשֶׁר, according
to our western mode of expression, equivalent to אֲשֶׁר בָּהֶם,
Ges. 123, 2*) it had been addicted to abundance of routine
from its youth upwards (יָגַעַתְּ with an auxiliary *pathach* for
יָגַעְתְּ) ; possibly it may be of some use, possibly it will terrify,
i.e. make itself so terrible to the approaching calamity, as to
cause it to keep off.   The prophet now sees in spirit how
Babylon draws near, and how it also harasses itself to no purpose ; he therefore follows up the עֲמָדִי־נָא, addressed *in pleno* to
Babylon, with a second challenge commencing with יַעַמְדוּ־נָא.

Their astrologers are to draw near, and try that power over the
future to which they lay claim, by bringing it to bear at once upon
the approaching destruction for the benefit of Babylon. עֲצָתַיִךְ
is a singular form connected with a feminine plural suffix, such
as we find in Ps. ix. 15, Ezek. xxxv. 11, Ezra ix. 15, connected
with a masculine plural suffix. Assuming the correctness of
the vowel-pointing, the singular appears in such cases as these
to have a collective meaning, like the Arabic *pl. fractus;* for
there is no ground to suppose that the Aramæan plural form
'*ētsâth* is used here in the place of the Hebrew. Instead of
הברו שמים (which would be equivalent to אשר הברו), the *keri*
reads הֹבְרֵי שָׁמַיִם, cutters up of the heavens, *i.e.* planners or
dissectors of them, from *hâbhar, dissecare, resecare* (compare
the rabbinical *hăbhârâh*, a syllable, *i.e. segmentum vocabuli,* and
possibly also the talmudic '*ēbhârīm*, limbs of a body). The
correction proposed by Knobel, viz. *chōbh'rē*, from *châbhār,* to
know, or be versed in, is unnecessary. *Châzâh b'* signifies here,
as it generally does, to look with pleasure or with interest at anything; hence Luther has rendered it correctly, *die Sternkucker*
(Eng. ver. star-gazers). They are described still further as those
who make known with every new moon (*lechŏdâshīm*, like
labb'qârīm, every morning, ch. xxxiii. 2, etc.), things which,
etc. מֵאֲשֶׁר is used in a partitive sense : out of the great mass
of events they select the most important, and prepare a calendar
or almanack (ἀλμενιχιακά in Plutarch) for the state every
month. But these very wise men cannot save themselves, to
say nothing of others, out of the power of that flame, which is
no comforting coal-fire to warm one's self by, no hearth-fire
(ch. xliv. 16) to sit in front of, but a devouring, eternal, *i.e.*
peremptory flame (ch. xxxiii. 14). The rendering adopted by
Grotius, Vitringa, Lowth, Gesenius, and others, " *non supererit
pruna ad calendum,*" is a false one, if only because it is not
in harmony with the figure. " Thus shall they be unto thee,"
he continues in ver. 15, *i.e.* such things shall be endured to
thy disgrace by those about whom thou hast wearied thyself
(אֲשֶׁר = בָּהֶם אֲשֶׁר). The learned orders of the Chaldeans had
their own quarter, and enjoyed all the distinction and privileges
of a priestly caste. What follows cannot possibly be understood as relating to these masters of astrology and witchcraft,
as Ewald supposes; for, according to the expression שְׁחַרָהּ in

ver. 11, they would be called שְׁחֲרָיִךְ. Moreover, if they became a prey of the flames, and therefore were unable to flee, we should have to assume that they were burned while taking flight (Umbreit). סֹחֲרָיִךְ are those who carried on commercial intercourse with the great "trading city" (Ezek. xvii. 4), as Berossos says, " In Babylon there was a great multitude of men of other nations who had settled in Chaldea, and they lived in disorder, like the wild beasts;" compare Æschylus, *Pers.* 52–3, Βαβυλὼν δ' ἡ πολύχρυσος πάμμικτον ὄχλον πέμπει. All of these are scattered in the wildest flight, אִישׁ אֶל־עֶבְרוֹ, every one on his own side, viz. in the direction of his own home, and do not trouble themselves about Babylon.

NINTH PROPHECY.—Chap. XLVIII.

DELIVERANCE FROM BABYLON.

This third portion of the trilogy (ch. xlvi. xlvii. xlviii.) stands in the same relation to ch. xlvii., as ch. xlvi. 3 sqq. to ch. xlvi. 1, 2. The prophecy is addressed to the great body of the captives. Vers. 1, 2. "*Hear ye this, O house of Jacob, who are called by the name of Israel, and have flowed out of the waters of Judah, who swear by the name of Jehovah, and extol the God of Israel, not in truth and not in righteousness! For they call themselves of the holy city, and stay themselves upon the God of Israel, Jehovah of hosts His name.*" The summons to hear is based upon the Israelitish nationality of those who are summoned, to which they still cling, and upon the relation in which they place themselves to the God of Israel. This gives to Jehovah the right to turn to them, and imposes upon them the duty to hearken to Him. The blame, inserted by the way, points at the same time to the reason for the address which follows, and to the form which it necessarily assumes. "The house of Jacob" is not all Israel, as the following words clearly show, but, as in ch. xlvi. 3, the house of Judah, which shared in the honourable name of Israel, but have flowed out of the waters, *i.e.* the source of Judah. The summons, therefore, is addressed to the Judæan exiles in Babylon, and that inasmuch as they swear by the name of Jehovah, and remember the God of Israel with praise (*hizkīr b'* as in Ps. xx. 8), though not in truth and not in righteousness (1 Kings iii. 6; Zech. viii. 8), *i.e.* without their state of mind (cf. ch. xxxviii. 3, Jer. xxxii. 41) or mode of action corresponding to their confession, so as to prove that it was sincerely and seriously meant. The praise bestowed upon the persons summoned, which is somewhat spoiled by this, is explained in ver. 2; they call themselves after the holy city (this title is applied to Jerusalem both here and in ch. lii. 1, as well as in the books of Daniel and Nehemiah). We may easily supply here, that the holiness of the city laid an obligation upon its citizens to be holy in their character and conduct. They also relied upon the God of Israel, whose name is Jehovah Zebaoth; and therefore He could require of them the fullest confidence and deepest reverence.

After this summons, and description of those who are summoned, the address of Jehovah begins. Vers. 3–5. "*The first I have long ago proclaimed, and it has gone forth out of my mouth, and I caused it to be heard. I carried it out suddenly, and it came to pass. Because I knew that thou art hard, and thy neck an iron clasp, and thy brow of brass; I proclaimed it to thee long ago; before it came to pass, I caused thee to hear it, that thou mightest not say, My idol has done it, and my graven image and molten image commanded it.*" The word הָרִאשׁוֹנוֹת in itself signifies simply *priora*; and then, according to the context, it signifies *prius facta* (ch. xlvi. 9), or *prius prædicta* (ch. xliii. 9), or *prius eventura* (ch. xli. 22, xlii. 9). In the present passage it refers to earlier occurrences, which Jehovah had foretold, and, when the time fixed for their accomplishment arrived, which He had immediately brought to pass. With a retrospective glance at this, we find plural masc. suffixes (cf. ch. xli. 27) used interchangeably with plural fem. (cf. ver. 7 and ch. xxxviii. 16); the prophet more frequently uses the sing. fem. in this neuter sense (ch. xli. 20, xlii. 23, etc.), and also, though very rarely, the sing. masc. (ch. xlv. 8). On *gîd*, a band, a sinew, but here a clasp (cf. Arab. *kaid*, a fetter), see *Psychology*, p. 233. *Nechûshâh* is a poetical equivalent for *nechôsheth*, as in ch. xlv. 2. The heathen cravings of Israel, which reached into the captivity, are here presupposed. Hengstenberg is mistaken in his supposition, that the prophet's standpoint is always anterior to the captivity when he speaks in condemnation of idolatry. We cannot draw any conclusion from the character of the community that returned, with regard to that of the people of the captivity generally. The great mass even of Judah, and still more of Israel, remained behind, and became absorbed into the heathen, to whom they became more and more assimilated. And does not Ezekiel expressly state in ch. xx. 30 sqq., that the *golah* by the Chaboras defiled themselves with the same abominations of idolatry as their fathers, and that the prevailing disposition was to combine the worship of Jehovah with heathenism, or else to exchange the former altogether for the latter? And we know that it was just the same with the exiles in Egypt, among whom the life and labours of Jeremiah terminated. Wherever the prophet speaks of פִּשְׁעִים and רְשָׁעִים, these names invariably include a tendency or falling away to Babylonian idolatry, to which he describes the exiles as having been addicted, both in ch. lxvi. 17 and elsewhere.

But in order to determine exactly what "the former things" were, which Jehovah had foretold in order that Israel might not ascribe them to this idol or the other, we must add vers. 6-8: "*Thou hast heard it, look then at it all; and ye, must ye not confess it? I give thee new things to hear from this time forth, and hidden things, and what thou didst not know. It is created now, and not long ago; and thou hast not heard it before, that thou mightest not say, Behold, I knew it. Thou hast neither heard it, nor known it, nor did thine ear open itself to it long ago: for I knew thou art altogether faithless, and thou art called rebellious from the womb.*" The meaning of the question in ver. 6*a* is very obvious: they must acknowledge and attest, even though against their will (ch. xliii. 10, xliv. 8), that Jehovah has foretold all that is now confirmed by the evident fulfilment. Consequently the "former things" are the events experienced by the people from the very earliest times (ch. xlvi. 9) down to the present times of Cyrus, and more especially the first half or epoch of this period itself, which expired at the time that formed the prophet's standpoint. And as the object of the prediction was to guard Israel against ascribing to its idols that which had taken place (which can only be understood of events that had occurred in favour of Israel), the "former things" must include the preparation for the redemption of Israel from the Babylonian captivity through the revolution brought to pass by Cyrus. Hence the " new things" will embrace the redemption of Israel with its attendant circumstances, and that not merely on its outward side, but on its spiritual side as well; also the glorification of the redeemed people in the midst of a world of nations converted to the God of Israel, and the creation of a new heaven and a new earth ; in short, the New Testament æon (compare לִבְרִית עָם, LXX. εἰς διαθήκην γένους, ch. xlii. 6), with the facts which contribute to its ultimate completion (cf. ch. xlii. 9). The announcement and realization of these absolutely new and hitherto secret things (cf. Rom. xvi. 25) take place from this time forward ; Israel has not heard of them " before to-day" (compare מִיּוֹם, "from this day forward," ch. xliii. 13), that it may not lay claim to the knowledge conveyed to it by prophecy, as something drawn from itself. This thought is carried to a climax in ver. 8 in three correlated sentences commencing with "yea" (gam). פִּתְּח signifies patescere here, as in ch. lx. 11 (Ewald, § 120, a). Jehovah had said nothing to them of this before, because it was to be feared that, with their faithlessness and tendency to idolatry, which had run through their entire history, they would only abuse it. This is strange! On the one hand, the rise of Cyrus is spoken of here as predicted from of old, because it belonged to the " former things," and as knowable through prophecy,—a statement which favours the opinion that these addresses were written before the captivity; and, on the other hand, a distinction is drawn between these " former things" and certain " new things" that were intentionally not predicted before the expiration of these " former things," which certainly seems to preclude the possibility of their having been composed before the captivity; since, as Ruetschi observes, if " the older Isaiah had predicted this, he would have acted in direct opposition to Jehovah's design." But in actual fact, the dilemma in which the opponents of the authenticity of these prophecies find themselves, is comparatively worse than this. For the principal objection—namely, that a prophet before the captivity could not possibly have known or predicted anything concerning Cyrus— cannot be satisfactorily removed by attributing these prophecies to a prophet of the time of the captivity, since they expressly and repeatedly affirm that the rise of Cyrus was an event foreknown and predicted by the God of prophecy. Now, if it is Isaiah who thus takes his stand directly in the midst of the captivity, we can understand both of these : viz. the retrospective glance at previous prophecies, which issued in the rise of Cyrus that prepared the way for the redemption from Babylon, since, so far as the prophet was concerned, such prophecies as ch. xiii.–xiv. 23, xxi. 1–10, and also ch. xi. 10–12 (Mic. iv. 10), are fused into one with his present predictions ; and also the prospective glance at prophecies which are now first to be uttered, and events which are now for the first time about to be accomplished ; inasmuch as the revelations contained in these prophecies concerning Israel's pathway through suffering to glory, more especially so far as they grew out of the idea of the " servant of Jehovah," might really be set down as absolutely new to the prophet himself, and never heard of before. Meanwhile our exposition is not affected by the critical question ; for even we most firmly maintain, that the prophet who is speaking here has his standpoint in the midst of the captivity, on the boundary line of the condition of suffering and punishment and its approaching termination.

The people now expiating its offences in exile has been from time immemorial faithless and inclined to apostasy ; nevertheless Jehovah will save it, and its salvation is therefore an unmerited work of His compassion. Vers. 9–11. "*For my name's sake I lengthen out my wrath, and for my praise I hold back towards thee, that I may not cut thee off. Behold, I have refined thee, and not in the manner of silver : I have proved thee in the furnace of affliction. For mine own sake, for mine own sake I accomplish it (for how is it profaned!), and my glory I give not to another.*" The futures in ver. 9 affirm what Jehovah continually does. He lengthens out His wrath, *i.e.* He retards its outbreak, and thus shows Himself long-suffering.

He tames or chains it (הֶחֱטַם, like خَبَلَ, root טם, compare *domare*,

root Sanscr. *dam*, possibly also to dam or damp) for the sake of Israel, that He may not exterminate it utterly by letting it loose, and that for the sake of His name and His praise, which require the carrying out of His plan of salvation, on which the existence of Israel depends. What Israel has

hitherto experienced has been a melting, the object of which
was not destruction, but testing and refinement.   The *Beth* of
וְלֹא בְכָסֶף is not *Beth pretii* in the sense of " not to gain silver,"
or " not so that I should have gained silver as *operæ pretium*,"
as Umbreit and Ewald maintain (and even Knobel, who
explains it however as meaning " in the accompaniment of
silver," though in the same sense).   Such a thought would be
out of place and purposeless here.   Nor is Rosenmüller's explanation admissible, viz. " not with silver, *i.e.* with that force
of fire which is necessary for the smelting out of silver."   This
is altogether unsuitable, because the sufferings inflicted upon
Israel did resemble the smelting out of the precious metal (see
ch. i. 25).   The *Beth* is rather the *Beth essentiæ*, which may be
rendered by *tanquam*, and introduces the accusative predicate
in this instance, just as it introduces the nominative predicate
in the substantive clause of Job xxiii. 13, and the verbal clause
of Ps. xxxix. 7.   Jehovah melted Israel, but not like silver
(not as men melt silver) ; the meaning of which is, not that
He melted it more severely, *i.e.* even more thoroughly, than
silver, as Stier explains it, but, as the thought is positively
expressed in ver. 10*b*, that the afflictions which fell upon
Israel served as a smelting furnace (*kūr* as in Deut. iv. 20).
It was, however, a smelting of a superior kind, a spiritual
refining and testing (*bâchar* is Aramaic in form, and equivalent to *bâchan*).   The manifestation of wrath, therefore, as
these expressions affirm, had a salutary object ; and in this very
object the intention was involved from the very first, that it
should only last for a time.   He therefore puts an end to it
now for His own sake, *i.e.* not because He is induced to do so
by the merits of Israel, but purely as an act of grace, to satisfy
a demand made upon Him by His own holiness, inasmuch as,
if it continued any longer, it would encourage the heathen to
blaspheme His name, and would make it appear as though He
cared nothing for His own honour, which was inseparably
bound up with the existence of Israel.   The expression here
is curt and harsh throughout.   In ver. 9*b*, לְמַעַן and אַפִּי are to
be supplied in thought from ver. 9*a* ; and in the parenthetical
exclamation, אֵיךְ יֵחָל (*niphal* of חָלַל, as in Ezek. xxii. 26), the
distant word שְׁמִי (my name), also from ver. 9*a*.   " I will do it "
refers to the carrying out of their redemption (cf. ch. xliv. 23).

In Ezek. xxxvi. 19–23 we have, as it were, a commentary upon ver. 11.

The prophecy opened with " Hear ye ;" and now the second half commences with " Hear." Three times is the appeal made to Israel : Hear ye ; Jehovah alone is God, Creator, shaper of history, God of prophecy and of fulfilment. Vers. 12–16. " *Hearken to me, O Jacob, and Israel my called ! I am it, I first, also I last. My hand also hath laid the foundation of the earth, and my right hand hath spanned the heavens : I call to them, and they stand there together. All ye, assemble yourselves, and hear : Who among them hath proclaimed this ? He whom Jehovah loveth will accomplish his will upon Babel, and his arm upon the Chaldeans. I, I have spoken, have also called him, have brought him here, and his way prospers. Come ye near to me ! Hear ye this ! I have not spoken in secret, from the beginning : from the time that it takes place, there am I : and now the Lord Jehovah hath sent me and His Spirit.*" Israel is to hearken to the call of Jehovah. The obligation to this exists, on the one hand, in the fact that it is the nation called to be the servant of Jehovah (ch. xli. 9), the people of sacred history ; and on the other hand, in the fact that Jehovah is הוא (ever since Deut. xxxii. 39, the fundamental clause of the Old Testament *credo*), *i.e.* the absolute and eternally unchangeable One, the Alpha and Omega of all history, more especially of that of Israel, the Creator of the earth and heavens (*tippach*, like *nâtâh* elsewhere, equivalent to the Syriac *t^e phach*, to spread out), at whose almighty call they stand ready to obey, with all the beings they contain. קֹרֵא אֲנִי is virtually a conditional sentence (Ewald, § 357, *b*). So far everything has explained the reason for the exhortation to listen to Jehovah. A further reason is now given, by His summoning the members of His nation to assemble together, to hear His own self-attestation, and to confirm it : Who among them (the gods of the heathen) has proclaimed this, or anything of the kind ? That which no one but Jehovah has ever predicted follows immediately, in the form of an independent sentence, the subject of which is יְהֹוָה אֲהֵבוֹ (cf. ch. xli. 24) : He whom Jehovah loveth will accomplish his will upon Babylon, and his arm (accomplish it) upon the Chaldeans. וּזְרֹעוֹ is not an accusative (as Hitzig, Ewald, Stier, and others maintain) ; for the expression " accom-

plish his arm" (? Jehovah's or his own) is a phrase that is
quite unintelligible, even if taken as zeugmatic; it is rather
the nominative of the subject, whilst בְּכַשְׂדִּים = בַּכַּשְׂדִּים, like
תִהְלָתִי = תְהִלָּתִי = לְמַעַן in ver. 9. Jehovah, He alone, is He who
has proclaimed such things; He also has raised up in Cyrus
the predicted conqueror of Babylon. The prosperity of his
career is Jehovah's work. As certainly now as הִקְבְּצוּ in ver.
14 is the word of Jehovah, so certain is it that קִרְבוּ אֵלַי is the
same. He summons to Himself the members of His nation,
that they may hear still further His own testimony concerning
Himself. From the beginning He has not spoken in secret
(see ch. xlv. 19); but from the time that all which now lies
before their eyes—namely, the victorious career of Cyrus—has
unfolded itself, He has been there, or has been by (shâm, there,
as in Prov. viii. 27), to regulate what was coming to pass, and
to cause it to result in the redemption of Israel. Hofmann
gives a different explanation, viz.: "I have not spoken in secret
from the beginning; not from the time when it came to pass
(not then for the first time, but long before); I was then
(when it occurred)." But the arrangement of the words is
opposed to this continued force of the לֹא, and the accents are
opposed to this breaking off of the שָׁם אֲנִי, which affirms that,
at the time when the revolution caused by Cyrus was preparing
in the distance, He caused it to be publicly foretold, and
thereby proclaimed Himself the present Author and Lord of
what was then occurring. Up to this point Jehovah is speaking;
but who is it that now proceeds to say, "And now—namely,
now that the redemption of Israel is about to appear (וְעַתָּה
being here, as in many other instances, e.g. ch. xxxiii. 10, the
turning-point of salvation)—now hath the Lord Jehovah sent
me and His Spirit?" The majority of the commentators assume that the prophet comes forward here in his own person,
behind Him whom he has introduced, and interrupts Him.
But although it is perfectly true, that in all prophecy, from
Deuteronomy onwards, words of Jehovah through the prophet
and words of the prophet of Jehovah alternate in constant,
and often harsh transitions, and that our prophet has this mark
of divine inspiration in common with all the other prophets
(cf. ch. lxii. 5, 6), it must also be borne in mind, that hitherto
he has not spoken once objectively of himself, except quite

indirectly (*vid.* ch. xl. 6, xliv. 26), to say nothing of actually coming forward in his own person. Whether this takes place further on, more especially in ch. lxi., we will leave for the present; but here, since the prophet has not spoken in his own person before, whereas, on the other hand, these words are followed in ch. xlix. 1 sqq. by an address concerning himself from that servant of Jehovah who announces himself as the restorer of Israel and light of the Gentiles, and who cannot therefore be either Israel as a nation or the author of these prophecies, nothing is more natural than to suppose that the words, " And now hath the Lord," etc., form a prelude to the words of the One unequalled servant of Jehovah concerning Himself which occur in ch. xlix. The surprisingly mysterious way in which the words of Jehovah suddenly pass into those of His messenger, which is only comparable to Zech. ii. 12 sqq., iv. 9 (where the speaker is also not the prophet, but a divine messenger exalted above him), can only be explained in this manner. And in no other way can we explain the וְעַתָּה, which means that, after Jehovah has prepared the way for the redemption of Israel by the raising up of Cyrus, in accordance with prophecy, and by his success in arms, He has sent him, the speaker in this case, to carry out, in a mediatorial capacity, the redemption thus prepared, and that not by force of arms, but in the power of the Spirit of God (ch. xlii. 1; cf. Zech. iv. 6). Consequently the Spirit is not spoken of here as joining in the sending (as Umbreit and Stier suppose, after Jerome and the Targum: the Septuagint is indefinite, καὶ τὸ πνεῦμα αὐτοῦ); nor do we ever find the Spirit mentioned in such co-ordination as this (see, on the other hand, Zech. vii. 12, *per spiritum suum*). The meaning is, that it is also sent, *i.e.* sent in and with the servant of Jehovah, who is speaking here. To convey this meaning, there was no necessity to write either שָׁלַח אֹתִי וְרוּחוֹ or שְׁלַחַנִי וְאֶת־רוּחוֹ, since the expression is just the same as that in ch. xxix. 7, צֹבֶיהָ וּמְצֹדָתָהּ; and the *Vav* may be regarded as the *Vav* of companionship (*Mitschaft*, lit. with-ship, as the Arabs call it; see at ch. xlii. 5).

The exhortation is now continued. Israel is to learn the incomparable nature of Jehovah from the work of redemption thus prepared in word and deed. The whole future depends upon the attitude which it henceforth assumes to His command-

ments. Vers. 17–19. " *Thus saith Jehovah, thy Redeemer, the
Holy One of Israel; I, Jehovah thy God, am He that teacheth
thee to do that which profiteth, and leadeth thee by the way that
thou shouldst go. O that thou hearkenedst to my commandments!
then thy peace becomes like the river, and thy righteousness like
waves of the sea; and thy seed becomes like the sand, and the
children of thy body like the grains thereof: its name will not be
cut off nor destroyed away from my countenance.*" Jehovah is
Israel's rightful and right teacher and leader. לְהוֹעִיל is used in
the same sense as in ch. xxx. 5 and xliv. 10, to furnish what
is useful, to produce what is beneficial or profitable. The
optative לוּא is followed, as in ch. lxiii. 19, by the preterite
utinam attenderis, the idea of reality being mixed up with the
wish. Instead of וַיְהִי in the apodosis, we should expect וִיהִי
(so would), as in Deut. xxxii. 29. The former points out the
consequence of the wish regarded as already realized. *Shâlōm*,
prosperity or health, will thereby come upon Israel in such
abundance, that it will, as it were, bathe therein ; and *ts͏eḏâqâh*,
rectitude acceptable to God, so abundantly, that it, the sinful
one, will be covered by it over and over again. Both of these,
shâlōm and *ts͏eḏâqâh*, are introduced here as a divine gift, not
merited by Israel, but only conditional upon that faith which
gives heed to the word of God, especially to the word which
promises redemption, and appropriates it to itself. Another
consequence of the obedience of faith is, that Israel thereby
becomes a numerous and eternally enduring nation. The play
upon the words in מֵעֶיךָ כִּמְעוֹתָיו is very conspicuous. Many
expositors (*e.g.* Rashi, Gesenius, Hitzig, and Knobel) regard
מְעוֹת as synonymous with מֵעִים, and therefore as signifying the
viscera, *i.e.* the beings that fill the heart of the sea ; but it is
much more natural to suppose that the suffix points back to *chōl*.
Moreover, no such metaphorical use of *viscera* can be pointed
out ; and since in other instances the feminine plural (such
as *k͏enâphōth, q͏erânōth*) denotes that which is artificial as distinguished from what is natural, it is impossible to see why the
interior of the sea, which is elsewhere called *lēbh* (*l͏ebhabh*, the
heart), and indirectly also *beten*, should be called מְעוֹת instead
of מֵעִים. To all appearance מְעוֹתָיו signifies the grains of sand
(LXX., Jerome, Targ.) ; and this is confirmed by the fact that
מְעָא (Neo-Heb. מֵעָה *numulus*) is the Targum word for גֵּרָה, and

the Semitic root מֵע, related to מֵג ; מֵק, melted, dissolved, signifies to be soft or tender. The conditional character of the concluding promise has its truth in the word מִלְּפָנַי. Israel remains a nation even in its apostasy, but fallen under the punishment of *kareth* (of cutting off), under which individuals perish when they wickedly transgress the commandment of circumcision, and others of a similar kind. It is still a people, but rooted out and swept away from the gracious countenance of God, who no more acknowledges it as His own people.

So far the address is hortatory. In the face of the approaching redemption, it demands fidelity and faith. But in the certainty that such a faithful and believing people will not be wanting within the outer Israel, the prophecy of redemption clothes itself in the form of a summons. Vers. 20–22. "*Go out of Babel, flee from Chaldœa with voice of shouting: declare ye, preach ye this, carry it out to the end of the earth! Say ye, Jehovah hath redeemed Jacob His servant. And they thirsted not: He led them through dry places; He caused water to trickle out of rocks for them; He split rocks, and waters gushed out. There is no peace, saith Jehovah, for the wicked.*" They are to go out of Babylon, and with speed and joy to leave the land of slavery and idolatry far behind. *Bârach* does not mean literally to flee in this instance, but to depart with all the rapidity of flight (compare Ex. xiv. 5). And what Jehovah has done to them, is to be published by them over the whole earth; the redemption experienced by Israel is to become a gospel to all mankind. The tidings which are to be sent forth (הוֹצִיא as in ch. xlii. 1), extend from גְּאַל to the second מַיִם, which is repeated palindromically. Jehovah has redeemed the nation that He chose to be the bearer of His salvation, amidst displays of love, in which the miracles of the Egyptian redemption have been renewed. This is what Israel has to experience, and to preach, so far as it has remained true to its God. But there is no peace, saith Jehovah, to the *r°shâ'îm :* this is the name given to *loose* men (for the primary meaning of the verbal root is laxity and looseness), *i.e.* to those whose inward moral nature is loosened, without firm hold, and therefore in a state of chaotic confusion, because they are without God. The reference is to the godless in Israel. The words express the same thought negatively which is expressed positively in Gal. vi. 16, "Peace upon the Israel of God." *Shâlôm* is the significant and comprehensive name given to the coming salvation. From this the godless exclude themselves; they have no part in the future inheritance; the sabbatical rest reserved for the people of God does not belong to them. With this divine utterance, which pierces the conscience like the point of an arrow, this ninth prophecy is brought to a close; and not that only, but also the trilogy concerning "Babel" in ch. xlvi.–xlix., and the whole of the first third of these 3×9 addresses to the exiles. From this time forth the name *Kōresh* (Cyrus), and also the name *Babel*, never occur again; the relation of the people of Jehovah to heathenism, and the redemption from Babylon, so far as it was foretold and accomplished by Jehovah, not only proving His sole deity, but leading to the overthrow of the idols and the destruction of their worshippers. This theme is now exhausted, and comes into the foreground no more. The expression שִׁמְעוּ אִיִּים, in its connection with נִחֲמוּ עַמִּי, points at once to the diversity in character of the second section, which commences here.

PART II.

FIRST PROPHECY.—Chap. xlix.

SELF-ATTESTATION OF THE SERVANT OF JEHOVAH. THE DESPONDENCY OF ZION REPROVED.

THE very same person who was introduced by Jehovah in ch. xlii. 1 sqq. here speaks for himself, commencing thus in vers. 1–3: "*Listen, O isles, unto me; and hearken, ye nations afar off: Jehovah hath called me from the womb; from my mother's lap hath He remembered my name. And He made my mouth like a sharp sword; in the shadow of His hand hath He hid me, and made me into a polished shaft; in His quiver hath He concealed me. And He said to me, Thou art my servant, O Israel, thou in whom I glorify myself.*" Although the speaker is called Israel in ver. 3b, he must not be regarded as either a collective person representing all Israel, or as the collective personality of the kernel of Israel, which answered to its true idea. It is not the former, because in ver. 5 he is expressly distinguished from the nation itself, which is the immediate object of his special work as restorer and (according to ver. 8 and ch. xlii. 6) covenant-mediator also; not the latter, because the nation, whose restoration he effects, according to ver. 5, was not something distinct from the collective personality of the "servant of Jehovah" in a national sense, but rather the entire body of the "servants of Jehovah" or remnant of Israel (see, for example, ch. lxv. 8–16). Moreover, it cannot be either of these, because what he affirms of himself is expressed in such terms of individuality, that they cannot be understood as employed in a collective sense at all, more especially where he speaks of his mother's womb. In every other case in which Israel is spoken of in this way, we find only "from the womb" (*mibbeten*, ch. xliv. 2, 24; xlvi. 3, along with *minnī-racham*; also ch. xlviii. 8), without the addition of אֵם (mother), which is quite unsuitable to the collective body of the nation (except in such allegorical connections as ch. li. 1, 2, and Ezek. xvi. 3). Is it then possibly the prophet, who is here speaking of himself and refers in ver. 1*b* to his own mother (compare אִמִּי in Jer. xv. 10, xx. 14, 17)? This is very improbable, if only because the prophet, who is the medium of the word of God in these prophecies, has never placed himself in the foreground before. In ch. xl. 6 he merely speaks of himself indirectly; in ch. xliv. 26, even if he refer to himself at all (which we greatly doubt), it is only objectively; and in ch. xlviii. 16, the other person, into whose words the words of Jehovah pass, cannot be the prophet, for the simple reason that the transition of the words of Jehovah into those of His messenger is essentially different in this instance from the otherwise frequent interchange of the words of Jehovah and those of His prophet, and also because the messenger of Jehovah speaks of himself there, after the "former things" have come to pass, as the mediator (either in word or deed) of the "new things" which were never heard of before, but are to be expected now; whereas the author of these addresses was also the prophet of the "former things," and therefore the messenger referred to rises up within the course of sacred history predicted by the author of these prophecies. Moreover, what the speaker in this case (ch. xlix. 1, 2) says of

himself is so unique, so glorious, that it reaches far beyond the
vocation and performance of any single prophet, or, in fact, of
any individual man subject to the limitations of human life and
human strength.   There is nothing else left, therefore, than
to suppose that the idea implied in the expression "servant of
Jehovah" is condensed in this instance, as in ch. xlii. 1 sqq.,
into that of a single person.   When it is expanded to its
widest circumference, the "servant of Jehovah" is all Israel;
when it only covers its smaller and inner circle, it is the true
people of Jehovah contained within the entire nation, like the
kernel in the shell (see the definition of this at ch. li. 7, lxv. 10;
Ps. xxiv. 6, lxxiii. 15); but here it goes back to its very centre.
The "servant of Jehovah," in this central sense, is the heart
of Israel.   From this heart of Israel the stream of salvation
flows out, first of all through the veins of the people of God,
and thence through the veins of the nations generally.   Just
as Cyrus is the world-power in person, as made subservient to
the people of God, so the servant of Jehovah, who is speaking here, is Israel in person, as promoting the glorification of
Jehovah in all Israel, and in all the world of nations : in other
words, it is He in whom the true nature of Israel is concentrated
like a sun, in whom the history of Israel is coiled up as into
a knot for a further and final development, in whom Israel's
world-wide calling to be the Saviour of mankind, including
Israel itself, is fully carried out; the very same who took up the
word of Jehovah in ch. xlviii. 16b, in the full consciousness of
His fellowship with Him, declaring Himself to be His messenger who had now appeared.   It must not be forgotten, moreover, that throughout these prophecies the breaking forth of
salvation, not for Israel only, but for all mankind, is regarded
as bound up with the termination of the captivity; and from
this its basis, the restoration of the people who were then in
exile, it is never separated.   This fact is of great importance in
relation to the question of authorship, and favours the conclusion that they emanated from a prophet who lived before the
captivity, and not in the midst of it.   Just as in ch. vii. Isaiah
sees the son of the virgin grow up in the time of the Assyrian
oppressions, and then sees his kingdom rising up on the ruins
of the Assyrian (cf. vol. i. p. 227); so does he here behold the
servant of Jehovah rising up in the second half of the captivity,

as if born in exile, in the midst of the punishment borne by his people, to effect the restoration of Israel. At the present time, when he begins to speak, coming forward without any further introduction, and speaking in his own name (a unique instance of dramatic style, which goes beyond even Ps. ii.), he has already left behind him the commencement of his work, which was directed towards the salvation of mankind. His appeal is addressed to the "isles," which had been frequently mentioned already when the evangelization of the heathen was spoken of (ch. xlii. 4, 10, 12; cf. ch. xxiv. 15), and to the "nations from afar," *i.e.* the distant nations (as in ch. v. 26; compare, on the other hand, Jer. xxiii. 23). They are to hear what he says, not merely what he says in the words that follow, but what he says generally. What follows is rather a vindication of his right to demand a hearing and obedience, than the discourse itself, which is to be received with the obedience of faith; at the same time, the two are most intimately connected. Jehovah has called him *ab utero,* has thought of his name from the bowels of his mother (מְעֵי as in Ps. lxxi. 6), *i.e.* even before he was born; ever since his conception has Jehovah assigned to him his calling, viz. his saving calling, and solemnly announced his name in relation to this calling. We call to mind here Jer. i. 5, Luke i. 41, Gal. i. 15, but above all the name Immanuel, which is given by anticipation to the Coming One in ch. vii. 14, and the name Jesus, which God appointed through the mouth of angels, when the human life of Him who was to bear that name was still ripening in the womb of the Virgin (Matt. i. 20-23). It is worthy of notice, however, that the great Coming One, though he is described in the Old Testament as one who is to be looked for "from the seed of David," is also spoken of as "born of a woman," whenever his entrance into the world is directly referred to. In the Protevangelium he is called, though not in an individual sense, "the seed of the woman;" Isaiah, in the time of Ahaz, mentions "the virgin" as his mother; Micah (v. 2) speaks of his יולדה; even the typical psalms, as in Ps. xxii. 10, 11, give prominence to the mother. And is not this a sign that prophecy is a work of the Spirit, who searches out the deep things of the counsel of God? In ver. 2 the speaker says still further, that Jehovah has made his mouth *k^echerebh*

chaddâh (like a sharp sword), namely, that he may overcome
everything that resists him as if with a sharp sword, and sever
asunder things that are bound up together in a pernicious
bond (ch. xi. 4; Rev. i. 16; Heb. iv. 12); also that He has
made him into *chêts bârûr* (not βέλος ἐκλεκτόν, LXX., but, as
in Jer. li. 11, cleaned,[1] polished, sharpened, pointed), namely, to
pierce the hearts (Ps. xlv. 6), and inflict upon them the most
wholesome wounds; and again, that Jehovah has hidden him
under the shadow of His almighty hand, and kept him concealed in the quiver of His loving counsel, just girt as men keep
their swords and arrows in sheaths and quivers ready for the
time when they want to use them, in order that in the fulness of
time He might draw out this His sword, and put this His arrow
to the bow. The question whether the allusion here is to the
time preceding the foreknown period of his coming, or whether
it is to eternity that the words refer, does not present any
great dilemma; at the same time, the prophecy in this instance
only traces back the being of the person, who now appears, to
the remotest point of his historical coming. Ver. 3 describes,
without any figure, what Jehovah has made him. He has said
to him (cf. Ps. ii. 7*b*): Thou art my servant; thou art Israel,
in whom (*in quo*, as in ch. xliv. 23) I glorify myself. Schenkel's
exposition is grammatically impossible: " (It is) in Israel that
I will glorify myself through thee." The servant himself is
called Israel. We call to mind here the expression in Matt.
xvi. 18, "Thou art Peter;" and the use of the name "Israel," as
the individuation of a generic name, reminds us of the fact that
the kings of a nation are sometimes called by the name of the
nation itself (*e.g.* Asshur, ch. x. 5 sqq.). But Israel was from
the very first the God-given name of an individual. Just as
the name Israel was first of all given to a man, and then after
that to a nation, so the name which sprang from a personal
root has also a personal crown. The servant of Jehovah is
Israel in person, inasmuch as the purpose of mercy, upon the
basis of which and for the accomplishment of which Jehovah
made Jacob the father of the twelve-tribed nation, is brought
by him into full and final realization. We have already seen
that Israel, as an entire nation, formed the basis of the idea

---

[1] The comparison to *purus* is one that naturally suggests itself; but
this, like *putus*, is derived from a root *pû*.

contained in the term "servant of Jehovah;" Israel, regarded as a people faithful to its calling, the centre; and the personal servant of Jehovah its apex. In the present instance, where he is called distinctly "Israel," the fact is clearly expressed, that the servant of Jehovah in these prophecies is regarded as the kernel of the kernel of Israel, as Israel's inmost centre, as Israel's highest head. He it is in whom (*i.e.* on whom and through whom) Jehovah glorifies Himself, inasmuch as He carries out through him the counsels of His love, which are the self-glorification of His holy love, its glory and its triumph.

In the next verse the speaker meets the words of divine calling and promise with a complaint, which immediately silences itself, however. Ver. 4. "*And I, I said, I have wearied myself in vain, and thrown away my strength for nothing and to no purpose; yet my right is with Jehovah, and my reward with my God.*" The *Vav* with which the verse opens introduces the apparent discrepancy between the calling he had received, and the apparent failure of his work. אֲבָל, however, denies the conclusion which might be drawn from this, that there was neither reality nor truth in his call. The relation between the clauses is exactly the same as that in Ps. xxxi. 23 and Jonah ii. 5 (where we find אַךְ, which is more rarely used in this adversative sense); compare also Ps. xxx. 7 (but I said), and the psalm of Hezekiah in ch. xxxviii. 10 with the antithesis in Ps. xxxviii. 15. In the midst of his activity no fruit was to be seen, and the thought came upon him, that it was a failure; but this disturbance of his rejoicing in his calling was soon quieted in the confident assurance that his *mishpât* (*i.e.* his good right in opposition to all contradiction and resistance) and his "work" (*i.e.* the result and fruit of the work, which is apparently in vain) are with Jehovah, and laid up with Him until the time when He will vindicate His servant's right, and crown his labour with success. We must not allow ourselves to be led astray by such parallels as ch. xl. 10, lxii. 11. The words are not spoken in a collective capacity any more than in the former part of the verse; the lamentation of Israel as a people, in ch. xl. 27, is expressed very differently.

The expression "and now" (וְעַתָּה), which follows, evidently indicates a fresh turn in the official life of the person speaking here. At the same time, it is evident that it is the failure of

his labours within his own people, which has forced out the
lamentation in ver. 4a. For his reason for addressing his
summons in ch. xlix. 1 to the world of nations, is that Jehovah
has not guaranteed to him, the undaunted one, success to his
labours among his own people, but has assigned him a mission
extending far beyond and reaching to all mankind. Vers. 5, 6.
"*And now, saith Jehovah, that formed me from the womb to be
His servant, to bring back Jacob to Him, and that Israel may
be gathered together to Him; and I am honoured in the eyes of
Jehovah, and my God has become my strength. He saith, It is
only a small thing that thou becomest my servant, to set up the
tribes of Jacob, and to bring back the preserved of Israel. I
have set thee for the light of the Gentiles, to become my salvation
to the end of the earth.*" Both *shōbhēbh* and *hāshībh* unite
within themselves the meanings *reducere* (Jer. l. 19) and *resti-
tuere*. On לֹא = לוֹ generally, see at ch. ix. 2, lxiii. 9. Jerome
is wrong in his rendering, *et Israel qui non congregabitur* (what
could a prophecy of the rejection of the Jews do here?); so
also is Hitzig's rendering, "since Israel is not swept away;"
and Hofmann's, "Israel, which is not swept away." In the
present instance, where the restoration of Israel is the event
referred to, אסף must signify "the gathering together of Israel,"
as in ch. xi. 12. לוֹ (parallel אֵלָיו) points to Jehovah as the
author of the gathering, and as the object of it also. The
transition from the infinitive of design to the finite verb of
desire, is the same as in ch. xiii. 9, xiv. 25. The attributive
clause, added to the name Jehovah, expresses the lofty mission
of the servant of God with regard to Israel. The parenthesis,
"I have honour in the eyes of Jehovah, and my God has become my strength, *i.e.* has become mighty in me, the apparently
weak one," looks beyond to the still loftier mission, by which
the former lofty one is far surpassed. On account of this
parenthetically inserted praise of Jehovah, the אָמַר is resumed
in וַיֹּאמֶר. Instead of נָקֵל הֱיוֹתְךָ (compare 1 Kings xvi. 31), *i.e.*
it is a small thing that thou shouldst be, we have it here, as
in Ezek. viii. 17, with a comparative *min*, which must not,
however, be logically pressed: "It is smaller than that," *i.e.*
it is too small a thing that thou shouldst be. The *nᵉtsīrē*
(*Keri, nᵉtsūrē*) of Israel are those who have been preserved
in exile (Ezek. vi. 12); in other cases, we find שְׁאָר, שְׁאֵרִית, or

פְּלֵטָה. Not only is the restoration of the remnant of Israel
the work of the servant of Jehovah; but Jehovah has appointed him for something higher than this. He has given
or set him for the light of the heathen ("a light to lighten
the Gentiles," Luke ii. 32), to become His salvation to the
end of the earth (LXX.: τοῦ εἶναί σε εἰς σωτηρίαν ἕως
ἐσχάτου τῆς γῆς). Those who regard Israel as a nation as
speaking here (*e.g.* Hitzig, Ewald, Umbreit, etc.) go right
away from this, which is the most natural sense of the words,
and explain them as meaning, "that my salvation may be,
reach, or penetrate to the end of the earth." But inasmuch as
the servant of Jehovah is the light of the world, he is through
that very fact the salvation of the world; and he is both of
these through Jehovah, whose counsels of יְשׁוּעָה are brought by
him into historical realization and visible manifestation.

The words of the servant of God, in which he enforces
his claim upon the nations, are now lost in words of Jehovah
to him, which are no longer reported by him, but are appended
as an independent address. His present condition is one of the
deepest humiliation. Ver. 7. "*Thus saith Jehovah, the Redeemer of Israel, His Holy One, to him of contemptible soul, to
the abhorrence of the people, to the servant of tyrants: kings shall
see and arise; princes, and prostrate themselves for the sake of
Jehovah, who is faithful, the Holy One of Israel, that He hath
chosen thee.*" As *bâzōh* with a changeable *kametz* (cf. *châmōts*, ch.
i. 17) has, if not exactly a passive force, yet something very like
a passive circumstantial meaning, בְּזֹה־נֶפֶשׁ must mean the man
who is contemptible as regards his soul, *i.e.* held in contempt,
or, as Hofmann explains it, whom men do not think worthy to
live (though he follows Ewald, and takes *b^ezōh* as an infinitive
treated as a substantive). Accordingly מְתָעֵב is also to be taken
personally. The meaning *abhorring* is unsuitable; but תִּעֵב is
also used in a causative sense, to cause to abhor, *i.e.* to make a
thing an abomination (Ezek. xvi. 25), or to excite abhorrence:
hence, "to him who excites the people's abhorrence," which is
the same, so far as the sense is concerned, as "to the object of
their abhorrence." But even as a participial substantive מְתָעֵב
would literally mean the thing exciting abhorrence, *i.e.* the
abhorrence, just as *m^ekhasseh* in ch. xxiii. 18 signifies the thing
covering, *i.e.* the covering. All these participial substantives

of the *piel* indicate the thing, place, or instrument accomplishing that which the *piel* affirms. We need not raise the question whether *gōi* refers to Israel or to the heathen. It signifies the mass of men, the people, like *'ām* in Ps. lxii. 9, and in those passages in which it is used by our prophet for the human race generally. The *mōsh*^e*līm*, of whom the person here addressed is the servant or enslaved one, are obviously heathen tyrants. What is here affirmed of the "one servant of Jehovah" was no doubt also applicable to the nation generally, and more especially to that portion of the nation which was true to its calling and confession. He in whom Israel's relation of servant to Jehovah was fully realized, did indeed spring out of His own nation, when it was under the oppression of the powers of this world; and all the shame and persecution which those who remained faithful among His people had to endure from the heathen oppressors, and also from the ungodly among their own countrymen (see, for example, ch. lxvi. 5), discharge their force like a violent storm upon Him as an individual. When, therefore, we find the sufferings of the people and the glory of which they became partakers described in other passages in just the same terms, we must not infer from this that "servant of Jehovah" is a collective epithet in the passage before us. The person addressed here is the Restorer of Israel, the Light of the Gentiles, the Salvation of Jehovah for all mankind. When kings and princes shall behold Him who was once brought so low, delivered from His humiliation, and exalted to the glorious height of the work to which He has been called, they will rise up with reverence from their thrones, and prostrate themselves upon the ground in worship for the sake of Jehovah, as before Him who (אֲשֶׁר emphatic, *utpote qui*) is faithful, showing Himself sincere in His promises, and for the sake of the Holy One of Israel, in that, as is now made manifest, "He hath chosen thee." The *fut. consec.* particularizes the general motive assigned, and carries it still further.

The next two verses describe (though only with reference to Israel, the immediate circle) what is the glory of the vocation to which Jehovah, in accordance with His promise, exalts His chosen One. Vers. 8, 9a. "*Thus saith Jehovah, In a time of favour have I heard thee, and in the day of salvation have I helped thee: and I form thee, and set thee for a covenant of the*

people, to raise up the land, to apportion again desolate inherit-
ances, saying to prisoners, Go ye out : to those who are in dark-
ness, Come ye to the light." Jehovah heard His servant, and
came to his help when he prayed to Him out of the condition
of bondage to the world, which he shared with his people. He
did it at the time for the active display of His good pleasure,
and for the realizing of salvation, which had been foreseen by
Him, and had now arrived. The futures which follow are to
be taken as such. The fact that Jehovah makes His servant
"a covenant of the people," *i.e.* the personal bond which unites
Israel and its God in a new fellowship (see ch. xlii. 6), is the
fruit of his being heard and helped. The infinitives with
Lamed affirm in what way the new covenant relation will be
made manifest. The land that has fallen into decay rises into
prosperity again, and the desolate possessions return to their
former owners. This manifestation of the covenant grace, that
has been restored to the nation again, is effected through the
medium of the servant of Jehovah. The rendering of the LXX.
is quite correct: τοῦ καταστῆσαι τὴν γῆν καὶ κληρονομῆσαι
κληρονομίας ἐρήμους λέγοντα. לֵאמֹר is a *dicendo* governed by
both infinitives. The prisoners in the darkness of the prison
and of affliction are the exiles (ch. xlii. 22). The mighty word
of the servant of Jehovah brings to them the light of liberty,
in connection with which (as has been already more than once
observed) the fact should be noticed, that the redemption is
viewed in connection with the termination of the captivity, and,
in accordance with the peculiar character of the Old Testament,
is regarded as possessing a national character, and therefore is
purely external.

The person of the servant of Jehovah now falls into the
background again, and the prophecy proceeds with a description of the return of the redeemed. Vers. 9*b*–12. " *They shall*
feed by the ways, and there is pasture for them upon all field-
hills. They shall not hunger nor thirst, and the mirage and sun
shall not blind them: for He that hath mercy on them shall lead
them, and guide them by bubbling water-springs. And I make
all my mountains ways, and my roads are exalted. Behold
these, they come from afar; and, behold, these from the north and
from the sea; and these from the land of the Sinese." The people
returning home are represented as a flock. By the roads that

they take to their homes, they are able to obtain sufficient pasture, without being obliged to go a long way round in order to
find a sufficient supply; and even upon bare sandy hills (ch.
xli. 18) there is pasture found for them.   Nothing is wanting;
even the *shârâbh* (see ch. xxxv. 7, p. 79) and the sun do not
hurt them, the former by deceiving and leading astray, the
latter by wearying them with its oppressive heat: for He
whose compassion has been excited by their long pining misery
(ch. xli. 17–20) is leading them, and bringing them along in
comfort by bubbling springs of real and refreshing water (יְנַחֵל,
as Petrarch once says of shepherds, *Move la schiêra sua soave-
mente*).   Jehovah also makes all the mountains into roads for
those who are returning home, and the paths of the desert are
lifted up, as it were, into well-made roads (*y⁰rumūn*, Ges. § 47,
Anm. 4).   They are called *my* mountains and *my* highways
(differently from ch. xiv. 25), because they are His creation;
and therefore He is also able to change them, and now really
does change them for the good of His people, who are returning
to the land of their forefathers out of every quarter of the globe.
Although in Ps. cvii. 3 *yâm* (the sea) appears to stand for the
south, as referring to the southern part of the Mediterranean,
which washes the coast of Egypt, there is no ground at all in
the present instance for regarding it as employed in any other
than its usual sense, namely the *west; mêrâchôq* (from far) is
therefore either the south (cf. ch. xliii. 6) or the east, according
to the interpretation that we give to 'erets Sīnīm, as signifying a
land to the east or to the south.   The Phœnician *Sinim* (Gen.
x. 17), the inhabitants of a fortified town in the neighbourhood
of Arca, which has now disappeared, but which was seen not
only by Jerome, but also by Marino Sanuto (*de castro Arachas
ad dimidiam leucam est oppidum Sin*), cannot be thought of, for
the simple reason that this Sin was too near, and was situated
to the west of Babylon and to the north of Jerusalem; whilst
Sin (= Pelusium) in Egypt, to which Ewald refers, did not
give its name to either a tribe or a land.   Arias Montanus was
among the first to suggest that the *Sinim* are the Sinese
(Chinese); and since the question has been so thoroughly discussed by Gesenius (in his *Commentary* and *Thesaurus*), most
of the commentators, and also such Orientalists as Langles (in
his *Recherches asiatiques*), Movers (in his *Phœnicians*), Lassen

(in his *Indische Alterthumskunde,* i. 856–7), have decided in favour of this opinion. The objection brought against the supposition, that the name of the Chinese was known to the nations of the west at so early a period as this, viz. that this could not have been the case till after the reign of the emperor *Shi-hoang-ti,* of the dynasty of *Thsin,* who restored the empire that had been broken up into seven smaller kingdoms (in the year 247 B.C.), and through whose celebrated reign the name of his dynasty came to be employed in the western nations as the name of China generally, is met by Lassen with the simple fact that the name occurs at a much earlier period than this, and in many different forms, as the name of smaller states into which the empire was broken up after the reign of *Wu-wang* (1122–1115 B.C.). "The name Θῖναι (Strabo), Σῖναι (Ptol.), Τζίνιτζα (Kosmas), says the Sinologist Neumann, did not obtain currency for the first time from the founder of the great dynasty of *Tsin;* but long before this, *Tsin* was the name of a feudal kingdom of some importance in *Shen-si,* one of the western provinces of the Sinese land, and *Fei-tse,* the first feudal king of Tsin, began to reign as early as 897 B.C." It is quite possible, therefore, that the prophet, whether he were Isaiah or any other, may have heard of the land of the Sinese in the far east, and this is all that we need assume; not that Sinese merchants visited the market of the world on the Euphrates (Movers and Lassen), but only that information concerning the strange people who were so wealthy in rare productions, had reached the remote parts of the East through the medium of commerce, possibly from Ophir, and through the Phœnicians. But Egli replies: "The seer on the streams of Babel certainly could not have described any exiles as returning home from China, if he had not known that some of his countrymen were pining there in misery, and I most positively affirm that this was not the case." What is here assumed—namely, that there must have been a Chinese *diaspora* in the prophet's own time—is overthrown by what has been already observed in ch. xi. 11; and we may also see that it is not purely by accident that the land of the Sinese is given as the farthest point to the east, from my communications concerning the Jews of China in the *History of the Post-biblical Poetry of the Jews* (1836, pp. 58–62, cf. p. 21). I have not yet seen Sionnet's work, which has appeared since, viz. *Essai sur les Juifs de la Chine et sur l'influence, qu'ils ont eue sur la littérature de ce vaste empire, avant l'ère chrétienne* ; but I have read the *Mission of Enquiry to the Jews in China* in the *Jewish Intelligence,* May 1851, where a fac-simile of their *thorah* is given. The immigration took place from Persia (cf. ʿ*Elâm,* ch. xi. 11), at the latest, under the *Han* dynasty (205 B.C.–220 A.D.), and certainly before the Christian era.

In this return of the exiles from every quarter of the globe to their fatherland, and for this mighty work of God on behalf of His church, which has been scattered in all directions, the whole creation is to praise Him. Ver. 13. " *Sing, O heavens ; and shout, O earth ; and break out into singing, O mountains ! for Jehovah hath comforted His people, and He hath compassion upon His afflicted ones.*" The phrase פָּצַח רִנָּה, like פָּצְחוּ וְרַנְּנוּ (which occurs in Ps. xcviii. 4 as well as in Isaiah), is peculiarly Isaiah's (ch. xiv. 7, and several times in ch. xl.–lxvi.). "The afflicted ones" (ʿ*ăniyyīm*) is the usual Old Testament name for the *ecclesia militans.* The future alternates with the perfect : the act of consolation takes place once for all, but the compassion lasts for ever. Here again the glorious liberty of the children of God appears as the focus from which the whole world is glorified. The joy of the Israel of God becomes the joy of heaven and earth. With the summons to this joy the first half of the prophecy closes ; for the word תֹּאמַר, which follows, shows clearly enough that the prophecy has merely reached a resting-point here, since this word is unsuitable for commencing a fresh prophecy.

The prophet, looking back at the period of suffering from the standpoint of the deliverance, exclaims from the midst of this train of thought : Ver. 14. " *Zion said, Jehovah hath forsaken me, and the Lord hath forgotten me.*" The period of suffering which forces out this lamentation still continues. What follows, therefore, applies to the church of the present, *i.e.* of the captivity. Vers. 15, 16. " *Does a woman forget her sucking child, so as not to have compassion upon the child of her womb ?   Even though mothers should forget, I will not forget thee.   Behold, I have graven thee upon the palms of my hands ; thy walls stand continually before me.*" In reply to the complaining church, which knows that her home is in Zion-

Jerusalem, and which has been kept so long away from her
home, Jehovah sets forth His love, which is as inalienable as a
mother's love, yea, far greater than even maternal love. On
עוּל, see vol. i. p. 139; the *min* in *mērachēm* is equivalent to
ὥστε μή, as in ch. xxiii. 1, xxiv. 10, xxxiii. 15, etc. גַּם, so far
as the actual sense is concerned, is equivalent to גַּם־כִּי (Ewald,
§ 362, *b*): "granted that such (mothers) should forget, *i.e.* disown, their love." The picture of Zion (not merely the name,
as ver. 16*b* clearly shows) is drawn in the inside of Jehovah's
hands, just as men are accustomed to burn or puncture ornamental figures and mementoes upon the hand, the arm, and the
forehead, and to colour the punctures with alhenna or indigo
(see Tafel, xii., in vol. ii. pp. 33–35 of Lane's *Manners and
Customs of the Modern Egyptians*). There is the figure of
Zion, unapproachable to every creature, as close to Him as He
is to Himself, and facing Him amidst all the emotions of His
divine life. There has He the walls of Zion constantly before
Him (on *neged*, see at ch. i. 16, xxiv. 23); and even if for a
time they are broken down here below, with Him they have an
eternal ideal existence, which must be realized again and again
in an increasingly glorious form.

It is this fact of a renewed glorification which presents itself
afresh to the prophet's mind. Vers. 17, 18. "*Thy children make
haste, thy destroyers and masters draw out from thee. Lift up
thine eyes round about, and see: all these assemble themselves
together, and come to thee. As truly as I live, saith Jehovah, thou
wilt put them all on like jewellery, and gird them round thee like
a bride.*" The pointing adopted by the LXX., Targ., Jer.,
and Saad., is בֹּנָיִךְ. The antithesis favours this reading; but
בָּנַיִךְ suits vers. 18, 19 better; and the thought that Zion's
children come and restore her fallen walls, follows of itself
from the very antithesis: her children come; and those who
destroyed their maternal home, and made it a desolate ruin,
have to depart from both city and land. Zion is to lift up her
eyes, that have been cast down till now, yea, to lift them up
round about; for on all sides those whom she thought she had
lost are coming in dense crowds לָךְ (cf. לֹא = לוֹ with אֵלָיו, ch.
xlix. 5), to her, *i.e.* henceforth to belong to her again. Jehovah
pledges His life (*chai 'ănī*, ζῶν ἐγώ, Ewald, § 329, *a*) that a
time of glory is coming for Zion and her children. כִּי in the

affirmative sense, springing out of the confirmative after an affirming oath, equivalent to אִם־לֹא elsewhere (*e.g.* ch. v. 9). The population which Zion recovers once more, will be to her like the ornaments which a woman puts on, like the ornamental girdle (ch. iii. 20) which a bride fastens round her wedding dress.

Thus will Zion shine forth once more with the multitude of her children as with a festal adorning. Vers. 19, 20. "*For thy ruins and thy waste places and thy land full of ruin,—yea, now thou wilt be too narrow for the inhabitants, and thy devourers are far away. Thy children, that were formerly taken from thee, shall say in thine ears, The space is too narrow for me ; give way for me, that I may have room.*" The word " for" (*kî*) introduces the explanatory reason for the figures just employed of jewellery and a bridal girdle. Instead of the three subjects, " thy ruins," etc., the comprehensive " thou" is employed permutatively, and the sentence commenced afresh. כִּי is repeated emphatically in כִּי עַתָּה (for now, or yea now) ; this has essentially the same meaning as in the apodosis of hypothetical protasis (*e.g.* Gen. xxxi. 42, xliii. 10), except that the sense is more decidedly affirmative than in the present instance, where one sees it spring out of the confirmative. Zion, that has been hitherto desolate, now becomes too small to hold her inhabitants ; and her devourers are far away, *i.e.* those who took forcible possession of the land and cities, and made them untenable. עוֹד is to be understood in accordance with Ps. xlii. 6, and בְּאָזְנָיִךְ in accordance with Ps. xliv. 2 (see at ch. v. 9). It will even come to this, that the children of which Zion was formerly robbed will call to one another, so that she becomes a witness with her ears to that which they have so clearly seen : the space is too narrow, give way (*geshâh*, from *nâgash*, to advance, then to move generally, also to move in an opposite direction, *i.e.* to fall back, as in Gen. xix. 9) for me, that I may be able to settle down.

The words that sound in the ears of Zion are now followed by the thought of astonishment and surprise, that rises up in her heart. Ver. 21. " *And thou wilt say in thy heart, Who hath borne me these, seeing I was robbed of children, and barren, banished, and thrust away ; and these, who hath brought them up ? Behold, I was left alone ; these, where were they ?*" She sees herself suddenly surrounded by a great multitude of children, and yet she was robbed of children, and *galmŭdâh* (lit. hard, stony, Arab. *'galmad, 'gulmûd, e.g. es-sachr el 'gulmûd*, the hardest stone, mostly as a substantive, stone or rock, from *gâlam*, from which comes the Syriac *g⁶lomo*, stony ground, related to *châlam*, whence *challâmīsh*, gravel, root *gal, gam*, to press together, or heap up in a lump or mass), *i.e.* one who seemed utterly incapacitated for bearing children any more. She therefore asks, Who hath borne me these (not, who hath begotten, which is an absurd question)? She cannot believe that they are the children of her body, and her children's children. As a tree, whose foliage is all faded away, is called *nōbheleth* itself in ch. i. 30, so she calls herself *gōlâh v⁶sūrâh, extorris et remota (sūr = mūsâr,* like *sūg* in Prov. xiv. 14 = *nâsōg* or *mussâg*), because her children have been carried away into exile. In the second question, the thought has dawned upon her mind, that those by whom she finds herself surrounded are her own children ; but as she was left alone, whilst they went forth, as she thought to die in a foreign land, she cannot comprehend where they have been hitherto concealed, or .where they have grown up into so numerous a people.

The prophecy now takes a step backward in the domain of the future, and describes the manner in which the children of Zion get back to their home. Ver. 22. *" Thus saith the Lord Jehovah, Behold, I lift up my hand to nations, and set up my standard to peoples : and they bring thy sons in their bosom ; and thy daughters, upon shoulders are they carried."* The setting up of a standard (ch. v. 26, xi. 12, xviii. 3, cf. lxii. 10) is a favourite figure with Isaiah, as well as swaying the hand. Jehovah gives a sign to the heathen nations with His hand, and points out to them the mark that they are to keep in view, with a signal pole which is set up. They understand it, and carry out His instructions, and bring Zion's sons and daughters thither, and that as a foster-father (*'ōmēn*) carries an infant in the bosom of his dress (*chōtsen*, as in Neh. v. 13 ; Arabic as in Ps. cxxix. 7, *hidn*, from *hadana*, to embrace, to press tenderly to one's self ; *vid.* Num. xi. 12), or upon his arms, so that it reclines upon his shoulder (*'al-kâthēph* ; cf. *'al-tsad*, ch. lx. 4, lxvi. 12).

Such affectionate treatment does the church receive, which is assembling once more upon its native soil, whilst kings and their consorts hasten to serve the re-assembled community.

Ver. 23. "*And kings become thy foster-fathers, and their princesses thy nurses: they bow down their face to thee to the earth,
and they lick the dust of thy feet; and thou learnest that I am
Jehovah, He whose hoping ones are not put to shame.*" As
foster-fathers devote all their strength and care to those entrusted to them, and nurses nourish children from the very
marrow of their own life, so will kings become the shelterers
of Zion, and princesses the sustainers of her growth. All that is
true in the regal headship of the church will be realized, and all
that is false in regal territorialism will condemn itself: "*vultu
in terram demisso adorabunt te et pulverem pedum tuorum lingent*"
(Jerome). They do homage to the church, and kiss the ground
upon which she stands and walks. According to ch. xlv. 14,
this adoration belongs to the God who is present in the church,
and points the church itself away from all thought of her own
merits to Jehovah, the God of salvation, *cui qui confidunt non
pudefient* (וְיָדַעְתָּ with an auxiliary *pathach*, like יָנַעְתָּ in ch. xlvii.
15; Ges. § 65, 2 : אֲשֶׁר with the first person made into a relative
as in ch. xli. 8; Ges. § 123, 1, Anm. 1). Observe, however,
that the state will not be swallowed up by the church,—a thing
which never will occur, and is never meant to occur; but by
the state becoming serviceable to the church, there is realized a
prelude of the perfected kingdom of God, in which the dualism
of the state and the church is entirely abolished.

There follows now a sceptical question prompted by weakness of faith; and the divine reply. The question, ver. 24:
"*Can the booty indeed be wrested from a giant, or will the captive host of the righteous escape?*" The question is logically
one, and only divided rhetorically into two (Ges. § 153, 2).
The giant, or gigantically strong one, is the Chaldean. Knobel,
in opposition to Hitzig, who supposes the Persian to be referred
to, points very properly to ch. li. 12, 13, and lii. 5. He is
mistaken, however, in thinking that we must read שְׁבִי עָרִיץ in
ver. 24*b*, as Ewald does after the Syriac and Jerome, on account
of the parallelism. The exiles are called *sh^ebhī tsaddīq*, not,
however, as captives wrested from the righteous (the congregation of the righteous), as Meier thinks, taking *tsaddīq* as the
gen. obj.; still less as captives carried off by the righteous one,
i.e. the Chaldean, for the Chaldean, even regarded as the
accomplisher of the righteous judgment of God, is not *tsaddīq*,

but "wicked" (Hab. i. 13); but merely as a host of captives consisting of righteous men (Hitzig). The divine answer, vers. 25, 26: " *Yea, thus saith Jehovah, Even the captive hosts of a giant are wrested-from him, and the booty of a tyrant escapes: and I will make war upon him that warreth with thee, and I will bring salvation to thy children. And I feed them that pain thee with their own flesh; and they shall be drunken with their own blood, as if with new wine; and all flesh sees that I Jehovah am thy Saviour, and that thy Redeemer is the Mighty One of Jacob.*" We might take the *kī* in ver. 25*a* as a simple affirmative, but it is really to be taken as preceded by a tacit intermediate thought. Rosenmüller's explanation is the correct one : " that which is hardly credible shall take place, for thus hath Jehovah said." He has also given the true interpretation of *gam*: " although this really seems incredible, yet I will give it effect." Ewald, on the contrary, has quite missed the sense of vers. 24, 25, which he gives as follows: " The booty in men which a hero has taken in war, may indeed be taken from him again; but Jehovah will never let the booty that He takes from the Chaldean (viz. Israel) be wrested from Him again." This is inadmissible, for the simple reason that it presupposes the emendation עָרִיץ שְׁבִי; and this *'ārīts* is quite unsuitable, partly because it would be Jehovah to whom the case supposed referred, and still more, because the correspondence in character between ver. 24 and ver. 14 is thereby destroyed. The *gibbōr* and *'ārīts* is called יְרִיבֵךְ in ver. 25*b*, with direct reference to Zion. This is a noun formed from the future, like *Jareb* in Hos. v. 13 and x. 6,—a name chosen as the distinctive epithet of the Asiatic emperor (probably a name signifying "king Fighting-cock"). The self-laceration threatened against the Chaldean empire recals to mind ch. ix. 19, 20, and Zech. xi. 9, and has as revolting a sound as Num. xxiii. 24 and Zech. ix. 15,—passages which Daumer and Ghillany understand in the cannibal sense which they appear to have, whereas what they understand literally is merely a hyperbolical figure. Moreover, it must not be forgotten that the Old Testament church was a nation, and that the spirit of revelation in the Old Testament assumed the national form, which it afterwards shattered to pieces. Knobel points to the revolt of the Hyrcanians and several satraps, who fought on the side of Cyrus against their former rulers (*Cyrop.* iv. 2, 6, v. 1-3) All this will be subservient to that salvation and redemption, which form the historical aim of Jehovah and the irresistible work of the Mighty One of Jacob. The name of God which we meet with here, viz. the Mighty One of Jacob, only occurs again in ch. i. 24, and shows who is the author of the prophecy which is concluded here. The first half set forth, in the servant of Jehovah, the mediator of Israel's restoration and of the conversion of the heathen, and closed with an appeal to the heaven and the earth to rejoice with the ransomed church. The second half (vers. 14–26) rebukes the despondency of Zion, which fancies itself forgotten of Jehovah, by pointing to Jehovah's more than maternal love, and the superabundant blessing to be expected from Him. It also rebukes the doubts of Zion as to the possibility of such a redemption, by pointing to the faithfulness and omnipotence of the God of Israel, who will cause the exiles to be wrested from the Chaldean, and their tormentors to devour one another. The following chapter commences a fresh train of ideas.

SECOND PROPHECY.—CHAP. L.

ISRAEL'S SELF-REJECTION; AND THE STEDFASTNESS OF THE
SERVANT OF JEHOVAH.

The words are no longer addressed to Zion, but to her children. Ver. 1. "*Thus saith Jehovah, Where is your mother's bill of divorce, with which I put her away? Or where is one of my creditors, to whom I sold you? Behold, for your iniquities are ye sold, and for your transgressions is your mother put away.*" It was not He who had broken off the relation in which He stood to Zion; for the mother of Israel, whom Jehovah had betrothed to Himself, had no bill of divorce to show, with which Jehovah had put her away and thus renounced for ever the possibility of receiving her again (according to Deut. xxiv. 1-4), provided she should in the meantime have married another. Moreover, He had not yielded to outward constraint, and therefore given her up to a foreign power; for where was there one of His creditors (there is not any one) to whom He would have been obliged to relinquish His sons, because

unable to pay His debts, and in this way to discharge them?
—a harsh demand, which was frequently made by unfeeling
creditors of insolvent debtors (Ex. xxi. 7; 2 Kings iv. 1; Matt.
xviii. 25). On *nōsheh*, a creditor, see at ch. xxiv. 2. Their
present condition was indeed that of being sold and put away;
but this was not the effect of despotic caprice, or the result of
compulsion on the part of Jehovah. It was Israel itself that
had broken off the relation in which it stood to Jehovah; they
had been sold through their own faults, and "for your transgressions is your mother put away." Instead of וּבְפִשְׁעֵיהָ we
have וּבְפִשְׁעֵיכֶם. This may be because the church, although on
the one hand standing higher and being older than her children
(*i.e.* her members at any particular time), is yet, on the other
hand, morally affected by those to whom she has given birth,
who have been trained by her, and recognised by her as her own.

The radical sin, however, which has lasted from the time
of the captivity down to the present time, is disobedience to the
word of God. This sin brought upon Zion and her children
the judgment of banishment, and it was this which made it
last so long. Vers. 2, 3. "*Why did I come, and there was no
one there? Why did I call, and there was no one who answered?
Is my hand too short to redeem? or is there no strength in me to
deliver? Behold, through my threatening I dry up the sea; turn
streams into a plain: their fish rot, because there is no water, and
die for thirst. I clothe the heavens in mourning, and make sackcloth their covering.*" Jehovah has come, and with what? It
follows, from the fact of His bidding them consider, that His
hand is not too short to set Israel loose and at liberty, that He
is not so powerless as to be unable to draw it out; that He is
the Almighty, who by His mere threatening word (Ps. cvi. 9,
civ. 7) can dry up the sea, and turn streams into a hard and
barren soil, so that the fishes putrefy for want of water (Ex.
vii. 18, etc.), and die from thirst (*thâmōth* a voluntative used as
an indicative, as in ch. xii. 1, and very frequently in poetical
composition); who can clothe the heavens in mourning, and
make sackcloth their (dull, dark) covering (for the expression
itself, compare ch. xxxvii. 1, 2); who therefore, *fiat applicatio*,
can annihilate the girdle of waters behind which Babylon
fancies herself concealed (see ch. xlii. 15, xliv. 27), and cover
the empire, which is now enslaving and torturing Israel, with

a sunless and starless night of destruction (ch. xiii. 10). It
follows from all this, that He has come with a gospel of deliverance from sin and punishment; but Israel has given no answer,
has not received this message of salvation with faith, since faith
is assent to the word of God. And in whom did Jehovah
come? Knobel and most of the commentators reply, "in His
prophets." This answer is not wrong, but it does not suffice
to show the connection between what follows and what goes
before. For there it is one person who speaks; and who is
that, but the servant of Jehovah, who is introduced in these
prophecies with dramatic directness, as speaking in his own
name? Jehovah has come to His people in His servant. We
know who was the servant of Jehovah in the historical fulfilment. It was He whom even the New Testament Scriptures
describe as τὸν παῖδα τοῦ κυρίου, especially in the Acts (iii.
13, 26, iv. 27, 30). It was not indeed during the Babylonian
captivity that the servant of Jehovah appeared in Israel with
the gospel of redemption; but, as we shall never be tired of
repeating, this is the human element in these prophecies, that
they regard the appearance of the "servant of Jehovah," the
Saviour of Israel and the heathen, as connected with the captivity: the punishment of Israel terminating, according to the
law of the perspective foreshortening of prophetic vision, with
the termination of the captivity; and the final glory of Israel
and the final salvation of all mankind beginning to dawn on
the border of the captivity,—a connection which we regard as
one of the strongest confirmations of the composition of these
addresses before the captivity, as well as of Isaiah's authorship.
But this ἀνθρώπινον does not destroy the θεῖον in them, inasmuch as the time at which Jesus appeared was not only similar
to that of the Babylonian captivity, but stood in a causal connection with it, since the Roman empire was the continuation
of the Babylonian, and the moral state of the people under the
iron arm of the Roman rule resembled that of the Babylonian
exiles (Ezek. ii. 6, 7). At the same time, whatever our opinion
on this point may be, it is perfectly certain that it is to the servant of Jehovah, who was seen by the prophet in connection
with the Babylonian captivity, that the words "wherefore did I
come" refer.

He in whom Jehovah came to His nation, and proclaimed

to it, in the midst of its self-induced misery, the way and work
of salvation, is He who speaks in ver. 4 : " *The Lord Jehovah
hath given me a disciple's tongue, that I may know how to set up
the wearied with words : He wakeneth every morning ; wakeneth
mine ear to attend in disciple's manner.*" The word *limmūdīm*,
which is used in the middle of the verse, and which is the older
word for the later *talmidīm*, μαθηταί, as in ch. viii. 16, liv. 13,
is repeated at the close of the verse, according to the figure of
palindromy, which is such a favourite figure in both parts of
the book of Isaiah ; and the train of thought, " He wakene'h
morning by morning, wakeneth mine ear," recals to mind the
parallelism with reservation which is very common in the
Psalms, and more especially the custom of a " triolet-like"
spinning out of the thoughts, from which the songs of " degrees " (or ascending steps, *shīr hamma'ălōth*) have obtained
their name. The servant of Jehovah affords us a deep insight
here into His hidden life. The prophets received special
revelations from God, for the most part in the night, either in
dreams or else in visions, which were shown them in a waking
condition, but yet in the more susceptible state of nocturnal
quiet and rest. Here, however, the servant of Jehovah receives the divine revelations neither in dreams nor visions of
the night ; but every morning (*babbōqer babbōqer* as in ch.
xxviii. 19), *i.e.* when his sleep is over, Jehovah comes to him,
awakens his ear, by making a sign to him to listen, and then
takes him as it were into the school after the manner of a
pupil, and teaches him what and how he is to preach. Nothing
indicates a tongue befitting the disciples of God, so much as
the gift of administering consolation ; and such a gift is possessed by the speaker here. " To help with words him that is

exhausted " (with suffering and self-torture) : עוּת, Arab. غاث

med. Vav, related to עיש, חוש, signifies to spring to a person
with words to help, Aq. ὑποστηρίσαι, Jer. *sustentare.* The

Arabic غاث *med. Je,* to rain upon or water (Ewald, Umbreit,

etc.), cannot possibly be thought of, since this has no support
in the Hebrew ; still less, however, can we take עוּת as a denom.
from עֵת, upon which Luther has founded his rendering, " to
speak to the weary in due season " (also Eng. ver.). דִּבֵּר is an

accusative of more precise definition, like אֲשֶׁר in ver. 1 (cf. ch.
xlii. 25, xliii. 23). Jerome has given the correct rendering:
"that I may know how to sustain him that is weary with a word."

His calling is to save, not to destroy; and for this calling
he has Jehovah as a teacher, and to Him he has submitted
himself in docile susceptibility and immoveable obedience.
Ver. 5. " *The Lord Jehovah hath opened mine ear; and I, I
was not rebellious, and did not turn back.*" He put him into a
position inwardly to discern His will, that he might become
the mediator of divine revelation; and he did not set himself
against this calling (*mârâh*, according to its radical meaning
stringere, to make one's self rigid against any one, ἀντιτείνειν),
and did not draw back from obeying the call, which, as he well
knew, would not bring him earthly honour and gain, but
rather shame and ill-treatment. Ever since he had taken the
path of his calling, he had not drawn timidly back from the
sufferings with which it was connected, but had rather cheerfully taken them upon him. Ver. 6. " *I offered my back to
smiters, and my cheeks to them that pluck off the hair; I hid
not my face from shame and spitting.*" He offered his back to
such as smote it, his cheeks to such as plucked out the hair
of his beard (*mârat* as in Neh. xiii. 25). He did not hide his
face, to cover it up from actual insults, or from being spit
upon (on *kelimmôth* with *rôq*, smiting on the cheek, κολαφίζειν,
strokes with rods, ῥαπίζειν, blows upon the head, τύπτειν εἰς
τὴν κεφαλήν with ἐμπτύειν, compare Matt. xxvi. 67, xxvii. 30,
John xviii. 22). The way of his calling leads through a
shameful condition of humiliation. What was typified in Job
(see ch. xxx. 10, xvii. 6), and prefigured typically and prophetically in the Psalms of David (see Ps. xxii. 7, lxix. 8),
finds in him its perfect antitypical fulfilment.

But no shame makes him faint-hearted; he trusts in Him
who hath called him, and looks to the end. Ver. 7. " *But the
Lord Jehovah will help me; therefore have I not suffered myself
to be overcome by mockery: therefore did I make my face like the
flint, and knew that I should not be put to shame.*" The ו introduces the thought with which his soul was filled amidst all
his sufferings. In לֹא נִכְלָמְתִּי he affirms, that he did not suffer
himself to be inwardly overcome and overpowered by *kelimmâh*.
The consciousness of his high calling remained undisturbed;

he was never ashamed of that, nor did he turn away from it.
The two עַל־כֵּן stand side by side upon the same line. He made
his face *kachallâmîsh* (from *châlam*, related to *gâlam* in ch.
xlix. 21, with the substantative termination *îsh*: see *Jeshurun*,
p. 229), *i.e.* he made it as unfeeling as a flint-stone to the
attacks of his foes (cf. Ezek. iii. 8, 9). The LXX. renders
this ἔθηκα τὸ πρόσωπον μου ὡς στερεὰν πέτραν; but ἐστήριξα
τὸ πρόσ., which is the rendering given to שִׂים פְּנֵי in Jer. xxi. 10,
would have been just the proper rendering here (see Luke
ix. 51). In "holy hardness of endurance," as Stier says, he
turned his face to his antagonists, without being subdued or
frightened away, and was well assured that He whose cause
he represented would never leave him in the lurch.

In the midst of his continued sufferings he was still
certain of victory, feeling himself exalted above every human
accusation, and knowing that Jehovah would acknowledge
him; whereas his opponents were on the way to that destruction, the germ of which they already carried within them.
Vers. 8, 9. "*He is near that justifieth me; who will contend with
me?! We will draw near together! Who is my adversary in
judgment?! Let him draw near to me! Behold, the Lord Jehovah
will help me; who is he that could condemn me?! Behold, they
all shall fall to pieces like a garment; the moth shall eat them up.*"
הַצְּדִּיק and הִרְשִׁיעַ are forensic antitheses: the former signifies
to set one forth, both practically and judicially, as righteous
(2 Sam. xv. 4; Ps. lxxxii. 3); the latter as guilty, רָשָׁע (Deut.
xxv. 1; Ps. cix. 7). נַעַמְדָה, which has lost the principal tone
on account of the following יָחַד (יַחַד), has *munach* instead of
metheg in the antepenultimate. *Ba'al mishpâtî* means, "he who
has a judicial cause or lawsuit against me," just as in Roman
law the *dominus litis* is distinguished from the *procurator*, *i.e.*
from the person who represents him in court (syn. *ba'al
d'bhârîm*, Ex. xxiv. 14, and *'ish ribhî* in Job xxxi. 35; compare
ch. xli. 11). מִי־הוּא are connected, and form an emphatic τίς,
Rom. viii. 34 (Ewald § 325, *a*). "All of them" (*kullâm*): this
refers to all who are hostile to him. They fall to pieces like a
worn-out garment, and fall a prey to the moth which they
already carry within them:— a figure which we meet with
again in ch. li. 8 (cf. Job xiii. 28, Hos. v. 12), and one which,
although apparently insignificant, is yet really a terrible one,

inasmuch as it points to a power of destruction working imperceptibly and slowly, but yet effecting the destruction of the object selected with all the greater certainty.

Thus far we have the words of the servant. The prophecy opened with words of Jehovah (vers. 1–3), and with such words it closes, as we may see from the expression, " this shall ye have at my hand," in ver. 11*b*. The first word of Jehovah is addressed to those who fear Him, and hearken to the voice of His servant. Ver. 10. " *Who among you is fearing Jehovah, hearkening to the voice of His servant?   He that walketh in darkness, and without a ray of light, let him trust in the name of Jehovah, and stay himself upon his God.*" The question is asked for the purpose of showing to any one who could reply, " I am one, or wish to be such an one," what his duty and his privileges are. In the midst of the apparent hopelessness of his situation (*chăshēkhīm* the accusative of the object, and plural to *chăshēkhâh*, ch. viii. 22), and of his consequent despondency of mind, he is to trust in the name of Jehovah, that firmest and surest of all grounds of trust, and to stay himself upon his God, who cannot forsake or deceive him. He is to *believe* (ch. vii. 9, xxviii. 16 ; Hab. ii. 4) in God and the word of salvation, for בטח and נשען are terms applied to that *fiducia fidei* which is the essence of faith. The second word of Jehovah is addressed to the despisers of His word, of which His servant is the bearer. Ver. 11. " *Behold, all ye that kindle fire, that equip yourselves with burning darts, away into the glow of your fire, and into the burning darts that ye have kindled !   This comes to you from my hand ; ye shall lie down in sorrow.*" The fire is not the fire of divine wrath (Jer. xvii. 4), but the fire of wickedness (*rish'âh*, ch. ix. 17), more especially that hellish fire with which an evil tongue is set on fire (Jas. iii. 6) ; for the *zīqōth* (equivalent to *ziqqōth*, from *zēq* = *zinq*, from *zânaq*, to spring, to let fly, Syr. to shoot or hurl), *i.e.* shots, and indeed burning arrows (Ps. vii. 14), are figurative, and stand for the blasphemies and anathemas which they cast at the servant of Jehovah. It is quite unnecessary to read מְאִירֵי instead of מְאַזְּרֵי, as Hitzig, Ewald, and Knobel propose, or even, contrary to all usage of speech, מְאוּרֵי. The former is the more pictorial : they gird burning darts, *accingunt malleolos, i.e.* they equip or arm themselves with them for the purpose of

attack (ch. xlv. 5). But the destruction which they prepare
for the servant of Jehovah becomes their own. They themselves have to go into the midst of the burning fire and the
burning darts, that they have set on fire. The hand of Jehovah
suddenly inverts the position; the fire of wrath becomes the
fire of divine judgment, and this fire becomes their bed of
torment. The LXX. has it correctly, ἐν λύπῃ κοιμηθήσεσθε.
The *Lamed* indicates the situation (Ewald, § 217, *d*). תִּשְׁכָּבוּן
with the tone upon the last syllable gives a dictatorial conclusion. It has a terrible sound, but still more terrible (apart
from the future state) is the historical fulfilment that presents
itself to the eye.

THIRD PROPHECY.—CHAP. LI.

THE BURSTING FORTH OF SALVATION, AND TURNING AWAY OF THE CUP OF WRATH.

The prophetic address now turns again from the despisers
of the word, whom it has threatened with the torment of fire,
to those who long for salvation. Vers. 1-3. "*Hearken to me,
ye that are in pursuit of righteousness, ye that seek Jehovah.
Look up to the rock whence ye are hewn, and to the hollow of the
pit whence ye are dug. Look up to Abraham your forefather,
and to Sara who bare you, that he was one when I called him,
and blessed him, and multiplied him. For Jehovah hath comforted Zion, comforted all her ruins, and turned her desert like
Eden, and her steppe as into the garden of God; joy and gladness
are found in her, thanksgiving and sounding music.*" The
prophecy is addressed to those who are striving after the right
kind of life and seeking Jehovah, and not turning from Him
to make earthly things and themselves the object of their pursuit; for such only are in a condition by faith to regard that as
possible, and in spirit to behold that as real, which seems impossible to human understanding, because the very opposite is
lying before the eye of the senses. Abraham and Sarah they
are mentally to set before them, for they are types of the salvation to be anticipated now. Abraham is the rock whence
the stones were hewn, of which the house of Jacob is composed;

and Sarah with her maternal womb the hollow of the pit out
of which Israel was brought to the light, just as peat is dug
out of a pit, or copper out of a mine. The marriage of Abraham and Sarah was for a long time unfruitful; it was, as it
were, out of hard stone that God raised up children to Himself
in Abraham and Sarah. The rise of Israel was a miracle of
divine power and grace. In antithesis to the masculine *tsūr*,
bōr is made into a feminine through *maqqebheth*, which is
chosen with reference to *neqēbhâh*. To חֻצַּבְתֶּם we must supply
אֲשֶׁר... מִמֶּנּוּ, and to נֻקַּרְתֶּם, מִמֶּנָּה... אֲשֶׁר. Ver. 2a informs
them who the rock and the hollow of the pit are, viz. Abraham
your forefather, and Sarah *techōlelkhem*, who bare you with all
the pains of childbirth: "*you*," for the birth of Isaac, the
son of promise, was the birth of the nation. The point to be
specially looked at in relation to Abraham (in comparison with
whom Sarah falls into the background) is given in the words
quod unum vocavi eum (that he was one when I called him).
The perfect קְרָאתִיו relates the single call of divine grace, which
removed Abraham from the midst of idolaters into the fellowship of Jehovah. The futures that follow (with *Vav cop.*)
point out the blessing and multiplication that were connected
with it (Gen. xii. 1, 2). He is called one ('*echád* as in Ezek.
xxxiii. 24, Mal. ii. 15), because he was one at the time of his
call, and yet through the might of the divine blessing became
the root of the whole genealogical tree of Israel, and of a great
multitude of people that branched off from it. This is what
those who are now longing for salvation are to remember,
strengthening themselves by means of the olden time in their
faith in the future which so greatly resembles it. The corresponding blessing is expressed in preterites (*nicham, vayyâsem*),
inasmuch as to the eye of faith and in prophetic vision the future
has the reality of a present and the certainty of a completed fact.
Zion, the mother of Israel (ch. l. 1), the counterpart of Sarah,
the ancestress of the nation,—Zion, which is now mourning so
bitterly, because she is lying waste and in ruins,—is comforted
by Jehovah. The comforting word of promise (ch. xl. 1)
becomes, in her case, the comforting fact of fulfilment (ch.
xlix. 13). Jehovah makes her waste like Eden (LXX. ὡς
παράδεισον), like a garden, as glorious as if it had been directly
planted by Himself (Gen. xiii. 10; Num. xxiv. 6). And this

paradise is not without human occupants; but when you enter it you find joy and gladness therein, and hear thanksgiving at the wondrous change that has taken place, as well as the voice of melody (zimrâh as in Amos v. 23). The pleasant land is therefore full of men in the midst of festal enjoyment and activity. As Sarah gave birth to Isaac after a long period of barrenness, so Zion, a second Sarah, will be surrounded by a joyous multitude of children after a long period of desolation.

But the great work of the future extends far beyond the restoration of Israel, which becomes the source of salvation to all the world. Vers. 4, 5. " *Hearken unto me, my people, and give ear unto me, O my congregation! for instruction will go forth from me, and I make a place for my right, to be a light of the nations. My righteousness is near, my salvation is drawn out, and my arms will judge nations : the hoping of the islands looks to me, and for mine arm is their waiting.*" It is Israel which is here summoned to hearken to the promise introduced with *kî.* לְאוּמִּי is only used here of Israel, like גּוֹי in Zeph. ii. 9; and the LXX. (καὶ οἱ βασιλεῖς) have quite misunderstood it. An address to the heathen would be quite out of harmony with the character of the whole prophecy, which is carried out quite consistently throughout. עַמִּי and לְאוּמִי, therefore, are not plurals, as the Syriac supposes, although it cannot be disputed that it is a rare thing to meet with the plural form apocopated thus, after the form of the talmudic Aramæan (see, for example, p. 89; and see also at Ps. xlv. 9). What ch. xlii. 1 sqq. describes as the calling of the servant of Jehovah, viz. to carry out justice among the nations, and to plant it on the earth, appears here as the act of Jehovah; but, as a comparison of מֵאִתִּי with מִצִּיּוֹן (ch. ii. 3) clearly shows, as the act of the God who is present in Israel, and works from Israel outwards. Out of Israel sprang the Saviour; out of Israel the apostleship; and when God shall have mercy upon Israel again, it will become to the whole world of nations " life from the dead." The *thorâh* referred to here is that of Sion, as distinguished from that of Sinai, the gospel of redemption, and *mishpât* the new order of life in which Israel and the nations are united. Jehovah makes for this a place of rest, a firm standing-place, from which its light to lighten the nations streams forth in all directions. הַרְגִּיעַ as in Jer. xxxi. 2, 1. 34,

from רָגַע, in the sense of the Arabic رجع, to return, to procure

return, entrance, and rest; a different word from רָגַע in ch. li.
15, which signifies the very opposite, viz. to disturb, literally to
throw into trembling.   צֶדֶק and יֵשַׁע, which occur in ver. 5a,
are synonyms throughout these prophecies.   The meaning of
the former is determined by the character of the *thorah*, which
gives " the knowledge of salvation" (Luke i. 77), and with that
" the righteousness of God" (Rom. i. 17; cf. Isa. liii. 11).
This righteousness is now upon the point of being revealed;
this salvation has started on the way towards the fullest realization.   The great mass of the nations fall under the judgment
which the arms of Jehovah inflict, as they cast down to the
ground on the right hand and on the left.   When it is stated
of the islands, therefore, that they hope for Jehovah, and
wait for His arm, the reference is evidently to the remnant of
the heathen nations which outlives the judgment, and not only
desires salvation, and is susceptible of it, but which actually
receives salvation (compare the view given in John xi. 52,
which agrees with that of Isaiah, and which, in fact, is the
biblical view generally, *e.g.* Joel iii. 5).   To these the saving
arm (the singular only was suitable here; cf. Ps. xvi. 11) now
brings that salvation, towards which their longing was more or
less consciously directed, and which satisfied their inmost need.
Observe in ver. 5 the majestic and self-conscious movement of
the rhythm, with the effective tone of *yᵉyachēlûn*.

The people of God are now summoned to turn their eyes
upwards and downwards : the old world above their heads and
under their feet is destined to destruction.   Ver. 6. " *Lift up
your eyes to the heavens, and look upon the earth beneath : for the
heavens will pass away like smoke, and the earth fall to pieces
like a garment, and its inhabitants die out like a nonentity ; and
my salvation will last for ever, and my righteousness does not go
to ruin.*"   The reason for the summons follows with *kī*.   The
heavens will be resolved into atoms, like smoke : *nimlâchū* from
mâlach, related to *mârach*, root *mal*, from which comes *mâlal*
(see at Job xiv. 2), to rub to pieces, to crumble to pieces, or
mangle ; Aquila, ἠλοήθησαν, from ἀλοᾶν, to thresh.   As
mᵉlâchīm signifies rags, the figure of a garment that has fallen

to pieces, which was then quite ready to hand (ch. l. 9), presented itself from the natural association of ideas. כְּמוֹ־כֵן, however, cannot mean "in like manner" (LXX., Targ., Jerome);
for if we keep to the figure of a garment falling to pieces, the
figure is a very insipid one; and if we refer it to the fate of
the earth generally, the thought which it offers is a very tame
one. The older expositors were not even acquainted with what
is now the favourite explanation, viz. "as gnats perish" (Hitzig,
Ewald, Umbreit, Knobel, Stier, etc.); since the singular of
kinnīm is no more *kēn* than the singular of בֵּיצִים is בֵּן. The
gnat (viz. a species of stinging gnat, probably the diminutive
but yet very troublesome species which is called *akol uskut*,
"eat and be silent," in Egyptian) is called *kinnâh*, as the
talmudic usage shows, where the singular, which does not
happen to be met with in the Old Testament, is found in the
case of *kinnīm* as well as in that of *bētsīm*.[1] We must explain
the word in the same manner as in 2 Sam. xxiii. 5, Num. xiii.
33, Job ix. 35. In all these passages *kēn* merely signifies
"so" (*ita, sic*); but just as in the classical languages, these
words often derive their meaning from the gesture with which
they are accompanied (*e.g.* in Terence's *Eunuch: Cape hoc
flabellum et ventulum sic facito*). This is probably Rückert's
opinion, when he adopts the rendering: and its inhabitants
"like so" (*so wie so*) do they die. But "like so" is here equivalent to "like nothing." That the heavens and the earth do
not perish without rising again in a renewed form, is a thought
which may naturally be supplied, and which is distinctly expressed in ver. 16, ch. lxv. 17, lxvi. 22. Righteousness
(*tsᵉdâqâh*) and salvation (*yᵉshū'âh*) are the heavenly powers,
which acquire dominion through the overthrow of the ancient
world, and become the foundations of the new (2 Pet. iii. 13).
That the *tsᵉdâqâh* will endure for ever, and the *yᵉshū'âh* will
not be broken (*yēchath*, as in ch. vii. 8, *confringetur*, whereas
in ver. 7 the meaning is *consternemini*), is a prospect that opens
after the restoration of the new world, and which indirectly

---

[1] *Kinnâm*, in Ex. viii. 13, 14, whether it be a collective plural or a singular, also proves nothing in support of *kēn*, any more than *middâh* in
Job xi. 9 (which see) in favour of *mad*, in the sense of measure. It does
not follow, that because a certain form lies at the foundation of a derivative, it must have been current in ordinary usage.

applies to men who survive the catastrophe, having become partakers of righteousness and salvation. For righteousness and salvation require beings in whom to exert their power.

Upon this magnificent promise of the final triumph of the counsel of God, an exhortation is founded to the persecuted church, not to be afraid of men. Vers. 7, 8. "*Hearken unto me, ye that know about righteousness, thou people with my law in the heart; fear ye not the reproach of mortals, and be ye not alarmed at their revilings. For the moth will devour them like a garment, and the worm devour them like woollen cloth; and my righteousness will stand for ever, and my salvation to distant generations.*" The idea of the "servant of Jehovah," in its middle sense, viz. as denoting the true Israel, is most clearly set forth in the address here. They that pursue after righteousness, and seek Jehovah (ch. li. 1), that is to say, the servants of Jehovah (ch. lxv. 8, 9), are embraced in the unity of a "people," as in ch. lxv. 10 (cf. ch. x. 24), *i.e.* of the true people of God in the people of His choice, and therefore of the kernel in the heart of the whole mass,—an integral intermediate link in the organism of the general idea, which Hävernick and, to a certain extent, Hofmann eliminate from it,[1] but not without thereby destroying the typical mirror in which the prophet beholds the passion of the One. The words are addressed to those who know from their own experience what righteousness

---

[1] Hävernick, in his *Lectures on the Theology of the Old Testament*, published by H. A. Hahn, 1848, and in a second edition by H. Schultz, 1863 ; Drechsler, in his article on the Servant of Jehovah, in the *Luth. Zeitschrift*, 1852 ; v. Hofmann, in his *Schriftbeweis*, ii. 1, 147. The first two understand by the servant of Jehovah as an individual, the true Israel personified : the idea has simply Israel as a whole at its base, *i.e.* Israel which did not answer to its ideal, and the Messiah as the summit, in whom the ideal of Israel was fully realized. Drechsler goes so far as to call the central link, viz. an Israel true to its vocation, a modern abstraction that has no support in the Scriptures. Hofmann, however, says that he has no wish to exclude this central idea, and merely wishes to guard against the notion that a number of individuals, whether Israelites generally or pious Israelites, are ever intended by the epithet "servant of Jehovah." "The nation," he says himself at p. 145, "was called as a nation to be the servant of God, but it fulfilled its calling as a church of believers." And so say we; but we also add that this church is a kernel always existing within the outer *ecclesia mixta*, and therefore always a number of individuals, though they are only known to God.

is as a gift of grace, and as conduct in harmony with the plan of salvation, *i.e.* to the nation, which bears in its heart the law of God as the standard and impulse of its life, the church which not only has it as a letter outside itself, but as a vital power within (cf. Ps. xl. 9). None of these need to be afraid of men. Their despisers and blasphemers are men (*'ĕnōsh;* cf. ver. 12, Ps. ix. 20, x. 18), whose pretended omnipotence, exaltation, and indestructibility, are an unnatural self-convicted lie. The double figure in ver. 8, which forms a play upon words that cannot well be reproduced, affirms that the smallest exertion of strength is quite sufficient to annihilate their sham greatness and sham power; and that long before they are actually destroyed, they carry the constantly increasing germ of it within themselves. The *sâs,* says a Jewish proverb, is brother to the *'âsh.* The latter (from *'âshēsh, collabi,* Arab. *'aththa,* trans. *corrodere*) signifies a moth; the former (like the Arabic *sûs, sûse,* Gr. σής) a moth, and also a weevil, *curculio.* The relative terms in Greek are σής (Armen. *tzetz*) and κίς. But whilst the persecutors of the church succumb to the powers of destruction, the righteousness and salvation of God, which are even now the confidence and hope of His church, and the full and manifest realization of which it will hereafter enjoy, stand for ever, and from " generation to generation," *lᵉdōr dōrīm, i.e.* to an age which embraces endless ages within itself.

But just as such an exhortation as this followed very naturally from the grand promises with which the prophecy commenced, so does a longing for the promised salvation spring out of this exhortation, together with the assurance of its eventual realization. Vers. 9–11. " *Awake, awake, clothe thyself in might, O arm of Jehovah; awake, as in the days of ancient time, the ages of the olden world! Was it not thou that didst split Rahab in pieces, and pierced the dragon? Was it not thou that didst dry up the sea, the waters of the great billow; that didst turn the depths of the sea into a way for redeemed to pass through? And the emancipated of Jehovah will return, and come to Zion with shouting, and everlasting joy upon their head: they grasp at gladness and joy, and sorrow and sighing flee away.*" The paradisaical restoration of Zion, the new world of righteousness and salvation, is a work of the arm of Jehovah, *i.e.* of the manifestation of His might. His arm is now in a sleeping state. It is not lifeless, indeed, but motionless. Therefore the church calls out to it three times, "Awake" ('ūrī: to avoid monotony, the *milra* and *milel* tones are interchanged, as in Judg. v. 12).[1] It is to arise and put on strength out of the fulness of omnipotence (*lábhēsh* as in Ps. xciii. 1; cf. λαμβάνειν δύναμιν, Rev. xi. 17, and δύσεο ἀλκήν, arm thyself with strength, in *Il.* xix. 36, ix. 231). The arm of Jehovah is able to accomplish what the prophecy affirms and the church hopes for; since it has already miraculously redeemed Israel once. *Rahabh* is Egypt represented as a monster of the waters (see ch. xxx. 7), and *tannīn* is the same (cf. xxvii. 1), but with particular reference to Pharaoh (Ezek. xxix. 3). אַתְּ־הִיא, *tu illud*, is equivalent to "thou, yea thou" (see at ch. xxxvii. 16). The Red Sea is described as the "waters of the great deep" (*tᵉhōm rabbāh*), because the great storehouse of waters that lie below the solid ground were partially manifested there (see *Genesis*, p. 259). הַשָּׂמָה has double *pashta;* it is therefore *milel*, and therefore the third pr. = אֲשֶׁר שָׂמָה (Ges. § 109, Anf.). Ch. xxxv. 10 is repeated in ver. 11, being attached to גְּאוּלִים of the previous verse, just as it is there. Instead of יְשִׂיגוּן נָסוּ, which we find here, we have there יַשִּׂיגוּ וְנָסוּ; in everything else the two passages are word for word the same. Hitzig, Ewald, and Knobel suppose that ver. 11 was not written by the author of these addresses, but was interpolated by some one else. But in ch. lxv. 25 we meet with just the same kind of repetition from ch. i.-xxxix.; and in the first part we find, at any rate, repetitions in the form of refrains and others of a smaller kind (like ch. xix. 15, cf. ch. ix. 13). And ver. 11 forms a conclusion here, just as it does in ch. xxxv. 10. An argument is founded upon the olden time with reference to the things to be expected now; the look into the future is cleared and strengthened by the look into the past. And thus will the emancipated of Jehovah return, being liberated from the present calamity as they were delivered from the Egyptian then. The first half of this prophecy is here brought to a close. It concludes with expressions of longing and of hope, the echo of promises that had gone before.

In the second half the promise commences again, but with more distinct reference to the oppression of the exiles and the

[1] See Norzi and Luzzatto's *Grammatica della Lingua Ebr.* § 513.

sufferings of Jerusalem. Jehovah Himself begins to speak now, setting His seal upon what is longed and hoped for. Vers. 12–15. " *I, I am your comforter: who art thou, that thou shouldst be afraid of a mortal who will die, and of a son of man who is made a blade of grass; that thou shouldst forget Jehovah thy Creator, who stretched out the heavens and founded the earth; that thou shouldst be afraid continually all the day of the fury of the tormentor, as he aims to destroy? and where is the fury of the tormentor left? He that is bowed down is quickly set loose, and does not die to the grave, and his bread does not fail him; as truly as I Jehovah am thy God, who frighteneth up the sea, so that its waves roar: Jehovah of hosts is His name.*" הוּא after אָנֹכִי אָנֹכִי is an emphatic repetition, and therefore a strengthening of the subject (αὐτὸς ἐγώ), as above, in ver. 10, in אֲתְּ־הִיא. From this major, that Jehovah is the comforter of His church, and by means of a minor, that whoever has Him for a comforter has no need to fear, the conclusion is drawn that the church has no cause to fear. Consequently we cannot adopt Knobel's explanation, " How small thou art, that thou art afraid." The meaning is rather, " Is it really the case with thee (*i.e.* art thou then so small, so forsaken), that thou hast any need to fear" (fut. consec., according to Ges. § 129, 1; cf. *ki*, Ex. iii. 11, Judg. ix. 28)? The attributive sentence *tâmūth* (who will die) brings out the meaning involved in the epithet applied to man, viz. *'ĕnōsh* (compare in the Persian myth *Gayomard*, from the old Persian *gaya meretan*, mortal life); חָצִיר = כֶּחָצִיר (Ps. xxxvii. 2, xc. 5, ciii. 15; compare above, ch. xl. 6–8) is an equation instead of a comparison. In ver. 12*b* the address is thrown into a feminine form, in ver. 13*a* into a masculine one; Zion being the object in the former, and (what is the same thing) Israel in the latter: that thou forgettest thy Creator, who is also the almighty Maker of the universe, and soarest about in constant endless alarm at the wrath of the tormentor, whilst he is aiming to destroy (*pichad, contremiscere,* as in Prov. xxviii. 14; *ka'ăsher* as in Ps. lvi. 7, Num. xxvii. 14, lit. according as; *kōnēn,* viz. his arrows, or even his bow, as in Ps. xi. 2, vii. 13, cf. xxi. 13). We must not translate this *quasi disposuisset,* which is opposed to the actual fact, although syntactically possible (Job x. 19; Zech. x. 6). The question with which the fear is met, " And where is the fury of the

tormentor ?" looks into the future : " There is not a trace of
him to be seen, he is utterly swept away." If *hammētsīq* signifies the Chaldean, ver. 14, in which the warning passes into
a promise, just as in the first half the promise passed into a
warning, is not to be understood as referring to oppression by
their own countrymen, who were more heathenish than Israelitish in their disposition, as Knobel supposes ; but *tsŏʿeh* (from
tsâʿâh, to stoop or bend) is an individualizing description of the
exiles, who were in captivity in Babylon, and some of them
actually in prison (see ch. xlii. 7, 22). Those who were lying
there in fetters, and were therefore obliged to bend, hastened
to be loosed, *i.e.* would speedily be set at liberty (the conquest
of Babylon by Cyrus may be referred to here) ; they would
not die and fall into the pit (*constr. prægnans*), nor would their
bread fail ; that is to say, if we regard the two clauses as the
dissection of one thought (which is not necessary, however,
though Hitzig supports it), " he will not die of starvation."
The pledge of this is to be found in the all-sufficiency of
Jehovah, who throws the sea into a state of trembling (even by
a threatening word, *geʿârâh ;* רֹגַע is the construct of the participle, with the tone upon the last syllable, as in Lev. xi. 7, Ps.
xciv. 9 : see Bär's *Psalter*, p. 132, from *râgaʿ, tremefacere*), *so
that its waves roar* (cf. Jer. xxxi. 35, and the original passage
in Job xxvi. 12).

The promise, as the pledge of which Jehovah has staked
His absolute power, to which everything must yield, now rises
up to an eschatological height, from the historical point at
which it began. Ver. 16. "*And I put my words into thy mouth,
and in the shadow of my hand have I covered thee, to plant
heavens, and to found an earth, and to say to Zion, Thou art my
people.*" It is a lofty calling, a glorious future, for the preparation and introduction of which Israel, although fallen as low
as ver. 7 describes, has been equipped and kept in the shadow
of unapproachable omnipotence. Jehovah has put His words
into the mouth of this Israel—His words, the force and certainty of which are measured by His all-determining absolute-
ness. And what is the exalted calling which it is to subserve
through the medium of these words, and for which it is preserved, without previously, or indeed at any time, passing
away ? We must not render it, " that thou mayest plant,"

etc., with which the conclusion does not harmonize, viz. " that thou mayest say," etc. ; for it is not Israel who says this to Israel, but Jehovah says it to Israel.   The planter, founder, speaker, is therefore Jehovah.   It is God's own work, to which Israel is merely instrumentally subservient, by means of the words of God placed in its mouth, viz. the new creation of the world, and the restoration of Israel to favour ; both of them, the former as well as the latter, *regalia* of God.   The reference is to the last times.   The Targum explains it thus : "to restore the people of whom it is said, They will be as numerous as the stars of heaven ; and to perfect the church, of which it is said, They will be as numerous as the dust of the earth." Knobel understands by this a completion of the theocracy, and a new arrangement of the condition of the world ; Ewald, a new spiritual creation, of which the liberation of Israel is the first corner-stone.   But the prophecy speaks of a new heaven and a new earth, in something more than a figurative sense, as a new creation of God (ch. lxv. 17).   Jehovah intends to create a new world of righteousness and salvation, and practically to acknowledge Zion as His people.   The preparation for this great and all-renewing work of the future is aided by the true Israel, which is now enslaved by the heathen, and disowned and persecuted by its own countrymen.   A future of salvation, embracing Israel and the heaven and the earth, is implied in the words placed by Jehovah in the mouth of His church, which was faithful to its calling.   These words in their mouth are the seed-corns of a new world in the midst of the old.   The fact that the very same thing is said here of the true spiritual Israel, as in ch. xlix. 2 of the one servant of Jehovah, may be explained in the same manner as when the apostles apply to themselves, in Acts xiii. 47, a word of God relating to the one Servant of Jehovah, by saying, "So hath the Lord commanded us."   The One is, in fact, one with this Israel ; He is this Israel in its highest potency ; He towers above it, but only as the head rises above the members of the body, with which it forms a living whole.   There is no necessity, therefore, to assume, as Hengstenberg and Philippi do, that ver. 13 contains an address from the One who then stood before the mind of the prophet.   " There is no proof," as Vitringa affirms, " of any change in the object in this passage, nor any solid reason for assuming it." The circumference of the idea is always the same. Here, however, it merely takes the direction towards the centre, and penetrates its smaller inner circle, but does not go back to the centre itself.

Just as we found above, that the exclamation "awake" (*'ūrī*), which the church addresses to the arm of Jehovah, grew out of the preceding great promises; so here there grows out of the same another "awake" (*hithʿ ōrʿrī*), which the prophet addresses to Jerusalem in the name of his God, and the reason for which is given in the form of new promises. Vers. 17–23. "*Wake thyself up, wake thyself up, stand up, O Jerusalem, thou that hast drunk out of the hand of Jehovah the goblet of His fury : the goblet cup of reeling hast thou drunk, sipped out. There was none who guided her of all the children that she had brought forth; and none who took her by the hand of all the children that she had brought up. There were two things that happened to thee; who should console thee? Devastation, and ruin, and famine, and the sword: how should I comfort thee? Thy children were benighted, lay at the corners of all the streets like a snared antelope : as those who were full of the fury of Jehovah, the rebuke of thy God. There-fore hearken to this, O wretched and drunken, but not with wine : Thus saith thy Lord, Jehovah, and thy God that defendeth His people, Behold, I take out of thine hand the goblet of reeling, the goblet cup of my fury : thou shalt not continue to drink it any more. And I put it into the hand of thy tormentors; who said to thy soul, Bow down, that we may go over; and thou madest thy back like the ground, and like a public way for those who go over it.*" In ver. 17, Jerusalem is regarded as a woman lying on the ground in the sleep of faintness and stupefaction. She has been obliged to drink, for her punishment, the goblet filled with the fury of the wrath of God, the goblet which throws those who drink it into unconscious reeling; and this goblet, which is called *qubbaʿath kōs* (κύπελλον ποτηρίου, a genitive construc-tion, though appositional in sense), for the purpose of giving greater prominence to its swelling sides, she has not only had to drink, but to drain quite clean (cf. Ps. lxxv. 9, and more especially Ezek. xxiii. 32–34). Observe the plaintive falling of the tone in *shâthīth mâtsīth*. In this state of unconscious stupefaction was Jerusalem lying, without any help on the part of her children; there was not one who came to guide the stupefied one, or took her by the hand to lift her up. The consciousness of the punishment that their sins had deserved, and the greatness of the sufferings that the punishment had brought, pressed so heavily upon all the members of the congregation, that not one of them showed the requisite cheerfulness and strength to rise up on her behalf, so as to make her fate at any rate tolerable to her, and ward off the worst calamities. What elegiac music we have here in the deep cadences: *mikkol-bânîm yâlâdâh, mikkol-bânîm giddēlâh!* So terrible was her calamity, that no one ventured to break the silence of the terror, or give expression to their sympathy. Even the prophet, humanly speaking, is obliged to exclaim, "How (*mî*, literally as who, as in Amos vii. 2, 5) should I comfort thee!" He knew of no equal or greater calamity, to which he could point Jerusalem, according to the principle which experience confirms, *solamen miseris socios habuisse malorum.* This is the real explanation, according to Lam. ii. 13, though we must not therefore take *mî* as an accusative = *bᵉmî*, as Hitzig does. The whole of the group is in the tone of the Lamentations of Jeremiah. There were two kinds of things (*i.e.* two kinds of evils: *mishpâchōth,* as in Jer. xv. 3) that had happened to her (קָרָא = קָרָה, with which it is used interchangeably even in the Pentateuch),—namely, the devastation and ruin of their city and their land, famine and the sword to her children, their inhabitants. In ver. 20 this is depicted with special reference to the famine. Her children were veiled ('*ullaph, deliquium pati, lit. obvelari*), and lay in a state of unconsciousness like corpses at the corner of every street, where this horrible spectacle presented itself on every hand. They lay *kᵉtho' mikhmâr* (rendered strangely and with very bad taste in the LXX., viz. like a half-cooked turnip; but given correctly by Jerome, *sicut oryx,* as in the LXX. at Deut. xiv. 5, *illaqueatus*), *i.e.* like a netted antelope (see at Job xxxix. 9), *i.e.* one that has been taken in a hunter's net and lies there exhausted, after having almost strangled itself by ineffectual attempts to release itself. The appositional הַמְלֵאִים וגו', which refers to בָּנַיִךְ, gives as a *quippe qui* the reason for all this suffering. It is the punishment decreed by God, which has pierced their very heart, and got them completely in its power. This clause assigning the reason, shows that the expression "thy children"

(*bânayikh*) is not to be taken here in the same manner as in
Lam. ii. 11, 12, iv. 3, 4, viz. as referring to children in distinction from adults; the subject is a general one, as in ch. v. 25.
With *lâkhēn* (therefore, ver. 21) the address turns from the
picture of sufferings to the promise, in the view of which the
cry was uttered, in ver. 17, to awake and arise. Therefore,
viz. because she had endured the full measure of God's wrath,
she is to hear what His mercy, that has now begun to move,
purposes to do. The connecting form *sh'khurath* stands here,
according to Ges. § 116, 1, notwithstanding the (epexegetical)
Vav which comes between. We may see from ch. xxix. 9
how thoroughly this " drunk, but not with wine," is in Isaiah's
own style (from this distinction between a higher and lower
sphere of related facts, compare ch. xlvii. 14, xlviii. 10). The
intensive plural *'ădōnīm* is only applied to human lords in
other places in the book of Isaiah; but in this passage, in which
Jerusalem is described as a woman, it is used once of Jehovah.
Yârībh 'ammō is an attributive clause, signifying " who conducts the cause of His people," *i.e.* their advocate or defender.
He takes the goblet of reeling and wrath, which Jerusalem has
emptied, for ever out of her hand, and forces it newly filled
upon her tormentors. There is no ground whatever for reading מוֹנַיִךְ (from יָנָה, to throw down, related to יֵן, whence comes
יֵן, a precipitate or sediment) in the place of מוֹגַיִךְ (*pret. hi.* of
יָגָה, (*laborare, dolere*), that favourite word of the Lamentations
of Jeremiah (ch. i. 5, 12, iii. 32, cf. i. 4), the tone of which we
recognise here throughout, as Lowth, Ewald, and Umbreit
propose after the Targum דַּהֲווֹ מוֹנָן לִיךְ. The words attributed
to the enemies, *sh'chī v'na' ăbhorâh* (from *shâchâh*, the *kal* of
which only occurs here), are to be understood figuratively, as
in Ps. cxxix. 3. Jerusalem has been obliged to let her children
be degraded into the defenceless objects of despotic tyranny
and caprice, both at home in their own conquered country, and
abroad in exile. But the relation is reversed now. Jerusalem
is delivered, after having been punished, and the instruments
of her punishment are given up to the punishment which their
pride deserved.

FOURTH PROPHECY.—Chap. lii. 1–12.

JERUSALEM EXCHANGES SERVITUDE FOR DOMINION, AND IMPRISONMENT FOR LIBERTY.

The same call, which was addressed in ch. li. 9 to the arm of Jehovah that was then represented as sleeping, is here addressed to Jerusalem, which is represented as a sleeping woman. Vers. 1, 2. "*Awake, awake; clothe thyself in thy might, O Zion; clothe thyself in thy state dresses, O Jerusalem, thou holy city: for henceforth there will no more enter into thee one uncircumcised and unclean! Shake thyself from the dust; arise, sit down, O Jerusalem: loose thyself from the chains of thy neck, O captive daughter of Zion!*" Jerusalem is lying upon the ground stupefied with the wrath of God, and exhausted with grief; but this shameful prostration and degradation will now come to an end. She is to rise up and put on her might, which has long been broken down, and apparently has altogether disappeared, but which can and must be constantly renewed, because it rests upon the foundation of an inviolable promise. She is to wake up and recover her ancient power, and put on her state robes, *i.e.* her priestly and royal ornaments, which belong to her as a "royal city," *i.e.* as the city of Jehovah and His anointed one. For henceforth she will be what she was always intended to be, and that without any further desecration. Heathen, uncircumcised, and those who were unclean in heart and flesh (Ezek. xliv. 9), had entered her by force, and desecrated her: heathen, who had no right to enter the congregation of Jehovah as they were (Lam. i. 10). But she should no longer be defiled, not to say conquered, by such invaders as these (Joel iv. 17; Nahum ii. 1*b*; compare ver. 7 with Nahum ii. 1*a*). On the construction *non perget intrabit = intrare*, see Ges. § 142, 3, c. In ver. 2 the idea of the city falls into the background, and that of the nation takes its place. שְׁבִי יְרוּשָׁלַם does not mean "captive people of Jerusalem," however, as Hitzig supposes, for this would require שְׁבִיָּה in accordance with the personification, as in ver. 2*b*. The rendering supported by the LXX. is the true one, "Sit down, O Jerusalem;" and this is also the way in which it is accentuated.

The exhortation is the counterpart of ch. xlvii. 1. Jerusalem is sitting upon the ground as a prisoner, having no seat to sit upon; but this is only that she may be the more highly exalted; —whereas the daughter of Babylon is seated as a queen upon a throne, but only to be the more deeply degraded. The former is now to shake herself free from the dust, and to rise up and sit down (viz. upon a throne, Targum). The captive daughter of Zion (*sh*ebhiyyâh*, αἰχμάλωτος, Ex. xii. 29, an adjective written first for the sake of emphasis, as in ch. x. 30, liii. 11) is to undo for herself (*sibi laxare* according to vol. i. p. 94 note, like *hithnachēl*, ch. xiv. 2, *sibi possidendo capere*) the chains of her neck (the *chethib* התפתחו, they loosen themselves, is opposed to the beautiful parallelism) ; for she who was mourning in her humiliation is to be restored to honour once more, and she who was so shamefully laden with fetters to liberty.

The reason for the address is now given in a well-sustained promise. Vers. 3-6. "*For thus saith Jehovah, Ye have been sold for nothing, and ye shall not be redeemed with silver. For thus saith the Lord Jehovah, My people went down to Egypt in the beginning to dwell there as guests; and Asshur has oppressed it for nothing. And now, what have I to do here? saith Jehovah: for my people are taken away for nothing; their oppressors shriek, saith Jehovah, and my name is continually blasphemed all the day. Therefore my people shall learn my name; therefore, in that day, that I am He who saith, There am I.*" Ye have been sold (this is the meaning of ver. 3) ; but this selling is merely a giving over to a foreign power, without the slightest advantage accruing to Him who had no other object in view than to cause them to atone for their sins (ch. l. 1), and without any other people taking their place, and serving Him in their stead as an equivalent for the loss He sustained. And there would be no need of silver to purchase the favour of Him who had given them up, since a manifestation of divine power would be all that would be required (ch. xlv. 13). For whether Jehovah show Himself to Israel as the Righteous One or as the Gracious One, as a Judge or as a Redeemer, He always acts as the Absolute One, exalted above all earthly affairs, having no need to receive anything, but able to give everything. He receives no recompense, and gives none. Whether punishing or redeeming, He always guards His people's honour, proving Himself in the one case to be all-sufficient, and in the other almighty, but acting in both cases freely from Himself. In the train of thought in vers. 4–6 the reason is given for the general statement in ver. 3. Israel went down to Egypt, the country of the Nile valley, with the innocent intention of sojourning, *i.e.* living as a guest (*gūr*) there in a foreign land ; and yet (as we may supply from the next clause, according to the law of a self-completing parallelism) there it fell into the bondage of the Pharaohs, who, whilst they did not fear Jehovah, but rather despised Him, were merely the blind instruments of His will. Asshur then oppressed it *bʻephes*, *i.e.* not " at last " (*ultimo tempore*, as Hävernick renders it), but (as אפס is the synonym of אין in ch. xl. 17, xli. 12) " for nothing," *i.e.* without having acquired any right to it, but rather serving in its unrighteousness simply as the blind instrument of the righteousness of Jehovah, who through the instrumentality of Asshur put an end first of all to the kingdom of Israel, and then to the kingdom of Judah. The two references to the Egyptian and Assyrian oppressions are expressed in as brief terms as possible. But with the words " now therefore " the prophecy passes on in a much more copious strain to the present oppression in Babylon. Jehovah inquires, *Quid mihi hic* (What have I to do here) ? Hitzig supposes *pōh* (here) to refer to heaven, in the sense of, " What pressing occupation have I here, that all this can take place without my interfering ? " But such a question as this would be far more appropriate to the Zeus of the Greek comedy than to the Jehovah of prophecy. Knobel, who takes *pōh* as referring to the captivity, in accordance with the context, gives a ridiculous turn to the question, viz., " What do I get here in Babylonia, from the fact that my people are carried off for nothing ? Only loss." He observes himself that there is a certain wit in the question. But it would be silly rather than witty, if, after Jehovah had just stated that He had given up His people for nothing, the prophet represented Him as preparing to redeem it by asking, " What have I gained by it ? " The question can have no other meaning, according to ch. xxii. 16, than " What have I to do here ? " Jehovah is thought of as present with His people (cf. Gen. xlvi. 4), and means to inquire whether He shall continue this penal condition of exile any

longer (Targum, Rashi, Rosenmüller, Ewald, Stier, etc.). The
question implies an intention to redeem Israel, and the reason
for this intention is introduced with *kī*. Israel is taken away
(*ablatus*), viz. from its own native home, *chinnâm*, *i.e.* without
the Chaldeans having any human claim upon them whatever.
The words יְהֵילִילוּ מֹשְׁלָיו (מֹשְׁלוֹ) are not to be rendered, " its
singers lament," as Ruetschi and Rosenmüller maintain, since
the singers of Israel are called *meshōrerīm*; nor " its (Israel's)
princes lament," as Vitringa and Hitzig supposed, since the
people of the captivity, although they had still their national
sârīm, had no other *mōshelīm* than the Chaldean oppressors
(ch. xlix. 7, xiv. 5). It is the intolerable tyranny of the oppressors of His people, that Jehovah assigns in this sentence as
the reason for His interposition, which cannot any longer be
deferred. It is true that we do meet with *hēlīl* (of which we
have the future here without any syncope of the first syllable)
in other passages in the sense of *ululare*, as a cry of pain; but
just as רָוַח, רָנַן, הֵרִיעַ signify a yelling utterance of either joy or
pain, so *hēlīl* may also be applied to the harsh shrieking of the
capricious tyrants, like Lucan's *lætis ululare triumphis*, and the
Syriac *ailel*, which is used to denote a war-cry and other noises
as well. In connection with this proud and haughty bluster,
there is also the practice of making Jehovah's name the butt of
their incessant blasphemy : מִנֹּאָץ is a *part. hithpoel* with an
assimilated ת and a pausal *ā* for *ē*, although it might also be a
passive *hithpoal* (for the *ō* in the middle syllable, compare מְגֹאָל,
Mal. i. 7; מְבֹהָל, Esth. viii. 14). In ver. 6 there follows the
closing sentence of the whole train of thought : therefore His
people are to get to learn His name, *i.e.* the self-manifestation
of its God, who is so despised by the heathen; therefore (*lákhēn*
repeated with emphasis, like בְּעַל in ch. lix. 18, and possibly
min in Ps. xlv. 9) in that day, the day of redemption, (supply
"it shall get to learn") that "I am he who saith, Here am I,"
i.e. that He who has promised redemption is now present as the
True and Omnipotent One to carry it into effect.

The first two turns in the prophecy (vers. 1–2, 3–6) close
here. The third turn (vers. 7–10) exults at the salvation which
is being carried into effect. The prophet sees in spirit, how
the tidings of the redemption, to which the fall of Babylon,
which is equivalent to the dismission of the prisoners, gives the

finishing stroke, are carried over the mountains of Judah to Jerusalem. Ver. 7. " *How lovely upon the mountains are the feet of them that bring good tidings, that publish peace, that bring tidings of good, that publish salvation, that say unto Zion, Thy God reigneth royally !* "   The words are addressed to Jerusalem, consequently the mountains are those of the Holy Land, and especially those to the north of Jerusalem : *m^ebhassēr* is collective (as in the primary passage, Nahum ii. 1; cf. xli. 27, Ps. lxviii. 12), " whoever brings the glad tidings to Jerusalem." The exclamation " how lovely " does not refer to the lovely sound of their footsteps, but to the lovely appearance presented by their feet, which spring over the mountains with all the swiftness of gazelles (Song of Sol. ii. 17, viii. 14).   Their feet look as if they had wings, because they are the messengers of good tidings of joy.   The joyful tidings that are left indefinite in *m^ebhassēr*, are afterwards more particularly described as a proclamation of *peace, good, salvation,* and also as containing the announcement " thy God reigneth," *i.e.* has risen to a right royal sway, or seized upon the government (מָלַךְ in an in-choative historical sense, as in the theocratic psalms which commence with the same watchword, or like ἐβασίλευσε in Rev. xix. 6, cf. xi. 17).   Up to this time, when His people were in bondage, He appeared to have lost His dominion (ch. lxiii. 19); but now He has ascended the throne as a Redeemer with greater glory than ever before (ch. xxiv. 23).   The gospel of the swift-footed messengers, therefore, is the gospel of the kingdom of God that is at hand ; and the application which the apostle makes of this passage of Isaiah in Rom. x. 15, is justified by the fact that the prophet saw the final and universal redemption as though in combination with the close of the captivity.

How will the prophets rejoice, when they see bodily before them what they have already seen from afar !   Ver. 8. " *Hark, thy watchers !   They lift up the voice together; they rejoice : for they see eye to eye, how Jehovah bringeth Zion home.*" קוֹל followed by a genitive formed an interjectional clause, and had almost become an interjection itself (see Gen. iv. 10). The prophets are here called *tsōphīm*, spies, as persons who looked into the distance as if from a watch-tower (*specula*, ch. xxi. 6, Hab. ii. 1), just as in ch. lvi. 10.   It is assumed that

the people of the captivity would still have prophets among
them : in fact, the very first word in these prophecies (ch. xl.
1) is addressed to them.   They who saw the redemption from
afar, and comforted the church therewith (different from
m⁶bhassēr, the evangelist of the fulfilment), lift up their voice
together with rejoicing; for they see Jehovah bringing back
Zion, as closely as one man is to another when he looks directly
into his eyes (Num. xiv. 14). בְּ is the same as in the construction בְּ רָאָה; and שׁוּב has the transitive meaning *reducere, resti-
tuere* (as in Ps. xiv. 7, cxxvi. 1, etc.), which is placed beyond all
doubt by שׁוּבֵנוּ in Ps. lxxxv. 5.

Zion is restored, inasmuch as Jehovah turns away her
misery, brings back her exiles, and causes the holy city to rise
again from her ruins.   Ver. 9. "*Break out into exultation, sing
together, ye ruins of Jerusalem : for Jehovah hath comforted His
people, He hath redeemed Jerusalem.*"   Because the word of
consolation has become an act of consolation, *i.e.* of redemption,
the ruins of Jerusalem are to break out into jubilant shouting
as they rise again from the ground.

Jehovah has wrought out salvation through judgment in the
sight of all the world.   Ver. 10. "*Jehovah hath made bare His
holy arm before the eyes of all nations, and all the ends of the
earth see the salvation of our God.*"   As a warrior is accustomed
to make bare his right arm up to the shoulder, that he may
fight without encumbrance (*exsertare humeros nudamque lacessere pugnan*, as Statius says in *Theb.* i. 413), so has Jehovah
made bare His holy arm, that arm in which holiness dwells,
which shines with holiness, and which acts in holiness, that
arm which has been hitherto concealed and therefore has
appeared to be powerless, and that in the sight of the whole
world of nations; so that all the ends of the earth come to see
the reality of the work, which this arm has already accomplished by showing itself in its unveiled glory—in other words,
"the salvation of our God."

This salvation in its immediate manifestation is the liberation of the exiles; and on the ground of what the prophet sees
in spirit, he exclaims to them (as in ch. xlviii. 20), in vers. 11,
12 : "*Go ye forth, go ye forth, go out from thence, lay hold of
no unclean thing; go ye out of the midst of her, cleanse yourselves, ye that bear the vessels of Jehovah.   For ye shall not go*

out in confusion, and ye shall not go forth in flight : for Jehovah
goeth before you, and the God of Israel is your rear-guard."
When they go out from thence, i.e. from Babylon, they are not
to touch anything unclean, i.e. they are not to enrich themselves with the property of their now subjugated oppressors, as
was the case at the exodus from Egypt (Ex. xii. 36). It is to
be a holy procession, at which they are to appear morally as
well as corporeally unstained. But those who bear the vessels
of Jehovah, i.e. the vessels of the temple, are not only not to
defile themselves, but are to purify themselves (hibbárū with
the tone upon the last syllable, a regular imperative niphal of
bárar). This is an indirect prophecy, and was fulfilled in the
fact that Cyrus directed the golden and silver vessels, which
Nebuchadnezzar had brought to Babylon, to be restored to the
returning exiles as their rightful property (Ezra i. 7–11).
It would thus be possible for them to put themselves into the
right attitude for their departure, since it would not take place
in precipitous haste (b᷎chippázon), as the departure from Egypt
did (Deut. xvi. 3, cf. Ex. xii. 39), nor like a flight, but they
would go forth under the guidance of Jehovah. מְאַסִּפְכֶם (with
the ē changed into the original ĭ) does not mean, " He bringeth
you, the scattered ones, together," but according to Num. x. 25,
Josh. vi. 9, 13, "He closes your procession,"—He not only goes
before you to lead you, but also behind you, to protect you (as
in Ex. xiv. 19). For the m᷎᷎asséph, or the rear-guard of an army,
is its keystone, and has to preserve the compactness of the whole.

The division of the chapters generally coincides with the
several prophetic addresses. But here it needs emendation.
Most of the commentators are agreed that the words " Behold
my servant," etc. (hinnēh yaskīl ʻabhdī) commence a new section, like hēn ʻabhdī (behold my servant) in ch. xlii. 1.

FIFTH PROPHECY.—CHAP. LII. 13–LIII.

GOLGOTHA AND SHEBLIMINI,[1] OR THE EXALTATION OF THE SERVANT OF JEHOVAH OUT OF DEEP DEGRADATION.

Victor F. Oehler has recently attempted to establish an
opinion, to which no one had given expression before, viz. that

[1] שֵׁב לִימִינִי: " sit thou at my right hand."—Tr.

the transition from the collective idea of the servant of God to the "Servant of God" as an individual takes place in ver. 14, where Israel is addressed in the first clause, and the Messiah referred to in the second. But our view is a totally different one. In every case, thus far, in which another than Jehovah has spoken, it has been the one "Servant of Jehovah" who was the centre of the circle, the heart and head of the body of Israel. And after having heard him speaking himself in ch. l. 4–9, xlix. 1–6, xlviii. 16b, and Jehovah speaking concerning him in ch. l. 10, 11, xlix. 7–9, xlii. 1–7, it does not come upon us at all unexpectedly, that Jehovah begins to speak of him again here. Nor does it surprise us, that the prophet should pass in so abrupt a manner, from the exaltation of the church to the exaltation of the servant of Jehovah. If we look back, we find that he has not omitted anything, that could preclude the possibility of our confounding this servant of Jehovah with Israel itself. For although Israel itself, in its relation to Jehovah, is spoken of frequently enough as "my servant" and "his servant;" yet the passage before us is preceded by the same representation of Israel the community as a female, which has been sustained from ch. li. 17 onwards; and although in ch. li. 1–16 the national idea of the "servant of Jehovah" is expressed in the most definite manner possible (more especially in ch. li. 7), the name employed is not that which the personal "Servant," whom no one can possibly mistake in ch. l. 4–9, already bears in ch. l. 10. It is this personal Servant who is spoken of here. It is his portrait that is here filled out and completed, and that as a side-piece to the liberation and restoration of Zion-Jerusalem as depicted just before. It is the servant of Jehovah who conducts His people through suffering to glory. It is in his heart, as we now most clearly discern, that the changing of Jehovah's wrath into love takes place. He suffers with his people, suffers for them, suffers in their stead; because he has not brought the suffering upon himself, like the great mass of the people, through sin, but has voluntarily submitted to it as the guiltless and righteous one, in order that he might entirely remove it, even to its roots, *i.e.* the guilt and the sin which occasioned it, by his own sacrifice of himself. Thus is Israel's glory concentrated in him like a sun. The glory of Israel has his glory for a focus. He is the seed-corn, which is buried in the earth, to bring forth much fruit; and this "much fruit" is the glory of Israel and the salvation of the nations.

"Christian scholars," says Abravanel, "interpret this prophecy as referring to that man who was crucified in Jerusalem about the end of the second temple, and who, according to their view, was the Son of God, who became man in the womb of the Virgin. But Jonathan ben Uziel explains it as relating to the Messiah who has yet to come; and this is the opinion of the ancients in many of their Midrashim." So that even the synagogue could not help acknowledging that the passage of the Messiah through death to glory is predicted here.[1] And what interest could we have in understanding by the "servant of Jehovah," in this section, the nation of Israel generally, as many Rabbis, both circumcised and uncircumcised, have done; whereas he is that One Israelite in whom Jehovah has effected the redemption of both Israel and the heathen, even through the medium of Israel itself? Or what interest could we have in persuading ourselves that Jeremiah, or some unknown martyr-prophet, is intended, as Grotius, Bunsen, and Ewald suppose; whereas it is rather the great unknown and misinterpreted One, whom Jewish and Judaizing exegesis still continues to misinterpret in its exposition of the figure before us, just as His contemporaries misinterpreted Him when He actually appeared among them. How many are there whose eyes have been opened when reading this "golden *passional* of the Old Testament evangelist," as Polycarp the Lysian calls it! In how many an Israelite has it melted the crust of his heart! It looks as if it had been written beneath the cross upon Golgotha, and was illuminated by the heavenly brightness of the full שֵׁב לִימִינִי. It is the unravelling of Ps. xxii. and Ps. cx. It forms the outer centre of this wonderful book of consolation (ch. xl.–lxvi.), and is the most central, the deepest, and the loftiest thing that the Old Testament prophecy, outstripping itself, has ever achieved.

And yet it does not belie its Old Testament origin. For the prophet sees the advent of "the servant of Jehovah," and

---

[1] See A. M. M'Caul's tract on Isa. liii., and the "Old Jewish Midrash of the Suffering Redeemer" in our Mag. *Saat auf Hoffnung*, i. 3, pp. 37-39.

His rejection by His own people, bound up as it were with the duration of the captivity. It is at the close of the captivity that he beholds the exaltation of the Servant of Jehovah, who has died and been buried, and yet lives for ever; and with His exaltation the inward and outward return of Israel, and the restoration of Jerusalem in its renewed and final glory; and with this restoration of the people of God, the conversion of the nations and the salvation of mankind.[1]

In this sense there follows here, immediately after the cry, "Go ye out from Babylon," an index pointing from the suffering of the Servant to His reward in glory. Ch. lii. 13. "*Behold, my servant will act wisely; he will come forth, and arise, and be very high.*" Even apart from ch. xlii. 1, *hinnēh* (*hēn*) is a favourite commencement with Isaiah; and this very first verse contains, according to Isaiah's custom, a brief, condensed explanation of the theme. The exaltation of the Servant of Jehovah is the theme of the prophecy which follows. In ver. 13*a* the way is shown, by which He reaches His greatness; in ver. 13*b* the increasing greatness itself. הִשְׂכִּיל by itself means simply to gain, prove, or act with intelligence (LXX. συνήσει);

---

[1] I cannot refrain from repeating here a passage taken from my closing remarks on Drechsler (iii. 376), simply because I cannot find any better way of expressing what I have to say upon this point: "When Isaiah sang his dying song on the border line of the reigns of Hezekiah and Manasseh, all the coming sufferings of his people appeared to be concentrated in the one view of the captivity in Babylon. And it was in the midst of this period of suffering, which formed the extreme limit of his range of vision, that he saw the redemption of Israel beginning to appear. He saw the servant of Jehovah working among the captives, just as at His coming He actually did appear in the midst of His people, when they were in bondage to the imperial power of the world; he also saw the Servant of Jehovah passing through death to glory, and Israel ascending with Him, as in fact the ascension of Jesus was the completion of the redemption of Israel; and it was only the unbelief of the great mass of Israel which occasioned the fact, that this redemption was at first merely the spiritual redemption of believers out of the nation, and not the spiritual and physical redemption of the nation as a whole. So far, therefore, a broad gap was made in point of time between the exaltation of the servant of Jehovah and the glorious restoration of Israel which is still in the future; and this gap was hidden from the prophet's view. It is only the coming of Christ in glory which will fully realize what was not yet realized when He entered into glory after the sufferings of death, on account of Israel's unbelief."

and then, since intelligent action, as a rule, is also effective, it is used as synonymous with הִכְשִׁיר, הִצְלִיחַ, to act with result, *i.e.* so as to be successful. Hence it is only by way of sequence that the idea of " prosperously" is connected with that of " prudently" (*e.g.* Josh. i. 8 ; Jer. x. 21). The word is never applied to such prosperity as a man enjoys without any effort of his own, but only to such as he attains by successful action, *i.e.* by such action as is appropriate to the desired and desirable result. In Jer. xxiii. 2, where *hiskīl* is one feature in the picture of the dominion exercised by the Messiah, the idea of intelligent action is quite sufficient, without any further subordinate meaning. But here, where the exaltation is derived from יַשְׂכִּיל as the immediate consequence, without any intervening עַל־כֵּן, there is naturally associated with the idea of wise action, *i.e.* of action suited to the great object of his call, that of effective execution or abundant success, which has as its natural sequel an ever-increasing exaltation. Rosenmüller observes, in ver. 13*b*, " There is no need to discuss, or even to inquire, what precise difference there is in the meaning of the separate words ;" but this is a very superficial remark. If we consider that *rūm* signifies not only to be high, but to rise up (Prov. xi. 11) and become exalted, and also to become manifest as exalted (Ps. xxi. 14), and that נִשָּׂא, according to the immediate and original reflective meaning of the *niphal*, signifies to raise one's self, whereas *gâbhah* expresses merely the condition, without the subordinate idea of activity, we obtain this chain of thought : he will rise up, he will raise himself still higher, he will stand on high. The three verbs (of which the two perfects are defined by the previous future) consequently denote the commencement, the continuation, and the result or climax of the exaltation ; and Stier is not wrong in recalling to mind the three principal steps of the *exaltatio* in the historical fulfilment, viz. the resurrection, the ascension, and the sitting down at the right hand of God. The addition of the word מְאֹד shows very clearly that וְגָבַהּ is intended to be taken as the final result : the servant of Jehovah, rising from stage to stage, reaches at last an immeasurable height, that towers above everything besides (comp. ὑπερύψωσε in Phil. ii. 9, with ὑψωθείς in Acts ii. 33, and for the nature of the ὑπερύψωσε, Eph. i. 20–23).

The prophecy concerning him passes now into an address to him, as in ch. xlix. 8 (cf. ver. 7), which sinks again immediately into an objective tone.   Vers. 14, 15. *" Just as many were astonished at thee : so disfigured, his appearance was not human, and his form not like that of the children of men : so will he make many nations to tremble ; kings will shut their mouth at him : for they see what has not been told them, and discover what they have not heard."*   Both Oehler and Hahn suppose that the first clause is addressed to Israel, and that it is here pointed away from its own degradation, which excited such astonishment, to the depth of suffering endured by the One man.   Hahn's principal reason, which Oehler adopts, is the sudden leap that we should otherwise have to assume from the second person to the third, — an example of " negligence" which we can hardly impute to the prophet.   But a single glance at ch. xlii. 20 and i. 29 is sufficient to show how little force there is in this principal argument.   We should no doubt expect עֲלֵיכֶם or עָלֶיךָ after what has gone before, if the nation were addressed; but it is difficult to see what end a comparison between the sufferings of the nation and those of the One man, which merely places the sufferings of the two in an external relation to one another, could be intended to answer; whilst the second *kēn* (so), which evidently introduces an antithesis, is altogether unexplained.   The words are certainly addressed to the servant of Jehovah ; and the meaning of the *sicut* (just as) in ver. 14, and of the *sic* (so) which introduces the principal sentence in ver. 15, is, that just as His degradation was the deepest degradation possible, so His glorification would be of the loftiest kind.   The height of the exaltation is held up as presenting a perfect contrast to the depth of the degradation.   The words, " so distorted was his face, more than that of a man," form, as has been almost unanimously admitted since the time of Vitringa, a parenthesis, containing the reason for the astonishment excited by the servant of Jehovah.   Stier is wrong in supposing that this first " so" (*kēn*) refers to *ka'ăsher* (just as), in the sense of " If men were astonished at thee, there was ground for the astonishment."   Ver. 15 would not stand out as an antithesis, if we adopted this explanation ; moreover, the thought that the fact corresponded to the impression which men received, is a very tame and unnecessary one; and the change of persons in sentences related to one another in this manner is intolerably harsh; whereas, with our view of the relation in which the sentences stand to one another, the parenthesis prepares the way for the sudden change from a direct address to a declaration. Hitherto many had been astonished at the servant of Jehovah: *shâmēm*, to be desolate or waste, to be thrown by anything into a desolate or benumbed condition, to be startled, confused, as it were petrified, by paralyzing astonishment (Lev. xxvi. 32; Ezek. xxvi. 16). To such a degree (*kēn, adeo*) was his appearance *mishchath mē'īsh*, and his form *mibb⁶nē 'âdâm* (*sc. mishchath*). We might take *mishchath* as the construct of *mishchâth*, as Hitzig does, since this connecting form is sometimes used (*e.g.* xxxiii. 6) even without any genitive relation; but it may also be the absolute, syncopated from מִשְׁחֶתֶת = מִשְׁחָת (Hävernick and Stier), like *moshchath* in Mal. i. 14, or, what we prefer, after the form *mirmas* (ch. x. 6), with the original *ă*, without the usual lengthening (Ewald, § 160, *c*, Anm. 4). His appearance and his form were altogether distortion (stronger than *moshchâth*, distorted), away from men, out beyond men, *i.e.* a distortion that destroys all likeness to a man;[1] *'īsh* does not signify man as distinguished from woman here, but a human being generally. The antithesis follows in ver. 15: viz. the state of glory in which this form of wretchedness has passed away. As a parallel to the "many" in ver. 14, we have here "many nations," indicating the excess of the glory by the greater fulness of the expression; and as a parallel to "were astonished at thee," "he shall make to tremble" (*yazzeh*), in other words, the effect which He produces by what He does to the effect produced by what He suffers. The *hiphil hizzâh* generally means to spirt or sprinkle (*adspergere*), and is applied to the sprinkling of the

[1] The church before the time of Constantine pictured to itself the Lord, as He walked on earth, as repulsive in His appearance; whereas the church after Constantine pictured Him as having quite an ideal beauty (see my tract, *Jesus and Hillel*, 1865, p. 4). They were both right: unattractive in appearance, though not deformed, He, no doubt was in the days of His flesh; but He is ideally beautiful in His glorification. The body in which He was born of Mary was no royal form, though faith could see the *doxa* shining through. It was no royal form, for the suffering of death was the portion of the Lamb of God, even from His mother's womb; but the glorified One is infinitely exalted above all the ideal of art.

blood with the finger, more especially upon the capporeth and
altar of incense on the day of atonement (differing in this respect from *zâraq*, the swinging of the blood out of a bowl),
also to the sprinkling of the water of purification upon a leper
with the bunch of hyssop (Lev. xiv. 7), and of the ashes of the
red heifer upon those defiled through touching a corpse (Num.
xix. 18) ; in fact, generally, to sprinkling for the purpose of
expiation and sanctification.   And Vitringa, Hengstenberg,
and others, accordingly follow the Syriac and Vulgate in adopting the rendering *adsperget* (he will sprinkle).   They have
the usage of the language in their favour ; and this explanation also commends itself from a reference to נָגוּעַ in ch. liii. 4,
and נֶגַע in ch. liii. 8 (words which are generally used of leprosy,
and on account of which the suffering Messiah is called in
b. Sanhedrin 98*b* by an emblematical name adopted from the
old synagogue, "the leper of Rabbi's school"), since it yields
the significant antithesis, that he who was himself regarded as
unclean, even as a second Job, would sprinkle and sanctify whole
nations, and thus abolish the wall of partition between Israel
and the heathen, and gather together into one holy church
with Israel those who had hitherto been pronounced "unclean"
(ch. lii. 1).   But, on the other hand, this explanation has so far
the usage of the language against it, that *hizzâh* is never construed with the accusative of the person or thing sprinkled (like
adspergere aliqua re aliquem ; since *'eth* in Lev. iv. 6, 17 is a
preposition like *'al*, *'el* elsewhere) ; moreover, there would be
something very abrupt in this sudden representation of the
servant as a priest.   Such explanations as "he will scatter
asunder" (*disperget*, Targum, etc.), or "he will spill" (*sc.* their
blood), are altogether out of the question ; such thoughts as
these would be quite out of place in a spiritual picture of salvation and glory, painted upon the dark ground we have here.
The verb *nâzâh* signified primarily to *leap* or *spring ;* hence
hizzâh, with the causative meaning to *sprinkle*.   The *kal* combines the intransitive and transitive meanings of the word
"spirt," and is used in the former sense in ch. lxiii. 3, to
signify the springing up or sprouting up of any liquid scattered
about in drops.   The Arabic *nazâ* (see Ges. *Thes.*) shows that
this verb may also be applied to the springing or leaping of
living beings, caused by excess of emotion.   And accordingly

we follow the majority of the commentators in adopting the rendering *exsilire faciet.* The fact that whole nations are the object, and not merely individuals, proves nothing to the contrary, as Hab. iii. 6 clearly shows. The reference is to their leaping up in amazement (LXX. θαυμάσονται); and the verb denotes less an external than an internal movement. They will tremble with astonishment within themselves (cf. *păchădū v'râg'zū* in Jer. xxxiii. 9), being electrified, as it were, by the surprising change that has taken place in the servant of Jehovah. The reason why kings " shut their mouths at him" is expressly stated, viz. what was never related they see, and what was never heard of they perceive ; *i.e.* it was something going far beyond all that had ever been reported to them outside the world of nations, or come to their knowledge within it. Hitzig's explanation, that they do not trust themselves to begin to speak before him or along with him, gives too feeble a sense, and would lead us rather to expect לִפְנֵי than עָלָיו. The shutting of the mouth is the involuntary effect of the overpowering impression, or the manifestation of their extreme amazement at one so suddenly brought out of the depths, and lifted up to so great a height. The strongest emotion is that which remains shut up within ourselves, because, from its very intensity, it throws the whole nature into a suffering state, and drowns all reflection in emotion (cf. *yachărīsh* in Zeph. iii. 17). The parallel in ch. xlix. 7 is not opposed to this ; the speechless astonishment, at what is unheard and inconceivable, changes into adoring homage, as soon as they have become to some extent familiar with it. The first turn in the prophecy closes here : The servant of Jehovah, whose inhuman sufferings excite such astonishment, is exalted on high ; so that from utter amazement the nations tremble, and their kings are struck dumb.

But, says the second turn in ch. liii. 1–3, the man of sorrows was despised among us, and the prophecy as to his future was not believed. We hear the first lamentation (the question is, From whose mouth does it come ?) in ver. 1 : " *Who hath believed our preaching; and the arm of Jehovah, over whom has it been revealed ?*" " I was formerly mistaken," says Hofmann (*Schriftbeweis*, ii. 1, 159, 160), " as to the connection between ch. liii. 1 and ch. lii. 13–15, and thought that the Gentiles were the speakers in the former, simply because it was to them

that the latter referred.   But I see now that I was in error.
It is affirmed of the heathen, that they have never heard before
the things which they now see with their eyes.   Consequently
it cannot be they who exclaim, or in whose name the inquiry is
made, Who hath believed our preaching?"   Moreover, it cannot be they, both because the redemption itself and the exaltation of the Mediator of the redemption are made known to
them from the midst of Israel as already accomplished facts,
and also because according to ch. lii. 15 (cf. ch. xlix. 7, xlii. 4,
li. 5) they hear the things unheard of before, with amazement
which passes into reverent awe, as the satisfaction of their own
desires, in other words, with the glad obedience of faith.   And
we may also add, that the expression in ch. liii. 8, "for the
transgression of my people," would be quite out of place in the
mouths of Gentiles, and that, as a general rule, words attributed to Gentiles ought to be expressly introduced as theirs.
Whenever we find a "we" introduced abruptly in the midst of
a prophecy, it is always Israel that speaks, including the prophet himself (ch. xlii. 24, lxiv. 5, xvi. 6, xxiv. 16, etc.).   Hofmann therefore very properly rejects the view advocated by
many, from Calvin down to Stier and Oehler, who suppose
that it is the prophet himself who is speaking here in connection with the other heralds of salvation; "for," as he says,
"how does all the rest which is expressed in the 1st pers.
plural tally with such a supposition?"   If it is really Israel,
which confesses in vers. 2 sqq. how blind it has been to the
calling of the servant of Jehovah, which was formerly hidden
in humiliation but is now manifested in glory; the mournful
inquiry in ver. 1 must also proceed from the mouth of Israel.
The references to this passage in John xii. 37, 38, and Rom.
x. 16, do not compel us to assign ver. 1 to the prophet and his
comrades in office.   It is Israel that speaks even in ver. 1.   The
nation, which acknowledges with penitence how shamefully it
has mistaken its own Saviour, laments that it has put no faith
in the tidings of the lofty and glorious calling of the servant of
God.   We need not assume, therefore, that there is any change
of subject in ver. 2 ; and (what is still more decisive) it is
necessary that we should not, if we would keep up any close
connection between ch. liii. 1 and ch. lii. 15.   The heathen
receive with faith tidings of things which had never been heard

of before; whereas Israel has to lament that it put no faith in
the tidings which it had heard long, long before, not only with
reference to the person and work of the servant of God, but
with regard to his lowly origin and glorious end. שְׁמוּעָה (a
noun after the form יְשׁוּעָה, שְׁבוּעָה, a different form from that of
גְּדֻלָּה, which is derived from the adjective גָּדֹל) signifies the hearsay (ἀκοή), i.e. the tidings, more especially the prophetic announcement in ch. xxviii. 9; and שְׁמֻעָתֵנוּ, according to the primary
subjective force of the suffix, is equivalent to שְׁמוּעָה אֲשֶׁר שָׁמַעְנוּ
(cf. Jer. xlix. 14), i.e. the hearsay which we have heard.
There were some, indeed, who did not refuse to believe the
tidings which Israel heard: ἀλλ' οὐ πάντες ὑπήκουσαν τῷ
εὐαγγελίῳ (Rom. x. 16); the number of the believers was
vanishingly small, when compared with the unbelieving mass of
the nation. And it is the latter, or rather its remnant which
had eventually come to its senses, that here inquires, Who hath
believed *our* preaching, i.e. the preaching that was common
among us? The substance of the preaching, which had not
been believed, was the exaltation of the servant of God from a
state of deep degradation. This is a work performed by the
"arm of Jehovah," namely, His holy arm that has been made
bare, and that now effects the salvation of His people, and of
the nations generally, according to His own counsel (ch. lii. 10,
li. 5). This arm works down from on high, exalted far above
all created things; men have it above them, and it is made
manifest to those who recognise it in what is passing around
them. Who, asks Israel, has had any faith in the coming
exaltation of the servant of God? who has recognised the omnipotence of Jehovah, which has set itself to effect his exaltation?
All that follows is the confession of the Israel of the last times,
to which this question is the introduction. We must not overlook the fact that this golden "passional" is also one of the
greatest prophecies of the future conversion of the nation,
which has rejected the servant of God, and allowed the Gentiles
to be the first to recognise him. At last, though very late, it
will feel remorse. And when this shall once take place, then
and not till then will this chapter—which, to use an old epithet,
will ever be *carnificina Rabbinorum*—receive its complete historical fulfilment.

The confession, which follows, grows out of the great

lamentation depicted by Zechariah in Zech. xii. 11 sqq. Ver.
2. "*And he sprang up like a layer-shoot before Him, and like a
root-sprout out of dry ground: he had no form, and no beauty; and
we looked, and there was no look, such that we could have found
pleasure in him.*" Ver. 2, as a sequel to ver. 1*b*, looks back to the
past, and describes how the arm of Jehovah manifested itself in
the servant's course of life from the very beginning, though imperceptibly at first, and unobserved by those who merely noticed
the outside. The suffix of לְפָנָיו cannot refer to the subject of
the interrogative sentence, as Hahn and Hofmann suppose, for
the answer to the *quis* there is *nemo;* it relates to Jehovah, by
which it is immediately preceded. Before Jehovah, namely,
so that He, whose counsel thus began to be fulfilled, fixed His
eye upon him with watchfulness and protecting care, he grew
up כַּיּוֹנֵק, like the suckling, *i.e.* (in a horticultural sense) the
tender twig which sucks up its nourishment from the root and
stem (not as Hitzig supposes, according to Ezek. xxxi. 16, from
the moisture in the soil); for the tender twig upon a tree, or
trunk, or stalk, is called יֶנֶקֶת (for which we have יוֹנֵק here):
vid. Ezek. xvii. 22, the twig of a cedar; Ps. lxxx. 12 (11), of a
vine; Job viii. 16, of a liana. It is thought of here as a layer,
as in Ezek. xvii. 22; and, indeed, as the second figure shows
when taken in connection with ch. xi. 1, as having been laid
down after the proud cedar of the Davidic monarchy from
which it sprang had been felled; for elsewhere it is compared
to a shoot which springs from the root left in the ground after
the tree has been felled. Both figures depict the lowly and
unattractive character of the small though vigorous beginning. The expression "out of dry ground," which belongs to
both figures, brings out, in addition, the miserable character of
the external circumstances in the midst of which the birth and
growth of the servant had taken place. The "dry ground"
is the existing state of the enslaved and degraded nation; *i.e.*
he was subject to all the conditions inseparable from a nation
that had been given up to the power of the world, and
was not only enduring all the consequent misery, but was
in utter ignorance as to its cause; in a word, the dry ground
is the corrupt character of the age. In what follows, the
majority of the commentators have departed from the accents,
and adopted the rendering, "he had no form and no beauty,

that we should look at Him" (should have looked at Him), viz.
with fixed looks that loved to dwell upon Him. This rendering
was adopted by Symmachus and Vitringa (ἵνα εἴδωμεν αὐτόν;
ut ipsum respiceremus). But Luther, Stier, and others, very
properly adhere to the existing punctuation; since the other
would lead us to expect וְנִרְאֶה בּוֹ instead of וְנִרְאֵהוּ, and the close
reciprocal relation of וְנִרְאֵהוּ וְלֹא־מַרְאֶה, which resembles a play
upon the words, is entirely expunged. The meaning therefore
is, " We saw Him, and there was nothing in His appearance
to make us desire Him, or feel attracted by Him." The literal
rendering of the Hebrew, with its lively method of transferring
you into the precise situation, is ut concupisceremus eum (delec-
taremur eo); whereas, in our oriental style, we should rather
have written ut concupivissemus, using the pluperfect instead of
the imperfect, or the tense of the associated past. Even in this
sense וְנִרְאֵהוּ is very far from being unmeaning: He dwelt in
Israel, so that they had Him bodily before their eyes, but in
His outward appearance there was nothing to attract or delight
the senses.

On the contrary, the impression produced by His appearance was rather repulsive, and, to those who measured the great
and noble by a merely worldly standard, contemptible. Ver. 3.
" He was despised and forsaken by men; a man of griefs, and
well acquainted with disease; and like one from whom men hide
their face: despised, and we esteemed Him not." All these different features are predicates of the erat that is latent in non
species ei neque decor and non adspectus. Nibhzeh is introduced
again palindromically at the close in Isaiah's peculiar style;
consequently Martini's conjecture נִבְזֶהוּ לֹא וגו' is to be rejected.
This nibhzeh (cf. bâzōh, ch. xlix. 7) is the keynote of the
description which looks back in this plaintive tone. The predicate chădal 'ishīm is misunderstood by nearly all the commentators, inasmuch as they take אִישִׁים as synonymous with
בְּנֵי־אָדָם, whereas it is rather used in the sense of בְּנֵי־אִישׁ (lords),
as distinguished from bᵉnē 'âdâm, or people generally (see ch.
ii. 9, 11, 17). The only other passages in which it occurs are
Prov. viii. 4 and Ps. cxli. 4; and in both instances it signifies
persons of rank. Hence Cocceius explains it thus: " wanting
in men, i.e. having no respectable men with Him, to support
Him with their authority." It might also be understood as

meaning the ending one among men, *i.e.* the one who takes the
last place (S. ἐλάχιστος, Jer. *novissimus*); but in this case
He Himself would be described as אִישׁ, whereas it is absolutely
affirmed that He had not the appearance or distinction of such
an one.   But the rendering *deficiens* (wanting) is quite correct;
compare Job xix. 14, " my kinsfolk have failed" (*defecerunt,
châdᵉlū, cognati mei*).   The Arabic *chadhalahu* or *chadhala
'anhu* (he left him in the lurch, kept back from him, forsook
him) also points to the true meaning; and from this we have
the derivatives *châdhil*, refusing assistance, leaving without
help; and *machdhûl*, helpless, forsaken (see Lane's *Arabic
Lexicon*).   In Hebrew, *châdal* has not only the transitive meaning to discontinue or leave off a thing, but the intransitive, to
cease or be in want, so that *chădal 'ishīm* may mean one in
want of men of rank, *i.e.* finding no sympathy from such men.
The chief men of His nation who towered above the multitude,
the great men of this world, withdrew their hands from Him,
drew back from Him : He had none of the men of any distinction at His side.   Moreover, He was אִישׁ מַכְאֹבוֹת, a man of sorrow
of heart in all its forms, *i.e.* a man whose chief distinction was,
that His life was one of constant painful endurance.   And He
was also יְדוּעַ חֹלִי, that is to say, not one known through His
sickness (according to Deut. i. 13, 15), which is hardly sufficient to express the genitive construction; nor an acquaintance
of disease (S. γνωστὸς νόσῳ, *familiaris morbo*), which would
be expressed by מְיֻדָּע or מוֹדָע; but *scitus morbi, i.e.* one who
was placed in a state to make the acquaintance of disease.
The deponent passive יָדוּעַ, acquainted (like *bâtuăch, confisus;
zâkhūr*, mindful; *peritus*, pervaded, experienced), is supported
by מַדּוּעַ = מַה־יָדוּעַ; Gr. τί μαθών.   The meaning is not, that
He had by nature a sickly body, falling out of one disease into
another; but that the wrath instigated by sin, and the zeal of
self-sacrifice (Ps. lxix. 10), burnt like the fire of a fever in His
soul and body, so that even if He had not died a violent death,
He would have succumbed to the force of the powers of destruction that were innate in humanity in consequence of sin, and of
His own self-consuming conflict with them.   Moreover, He was
kᵉmastēr pânīm mimmennū.   This cannot mean, " like one
hiding his face from us," as Hengstenberg supposes (with an
allusion to Lev. xiii. 45); or, what is comparatively better,

"like one causing the hiding of the face from him:" for although
the feminine of the participle is written מַסְתֶּרֶת, and in the plural
מַסְתִּרִים for מַסְתִּירִים is quite possible, we never meet with *mastēr*
for *mastīr*, like *hastēr* for *hastīr* in the infinitive (ch. xxix. 15,
cf. Deut. xxvi. 12). Hence *mastēr* must be a noun (of the form
marbēts, *marbēq*, *mashchēth*); and the words mean either "like
the hiding of the face on our part," or like one who met with
this from us, or (what is more natural) like the hiding of the
face before his presence (according to ch. viii. 17, l. 6, liv. 8,
lix. 2, and many other passages), *i.e.* like one whose repulsive
face it is impossible to endure, so that men turn away their
face or cover it with their dress (compare ch. l. 6 with Job
xxx. 10). And lastly, all the predicates are summed up in the
expressive word *nibhzeh*: He was despised, and we did not think
Him dear and worthy, but rather "esteemed Him not," or rather
did not estimate Him at all, or as Luther expresses it, "esti-
mated Him at nothing" (*châshabh*, to reckon, value, esteem, as
in ch. xiii. 17, xxxiii. 8, Mal. iii. 16).

The second turn closes here. The preaching concerning
His calling and His future was not believed; but the Man of
sorrows was greatly despised among us.

Those who formerly mistook and despised the Servant of
Jehovah on account of His miserable condition, now confess
that His sufferings were altogether of a different character
from what they had supposed. Ver. 4. "*Verily He hath
borne our diseases and our pains: He hath laden them upon
Himself; but we regarded Him as one stricken, smitten of God,
and afflicted.*" It might appear doubtful whether אָכֵן (the
fuller form of אַךְ) is affirmative here, as in ch. xl. 7, xlv. 15,
or adversative, as in ch. xlix. 4. The latter meaning grows
out of the former, inasmuch as it is the opposite which is
strongly affirmed. We have rendered it affirmatively (Jer.
vere), not adversatively (*verum, ut vero*), because ver. 4 itself
consists of two antithetical halves,—a relation which is expressed in the independent pronouns הוּא and אֲנַחְנוּ, that answer
to one another. The penitents contrast themselves and their
false notion with Him and His real achievement. In Matthew
(viii. 17) the words are rendered freely and faithfully thus:
αὐτὸς τὰς ἀσθενείας ἡμῶν ἔλαβε, καὶ τὰς νόσους ἐβάστασεν.
Even the fact that the relief which Jesus afforded to all kinds

of bodily diseases is regarded as a fulfilment of what is here
affirmed of the Servant of Jehovah, is an exegetical index
worth noticing. In 4a it is not really sin that is spoken of,
but the evil which is consequent upon human sin, although not
always the direct consequence of the sins of individuals (John
ix. 3). But in the fact that He was concerned to relieve this
evil in all its forms, whenever it came in His way in the exercise of His calling, the relief implied as a consequence in ver.
4a was brought distinctly into view, though not the bearing
and lading that are primarily noticed here. Matthew has
very aptly rendered נָשָׂא by ἔλαβε, and סָבַל by ἐβάστασε. For
whilst סָבַל denotes the toilsome bearing of a burden that has
been taken up, נָשָׂא combines in itself the ideas of *tollere* and
ferre. When construed with the accusative of the sin, it signifies to take the debt of sin upon one's self, and carry it as one's
own, *i.e.* to look at it and feel it as one's own (*e.g.* Lev. v. 1, 17),
or more frequently to bear the punishment occasioned by sin,
i.e. to make expiation for it (Lev. xvii. 16, xx. 19, 20, xxiv. 15),
and in any case in which the person bearing it is not himself
the guilty person, to bear sin in a mediatorial capacity, for the
purpose of making expiation for it (Lev. x. 17). The LXX.
render this נשא both in the Pentateuch and Ezekiel λαβεῖν
ἁμαρτίαν, once ἀναφέρειν; and it is evident that both of these
are to be understood in the sense of an expiatory bearing, and
not merely of taking away, as has been recently maintained
in opposition to the *satisfactio vicaria*, as we may see clearly
enough from Ezek. iv. 4–8, where the שְׂאת עָוֹן is represented
by the prophet in a symbolical action. But in the case before
us, where it is not the sins, but "our diseases" (חֳלָיֵנוּ is a defective plural, as the singular would be written חָלְיֵנוּ) and "our
pains" that are the object, this mediatorial sense remains
essentially the same. The meaning is not merely that the Servant of God entered into the fellowship of our sufferings, but
that He took upon Himself the sufferings which we had to
bear and deserved to bear, and therefore not only took them
away (as Matt. viii. 17 might make it appear), but bore them
in His own person, that He might deliver us from them. But
when one person takes upon himself suffering which another
would have had to bear, and therefore not only endures it with
him, but in his stead, this is called *substitution* or representation,

—an idea which, however unintelligible to the understanding,
belongs to the actual substance of the common consciousness
of man, and the realities of the divine government of the world
as brought within the range of our experience, and one which
has continued even down to the present time to have much
greater vigour in the Jewish nation, where it has found its
true expression in sacrifice and the kindred institutions, than
in any other, at least so far as its nationality has not been
entirely annulled.[1] Here again it is Israel, which, having been
at length better instructed, and now bearing witness against
itself, laments its former blindness to the mediatorially vicarious character of the deep agonies, both of soul and body, that
were endured by the great Sufferer. They looked upon them
as the punishment of His own sins, and indeed—inasmuch as,
like the friends of Job, they measured the sin of the Sufferer
by the sufferings that He endured—of peculiarly great sins.
They saw in Him נָגוּעַ, "*one stricken*," *i.e.* afflicted with a
hateful, shocking disease (Gen. xii. 17 ; 1 Sam. vi. 9),—such,
for example, as leprosy, which was called נֶגַע κατ' ἐξ. (2 Kings
xv. 5, A. ἀφήμενον, S. ἐν ἁφῇ ὄντα = *leprosum*, Th. μεμαστιγω-
μένον, cf. μάστιγες, Mark iii. 10, scourges, *i.e.* bad attacks);
also מֻכֵּה אֱלֹהִים, "*one smitten of God*" (from *nâkhâh*, root
נכ, נג ; see *Job*, vol. ii. p. 146), and מְעֻנֶּה, *bowed down* (by
God), *i.e.* afflicted with sufferings. The name Jehovah would
have been out of place here, where the evident intention is to
point to the all-determining divine power generally, whose
vengeance appeared to have fallen upon this particular sufferer. The construction *mukkēh 'Elōhīm* signifies, like the
Arabic *muqâtal rabbuh*, one who has been defeated in conflict
with God his Lord (see *Job*, vol. i. p. 267) ; and *'Elōhīm* has
the syntactic position between the two adjectives, which it
necessarily must have in order to be logically connected with
them both.

In ver. 5, וְהוּא, as contrasted with וַאֲנַחְנוּ, continues the true
state of the case as contrasted with their false judgment.
Ver. 5. "*Whereas He was pierced for our sins, bruised for our
iniquities: the punishment was laid upon Him for our peace; and
through His stripes we were healed.*" The question is, whether
ver. 5*a* describes what He was during His life, or what He was

[1] See my *Jesus und Hillel*, pp. 26, 27.

in His death.   The words decide in favour of the latter.   For
although *châlâl* is applied to a person mortally wounded but
not yet dead (Jer. li. 52 ; Ps. lxix. 27), and *châlal* to a heart
wounded to death (Ps. cix. 22) ; the pure passives used here,
which denote a calamity inflicted by violence from without,
more especially *m^echōlâl*, which is not the participle *polal* of
chīl (made to twist one's self with pain), but the participle *poal*
of *châlal* (pierced, *transfossus*, the passive of *m^echōlēl*, ch. li. 9),
and the substantive clauses, which express a fact that has
become complete in all its circumstances, can hardly be understood in any other way than as denoting, that "the servant of
God" floated before the mind of the speaker in all the sufferings of death, just as was the case with Zechariah in Zech.
xii. 10.   There were no stronger expressions to be found in
the language, to denote a violent and painful death.   As *min*,
with the passive, does not answer to the Greek ὑπό, but to
ἀπό, the meaning is not that it was our sins and iniquities that
had pierced Him through like swords, and crushed Him like
heavy burdens, but that He was pierced and crushed on account
of our sins and iniquities.   It was not His own sins and iniquities, but *ours*, which He had taken upon Himself, that He
might make atonement for them in our stead, that were the
cause of His having to suffer so cruel and painful a death.
The ultimate cause is not mentioned; but מוּסַר שְׁלוֹמֵנוּ עָלָיו which
follows points to it.   His suffering was a *mūsâr*, which is an
indirect affirmation that it was God who had inflicted it upon
Him, for who else could the *yōsēr* (*m^eyassēr*) be ?   We have
rendered *mūsâr* "punishment;" and there was no other word in
the language for this idea ; for though נָקָם and פְּקֻדָּה (to which
Hofmann refers) have indeed the idea of punishment associated
with them, the former signifies ἐκδίκησις, the latter ἐπίσκεψις,
whereas *mūsâr* not only denotes παιδεία, as the chastisement
of love (Prov. iii. 11), but also as the infliction of punishment
(= τιμωρία, κόλασις, Prov. vii. 22, Jer. xxx. 14), just as
David, when he prayed that God might not punish him in His
anger and hot displeasure (Ps. vi. 2), could not find a more
suitable expression for punishment, regarded as the execution
of judgment, than יִפֵּר (הוֹכִיחַ).   The word itself, which follows
the form of *mūsâd* (ch. xxviii. 16), signified primarily being
chastised (from *yâsar* = *vâsar*, *constringere*, *coercere*), and

included from the very outset the idea of practical chastisement, which then passed over into that of admonition in words,
of warning by example, and of chastity as a moral quality.
In the case before us, in which the reference is to a sufferer,
and to a *mūsâr* resting upon him, this can only mean actual
chastisement. If the expression had been מוּסָרֵנוּ עָלָיו, it would
merely mean that God had caused Him, who had taken upon
Himself our sins and iniquities and thus made Himself repre-
sentatively or vicariously guilty, to endure the chastisement
which those sins deserved. But it is מוּסַר שְׁלוֹמֵנוּ. The connection of the words is the same as that of תּוֹכַחַת חַיִּים in Prov.
xv. 31. As the latter signifies " reproof leading to life," so
the former signifies " the chastisement which leads to our
peace." It is true that the suffix belongs to the one idea, that
that has grown up through this combination of the words, like
bʳîth shʳlōmî, " my peace-covenant" (ch. liv. 10); but what else
could our " peace-chastisement" be, than the chastisement that
brings us peace, or puts us into a state of salvation? This is
the idea involved in Stier's rendering, " restoring chastisement,"
and Hofmann's, " the chastisement wholesome for us." The
difference in the exposition simply lies in the view entertained
of the *mūsâr*, in which neither of these commentators will
allow that there is any idea of a visitation of justice here.
But according to our interpretation, the genitive שְׁלוֹמֵנוּ, which
defines the *mūsâr* so far as its object and results are concerned,
clearly shows that this manifestation of the justice of God, this
satisfaction procured by His holiness, had His love for its
foundation and end. It was our peace, or, what is more in
accordance with the full idea of the word, our general well-
being, our blessedness, which these sufferings arrived at and
secured (the synonyms of *shâlōm* are *tōbh* and *yʳshûʿâh*, ch.
lii. 7). In what follows, " and by His stripes (*chăbhûrâh* =
chabbûrâh, ch. i. 6) we have been healed," *shâlōm* is defined as
a condition of salvation brought about by healing. " *Venustis-
simum* 'ὀξύμωρον," exclaims Vitringa here. He means the
same as Jerome when he says, *suo vulnere vulnera nostra
curavit.* The stripes and weals that were inflicted upon Him
have made us sound and well (the LXX. keeps the collective
singular, and renders it very aptly τῷ μώλωπι αὐτοῦ; cf. 1 Pet.
ii. 24). We were sick unto death because of our sins; but He,

the sinless one, took upon Himself a suffering unto death, which was, as it were, the concentration and essence of the woes that we had deserved; and this voluntary endurance, this submission to the justice of the Holy One, in accordance with the counsels of divine love, became the source of our healing.

Thus does the whole body of the restored Israel confess with penitence, that it has so long mistaken Him whom Jehovah, as is now distinctly affirmed, had made a curse for their good, when they had gone astray to their own ruin. Ver. 6. "*All we like sheep went astray; we had turned every one to his own way; and Jehovah caused the iniquity of us all to fall on Him.*" It is the state of exile, upon which the penitent Israel is here looking back; but exile as being, in the prophet's view, the final state of punishment before the final deliverance. Israel in its exile resembled a scattered flock without a shepherd; it had lost the way of Jehovah (ch. lxiii. 17), and every one had turned to his own way, in utter selfishness and estrangement from God (ch. lvi. 11). But whereas Israel thus heaped up guilt upon guilt, the Servant of Jehovah was He upon whom Jehovah Himself caused the punishment of their guilt to fall, that He might make atonement for it through His own suffering. Many of the more modern expositors endeavour to set aside the *pœna vicaria* here, by giving to הִפְגִּיעַ a meaning which it never has. Thus Stier renders it, "Jehovah caused the iniquity of all to strike or break upon Him." Others, again, give a meaning to the statement which is directly at variance with the words themselves. Thus Hahn renders it: Jehovah took the guilt of the whole into His service, causing Him to die a violent death through their crime. Hofmann very properly rejects both explanations, and holds fast to the fact that הִפְגִּיעַ בְּ, regarded as a causative of פָּגַע בְּ, signifies "to cause anything to strike or fall upon a person," which is the rendering adopted by Symmachus: κύριος καταντῆσαι ἐποίησεν εἰς αὐτὸν τὴν ἀνομίαν πάντων ἡμῶν. "Just as the blood of a murdered man comes upon the murderer, when the bloody deed committed comes back upon him in the form of blood-guiltiness inflicting vengeance; so does sin come upon, overtake (Ps. xl. 13), or meet with the sinner. It went forth from him as his own act; it returns with destructive effect, as a fact by which he is condemned. But in this case God does not suffer those who have

sinned to be overtaken by the sin they have committed; but it
falls upon His servant, the righteous One." These are Hofmann's words. But if the sin turns back upon the sinner in
the shape of punishment, why should the sin of all men, which
the Servant of God has taken upon Himself as His own, overtake Him in the form of an evil, which, even if it be a punishment, is not punishment inflicted upon Him? For this is just
the characteristic of Hofmann's doctrine of the atonement,
that it altogether eliminates from the atoning work the reconciliation of the purposes of love with the demands of righteousness. Now it is indeed perfectly true, that the Servant of
God cannot become the object of punishment, either as a servant of God or as an atoning Saviour; for as servant of God
He is the beloved of God, and as atoning Saviour He undertakes
a work which is well pleasing to God, and ordained in God's
eternal counsel. So that the wrath which pours out upon
Him is not meant for Him as the righteous One who voluntarily
offers up Himself; but indirectly it relates to Him, so far as He
has vicariously identified Himself with sinners, who are deserving of wrath. How could He have made expiation for sin, if
He had simply subjected Himself to its cosmical effects, and not
directly subjected Himself to that wrath which is the invariable
divine correlative of human sin? And what other reason could
there be for God's not rescuing Him from this the bitterest cup
of death, than the ethical impossibility of acknowledging the
atonement as really made, without having left the representative of the guilty, who had presented Himself to Him as though
guilty Himself, to taste of the punishment which they had
deserved? It is true that vicarious expiation and *pœna vicaria*
are not coincident ideas. The punishment is but one element
in the expiation, and it derives a peculiar character from the
fact that one innocent person voluntarily submits to it in His
own person. It does not stand in a thoroughly external relation of identity to that deserved by the many who are guilty;
but the latter cannot be set aside without the atoning individual enduring an intensive equivalent to it, and that in such
a manner, that this endurance is no less a self-cancelling of
wrath on the part of God, than an absorption of wrath on the
part of the Mediator; and in this central point of the atoning
work, the voluntarily forgiving love of God and the voluntarily

self-sacrificing love of the Mediator meet together, like hands stretched out to grasp one another from the midst of a dark cloud. Hermann Schultz also maintains that the suffering, which was the consequence of sin and therefore punishment to the guilty, is borne by the Redeemer as suffering, without being punishment. But in this way the true mystery is wiped out of the heart of the atoning work; and this explanation is also at variance with the expression " the chastisement of our peace" in ver. 5*b*, and the equally distinct statement in ver. 6*b*, " He hath laid on Him the iniquity of us all." It was the sin of all Israel, as the palindromically repeated *kullânû* emphatically declares, which pressed upon Him with such force when His atoning work was about to be decided. But עָוֹן is used to denote not only the transgression itself, but also the guilt incurred thereby, and the punishment to which it gives rise. All this great multitude of sins, and mass of guilt, and weight of punishment, came upon the Servant of Jehovah according to the appointment of the God of salvation, who is gracious in holiness. The third turn ends here. It was our sins that He bore, and for our salvation that God caused Him to suffer on our account.

The fourth turn describes how He suffered and died and was buried. Ver. 7. "*He was ill treated; whilst He suffered willingly, and opened not His mouth, like the sheep that is led to the slaughter-bench, and like a lamb that is dumb before its shearers, and opened not His mouth.*" The third pers. *niphal* stands first in a passive sense: He has been hard pressed (1 Sam. xiii. 6): He is driven, or hunted (1 Sam. xiv. 24), treated tyrannically and unsparingly; in a word, plagued (*vexatus*; compare the *niphal* in a reciprocal sense in ch. iii. 5, and according to the reading נגשׂ in ch. xxix. 13 in a reflective sense, to torment one's self). Hitzig renders the next clause, " and although tormented, He opened not His mouth." But although an explanatory subordinate clause may precede the principal clause which it more fully explains, no example can be found of such a clause with (a retrospective) וְהוּא explaining what follows; for in Job ii. 8 the circumstantial clause, " sitting down among the ashes," belongs to the principal fact which stands before. And so here, where נַעֲנָה (from which comes the participle נַעֲנֶה, usually met with in circum-

stantial clauses) has not a passive, but a reflective meaning, as
in Ex. x. 3: "He was ill treated, whilst He bowed Himself
(= suffered voluntarily), and opened not His mouth" (the
regular leap from the participle to the finite). The voluntary
endurance is then explained by the simile "like a sheep that is
led to the slaughter" (an attributive clause, like Jer. xi. 19);
and the submissive quiet bearing, by the simile "like a lamb
that is dumb before its shearers." The commentators regard
נֶאֱלָמָה as a participle; but this would have the tone upon the
last syllable (see ch. i. 21, 26, Nah. iii. 11; cf. *Job*, vol. i.
p. 393, note). The tone shows it to be the pausal form for
נֶאֱלָמָה, and so we have rendered it; and, indeed, as the interchange of the perfect with the future in the attributive clause
must be intentional, not *quæ obmutescit*, but *obmutuit*. The
following words, וְלֹא יִפְתַּח פִּיו, do not form part of the simile,
which would require *tiphtach*, for nothing but absolute necessity
would warrant us in assuming that it points back beyond רָחֵל
to שֶׂה, as Rashi and others suppose. The palindromical repetition also favours the unity of the subject with that of the
previous יפתח and the correctness of the delicate accentuation, with which the rendering in the LXX. and Acts viii. 32
coincides. All the references in the New Testament to the
Lamb of God (with which the corresponding allusions to the
passover are interwoven) spring from this passage in the book
of Isaiah.

The description of the closing portion of the life of the
Servant of Jehovah is continued in ver. 8. "*He has been taken
away from prison and from judgment; and of His generation
who considered: 'He was snatched away out of the land of the
living; for the wickedness of my people punishment fell upon
Him'?*" The principal emphasis is not laid upon the fact that
He was *taken away* from suffering, but that it was out of the
midst of suffering that He was carried off. The idea that is
most prominent in *luqqâch* (with *â* in half pause) is not that of
being translated (as in the accounts of Enoch and Elijah), but
of being snatched or hurried away (*abreptus est*, ch. lii. 5,
Ezek. xxxiii. 4, etc.). The parallel is *abscissus* (cf. *nikhrath*,
Jer. xi. 19) *a terra viventium*, for which נִגְזַר by itself is supposed
to be used in the sense of carried away (*i.e.* out of the sphere
of the living into that of the dead, Lam. iii. 54; cf. Ezek.

xxxvii. 11, "It is all over with us"). עֹצֶר (from עָצַר, *compescere*) is a violent constraint; here, as in Ps. cvii. 39, it signifies a persecuting treatment which restrains by outward force, such as that of prison or bonds; and *mishpât* refers to the judicial proceedings, in which He was put upon His trial, accused and convicted as worthy of death,—in other words, to His unjust judgment. The *min* might indeed be understood, as in ver. 5*a*, not as referring to the persons who swept Him away (= ὑπό), but, as in Ps. cvii. 39, as relating to the ground and cause of the sweeping away. But the local sense, which is the one most naturally suggested by *luqqach* (*e.g.* ch. xlix. 24), is to be preferred: hostile oppression and judicial persecution were the circumstances out of which He was carried away by death. With regard to what follows, we must in any case adhere to the ordinary usage, according to which *dōr* (= Arab. *daur, dahr*, a revolution or period of time) signifies an age, or the men living in a particular age; also, in an ethical sense, the entire body of those who are connected together by similarity of disposition (see, for example, Ps. xiv. 5); or again (= Arab. *dâr*) a dwelling, as in ch. xxxviii. 12, and possibly also (of the grave) in Ps. xlix. 20. Such meanings as length of life (Luther and Grotius), course of life (Vitringa), or fate (Hitzig), it is impossible to sustain. Hence the Sept. rendering, τὴν γενεὰν αὐτοῦ τίς διηγήσεται, which Jerome also adopts, can only mean, so far as the usage of the language is concerned, "who can declare the number of His generation" (*i.e.* of those inspired by His spirit, or filled with His life); but in this connection such a thought would be premature. Moreover, the generation intended would be called זַרְעוֹ rather than דּוֹרוֹ, as springing from Him. Still less can we adopt the meaning "dwelling," as Knobel does, who explains the passage thus: "who considers how little the grave becomes Him, which He has received as His dwelling-place." The words do not admit of this explanation. Hofmann formerly explained the passage as meaning, "No one takes His dwelling-place into his mind or mouth, so as even to think of it, or inquire what had become of Him;" but in His *Schriftbeweis* he has decided in favour of the meaning, His contemporaries, or the men of His generation. It is only with this rendering that we obtain a thought at all suitable to the picture of suffering given here, or to the words

which follow (compare Jer. ii. 31, O ye men of this generation).
וְאֶת־דּוֹרוֹ in that case is not the object to יְשׂוֹחֵחַ, the real object to
which is rather the clause introduced by כִּי, but an adverbial
accusative, which may serve to give emphatic prominence to
the subject, as we may see from ch. lvii. 12, Ezek. xvii. 21,
Neh. ix. 34 (Ges. § 117, Anm.) ; for אֶת cannot be a preposition, since *inter æquales ejus* would not be expressed in Hebrew
by אֶת־דּוֹרוֹ, but by בְדוֹרוֹ. The *pilel sōchĕăch* with b^e signifies
in Ps. cxliii. 5 a thoughtful consideration or deliberation, in
a word, *meditationem alicujus rei* (compare the *kal* with the
accusative, Ps. cxlv. 5). The following *kī* is an explanatory
quod : with regard to His contemporaries, who considered that,
etc. The words introduced with *kī* are spoken, as it were, out
of the heart of His contemporaries, who ought to have considered, but did not. We may see from עַמִּי that it is intended
to introduce a direct address ; and again, if we leave *kī* untrans-
lated, like ὅτι *recitativum* (see, for example, Josh. ii. 24 ; compare *di*, Dan. ii. 25), we can understand why the address, which
has been carried on thus far in such general terms, assumes all
at once an individual form. It cannot be denied, indeed, that
we obtain a suitable object for the missing consideration, if we
adopt this rendering: " He was torn away (3*d præt.*) out of the
land of the living, through (*min* denoting the mediating cause)
the wicked conduct of my people (in bringing Him to death),
to their own punishment ; *i.e.* none of the men of His age
(like *mī* in ver. 1, no one = only a very few) discerned what
had befallen them on account of their sin, in ridding themselves of Him by a violent death." Hofmann and V. F.
Oehler both adopt this explanation, saying, "Can the prophet
have had the person of the *Ecce Homo* before his eye, without
intimating that his people called down judgment upon themselves, by laying violent hands upon the Servant of God?"
We cannot, however, decide in favour of this explanation ; since
the impression produced by this מִפֶּשַׁע עַמִּי נֶגַע לָמוֹ is, that it is
intended to be taken as a rectification of וַאֲנַחְנוּ חֲשַׁבְנֻהוּ נָגוּעַ in ver.
4*b*, to which it stands in a reciprocal relation. This reciprocal
relation is brought out more fully, if we regard the force of
the *min* as still continued (*ob plagam quæ illis debebatur*, Seb.
Schmid, Kleinert, etc.) ; though not in the sense of "through
the stroke proceeding from them, my people " (Hahn), which

would be opposed to the general usage of נֶגַע ; or taking נגע למו
as a relative clause, *populi mei quibus plaga debebatur* (Hengstenberg, Hävernick). But the most natural course is to take
lâmō as referring to the Servant of God, more especially as our
prophet uses *lâmō* pathetically for *lō*, as ch. xliv. 15 unquestionably shows (notwithstanding the remonstrance of Stier,
who renders the passage, " He was all plague, or smiting, for
them"). נֶגַע always signifies suffering as a calamity proceeding
from God (*e.g.* Ex. xi. 1, Ps. xxxix. 11, and in every other
passage in which it does not occur in the special sense of
leprosy, which also points back, however, to the generic idea of
a plague divinely sent) ; hence Jerome renders it, " for the sin
of my people have I smitten Him." The text does not read so;
but the smiter is really Jehovah. Men looked upon His Servant as a נגוע ; and so He really was, but not in the sense in
which men regarded Him as such. Yet, even if they had been
mistaken concerning Him during His lifetime; now that He
no longer dwelt among the living, they ought to see, as they
looked back upon His actions and His sufferings, that it was
not for His own wickedness, but for that of Israel, viz. to make
atonement for it, that such a visitation from God had fallen
upon Him (לֹ as in ch. xxiv. 16 and ch. xxvi. 16, where the
sentence is in the same logical subordination to the previous one
as it is here, where Dachselt gives this interpretation, which is
logically quite correct: *propter prævaricationem populi mei
plaga ei contingente*).

After this description in ver. 7 of the patience with which
He suffered, and in ver. 8 of the manner in which He died,
there follows a retrospective glance at His burial. Ver. 9.
" *And they assigned Him His grave with sinners, and with a rich
man in His martyrdom, because He had done no wrong, and there
was no deceit in His mouth.*" The subject to וַיִּתֵּן (assigned) is
not Jehovah, although this would not be impossible, since נֶגַע has
Jehovah as the latent subject; but it would be irreconcilable
with ver. 10, where Jehovah is introduced as the subject with
antithetical prominence. It would be better to assume that " my
people" is the subject; but as this would make it appear as if the
statement introduced in ver. 8*b* with *kī* (for) were continued here,
we seem compelled to refer it to *dōrō* (His generation), which
occurs in the principal clause. No objection could be offered

to our regarding " His own generation" as the subject; but
dōrō is somewhat too far removed for this; and if the prophet
had had the contemporaries of the sufferer in his mind, he
would most likely have used a plural verb (*vayyitt*e*nū*). Some,
therefore, supply a personal subject of the most general kind
to *yittēn* (which occurs even with a neuter subject, like the
German *es gibt*, Fr. *il y a*, Eng. " there is;" cf. Prov. xiii.
10): " they (*on*) gave;" and looking at the history of the
fulfilment, we confess that this is the rendering we prefer.   In
fact, without the commentary supplied by the fulfilment, it
would be impossible to understand ver. 9*a* at all.   The earlier
translators did great violence to the text, and yet failed to bring
out any admissible thought. And the explanation which is most
generally adopted now, viz. that עָשִׁיר is the synonymous parallel
to רְשָׁעִים (as even Luther rendered it, " and died like a rich
man," with the marginal gloss, " a rich man who sets all his
heart upon riches, *i.e.* a wicked man"), is also untenable; for
even granting that *'áshīr* could be proved by examples to be
sometimes used as synonymous with רשע, as עָנִי and אֶבְיוֹן are
as synonyms of צַדִּיק, this would be just the passage in which
it would be least possible to sustain any such use of the word;
since he who finds his grave with rich men, whether with the
godly or the ungodly, would thereby have received a decent,
and even honourable burial.   This is so thoroughly sustained
by experience, as to need no confirmation from such passages
as Job xxi. 32.   Hitzig has very good ground, therefore, for
opposing this " synonymous" explanation; but when he adopts

the rendering *lapsator*, after the Arabic عَثُور, this is quite as

much in opposition to Arabic usage (according to which
this word merely signifies a person who falls into error, and
makes a mistake in speaking), as it is to the Hebrew. Ewald
changes עשיר into עָשִׁיק (a word which has no existence); and
Böttcher alters it into עֹשֵׂי רָע, which is comparatively the best
suggestion of all. Hofmann connects the two words עָשִׁיר בְּמוֹתָיו,
" men who have become rich through the murders that they
have treacherously caused" (though without being able to ad-
duce any proof that *mōth* is ever applied to the death which one
person inflicts upon another). At any rate, all these attempts
spring from the indisputable assumption, that to be rich is not

in itself a sin which deserves a dishonourable burial, to say
nothing of its receiving one. If, therefore, רשעים and עשיר are
not kindred ideas, they must be antithetical; but it is no easier
to establish a purely ethical antithesis than an ethical coincidence. If, however, we take the word רשעים as suggesting the
idea of persons found guilty, or criminals (an explanation which
the juridical context of the passage well sustains; see at ch.
l. 9), we get a contrast which our own usage of speech also
draws between a rich man who is living in the enjoyment of
his own possessions, and a delinquent who has become impoverished to the utmost, through hatred, condemnation, ruin.
And if we reflect that the Jewish rulers would have given to
Jesus the same dishonourable burial as to the two thieves, but
that the Roman authorities handed over the body to Joseph the
Arimathæan, a " rich man" (Matt. xxvii. 57), who placed it
in the sepulchre in his own garden, we see an agreement at
once between the gospel history and the prophetic words, which
could only be the work of the God of both the prophecy and
its fulfilment, inasmuch as no suspicion could possibly arise of
there having been any human design of bringing the former
into conformity with the latter. But if it be objected, that
according to the parallel the 'âshīr must be regarded as dead,
quite as much as the rᵉshâ'īm, we admit the force of this
objection, and should explain it in this way: " They assigned
Him His grave with criminals, and after He had actually died
a martyr's death, with a rich man;" i.e. He was to have lain
where the bodies of criminals lie, but He was really laid in a
grave that was intended for the corpse of a rich man.[1] The
rendering adopted by Vitringa and others, " and He was with
a rich man in his death," is open to this objection, that such a
clause, to be quite free from ambiguity, would require ואת־עשיר
הוא במותיו. Hengstenberg and Stier very properly refer both
ויתן and קברו, which must be repeated in thought, to the second
clause as well as the first. The rendering tumulum ejus must
be rejected, since bâmâh never has this meaning; and בָּמֹתָיו,
which is the pointing sustained by three Codd., would not be
mausolea, but a lofty burial-hill, after the fashion of the
Hünengräber (certain " giants' graves," or barrows, in Holstein

[1] A clairvoyant once said of the Lord: " Died like a criminal; buried
like a prince of the earth" (vid. Psychol. pp. 262, 364).

and Saxony).[1] מוֹתֵי is a *plur. exaggerativus* here, as in Ezek.
xxviii. 10 (compare *m^emōthē* in Ezek. xxviii. 8 and Jer. xvi. 4);
it is applied to a violent death, the very pain of which makes it
like dying again and again. The first clause states with whom
they at first assigned Him His grave ; the second with whom it
was assigned Him, after He had really died a painful death.
"Of course," as F. Philippi observes, "this was not a thorough
compensation for the ignominy of having died the death of a
criminal ; but the honourable burial, granted to one who had
been ignominiously put to death, showed that there must be
something very remarkable about Him. It was the beginning
of the glorification which commenced with His death." If we
have correctly interpreted the second clause, there can be no
doubt in our minds, since we cannot shake the word of God
like a kaleidoscope, and multiply the *sensus complex*, as Stier
does, that עַל לֹא (= עַל־אֲשֶׁר לֹא) does not mean "notwithstanding
that not," as in Job xvi. 17, but " because not," like עַל־בְּלִי in
Gen. xxxi. 20. The reason why the Servant of God received
such honourable treatment immediately after His ignominious
martyrdom, was to be found in His freedom from sin, in the
fact that He had done no wrong, and there was no deceit in
His mouth (LXX. and 1 Pet. ii. 22, where the clause is
correctly rendered οὐδὲ εὑρέθη δόλος ἐν τῷ στόματι αὐτοῦ).
His actions were invariably prompted by pure love, and His
speech consisted of unclouded sincerity and truth.

The last turn in the prophecy, which commences here, carries
out ver. 6*b* still further, and opens up the background of His
fate.   The gracious counsel of God for our salvation was
accomplished thus. Ver. 10. "*And it pleased Jehovah to bruise
Him, to afflict Him with disease ; if His soul would pay a trespass-offering, He should see posterity, should live long days, and*

---

[1] The usage of the language shows clearly that *bâmâh* had originally
the meaning of "height" (*e.g.* 2 Sam. i. 19). The primary meaning suggested by Böttcher, of *locus clausus, septus* (from בום = בהם, יָשֵׁם), cannot
be sustained. We still hold that בם is the expanded בא, and במה an
ascent, steep place, or stair. In the Talmud, *bâmâh* is equivalent to βωμός,
an altar, and בִּימָה (Syr. *bim*) equivalent to the βῆμα of the orator and
judge ; βωμός, root βα, like the Hebrew *bâmâh*, signifies literally an elevation, and actually occurs in the sense of a sepulchral hill, which this never
has, not even in Ezek. xliii. 7.

the purpose of Jehovah should prosper through His hand. הֶחֱלִי
cannot possibly be equivalent to הֶחֱלִיּ, as Hitzig supposes. An
article appended to a noun never obliterates the fundamental
character of its form (not even in הָאָרֶץ). Nor does Böttcher's
suggestion, that we should read הֶחֱלִי as an accusative of more
precise definition, commend itself; for what would the article
do in that case? It is the *hiphil* of חָלָה, like the Syriac *agli*
from g^elo; or rather, as even in Syriac this אַגְלִי is equivalent to
אַגְלִיא, of חֶלָא, 2 Chron. xvi. 12 (cf. תֶּחֱלוּאִים), like הֶחֱטִי in 2 Kings
xiii. 6 and Jer. xxxii. 35, from חָטָא. דַּכְּאוֹ is placed under דְּכָא
(=דַּכָּאוֹ with *Dag. dirimens*) in Gesenius' *Lexicon;* but this
substantive is a needless fiction. דכאו is an inf. *piel: conterere
eum* (Jerome), not καθαρίσαι αὐτόν (LXX. from זָכָה=דְּכָא).
According to Mic. vi. 13 (הֶחֱלֵיתִי הַכּוֹתֶךָ, I hurt to smite thee, *i.e.*
I smite thee with a painful blow), דַּכְּאוֹ הֶחֱלִי are apparently connected, in the sense of "And it pleased Jehovah to bruise Him
painfully." But both logically and syntactically this would
require the opposite construction, viz. החלי דכאו. דַּכְּאוֹ must
therefore be an infinitive, depending upon חָפֵץ, according to
Job xxxiii. 32 (=εὐδόκησε; the LXX. thoughtlessly renders it
βούλεται). The infinitive construction is then changed into the
finite; for even החלי is subordinate to חפץ, as in Hos. v. 11 (cf. ch.
xlii. 21; Ges. § 142, 3); "he would, made ill," being equivalent to "he would make ill," *i.e.* he would plunge into distress.
There is no necessity to repeat דכאו after החלי, in the sense of
"he caused sore evil therewith," viz. with the דכאו. It was
men who inflicted upon the Servant of God such crushing
suffering, such deep sorrow; but the supreme *causa efficiens* in
the whole was *God*, who made the sin of men subservient to
His pleasure, His will, and predetermined counsel. The suffering of His Servant was to be to Him the way to glory, and this
way of His through suffering to glory was to lead to the establishment of a church of the redeemed, which would spring
from Him; in other words, it would become the commencement
of that fulfilment of the divine plan of salvation which He, the
ever-living, ever-working One, would carry out to completion.
We give up the idea that תִּשִׂים is to be taken as addressed by
Jehovah to "His Servant." The person acting is the Servant,
and it is to Jehovah that the action refers. But Hofmann's
present view, viz. that *tâsîm* is addressed to the people, is still

less admissible. It is the people who are speaking here; and although the confession of the penitent Israel runs on from ver. 11 (where the confessing retrospective view of the past becomes a prospective and prophetic glance at the future) in a direct prophetic tone, and ver. 10 might form the transition to this; yet, if the people were addressed in this word *tâsîm*, it would be absolutely necessary that it should be distinctly mentioned in this connection. And is it really Israel which makes the soul of the Servant an *'âshâm*, and not rather the Servant Himself? No doubt it is true, that if nothing further were stated here than that " the people made the life of the Servant of God an *'âshâm*, inasmuch as it treated Him just as if it had a pricking in its conscience so long as it suffered Him to live,"—which is a natural sequel in Hofmann's case to his false assumption, that the passion described in ch. liii. was merely the culminating point in the sufferings which the Servant was called to endure *as a prophet*, whereas the prophet falls into the background here behind the sacrifice and the priest,—we should no doubt have one scriptural testimony less to support the *satisfactio vicaria*.[1] But if we adopt the following rendering, which is the simplest, and the one least open to exception : if His soul offered (placed, *i.e.* should have placed; cf. Job xiv. 14, *si mortuus fuerit*) an *'âshâm*,—it is evident that *'âshâm* has here a sacrificial meaning, and indeed a very definite one, inasmuch as the *'âshâm* (the trespass-offering) was a sacrifice, the character of which was very sharply defined. It is self-evident, however, that the *'âshâm* paid by the soul of the Servant must consist in the sacrifice of itself, since He pays it by submitting to a violent death; and a sacrifice presented by the *nephesh* (the soul, the life, the very self) must be not only one which pro-

---

[1] In the first edition of Hofmann's *Schriftbeweis* (i. 2, 137), in which he regarded *tâsîm* as addressed to God, he set aside the orthodox view with the remark, that God Himself makes good the injury that men have done to Him by giving up the life of His Servant. In the second edition (i. 2, 208) he supposes the people to be addressed, and it is therefore the people who make the Servant's life an *'âshâm*. The first edition contained the following correct definition of *'âshâm*: " In general, it denotes what one person pays to make good an injury done by him to another." The exposition which follows above will show how we are forced to adopt the orthodox view, if we adhere to this definition and regard the Servant Himself as presenting the *'âshâm*.

ceeds from itself, but one which consists in itself. If, then, we would understand the point of view in which the self-sacrifice of the Servant of God is placed when it is called an *'âshâm*, we must notice very clearly the characteristic distinction between this kind of sacrifice and every other. Many of the ritual distinctions, however, may be indicated superficially, inasmuch as they have no bearing upon the present subject, where we have to do with an antitypical and personal sacrifice, and not with a typical and animal one. The *'âshâm* was a *sanctissimum*, like that of the sin-offering (Lev. vi. 10, 17, and xiv. 13), and according to Lev. vii. 7 there was "one law" for them both. This similarity in the treatment was restricted simply to the fact, that the fat portions of the trespass-offering, as well as of the sin-offering, were placed upon the altar, and that the remainder, as in the case of those sin-offerings the blood of which was not taken into the interior of the holy place, was assigned to the priests and to the male members of the priestly families (see Lev. vi. 22, vii. 6). There were the following points of contrast, however, between these two kinds of sacrifice: (1.) The material of the *sin-offerings* varied considerably, consisting sometimes of a bullock, sometimes of a pair of doves, and even of meal without oil or incense; whereas the *trespass-offering* always consisted of a ram, or at any rate of a male sheep. (2.) The choice of the victim, and the course adopted with its blood, was regulated in the case of the *sin-offering* according to the condition of the offerer; but in the case of the *trespass-offering* they were neither of them affected by this in the slightest degree. (3.) *Sin-offerings* were presented by the congregation, and upon holy days, whereas *trespass-offerings* were only presented by individuals, and never upon holy days. (4.) In connection with the *trespass-offering* there was none of the smearing of the blood (*n^ethînâh*) or of the sprinkling of the blood (*hazzâ'âh*) connected with the *sin-offering*, and the pouring out of the blood at the foot of the altar (*sh^ephîkhâh*) is never mentioned. The ritual for the blood consisted purely in the swinging out of the blood (*z^erîqâh*), as in the case of the whole offering and of the peace-offerings. There is only one instance in which the blood of the trespass-offering is ordered to be smeared, viz. upon certain portions of the body of the leper (Lev. xiv. 14), for which the blood of the sin-offering that was to be applied exclusively to the altar could not be used. And in general we find that, in the case of the trespass-offering, instead of the altar-ritual, concerning which the law is very brief (Lev. vii. 1–7), other acts that are altogether peculiar to it are brought prominently into the foreground (Lev. v. 14 sqq.; Num. v. 5–8). These are all to be accounted for from the fact that a trespass-offering was to be presented by the man who had un-intentionally laid hands upon anything holy, e.g. the tithes or first-fruits, or who had broken any commandment of God "in ignorance" (if indeed this is to be taken as the meaning of the expression "and wist it not" in Lev. v. 17–19); also by the man who had in any way defrauded his neighbour (which was re-garded as unfaithfulness towards Jehovah), provided he antici-pated it by a voluntary confession,—this included the violation of another's conjugal rights in the case of a bondmaid (Lev. xix. 20–22); also by a leper or a Nazarite defiled by contact with a corpse, at the time of their purification, because their uncleanness involved the neglect and interruption of the duties of worship which they were bound to observe. Wherever a material restitution was possible, it was to be made with the addition of a fifth; and in the one case mentioned in Lev. xix. 20–22, the trespass-offering was admissible even after a judicial punishment had been inflicted. But in every case the guilty person had to present the animal of the trespass-offering "ac-cording to thy valuation, O priest, in silver shekels," i.e. accord-ing to the priest's taxation, and in holy coin. Such was the prominence given to the person of the priest in the ritual of the trespass-offering. In the sin-offering the priest is always the representative of the offerer; but in the trespass-offering he is generally the representative of God. The trespass-offer-ing was a restitution or compensation made to God in the person of the priest, a payment or penance which made amends for the wrong done, a satisfactio in a disciplinary sense. And this is implied in the name; for just as חטאת denotes first the sin, then the punishment of the sin and the expiation of the sin, and hence the sacrifice which cancels the sin; so 'áshâm signifies first the guilt or debt, then the compensation or penance, and hence (cf. Lev. v. 15) the sacrifice which dis-charges the debt or guilt, and sets the man free. Every species of sacrifice had its own primary idea. The fundamental idea of the 'ōláh (burnt-offering) was *oblatio*, or the offering of worship; that of the *sh*e*lámīm* (peace-offerings), *conciliatio*, or the knitting of fellowship; that of the *minchâh* (meat-offering), *donatio*, or sanctifying consecration; that of the *chattâ'th* (sin-offering), *expiatio*, or atonement; that of the *'ashâm* (trespass-offering), *mulcta* (*satisfactio*), or a compensatory payment. The self-sacrifice of the Servant of Jehovah may be presented under all these points of view. It is the complete antitype, the truth, the object, and the end of all the sacrifices. So far as it is the antitype of the "whole offering," the central point in its anti-typical character is to be found in the offering of His entire personality ($\pi\rho o\sigma\phi o\rho\grave{a}$ $\tau o\hat{u}$ $\sigma\acute{\omega}\mu a\tau o\varsigma$, Heb. x. 10) to God for a sweet smelling savour (Eph. v. 2); so far as it is the antitype of the sin-offering, in the shedding of His blood (Heb. ix. 13, 14), the "blood of sprinkling" (Heb. xii. 24; 1 Pet. i. 2); so far as it is the antitype of the *sh*e*lámīm*, and especially of the passover, in the sacramental participation in His one self-sacri-fice, which He grants to us in His courts, thus applying to us His own redeeming work, and confirming our fellowship of peace with God (Heb. xiii. 10; 1 Cor. v. 7), since the *sh*e*lámīm* derive their name from *shâlōm*, *pax*, *communio*; so far as it is the antitype of the trespass-offering, in the equivalent rendered to the justice of God for the sacrileges of our sins. The idea of compensatory payment, which Hofmann extends to the whole sacrifice, understanding by *kipper* the covering of the guilt in the sense of a debt (*debitum*), is peculiar to the *'ashâm*; and at the same time an idea, which Hofmann cannot find in the sacrifices, is expressed here in the most specific manner, viz. that of *satisfaction* demanded by the justice of God, and of *poena* outweighing the guilt contracted (cf. *nirtsâh*, ch. xl. 2); in other words, the idea of *satisfactio vicaria* in the sense of Anselm is brought out most distinctly here, where the soul of the Servant of God is said to present such an atoning sacri-fice for the whole, that is to say, where He offers Himself as such a sacrifice by laying down the life so highly valued by God (ch. xlii. 1, xlix. 5). As the verb most suitable to the idea of the *'ashâm* the writer selects the verb *sīm*, which is generally used to denote the giving of a pledge (Job xvii. 3), and is therefore the most suitable word for every kind of *satis-factio* that represents a direct *solutio*. The apodoses to "if His

soul shall have paid the penalty (*pœnam* or *mulctam*)" are expressed in the future, and therefore state what would take
place when the former should have been done. He should see
posterity (*vid.* Gen. 1. 23; Job xlii. 16), *i.e.* should become
possessed of a large family of descendants stretching far and
wide. The reference here is to the new "seed of Israel," the
people redeemed by Him, the church of the redeemed out of
Israel and all nations, of which He would lay the foundation.
Again, He should live long days, as He says in Rev. i. 18, "I
was dead; and, behold, I am alive for evermore."[1] Thirdly,
the pleasure of Jehovah should prosper "in His hand," *i.e.*
through the service of His mediation, or (according to the
primary meaning of *tsâlach*) should go on advancing incessantly, and pressing on to the final goal. His self-sacrifice,
therefore, merely lays the foundation for a progressively self-
realizing "pleasure of the Lord," *i.e.* (cf. ch. xliv. 28) for the
realization of the purpose of God according to His determinate
counsel, the fuller description of which we had in ch. xlii. and
xlix., where it was stated that He should be the mediator of a
new covenant, and the restorer of Israel, the light of the Gentiles and salvation of Jehovah even to the ends of the earth.

This great work of salvation lies as the great object of His
calling in the hand of the deceased and yet eternally living One,
and goes on victoriously through His mediation. He now reaps
the fruit of His self-sacrifice in a continuous priestly course.
Ver. 11. "*Because of the travail of His soul, He will see, and
be refreshed; through His knowledge will He procure justice,
my righteous servant, for the many, and will take their iniquities
upon Himself.*" The prophecy now leaves the standpoint of
Israel's retrospective acknowledgment of the long rejected Servant of God, and becomes once more the prophetic organ of
God Himself, who acknowledges the servant as His own. The
min of מֵעֲמַל might be used here in its primary local signification, "far away from the trouble" (as in Job xxi. 9, for
example); or the temporal meaning which is derived from the

---

[1] Knobel observes here: "The statement that a person first offers
himself as a trespass-offering, and then still lives for a long time, and still
continues working, is a very striking one; but it may be explained on the
ground that the offerer is a plurality." But how are we to explain the
striking expression in our creed, "rose again from the dead?"

local would be also admissible, viz. "from the time of the
trouble," *i.e.* immediately after it (as in Ps. lxxiii. 20); but
the causal sense is the most natural, viz. on account of, in
consequence of (as in Ex. ii. 23), which not only separates
locally and links together temporarily, but brings into intimate
connection. The meaning therefore is, "In consequence of the
trouble of His soul (*i.e.* trouble experienced not only in His
body, but into the inmost recesses of His soul), He will see,
satisfy Himself." Hitzig supplies בְּטוֹב (Jer. xxix. 32); Knobel
connects בְּדַעְתּוֹ, in opposition to the accents (like A. S. Th.
ἐμπλησθήσεται ἐν τῇ γνώσει αὐτοῦ), thus: "He looks at His
prudent work, and has full satisfaction therewith." But there
is nothing to supply, and no necessity to alter the existing
punctuation. The second verb receives its colouring from the
first; the expression "He will see, will satisfy Himself," being
equivalent to "He will enjoy a satisfying or pleasing sight"
(cf. Ps. xvii. 15), which will consist, as ver. 10*b* clearly shows,
in the successful progress of the divine work of salvation, of
which He is the Mediator. בדעתו belongs to יַצְדִּיק as the medium
of setting right (cf. Prov. xi. 9). This is connected with לְ in
the sense of "procure justice," like רְפָא לְ (ch. vi. 10); הֵנִיחַ לְ in
ch. xiv. 3, xxviii. 12 (cf. Dan. xi. 33, הֵבִין לְ, to procure intelligence; Gen. xlv. 7, הֶחֱיָה לְ, to prolong life,—a usage which leads
on to the Aramæan combination of the dative with the accusative, *e.g.* Job xxxvii. 18, compare v. 2). *Tsaddîq 'abhdî* do not
stand to one another in the relation of a proper name and a
noun in apposition, as Hofmann thinks, nor is this expression
to be interpreted according to הַמֶּלֶךְ דָּוִד (Ges. § 113); but "a
righteous man, my servant," with the emphatic prominence
given to the attribute (cf. ch. x. 30, xxiii. 12, Ps. lxxxix. 51), is
equivalent to "my righteous servant." But does בדעתו mean
per cognitionem sui, or *per cognitionem suam?* The former
gives a sense which is both doctrinally satisfying and practically correct: the Righteous One makes others partakers of
righteousness, through their knowledge of Him, His person,
and His work, and (as the biblical יָדַע, which has reference not
only to the understanding, but to personal experience also,
clearly signifies) through their entrance into living fellowship
with Him. Nearly all the commentators, who understand by
the servant of God the Divine Redeemer, give the preference

to this explanation (*e.g.* Vitringa, Hengstenberg, and Stier).
But the meaning preferred is not always the correct one. The
subjective rendering of the suffix (cf. Prov. xxii. 17) is favoured
by Mal. ii. 7, where it is said that "the priest's lips should keep
da'ath (knowledge);" by Dan. xii. 3, where faithful teachers are
called *matsdīqē hârabbīm* (they that turn many to righteousness); and by ch. xi. 2, according to which "the spirit of
knowledge" (*rŭăch da'ath*) is one of the seven spirits that descend upon the sprout of Jesse; so that "knowledge" (*da'ath*)
is represented as equally the qualification for the priestly, the
prophetic, and the regal calling. It is a very unseemly remark,
therefore, on the part of a modern commentator, when he
speaks of the subjective knowledge of the Servant as "halting
weakly behind in the picture, after His sacrificial death has
already been described." We need only recal to mind the
words of the Lord in Matt. xi. 27, which are not only recorded
both by the synoptists and by John, but supported by testimony outside the Gospels also: "No man knoweth the Son, but
the Father; neither knoweth any man the Father, save the Son,
and he to whomsoever the Son will reveal Him." Let us
remember also, that the Servant of Jehovah, whose priestly
mediatorial work is unfolded before us here in ch. liii., upon
the ground of which He rises to more than regal glory (ch. lii.
15, compare liii. 12), is no other than He to whom His God has
given the tongue of the learned, "to know how to speak a word
in season to him that is weary, *i.e.* to raise up the weary and
heavy laden" (ch. l. 4). He knows God, with whom He
stands in loving fellowship; He knows the counsels of His
love and the will of His grace, in the fulfilment of which His
own life ascends, after having gone down into death and come
forth from death; and by virtue of this knowledge, which rests
upon His own truest and most direct experience, He, the
righteous One, will help "the many," *i.e.* the great mass
(*hârabbīm* as in Dan. ix. 27, xi. 33, 39, xii. 3; cf. Ex. xxiii. 2,
where *rabbīm* is used in the same sense without the article),
hence all His own nation, and beyond that, all mankind (so far
as they were susceptible of salvation; == τοῖς πολλοῖς, Rom.
v. 19, cf. πολλῶν, Matt. xxvi. 28), to a right state of life and
conduct, and one that should be well-pleasing to God. The
primary reference is to the righteousness of faith, which is the

consequence of justification on the ground of His atoning work, when this is believingly appropriated; but the expression also includes that righteousness of life, which springs by an inward necessity out of those sanctifying powers, that are bound up with the atoning work which we have made our own (see Dan. ix. 24). The ancients recognised this connection between the *justitia fidei et vitæ* better than many of the moderns, who look askance at the Romish *justitia infusa*, and therewith boast of advancing knowledge. Because our righteousness has its roots in the forgiveness of sins, as an absolutely unmerited gift of grace without works, the prophecy returns once more from the justifying work of the Servant of God to His sin-expunging work as the basis of all righteousness: "He shall bear their iniquities." This *yisbōl* (He shall bear), which stands along with futures, and therefore, being also future itself, refers to something to be done after the completion of the work to which He is called in this life (with which Hofmann connects it), denotes the continued operation of His *s°bhâlâm* (ver. 4), through His own active mediation. His continued lading of our trespasses upon Himself is merely the constant presence and presentation of His atonement, which has been offered once for all. The dead yet living One, because of His one self-sacrifice, is an eternal Priest, who now lives to distribute the blessings that He has acquired.

The last reward of His thus working after this life for the salvation of sinners, and also of His work in this life upon which the former is founded, is victorious dominion. Ver: 12. "*Therefore I give Him a portion among the great, and with strong ones will He divide spoil; because He has poured out His soul into death: and He let Himself be reckoned among transgressors; whilst He bare the sin of many, and made intercession for the transgressors.*" The promise takes its stand between humiliation and exaltation, and rests partly upon the working of the exalted One, and partly upon the doing and suffering of One who was so ready to sacrifice Himself. Luther follows the LXX. and Vulgate, and adopts the rendering, "Therefore will I give Him a great multitude for booty;" and Hävernick, Stier, and others adopt essentially the same rendering, "Therefore will I apportion to Him the many." But, as Job xxxix. 17 clearly shows, this clause can only mean, "Therefore will I give Him a portion in the many." If, however, *chillēq b'* means to have a portion in anything, and not to give the thing itself as a portion, it is evident that *hârabbīm* here are not the many, but the great; and this is favoured by the parallel clause. The ideas of greatness and force, both in multitude and might, are bound up together in *rabh* and *'âtsūm* (see ch. viii. 7), and the context only can decide which rendering is to be adopted when these ideas are separated from one another. What is meant by "giving a portion *bârabbīm*," is clearly seen from such passages as ch. lii. 15, xlix. 7, according to which the great ones of the earth will be brought to do homage to Him, or at all events to submit to Him. The second clause is rendered by Luther, "and He shall have the strong for a prey." This is at any rate better than the rendering of the LXX. and Vulgate, "*et fortium dividet spolia.*" But Prov. xvi. 19 shows that אֶת is a preposition. Strong ones surround Him, and fight along with Him. The reference here is to the people of which it is said in Ps. cx. 3, "Thy people are thorough devotion in the day of Thy power;" and this people, which goes with Him to battle, and joins with Him in the conquest of the hostile powers of the world (Rev. xix. 14), also participates in the enjoyment of the spoils of His victory. With this victorious sway is He rewarded, because He has poured out His soul unto death, having not only exposed His life to death, but "poured out" (*he'ĕrâh*, to strip or empty, or pour clean out, even to the very last remnant) His life-blood into death (*lammâveth* like the *Lamed* in Ps. xxii. 16), and also because He has suffered Himself to be reckoned with transgressors, *i.e.* numbered among them (*niph. tolerativum*), namely, in the judgment of His countrymen, and in the unjust judgment (*mishpât*) by which He was delivered up to death as a wicked apostate and transgressor of the law. With וְהוּא there is attached to וְאֶת־פֹּשְׁעִים נִמְנָה (He was numbered with the transgressors), if not in a subordinate connection (like והוא in ver. 5; compare ch. x. 7), the following antithesis: He submitted cheerfully to the death of a sinner, and yet He was no sinner, but "bare the sin of many (cf. Heb. ix. 28), and made intercession for the transgressors." Many adopt the rendering, "and He takes away the sin of many, and intervenes on behalf of the transgressors." But in this connection the preterite נָשָׂא can only relate to some-

thing antecedent to the foregoing future, so that יַפְגִּיעַ denotes a
connected past; and thus have the LXX. and Vulg. correctly
rendered it. Just as הִפְגִּיעַ בְּ in ver. 6*b* signifies to cause to fall
upon a person, so in Jer. xv. 11 it signifies to make one approach another (in supplication). Here, however, as in ch. lix.
16, the *hiphil* is not a causative, but has the intensive force of
the *kal*, viz. to press forward with entreaty, hence to intercede
(with a *Lâmed* of the person on whose behalf it occurs). According to the *cons. temporum*, the reference is not to the intercession (ἔντευξις) of the glorified One, but to that of the suffering
One, on behalf of His foes. Every word stands here as if
written beneath the cross on Golgotha. And this is the case
with the clause before us, which was fulfilled (though not exclusively) in the prayer of the crucified Saviour: "Father, forgive
them; for they know not what they do" (Luke xxiii. 34).

"The prophetic view," says Oehler, who agrees with us in
the general opinion that the idea of the Servant of Jehovah has
three distinct stages, "ascends in these discourses step by step,
as it were, from the one broad space covered by the foundation-
walls of a cathedral up to the very summit with its giddy height,
on which the cross is planted; and the nearer it reaches the
summit, the more conspicuous do the outlines of the cross
itself become, until at last, when the summit is reached, it rests
in peace, having attained what it desired when it set its foot
upon the first steps of the temple tower." There is something
very striking in this figure. Here, in the very centre of this
book of consolation, we find the idea of the Servant of Jehovah
at the very summit of its ascent. It has reached the goal. The
Messianic idea, which was hidden in the general idea of the
nation regarded as "the servant of Jehovah," has gradually
risen up in the most magnificent metamorphosis from the
depths in which it was thus concealed. And this fusion has
generated what was hitherto altogether strange to the figure of
the Messiah, viz. the *unio mystica capitis et corporis*. Hitherto
Israel has appeared simply as the nation governed by the
Messiah, the army which He conducted into battle, the commonwealth ordered by Him. But now, in the person of the
Servant of Jehovah, we see Israel itself in personal self-manifestation: the idea of Israel is fully realized, and the true
nature of Israel shines forth in all its brilliancy. Israel is

the body, and He the head, towering above it.   Another
element, with which we found the Messianic idea enriched
even before ch. liii., was the *munus triplex*.   As early as
ch. vii.–xii. the figure of the Messiah stood forth as the
figure of a King; but the Prophet like unto Moses, promised
in Deut. xviii. 15, was still wanting.   But, according to ch.
xlii., xlix., l., the servant of Jehovah is first a prophet, and as
the proclaimer of a new law, and the mediator of a new covenant, really a second Moses; at the close of the work appointed
Him, however, He receives the homage of kings, whilst, as
ch. liii. clearly shows, that self-sacrifice lies between, on the
ground of which He rules above as a Priest after the order of
Melchizedek,—in other words, a Priest and also a King.   From
this point onward there are added to the Messianic idea the
further elements of the *status duplex* and the *satisfactio vicaria.*
David was indeed the type of the twofold state of his antitype,
inasmuch as it was through suffering that he reached the
throne; but where have we found, in all the direct Messianic
prophecies anterior to this, the suffering path of the *Ecce Homo*
even to the grave?   But the Servant of Jehovah goes through
shame to glory, and through death to life.   He conquers when
He falls; He rules after being enslaved; He lives after He
has died; He completes His work after He Himself has been
apparently cut off.   His glory streams upon the dark ground of
the deepest humiliation, to set forth which the dark colours were
supplied by the pictures of suffering contained in the Psalms
and in the book of Job.   And these sufferings of His are
not merely the sufferings of a confessor or a martyr, like those
of the *ecclesia pressa,* but a vicarious atoning suffering, a sacrifice for sin.   To this the chapter before us returns again and
again, being never tired of repeating it.   " *Spiritus Sanctus,*"
says Brentius, " *non delectatur inani βαττολογίᾳ, et tamen quum
in hoc cap. videatur βαττολόγος καὶ ταυτολόγος esse, dubium non
est, quin tractet rem cognitu maxime necessariam.*"   The banner
of the cross is here set up.   The curtain of the most holy is
lifted higher and higher.   The blood of the typical sacrifice,
which has been hitherto dumb, begins to speak.   Faith, which
penetrates to the true meaning of the prophecy, hopes on not
only for the Lion of the tribe of Judah, but also for the Lamb
of God, which beareth the sin of the world.   And in pro-

phecy itself we see the after-effect of this gigantic advance. Zechariah no longer prophesies of the Messiah merely as a king (ch. vi. 13); He not only rules upon His throne, but is also a priest upon His throne: sovereignty and priesthood go hand in hand, being peacefully united in Him. And in Zech. xii. 13 the same prophet predicts in Him the good Divine Shepherd, whom His people pierce, though not without thereby fulfilling the counsel of God, and whom they afterwards long for with bitter lamentation and weeping. The penitential and believing confession which would then be made by Israel is prophetically depicted by Isaiah's pen—"mourning in bitter sorrow the lateness of its love."

SIXTH PROPHECY.—CHAP. LIV.

THE GLORY OF JERUSALEM, THE CHURCH OF THE SERVANTS OF JEHOVAH.

After the "Servant of God" has expiated the sin of His people by the sacrifice of Himself, and Israel has acknowledged its fault in connection with the rejected One, and entered into the possession and enjoyment of the salvation procured by Him, the glory of the church, which has thus become a partaker of salvation through repentance and faith, is quite ready to burst forth. Hence the prophet can now exclaim, ver. 1: "*Exult, O barren one, thou that didst not bear; break forth into exulting, and cry aloud, thou that didst not travail with child: for there are more children of the solitary one than children of the married wife, saith Jehovah.*" The words are addressed to Jerusalem, which was a counterpart of Sarah in her barrenness at first, and her fruitfulness afterwards (ch. li. 1–3). She is not עֲקָרָה לֹא חֵלֵר (Job xxiv. 21), but עֲקָרָה לֹא יָלָדָה (Judg. xiii. 2); not indeed that she had never had any children, but during her captivity and exile she had been robbed of her children, and as a holy city had given birth to no more (ch. xlix. 21). She was *shōmēmâh*, rendered *solitary* (2 Sam. xiii. 20; the allusion is to her depopulation as a city), whereas formerly she was בְּעוּלָה, *i.e.* enjoyed the fellowship of Jehovah her husband (*baʿal*). But this condition would not last (for Jehovah had not given her a divorce): she was therefore to exult and shout, since the

number of children which she would now have, as one desolate
and solitary, would be greater than the number of those which
she had as a married wife.

With this prospect before her, even her dwelling-place
would need enlarging. Ver. 2. "*Enlarge the space of thy tent,
and let them stretch out the curtains of thy habitations; forbid
not! lengthen thy cords, and fasten thy plugs.*" She is to widen
out the space inside her tent, and they (יַטּוּ has no definite subject, which is often the case where some subordinate servant is
to be thought of) are to spread out far and wide the coverings
of the framework of her dwelling, which is called *mishk^enōth*
(in the plural) on account of its roominess and magnificence:
she is not to forbid it, thinking in her weakness of faith, "It is
good enough as it is; it would be too large." The cords which
hold up the walls, she is to lengthen; and the plugs, to which
the cords are fastened, she is to ram fast into the earth: the
former because the tent (*i.e.* the holy city, Jer. xxxi. 38–40,
and the dwelling-place of the church generally, ch. xxvi. 15)
has to receive a large number of inhabitants; the latter because it will not be broken up so soon again (ch. xxxiii. 20).

The reason why the tent is to be so large and strong is
given in ver. 3: "*For thou wilt break forth on the right and on
the left; and thy seed will take possession of nations, and they
will people desolate cities.*" "On the right and on the left" is
equivalent to "on the south and north" (Ps. lxxxix. 13, the
speaker being supposed to have his face turned towards the
east: compare the Sanscrit *apân*, situated at the back, *i.e.*
towards the west). We must supply both west and east, since
the promises contained in such passages as Gen. xv. 18–21
remained unfulfilled even in the age of David and Solomon.
Jerusalem will now spread out, and break through all her
former bounds (*pârats* is used in the same sense in Gen.
xxviii. 14); and her seed (*i.e.* the seed acquired by the Servant
of Jehovah, the dead yet eternally living One, the σπέρμα,
whose σπέρμα He Himself is) will take possession of nations
(*yârash, yârēsh, capessere, occupare;* more especially κληρονο-
μεῖν, syn. *nâchal*); and *they* (*i.e.* the children born to her) will
people desolate cities (*hōshībh*, the causative of *yâshabh*, to be
inhabited, ch. xiii. 20). Thus will the promise be fulfilled, that
"the meek shall inherit the earth,"—a promise not confined to

the Preacher on the mount, but found also in Ps. xxxvii. 9–11,
and uttered by our own prophet in ch. lx. 21, lxv. 9.

The encouraging promise is continued in ver. 4 : " *Fear
not, for thou wilt not be put to shame; and bid defiance to
reproach, for thou wilt not blush : no, thou wilt forget the shame
of thy youth, and wilt no more remember the reproach of thy
widowhood.*" Now that redemption was before the door, Israel
was not to fear any more, or to be overcome (as the *niphal
nikhlam* implies) by a feeling of the shame consequent upon
her state of punishment, or so to behave herself as to leave no
room for hope. For a state of things was about to commence,
in which she would have no need to be ashamed (on *bōsh* and
châphēr or *hechpīr*, see vol. i. p. 108, note), but which, on the
contrary (כִּי, *imo*, as in ch. x. 7, lv. 9), would be so glorious
that she would forget the shame of her youth, *i.e.* of the Egyptian bondage, in which the national community of Israel was
still but like a virgin (*'almâh*), who entered into a betrothal
when redeemed by Jehovah, and became His youthful wife
through a covenant of love (*ehe* = *b⁰rīth*) when the law was
given at Sinai (Jer. ii. 2 ; Ezek. xvi. 60) ; so glorious indeed,
that she would never again remember the shame of her widowhood, *i.e.* of the Babylonian captivity, in which she, the wife
whom Jehovah had taken to Himself, was like a widow whose
husband had died.

It was no real widowhood, however, but only an apparent
one (Jer. li. 5), for the husband of Jerusalem was living still.
Ver. 5. " *For thy husband is thy Creator ; Jehovah of hosts is
His name ; and thy Redeemer the Holy One of Israel ; God of
the whole earth is He called.*" The plurals בֹּעֲלַיִךְ and עֹשַׂיִךְ (see
at ch. xxii. 11) are to be explained from the plural '*Elōhīm*,
which is connected with plural attributes in Josh. xxiv. 19,
1 Sam. xvii. 26, Ps. lviii. 12 (compare מְרִימָיו in ch. x. 15),
and with plural predicates in Gen. xx. 13, xxxv. 7, and 2 Sam.
vii. 23. By such expressions as these, which represent all
the plurality of the divine nature as inherent in the One, the
religion of revelation, both Israelitish and Christian, exhibits
itself as embodying all that is true in polytheism. He who
has entered into the relation of husband to Jerusalem (בֹּעֲלַיִךְ,
not בְּעָלַיִךְ, ch. i. 3) is the very same through whom she first
came into existence, the God whose bidding the heavenly

hosts obey; and the Redeemer of Jerusalem, the Holy One of Israel, is called the God of the whole earth, and therefore has both the power and the means to help her, as prompted by the relation of love which exists between them.

And this relation He now renews. Ver. 6. "*For Jehovah calleth thee as a wife forsaken and burdened with sorrow, and as a wife of youth, when once she is despised, saith thy God.*" The verb קָרָא, which is the one commonly used in these prophecies to denote the call of grace, on the ground of the election of grace, is used here to signify the call into that relation, which did indeed exist before, but had apparently been dissolved. קְרָאָךְ is used here out of pause (cf. ch. lx. 9); it stands, however, quite irregularly for the form in *ēkh*, which is the one commonly employed (Judg. iv. 20; Ezek. xxvii. 26). "And as a wife :" וְאֵשֶׁת is equivalent to וּכְאֵשֶׁת. The hypothetical כִּי תִמָּאֵס belongs to the figure. Jehovah calls His church back to Himself, as a husband takes back the wife he loved in his youth, even though he may once have been angry with her. It is with intention that the word נִמְאָסָה is not used. The future (imperfect) indicates what partially happens, but does not become an accomplished or completed fact: He is displeased with her, but He has not cherished aversion or hatred towards her.

Thus does Jehovah's displeasure towards Jerusalem pass quickly away; and all the more intense is the manifestation of love which follows His merely momentary anger. Vers. 7, 8. "*For a small moment have I forsaken thee, and with great mercy will I gather thee. In an effusion of anger I hid my face from thee for a moment, and with everlasting grace I have compassion upon thee, saith Jehovah thy Redeemer.*" "For a small moment" carries us to the time of the captivity, which was a small moment in comparison with the duration of the tender and merciful love, with which Jehovah once more received the church into His fellowship in the person of its members. רֶגַע in ver. 8a is not an adverb, meaning momentarily, as in ch. xlvii. 9, but an accusative of duration, signifying a single moment long. *Ketseph* signifies wrath regarded as an outburst (*fragor*), like the violence of a storm or a clap of thunder; *shetseph*, which rhymes with it, is explained by A. Schultens, after the Arabic, as signifying *durum et asperum esse* : and hence the rendering

adopted by Hitzig, " in hard harshness." But this yields no
antithesis to "everlasting kindness," which requires that *shetseph*
should be rendered in some way that expresses the idea of something transitory or of short duration. The earlier translators
felt this, when, like the LXX. for example, they adopted the
rendering ἐν θυμῷ μικρῷ, and others of a similar kind ; and
Ibn Labrât, in his writing against Menahem b. Zerûk, who
gives *chŏrî*, burning heat, as a gloss to *shetseph*, explains it by
מְעַט (as Kimchi and others did afterwards). But, as Jakob Tam
correctly observes, " this makes the sense purely tautological."
In all probability, *shâtsaph* is a form allied to *shâtaph*, as
nâshabh (ch. xl. 7) is to *nâshaph* (ch. xl. 24), and *qâmat* (Job
xvi. 8) to *qâmats*, which stand in the same relation to one
another, so far as the sense is concerned, as bubbling over to
flowing over : so that the proper rendering would not be " in
the overflowing of glowing heat," as Umbreit thinks, which
would require בְּשֶׁצֶף קֶצֶף (Prov. xxvii. 4), but in the gushing up
of displeasure, the overflowing of indignation (Meier). The
ketseph is only a *shetseph*, a vanishing moment (Jer. *in momento
indignationis*), when compared with the true feeling of Jehovah
towards Jerusalem, which is *chesed ʿôlâm*, everlasting kindness.

The ground of this " everlasting kindness" is given in
ver. 9 : " *For it is now as at the waters of Noah, when I swore
that the waters of Noah should not overflow the earth any more ;
so have I sworn not to be wroth with thee, and not to threaten
thee.*" The commencement of this verse has been a fluctuating
one from the earliest times. The Sept. reading is מִמֵּי ; that of
the Targ., S., Jerome, Syriac, and Saad., כִּימֵי ; and even the
Codd. read sometimes כִּי־מֵי, sometimes כִּימֵי (compare Matt.
xxiv. 37, ὥσπερ αἱ ἡμέραι τοῦ Νῶε, οὕτως, κ.τ.λ.,—a passage
which appears to derive its shape from the one before us, with
the reading כימי, and which is expounded in Luke xvii. 26).
If we read כימי, the word זאת must refer to the present, as the
turning-point between wrath and mercy ; but if we read כי־מי,
זאת denotes the pouring out of wrath in connection with the
captivity. Both readings are admissible ; and as even the
Septuagint, with its ἀπὸ τοῦ ὕδατος (from the water), gives an
indirect support to the reading כִּימֵי as one word, this may
probably merit the preference, as the one best sustained. אֲשֶׁר
is *ubi*, *quum*, as in Num. xx. 13, Ps. xcv. 9, etc., although it

might also be taken as the correlate of the *kēn* which follows, as in Jer. xxxiii. 22 (cf. xlviii. 8) ; and in accordance with the accents, we prefer the former.   The present turning-point resembles, in Jehovah's esteem, the days of Noah,—those days in which He swore that a flood should not any more come upon the earth (*min* as in ch. v. 6 and many other passages) : for so does He now confirm with an oath His fixed purpose that no such judgment of wrath as that which has just been endured shall ever fall upon Jerusalem again (גָּעַר denotes threatening with a judicial word, which passes at once into effect, as in ch. li. 20). Hendewerk has the following quibbling remark here : " What the comparison with the flood is worth, we may gather from the later history, which shows how soon the new Jerusalem and the renovated state succumbed to the judicial wrath of God again." To this we reply : (1.) That the prophecy refers to the converted Israel of the last days, whose Jerusalem will never be destroyed again.   These last days appear to the prophet, according to the general character of all prophecy, as though linked on to the close of the captivity.   For throughout all prophecy, along with the far-sightedness imparted by the Spirit, there was also a short-sightedness which the Spirit did not remove; that is to say, the directly divine element of *insight* into the future was associated with a human element of *hope*, which was nevertheless also indirectly divine, inasmuch as it subserved the divine plan of salvation ; and this hope brought, as it were, the far distant future into the closest proximity with the troubled present.   If, then, we keep this in mind, we shall see that it was quite in order for the prophet to behold the final future on the very edge of the present, and not to see the long and undulating way between.   (2.) The Israel which has been plunged by the Romans into the present exile of a thousand years is that part of the nation (Rom. xi. 25), which has thrust away the eternal mercy and the unchangeable covenant of peace ; but this rejection has simply postponed, and not pre-vented, the full realization of the salvation promised to Israel as a people.   The *covenant* still exists, primarily indeed as an offer on the part of Jehovah, so that it rests with Israel whether it shall continue one-sided or not ; but all that is wanted on the part of Israel is faith, to enable it to exchange the shifting soil of its present exile for the rocky foundation of that covenant

of peace which has encircled the ages since the captivity (see
Hag. ii. 9), as the covenant with Noah encircled those after
the flood with the covenant sign of the rainbow in the cloud.

Ver. 10. *"For the mountains may depart, and the hills may
shake; my grace will not depart from thee, and my covenant of
peace will not shake, saith Jehovah who hath compassion on
thee."* Jehovah's grace and covenant of peace (cf. Num.
xxv. 12) stand as firm as the mountains of God (Ps. xxxvi. 7),
without departing from Jerusalem (מֵאִתֵּךְ instead of the usual
מֵאִתָּךְ) and without shaking; and they will be fulfilled. This
fulfilment will not take place either by force or by enchant-
ment; but the church which is to be glorified must pass through
sufferings, until it has attained the form which answers to the
glory promised to it on oath. And this will also take place; for
the old Jerusalem will come forth as a new one out of the
furnace of affliction. Vers. 11, 12. *" O thou afflicted, tossed
with tempest, not comforted, behold, I lay thy stones in stibium,
and lay thy foundations with sapphires; and make thy minarets
of ruby, and thy gates into carbuncles, and all thy boundary into
jewels."* At the present time the church, of which Jerusalem
is the metropolis, is sunk in misery, driven with tempest like
chaff of the threshing-floor (Hos. xiii. 3), without comfort;
because till now it has waited in vain for any act of consolation
on the part of God, and has been scorned rather than comforted by man (סֹעֲרָה is a *part. kal,* not *pual;* and נֻחָמָה 3d pers.
præt. like נֶעֱזָבָה, ch. lxii. 12, and רֻחָמָה, Hos. i. 6, ii. 3). But
this will be altered; Jerusalem will rise again from the dust,
like a glorious building of God. Jerome makes the following
apt remark on ver. 11*b*: *"in stibio, i.e.* in the likeness of an
elegant woman, who paints her eyes with *stibium;* referring
to the beauty of the city." *Pūkh* is eye-black (*kohl,* cf. *kâchal,*
Ezek. xxiii. 40), *i.e.* a sooty compound, the chief component of
which was powdered antimony, or else manganese or lead, and
with which oriental women coloured their eyebrows, and more
particularly the eyelids both above and below the eyes, that the
beauty of the latter might be all the more conspicuous (2 Kings
ix. 30). The classic φῦκος, *fucus,* has a meaning foreign to the
Hebrew word, viz. that of rouge for the cheeks. If, then,
stibium (antimony), or any blackening collyrium generally,
served the purpose of mortar in the rebuilding of Jerusalem,

the stones of its walls (not its foundation-stones, אֲדָנַיִךְ, which is
the reading adopted by Ewald, but, on the contrary, the visible
stones of its towering walls) would look like the eyes of a
woman shining forth from the black framework of their
painted lids, *i.e.* they would stand out in splendour from their
dark ground.   The *Beth* in *bassappīrīm* indicates the means
employed.   Sapphires serve as foundation-stones, for the
foundation of Jerusalem stands as immoveably firm as the
covenant of God.   The sapphire blue is the colour of the
heaven, of revelation, and of the covenant.   The *sh°māshōth*,
however, *i.e.* the minarets which stand out like rays of the sun,
and also the gates, have a red appearance.   Red is the colour
of blood, and hence of life and of imperishableness; also the
colour of fire and of lightning, and hence of wrath and victory.
Jehovah makes the minarets of " ruby."   The Sept. and
Jerome adopt the rendering *iaspidem* (a jasper); at any rate,
כַּדְכֹּד (which is the proper way of writing the word: Ewald,
§ 48, *c*[1]) is a red sparkling jewel (from *kidkēd*; cf. *kīdōd, scin-
tilla*).   The arches of the gates He forms of אַבְנֵי אֶקְדָּח, stones
of fiery splendour (from *qâdach*, to burn: hence *qaddachath*,
πυρετός), that is to say, of carbuncle stones (from *carbunculus*,
a small red-hot coal), like ruby, garnet, etc.   Jerome has
adopted the false rendering *lapides sculptos*, after Symm. λίθοι
γλυφῆς (from קדח = קדר, *findere?*).   The accusative of the
predicate כדכד is interchanged with לאבני אקדח, and then with
לְאַבְנֵי־חֵפֶץ, to denote the *materia ex qua*.   The whole territory
(precinct) of Jerusalem is turned by Jehovah into precious
stones, that is to say, it appears to be paved with such stones,
just as in Tobit xiii. 17 the streets are said to be " paved with
beryl, and carbuncle, and stones of Ophir," *i.e.* to be covered
with a mosaic formed of precious stones.   It is upon the
passage before us that Tobit xiii. 16, 17, and Rev. xxi. 18–21,
are founded.   The motley colours of the precious stones, with
which the new Jerusalem is adorned, are something more than

---

[1] The first ב is *dagessatum*, the second *raphatum:* see Norzi. The word
forms one of the eighteen which have a *dagesh* after a word ending with
a vowel sound (דנשין בתר יה"וא בלא מבטל): see *Masora Magna* on Dan.
v. 11, and Heidenheim's משפטי הטעמים, 41*a*. The object is to secure
greater euphony, as in כְּבִרְכְּמִישׁ (הלא), ch. x. 9, which is one of the
eighteen words.

a mere childish fancy. Whence, then, do the precious stones derive their charm? The ultimate ground of this charm is the fact, that in universal nature everything presses to the light, and that in the mineral world the jewels represent the highest stage of this ascending process. It is the self-unfolding process of the divine glory itself, which is reflected typologically in the several gradations of the manifold play of colours and the transparency of the precious stones. For this reason, the high priest wore a breastplate with twelve precious stones, upon which were the names of the twelve tribes of Israel; and for this same reason, the author of the Apocalypse carries out into detail in ch. xxi. the picture of the new Jerusalem, which is here sketched by the prophet of the Old Testament (without distinguishing time from eternity), adding crystals and pearls to the precious stones which he there mentions one by one. How can all this be explained, except on the ground that even the mineral world reflects the glory of those eternal lights from which God is called the "Father of lights," or except on the assumption that the saints in light will one day be able to translate these stony types into the words of God, out of which they have their being?

The outward glory of the city is only the manifestation, which strikes the senses, of the spiritual glory of the church dwelling therein. Ver. 13. "*And all thy children will be the learned of Jehovah; and great the peace of thy children.*" We translate both halves of the verse as substantive clauses, although they might be accusatives of both the object and predicate, dependent upon שַׂמְתִּי. לִמּוּדֵי ה׳ are disciples of Jehovah, but, as in ch. l. 4, with the subordinate idea of both docility and learning. The children of Jerusalem will need no instruction from man, but carry within them the teaching of heaven, as those who are "taught of God" (διδακτοὶ Θεοῦ, John vi. 45; θεοδίδακτοι, 1 Thess. iv. 9). Essentially the same promise is given in Joel iii. 1, 2, and Jer. xxxi. 34; and represented in 1 John ii. 20 ("Ye have the anointing of the Holy One, and know all things") as already fulfilled. In the place of the former inward and outward distress, there has now entered *shâlôm*, perfect inward and outward peace, complete salvation, and blessedness as its result. רַב is an adjective, for this form cannot be shown to have existed as a syncopated third pers. *præt.*, like שָׁח, חַי (= חָיַי). The verse closes palin-dromically.

In perfect keeping with this grace through righteousness, Jerusalem will then stand firm and impregnable. Vers. 14, 15. "*Through righteousness wilt thou be fortified: be far from anxiety, for thou hast nothing to fear; and from terror, for it will not come near thee. Behold, men crowd together in crowds; my will is not there. Who crowd together against thee?—he shall fall by thee.*" Both the thought and action of Jerusalem will be righteousness then, and it will thereby acquire strength; תִּכּוֹנָנִי is a pausal future *hithpalel*, with the ת of the reflective opening syllable assimilated (Ges. § 53, 2, *b*). With this reciprocal influence of its moral character and imparted glory, it can, and is to keep far away from all thought of oppression and terror; for, through divine grace and a corresponding divine nature, it has nothing to fear. הֵן (ver. 15*a*), when pointing to any transaction as possible (as, for example, in Job xii. 14, xxiii. 8), acquires almost the significance of a conditional particle (Ewald, § 103, *g*). The equally hypothetical parallel clause is clothed in the form of an interrogative. For the verb *gūr*, the meaning "to gather together" (related to אָגַר), more especially to join together with hostile intention (cf. συνάγεσθαι, Rev. xix. 19, xx. 8), is sustained by Ps. lvi. 7, lix. 4; and with גָּרָה, *lacessere*, it has nothing to do (Hitzig and Ewald). אִתָּךְ has the force of *contra te*, as in the case of verbs of combat. The first apodosis is this: "but it takes place entirely away from me," *i.e.* without and against my will; מֵאוֹתִי = מֵאִתִּי (as in ch. lix. 21), and אִתָּם = אוֹתָם, are no sure signs of a later usage; for this alternation of the two forms of אֵת is met with as early as Josh. xiv. 12. The second apodosis is, "he will fall upon (or against) thee," or, as we should say, "founder," or "be wrecked." It is far more likely that this is the meaning of the words, than that they mean "he will fall to thy lot" (נָפַל עַל, like נָפַל לְ elsewhere, to fall to a person); for the context here is a totally different one from ch. xlv. 14, and we look for nothing more than a declaration of the utter failure and ruin of the undertaking.

Jerusalem will be thus invincible, because Jehovah, the Almighty One, is its protector. Vers. 16, 17. "*Behold, I have created the smith who bloweth the coal-fire, and brings to the light a weapon according to his trade; and I have created the destroyer*

*to destroy. Every weapon formed against thee has no success,
and every tongue that cometh before the judgment with thee thou
wilt condemn. This the inheritance of the servants of Jehovah; and
their righteousness from me, saith Jehovah.*" If Jehovah has
created the armourer, who forges a weapon לְמַעֲשֵׂהוּ (*i.e.* according to his trade, or according to the thing he has to finish,
whether an arrow, or a sword, or a spear ; not "for his own
use," as Kimchi supposes), to be used in the hostile army
against Jerusalem, He has also created a destroyer (לְחַבֵּל) to
destroy. The very same creative might, to which the origin of
the weapon is to be traced as its primary cause, has opposed
to it beforehand a defender of Jerusalem. And as every
hostile weapon fails, Jerusalem, in the consciousness of its
divine right, will convict every accusing tongue as guilty and
deserving of utter condemnation (הִרְשִׁיעַ as in ch. l. 9, cf. 1
Sam. xiv. 47, where it denotes the punishment of the guilty).
The epiphonem in ver. 17*b*, with the retrospective זאת and the
words "saith the Lord," which confirm the certainty of the
fulfilment, forms an unmistakeable close to the prophecy.
This is the position in which Jehovah has placed His servants
as heirs of the future salvation ; and this the righteousness
which they have received as His gift, and which makes them
strong within and victorious without. The individual idea of
the church, which we find elsewhere personified as "the servant
of Jehovah," equivalent to "the people in whose heart is my
law" (ch. li. 7), or "my people that have sought me" (ch. lxv.
10), is here expanded into "the servants of Jehovah" (as in
ch. lxv. 8, 9 ; compare ch. lix. 21 with ch. li. 16). But totally
different colours are employed in ch. lii. 13–ch. liii. to depict
the exaltation of the one "Servant of Jehovah," from those
used here to paint the glory of the church of the "servants of
Jehovah,"—a proof that the ideas do not cover one another.
That which is the reward of suffering in the case of the former,
is the experience of divine mercy in that of the latter: it becomes
a partaker of the salvation purchased by the other. The one
"Servant of Jehovah" is the heart of the church, in which the
crisis which bursts forth into life is passing ; the righteousness
of the "servants of Jehovah" is the fruit of the sufferings
of this one "Servant of Jehovah," who is Himself צדיק and
מצדיק. He is the Mediator of all the salvation of the

church. He is not only its "head," but its "fulness" (πλήρωμα) also.

SEVENTH PROPHECY.—Chap. LV.

COME AND TAKE THE SURE SALVATION OF JEHOVAH.

All things are ready; the guests are invited; and nothing is required of them except to come. Vers. 1, 2. *"Alas, all ye thirsty ones, come ye to the water; and ye that have no silver, come ye, buy, and eat! Yea, come, buy wine and milk without money and without payment! Wherefore do ye weigh silver for that which is not bread, and the result of your labour for that which satisfieth not? O hearken ye to me, and eat the good, and let your soul delight itself in fat."* Hitzig and Knobel understand by water, wine, and milk, the rich material blessings which awaited the exiles on their return to their fatherland, whereas they were now paying tribute and performing service in Babylon without receiving anything in return. But the prophet was acquainted with something higher than either natural water (ch. xliv. 3, cf. xli. 17) or natural wine (ch. xxv. 6). He knew of an eating and drinking which reached beyond the mere material enjoyment (ch. lxv. 13); and the expression טוּב ה׳, whilst it includes material blessings (Jer. xxxi. 12), is not exhausted by them (ch. lxiii. 7, cf. Ps. xxvii. 13), just as הִתְעַנֵּג in ch. lviii. 14 (cf. Ps. xxxvii. 4, 11) does not denote a feeling of worldly, but of spiritual joy. Water, wine, and milk, as the fact that water is placed first clearly shows, are not the produce of the Holy Land, but figurative representations of spiritual revival, recreation, and nourishment (cf. 1 Pet. ii. 2, "the sincere milk of the word"). The whole appeal is framed accordingly. When Jehovah summons the thirsty ones of His people to come to the water, the summons must have reference to something more than the water to which a shepherd leads his flock. And as buying without money or any other medium of exchange is an idea which neutralizes itself in the sphere of natural objects, wine and milk are here blessings and gifts of divine grace, which are obtained by grace (χάριτι, *gratis*), their reception being dependent upon nothing but a sense of need, and a readiness to accept the blessings offered. Again,

the use of the verb שָׁבְרוּ, which is confined in other passages to
the purchase of cereals, is a sufficient proof that the reference is
not to natural objects, but to such objects as could properly be
compared to cereals. The bread and other provisions, which Israel
obtained in its present state of punishment, are called "not
bread," and "not serving to satisfy," because that which truly
satisfies the soul comes from above, and being of no earthly
nature, is to be obtained by those who are the most destitute of
earthly supplies. Can any Christian reader fail to recal, when
reading the invitation in ver. 1, the words of the parable in
Matt. xxii. 4, "All things are now ready?" And does not
ver. 2 equally suggest the words of Paul in Rom. xi. 6, "If
by grace, then is it no more of works?" Even the exclamation *hoi* (alas! see ch. xviii. 1), with which the passage commences, expresses deep sorrow on account of the unsatisfied
thirst, and the toilsome labour which affords nothing but
seeming satisfaction. The way to true satisfaction is indicated
in the words, "Hearken unto me:" it is the way of the obedience of faith. In this way alone can the satisfaction of the
soul be obtained.

And in this way it is possible to obtain not only the satisfaction of absolute need, but a superabundant enjoyment, and
an overflowing fulfilment of the promise. Vers. 3–5. "*Incline
your ear, and come to me : hear, and let your soul revive ; and I
will make an everlasting covenant with you, the true mercies of
David. Behold, I have set him as a witness for nations, a prince
and commander of nations. Behold, thou wilt call a mass of
people that thou knowest not ; and a mass of people that knoweth
thee not will hasten to thee, for the sake of Jehovah thy God, and
for the Holy One of Israel, that He hath made thee glorious.*"
The expression "make a covenant" (*kârath b'rîth*) is not
always applied to a superior in relation to an inferior (compare,
on the contrary, Ezra x. 3) ; but here the double-sided idea
implied in *pactio* is confined to one-side alone, in the sense of a
spontaneous *sponsio* having 'all the force of a covenant (ch.
lxi. 8; compare 2 Chron. vii. 18, where *kârath* by itself signifies
"to promise with the force of a covenant"), and also of the
offer of a covenant or anticipated conclusion of a covenant, as
in Ezek. xxxiv. 25, and in the case before us, where "the true
mercies of David" are attached to the idea of offering or grant-

ing involved in the expression, "I will make an everlasting
covenant with you," as a more precise definition of the object.
All that is required on the part of Israel is hearing, and coming,
and taking : let it do this, and it will be pervaded by new
life; and Jehovah will meet it with an everlasting covenant,
viz. the unchangeable mercies of David. Our interpretation
of this must be dependent chiefly upon whether ver. 4 is regarded as looking back to the history of David, or looking forward to something future. In the latter case we are either to
understand by "David" the second David (according to Hos.
iii. 5, Jer. xxx. 9, Ezek. xxxiv. 24), so that the allusion is to
the mercies granted in the Messiah, and according to ch. ix. 7,
enduring "from henceforth even for ever;" or else David is
the son of Jesse, and "the mercies of David" are the mercies
bestowed upon him, which are called "the true mercies" as
mercies promised and running into the future (Ps. lxxxix. 50;
2 Chron. vi. 42), in which case ver. 4 explains what David
will become in the person of his antitype the second David.
The directly Messianic application of the name "David" is to
be objected to, on the ground that the Messiah is never so
called without further remark; whilst the following objections
may be adduced to the indirectly Messianic interpretation of
ver. 4 (David in the Messiah) : (1.) The change of the tense in
vers. 4, 5, which requires that we should assume that ver. 4
points backwards into the past, and ver. 5 forwards into the
future : [1] (2.) That the choice of the expression in vers. 4, 5
is designed to represent what Israel has to look for in the future
as going beyond what was historically realized in David; for in
ver. 5 the mass of the heathen world, which has hitherto stood

---

[1] F. Philippi observes that הֵן, which refers to the future in ver. 5 at
any rate, must be taken as referring to the same sphere of time as that
which immediately precedes. But *hēn* in Isaiah points sometimes backwards (ch. l. 1, lxiv. 4), sometimes forwards; and where two follow
one another, of which the one points backwards and the other forwards,
the former is followed by the perfect, the latter by the future (ch. l. 1, 2).
But if they both point to the future, the future tense is used in both
instances (ch. l. 9). A better argument in favour of the prophetic interpretation of ver. 4 might be drawn from the fact that הֵן נְתַתִּי may mean
"I give (set, lay, or make) even now" (*e.g.* Jer. i. 9). But what we have
said above is sufficient proof that this is not the meaning here (if this were
the meaning, we should rather expect הֵן נְתַתִּיו).

out of all relation to Israel, answers to the לְאֻמִּים: (3.) That
the juxtaposition of the Messiah and Israel would be altogether
without parallel in these prophecies (ch. xl.–lxvi.), and contrary
to their peculiar character; for the earlier stereotype idea of
the Messiah is here resolved into the idea of the "servant of
Jehovah," from which it returns again to its primary use, *i.e.*
from the national basis to the individual, by means of the
ascending variations through which this expression passes, and
thus reaches a more comprehensive, spiritual, and glorified
form.   The personal "servant of Jehovah" is undoubtedly
no other than the "Son of David" of the earlier prophecy;
but the premises, from which we arrive at this conclusion in
connection with our prophet, are not that the "servant of
Jehovah" is of the seed of David and the final personal realization of the promise of a future king, but that he is of the
nation of Israel, and the final personal realization of the idea
of Israel, both in its inward nature, and in its calling in relation
to the whole world of nations.   Consequently vers. 4 and 5 stand
to one another in the relation of type and antitype, and the
"mercies of David" are called "the true mercies" (probably
with an allusion to 2 Sam. vii. 16; cf. Ps. lxxxix. 29, 30), as
being inviolable,—mercies which had both been realized in
the case of David himself, and would be realized still further,
inasmuch as they must endure for an everlasting future, and
therefore be further and further fulfilled, until they have
reached that lofty height, on the summit of which they will
remain unchangeable for ever.   It is of David the son of
Jesse that Jehovah says in ver. 4, "I have given him for a
witness to peoples, a leader and commander to the peoples."
So far as the sense is concerned, נָגִיד is as much a construct as
מְצַוֶּה.   In the application to David of the term עֵד, which never
means anything but *testis*, witness, in these prophecies, we may
clearly see the bent of the prophet's mind towards what is
spiritual.   David had subdued nations by the force of arms,
but his true and loftiest greatness consisted in the fact that he
was a witness of the nations,—a witness by the victorious power
of his word, the conquering might of his Psalms, the attractive
force of his typical life.   What he expresses so frequently in
the Psalms as a resolution and a vow, viz. that he will proclaim
the name of Jehovah among the nations (Ps. xviii. 50, lvii. 10),

he has really fulfilled : he has not only overcome them by bloody warfare, but by the might of his testimony, more especially as " the sweet psalmist of Israel " (2 Sam. xxiii. 1). What David himself was able to say in Ps. xviii. 43, " People that I did not know served me," will be fulfilled to a still wider extent in the experience of Israel. Having been presented with the promised " inviolable mercies of David," it will effect a spiritual conquest over the heathen world, even over that portion which has hitherto stood in no reciprocal relation to it, and gain possession of it for itself for the sake of Jehovah, whom it has for its God, and to the Holy One of Israel (לְ of the object, in relation to which, or at the instigation of which, anything is done), because He hath glorified it (His people : פֵּאֲרָךְ is not a pausal form for פֵּאֲרֵךְ, cf. ch. liv. 6, but for פֵּאֲרֵךְ, פֵּאֲרָךְ, hence = פֵּאֲרֵךְ, cf. עָנָךְ, ch. xxx. 19) ; so that joining themselves to Israel is the same as joining themselves to God and to the church of the God of revelation (cf. ch. lx. 9, where ver. 5b is repeated almost word for word).

So gracious is the offer which Jehovah now makes to His people, so great are the promises that He makes to it, viz. the regal glory of David, and the government of the world by virtue of the religion of Jehovah. Hence the exhortation is addressed to it in vers. 6 and 7 : " *Seek ye Jehovah while He may be found, call ye upon Him while He is near. Let the wicked forsake his way, and the unrighteous man his thoughts : and let him return to Jehovah, and He will have compassion upon him ; and to our God, for He will abundantly pardon.*" They are to seek to press into the fellowship of Jehovah (*dârash* with the radical meaning *terere*, to acquire experimental knowledge or confidential acquaintance with anything) now that He is to be found (ch. lxv. 1, compare the parallelism of words and things in Jer. xxix. 14), and to call upon Him, viz. for a share in that superabundant grace, now that He is near, *i.e.* now that He approaches Israel, and offers it. In the admonition to repentance introduced in ver. 7, both sides of the μετάνοια find expression, viz. turning away from sinful self-will, and turning to the God of salvation. The apodosis with its promises commences with וִירַחֲמֵהוּ—then will He have compassion upon such a man ; and consequently כִּי־יַרְבֶּה לִסְלוֹחַ (with כִּי because the fragmentary sentence וְאֶל־אֱלֹהֵינוּ did not admit of the

continuation with וֹ) has not a general, but an individual meaning (*vid.* Ps. cxxx. 4, 7), and is to be translated as a future (for
the expression, compare ch. xxvi. 17).

The appeal, to leave their own way and their own thoughts,
and yield themselves to God the Redeemer, and to His word,
is now urged on the ground of the heaven-wide difference between the ways and thoughts of this God and the despairing
thoughts of men (ch. xl. 27, xlix. 24), and their aimless laby-
rinthine ways. Vers. 8, 9. "*For my thoughts are not your
thoughts, neither are your ways my ways, saith Jehovah: no,
heaven is high above the earth; so high are my ways above your
ways, and my thoughts above your thoughts.*" The *kî* (*imo*)
introduces the undeniable statement of a fact patent to the
senses, for the purpose of clearly setting forth, by way of comparison, the relation in which the ways and thoughts of God
stand to those of man. There is no necessity to supply כַּאֲשֶׁר after
כִּי, as Hitzig and Knobel do. It is simply omitted, as in ch. lxii. 5
and Jer. iii. 20, or like כֵּן in Prov. xxvi. 11, etc. On what side
the heaven-wide elevation is to be seen, is shown in what follows.
They are not so fickle, so unreliable, or so powerless.

This is set forth under a figure drawn from the rain and the
snow. Vers. 10, 11. "*For as the rain cometh down, and the snow
from heaven, and returneth not thither, till it has moistened the
earth, and fertilized it, and made it green, and offered seed to the
sower and bread to the eater; so will my word be which goeth forth
out of my mouth: it will not return to me fruitless, till it has
accomplished that which I willed, and prosperously carried out that
for which I sent it.*" The rain and snow come down from the
sky, and return not thither till they have . . . The perfects
after כִּי אִם are all to be understood as such (Ewald, § 356, *a*).
Rain and snow return as vapour to the sky, but not without
having first of all accomplished the purpose of their descent.
And so with the word of Jehovah, which goeth forth out of His
mouth (יֵצֵא, not יָצָא, ch. xlv. 23, because it is thought of as still
going on in the preaching of the prophet): it will not return without having effected its object, *i.e.* without having accomplished
what was Jehovah's counsel, or "good pleasure"—without having
attained the end for which it was sent by Jehovah (constr. as
in 2 Sam. xi. 22, 1 Kings xiv. 6). The word is represented in
other places as the messenger of God (ch. ix. 8; Ps. cvii. 20.

cxlvii. 15 sqq.). The personification presupposes that it is not a mere sound or letter. As it goeth forth out of the mouth of God it acquires shape, and in this shape is hidden a divine life, because of its divine origin; ˊand so it runs, with life from God, endowed with divine power, supplied with divine commissions, like a swift messenger through nature and the world of man, there to melt the ice, as it were, and here to heal and to save; and does not return from its course till it has given effect to the will of the sender. This return of the word to God also presupposes its divine nature. The will of God, which becomes concrete and audible in the word, is the utterance of His nature, and is resolved into that nature again as soon as it is fulfilled. The figures chosen are rich in analogies. As snow and rain are the mediating causes of growth, and therefore the enjoyment of what is reaped; so is the soil of the human heart softened, refreshed, and rendered productive or prolific by the word out of the mouth of Jehovah; and this word furnishes the prophet, who resembles the sower, with the seed which he scatters, and brings with it bread which feeds the souls: for every word that proceedeth out of the mouth of God is bread (Deut. viii. 3).

The true point of comparison, however, is the energy with which the word is realized. Assuredly and irresistibly will the word of redemption be fulfilled. Vers. 12, 13. "*For ye will go out with joy, and be led forth in peace: the mountains and the hills will break out before you into shouting, and all the trees of the field will clap their hands. Instead of the thorn will cypresses shoot up, and instead of the fleabane will myrtles shoot up: and it will be to Jehovah for a name, for an everlasting memorial that will not be swept away.*" "With joy," *i.e.* without the hurry of fear (ch. lii. 12); "in peace," *i.e.* without having to fight their way through or flee. The idea of the sufferer falls back in הוּבָל behind that of a festal procession (Ps. xlv. 15, 16). In applying the term *kaph* (hand) to the trees, the prophet had in his mind their *kippōth*, or branches. The psalmist in Ps. xcviii. 8 transfers the figure created by our prophet to the waves of the streams. *Naʿătsūts* (from *năˊats*, to sting) is probably no particular kind of thorn, such, for example, as the fuller's thistle, but, as in ch. vii. 19, briers and thorns generally. On *sirpad*, see Ges. *Thes.;* we have followed the rendering, κόνυζα, of the **LXX**. That this transformation of the vegetation of the desert is not to be taken literally, any more than in ch. xli. 17–20, is evident from the shouting of the mountains, and the clapping of hands on the part of the trees. On the other hand, however, the prophet says something more than that Israel will return home with such feelings of joy as will cause everything to appear transformed. Such promises as those which we find here and in ch. xli. 19 and xxxv. 1, 2, and such exhortations as those which we find in ch. xliv. 23, xlix. 13, and lii. 9, arise from the consciousness, which was common to both prophets and apostles, that the whole creation will one day share in the liberty and glory of the children of God (Rom. viii. 21). This thought is dressed up sometimes in one form, and sometimes in another. The psalmists after the captivity borrowed the colours in which they painted it from our prophet (see at Ps. xcvi. and xcviii.). וְהָיָה is construed as a neuter (cf. בְּרָאתִיו, ch. xlv. 8), referring to this festal transformation of the outer world on the festive return of the redeemed. אוֹת is treated in the attributive clause as a masculine, as if it came from אוּת, to make an incision, to crimp, as we have already indicated in vol. i. p. 213; but the Arabic آيَة, *âyat*, shows that it comes from אָוָה, to point out, and is contracted from *âwâyat*, and therefore was originally a feminine.

EIGHTH PROPHECY.—Chap. lvi. 1–8.

SABBATICAL ADMONITIONS, AND CONSOLATION FOR PROSELYTES AND EUNUCHS.

The note of admonition struck in the foregoing prophecy is continued here, the sabbatical duties being enforced with especial emphasis as part of the general righteousness of life. Vers. 1, 2. " *Thus saith Jehovah, Keep ye right, and do righteousness: for my salvation is near to come, and my righteousness to reveal itself. Blessed is the mortal that doeth this, and the son of man that layeth fast hold thereon; who keepeth the Sabbath, that he doth not desecrate it, and keepeth his hand from doing any kind of evil.*" Jehovah and Israel have both an objective standard in the covenant relation into which they have entered: מִשְׁפָּט

(right) is practice answering to this; יְשׁוּעָה (salvation) the performance promised by God; צְדָקָה (righteousness) on both sides such personal activity as is in accordance with the covenant relation, or what is the same thing, with the purpose and plan of salvation. The nearer the full realization on the part of Jehovah of what He has promised, the more faithful ought Israel to be in everything to which it is bound by its relation to Jehovah. זאת (this) points, as in Ps. vii. 4, to what follows; and so also does בָּהּ, which points back to זאת. Instead of שָׁמוֹר or לִשְׁמֹר we have here שֹׁמֵר, the זאת being described personally instead of objectively. שַׁבָּת is used as a masculine in vers. 2 and 6 (cf. ch. lviii. 13), although the word is not formed after the same manner as קַטָּל, but is rather contracted from שַׁבֶּתֶת (a festive time, possibly with עֶרֶת=עֵת understood), and therefore was originally a feminine; and it is so personified in the language employed in the worship of the synagogue.[1] The prophet here thinks of שַׁבָּת as יוֹם הַשַּׁבָּת, and gives it the gender of יוֹם.

The אשרי (blessed) of ver. 2 is now extended to those who might imagine that they had no right to console themselves with the promises which it contained. Ver. 3. "*And let not the foreigner, who hath not joined himself to Jehovah, speak thus: Assuredly Jehovah will cut me off from His people; and let not the eunuch say, I am only a dry tree.*" As נלוה is not pointed as a participle (נִלְוָה), but as a 3d pers. pres., the ה of הַנִּלְוָה is equivalent to אֲשֶׁר, as in Josh. x. 24, Gen. xviii. 21, xxi. 3, xlvi. 27, 1 Kings xi. 9 (Ges. § 109). By the eunuchs we are to understand those of Israelitish descent, as the attributive clause is not repeated in their case. Heathen, who professed the religion of Jehovah, and had attached themselves to Israel, might be afraid lest, when Israel should be restored to its native land, according to the promise, as a holy and glorious community with a thoroughly priestly character, Jehovah would no longer tolerate them, *i.e.* would forbid their receiving full citizenship. יַבְדִּילַנִי has the connecting vowel *á*, as in Gen. xix. 19, xxix. 32, instead of the usual *ē*. And the Israelitish

---

[1] According to b. *Sabbath* 119a, R. Chanina dressed himself on Friday evening in his sabbath-clothes, and said, "Come, and let us go to meet Queen Sabbath." And so did also Jannai, saying, "Come, O bride; come, O bride." Hence the customary song with which the Sabbath was greeted had לְכָה דוֹדִי לִקְרַאת כַּלָּה פְּנֵי שַׁבָּת נְקַבְּלָה as its commencement and refrain.

eunuchs, who had been mutilated against their will, that they might serve at heathen courts or in the houses of foreign lords, and therefore had not been unfaithful to Jehovah, might be afraid lest, as unfruitful trees, they should be pronounced unworthy of standing in the congregation of Jehovah. There was more ground for the anxiety of the latter than for that of the former. For the law in Deut. xxiii. 4–7 merely prohibits Ammonites and Moabites for all time to come from reception into the congregation, on account of their unbrotherly conduct towards the Israelites as they came out of Egypt, whilst that in Deut. xxiii. 8, 9 prohibits the reception of Edomites and Egyptians to the third generation ; so that there was no prohibition as to other allies—such, for example, as the Babylonians. On the other hand, the law in Deut. xxiii. 2 expressly declares, as an expression of the horror of God at any such mutilation of nature, and for the purpose of precluding it, that no kind of emasculated person is to enter the congregation of Jehovah. But prophecy breaks through these limits of the law. Vers. 4, 5. "*For thus saith Jehovah to the circumcised, Those who keep my Sabbaths, and decide for that in which I take pleasure, and take fast hold of my covenant; I give to them in my house and within my walls a memorial and a name better than sons and daughters : I give such a man an everlasting name, that shall not be cut off*." The second condition after the sanctification of the Sabbath has reference to the regulation of life according to the revealed will of God; the third to fidelity with regard to the covenant of circumcision. יָד also means a side, and hence a place (Deut. xxiii. 13) ; but in the passage before us, where יָד וָשֵׁם form a closely connected pair of words, to which מִבָּנִים וּמִבָּנוֹת is appended, it signifies the memorial, equivalent to מַצֶּבֶת (2 Sam. xviii. 18 ; 1 Sam. xv. 12), as an index lifted up on high (Ezek. xxi. 24), which strikes the eye and arrests attention, pointing like a signpost to the person upon whom it is placed, like *monumentum a monendo*. They are assured that they will not be excluded from close fellowship with the church ("in my house and within my walls"), and also promised, as a superabundant compensation for the want of posterity, long life in the memory of future ages, by whom their long tried attachment to Jehovah and His people in circumstances of great temptation will not be forgotten.

The fears of proselytes from among the heathen are also removed. Vers. 6, 7. "*And the foreigners, who have joined themselves to Jehovah, to serve Him, and to love the name of Jehovah, to be His servants, whoever keepeth the Sabbath from desecrating it, and those who hold fast to my covenant, I bring them to my holy mountain, and make them joyful in my house of prayer; their whole-offerings and their slain-offerings are well-pleasing upon mine altar: for my house, a house of prayer shall it be called for all nations.*" The proselytes, who have attached themselves to Jehovah (עַל־ה'),[1] the God of Israel, with the pure intention of serving Him with love, are not to be left behind in the strange land. Jehovah will bring them along with His people to the holy mountain, upon which His temple rises once more; there will He cause them to rejoice, and all that they place upon His altar will find a most gracious acceptance. It is impossible that the prophet should be thinking here of the worship of the future without sacrifice, although in ch. liii. he predicts the self-sacrifice of the " Servant of Jehovah," which puts an end to all animal sacrifices. But here the temple is called " the house of prayer," from the prayer which is the soul of all worship. It will be called a house of prayer for all nations; and therefore its nature will correspond to its name. This ultimate intention is already indicated in Solomon's dedicatory prayer (1 Kings viii. 41–43); but our prophet was the first to give it this definite universal expression. Throughout this passage the spirit of the law is striving to liberate itself from its bondage. Nor is there anything to surprise us in the breaking down of the party wall, built up so absolutely between the eunuchs on the one hand and the congregation on the other, or the one partially erected between the heathen and the congregation of Israel; as we may see from ch. lxvi. 21, where it is affirmed that Jehovah will even take priests and Levites out of the midst of the heathen whom Israel will bring back with it into its own land.

The expression " *saying of the Lord*" (*Ne'um Jehovah*), which is so solemn an expression in itself, and which stands

---

[1] The oriental reading, not in ver. 3, but here in ver. 6, is עַל־ה'; the western, אֶל־ה'. The Masora follows the western (מערבאי), *i.e.* the Palestinian, and reckons this passage as one of the 31 עַל־ה' in the Old Testament Scriptures.

here at the head of the following declaration, is a proof that it contains not only something great, but something which needs a solemn confirmation because of its strangeness. Not only is there no ground for supposing that Gentiles who love Jehovah will be excluded from the congregation; but it is really Jehovah's intention to gather some out of the heathen, and add them to the assembled *diaspora* of Israel. Ver. 8. " *Word of the Lord, Jehovah : gathering the outcasts of Israel, I will also gather beyond itself to its gathered ones.*" We only find נְאֻם ה׳ at the commencement of a sentence, in this passage and Zech. xii. 1. The double name of God, *Adonai Jehovah*, also indicates something great. עָלָיו (to it) refers to Israel, and לְנִקְבָּצָיו is an explanatory permutative, equivalent to עַל־נִקְבָּצָיו; or else עַל denotes the fact that the gathering will exceed the limits of Israel (cf. Gen. xlviii. 22), and לְ the addition that will be made to the gathered ones of Israel. The meaning in either case remains the same. Jehovah here declares what Jesus says in John x. 16 : "Other sheep I have which are not of this fold : them also I must bring, and they shall hear my voice; and there shall be one fold and one Shepherd ;" " Jehovah one, and His name one," as it is expressed in Zech. xiv. 9. Such are the views and hopes that have grown up out of the chastisement inflicted by their captivity. God has made it a preparatory school for New Testament times. It has been made subservient to the bursting of the fetters of the law, the liberation of the spirit of the law, and the establishment of friendship between Israel and the Gentile world as called to one common salvation.

NINTH PROPHECY.—CHAP. LVI. 9–LVII. 21.

NEGLECT OF DUTY BY THE LEADERS OF ISRAEL; AND ERRORS OF THE PEOPLE.

It is a question whether ch. lvi. 9 forms the commencement of a fresh prophecy, or merely the second half of the prophecy contained in ch. lvi. 1–8. We decide, for our part, in favour of the former. If ch. lvi. 9 sqq. formed an antithetical second half to the promising first half in ch. lvi. 1–8, we should expect to find the prophets and leaders of Israel, whose licentiousness and want of principle are here so severely condemned, threatened with destruction in the heathen land, whilst true proselytes and even eunuchs were brought to the holy mountain. But we meet with this antithesis for the first time in ch. lvii. 13, where we evidently find ourselves in the midst of another prophetic address. And where can that address commence, if not at ch. lvi. 9, from which point onwards we have that hard, dull, sharp, and concise language of strong indignation (see p. 130), which recals to mind psalms written "in a thundering style" (*Psalter*, i. 80) and the reproachful addresses of Jeremiah, and which passes again in ch. lvii. 11 sqq. into the lofty crystalline language peculiar to our prophet's "book of consolation?" The new prophetic address commences, like ch. lv. 1, with a summons. Ver. 9. "*All ye beasts of the field, come near! To devour, all ye beasts in the forest!*" According to the accentuation before us (לאכל *mercha*, כל־חיתו *tiphchah*), the beasts of the field are summoned to devour the beasts in the forest. This accentuation, however, is false, and must be exchanged for another which is supported by some MSS., viz. לאכל *tiphchah*, כל־חיתו *mercha*, and ביער *Beth raphatum*. It is true that even with these accents we might still adhere to the view favoured by Jewish commentators, viz. that the beasts of the field are to be devoured by the beasts of the forest, if this view yielded any admissible sense (compare, for example, that supported by Meyer, "Ye enemies, devour the scattered ones of my congregation"), and had not against it the synonymous parallelism of חיתו שדי and חיתו ביער (ch. xliii. 20; Ps. civ. 11, 20; cf. Gen. iii. 14). But there remains another view, according to which כל־חיתו ביער is a second vocative answering to כל־חיתו שדי. According to the Targum, what is to be devoured is the great body of heathen kings attacking Jerusalem; according to Jerome, Cyril, Stier, etc., the pasture and food provided by the grace of God. But what follows teaches us something different from this. Israel has prophets and shepherds, who are blind to every coming danger, and therefore fail to give warning of its approach, because they are sunken in selfishness and debauchery. It resembles a flock without a keeper, and therefore an easy prey (Ezek. xxxiv. 5); and the meaning of the appeal, which is certainly addressed to the nations of the world, the enemies of the people of God, is this:

"Ye have only to draw near; ye can feed undisturbed, and devour as much as ye please." This is the explanation adopted by most of the more modern commentators. In Jer. xii. 9, which is founded upon this ("Assemble all ye beasts of the field, bring them hither to devour"), it is also Jerusalem which is assigned as food to the heathen. The parallel in ver. 9 is both synonymous and progressive. The writer seeks for rare forms, because he is about to depict a rare inversion of the proper state of things. חִיְתוֹ (with the first syllable loosely closed) is the antiquated form of connection, which was admissible even with בְיַעַר following (cf. ch. v. 11, ix. 1, 2; 2 Sam. i. 21). On אֱתָיוּ (=אָתוּ), see at ch. xxi. 12 (cf. ver. 14).

The prophet now proceeds with צפו (צֹפָיו) : the suffix refers to Israel, which was also the object to לֶאֱכֹל. Vers. 10, 11. "*His watchmen are blind: they* (are) *all ignorant, they* (are) *all dumb dogs that cannot bark; raving, lying down, loving to slumber. And the dogs are mightily greedy, they know no satiety; and such are shepherds! They know no understanding; they have all turned to their own ways, every one for his own gain throughout his border.*" The "watchmen" are the prophets here, as everywhere else (ch. lii. 8, cf. ch. xxi. 6, Hab. ii. 1; Jer. vi. 17; Ezek. iii. 17). The prophet is like a watchman ('*tsōpheh*) stationed upon his watch-tower (*specula*), whose duty it is, when he sees the sword come upon the land, to blow the *shōphâr*, and warn the people (Ezek. xxxiii. 1–9). But just as Jeremiah speaks of bad prophets among the captives (Jer. xxix. 1–32), and the book of Ezekiel is full of reproaches at the existing neglect of the office of watchman and shepherd; so does the prophet here complain that the watchmen of the nation are blind, in direct opposition to both their title and their calling; they are all without either knowledge or the capacity for knowledge (*vid.* ch. xliv. 9, xlv. 20). They ought to resemble watchful sheep-dogs (Job xxx. 1), which bark when the flock is threatened; but they are dumb, and cannot bark (*nâbhach*, root *nab*), and leave the flock to all its danger. Instead of being "seers" (*chōzīm*), they are ravers (*hōzīm*; cf. ch. xix. 18, where we have a play upon הַחֶרֶס in הַחֶרֶם). הֹזִים, from הָזָה, to rave in sickness, *n. act.* hadhajan (which Kimchi compares to *parlare in sónno*); hence the Targum נְיְמִין, LXX.

ἐνυπνιαζόμενοι, A φαντάζομενοι, S ὁραματισταί, Jer. *videntes vana*. The predicates which follow are attached to the leading word *hōzīm* (raving), if not precisely as adjectives, yet as more minutely descriptive. Instead of watching, praying, wrestling, to render themselves susceptible of visions of divine revelations for the good of their people, and to keep themselves in readiness to receive them, they are idle, loving comfortable ease, talkers in their sleep. And the dogs, viz. those prophets who resemble the worst of them (see at ch. xl. 8, p. 144), are עַזֵּי נֶפֶשׁ, of violent, unrestrained soul, insatiable. Their soul lives and moves in the lowest parts of their nature; it is nothing but selfish avarice, self-indulgent greediness, violent restlessness of passion, that revolves perpetually around itself. With the words "and these are shepherds," the range of the prophet's vision is extended to the leaders of the nation generally; for when the prophet adds as an exclamation, "And such (*hi = tales*) are shepherds!" he applies the glaring contrast between calling and conduct to the holders of both offices, that of teacher and that of ruler alike. For, apart from the accents, it would be quite at variance with the general use of the personal pronoun המה, to apply it to any other persons than those just described (viz. in any such sense as this: "And those, who ought to be shepherds, do not know"). Nor is it admissible to commence an adversative minor clause with והמה, as Knobel does, "whereas they are shepherds;" for, since the principal clause has הכלבים (dogs) as the subject, this would introduce a heterogeneous mixture of the two figures, shepherds' dogs and shepherds. We therefore take והמה רעים as an independent clause: "And it is upon men of such a kind, that the duty of watching and tending the nation devolves!" These רֹעִים (for which the Targum reads רָעִים) are then still further described: they know not to understand, *i.e.* they are without spiritual capacity to pass an intelligible judgment (compare the opposite combination of the two verbs in ch. xxxii. 4); instead of caring for the general good, they have all turned to their own way (*l'darkâm*), *i.e.* to their own selfish interests, every one bent upon his own advantage (בְּצַע from בָּצַע, *abscindere*, as we say, *seinen Schnitt zu machen*, to reap an advantage, lit. to make an incision). מִקָּצֵהוּ, from his utmost extremity (*i.e.* from that of his own station, including all its members), in other words,

"throughout the length and breadth of his own circle;" *qâtseh*,
the end, being regarded not as the terminal point, but as the
circumference (as in Gen. xix. 4, xlvii. 21, and Jer. li. 31).

An office-bearer of the kind described is now introduced
per mimesin as speaking. Ver. 12. " *Come here, I will fetch
wine, and let us drink meth ; and to-morrow shall be like to-day,
great, excessively abundant.*" He gives a banquet, and promises the guests that the revelry shall be as great to-morrow
as to-day, or rather much more glorious. יוֹם מָחָר is the day of
to-morrow, τὸ ἐπαύριον, for *mâchâr* is always without an article;
hence *et fiet uti hic* (*dies*) *dies crastinus*, viz. *magnus supra
modum valde*. יֶתֶר, or יָתֵר (as it is to be pointed here according
to Kimchi, *Michlol* 167*b*, and *Wörterbuch*), signifies superabundance ; it is used here adverbially in the sense of extra-
ordinarily, beyond all bounds (differing therefore from יוֹתֵר,
" more," or " singularly," in the book of Ecclesiastes).

Whilst watchmen and shepherds, prophets and rulers,
without troubling themselves about the flock which they have
to watch and feed, are thus indulging their own selfish desires,
and living in debauchery, the righteous man is saved by early
death from the judgment, which cannot fail to come with such
corruption as this. Ch. lvii. 1, 2. " *The righteous perisheth,
and no man taketh it to heart; and pious men are swept away,
without any one considering that the righteous is swept away from
misfortune. He entereth into peace : they rest upon their beds,
whoever has walked straight before him.*" With " the righteous"
the prophet introduces, in glaring contrast to this luxurious
living on the part of the leading men of the nation, the standing
figure used to denote the fate of its best men. With this prevailing demoralization and worldliness, the righteous succumbs
to the violence of both external and internal sufferings. אָבַד,
he dies before his time (Eccles. vii. 15) ; from the midst of
the men of his generation he is carried away from this world
(Ps. xii. 2 ; Mic. vii. 2), and no one lays it to heart, viz. the
divine accusation and threat involved in this early death. Men
of piety (*chesed*, the love of God and man) are swept away,
without there being any one to understand or consider that
(*kî* unfolds the object to be considered and laid to heart, viz.
what is involved in this carrying away when regarded as a
providential event) the righteous is swept away " from the

evil," *i.e.* that he may be saved from the approaching punishment (compare 2 Kings xxii. 20). For the prevailing corruption calls for punishment from God; and what is first of all to be expected is severe judgment, through which the coming salvation will force its way. In ver. 2 it is intimated that the righteous man and the pious do not lose the blessings of this salvation because they lose this life: for whereas, according to the prophet's watchword, there is no peace to the wicked, it is true, on the other hand, of the departing righteous man, that "he enters into peace" (*shâlōm, acc. loci s. status;* Ges. 118, 1); "they rest upon their beds," viz. the bottom of the grave, which has become their *mishkábh* (Job xvii. 13, xxi. 26), "whoever has walked in that which lay straight before him," *i.e.* the one straight plain path which he had set before him (נכחו *acc. obj.* as in ch. xxxiii. 15, l. 10, Ewald, § 172, *b,* from נָכֹחַ, that which lies straight before a person; whereas נֹכַח with נִכְחוֹ נֶכַח, signifying probably fixedness, steadiness of look, related to نَكَا, to pierce, נָכָה, *percutere,* is used as a preposition: compare Prov. iv. 25, לְנֹכַח, straight or exactly before him). The grave, when compared with the restlessness of this life, is therefore "peace." He who has died in faith rests in God, to whom he has committed himself and entrusted his future. We have here the glimmering light of the New Testament consolation, that the death of the righteous is better than life in this world, because it is the entrance into peace.

The reproachful language of the prophet is now directed against the mass of the nation, who have occasioned the "evil" from which the righteous is swept away, *i.e.* the generation that is hostile to the servants of Jehovah, and by whom those sins of idolatry are still so shamelessly carried on, which first led to the captivity. Vers. 3, 4. "*And ye, draw nearer hither, children of the sorceress, seed of the adulterer, and of her that committed whoredom! Over whom do ye make yourselves merry? Over whom do ye open the mouth wide, and put the tongue out long? Are ye not the brood of apostasy, seed of lying?*" They are to draw nearer hither (*hennáh* as in Gen. xv. 16), to the place where God is speaking through His prophet, to have themselves painted, and to hear their sentence. Just as elsewhere the moral character of a man is frequently indicated by the mention of his father (2 Kings vi. 32), or his mother (1 Sam. xx. 30), or both parents (Job xxx. 8), so here the generation of the captivity, so far as it continued· to practise the idolatry by which its ancestors had brought upon themselves the Chaldean catastrophe, is called *first* בְּנֵי עֹנְנָה (or more correctly עֹנֵנָה), sons of the sorceress (possibly the maker of clouds or storm, ch. ii. 6, vol. i. 118 : Jer. *auguratricis*), one who made heathen and superstitious customs her means of livelihood, viz. the community as it existed before the captivity, which really deserved no better name, on account of the crying contradiction between its calling and its conduct; and *secondly*, with regard to both the male and female members of the community, זֶרַע מְנָאֵף וַתִּזְנֶה, *semen adulteri et fornicariæ* (Jer.), though Stier, Hahn, and others adopt the rendering *semen adulterum et quod* (*qui*) *scortaris*. A better rendering than this would be, "Seed of an adulterer, and one who committest adultery thyself," viz. (what would be indicated with this explanation by the *fut. consec.*) in consequence of this descent from an adulterer. But as זֶרַע (seed, posterity), wherever it is more minutely defined, is connected with a genitive, and not with an adjective, the presumption is that מנאף ותזנה denotes the father and mother. וַתִּזְנֶה is an attributive clause regarded as a genitive (Ges. § 123, 3, Anm. 1), and more closely connected with מנאף than if it was written וְתִזְנֶה (= וְזוֹנָה, ch. i. 21): Seed of an adulterer, and consequently (Ewald, § 351, *b*), or similarly, of one who gave herself up to whoredom. Idolatry, prostitution, and magic are most closely allied. The prophet now asks, "Over whom do ye find your pleasure? For whom are your common contemptuous actions intended?" הִתְעַנָּג is only used here, and denotes the feeling which finds pleasure in the sufferings of another. The objects of this malicious contemptuous pleasure (Ps. xxii. 8 sqq., xxxv. 21) are the servants of Jehovah; and the question, as in ch. xxxvii. 23, is one of amazement at their impudence, since the men over whom they make merry are really deserving of esteem, whereas they themselves are the refuse of Israel : Are ye not a brood of apostasy, seed of lying? As apostasy and lying, when regarded as parents, can only produce something resembling themselves; the character of those from whom they are descended is here imputed to the men themselves, even more clearly than before. The genitives of origin

are also genitives of attribute. Instead of יַלְדֵי (*e.g.* ch. ii. 6)
we have here יַלְדֵי־ before *makkeph,* with the shortening of *a*
into *i.*

The participles which follow in the next verse are in apposition to אַתֶּם, and confirm the predicates already applied to
them. They soon give place, however, to independent sentences. Vers. 5, 6. " *Ye that inflame yourselves by the tere-*
binths, under every green tree, ye slayers of children in the valleys
under the clefts of the rocks. By the smooth ones of the brook
was thy portion; they, they were thy lot: thou also pouredst out
libations to them, thou laidst meat-offerings upon them. Shall I
be contented with this?" The people of the captivity are addressed, and the idolatry handed down to them from their
ancestors depicted. The prophet looks back from the standpoint of the captivity, and takes his colours from the time in
which he himself lived, possibly from the commencement of
Manasseh's reign, when the heathenism that had for a long
time been suppressed burst forth again in all its force, and the
measure of iniquity became full. The *part. niphal* הַנֵּחָמִים is
formed like נֵחַ in Jer. xxii. 23, if the latter signifies *miserandum*
esse. The primary form is נָחָם, which is doubled like נְּוַּר from
נָרַר in Job xx. 28, and from which נֵחַם is formed by the resolution of the latent reduplication. Stier derives it from יָחַם;
but even if formed from this, נֵחַם would still have to be explained from נָחַם, after the form נִצֵּת. '*Elim* signifies either
gods or terebinths (see vol. i. 108, note 1). But although
it might certainly mean idols, according to Ex. xv. 11, Dan.
xi. 36 (LXX., Targ., and Jerome), it is never used directly
in this sense, and Isaiah always uses the word as the name of
a tree (ch. i. 29, lxi. 3). The terebinths are introduced here,
exactly as in ch. i. 29, as an object of idolatrous lust: " who
inflame themselves with the terebinths;" בְּ denotes the object
with which the lust is excited and inflamed. The terebinth
(*'ēlâh*) held the chief place in tree-worship (hence אַלָּנִם, lit.
oak-trees, together with אַלֻם, is the name of one of the Phœnician gods[1]), possibly as being the tree sacred to Astarte; just
as the *Samura Acacia* among the heathen Arabs was the tree
sacred to the goddess '*Uzza.*[2] The following expression, "under

[1] See Levy, *Phönizische Studien,* i. 19.
[2] Krehl, *Religion der vorisl. Araber,* p. 74 sqq.

every green tree," is simply a permutative of the words "with
the terebinths" in the sense of "with the terebinths, yea, under
every green tree" (a standing expression from Deut. xii. 2 downwards),—one tree being regarded as the abode and favourite of
this deity, and another of that, and all alluring you to your
carnal worship. From the tree-worship with its orgies, which
was so widely spread in antiquity generally, the prophet passes
to the leading Canaanitish abomination, viz. human sacrifices,
which had been adopted by the Israelites (along with שֹׁחֲטֵי we
find the false reading שֹׁחֲטֵי, which is interpreted as signifying
self-abuse). Judging from the locality named, "under the
clefts of the rocks," the reference is not to the slaying of children sacrificed to Moloch in the valley of Hinnom, but to those
offered to Baal upon his *bâmōth* or high places (Jer. xix. 5;
Ezek. xvi. 20, 21; Hos. xiii. 2; Ps. cvi. 37, 38). As we
learn from the *chronique scandaleuse* many things connected
with the religious history of Israel, which cannot be found
in its historical books, there is nothing to surprise us in the
stone-worship condemned in ver. 6. The *dagesh* of חַלְּקֵי is in
any case *dagesh dirimens*. The singular is either חֵלֶק after the
form חַכְמֵי (cf. עַצְבֵי, ch. lviii. 3), or חֵלֶק after the form יַלְדֵי.
But חָלָק, smoothness, never occurs; and the explanation, "in
the smoothnesses, *i.e.* the smooth places of the valley, is thy
portion," has this also against it, that it does not do justice to
the connection בְּ חֵלֶק, in which the preposition is not used in a
local sense, and that it leaves the emphatic הֵם הֵם quite unexplained. The latter does not point to places, but to objects of
worship for which they had exchanged Jehovah, of whom the
true Israelite could say חֶלְקִי ה', Ps. cxix. 57, etc., or חֵלֶק לִי בָּהּ,
Josh. xxii. 25, and אַתָּה תּוֹמִיךְ גּוֹרָלִי (Thou art He that maintaineth
my lot), Ps. xvi. 5. The prophet had such expressions as these
in his mind, and possibly also the primary meaning of גורל =
κλῆρος, which may be gathered from the rare Arabic word
'*garal*, gravel, stones worn smooth by rolling, when he said, "In
the smooth ones of the valley is thy portion; they, they are thy
lot." In the Arabic also, *achlaq* (equivalent to *châlâq*, smooth,
which forms here a play upon the word with חֵלֶק, *châlâq*)
is a favourite word for stones and rocks. חַלְקֵי-נַחַל, however,
according to 1 Sam. xvii. 40 (where the intensive form חַלֻּק,
like שָׂבֻּל, is used), are stones which the stream in the valley

has washed smooth with time, and rounded into a pleasing shape. The mode of the worship, the pouring out of libations,[1] and the laying of meat-offerings upon them, confirm this view. In Carthage such stones were called *abbadires* (= אדיר, אבן) ; and among the ancient Arabs, the *asnâm* or idols consisted for the most part of rude blocks of stone of this description. Herodotus (iii. 8) speaks of seven stones which the Arabs anointed, calling upon the god Orotal. Suidas (*s.v. Θεὺς ἄρης*) states that the idol of Ares in Petra was a black square stone; and the black stone of the Ka'aba was, according to a very inconvenient tradition for the Mohammedans, an idol of Saturn (*zuhal*).[2] Stone-worship of this kind had been practised by the Israelites before the captivity, and their heathenish practices had been transmitted to the exiles in Babylon. The meaning of the question, Shall I comfort myself concerning such things?—*i.e.* Shall I be contented with them (אֶנָּחֵם *niphal,* not *hithpael*)?—is, that it was impossible that descendants who so resembled their fathers should remain unpunished.

The prophet now proceeds with perfects, like שָׁפַכְתְּ and הֶעֱלִית (addressed to the national community generally, the congregation regarded as a woman). The description is mostly retrospective. Vers. 7, 8. *" Upon a lofty and high mountain hast thou set up thy bed; thou also ascendedst thither to offer slain offerings.*

---

[1] Compare the remarks made in the *Comm. on the Pentateuch*, vol. i. p. 283, on the heathen worship of anointed stones, and the Bætulian worship.

[2] See Krehl, p. 72. In the East Indies also we find stone-worship not only among the Vindya tribes (Lassen, *A.K.* i. 376), but also among the Vaishnavas, who worship Vishnu in the form of a stone, viz. the *sâlagrâma*, a kind of stone from the river Gandak (see Wilson's *Sanscrit Lexicon s.h.v.* and *Vishnu-Purâna*, p. 163). The fact of the great antiquity of stone and tree worship has been used in the most ridiculous manner by Dozy in his work on the Israelites at Mecca (1864). He draws the following conclusion from Deut. xxxii. 18: " Thus the Israelites sprang from a divine block of stone; and this is, in reality, the true old version of the origin of the nation." From Isa. li. 1, 2, he infers that Abraham and Sara were not historical persons at all, but that the former was a block of stone, and the latter a hollow; and that the two together were a block of stone in a hollow, to which divine worship was paid. "This fact," he says, " viz. that Abraham and Sarah in the second Isaiah are not historical persons, but a block of stone and a hollow, is one of great worth, as enabling us to determine the time at which the stories of Abraham in Genesis were written, and to form a correct idea of the spirit of those stories."

*And behind the door and the post thou didst place thy reminder:
for thou uncoveredst away from me, and ascendedst; thou madest
thy bed broad, and didst stipulate for thyself what they had to
do: thou lovedst their lying with thee; thou sawest their manhood."*
The lovers that she sought for herself are the gods of the
heathen.   Upon lofty mountains, where they are generally
worshipped, did she set up her bed, and did all that was needed
to win their favour.   The *zikkârōn, i.e.* the declaration that
Jehovah is the only God, which the Israelites were to write
upon the posts of their houses, and upon the entrances (Deut.
vi. 9, xi. 20), for a constant reminder, she had put behind the
door and post, that she might not be reminded, to her shame,
of her unfaithfulness.   That this explanation, which most of
the commentators adopt, is the true one, is proved by the
expression כִּי מֵאִתִּי which follows, and according to which זִכְרוֹנֵךְ
is something inconvenient, which might and was intended to
remind them of Jehovah.   מֵאִתִּי, away, far from me, as in Jer.
iii. 1, and like מִתַּחְתִּי, which is still more frequently used.   It
is unnecessary to take *gillīth* with עֶרְוָתֵךְ understood (Ezek.
xxiii. 18) as equivalent to "thou makest thyself naked," or
with reference to the clothes = ἀνασύρεις.   מִשְׁכָּבֵךְ is the common
object of all three verbs, even of וַתַּעֲלִי (with double *metheg*),
after Gen. xlix. 4.   On וַתִּכְרָת for וַתִּכְרְתִי (cf. Jer. iii. 5), see
Ewald, § 191, *b.*   The explanation "thou didst bind," or "thou
didst choose (some) of them to thyself," is contrary to the
general usage, according to which כָּרַת לְ signifies *spondere*
(2 Chron. vii. 18), and כָּרַת עִם *pacisci* (1 Sam. xxii. 8), in both
cases with בְּרִית to be supplied, so that כָּרַת (בְּרִית) מִן would
mean *stipulari ab aliquo, i.e.* to obtain from a person a solemn
promise, with all the force of a covenant.   What she stipulated
from them was, either the wages of adultery, or the satisfaction
of her wanton lust.   What follows agrees with this; for it is
there distinctly stated, that the lovers to whom she offered
herself gratified her lust abundantly: *adamasti concubitum
eorum (mishkâbh, cubile, e.g.* Prov. vii. 17, and *concubitus, e.g.*
Ezra xxiii. 17), *manum conspexisti.*   The Targum and Jewish
commentators adopt this explanation, *loco quem delegisti,* or
(*postquam*) *locum delegisti.*   This also is apparently the meaning
of the accents, and most of the more modern commentators
have adopted it, taking יָד in the sense of place or side.   But

this yields only a very lame and unmeaning thought.   Dœderlein conjectured that יָד was employed here in the sense of
ἰθύφαλλος; and this is the explanation adopted by Hitzig,
Ewald, and others.   The Arabic furnishes several analogies to
this obscene use of the word; and by the side of Ezek. xvi. 26
and xxiii. 20, where the same thing is affirmed in even plainer
language, there is nothing to astonish in the passage before us.
The meaning is, that after the church of Jehovah had turned
away from its God to the world and its pleasures, it took more
and more delight in the pleasures afforded it by idolatry, and
indulged its tastes to the full.

In the closest reciprocal connection with this God-forgetting,
adulterous craving for the favour of heathen gods, stood their
coquetting with the heathen power of the world.   Vers. 9, 10.
" And thou wentest to the king with oil, and didst measure
copiously thy spices, and didst send thy messengers to a great
distance, and didst deeply abase thyself, even to Hades.   Thou
didst become weary of the greatness of thy way; yet thou saidst
not, It is unattainable: thou obtainedst the revival of thy strength:
therefore thou wast not pained."   The first thing to be noticed
here, is one that has been overlooked by nearly all the modern
commentators, viz. that we have here a historical retrospect
before us.   And secondly, a single glance at ver. 11 is sufficient to show that the words refer to a servile coquetry from
the fear of man, and therefore to a wicked craving for the
favour of man; so that " the king" is not Baal, or any heathen
god whatever (according to ch. viii. 21 and Zeph. i. 5), but the
Asiatic ruler of the world.   Ahaz sent messengers, as we read
in 2 Kings xvi. 7 sqq., to Tiglath-pileser, the king of Assyria,
to say to him, " I am thy servant and thy son."   And Ahaz
took the silver and gold that were in the house of Jehovah, and
in the treasures of the palace, and sent a bribe to the king of
Assyria.   And again, at vers. 10 sqq., Ahaz went to Damascus
to meet the king of Assyria, and there he saw an altar, and
sent a model of it to Jerusalem, and had one like it put in the
place of the altar of burnt-offering.   Such acts as these are
here described in the figure of Israel travelling with oil to the
king, and taking a quantity of choice spices with it to gain his
favour, and also sending messengers, and not only bowing
itself to the earth, but even stooping to Hades, that is to say,

standing as it were on its head in its excessive servility, for
the purpose of obtaining allies. It seems most natural to take
בַּשֶּׁמֶן as equivalent to מָשׁוּחָה בשמן: thou wentest in oil (dripping
with pomade), and didst apply to thyself many spices; but
Beth after verbs of going signifies to go with anything, to take
it with one and bring it, so that the oil and spices are thought
of here as presents, which she took with her as sensual stimu-
lants, with a view to the amorous pleasures she was seeking
(Ezek. xxiii. 41, cf. Hos. xii. 2). הִשְׁפִּיל signifies to go deep
down in Jer. xiii. 18; the meaning here is, to bow very low,
or to degrade one's self. By " the greatness or breadth of the
way" (a similar expression to that in Josh. ix. 13), all the great
sacrifices are intended which it cost her to purchase the favour
of the heathen ruler. Although they were a great trouble to
her, yet she did not say נוֹאָשׁ, " it is hopeless;" the *niphal* of
יָאַשׁ signifies in 1 Sam. xxvii. 1, to betake one's self to a thing with
despair of its success. The participle in Job vi. 26 means a
despairing person; it also occurs in a neuter sense in Jer.
ii. 25, xviii. 12, viz. given up, *i.e.* absolutely in vain. She did
not give up hope, although the offerings nearly exhausted her
strength; on the contrary, she gained חַיַּת יָד, " life of her arm,"
i.e. (according to the use of חָיָה in the sense of reviving, and
הֶחֱיָה, to bring to life again) new life in her arm, in other words,
" the renewing of her strength" (*recentem vigorem virium
suarum*). Thus, without noticing the sighs and groans forced
from her by the excessive toil and fatigue, but stirring herself
up again and again, she pursued the plan of strengthening her
alliances with the heathen. Ezekiel's picture of Aholah and
Aholibah is like a commentary on vers. 3–10 (see Ezek. xxiii.).

From fear of man, Israel, and still more Judah, had given
up the fear of Jehovah. Ver. 11a. "*And of whom hast thou
been afraid, and (whom) didst thou fear, that thou becamest a liar,
and didst not continue mindful of me, and didst not take it to
heart?*" It was of men—only mortal men, with no real power
(ch. li. 12)—that Israel was so needlessly afraid, that it resorted
to lies and treachery to Jehovah (*kî, ut*, an interrogative sentence, as in 2 Sam. vii. 18, Ps. viii. 5): purchasing the favour
of man out of the fear of man, and throwing itself into the
arms of false tutelar deities, it banished Jehovah its true
shelter out of its memory, and did not take it to heart, viz. the

sinfulness of such infidelity, and the eventful consequences by which it was punished (compare ch. xlvii. 7 and xlii. 25).

With ver. 11*b* the reproaches are addressed to the present. The treachery of Israel had been severely punished in the catastrophe of which the captivity was the result, but without effecting any improvement. The great mass of the people were as forgetful of God as ever, and would not be led to repentance by the long-suffering of God, which had hitherto spared them from other well-merited punishments. Ver. 11*b*. *"Am I not silent, and that for a long time, whereas thou wast not afraid of me?"* A comparison with ch. xlii. 14 will show that the prophecy returns here to its ordinary style. The LXX. and Jerome render the passage as if the reading were מֵעֹלָם (viz. עֵינַי = παρορῶν, *quasi non videns*), and this is the reading which Lowth adopts. We may see from this, that the original text had a defective וּמֵעֹלָם, which was intended, however, to be read וּמֵעֹלָם. The prophet applies the term *'ôlâm* (see ch. xlii. 14) to the captivity, which had already lasted a long time—a time of divine silence : the silence of His help so far as the servants of Jehovah were concerned, but the silence of His wrath as to the great mass of the people.

But this silence would not last for ever. Vers. 12, 13. *"I, I will proclaim thy righteousness ; and thy works, they will not profit thee. When thou criest, let thy heaps of idols save thee : but a wind carries them all away ; a breath takes them off ; and whoever putteth trust in me will inherit the land, and take possession of my holy mountain."* According to the context, צִדְקָתֵךְ cannot be a synonym of יְשׁוּעָה here. It is neither salvation nor the way of salvation that is intended ; nor is this even included, as Stier supposes. But the simple reference is to what Israel in its blindness regarded as righteousness ; whereas, if it had known itself, it would have seen that it was the most glaring opposite. This lying-righteousness of Israel would be brought to a judicial exposure by Jehovah. וְאֶת־מַעֲשַׂיִךְ is not a second accusative to אַגִּיד, for in that case we should have אֶת־צִדְקָתֵךְ וּמַעֲשַׂיִךְ ; but it commences a second sentence, as the accents really indicate. When Jehovah begins thus to speak and act, the impotence of the false gods which His people have made for themselves will soon be exposed ; and " as for thy works (*i.e.* thine idols, ch. xli. 29, cf. ch. i. 31), they will do thee no good"

(ch. xliv. 9, 10, compare Jer. xxiii. 33; for the question
מַה־מִּשָּׂא, here an emphatic elevation of the subject, compare ch.
liii. 8, וְאֶת־דּוֹרוֹ, Ewald, § 277, p. 683). This determines the
meaning of קִבּוּצַיִךְ, which Knobel supposes to refer to the large
army of the Babylonians, with which the apostates among the
exiles had formed an offensive and defensive alliance. But the
term is really applied to the heaps (qibbûts, collectio, not an adjective of the form limmūd) of different idols, with which Israel
had furnished itself even in its captivity (compare qibbâtsâh in
Mic. i. 17). It was in vain for them to turn to these pan-
theons of theirs; a single rūăch would carry them all away, a
hebhel would sweep them off, for they themselves were nothing
but hebhel and rūăch (ch. xli. 29). The proper punctuation
here is יִקַּֽח־הָבֶל; the first syllable of יקח, which is attached to a
word with a disjunctive accent, has a so-called heavy Gaya, the
second a euphonic Gaya, according to rules which are too little
discussed in our grammars. When Knobel supports his explanation of קבוציך on the ground that the idols in ver. 13a and
the worshippers of Jehovah in ver. 13b do not form a fitting
antithesis, the simple reply is, that the contrast lies between
the idols, which cannot save, and Jehovah, who not only saves
those who trust in Him, but sends them prosperity according
to His promises. With the promise, "Whoso trusts in me will
inherit the land," this prophecy reaches the thought with
which the previous prophecy (ch. lvi. 7, 8) closed; and possibly
what is here affirmed of קִבּוּצַיִךְ forms an intentional antithesis
to the promise there, עוֹד אֲקַבֵּץ עָלָיו לְנִקְבָּצָיו: when Jehovah gathers
His faithful ones from the dispersion, and gathers others to
them (from among the heathen), then will the plunder which
the faithless have gathered together be all scattered to the
winds. And whilst the latter stand forsaken by their powerless works, the former will be established in the peaceful inheritance of the promised land.

The first half of the prophecy closes here. It is full of
reproach, and closes with a brief word of promise, which is
merely the obverse of the threat. The second half follows an
opposite course. Jehovah will redeem His people, provided it
has been truly humbled by the sufferings appointed, for He
has seen into what errors it has fallen since He has withdrawn
His mercy from it. "But the wicked," etc. The whole closes

here with words of threatening, which are the obverse of the promise. Ver. 13*b* forms the transition from the first half to the second.

The promise is now followed by an appeal to make ready the way which the redeemed people have to take. Ver. 14. "*And He saith, Heap up, heap up, prepare a way, take away every obstruction from the way of my people.*" This is the very same appeal which occurs once in all three books of these prophecies (ch. xl. 3, 4, lvii. 14, lxii. 10). The subject of the verb ('*âmar*) is not Jehovah ; but the prophet intentionally leaves it obscure, as in ch. xl. 3, 6 (cf. xxvi. 2). It is a heavenly cry ; and the crier is not to be more precisely named.

The primary ground for this voice being heard at all is, that the Holy One is also the Merciful One, and not only has a manifestation of glory on high, but also a manifestation of grace below. Ver. 15. "*For thus saith the high and lofty One, the eternally dwelling One, He whose name is Holy One; I dwell on high and in the holy place, and with the contrite one and him that is of a humbled spirit, to revive the spirit of humbled ones, and to revive the heart of contrite ones.*" He inflicts punishment in His wrath; but to those who suffer themselves to be urged thereby to repentance and the desire for salvation, He is most inwardly and most effectually near with His grace. For the heaven of heavens is not too great for Him, and a human heart is not too small for Him to dwell in. And He who dwells upon cherubim, and among the praises of seraphim, does not scorn to dwell among the sighs of a poor human soul. He is called *râm* (high), as being high and exalted in Himself ; נִשָּׂא (the lofty One), as towering above all besides ; and עַד שֹׁכֵן. This does not mean the dweller in eternity, which is a thought quite outside the biblical range of ideas ; but, since עַד stands to שׁכן not in an objective, but in an attributive or adverbial relation (Ps. xlv. 7, cf. Prov. i. 33), and שָׁכֵן, as opposed to being violently wrested from the ordinary sphere of life and work (cf. Ps. xvi. 9, cii. 29), denotes a continuing life, a life having its root in itself, שֹׁכֵן עַד must mean the eternally (= לְעַד) dwelling One, *i.e.* He whose life lasts for ever and is always the same. He is also called *qâdōsh*, as One who is absolutely pure and good, separated from all the uncleanness and imperfection by which creatures are characterized. This is not to be rendered *sanctum nomen ejus*, but *sanctus ;* this name is the *facit* of His revelation of Himself in the history of salvation, which is accomplished in love and wrath, grace and judgment. This God inhabits *mârōm vᵉqâdōsh*, the height and the Holy Place (accusatives of the object, like *mârōm* in ch. xxxiii. 5, and *mᵉrōmīm* in ch. xxxiii. 16), both together being equivalent to φῶς ἀπρόσιτον (1 Tim. vi. 16), since *qâdōsh* (neuter, as in Ps. xlvi. 5, lxv. 5) answers to φῶς, and *mârōm* to ἀπρόσιτον. But He also dwells with (אֶת as in Lev. xvi. 16) the crushed and lowly of spirit. To these He is most intimately near, and that for a salutary and gracious purpose, namely " to revive . . ." הֶחֱיָה and חָיָה always signify either to keep that which is living alive, or to restore to life that which is dead. The spirit is the seat of pride and humility, the heart the seat of all feeling of joy and sorrow; we have therefore *spiritum humilium* and *cor contritorum*. The selfish egotism which repentance breaks has its root in the heart; and the self-consciousness, from whose false elevation repentance brings down, has its seat in the spirit (*Psychol.* p. 199).

The compassion, by virtue of which God has His abode and His work of grace in the spirit and heart of the penitent, is founded in that free anticipating love which called man and his self-conscious spirit-soul into being at the first. Ver. 16. " *For I do not contend for ever, and I am not angry for ever: for the spirit would pine away before me, and the souls of men which I have created.*" The early translators (LXX., Syr., Jer., possibly also the Targum) give to יַעֲטֹף the meaning *egredietur*, which certainly cannot be established. And so also does Stier, so far as the thought is concerned, when he adopts the rendering, " A spirit from me will cover over, and breath of life will I make;" and so Hahn, " When the spirit pines away before me, I create breath in abundance." But in both cases the writer would at any rate have used the *perf. consec.* וְעָשִׂיתִי, and the last clause of the verse has not the syntactic form of an apodosis. The rendering given above is the only one that is unassailable both grammatically and in fact. כִּי introduces the reason for the self-limitation of the divine wrath, just as in Ps. lxxviii. 38, 39 (cf. Ps. ciii. 14): if God should put no restraint upon His wrath, the consequence would be the entire destruction of human life, which was His creative work at first. The verb עָטַף, from its primary meaning to bend round (*Job,*

ii. p. 8), has sometimes the transitive meaning to cover, and
sometimes the meaning to wrap one's self round, *i.e.* to become
faint or weak (compare עָטוּף, fainted away, Lam. ii. 19 ; and
הִתְעַטֵּף in Ps. cxlii. 4, which is applied to the spirit, like the *kal*
here). מִלְּפָנַי is equivalent to " in consequence of the wrath
proceeding from me." נְשָׁמוֹת (a plural only met with here)
signifies, according to the fixed usage of the Old Testament
(ii. 22, xlii. 5), the souls of men, the origin of which is described as a *creation* in the attributive clause (with an emphatic
אֲנִי), just as in Jer. xxxviii. 16 (cf. Zech. xii. 1). Whether the
accents are intended to take אֲנִי עָשִׂיתִי in this attributive sense
or not, cannot be decided from the *tiphchah* attached to וּנְשָׁמוֹת.
The prophet, who refers to the flood in other passages also (*e.g.*
ch. liv. 9), had probably in his mind the promise given after
the flood, according to which God would not make the existing
and inherited moral depravity an occasion for utterly destroying the human race.

This general law of His action is most especially the law of
His conduct towards Israel, in which such grievous effects of
its well-deserved punishment are apparent, and effects so different from those intended, that the compassion of God feels
impelled to put an end to the punishment for the good of all
that are susceptible of salvation. Vers. 17, 18. *" And because
of the iniquity of its selfishness, I was wroth, and smote it; hiding
myself, and being angry : then it went on, turning away in the
way of its own heart. I have seen its ways, and will heal it ;
and will lead it, and afford consolations to it, and to its mourning
ones."* The fundamental and chief sin of Israel is here called
בֶּצַע, lit. a cut or slice (= gain, ch. lvi. 11); then, like πλεονεξία,
which is "idolatry" according to Col. iii. 5, or like φιλαργυρία,
which is " the root of all evil" according to 1 Tim. vi. 10, greedy
desire for worldly possession, self-seeking, or worldliness generally. The future וָאַכֵּהוּ, standing as it does by the side of the
perfect here, indicates that which is also past ; and וָאֶקְצֹף stands
in the place of a second gerund : *abscondendo* (viz. *pánai*, my
face, ch. liv. 8) *et stomachando.* When Jehovah had thus
wrathfully hidden His gracious countenance from Israel, and
withdrawn His gracious presence out of the midst of Israel
(Hos. v. 6, חָלַץ מֵהֶם), it went away from Him (שׁוֹבָב with שׁוֹבֵב,
like עֹלֵל with עֹלָל), going its own ways like the world of nations

that had been left to themselves. But Jehovah had not seen
these wanderings without pity. The futures which follow are
promising, not by virtue of any syntactic necessity, but by
virtue of an inward necessity. He will heal His wounded (ch.
i. 4–6) and languishing people, and lead in the right way those
that are going astray, and afford them consolation as a recompense for their long sufferings (נִחוּמִים is derived from the *piel*
נִחֵם, and not, as in Hos. xi. 8, from the *niphal hinnáchēm*, in the
sense of "feelings of sympathy"), especially (*Vav epexeget.*;
Ges. § 155, 1) its mourning ones (ch. lxi. 2, 3, lxvi. 10), *i.e.*
those whom punishment has brought to repentance, and rendered desirous of salvation.

But when the redemption comes, it will divide Israel into
two halves, with very different prospects. Vers. 19–21.
"*Creating fruit of the lips; Jehovah saith, 'Peace, peace to
those that are far off, and to those that are near; and I heal it.'
But the wicked are like the sea that is cast up; for it cannot rest,
and its waters cast out slime and mud. There is no peace, saith
my God, for the wicked.*" The words of God in ver. 19 are
introduced with an interpolated "*inquit Jehova*" (cf. ch. xlv.
24, and the ellipsis in ch. xli. 27); and what Jehovah effects by
speaking thus is placed first in a determining participial clause:
"Creating fruit (נוב = נוּב, נוֹב, *keri* נִיב) of the lips," καρπὸν
χειλέων (LXX., Heb. xiii. 15), *i.e.* not of His own lips, to
which בּוֹרֵא would be inapplicable, but the offering of praise
and thanksgiving springing from human lips (for the figure,
see *Psychol.* p. 214, transl.; and on the root נב, to press upon
forward, *Gen.* p. 635): "Jehovah saith *shálōm, shálōm*," *i.e.*
lasting and perfect peace (as in ch. xxvi. 3), "be the portion
of those of my people who are scattered far and near" (ch. xliii.
5–7, xlix. 12; compare the application to heathen and Jews in
Eph. ii. 17); "and I heal *it*" (viz. the nation, which, although
scattered, is like one person in the sight of God). But the
wicked, who persist in the alienation from God inherited from
the fathers, are incapable of the peace which God brings to
His people: they are like the sea in its tossed and stormy state
(נִגְרָשׁ pausal third pers. as an attributive clause). As this cannot
rest, and as its waters cast out slime and mud, so has their
natural state become one of perpetual disturbance, leading to
the uninterrupted production of unclean and ungodly thoughts,

words, and works. Thus, then, there is no peace for them, saith my God. With these words, which have even a more pathetic sound here than in ch. xlviii. 22, the prophet seals the second book of his prophecies. The "wicked" referred to are not the heathen outside Israel, but the heathen, *i.e.* those estranged from God, within Israel itself.

The transition from the first to the second half of this closing prophecy is formed by וַיֹּאמֶר in ch. lvii. 14. In the second half, from ch. lvii. 11*b*, we find the accustomed style of our prophet; but in ch. lvi. 9–lvii. 11*a* the style is so thoroughly different, that Ewald maintains that the prophet has here inserted in his book a fragment from some earlier writer of the time of Manasseh. But we regard this as very improbable. It is not required by what is stated concerning the prophets and shepherds, for the book of Ezekiel clearly shows that the prophets and shepherds of the captivity were thus debased. Still less does what is stated concerning the early death of the righteous require it; for the fundamental idea of the suffering servant of Jehovah, which is peculiar to the second book, is shadowed forth therein. Nor by what is affirmed as to the idolatrous conduct of the people; for in the very centre (ver. 4) the great mass of the people are reproached for their contemptuous treatment of the servants of Jehovah. Nor does the language itself force us to any such conjecture, for ch. liii. also differs from the style met with elsewhere; and yet (although Ewald regards it as an earlier, borrowed fragment) it must be written by the author of the whole, since its grandest idea finds its fullest expression there. At the same time, we may assume that the prophet described the idolatry of the people under the influence of earlier models. If he had been a prophet of the captives after the time of Isaiah, he would have rested his prophecies on Jeremiah and Ezekiel. For just as ch. li. 18 sqq. has the ring of the Lamentations of Jeremiah, so does ch. lvii. 3 sqq. resemble in many respects the earlier reproaches of Jeremiah (compare Jer. v. 7–9, 29, ix. 8, with the expression, "Should I rest satisfied with this?"); also ch. ii. 25 (נוֹאָשׁ), ii. 20, iii. 6, 13 ("upon lofty mountains and under green trees"); also the night scene in Ezek. xxiii.

PART III.

FIRST PROPHECY.—Chap. LVIII.

THE FALSE WORSHIP AND THE TRUE, WITH THE PROMISES BELONGING TO THE LATTER.

As the last prophecy of the second book contained all the three elements of prophetic addresses—reproach, threat, and promise, —so this, the first prophecy of the third book, cannot open in any other way than with a rehearsal of one of these. The prophet receives the commission to appear as the preacher of condemnation; and whilst Jehovah is giving the reason for this commission, the preaching itself commences. Vers. 1, 2. *"Cry with full throat, hold not back; lift up thy voice like a bugle, and proclaim to my people their apostasy, and to the house of Jacob their sins. And they seek me day by day, and desire to learn my ways, like a nation which has done righteousness, and has not forsaken the right of their God: they ask of me judgments of righteousness; they desire the drawing near of Elohim."* As the second prophecy of the first part takes as its basis a text from Micah (ch. ii. 1–4), so have we here in ver. 1*b* the echo of Mic. iii. 8. Not only with lisping lips (1 Sam. i. 13), but with the throat (Ps. cxv. 7, cxlix. 6); that is to say, with all the strength of the voice, lifting up the voice like the *shôphâr* (not a trumpet, which is called חֲצֹצְרָה, nor in fact any metallic instrument, but a bugle or signal horn, like that blown on new year's day : see at Ps. lxxxi. 4), *i.e.* in a shrill shouting tone. With a loud voice that must be heard, with the most unsparing publicity, the prophet is to point out to the people their deep moral wounds, which they may indeed hide from themselves with hypocritical *opus operatum*, but cannot conceal from the all-seeing God. The ו of וְאֹותִי does not stand for an explanatory particle, but for an adversative one : "their apostasy . . . their sins; and yet (although they are to be punished for these) they approach Jehovah every day" (יֹום יֹום with *mahpach* under the first יֹום, and *pasek* after it, as is the general rule between two like-sounding words), "that He would now speedily interpose." They also desire to know the ways which He intends to take for their deliverance, and by which He desires to lead them. This reminds us of the occurrence between Ezekiel and the elders of Gola (Ezek. xx. 1 sqq.; compare also Ezek. xxxiii. 30 sqq.). As if they had been a people whose rectitude of action and fidelity to the commands of God warranted them in expecting nothing but what was good in the future, they ask God (viz. in prayer and by inquiring of the prophet) for *mishpᵉtē tsedeq*, "righteous manifestations of judgment," *i.e.* such as will save them and destroy their foes, and desire *qirbath 'Elōhīm*, the coming of God, *i.e.* His saving *parousia*. The energetic futures, with the tone upon the last syllable, answer to their self-righteous presumption; and יֶחְפָּצוּן is repeated, according to Isaiah's most favourite oratorical figure (see p. 134), at the close of the verse.

There follow now the words of the work-righteous themselves, who hold up their fasting before the eyes of God, and complain that He takes no notice of it. And how could He?! Vers. 3, 4. "*'Wherefore do we fast and Thou seest not, afflict our soul and Thou regardest not?' Behold, on the day of your fasting ye carry on your business, and ye oppress all your labourers. Behold, ye fast with strife and quarrelling, and with smiting with the fist maliciously closed: ye do not fast now to make your voice audible on high.*" By the side of צוּם (root צָם, to press, tie up, constrain) we have here the older expression found in the Pentateuch, עִנָּה נֶפֶשׁ, to do violence to the natural life. In addition to the fasting on the day of atonement (the tenth of the seventh month Tizri), the only fast prescribed by the law, other fasts were observed according to Zech. vii. 3, viii. 19, viz. fasts to commemorate the commencement of the siege of Jerusalem (10th Tebeth), its capture (17th Tammuz), its destruction (9th Abib), and the murder of Gedaliah (3d Tizri). The exiles boast of this fasting here; but it is a heartless, dead work, and therefore worthless in the sight of God. There is the most glaring contrast between the object of the fast and their conduct on the fast-day: for they carry on their work-day occupation; they are then, more than at any other time, true taskmasters to their work-people (lest the service of the master should suffer from the service of God); and because when fasting they are doubly irritable and ill-tempered, this leads to quarrelling and strife, and even to striking with angry fist (בְּאֶגְרֹף, from גָּרַף, to collect together, make into a ball, clench). Hence in their present state the true purpose of fasting is quite unknown to them, viz. to enable them to draw near with importunate prayer to God, who is enthroned on high (ch. lvii. 15).[1] The only difficulty here is the phrase מְצֹא חֵפֶץ. In the face of ver. 13, this cannot have any other meaning than to stretch one's hand after occupation, to carry on business, to occupy one's self with it,—חֵפֶץ combining the three meanings, application or affairs, striving, and trade or occupation. מְצֹא, however, maintains its primary meaning, to lay hold of or grasp (cf. ch. x. 14; Targ. אַתּוּן תִּבְעִין צָרְכֵיכוֹן, ye seek your livelihood). This is sustained by what follows, whether we derive עַצְּבֵיכֶם (cf. חַלְּקֵי, ch. lvii. 6) from עָצַב (et omnes labores vestros graves rigide exigitis), נָגַשׂ (from which we have here תִּנְגֹּשׂוּ for תִּגֹּשׂ, Deut. xv. 3) being construed as in 2 Kings xxiii. 35 with the accusative of what is peremptorily demanded; or (what we certainly prefer) from עָצָב; or better still from עָצַב (like עָמָל): omnes operarios vestros adigitis (urgetis), נָגַשׂ being construed with the accusative of the person oppressed, as in Deut. xv. 2, where it is applied to the oppression of a debtor. Here, however, the reference is not to those who owe money, but to those who owe labour, or to obligations to labour; and עָצָב does not signify a debtor (an idea quite foreign to this verbal root), but a labourer, one who eats the bread of sorrows, or of hard toil (Ps. cxxvii. 2). The prophet paints throughout from the life; and we cannot be persuaded by Stier's false zeal for Isaiah's authorship to give up the opinion, that we have here a figure drawn from the life of the exiles in Babylon.

Whilst the people on the fast-day are carrying on their worldly, selfish, everyday business, the fasting is perverted from a means of divine worship and absorption in the spiritual character of the day to the most thoroughly selfish purposes: it is supposed to be of some worth and to merit some reward.

---

[1] The ancient church called a fast *statio*, because he who fasted had to wait in prayer day and night like a soldier at his post. See on this and what follows, the *Shepherd of Hermas*, iii. Sim. 5, and the *Epistle of Barnabas*, c. iii.

This work-holy delusion, behind which self-righteousness and unrighteousness were concealed, is met thus by Jehovah through His prophet: Vers. 5-7. *" Can such things as these pass for a fast that I have pleasure in, as a day for a man to afflict his soul? To bow down his head like a bulrush, and spread sackcloth and ashes under him—dost thou call this a fast and an acceptable day for Jehovah? Is not this a fast that I have pleasure in: To loose coils of wickedness, to untie the bands of the yoke, and for sending away the oppressed as free, and that ye break every kind of yoke? Is it not this, to break thy bread to the hungry, and to take the poor and houseless to thy home; when thou seest a naked man that thou clothest him, and dost not deny thyself before thine own flesh?"* The second part of the address commences with ver. 5. The true worship, which consists in works of merciful love to one's brethren, and its great promises are here placed in contrast with the false worship just described. הֲכָזֶה points backwards: is such a fast as this a fast after Jehovah's mind, a day on which it can be said in truth that a man afflicts his soul (Lev. xvi. 29)? The הֲ of הֲלָכֹף is resumed in הֲלָזֶה; the second לְ is the object to תִּקְרָא expressed as a dative. The first לְ answers to our preposition "to" with the infinitive, which stands here at the beginning like a *casus absol.* (to hang down; for which the *inf. abs.* הַכְפוֹף might also be used), and as in most other cases passes over into the finite (*et quod saccum et cinerem substernit*, viz. *sibi*: Ges. § 132, Anm. 2). To hang down the head and sit in sackcloth and ashes—this does not in itself deserve the name of fasting and of a day of gracious reception (ch. lvi. 7, lxi. 2) on the part of Jehovah (לַיהוה for a subjective genitive). Vers. 6 and 7 affirm that the fasting which is pleasant to Jehovah consists in something very different from this, namely, in releasing the oppressed, and in kindness to the helpless; not in abstinence from eating as such, but in sympathetic acts of that self-denying love, which gives up bread or any other possession for the sake of doing good to the needy.[1] There is a bitter irony in these words, just as when the ancients said, " not eating is a natural fast, but abstaining from sin is a spiritual fast." During the siege of Jerusalem by the Chaldeans a general

---

[1] The ancient church connected fasting with almsgiving by law. Dressel, *Patr. Ap.* p. 493.

emancipation of the slaves of Israelitish descent (who were to
be set free, according to the law, every three years) was resolved
upon and carried out; but as soon as the Chaldeans were gone,
the masters fetched their liberated slaves back into servitude
again (Jer. xxxiv. 8–22). And as ver. 6 shows, they carried
the same selfish and despotic disposition with them into
captivity. The זֶה which points forwards is expanded into infin.
absolutes, which are carried on quite regularly in the finite
tense. *Mōtâh*, which is repeated palindromically, signifies in
both cases a yoke, lit. *vectis*, the cross wood which formed the
most important part of the yoke, and which was fastened to the
animal's head, and so connected with the plough by means of
a cord or strap (Sir. xxx. 35, xxxiii. 27).[1] It is to this that
אֲגֻדּוֹת, knots, refers. We cannot connect it with *mutteh*, a state
of perverted right (Ezek. ix. 9), as Hitzig does. רְצוּצִים are
persons unjustly and forcibly oppressed even with cruelty; רָצַץ
is a stronger synonym to עָשַׁק (*e.g.* Amos iv. 1). In ver. 7 we
have the same spirit of general humanity as in Job xxxi. 13–23,
Ezek. xviii. 7, 8 (compare what James describes in ch. i. 27 as
"pure religion and undefiled"). פָּרַס (פָּרַשׂ) לֶחֶם is the usual
phrase for κλᾶν (κλάζειν) ἄρτον. מְרוּדִים is the adjective to
עֲנִיִּים, and apparently therefore must be derived from מָרַד:
miserable men who have shown themselves refractory towards
despotic rulers. But the participle *mârūd* cannot be found
elsewhere; and the recommendation to receive political fugitives
has a modern look. The parallels in Lam. i. 7 and iii. 19 are
conclusive evidence, that the word is intended as a derivative
of רוּד, to wander about, and it is so rendered in the LXX.,
Targ., and Jerome (*vagos*). But מָרוֹד, pl. מְרוּדִים, is no adjective;
and there is nothing to recommend the opinion, that by "wan-
derers" we are to understand Israelitish men. Ewald supposes
that מְרוּדִים may be taken as a *part. hoph.* for מוּרָדִים, hunted
away, like הממותים in 2 Kings xi. 2 (*keri* הַמֻּמָתִים); but it cannot

---

[1] I have already observed at ch. xlvii. 6, in vindication of what was
stated at ch. x. 27, that the yoke was not in the form of a collar. I
brought the subject under the notice of Prof. Schegg, who wrote to me
immediately after his return from his journey to Palestine to the following
effect: "I saw many oxen ploughing in Egypt, Palestine, Syria, and the
neighbourhood of Ephesus; and in every case the yoke was a cross piece
of wood laid upon the neck of the animal, and fastened to the pole of the
plough by a cord which passed under the neck of the animal."

be shown that the language allowed of this shifting of a vowel-sound. We prefer to assume that מְרוּדִים (persecuted) is re-garded as *part..pass.*, even if only *per metaplasmum*, from מָרַד, a secondary form of רוּד (cf. מָכַס, מָלַן, מָצַח, *makuna*). Ver. 7b is still the virtual subject to צוֹם אֶבְחָרֵהוּ. The apodosis to the hypothetical כִּי commences with a *perf. consec.*, which then passes into the pausal future תִּתְעַלָּם. In מִבְּשָׂרֶךָ (from thine own flesh) it is presupposed that all men form one united whole as being of the same flesh and blood, and that they form one family, owing to one another mutual love.

The prophet now proceeds to point out the reward of divine grace, which would follow such a fast as this, consisting of self-renouncing, self-sacrificing love; and in the midst of the promise he once more reminds of the fact, that this love is the condition of the promise. This divides the promises into two. The middle promise is linked on to the first; the morning dawn giving promise of the "perfect day" (Prov. iv. 18). The first series of promises we have in vers. 8, 9a. "*Then will thy light break forth as the morning dawn, and thy healing will sprout up speedily, and thy righteousness will go before thee, the glory of Jehovah will follow thee. Then wilt thou call and Jehovah will answer; thou wilt beseech, and He will say, Here am I!*" The love of God is called "light" in contrast with His wrath; and a quiet cheerful life in God's love is so called, in contrast with a wild troubled life spent in God's wrath. This life in God's love has its dawn and its noon-day. When it is night both within and around a man, and he suffers himself to be awakened by the love of God to a reciprocity of love; then does the love of God, like the rising sun, open for itself a way through the man's dark night and overcome the darkness of wrath, but so gradually that the sky within is at first only streaked as it were with the red of the morning dawn, the herald of the sun. A second figure of a promising character follows. The man is sick unto death; but when the love of God stimulates him to reciprocal love, he is filled with new vigour, and his recovery springs up suddenly; he feels within him a new life working through with energetic force like a miraculous springing up of verdure from the earth, or of growing and flowering plants. The only other passages in which אֲרוּכָה occurs are in the books of Jeremiah, Chronicles, and Nehemiah. It signifies recovery (LXX. here, τὰ ἰάματά σου ταχὺ ἀνατελεῖ, an old mistake for ἱμάτια, vestimenta), and hence general prosperity (2 Chron. xxiv. 13). It always occurs with the predicate עָלְתָה (causative הֶעֱלָה, cf. Targ. Ps. cxlvii. 3, אָסֵף אַרְכָּא, another reading אֲרוּכִין), oritur (for which we have here poetically germinat) alicui sanitas; hence Gesenius and others have inferred, that the word originally meant the binding up of a wound, bandage (imponitur alicui fascia). But the primary word is אָרַךְ = אָרַן, to set to rights, to restore or put into the right condition (e.g. b. Sabbath 33b, "he cured his wounded flesh"), connected with אָרֵיךְ, Arab. árak, accommodatus; so that אֲרוּכָה, after the form מְלוּכָה, Arab. (though rarely) arika, signifies properly, setting to rights, i.e. restoration.

The third promise is: "thy righteousness will go before thee, the glory of Jehovah will gather thee, or keep thee together," i.e. be thy rear-guard (LXX. περιστελεῖ σε, enclose thee with its protection; אָסַף as in מְאַסֵּף, ch. lii. 12). The figure is a significant one: the first of the mercies of God is δικαιοῦν, and the last δοξάζειν. When Israel is diligent in the performance of works of compassionate love, it is like an army on the march or a travelling caravan, for which righteousness clears and shows the way as being the most appropriate gift of God, and whose rear is closed by the glory of God, which so conducts it to its goal that not one is left behind. The fourth promise assures them of the immediate hearing of prayer, of every appeal to God, every cry for help.

But before the prophet brings his promises up to their culminating point, he once more lays down the condition upon which they rest. Vers. 9b–12. "*If thou put away from the midst of thee the yoke, the pointing of the finger, and speaking of evil, and offerest up thy gluttony to the hungry, and satisfiest the soul that is bowed down: thy light will stream out in the darkness, and thy darkness become like the brightness of noon-day. And Jehovah will guide thee continually, and satisfy thy soul in droughts, and refresh thy bones; and thou wilt become like a well-watered garden, and like a fountain, whose waters never deceive. And thy people will build ruins of the olden time, foundations of earlier generations wilt thou erect; and men will call thee repairers of breaches, restorers of habitable streets.*" מוֹטָה, a yoke, is here equivalent to yoking or oppression, as in ver. 6a, where it

stands by the side of רֶשַׁע. שְׁלַח־אֶצְבַּע (only met with here, for
שְׁלֹחַ, Ges. § 65, 1, a), the stretching out of the finger, signifies
a scornful pointing with the fingers (Prov. vi. 13, δακτυλο-
δεικτεῖν) at humbler men, and especially at such as are
godly (ch. lvii. 4). דַּבֶּר־אָוֶן, the utterance of things which are
wicked in themselves and injurious to one's neighbour, hence
sinful conversation in general. The early commentators looked
for more under נַפְשֶׁךָ, than is really meant (and so does even
Stier: "thy soul, thy heart, all thy sympathetic feelings," etc.).
The name of the soul, which is regarded here as greedily longing (ch. lvi. 11), is used in Deut. xxiv. 6 for that which nourishes
it, and here for that which it longs for; the longing itself
(appetitus) for the object of the longing (Psychol. p. 204).
We may see this very clearly from the choice of the verb תָּפֵק
(a voluntative in a conditional clause, Ges. § 128, 2), which,
starting from the primary meaning educere (related to נָפַק, Arabic
anfaqa, to give out, distribute, nafaqa, distribution, especially
of alms), signifies both to work out, acquire, carry off (Prov.
iii. 13, viii. 35, etc.), and also to take out, deliver, offer, ex-
promere (as in this instance and Ps. cxl. 9, cxliv. 13). The
soul "bowed down" is bowed down in this instance through
abstinence. The apodoses commence with the perf. cons. וְזָרַח.
אֲפֵלָה is the darkness caused by the utter absence of light (Arab.
afalat esh-shemsu, "the sun has become invisible"); see at
Job x. 22. This, as the substantive clause affirms, is like the
noon-day, which is called צָהֳרַיִם, because at that point the daylight of both the forenoon and afternoon, the rising and setting
light, is divided as it were into two by the climax which it has
attained. A new promise points to the fact, that such a man
may enjoy without intermission the mild and safe guidance of
divine grace, for which נָחָה (הִנְחָה, syn. נָהֵל) is the word commonly employed; and another to the communication of the
most copious supply of strength. The ἅπαξ γεγρ. בְּצַחְצָחוֹת
does not state with what God will satisfy the soul, as Hahn
supposes (after Jerome, "splendoribus"), but according to צְחִיחָה
(Ps. lxviii. 7) and such promises as ch. xliii. 20, xlviii. 21,
xlix. 10, the kind of satisfaction and the circumstances under
which it occurs, viz. in extreme droughts (Targ. "years of
drought"). In the place of the perf. cons. we have then the
future, which facilitates the elevation of the object: "and thy

bones will He make strong," יַחֲלִיץ, for which Hupfeld would
read יְחַלִּיף, "will He rejuvenate." הֶחֱלִיץ is a denom. of חָלִץ,
expeditus; it may, however, be directly derived from a verb חָלַץ,
presupposed by חֲלָצִים, not, however, in the meaning "to be fat"
(LXX. πιανθήσεται, and so also Kimchi), but "to be strong,"
lit. to be loose or ready for action; and *b. Jebamoth* 102*b*
has the very suitable gloss זרוזי גרמי (making the bones strong).
This idea of invigorating is then unfolded in two different
figures, of which that of a well-watered garden sets forth the
abundance received, that of a spring the abundance possessed.
Natural objects are promised, but as a gift of grace; for this
is the difference between the two testaments, that in the Old
Testament the natural is ever striving to reach the spiritual,
whereas in the New Testament the spiritual lifts up the natural
to its own level. The Old Testament is ever striving to give
inwardness to what was outward; in the New Testament this
object is attained, and the further object now is to make the
outward conformed to the inward, the natural life to the
spiritual. The last promise (whether the seventh or eighth,
depends upon whether we include the growing of the morning
light into the light of noon, or not) takes its form from the
pining of the exiles for their home: "and thy people (מִמְּךָ)
build" (Ewald, § 295, *c*); and Böttcher would read וּבָנוּ מִמָּךְ; but
מִן with a passive, although more admissible in Hebrew than in
Arabic, is very rarely met with, and then more frequently in the
sense of ἀπό than in that of ὑπό, and בְּנֵי followed by a plural
of the thing would be more exact than customary. Moreover,
there is no force in the objection that מִמְּךָ with the active can
only signify "some of thee," since it is equivalent to אֲשֶׁר מִמָּךְ,
those who sprang from thee and belong to thee by kindred
descent. The members born to the congregation in exile will
begin, as soon as they return to their home, to build up again
the ruins of olden time, the foundations of earlier generations,
i.e. houses and cities of which only the foundations are left
(ch. lxi. 4); therefore Israel restored to its fatherland receives
the honourable title of "builder of breaches," "restorer of streets
(*i.e.* of places much frequented once) לָשֶׁבֶת" (for inhabiting),
i.e. so that, although so desolate now (ch. xxxiii. 8), they become
habitable and populous once more.

The third part of the prophecy now adds to the duties of

human love the duty of keeping the Sabbath, together with equally great promises; *i.e.* it adds the duties of the first table to those of the second, for the service of works is sanctified by the service of worship. Vers. 13, 14. " *If thou hold back thy foot from the Sabbath, from doing thy business on my holy day, and callest the Sabbath a delight, the holy of Jehovah, reverer, and honourest it, not doing thine own ways, not pursuing thy business and speaking words : then wilt thou have delight in Jehovah, and I will cause thee to ride upon the high places of the land, and make thee enjoy the inheritance of Jacob thy forefather, for the mouth of Jehovah hath spoken it.*" The duty of keeping the Sabbath is also enforced by Jeremiah (ch. xvii. 19 sqq.) and Ezekiel (ch. xx. 12 sqq., xxii. 8, 26), and the neglect of this duty severely condemned. Ch. lvi. has already shown the importance attached to it by our prophet. The Sabbath, above all other institutions appointed by the law, was the true means of uniting and sustaining Israel as a religious community, more especially in exile, where a great part of the worship necessarily fell into abeyance on account of its intimate connection with Jerusalem and the holy land ; but whilst it was a Mosaic institution so far as its legal appointments were concerned, it rested, in a way which reached even beyond the rite of circumcision, upon a basis much older than that of the law, being a ceremonial copy of the Sabbath of creation, which was the divine rest established by God as the true object of all motion; for God entered into Himself again after He had created the world out of Himself, that all created things might enter into Him. In order that this, the great end set before all creation, and especially before mankind, viz. entrance into the rest of God, might be secured, the keeping of the Sabbath prescribed by the law was a divine method of education, which put an end every week to the ordinary avocations of the people, with their secular influence and their tendency to fix the mind on outward things, and was designed by the strict prohibition of all work to force them to enter into themselves and occupy their minds with God and His word. The prophet does not hedge round this commandment to keep the Sabbath with any new precepts, but merely demands for its observance full truth answering to the spirit of the letter. " If thou turn away thy foot from the Sabbath " is equivalent to, if thou do not tread upon its holy

ground with a foot occupied with its everyday work. עֲשׂוֹת
which follows is not elliptical (= מֵעֲשׂוֹת answering to מִשַּׁבָּת,
an unnecessary and mistaken assumption), but an explanatory
permutative of the object "thy foot:" "turn away thy foot,"
viz. from attending to thy business (a defective plural) on my
holy day. Again, if thou call (*i.e.* from inward contemplation
and esteem) the Sabbath a pleasure (ʿōneg, because it leads thee
to God, and not a burden because it leads thee away from
thine everyday life; cf. Amos viii. 5) and the holy one of
Jehovah (on this masculine personification of the Sabbath, see
ch. lvi. 2), "mᵉkhubbâd," honoured = honourable, *honorandus*
(see vol. i. p. 128), and if thou truly honourest him, whom
Jehovah has invested with the splendour of His own glory
(Gen. ii. 3 : " and sanctified it "), "not" (מֵן = ὥστε μή) " to
perform thy ways" (the ordinary ways which relate to self-
preservation, not to God), " not to attend to thine own business"
(see at ver. 3) " and make words," viz. words of vain useless
character and needless multitude (דַּבֵּר־דָּבָר as in Hos. x. 4,
denoting unspiritual gossip and boasting) ;[1] then, just as the
Sabbath is thy pleasure, so wilt thou have thy pleasure in
Jehovah, *i.e.* enjoy His delightful fellowship (תִּתְעַנַּג עַל־ה', a
promise as in Job xxii. 26), and He will reward thee for thy

---

[1] Hitzig observes, that " the law of the Sabbath has already received
the Jewish addition, ʿ speaking is work.ʾ " But from the premiss that the
sabbatical rest of God was rest from speaking His creating word (Ps.
xxxiii. 6), all the conclusion that tradition has ever drawn is, that on the
Sabbath men must *to a certain extent* rest מהדבור as well as ממעשה ; and
when R. Simon b. Jochai exclaimed to his loquacious old mother on the
Sabbath, "Keeping the Sabbath means keeping silence," his meaning was
not that talking in itself was working and therefore all conversation was
forbidden on the Sabbath. Tradition never went as far as this. The
rabbinical exposition of the passage before us is the following : " Let not
thy talking on the Sabbath be the same as that on working days ;" and
when it is stated once in the Jerusalem Talmud that the Rabbins could
hardly bring themselves to allow of friendly greetings on the Sabbath, it
certainly follows from this, that they did not forbid them. Even the
author of the שׁ"לה (שׁני לוחות הברית) with its excessive ceremonial stringency goes no further than this, that on the Sabbath men must abstain
from דברי חול. And is it possible that our prophet can have been more
stringent than the strictest traditionalists, and wished to make the keeper
of the Sabbath a Carthusian monk ? There could not be a more thorough
perversion of the spirit of prophecy than this.

renunciation of earthly advantages with a victorious reign, with an unapproachable possession of the high places of the land— *i.e.* chiefly, though not exclusively, of the promised land, which shall then be restored to thee,—and with the free and undisputed usufruct of the inheritance promised to thy forefather Jacob (Ps. cv. 10, 11; Deut. xxxii. 13 and xxxiii. 29);—this will be thy glorious reward, for the mouth of Jehovah hath spoken it. Thus does Isaiah confirm the predictions of ch. i. 20 and xl. 25 (compare ch. xxiv. 3 and the passages quoted at vol. i. p. 425).

SECOND PROPHECY.—Chap. LIX.

THE EXISTING WALL OF PARTITION BROKEN DOWN AT LAST.

This second prophetic address continues the reproachful theme of the first. In the previous prophecy we found the virtues which are well-pleasing to God, and to which He promises redemption as a reward of grace, set in contrast with those false means, upon which the people rested their claim to redemption. In the prophecy before us the sins which retard redemption are still more directly exposed. Vers. 1, 2. " *Behold, Jehovah's hand is not too short to help, nor His ear too heavy to hear; but your iniquities have become a party-wall between you and your God, and your sins have hidden His face from you, so that He does not hear.*" The reason why redemption is delayed, is not that the power of Jehovah has not been sufficient for it (cf. ch. l. 2), or that He has not been aware of their desire for it, but that their iniquities (עֲוֹנֹתֵיכֶם with the second syllable defective) have become dividers (מַבְדִּלִים, defective), have grown into a party-wall between them and their God, and their sins (cf. Jer. v. 25) have hidden *pânīm* from them. As the " hand" (*yâd*) in ch. xxviii. 2 is the *absolute* hand; so here the " face" (*pânīm*) is that face which sees everything, which is everywhere present, whether uncovered or concealed; which diffuses light when it unveils itself, and leaves darkness when it is veiled; the sight of which is blessedness, and not to see which is damnation. This absolute countenance is never to be seen in this life without a veil; but the rejection and abuse of grace make this veil a perfectly impenetrable covering. And Israel had forfeited in this way the

light and sight of this countenance of God, and had raised a
party-wall between itself and Him, and that מִשְּׁמוֹעַ, so that He
did not hear, *i.e.* so that their prayer did not reach Him (Lam.
iii. 44) or bring down an answer from Him.

The sins of Israel are sins in words and deeds. Ver. 3.
" *For your hands are defiled with blood, and your fingers with
iniquity; your lips speak lies, your tongue murmurs wickedness.*"
The verb גָּאַל, to spot (see ch. lxiii. 3), is a later softening down
of גָּעַל (*e.g.* 2 Sam. i. 21); and in the place of the niphal נִגְאַל
(Zeph. iii. 1), we have here, as in Lam. iv. 14, the double passive
form נְגֹאַל, compounded of niphal and pual. The post-biblical
nithpaël, compounded of the *niphal* and the *hithpael,* is a mixed
form of the same kind, though we also meet with it in a few
biblical passages (Deut. xxi. 8; Prov. xxvii. 15; Ezek. xxiii.
48). The verb *hâgâh* (LXX. μελετᾶ) combines the two
meanings of " thought" (meditation or reflection), and of a
light low " expression," half inward half outward.

The description now passes over to the social and judicial
life. Lying and oppression universally prevail. Vers. 4–6.
" *No one speaks with justice, and no one pleads with faithfulness;
men trust in vanity, and speak with deception; they conceive
trouble, and bring forth ruin. They hatch basilisks' eggs, and
weave spiders' webs. He that eateth of their eggs must die; and
if one is trodden upon, it splits into an adder. Their webs do
not suffice for clothing, and men cannot cover themselves with
their works: their works are works of ruin, and the practice of
injustice is in their hands.*" As קָרָא is generally used in these
prophetic addresses in the sense of κηρύσσειν, and the judicial
meaning, *citare, in jus vocare, litem intendere,* cannot be sustained, we must adopt this explanation, " no one gives public
evidence with justice" (LXX. οὐδεὶς λαλεῖ δίκαια). צֶדֶק is firm
adherence to the rule of right and truth; אֱמוּנָה a conscientious
reliance which awakens trust; מִשְׁפָּט (in a reciprocal sense, as
in ch. xliii. 26, lxvi. 16) signifies the commencement and pursuit of a law-suit with any one. The abstract infinitives which
follow in ver. 4*b* express the general characteristics of the
social life of that time, after the manner of the historical infinitive in Latin (cf. ch. xxi. 5; Ges. § 131, 4, *b*). Men trust
in *tôhū,* that which is perfectly destitute of truth, and speak
שָׁוְא, what is morally corrupt and worthless. The double figure

הָרוּ עָמָל וְהוֹלֵיד אָוֶן is taken from Job xv. 35 (cf. Ps. vii. 15). הָרוּ (compare the *poel* in ver. 13) is only another form for הָרָה (Ges. § 131, 4, *b*); and הוֹלֵיד (the western or Palestinian reading here), or הוֹלֵד (the oriental or Babylonian reading), is the usual form of the *inf. abs. hiph.* (Ges. § 53, Anm. 2). What they carry about with them and set in operation is compared in ver. 5*a* to basilisks' eggs (צִפְעוֹנִי, *serpens regulus*, as in ch. xi. 8) and spiders' webs (עַכָּבִישׁ, as in Job viii. 14, from עָכַב, possibly in the sense of squatter, sitter still, with the substantive ending *îsh;* see Jeshurun, p. 228). They hatch basilisks' eggs (בִּקֵּעַ like בָּקַע, ch. xxxiv. 15, a perfect, denoting that which has hitherto always taken place and therefore is a customary thing); and they spin spiders' webs (אֶרֶג possibly related to ἀράχ-νη;[1] the future denoting that which goes on occurring). The point of comparison in the first figure is the injurious nature of all they do, whether men rely upon it, in which case "he that eateth of their eggs dieth," or whether they are bold or imprudent enough to try and frustrate their plans and performances, when that (the egg) which is crushed or trodden upon splits into an adder, *i.e.* sends out an adder, which snaps at the heel of the disturber of its rest. זוּר as in Job xxxix. 15, here the *part. pass. fem.* like סוּרָה (ch. xlix. 21), with ־ָ instead of ־ָ, like לְנֶה, the original *ă* of the feminine (*zûrăth*) having returned from its lengthening into *ā* to the weaker lengthening into *ĕ*. The point of comparison in the second figure is the worthlessness and deceptive character of their works. What they spin and make does not serve for a covering to any man (יִתְכַּפּוּ with the most general subject: Ges. § 137, 3), but has simply the appearance of usefulness; their works are מַעֲשֵׂי־אָוֶן (with *metheg*, not *munach*, under the *Mem*), evil works, and their acts are all directed to the injury of their neighbour, in his right and his possession.

This evil doing of theirs rises even to hatred, the very opposite of that love which is well-pleasing to God. Ver. 7. "*Their feet run to evil, and make haste to shed innocent blood:*

---

[1] Neither χαῖρος nor ἀράχνη has hitherto been traced to an Indian root in any admissible way. Benfey deduces the former from the root *dhvri* (to twist); but this root has to perform an immense number of services M. Müller deduces the latter from *rak;* but this means to make, not to spin.

their thoughts are thoughts of wickedness; wasting and destruction are in their paths." Paul has interwoven this passage into his description of the universal corruption of morals, in Rom. iii. 15–17. The comparison of life to a road, and of a man's conduct to walking, is very common in proverbial sayings. The prophet has here taken from them both his simile and his expressions. We may see from ver. 7*a*, that during the captivity the true believers were persecuted even to death by their countrymen, who had forgotten God. The verbs יָרֻצּוּ and וִימַהֲרוּ (the proper reading, with *metheg*, not *munach*, under the מ) depict the pleasure taken in wickedness, when the conscience is thoroughly lulled to sleep.

Their whole nature is broken up into discord. Ver. 8. " *The way of peace they know not, and there is no right in their roads: they make their paths crooked: every one who treads upon them knows no peace.*" With דֶּרֶךְ, the way upon which a man goes, the prophet uses interchangeably (here and in ver. 7) מְסִלָּה, a high-road thrown up with an embankment; מַעְגָּל (with the plural in *îm* and *ôth*), a carriage-road; and נְתִיבָה, a footpath formed by the constant passing to and fro of travellers. Peaceable conduct, springing from a love of peace, and aiming at producing peace, is altogether strange to them; no such thing is to be met with in their path as the recognition or practice of right: they make their paths for themselves (לָהֶם, *dat. ethicus*), *i.e.* most diligently, twisting about; and whoever treads upon them (*bâh*, neuter, as in ch. xxvii. 4), forfeits all enjoyment of either inward or outward peace. *Shâlôm* is repeated significantly, in Isaiah's peculiar style, at the end of the verse. The first strophe of the prophecy closes here: it was from no want of power or willingness on the part of God, that He had not come to the help of His people; the fault lay in their own sins.

In the second strophe the prophet includes himself when speaking of the people. They now mourn over that state of exhaustion into which they have been brought through the perpetual straining and disappointment of expectation, and confess those sins on account of which the righteousness and salvation of Jehovah have been withheld. The prophet is speaking communicatively here; for even the better portion of the nation was involved in the guilt and consequences of the

corruption which prevailed among the exiles, inasmuch as a
nation forms an organized whole, and the delay of redemption
really affected them. Vers. 9–11. " *Therefore right remains
far from us, and righteousness does not overtake us ; we hope for
light, and behold darkness ; for brightness—we walk in thick darkness. We grope along the wall like the blind, and like eyeless
men we grope : we stumble in the light of noon-day as in the darkness, and among the living like the dead. We roar all like bears,
and moan deeply like doves : we hope for right, and it cometh not ;
for salvation—it remaineth far off from us.*" At the end of this
group of verses, again, the thought with which it sets out is
palindromically repeated. The perfect רָחֲקָה denotes a state of
things reaching from the past into the present ; the future
תַשִּׂיגֵנוּ a state of things continuing unchangeable in the present.
By *mishpât* we understand a solution of existing inequalities or
incongruities through the judicial interposition of God ; by
ts͏ᵉdâqâh the manifestation of justice, which bestows upon Israel
grace as its right in accordance with the plan of salvation
after the long continuance of punishment, and pours out
merited punishment upon the instruments employed in punishing Israel. The prophet's standpoint, whether a real or an
ideal one, is the last decade of the captivity. At that time,
about the period of the Lydian war, when Cyrus was making
one prosperous stroke after another, and yet waited so long
before he turned his arms against Babylon, it may easily be
supposed that hope and despondency alternated incessantly in
the minds of the exiles. The dark future, which the prophet
penetrated in the light of the Spirit, was indeed broken up by
rays of hope, but it did not amount to light, *i.e.* to a perfect
lighting up (*nᵉgōhōth*, an intensified plural of *nᵉgōhâh*, like
nᵉkhōchōth in ch. xxvi. 10, pl. of *nᵉkhōchâh* in ver. 14) ; on the
contrary, darkness was still the prevailing state, and in the deep
thick darkness (*'ăphēlōth*) the exiles pined away, without the
promised release being effected for them by the oppressor of
the nations. "We grope," they here complain, "like blind
men by a wall, in which there is no opening, and like eyeless
men we grope." נְגַשֵּׁשׁ (only used here) is a synonym of the
older מִשֵּׁשׁ (Deut. xxviii. 29) ; נִגְשְׁשָׁה (with the elision of the
reduplication, which it is hardly possible to render audible, and
which comes up again in the pausal נְגַשֵּׁשָׁה) has the *ah* of force,

here of the impulse to self-preservation, which leads them to grope for an outlet in this ἀπορία; and עֵינַיִם אֵין is not quite synonymous with עִוְרִים, for there is such a thing as blindness with apparently sound eyes (cf. ch. xliii. 8); and there is also a real absence of eyes, on account of either a natural malformation, or the actual loss of the eyes through either external injury or disease. In the lamentation which follows, " we stumble in the light of noon-day (צָהֳרַיִם, *meridies* = *mesidies*, the culminating point at which the eastern light is separated from the western) as if it were darkness, and בָּאִשְׁמַנִּים, as if we were dead men," we may infer from the parallelism that since בָּאִשְׁמַנִּים must express some antithesis to כַּמֵּתִים, it cannot mean either *in caliginosis* (Jer., Luther, etc.), or "in the graves" (Targ., D. Kimchi, etc.), or " in desolate places" (J. Kimchi). Moreover, there is no such word in Hebrew as אָשֵׁם, to be dark, although the lexicographers give a Syriac word אוּתְמָנָא, thick darkness (possibly related to عَتَمَة, which does not mean the dark night, but late in the night); and the verb *shâmēn*, to be fat, is never applied to "fat, *i.e.* thick darkness," as Knobel assumes, whilst the form of the word with נ *c. dagesh* precludes the meaning a solitary place or desert (from אָשֵׁם = שָׁמֵם). The form in question points rather to the verbal stem שָׁמֵן, which yields a fitting antithesis to כמתים, whether we explain it as meaning "in luxuriant fields," or "among the fat ones, *i.e.* those who glory in their abundant health." We prefer the latter, since the word *mishmannīm* (Dan. xi. 24; cf. Gen. xxvii. 28) had already been coined to express the other idea; and as a rule, words formed with א *prosth.* point rather to an attributive than to a substantive idea. אָשְׁמָן is a more emphatic form of שָׁמֵן (Judg. iii. 29); [1] and אַשְׁמַנִּים indicates indirectly the very same thing which is directly expressed by מִשְׁמַנִּים in ch. x. 16. Such explanations as "*in opimis rebus*" (Stier, etc.), or "in fat-

---

[1] The name of the Phœnician god of health and prosperity, viz. Esmoun, which Alois Müller (Esmun, *ein Beitrag zur Mythologie des orient. Alterthums.* 1864) traces to חַשְׁמָן (Ps. lxviii. 32) from אשם = חשם, "the splendid one (*illustris*)," probably means "the healthy one, or one of full health" (after the form אֶשְׁחוּר, אֲשְׁמוּרָה), which agrees somewhat better with the account of Photios : Ἐσμουνον ὑπὸ Φοινίκων ὠνομασμένον ἐπὶ τῇ θέρμῃ τῆς ζωῆς.

ness of body, *i.e.* fulness of life" (Böttcher), are neither so
suitable to the form of the word, nor do they answer to the
circumstances referred to here, where all the people in exile
are speaking. The true meaning therefore is, "we stumble
(reel about) among fat ones, or those who lead a merry life," as
if we were dead. "And what," as Dœderlein observes, "can
be imagined more gloomy and sad, than to be wandering about
like shades, while others are fat and flourishing?" The growl-
ing and moaning in ver. 11 are expressions of impatience and
pain produced by longing. The people now fall into a state of
impatience, and roar like bears (*hámáh* like *fremere*), as when,
for example, a bear scents a flock, and prowls about it (*vesper-
tinus circumgemit ursus ovile :* Hor. *Ep.* xvi. 51); and now
again they give themselves up to melancholy, and moan in a
low and mournful tone like the doves, *quarum blanditias ver-
baque murmur habet* (Ovid). הָגָה, like *murmurare*, expresses
less depth of tone or *raucitas* than הָמָה. All their looking
for righteousness and salvation turns out again and again to
be nothing but self-deception, when the time for their coming
seems close at hand.

The people have already indicated by עַל־כֵּן in ver. 9 that
this benighted, hopeless state is the consequence of their prevailing sins; they now come back to this, and strike the note
of penitence (*viddui*), which is easily recognised by the recurring rhymes *ánu* and *ênu*. The prophet makes the confession
(as in Jer. xiv. 19, 20, cf. iii. 21 sqq.), standing at the head of
the people as the leader of their prayer (*ba‘al tᵉphillâh*) : Vers.
12, 13. "*For our transgressions are many before Thee, and our
sins testify against us; for our transgressions are known to us, and
our evil deeds well known : apostasy and denial of Jehovah, and
turning back from following our God, oppressive and false speaking, receiving and giving out from the heart words of falsehood.*"
The people acknowledge the multitude and magnitude of their
apostate deeds, which are the object of the omniscience of
God, and their sins which bear witness against them (עָנְתָה the
predicate of a neuter plural; Ges. § 146, 3). The second כִּי
resumes the first : "our apostate deeds are with us (אֵת as in
Job xii. 3 ; cf. עִם, Job xv. 9), *i.e.* we are conscious of them ;
and our misdeeds, we know them " (יְדַעֲנוּם for ידענן, as in Gen.
xli. 23, cf. 6, and with עֲ, as is always the case with verbs ל״ע

before ב, and with a suffix; Ewald, § 60). The sins are now enumerated in ver. 13 in abstract infinitive forms. At the head stands apostasy in thought and deed, which is expressed as a threefold sin. בַּה׳ (of Jehovah) belongs to both the "apostasy" (treachery; e.g. ch. i. 2) and the "denial" (Jer. v. 12). נָסוֹג is an inf. abs. (different from Ps. lxxx. 19). Then follow sins against the neighbour: viz. such speaking as leads to oppression, and consists of sârâh, that which deviates from or is opposed to the law and truth (Deut. xix. 16); also the conception (concipere) of lying words, and the utterance of them from the heart in which they are conceived (Matt. xv. 18, xii. 35). הֹרוֹ and הֹגוֹ are the only poel infinitives which occur in the Old Testament, just as שׁוֹשֵׂתִי (ch. x. 13) is the only example of a poel perfect of a verb ל״ה. The poël is suitable throughout this passage, because the action expressed affects others, and is intended to do them harm. According to Ewald, the poel indicates the object or tendency: it is the conjugation employed to denote seeking, attacking, or laying hold of; e.g. לוֹשֵׁן, lingua petere, i.e. to calumniate; עֹיֵן, oculo petere, i.e. to envy.

The confession of personal sins is followed by that of the sinful state of society. Vers. 14, 15a. "And right is forced back, and righteousness stands afar off; for truth has fallen in the market-place, and honesty finds no admission. And truth became missing, and he who avoids evil is outlawed." In connection with mishpât and tsᵉdâqâh here, we have not to think of the manifestation of divine judgment and justice which is prevented from being realized; but the people are here continuing the confession of their own moral depravity. Right has been forced back from the place which it ought to occupy (hissîg is the word applied in the law to the removal of boundaries), and righteousness has to look from afar off at the unjust habits of the people, without being able to interpose. And why are right and righteousness—that united pair so pleasing to God and beneficial to man—thrust out of the nation, and why do they stand without? Because there is no truth or uprightness in the nation. Truth wanders about, and stands no longer in the midst of the nation; but upon the open street, the broad market-place, where justice is administered, and where she ought above all to stand upright and be preserved upright, she has stumbled and fallen down (cf. ch. iii. 8) ; and honesty (*n°khochah*), which goes straight forward, would gladly enter the limits of the forum, but she cannot : people and judges alike form a barrier which keeps her back. The consequence of this is indicated in ver. 15*a* : truth in its manifold practical forms has become a missing thing; and whoever avoids the existing voice is *mishtolēl* (*part. hithpoel*, not *hithpoal*), one who is obliged to let himself be plundered and stripped (Ps. lxxvi. 6), to be made a *sholal* (Mic. i. 8), Arab. *maslub*, with a passive turn given to the reflective meaning, as in הִתְחַפֵּשׂ, to cause one's self to be spied out = to disguise one's self, and as in the so-called *niphal tolerativum* (Ewald, 133, *b*, 2).

The third strophe of the prophecy commences at ver. 15*b* or ver. 16. It begins with threatening, and closes with promises ; for the true nature of God is love, and every manifestation of wrath is merely one phase in its development. In consideration of the fact that this corrupt state of things furnishes no prospect of self-improvement, Jehovah has already equipped Himself for judicial interposition. Vers. 15*b*–18. "*And Jehovah saw it, and it was displeasing in His eyes, that there was no right. And He saw that there was not a man anywhere, and was astonished that there was nowhere an intercessor : then His arm brought Him help, and His righteousness became His stay. And He put on righteousness as a coat of mail, and the helmet of salvation upon His head ; and put on garments of vengeance as armour, and clothed Himself in zeal as in a cloak. According to the deeds, accordingly He will repay : burning wrath to His adversaries, punishment to His foes ; the islands He will repay with chastisement.*" The prophet's language has now toilsomely worked its way through the underwood of keen reproach, of dark descriptions of character, and of mournful confession which has brought up the apostasy of the great mass in all the blacker colours before his mind, from the fact that the confession proceeds from those who are ready for salvation. And now, having come to the description of the approaching judgment, out of whose furnace the church of the future is to spring, it rises again like a palm-tree that has been violently hurled to the ground, and shakes its head as if restored to itself in the transforming ether of the future.

Jehovah saw, and it excited His displeasure ("it was evil in
His eyes," an antiquated phrase from the Pentateuch, *e.g.*
Gen. xxxviii. 10) to see that right (which He loves, ch. lxi. 8;
Ps. xxxvii. 28) had vanished from the life of His nation. He
saw that there was no man there, no man possessing either the
disposition or the power to stem this corruption (אִישׁ as in Jer.
v. 1, cf. 1 Sam. iv. 9, 1 Kings ii. 2, and the old Jewish saying, "Where there is no man, I strive to be a man"). He was
astonished (the sight of such total depravity exciting in Him
the highest degree of compassion and displeasure) that there
was no מַפְגִּיעַ, *i.e.* no one to step in between God and the people,
and by his intercession to press this disastrous condition of the
people upon the attention of God (see ch. liii. 12) ; no one to
form a wall against the coming ruin, and cover the rent with
his body ; no one to appease the wrath, like Aaron (Num. xvii.
12, 13) or Phinehas (Num. xxv. 7). What the *fut. consec.*
affirms from וַתּוֹשַׁע onwards, is not something to come, but
something past, as distinguished from the coming events announced from ver. 18 onwards. Because the nation was so
utterly and deeply corrupt, Jehovah had equipped Himself
for judicial interposition. The equipment was already completed ; only the taking of vengeance remained to be effected.
Jehovah saw no man at His side who was either able or willing
to help Him to His right in opposition to the prevailing abominations, or to support His cause. Then His own arm became
His help, and His righteousness His support (cf. ch. lxiii. 5) ;
so that He did not desist from the judgment to which He felt
Himself impelled, until He had procured the fullest satisfaction for the honour of His holiness (ch. v. 16). The armour
which Jehovah puts on is now described. According to the
scriptural view, Jehovah is never unclothed ; but the free
radiation of His own nature shapes itself into a garment of
light. Light is the robe He wears (Ps. civ. 2). When the
prophet describes this garment of light as changed into a suit
of armour, this must be understood in the same sense as when
the apostle in Eph. vi. speaks of a Christian's panoply. Just
as there the separate pieces of armour represent the manifold
self-manifestations of the inward spiritual life, so here the
pieces of Jehovah's armour stand for the manifold self-manifestations of His holy nature, which consist of a mixture of

wrath and love. He does not arm Himself from any outward
armoury; but the armoury is His infinite wrath and His
infinite love, and the might in which He manifests Himself
in such and such a way to His creatures is His infinite will.
He puts on righteousness as a coat of mail (שִׁרְיָן in half pause,
as in 1 Kings xxii. 34 in full pause, for שִׁרְיוֹן, ō passing into
the broader â, as is generally the case in יַחְפֹּן, יַחְבֹּשׁ; also in
Gen. xliii. 14, שִׁכֻּלְתִּי; xlix. 3, עָז; xlix. 27, יִטְרָף), so that His
appearance on every side is righteousness; and on His head
He sets the helmet of salvation: for the ultimate object for
which He goes into the conflict is the redemption of the
oppressed, salvation as the fruit of the victory gained by
righteousness. And over the coat of mail He draws on clothes
of vengeance as a tabard (LXX. περιβόλαιον), and wraps
Himself in zeal as in a war-cloak. The inexorable justice of
God is compared to an impenetrable brazen coat of mail; His
joyful salvation, to a helmet which glitters from afar; His
vengeance, with its manifold inflictions of punishment, to the
clothes worn above the coat of mail; and His wrathful zeal
(קִנְאָה from קָנָא, to be deep red) with the fiery-looking chlamys.
No weapon is mentioned, neither sword nor bow; for His
own arm procures Him help, and this alone. But what will
Jehovah do, when He has armed Himself thus with justice
and salvation, vengeance and zeal? As ver. 18 affirms, He
will carry out a severe and general retributive judgment. גְּמוּל
and גְּמֻלָה signify accomplishment of (on gâmal, see at ch. iii. 9)
a ῥῆμα μέσον; גְּמֻלוֹת, which may signify, according to the context, either manifestations of love or manifestations of wrath,
and either retribution as looked at from the side of God, or
forfeiture as regarded from the side of man, has the latter
meaning here, viz. the works of men and the double-sided
gᵉmūl, i.e. repayment, and that in the infliction of punishment. כְּעַל, as if, as on account of, signifies, according to its
Semitic use, in the measure (כְּ) of that which is fitting (עַל);
cf. ch. lxiii. 7, uti par est propter. It is repeated with emphasis (like לְכֵן in ch. lii. 6); the second stands without rectum,
as the correlate of the first. By the adversaries and enemies,
we naturally understand, after what goes before, the rebellious
Israelites. The prophet does not mention these, however, but
"the islands," that is to say, the heathen world. He hides the

special judgment upon Israel in the general judgment upon
the nations. The very same fate falls upon Israel, the salt of
the world which has lost its savour, as upon the whole of the
ungodly world. The purified church will have its place in the
midst of a world out of which the crying injustice has been
swept away.

The prophet now proceeds to depict the יְשׁוּעָה, the symbol
of which is the helmet upon Jehovah's head. Vers. 19, 20.
"*And they will fear the name of Jehovah from the west, and
His glory from the rising of the sun: for He will come like a
stream dammed up, which a tempest of Jehovah drives away.
And a Redeemer comes for Zion, and for those who turn from
apostasy in Jacob, saith Jehovah.*" Instead of וְיִרְאוּ, Knobel
would strike out the *metheg*, and read וְיִרְאוּ, "and they will see;"
but "seeing the name of Jehovah" (the usual expression is
"seeing His glory") is a phrase that cannot be met with,
though it is certainly a passable one; and the relation in
which ver. 19*b* stands to 19*a* does not recommend the altera-
tion, since ver. 19*b* attributes that general fear of the name of
Jehovah (cf. Deut. xxviii. 58) and of His glory (see the parallel
overlooked by Knobel, Ps. cii. 16), which follows the manifestation of judgment on the part of Jehovah, to the manner in
which this manifestation occurs. Moreover, the true Masoretic
reading in this passage is not וְיִרְאוּ (as in Mic. vii. 17), but
וְיִירְאוּ (see Norzi). The two מִן in מִמַּעֲרָב (with the indispensable *metheg* before the *chateph*, and a second to ensure clearness of pronunciation) [1] and וּמִמִּזְרַח־שֶׁמֶשׁ (also with the so-called
strong *metheg*) [2] indicate the *terminus a quo*. From all quarters
of the globe will fear of the name and of the glory of Jehovah
become naturalized among the nations of the world. For
when God has withdrawn His name and His glory from the
world's history, as during the Babylonian captivity (and also at
the present time), the return of both is all the more intense and
extraordinary; and this is represented here in a figure which
recals ch. xxx. 27, 28, x. 22, 23 (cf. Ezek. xliii. 2). The
accentuation, which gives *pashta* to בַּנָּהָר, does indeed appear to
make צָר the subject, either in the sense of oppressor or adversary, as in Lam. iv. 12, or in that of oppression, as in ch. xxv. 4,

---

[1] See the law in Bär's *Metheg-Setzung*, § 29.
[2] See *idem*, § 28.

xxvi. 16, xxx. 20. The former is quite out of the question, since no such transition to a human instrument of the retributive judgment could well take place after the חֵמָה לְצָרָיו in ver. 18. In support of the latter, it would be possible to quote ch. xlviii. 18 and lxvi. 12, since צר is the antithesis to *shâlōm*. But according to such parallels as ch. xxx. 27, 28, it is incomparably more natural to take Jehovah (His name, His glory) as the subject. Moreover, בּוֹ, which must in any case refer to כנהר, is opposed to the idea that צר is the subject, to which בו would have the most natural claim to be referred,—an explanation indeed which Stier and Hahn have really tried, taking נוססה as in Ps. lx. 4, and rendering it "The Spirit of Jehovah holds up a banner against him, viz. the enemy." If, however, Jehovah is the subject to יָבֹא, כַּנָּהָר צָר must be taken together (like מְכַסִּים . . . כַּמַּיִם, ch. xi. 9; רוּחֲךָ טוֹבָה, Ps. cxliii. 10; Ges. § 111, 2, *b*), either in the sense of "a hemming stream," one causing as it were a state of siege (from *tsūr*, ch. xxi. 2, xxix. 3), or, better still, according to the adjective use of the noun צָר (here with *tzakeph*, צָר from צָרַר) in ch. xxviii. 20, Job xli. 7, 2 Kings vi. 1, a closely confined stream, to whose waters the banks form a compressing dam, which it bursts through when agitated by a tempest, carrying everything away with it. Accordingly, the explanation we adopt is this: Jehovah will come like the stream, a stream hemmed in, which a wind of Jehovah, *i.e.* (like "the mountains of God," "cedars of God," "garden of Jehovah," ch. li. 3, cf. Num. xxiv. 6) a strong tempestuous wind, sweeps away (נֹסְסָה בּוֹ, *nōsᵉsa-b-bô*, with the tone drawn back and *dagesh forte conj.* in the monosyllable, the *pilel* of *nūs* with *Beth*: to hunt into, to press upon and put to flight),—a figure which also indicates that the Spirit of Jehovah is the driving force in this His judicially gracious revelation of Himself. Then, when the name of Jehovah makes itself legible once more as with letters of fire, when His glory comes like a sea of fire within the horizon of the world's history, all the world from west to east, from east to west, will begin to fear Him. But the true object of the love, which bursts forth through this revelation of wrath, is His church, which includes not only those who have retained their faith, but all who have been truly converted to Him. And He comes (וּבָא a continuation of יָבֹא) for Zion a Redeemer, *i.e.* as a Redeemer (a closer definition of the predicate), and·for those who turn away from apostasy (שָׁבֵי פֶּשַׁע, compare ch. i. 27, and for the genitive connection Mic. ii. 8, שׁוּבֵי מִלְחָמָה, those who have turned away from the war). The *Vav* here does not signify "and indeed," as in ch. lvii. 18, but "more especially." He comes as a Redeemer for Zion, *i.e.* His church which has remained true, including those who turn again to Jehovah from their previous apostasy. In Rom. xi. 26 the apostle quotes this word of God, which is sealed with " Thus saith Jehovah," as a proof of the final restoration of all Israel; for יהוה (according to the Apocalypse, ὁ ὢν καὶ ὁ ἦν καὶ ὁ ἐρχόμενος) is to him the God who moves on through the Old Testament towards the goal of His incarnation, and through the New Testament towards that of His *parousia* in Christ, which will bring the world's history to a close. But this final close does not take place without its having become apparent at the same time that God "has concluded all in unbelief, that He may have compassion upon all" (Rom. xi. 32).

Jehovah, having thus come as a Redeemer to His people, who have hitherto been lying under the curse, makes an everlasting covenant with them. Ver. 21. " *And I, this is my covenant with them, saith Jehovah: My Spirit which is upon thee, and my word which I have put in thy mouth, shall not depart out of thy mouth, and out of the mouth of thy seed, and out of the mouth of thy seed's seed, saith Jehovah, from henceforth and for ever.*" In the words, "And I, this is my covenant with them," we have a renewal of the words of God to Abram in Gen. xvii. 4, " As for me, behold, my covenant is with thee." Instead of אַתָּה we have in the same sense אֹתָם (not אוֹתָם, as in ch. liv. 15); we find this very frequently in Jeremiah. The following prophecy is addressed to Israel, the " servant of Jehovah," which has been hitherto partially faithful and partially unfaithful, but which has now returned to fidelity, viz. the " remnant of Israel," which has been rescued through the medium of a general judgment upon the nations, and to which the great body of all who fear God from east to west attach themselves. This church of the new covenant has the Spirit of God over it, for it comes down upon it from above; and the comforting saving words of God are not only the blessed treasure of its heart, but the confession of its mouth which spreads salvation all around. The words intended are those which prove, according to ch. li. 16, the seeds of the new heaven and the new earth. The church of the last days, endowed with the Spirit of God, and never again forsaking its calling, carries them as the evangelist of God in her apostolic mouth. The subject of the following prophecy is the new Jerusalem, the glorious centre of this holy church.

THIRD PROPHECY.—Chap. lx.

THE GLORY OF THE JERUSALEM OF THE LAST DAYS.

It is still night. The inward and outward condition of the church is night ; and if it is night followed by a morning, it is so only for those who " against hope believe in hope." The reality which strikes the senses is the night of sin, of punishment, of suffering, and of mourning,—a long night of nearly seventy years. In this night, the prophet, according to the command of God, has been prophesying of the coming light. In his inward penetration of the substance of his own preaching, he has come close to the time when faith is to be turned to sight. And now in the strength of God, who has made him the mouthpiece of His own creative fiat, he exclaims to the church, ver. 1 : " *Arise, grow light ; for thy light cometh, and the glory of Jehovah riseth upon thee.*" The appeal is addressed to Zion-Jerusalem, which is regarded (as in ch. xlix. 18, l. 1, lii. 1, 2, liv. 1) as a woman, and indeed as the mother of Israel. Here, however, it is regarded as the church redeemed from banishment, and settled once more in the holy city and the holy land, the church of salvation, which is now about to become the church of glory. Zion lies prostrate on the ground, smitten down by the judgment of God, brought down to the ground by inward prostration, and partly overcome by the sleep of self-security. She now hears the cry, "Arise" (*qūmī*). This is not a mere admonition, but a word of power which puts new life into her limbs, so that she is able to rise from the ground, on which she has lain, as it were, under the ban. The night, which has brought her to the ground mourning, and faint, and intoxicated with sleep, is now at an end. The mighty word *qūmī*, " arise," is supplemented by a second word : '*ōrī*. What creative force there is in these two

trochees, *qūmī 'ōrī*, which hold on, as it were, till what they
express is accomplished; and what force of consolation in the
two *iambi, ki-bhâ 'ōrēkh*, which affix, as it were, to the acts of
Zion the seal of the divine act, and add to the ἄρσις (or elevation) its θέσις (or foundation)! Zion is to become light; it is
to, because it can. But it cannot of itself, for in itself it has
no light, because it has so absolutely given itself up to sin; but
there is a light which will communicate itself to her, viz. the
light which radiates from the holy nature of God Himself.
And this light is salvation, because the Holy One loves Zion: it
is also glory, because it not only dispels the darkness, but sets
itself, all glorious as it is, in the place of the darkness. *Zârach*
is the word commonly applied to the rising of the sun (Mal.
iii. 20). The sun of suns is Jehovah (Ps. lxxxiv. 12), the God
who is coming (ch. lix. 20).

It is now all darkness over mankind; but Zion is the east,
in which this sun of suns will rise. Ver. 2. "*For, behold, the
darkness covereth the earth, and deep darkness the nations; and
Jehovah riseth over thee, and His glory becomes visible over thee.*"
The night which settles upon the world of nations is not to be
understood as meaning a night of ignorance and enmity against
God. This prophecy no doubt stands in progressive connection
with the previous one; but, according to ch. lix. 19, the manifestation of judgment, through which Zion is redeemed, brings
even the heathen from west to east, *i.e.* those who survive the
judgment, to the fear of Jehovah. The idea is rather the
following: After the judgments of God have passed, darkness
in its greatest depth still covers the earth, and a night of clouds
the nations. It is still night as on the first day, but a night
which is to give place to light. Where, then, will the sun rise,
by which this darkness is to be lighted up? The answer is,
"Over Zion, the redeemed church of Israel." But whilst darkness still covers the nations, it is getting light in the Holy
Land, for a sun is rising over Zion, viz. Jehovah in His
unveiled glory. The consequence of this is, that Zion itself
becomes thoroughly light, and that not for itself only, but for
all mankind. When Jehovah has transformed Zion into the
likeness of His own glory, Zion transforms all nations into the
likeness of her own. Ver. 3. "*And nations walk to thy light,
and kings to the shining of thy rays.*" Zion exerts such an

attractive force, that nations move towards her light (לְ הָלַךְ as
in הָלַךְ לְבֵיתוֹ and other similar expressions), and kings to the
splendour of her rays, to share in them for themselves, and
enjoy them with her. All earthly might and majesty station
themselves in the light of the divine glory, which is reflected
by the church.

Zion is now exhorted, as in ch. xlix. 18, to lift up her eyes,
and turn them in all directions; for she is the object sought by
an approaching multitude. Ver. 4. " *Lift up thine eyes round
about, and see: they all crowd together, they come to thee : thy
sons come from afar, and thy daughters are carried hither upon
arms.*" The multitude that are crowding together and coming
near are the *diaspora* of her sons and daughters that have been
scattered far away (ch. xi. 12), and whom the heathen that are
now drawing near to her bring with them, conducting them
and carrying them, so that they cling " to the side" (ch. lxvi.
12) of those who are carrying them upon their arms and
shoulders (ch. xlix. 22). תֵּאָמַנָה is softened from תֵּאָמַמְנָה, the
pausal form for תֵּאָמַמְנָה (compare the softening in Ruth i. 13),
from אָמַן, to keep, fasten, support; whence אֹמֵן, אֹמֶנֶת, a foster-
father, a nurse who has a child in safe keeping.

When this takes place, Zion will be seized with the greatest
delight, mingled with some trembling. Ver. 5. " *Then wilt
thou see and shine, and thine heart will tremble and expand ; for
the abundance of the sea will be turned to thee, the wealth of the
nations cometh to thee.*" It is a disputed question whether the
proper reading is תִּרְאִי, תֵּרְאִי, or תִּירְאִי—all three point to יָרֵא—
or תֵּרְאִי, from רָאָה. The last is favoured by the LXX., Targ.,
Syr., Jerome, Saad., and all the earlier Jewish commentators
except AE, and is also the Masoretic reading; for the *Masora
finalis* (f. 1, col. 6) observes that this תראי is the only instance
of such a form from רָאָה (differing therefore from תֵּרְאִי in Zeph.
iii. 15, where we also find the readings תִּירְאִי and תֵּרְאִי); and
there is a note in the margin of the Masora, לית חטף, to the
effect that this תראי is the only one with *chateph, i.e. Sheva.*
Moreover, תֵּרְאִי (thou shalt see) is the more natural reading,
according to ch. lxvi. 14 and Zech. x. 7; more especially as יָרֵא
is not a suitable word to use (like *pâchad* and *râgaz* in Jer.
xxxiii. 9) in the sense of trembling for joy (compare, on the
contrary, יָרֵע, ch. xv. 4, and רָהֲה in ch. xliv. 8). The true ren-

dering therefore is, "Then wilt thou see and shine," *i.e.* when
thou seest this thou wilt shine, thy face will light up with joy;
nâhar as in Ps. xxxiv. 6. Luther renders it, "Then wilt thou
see thy desire, and break out," viz. into shouting; Jerome, on
the contrary, has, "Thou wilt overflow, *i.e.* thou wilt be inun-
dated with waters coming suddenly like rivers."

The impression produced by this revolution is so overpowering, that Zion's heart trembles; yet at the same time it
is so elevating, that the straitened heart expands (וְרָחַב, a figure
quite unknown to the classical languages, although they have
angor and *angustia;* the LXX. renders it καὶ ἐκστήσῃ, after
the reading וְרָהַב in Chayug, and Isaac Nathan in his *Con-
cordance,* entitled מאיר נתיב): for *hămōn yâm, i.e.* everything
of value that is possessed by islands and coast lands (*hâmōn,*
groaning, a groaning multitude, more especially of possessions,
Ps. xxxvii. 16, etc.), is brought to her; and *chēl gōyim,* the
property, *i.e.* (looking at the plural of the predicate which
follows; cf. Hag. ii. 7) the riches (gold, silver, etc., Zech. xiv.
14) of the heathen, are brought into her, that she may dispose
of them to the glory of her God.

The nations engaged in commerce, and those possessing
cattle, vie with one another in enriching the church. Vers. 6, 7.
"*A swarm of camels will cover thee, the foals of Midian and
Ephah: they come all together from Saba; they bring gold and
incense, and they joyfully make known the praises of Jehovah. All
the flocks of Kedar gather together unto thee, the rams of Nebaioth
will serve thee: they will come up with acceptance upon mine
altar, and I will adorn the house of my adorning.*" The trading
nations bring their wares to the church. The tribe of *Midian,*
which sprang from Abraham and Keturah (Gen. xxv. 2), and
of which Ephah (Targ. *Hōlâd,* the Hutheilites?) formed one
of the several branches (Gen. xxv. 4), had its seat on the
eastern coast of the Elanitic Gulf, which is still indicated by
the town of *Madyan,* situated, according to the geographers of
Arabia, five days' journey to the south of Aila. These come
in such long and numerous caravans, that all the country round
Jerusalem swarms with camels. שִׁפְעַת as in Job xxii. 11; and
בִּכְרֵי (parallel to גְּמַלִּים) from בֶּכֶר = Arabic *bakr* or *bikr,* a young
male camel, or generally a camel's foal (up to the age of not
more than nine years; see Lane's *Lexicon,* i. 240). All of these,

both Midianites and Ephæans, come out of Sheba, which Strabo (xvi. 4, 19) describes as " the highly blessed land of the Sabæans, in which myrrh, frankincense, and cinnamon grow." There, viz. in Yemen,[1] where spices, jewels, and gold abound, they have purchased gold and frankincense, and these valuable gifts they now bring to Jerusalem, not as unwilling tribute, but with the joyful proclamation of the glorious deeds and attributes of Jehovah, the God of Israel. And not only do the trading nations come, but the nomad tribes also: viz. *Kedar*, the Kedarenes, with their bows (ch. xxi. 17), who lived in the desert, between Babylonia and Syria, in חֲצֵרִים (ch. xlii. 11), *i.e.* fixed settlements ; and *Nebaioth*, also an Ishmaelitish tribe (according to the incontrovertible account of Gen. xxv. 13), a nomad tribe, which was still of no note even in the time of the kings of Israel, but which rose into a highly cultivated nation in the centuries just before Christ, and had a kingdom extending from the Elanitic Gulf to the land on the east of the Jordan, and across Belka as far as Hauran ; for the monuments reach from Egypt to Babylonia, though Arabia Petræa is the place where they chiefly abound.[2] The Kedarenes drive their collected flocks to Jerusalem, and the rams (אֵילֵי, *arietes*, not *principes*) of the Nabatæans, being brought by them, are at the service of the church (יְשָׁרְתוּנֶךְ, a verbal form with a

---

[1] *Seba* (סְבָא, ch. xliii. 3, xlv. 14) is Meroe generally, or (according to Strabo and Steph. Byz.) more especially a port in northern Ethiopia ; *Sheba* (שְׁבָא), the principal tribe of southern Arabia, more especially its capital Marib (*Mariaba*), which, according to an Arabian legend, contained the palace of Bilkis, the מַלְכַּת שְׁבָא (see Exc. iv. in Krüger's *Feldzug von Ælius Gallus*, 1862). It is true that the following passage of Strabo (xvi. 14, 21) is apparently at variance with the opinion that the seat of the Sabæans was in southern Arabia. " First of all," he says, "above Syria, Arabia Felix is inhabited by the Nabatæans and Sabæans, who frequently marched through the former before it belonged to the Romans." But as, according to every other account given by Strabo, the Sabæans had their home in Arabia Felix, and the Nabatæans at the northern extremity of the Red Sea, in Arabia Petræa, all that this passage can imply is, that at that part of Arabia which stretches towards the Syrian boundary, the expeditions of the Sabæans came upon the Nabatæans.

[2] Quatremère rejects the identity of the Nabatæans and the Ishmaelitish *Nebaioth ;* but it has been justly defended by Winer, Kless, Knobel, and Krehl (*Religion der vorisl. Araber*, p. 51).

toneless contracted suffix, as in ch. xlvii. 10), and ascend עַל־רָצוֹן,
according to good pleasure = acceptably (with the עַל used to
form adverbs, Ewald, § 217, i; cf. l'râtsōn in ch. lvi. 7), the
altar of Jehovah ('âlâh with the local object in the accusative,
as in Gen. xlix. 4, Num. xiii. 17). The meaning is, that
Jehovah will graciously accept the sacrifices which the church
offers from the gifts of the Nabatæans (and Kedarenes) upon
His altar. It would be quite wrong to follow Antistes Hess
and Baumgarten, and draw the conclusion from such prophecies as these, that animal sacrifices will be revived again. The
sacrifice of animals has been abolished once for all by the self-
sacrifice of the " Servant of Jehovah;" and by the spiritual
revolution which Christianity, i.e. the Messianic religion, has
produced, so far as the consciousness of modern times is concerned, even in Israel itself, it is once for all condemned (see
Holdheim's Schrift über das Ceremonial-gesetz im Messiasreich,
1845). The prophet, indeed, cannot describe even what belongs
to the New Testament in any other than Old Testament
colours, because he is still within the Old Testament limits.
But from the standpoint of the New Testament fulfilment, that
which was merely educational and preparatory, and of which
there will be no revival, is naturally transformed into the truly
essential purpose at which the former aimed; so that all that
was real in the prophecy remains unaffected and pure, after
the deduction of what was merely the unessential medium employed to depict it. The very same Paul who preaches Christ
as the end of the law, predicts the conversion of Israel as the
topstone of the gracious counsels of God as they unfold themselves in the history of salvation, and describes the restoration
of Israel as " the riches of the Gentiles;" and the very same
John who wrote the Gospel was also the apocalyptist, by whom
the distinction between Israel and the Gentiles was seen in
vision as still maintained even in the New Jerusalem. It
must therefore be possible (though we cannot form any clear
idea of the manner in which it will be carried out), that the
Israel of the future may have a very prominent position in the
perfect church, and be, as it were, the central leader of its
worship, though without the restoration of the party-wall of
particularism and ceremonial shadows, which the blood of the
crucified One has entirely washed away. The house of God

in Jerusalem, as the prophet has already stated in ch. lvi. 7, will be a house of prayer (*bēth tᵉphilláh*) for all nations. Here Jehovah calls the house built in His honour, and filled with His gracious presence, "the house of my glory." He will make its inward glory like the outward, by adorning it with the gifts presented by the converted Gentile world.

From the mainland, over which caravans and flocks are coming, the prophet now turns his eyes to the sea. Vers. 8, 9. "*Who are these who fly hither as a cloud, and like the doves to their windows? Yea, the islands wait for me; and the ships of Tarshish come first, to bring thy children from far, their silver and gold with them, to the name of thy God, and to the holy One of Israel, because He hath ornamented thee.*" Upon the sea there appear first of all enigmatical shapes, driving along as swiftly as if they were light clouds flying before the wind (ch. xix. 1, xliv. 22), or like doves flying to their dovecots (*celeres cavis se turribus abdunt*, as Ovid says), *i.e.* to the round towers with their numerous pigeon-holes, which are provided for their shelter. The question is addressed to Zion, and the answer may easily be anticipated,—namely, that this swarm of swiftly flying figures are hurrying to a house which they long to reach, as much as pigeons do to reach their pigeon-house. The *kī* which follows is explanatory: this hurrying presents itself to thine eyes, because the isles wait for me. The reason for all this haste is to be found in the faith of those who are hurrying on. The Old Testament generally speaks of faith as hope (קָוָה ? as in ch. li. 5, xlii. 4); not that faith is the same as hope, but it is the support of hope, just as hope is the comfort of faith. In the Old Testament, when the true salvation existed only in promise, this epithet, for which there were many synonyms in the language, was the most appropriate one. The faith of the distant lands of the west is now beginning to work. The object of all this activity is expressed in the word לְהָבִיא. The things thus flying along like clouds and doves are ships; with the Tartessus ships, which come from the farthest extremity of the European insular quarter of the globe, at their head (בְּרִאשֹׁנָה with *munach* instead of *metheg*, in the same sense as in Num. x. 14; LXX. ἐν πρώτοις; Jerome, *in principio*, in the foremost rank), *i.e.* acting as the leaders of the fleet which is sailing to Zion and bringing Zion's children from afar, and along with them the gold and silver of the owners of the vessels themselves, to the name (לְשֵׁם, to the name, dative, not equivalent to לְמַעַן ; LXX. διὰ, as in ch. lv. 5) of thy God, whom they adore, and to the Holy One of Israel, because He hath ornamented thee, and thereby inspired them with reverence and love to thee (פֵּאֲרֵךְ for פֵּאֲרֵךְ, as in ch. liv. 6, where it even stands out of pause).

The first turn (vers. 1–3) described the glorification of Zion through the rising of the glory of Jehovah; the second (vers. 4–9) her glorification through the recovery of her scattered children, and the gifts of the Gentiles who bring them home; and now the third depicts her glorification through the service of the nations, especially of her former persecutors, and generally through the service of all that is great and glorious in the world of nature and the world of men. Not only do the converted heathen offer their possessions to the church on Zion, but they offer up themselves and their kings to pay her homage and render service to her. Vers. 10–12. *"And sons of strangers build thy walls, and their kings serve thee: for in my wrath I have smitten thee, and in my favour I have had mercy upon thee. And thy gates remain open continually day and night, they shall not be shut, to bring in to thee the possessions of the nations and their kings in triumph. For the nation and the kingdom which will not serve thee will perish, and the nations be certainly laid waste."* The walls of Zion (הֹמְתַיִךְ doubly defective) rise up from their ruins through the willing co-operation of converted foreigners (ch. lvi. 6, 7), and foreign kings place themselves at the service of Zion (ch. xlix. 23); the help rendered by the edicts of Cyrus, Darius, and Artaxerxes Longimanus being only a prelude to events stretching on to the end of time, though indeed, in the view of the prophet himself, the period immediately succeeding the captivity really would be the end of time. Of the two perfects in ver. 10*b*, הִכִּיתִיךְ points to the more remote past; רִחַמְתִּיךְ to the nearer past, stretching forward into the present (cf. ch. liv. 8). On *pittēăch, patescere, hiscere,* see ch. xlviii. 8, where it is applied to the ear, as in Song of Sol. vii. 13 to a bud. The first clause of ver. 11*a* closes with וָלַיְלָה; *tiphchah* divides more strongly than *tebir,* which is subordinate to it. At the same time, "day and night" may be connected with "shall not be shut," as in Rev. xxi.

25, 26. The gates of Zion may always be left open, for there is no more fear of a hostile attack; and they must be left open *ad importandum*, that men may bring in the possession of the heathen through them (a thing which goes on uninterruptedly), וּמַלְכֵיהֶם נְהוּגִים. The last words are rendered by Knobel, " and their kings are leaders (of the procession) ;" but *nâhûg* would be a strange substantive, having nothing to support it but the obscure יָקוֹשׁ from יָקוֹשׁ, for אָחוּז in Cant. iii. 8 does not mean a support, but *amplexus* (Ewald, § 149, *d*). The rendering " and their kings escorted," *i.e.* attended by an escort, commends itself more than this; but in the passage quoted in support of this use of *nâhag*, viz. Nah. ii. 8, it is used as a synonym of *hâgâh*, signifying *gemere*. It is better to follow the LXX. and Jerome, and render it, " and their kings brought," viz., according to ch. xx. 4, 1 Sam. xxx. 2, as prisoners (Targ. *zᵉqîqîn, i.e. bᵉziqqîm*, in fetters),—brought, however, not by their several nations who are tired of their government and deliver them up (as Hitzig supposes), but by the church, by which they have been irresistibly bound in fetters, *i.e.* inwardly conquered (compare ch. xlv. 14 with Ps. cxlix. 8), and thus suffer themselves to be brought in a triumphal procession to the holy city as the captives of the church and her God. Ver. 12 is connected with this *nᵉhûgîm;* for the state of every nation and kingdom is henceforth to be determined by its subjection to the church of the God of sacred history (עָבַד, δουλεύειν, in distinction from *shērēth*, διακονεῖν, θεραπεύειν), and by its entrance into this church—the very same thought which Zechariah carries out in ch. xiv. 16 sqq. Instead of כִּי־הַגּוֹי, כִּי is more properly pointed according to certain MSS. with *munach* (without *makkeph*) ; the article before *haggôyim* is remonstrative, and the inf. intens. *chârôbh* makes the thing threatened unquestionable.

From the thought that everything great in the world of man is to be made to serve the Holy One and His church, the prophet passes to what is great in the world of nature. Ver. 13. *" The glory of Lebanon will come to thee, cypresses, plane-trees and Sherbin-trees all together, to beautify the place of my sanctuary, and to make the place of my feet glorious."* The splendid cedars, which are the glory of Lebanon, and in fact the finest trees of all kinds, will be brought to Zion, not as

trunks felled to be used as building materials, but dug up with
their roots, to ornament the holy place of the temple (Jer. xvii.
12), and also to this end, that Jehovah may glorify the "holy
place of His feet," *i.e.* the place where He, who towers above
the heaven of all heavens, has as it were to place His feet.
The temple is frequently called His footstool (*hădōm raglâiv*),
with especial reference to the ark of the covenant (Ps. xcix. 5,
cxxxii. 7 ; Lam. ii. 1 ; 1 Chron. xxviii. 2) as being the central
point of the earthly presence of God (cf. ch. lxvi. 1). The
trees, that is to say, which tower in regal glory above all the rest
of the vegetable world, are to adorn the environs of the temple,
so that avenues of cedars and plane-trees lead into it; a proof
that there is no more fear of any further falling away to
idolatry. On the names of the trees, see ch. xli. 19. Three
kinds are mentioned here ; we found seven there. The words
ברוֹשׁ תדהר ותאשׁור יחדו are repeated *verbatim* from ch. xli. 19 (on
these repetitions of himself, see p. 288).

The prophecy now returns to the world of man. Ver. 14.
"*The children also of thy tormentors come bending unto thee, and
all thy despisers stretch themselves at the soles of thy feet, and call
thee 'City of Jehovah, Zion of the Holy One of Israel.'*" The
persecutors of the church both in work and word are now no
more (ch. xxvi. 14), and their children feel themselves dis-
armed. They are seized with shame and repentance, when
they see the church which was formerly tormented and despised
so highly exalted. They come *shechŏăch* (an inf. noun of the
form מָחוֹן, Lam. v. 13; used here as an accusative of more precise definition, just as nouns of this kind are frequently connected directly with the verb הָלַךְ, Ewald, § 279, *c*), literally a
bow or stoop, equivalent to bowing or stooping (the opposite to
rōmâh in Micah ii. 3), and stretch themselves "at the soles of
thy feet," *i.e.* clinging to thee as imploringly and obsequiously
as if they would lay themselves down under thy very feet, and
were not worthy to lie anywhere but there (as in ch. xlix. 23) ;
and whereas formerly they called thee by nicknames, they now
give thee the honourable name of "City of Jehovah, Zion of
the Holy One of Israel," not "Sanctuary of Israel," as Meier
supposes, since *qedōsh Israel* is always a name of Jehovah in
the book of Isaiah. It is a genitive construction like Bethlehem of Judah, Gibeah of Saul, and others.

The fourth turn (vers. 15–18) describes the glorification of Zion through the growth and stability of its community both without and within. A glorious change takes place in the church, not only in itself, but also in the judgment of the nations. Vers. 15, 16. " *Whereas thou wast forsaken, and hated, and no one walked through thee, I make thee now into eternal splendour, a rapture from generation to generation. And thou suckest the milk of nations, and the breast of kings thou wilt suck, and learn that I Jehovah am thy Saviour and thy Redeemer, the Mighty One of Jacob.*" Of the two ideas of a church (the mother of Israel) and a city (metropolis) involved in the term Zion, the former prevails in ver. 15, the latter in ver. 16. For although עֲזוּבָה and שְׂנוּאָה are equally applicable to a city and a church (ch. liv. 6, 11), the expression "no one walked through thee" applies only to the desolate city as she lay in ruins (see ch. xxxiv. 10). The fusion of the two ideas in ver. 15 is similar to ch. xlix. 21. Jerusalem will now become thoroughly a splendour, and in fact an eternal splendour, a rapture of successive generations so long as the history of this world continues. The nations and their kings give up their own vital energy to the church, just as a mother or nurse gives the milk of her breasts to a child ; and the church has thereby rich food for a prosperous growth, and a constant supply of fresh material for grateful joy. We cannot for a moment think of enriching by means of conquest, as Hitzig does ; the sucking is that of a child, not of a vampyre. We should expect *mᵉlâkhōth* (ch. xlix. 23) instead of *mᵉlâkhīm* (kings) ; but by שֹׁד (as in ch. lxvi. 11 for שַׁד) the natural character of what is promised is intentionally spiritualized. The figure proves itself to be only a figure, and requires an ideal interpretation. The church sees in all this the gracious superintendence of her God ; she learns from experience that Jehovah is her Saviour, that He is her Redeemer, He the Mighty One of Jacob, who has conquered for her, and now causes her to triumph (כִּי אֲנִי with *munach yethib*, as in ch. xlix. 26b, which passage is repeated almost *verbatim* here, and ch. lxi. 8).

The outward and inward beauty of the new Jerusalem is now depicted by the materials of her structure, and the powers which prevail within her. Vers. 17, 18. " *For copper I bring gold, and for iron I bring silver, and for wood copper, and for*

*stones iron, and make peace thy magistracy, and righteousness
thy bailiffs. Injustice is no more seen in thy land, wasting and
destruction in thy borders; and thou callest salvation thy walls,
and renown thy gates.*" Wood and stone are not used at all in
the building of the new Jerusalem. Just as in the time of
Solomon silver was counted as nothing (1 Kings x. 21) and
had only the value of stones (1 Kings x. 27), so here Jehovah
gives her gold instead of copper, silver instead of iron; whilst
copper and iron are so despised with this superabundance of
the precious metals, that they take the place of such building
materials as wood and stones. Thus the city will be a massive
one, and not even all of stone, but entirely built of metal, and
indestructible not only by the elements, but by all kinds of foes.
The allegorical continuation of the prophecy shows very clearly
that the prophet does not mean his words to be taken literally.
The LXX., Saad., and others, are wrong in adopting the rendering, "I make thy magistracy peace," etc.; since *shâlōm* and
ts⁼dâqâh are not accusatives of either the predicate or the object,
but such personifications as we are accustomed to in Isaiah (*vid.*
ch. xxxii. 16, 17, lix. 14; cf. ch. xlv. 8). Jehovah makes
peace its *p⁼quddâh, i.e.* its "overseership" (like *g⁼bhūrâh*, hero-
ship, in ch. iii. 25, and *'ezrâh*, helpership, in ch. xxxi. 2), or
magistracy; and righteousness its bailiffs. The plural נֹגְשַׂיִךְ
is no disproof of the personification; the meaning is, that
ts⁼dâqâh (righteousness) is to Jerusalem what the whole body
of civil officers together are: that is to say, righteousness is a
substitute for the police force in every form. Under such
magistracy and such police, nothing is ever heard within the
land, of which Jerusalem is the capital, of either *châmâs, i.e.* a
rude and unjust attack of the stronger upon the weaker, or of
shōd, i.e. conquest and devastation, and *shebher, i.e.* dashing to
pieces, or breaking in two. It has walls (ver. 10); but in truth
"salvation," the salvation of its God, is regarded as its impregnable fortifications. It has gates (ver. 11); but *t⁼hillâh*, the
renown that commands respect, with which Jehovah has invested it, is really better than any gate, whether for ornament
or protection.

The fifth turn celebrates the glorifying of Jerusalem,
through the shining of Jehovah as its everlasting light and
through the form of its ever-growing membership, which is so

well-pleasing to God. The prophecy returns to the thought
with which it set out, and by which the whole is regulated, viz.
that Jerusalem will be light.   This leading thought is now unfolded in the most majestic manner, and opened up in all its
eschatological depth. Vers. 1, 20. "*The sun will be no more
thy light by day, neither for brightness will the moon shine upon
thee : Jehovah will be to thee an everlasting light, and thy God
thy glory.   Thy sun will no more go down, and thy moon will
not be withdrawn; for Jehovah will be to thee an everlasting
light, and the days of thy mourning will be fulfilled.*" Although,
in the prophet's view, the Jerusalem of the period of glory in
this world and the Jerusalem of the eternal glory beyond
flow into one another; the meaning of this prophecy is not
that the sun and moon will no longer exist.   Even of the
Jerusalem which is not to be built by Israel with the help of
converted heathen, but which comes down from heaven to
earth, the seer in Rev. xxi. 23 merely says, that the city needs
neither the shining of the sun nor of the moon (as the Targum
renders the passage before us, " thou wilt not need the shining
of the sun by day"), for the glory of God lightens it, and the
Lamb is the light thereof, *i.e.* God Himself is instead of a sun
to her, and the Lamb instead of a moon.   Consequently we
do not agree with Stier, who infers from this passage that
" there is a final new creation approaching, when there will be
no more turning round into the shadow (Jas. i. 17), when the
whole planetary system, including the earth, will be changed,
and when the earth itself will become a sun, yea, will become
even more than that, in the direct and primary light which
streams down upon it from God Himself." We rather agree
with Hofmann, that " there will still be both sun and moon, but
the Holy Place will be illumined without interruption by the
manifestation of the presence of God, which outshines all
besides."   The prophet has here found the most complete
expression, for that which has already been hinted at in such
prophecies in ch. iv. 5, xxx. 26, xxiv. 23.   As the city receives
its light neither from the sun nor from the moon, this implies,
what Rev. xxi. 25 distinctly affirms, that there will be no
more night there.   The prophet intentionally avoids a לְאוֹר לַיְלָה
parallel to לְאוֹר יוֹמָם. We must not render the second clause in
ver. 19, " and it will not become light to thee with the shining

of the moon," for הֵאִיר never means to get light; nor "and as for the shining of the moon, it does not give the light," as Hitzig and Knobel propose, for וְלֹנַהּ is used alone, and not וּלְנֹגַהּ הַיָּרֵחַ as the antithesis to לְאוֹר יוֹמָם, in the sense of "to light up the night" (compare נֹגַהּ as applied to the shining of the moon in ch. xiii. 10, and נֹגַהּ to the glittering of the stars in Joel ii. 10), and even the use of הַלַּיְלָה is avoided. The true rendering is either, "and for lighting, the moon will not shine upon thee" (Stier, Hahn, etc.); or, what is more in accordance with the accentuation, which would have given וּלְנֹגַהּ *tifchah* and not *tsakeph gadol,* if it had been intended to indicate the object, "and as for the lighting" (לְ as in ch. xxxii. 1b). The glory of Jehovah, which soars above Jerusalem, and has come down into her, is henceforth her sun and her moon,—a sun that never sets, a moon לֹא יֵאָסֵף which is not taken in towards morning, like a lamp that has been hung out at night (compare נֶאֱסָף, ch. xvi. 10, withdrawn, disappeared). The triumph of light over darkness, which is the object of the world's history, is concentrated in the new Jerusalem. How this is to be understood, is explained in the closing clause of ver. 20. The sum of the days of mourning allotted to the church is complete. The darkness of the corruption of sin and state of punishment is overcome, and the church is nothing but holy blessed joy without change or disturbance; for it walks no longer in sidereal light, but in the eternally unchangeable light of Jehovah, which with its peaceful gentleness and perfect purity illumines within as well as without. The seer of the Apocalypse also mentions the Lamb. The Lamb is also known to our prophet; for the "Servant of Jehovah" is the Lamb. But the light of transfiguration, in which he sees this exalted Lamb, is not great enough to admit of its being combined with the light of the Divine Nature itself.

The next verse shows how deep was his consciousness of the close connection between darkness, wrath, and sin. Ver. 21. "*And thy people, they are all righteous; they possess the land for ever, a sprout of my plantations, a work of my hands for glorification.*" The church of the new Jerusalem consists of none but righteous ones, who have been cleansed from guilt, and keep themselves henceforth pure from sinning, and therefore possess the land of promise for ever, without having to fear repeated destruction and banishment: a "sprout" (*nētser* as in ch. xi. 1, xiv. 19; Arab. *nadr*, the green branch) "of my plantations" (מַטָּעַי *chethib*, erroneously מַטָּעוֹ or מַטָּעָו), *i.e.* of my creative acts of grace (cf. ch. v. 7), a "work of my hands" (cf. ch. xix. 25), "to glorify me," *i.e.* in which I possess that in which I glory (לְהִתְפָּאֵר as in ch. lxi. 3).

The life of this church, which is newly created, new-born, through judgment and grace, gradually expands from the most unassuming centre in ever widening circles until it has attained the broadest dimensions. Ver. 22a. "*The smallest one will become thousands, and the meanest one a powerful nation.*" "The small and mean one," or, as the idea is a relative one, "the smallest and meanest one" (Ges. § 119, 2), is either a childless one, or one blessed with very few children. At the same time, the reference is not exclusively to growth through the blessing of children, but also to growth through the extension of fellowship. We have a similar expression in Mic. iv. 7 (cf. v. 1), where *'eleph* is employed, just as it is here, in the sense of לְאֶלֶף, "to thousands (or chiliads)."

The whole of the prophetic address is now sealed with this declaration: Ver. 22b. "*I, Jehovah, will hasten it in His time.*" The neuter זֹּה (as in ch. xliii. 13, xlvi. 11) refers to everything that has been predicted from ver. 1 downwards. Jehovah will fulfil it rapidly, when the point of time (καιρός) which He has fixed for it shall have arrived. As this point of time is known to Him only, the predicted glory will burst all at once with startling suddenness upon the eyes of those who have waited believingly for Him.

This chapter forms a connected and self-contained whole, as we may see very clearly from the address to Zion-Jerusalem, which is sustained throughout. If we compare together such passages as ch. li. 17–23 ("Awake, awake, stand up, O Jerusalem"), ch. lii. 1, 2 ("Awake, awake, put on thy strength, O Zion"), and ch. liv. ("Sing, O barren"), which are all closely related so far as their contents are concerned, we shall find that these addresses to Zion form an ascending series, ch. lx. being the summit to which they rise, and that the whole is a complete counterpart to the address to the daughter of Babylon in ch. xlvii.

FOURTH PROPHECY.—CHAP. LXI.

THE GLORY OF THE OFFICE COMMITTED TO THE SERVANT OF JEHOVAH.

The words of Jehovah Himself pass over here into the words of another, whom He has appointed as the Mediator of His gracious counsel. Vers. 1–3. " *The Spirit of the Lord Jehovah is over me, because Jehovah hath anointed me, to bring glad tidings to sufferers, hath sent me to bind up broken-hearted ones, to proclaim liberty to those led captive, and emancipation to the fettered ; to proclaim a year of grace from Jehovah, and a day of vengeance from our God; to comfort all that mourn ; to put upon the mourners of Zion, to give them a head-dress for ashes, oil of joy for mourning, a wrapper of renown for an expiring spirit, that they may be called terebinths of righteousness, a planting of Jehovah for glorification.*" Who is the person speaking here ? The Targum introduces the passage with אֲמַר נְבִיָּא. Nearly all the modern commentators support this view. Even the closing remarks to Drechsler (iii. 381) express the opinion, that the prophet who exhibited to the church the summit of its glory in ch. lx., an evangelist of the rising from on high, an apocalyptist who sketches the painting which the New Testament apocalyptist is to carry out in detail, is here looking up to Jehovah with a grateful eye, and praising Him with joyful heart for his exalted commission. But this view, when looked at more closely, cannot possibly be sustained. It is open to the following objections : (1.) The prophet never speaks of himself as a prophet at any such length as this ; on the contrary, with the exception of the closing words of ch. lvii. 21, " saith my God," he has always most studiously let his own person fall back into the shade. (2.) Wherever any other than Jehovah is represented as speaking, and as referring to his own calling, or his experience in connection with that calling, as in ch. xlix. 1 sqq., l. 4 sqq., it is the very same " servant of Jehovah" of whom and to whom Jehovah speaks in ch. xlii. 1 sqq., lii. 13–liii., and therefore not the prophet himself, but He who had been appointed to be the Mediator of a new covenant, the light of the Gentiles, the salvation of

Jehovah for the whole world, and who would reach this glorious height, to which He had been called, through self-abasement even to death. (3.) All that the person speaking here says of himself is to be found in the picture of the unequalled " Servant of Jehovah," who is highly exalted above the prophet. He is endowed with the Spirit of Jehovah (ch. xlii. 1); Jehovah has sent Him, and with Him His Spirit (ch. xlviii. 16*b*); He has a tongue taught of God, to help the exhausted with words (ch. l. 4); He spares and rescues those who are almost despairing and destroyed, the bruised reed and expiring wick (ch. xlii. 7). " To open blind eyes, to bring out prisoners from the prison, and them that sit in darkness out of the prison-house :" this is what He has chiefly to do for His people, both in word and deed (ch. xlii. 7, xlix. 9). (4.) We can hardly expect that, after the prophet has described the Servant of Jehovah, of whom he prophesied, as coming forward to speak with such dramatic directness as in ch. xlix. 1 sqq., l. 4 sqq. (and even ch. xlviii. 16*b*), he will now proceed to put himself in the foreground, and ascribe to himself those very same official attributes which he has already set forth as characteristic features in his portrait of the predicted One. For these reasons we have no doubt that we have here the words of the Servant of Jehovah. The glory of Jerusalem is depicted in ch. lx. in the direct words of Jehovah Himself, which are well sustained throughout. And now, just as in ch. xlviii. 16*b*, though still more elaborately, we have by their side the words of His servant, who is the mediator of this glory, and who above all others is the pioneer thereof in his evangelical predictions. Just as Jehovah says of him in ch. xlii. 1, " I have put my Spirit upon him;" so here he says of himself, " The Spirit of Jehovah is upon me." And when he continues to explain this still further by saying, "because" (יַעַן from עָנָה, intention, purpose; here equivalent to יַעַן אֲשֶׁר) "Jehovah hath anointed me" (*mâshach 'ōthī*, more emphatic than *m⁰shâchănī*), notwithstanding the fact that *mâshach* is used here in the sense of prophetic and not regal anointing (1 Kings xix. 16), we may find in the choice of this particular word a hint at the fact, that the Servant of Jehovah and the Messiah are one and the same person. So also the account given in Luke iv. 16–22—viz. that when Jesus was in the synagogue at Nazareth, after reading the opening

words of this address, He closed the book with these words,
" This day is this scripture fulfilled in your ears "—cannot be
interpreted more simply in any other way, than on the supposition that Jesus here declares Himself to be the predicted and
divinely anointed Servant of Jehovah, who brings the gospel
of redemption to His people. Moreover, though it is not
decisive in favour of our explanation, yet this explanation is
favoured by the fact that the speaker not only appears as the
herald of the new and great gifts of God, but also as the
dispenser of them (" *non præco tantum, sed et dispensator,*"
Vitringa). The combination of the names of God ('Adonai
Yehovâh) is the same as in ch. l. 4–9. On *bissēr*, εὐαγγελίζειν
(-εσθαι), see p. 145. He comes to put a bandage on the
hearts' wounds of those who are broken-hearted : לְ חָבַשׁ (חִבֵּשׁ)
as in Ezek. xxxiv. 4, Ps. cxlvii. 3 ; cf. רָפָא לְ (רִפֵּא), vol. i. p. 200;
לְ הַצַּדִּיק, p. 336. קָרָא דְרוֹר is the phrase used in the law for
the proclamation of the freedom brought by the year of jubilee,
which occurred every fiftieth year after seven sabbatical periods,
and was called *sh^enath hadd^erōr* (Ezek. xlvi. 17) ; *d^eror* from
dârar, a verbal stem, denoting the straight, swift flight of a
swallow (see at Ps. lxxxiv. 4), and free motion in general, such
as that of a flash of lightning, a liberal self-diffusion, like that
of a superabundant fulness. *P^eqach-qōăch* is written like two
words (see at ch. ii. 20). The Targum translates it as if *p^eqach*
were an imperative : " Come to the light," probably meaning
undo the bands. But *qōăch* is not a Hebrew word ; for the
qīchōth of the Mishna (the loops through which the strings of
a purse are drawn, for the purpose of lacing it up) cannot be
adduced as a comparison. Parchon, AE, and A, take *p^eqach-*
qōăch as one word (of the form שְׁחַרְחֹר, פְּתַלְתֹּל), in the sense of
throwing open, viz. the prison. But as *páqach* is never used
like *páthach* (ch. xiv. 17, li. 14), to signify the opening of a
room, but is always applied to the opening of the eyes (ch.
xxxv. 5, xlii. 7, etc.), except in ch. xlii. 20, where it is used for
the opening of the ears, we adhere to the strict usage of the
language, if we understand by *p^eqachqōăch* the opening up of
the eyes (as contrasted with the dense darkness of the prison) ;
and this is how it has been taken even by the LXX., who
have rendered it καὶ τυφλοῖς ἀνάβλεψιν, as if the reading had
been וְלָעִוְרִים (Ps. cxlvi. 8). Again, he is sent to promise with

a loud proclamation a year of good pleasure (*râtsōn*: syn.
yeshū‛áh) and a day of vengeance, which Jehovah has appointed; a promise which assigns the length of a year for the
thorough accomplishment of the work of grace, and only the
length of a day for the work of vengeance. The vengeance
applies to those who hold the people of God in fetters, and
oppress them; the grace to all those whom the infliction of
punishment has inwardly humbled, though they have been
strongly agitated by its long continuance (ch. lvii. 15). The
'ăbhēlīm, whom the Servant of Jehovah has to comfort, are the
" mourners of Zion," those who take to heart the fall of Zion.
In ver. 3, לָשׂוּם . . . לָתֵת, he corrects himself, because what he
brings is not merely a diadem, to which the word *sūm* (to set)
would apply, but an abundant supply of manifold gifts, to
which only a general word like *nâthan* (to give) is appropriate.
Instead of אֵפֶר, the ashes of mourning or repentance laid upon
the head, he brings פְּאֵר, a diadem to adorn the head (a transposition even so far as the letters are concerned, and therefore
the counterpart of אפר); the " oil of joy" (from Ps. xlv. 8;
compare also מְשָׁחֶךָ there with מָשַׁח אֹתִי here) instead of mourning; " a wrapper (cloak) of renown" instead of a faint and
almost extinguished spirit. The oil with which they henceforth
anoint themselves is to be joy or gladness, and renown the
cloak in which they wrap themselves (a genitive connection, as
in ch. lix. 17). And whence is all this? The gifts of God,
though represented in outward figures, are really spiritual, and
take effect within, rejuvenating and sanctifying the inward
man; they are the sap and strength, the marrow and impulse
of a new life. The church thereby becomes " terebinths of
righteousness" (אֵילֵי: Targ., Symm., Jer., render this, strong
ones, mighty ones; Syr. *dechre*, rams; but though both of these
are possible, so far as the letters are concerned, they are unsuitable here), *i.e.* possessors of righteousness, produced by God
and acceptable with God, having all the firmness and fulness
of terebinths, with their strong trunks, their luxuriant verdure,
and their perennial foliage,—a planting of Jehovah, to the
end that He may get glory out of it (a repetition of ch. lx. 21).

Even in ver. 3*b* with וְקֹרָא לָהֶם a perfect was introduced in
the place of the infinitives of the object, and affirmed what was
to be accomplished through the mediation of the Servant of

Jehovah. The second turn in the address, which follows in vers. 4–9, continues the use of such perfects, which afterwards pass into futures. But the whole is still governed by the commencement in ver. 1. The Servant of Jehovah celebrates the glorious office committed to him, and expounds the substance of the gospel given him to proclaim. It points to the restoration of the promised land, and to the elevation of Israel, after its purification in the furnace of judgment, to great honour and dignity in the midst of the world of nations. Vers. 4–6. *"And they will build up wastes of the olden time, raise up desolations of the forefathers, and renew desolate cities, desolations of former generations. And strangers stand and feed your flocks, and foreigners become your ploughmen and vinedressers. But ye will be called priests of Jehovah; Servants of our God, will men say to you: ye will eat the riches of the nations, and pride yourselves in their glory."* The desolations and wastes of *'ōlâm* and *dōr vâdōr, i.e.* of ages remote and near (ch. lviii. 12), are not confined to what had lain in ruins during the seventy years of the captivity. The land will be so thickly populated, that the former places of abode will not suffice (ch. xlix. 19, 20); so that places must be referred to which are lying waste beyond the present bounds of the promised land (ch. liv. 3), and which will be rebuilt, raised up, and renewed by those who return from exile, and indeed by the latest generations (ch. lviii. 12, מִמְּךָ; cf. ch. lx. 14). *Chōrebh,* in the sense of desolation, is a word belonging to the later period of the language (Zeph., Jer., and Ezek.). The rebuilding naturally suggests the thought of assistance on the part of the heathen (ch. lx. 10). But the prophet expresses the fact that they will enter into the service of Israel (ver. 5), in a new and different form. They " stand there" (viz. at their posts ready for service, *'al-mishmartâm,* 2 Chron. vii. 6), "and feed your flocks" (צֹאן *singularetantum,* cf. Gen. xxx. 43), and foreigners are your ploughmen and vinedressers. Israel is now, in the midst of the heathen who have entered into the congregation of Jehovah and become the people of God (ch. xix. 25), what the Aaronites formerly were in the midst of Israel itself. It stands upon the height of its primary destination to be a kingdom of priests (Ex. xix. 6). They are called " priests of Jehovah," and the heathen call them "servants of our God;" for even the heathen speak with

believing reverence of the God, to whom Israel renders priestly
service, as " our God." This reads as if the restored Israelites
were to stand in the same relation to the converted heathen as
the clergy to the laity; but it is evident, from ch. lxvi. 21, that
the prophet has no such hierarchical separation as this in his
mind. All that we can safely infer from his prophecy is, that
the nationality of Israel will not be swallowed up by the
entrance of the heathen into the community of the God of
revelation. The people created by Jehovah, to serve as the
vehicle of the promise of salvation and the instrument in preparing the way for salvation, will also render Him special service,
even after that salvation has been really effected. At the same
time, we cannot take the attitude, which is here assigned to the
people of sacred history after it has become the teacher of the
nations, viz. as the leader of its worship also, and shape it into
any clear and definite form that shall be reconcilable with the
New Testament spirit of liberty and the abolition of all national
party-walls. The Old Testament prophet utters New Testament prophecies in an Old Testament form. Even when he
continues to say, " Ye will eat the riches of the Gentiles, and
pride yourselves in their glory," i.e. be proud of the glorious
things which have passed from their possession into yours, this
is merely colouring intended to strike the eye, which admits of
explanation on the ground that he saw the future in the mirror
of the present, as a complete inversion of the relation in which
the two had stood before. The figures present themselves to
him in the form of contrasts. The New Testament apostle, on
the other hand, says in Rom. xi. 12 that the conversion of all
Israel to Christ will be " the riches of the Gentiles." But if
even then the Gentile church should act according to the words
of the same apostle in Rom. xv. 27, and show her gratitude to
the people whose spiritual debtor she is, by ministering to them
in carnal things, all that the prophet has promised here will be
amply fulfilled. We cannot adopt the explanation proposed by
Hitzig, Stier, etc., " and changing with them, ye enter into
their glory" (*hithyammēr* from *yâmar = mûr, Hiph.: hēmīr*, Jer.
ii. 11; lit. to exchange with one another, to enter into one
another's places); for *yâmar = 'âmar* (cf. *yâchad = 'âchad;
yâsham = 'âsham; yâlaph = 'âlaph*), to press upwards, to rise
up (related to *tâmar*, see at ch. xvii. 9; *sâmar*, Symm. ὀρθοτρι-

χεῖν, possibly also *'ámar* with the *hithpael hith'ammēr*, LXX. καταδυναστεύειν), yields a much simpler and more appropriate meaning. From this verb we have *hith'ammēr* in Ps. xciv. 4, " to lift one's self up (proudly)," and here *hithyammēr;* and it is in this way that the word has been explained by Jerome (*superbietis*), and possibly by the LXX. (θαυμασθήσεσθε, in the sense of *spectabiles eritis*), by the Targum, and the Syriac, as well as by most of the ancient and modern expositors.

The shame of banishment will then be changed into an excess of joy, and honourable distinction. Vers. 7–9. " *Instead of shame ye will have double, and (instead) of insult they rejoice at their portion : thus in their land they will possess double ; everlasting joy will they have. For I Jehovah love right, hate robbery in wickedness ; and give them their reward in faithfulness, and conclude an everlasting covenant with them. And their family will be known among the nations, and their offspring in the midst of the nations : all who see them will recognise them, for they are a family that Jehovah hath blessed.*" The enigmatical first half of ver. 7 is explained in ver. 2, where *mishneh* is shown to consist of double possession in the land of their inheritance, which has not only been restored to them, but extended far beyond the borders of their former possession ; and *yârōnnū chelqâm* (cf. ch. lxiv. 14) denotes excessive rejoicing in the ground and soil belonging to them (according to the appointment of Jehovah) : *chelqâm* as in Mic. ii. 4 ; and *mishneh* as equivalent not to מִשְׁנֶה כָבוֹד, but to מִשְׁנֶה יְרֻשָּׁה. Taking this to be the relation between ver. 7*b* and 7*a*, the meaning of *lâkhēn* is not, " therefore, because they have hitherto suffered shame and reproach ;" but what is promised in ver. 7*a* is unfolded according to its practical results, the effects consequent upon its fulfilment being placed in the foreground (cf. vol. i. p. 448) ; so that there is less to astonish us in the elliptically brief form of ver. 7*a* which needed explanation. The transition from the form of address to that of declaration is the same as in ch. i. 29, xxxi. 6, lii. 14, 15. וּכְלִמָּה is a concise expression for וְתַחַת כְּלִמָּה, just as וּתְהִלָּתִי in ch. xlviii. 9 is for וּלְמַעַן תְּהִלָּתִי. *Chelqâm* is either the accusative of the object, according to the construction of רָנַן, which occurs in Ps. li. 16 ; or what I prefer, looking at חֵמָה in ch. xlii. 25, and וּבְכָיִךְ in ch. xliii. 23, an adverbial accusative = בְּחֶלְקָם. The LXX.,

Jerome, and Saad. render the clause, in opposition to the accents, "instead of your double shame and reproach;" but in that case the principal words of the clause would read תָּרֹנּוּ הֶלְקְכֶם. The explanation adopted by the Targum, Saad., and Jerome, "shame on the part of those who rejoice in their portion," is absolutely impossible. The great majority of the modern commentators adopt essentially the same explanation of ver. 7a as we have done, and even A. E. Kimchi does the same. Hahn's modification, "instead of your shame is the double their portion, and (instead) of the insult this, that they will rejoice," forces a meaning upon the syntax which is absolutely impossible. The reason for the gracious recompense for the wrong endured is given in ver. 8, "Jehovah loves the right," which the enemies of Israel have so shamefully abused. "He hates גָּזֵל בְּעוֹלָה, i.e. not *rapinam in holocausto* (as Jerome, Talmud b. Succa 30a, Luther, and others render it; Eng. ver. "robbery for burnt-offering"),—for what object could there be in mentioning sacrifices here, seeing that only heathen sacrifices could be intended, and there would be something worse than *gâzēl* to condemn in them?—but *robbery*, or, strictly speaking, "something robbed in or with knavery" (LXX., Targ., Syr., Saad.), which calls to mind at once the cruel robbery or spoiling that Israel had sustained from the Chaldeans, its *bōzᵉzīm* (ch. xlii. 24),—a robbery which passed all bounds. עוֹלָה is softened from עַוְלָה (from עָוַל, עַוֵּל), like עֹלָתָה in Job v. 16, and עֹלֹת in Ps. lviii. 3 and lxiv. 7; though it is doubtful whether the punctuation assumes the latter, as the Targum does, and not rather the meaning *holocaustum* supported by the Talmud. For the very reason, therefore, that Israel had been so grievously ill-treated by the instruments of punishment employed by Jehovah, He would give those who had been ill-treated their due reward, after He had made the evil, which He had not approved, subservient to His own salutary purposes. פְּעֻלָּה is the reward of work in Lev. xix. 13, of hardship in Ezek. xxix. 20; here it is the reward of suffering. This reward He would give בֶּאֱמֶת, exactly as He had promised, without the slightest deduction. The posterity of those who have been ill-treated and insulted will be honourably known (נוֹדָע as in Prov. xxxi. 23) in the world of nations, and men will need only to catch sight of them to recognise them (by prominent marks of blessing), for they are a family blessed of God. כִּי, not *quod* (because), although it might have this meaning, but *nam* (for), as in Gen. xxvii. 23, since *hikkīr* includes the meaning *agnoscere* (to recognise).

This is the joyful calling of the Servant of Jehovah to be the messenger of such promises of God to His people. Vers. 10, 11. "*Joyfully I rejoice in Jehovah; my soul shall be joyful in my God, that He hath given me garments of salvation to put on, hath wrapped me in the robe of righteousness, as a bridegroom who wears the turban like a priest, and as a bride who puts on her jewellery. For like the land which brings forth its sprouts, and as a garden which causes the things sown in it to sprout up; so the Lord Jehovah bringeth righteousness to sprouting, and renown before all nations.*" The Targum precedes this last turn with "Thus saith Jerusalem." But as vers. 4–9 are a development of the glorious prospects, the realization of which has to be effected through the instrumentality of the person speaking in vers. 1–3 both in word and deed, the speaker here is certainly the same as there. Nor is it even the fact that he is here supposed to commence speaking again; but he is simply continuing his address by expressing at the close, as he did at the beginning, the relation in which he stands in his own person to the approaching elevation of His people. Exalted joy, which impels him to exult, is what he experiences in Jehovah his God (בְּ denoting the ground and orbit of his experience): for the future, which so abounds in grace, and which he has to proclaim as a prophet and as the evangelist of Israel, and of which he has to lay the foundation as the mediator of Israel, and in which he is destined to participate as being himself an Israelite, consists entirely of salvation and righteousness; so that he, the bearer and messenger of the divine counsels of grace, appears to himself as one to whom Jehovah has given clothes of salvation to put on, and whom He has wrapped in the robe of righteousness. *Tsᵉdâqâh* (righteousness), looked at from the evangelical side of the idea which it expresses, is here the parallel word to *yᵉshū'âh* (salvation). The figurative representation of both by different articles of dress is similar to ch. lix. 17; *yâ'at*, which only occurs here, is synonymous with *'âtâh*, from which comes *ma'âteh*, a wrapper or cloak (ver. 3). He appears to himself, as he stands there hoping such things for his people, and preaching such things to his people, to resemble a bridegroom, who makes his turban in priestly style, *i.e.* who winds it round his head after the fashion of the priestly *migbâʿōth* (Ex. xxix. 9), which are called פְּאָרִים in Ex. xxxix. 28 (cf. Ezek. xliv. 18). Rashi and others think of the *mitsnepheth* of the high priest, which was of purple-blue; but יכהן does not imply anything beyond the *migbâʿâh*, a tall mitra, which was formed by twisting a long linen band round the head so as to make it stand up in a point. כָּהֵן is by no means equivalent to *kōnēn*, or *hēkhīn*, as Hitzig and Hahn suppose, since the verb *kâhan = kūn* only survives in *kōhēn*. *Kīhēn* is a denom., and signifies to act or play the priest; it is construed here with the accusative פְּאֵר, which is either the accusative of more precise definition ("who play the priest in a turban;" A. ὡς νύμφιον ἱερατευόμενον στεφάνῳ), or what would answer better to the parallel member, "who makes the turban like a priest." As often as he receives the word of promise into his heart and takes it into his mouth, it is to him like the turban of a bridegroom, or like the jewellery which a bride puts on (*taʿdeh, kal*, as in Hos. ii. 15). For the substance of the promise is nothing but salvation and renown, which Jehovah causes to sprout up before all nations, just as the earth causes its vegetation to sprout, or a garden its seed (כ as a preposition in both instances, *instar* followed by attributive clauses; see ch. viii. 23). The word in the mouth of the servant of Jehovah is the seed, out of which great things are developed before all the world. The ground and soil (*'erets*) of this development is mankind; the enclosed garden therein (*gannâh*) is the church; and the great things themselves are *tsᵉdâqâh*, as the true inward nature of His church, and *tᵉhillâh* as its outward manifestation. The force which causes the seed to germinate is Jehovah; but the bearer of the seed is the servant of Jehovah, and the ground of his festive rejoicing is the fact that he is able to scatter the seed of so gracious and glorious a future.

FIFTH PROPHECY.—CHAP. LXII.

THE GRADUAL EXTENSION OF THE GLORY OF JERUSALEM.

Nearly all the more recent commentators regard the prophet himself as speaking here. Having given himself up to
praying to Jehovah and preaching to the people, he will not
rest or hold his peace till the salvation, which has begun to be
realized, has been brought fully out to the light of day. It is,
however, really Jehovah who commences thus: Vers. 1–3.
"*For Zion's sake I shall not be silent, and for Jerusalem's sake
I shall not rest, till her righteousness breaks forth like morning
brightness, and her salvation like a blazing torch. And nations
will see thy righteousness, and all kings thy glory; and men
will call thee by a new name, which the mouth of Jehovah will
determine. And thou wilt be an adorning coronet in the hand
of Jehovah, and a royal diadem in the lap of thy God.*" It is
evident that Jehovah is the speaker here, both from ver. 6 and
also from the expression used; for *châshâh* is the word commonly employed in such utterances of Jehovah concerning
Himself, to denote His leaving things in their existing state
without interposing (ch. lxv. 6, lvii. 11, lxiv. 11). Moreover,
the arguments which may be adduced to prove that the author
of ch. xl.–lxvi. is not the speaker in ch. lxi., also prove that it
is not he who is continuing to speak of himself in ch. lxii.
Jehovah, having now begun to speak and move on behalf of
Zion, will "for Zion's sake," *i.e.* just because it is Zion, His
own church, neither be silent nor give Himself rest, till He
has gloriously executed His work of grace. Zion is now in
the shade, but the time will come when her righteousness will
go forth as *nōgah*, the light which bursts through the night
(ch. lx. 19, lix. 9; here the morning sunlight, Prov. iv. 18;
compare *shachar*, the morning red, ch. lviii. 8); or till her
salvation is like a torch which blazes. יִבְעָר belongs to כְּלַפִּיד
(*mercha*) in the form of an attributive clause = בֹּעֵר, although
it might also be assumed that יבער stands by attraction for
תבער (cf. ch. ii. 11; Ewald, § 317, *c*). The verb בָּעַר, which
is generally applied to wrath (*e.g.* ch. xxx. 27), is here used in
connection with salvation, which has wrath towards the enemies

of Zion as its obverse side: Zion's *tsedeq* (righteousness) shall become like the morning sunlight, before which even the last twilight has vanished; and Zion's *yᵉshûʿâh* is like a nightly torch, which sets fire to its own material, and everything that comes near it. The force of the conjunction עַד (until) does not extend beyond ver. 1. From ver. 2 onwards, the condition of things in the object indicated by עד is more fully described. The eyes of the nations will be directed to the righteousness of Zion, the impress of which is now their common property; the eyes of all kings to her glory, with which the glory of none of them, nor even of all together, can possibly compare. And because this state of Zion is a new one, which has never existed before, her old name is not sufficient to indicate her nature. She is called by a new name; and who could determine this new name? He who makes the church righteous and glorious, He, and He alone, is able to utter a name answering to her new nature, just as it was He who called Abram *Abraham*, and Jacob *Israel*. The mouth of Jehovah will determine it (נָקַב, to pierce, to mark, to designate in a signal and distinguishing manner, *nuncupare*; cf. Amos vi. 1, Num. i. 17). It is only in imagery that prophecy here sees what Zion will be in the future: she will be "a crown of glory," "a diadem," or rather a tiara (*tsᵉnîph*; *Chethib tsᵉnûph* = *mitsnepheth*, the head-dress of the high priest, Ex. xxviii. 4, Zech. iii. 5; and that of the king, Ezek. xxi. 31) "of regal dignity," in the hand of her God (for want of a synonym of "hand," we have adopted the rendering "in the lap" the second time that it occurs). Meier renders בְּכַף (בְּיַד יהוה) *Jovæ sub præsidio*, as though it did not form part of the figure. But it is a main feature in the figure, that Jehovah holds the crown in His hand. Zion is not the ancient crown which the Eternal wears upon His head, but the crown wrought out in time, which He holds in His hand, because He is seen in Zion by all creation. The whole history of salvation is the history of the taking of the kingdom, and the perfecting of the kingdom by Jehovah; in other words, the history of the working out of this crown.

Zion will be once more the beloved of God, and her home the bride of her children. Vers. 4, 5. "*Men will no more call thee 'Forsaken one;' and thy land they will no more call 'Desert:' but men will name thee 'My delight in her,' and thy* home ' *Married one :*' *for Jehovah hath delight in thee, and thy land is married. For the young man marrieth the maiden, thy children will marry thee; and as the bridegroom rejoiceth in the bride, thy God will rejoice in thee.*" The prophecy mentions new names, which will now take the place of the old ones; but these names indicate what Zion appears to be, not her true nature which is brought to the light.   In the explanatory clause לָךְ stands at the head, because the name of Zion is given first in distinction from the name of her land. Zion has hitherto been called *'ăzūbhâh,* forsaken by Jehovah, who formerly loved her; but she now receives instead the name of *chephtsî-bhâh* (really the name of a woman, viz. the wife of Hezekiah, and mother of Manasseh, 2 Kings xxi. 1), for she is now the object of true affection on the part of Jehovah. With the rejoicing of a bridegroom in his bride (the accusative is used here in the same sense as in שֹׂמֵחַ שִׂמְחָה גְדֹלָה; Ges. § 138, 1) will her God rejoice in her, turning to her again with a love as strong and deep as the first love of a bridal pair. And the land of Zion's abode, the fatherland of her children, was hitherto called *sh^emâmâh;* it was turned into a desert by the heathen, and the connection that existed between it and the children of the land was severed; but now it shall be called *b^e'ûlâh,* for it will be newly married. A young man marries a virgin, thy children will marry *thee :* the figure and the fact are placed side by side in the form of an emblematical proverb, the particle of comparison being omitted (see Herzog's *Cyclopædia,* xiv. 696, and Ges. § 155, 2, *h*). The church in its relation to Jehovah is a weak but beloved woman, which has Him for its Lord and Husband (ch. liv. 5); but in relation to her home she is the totality of those who are lords or possessors (*ba'ălē,* 2 Sam. vi. 2) of the land, and who call the land their own as it were by right of marriage. Out of the loving relation in which the church stands to its God, there flows its relation of authority over every earthly thing of which it stands in need. In some MSS. there is a break here.

Watchmen stationed upon the walls of Zion (says the third strophe) do not forsake Jehovah till He has fulfilled all His promise. Vers. 6, 7. " *Upon thy walls, O Jerusalem, have I stationed watchmen; all the day and all the night continually they are not silent. O ye who remember Jehovah, leave yourselves no rest!* And give *Him* no rest, till He raise up, and till He set Jerusalem for a praise in the earth." As the phrase *hiphqīd 'al* signifies to make a person an overseer (president) over any-thing, it seems as though we ought to render the sentence before us, " I have set watchmen over thy walls." But *hiphqīd* by itself may also mean " to appoint" (2 Kings xxv. 23), and therefore עַל־חוֹמֹתַיִךְ may indicate the place of appointment (LXX. ἐπὶ τῶν τειχέων σου, upon thy walls; Ἰερουσαλήμ, κατέστησα φύλακας). Those who are stationed upon the walls are no doubt keepers of the walls; not, however, as persons whose exclusive duty it is to keep the walls, but as those who have committed to them the guarding of the city both within and without (Song of Sol. v. 7). The appointment of such watchmen presupposes the existence of the city, which is thus to be watched from the walls. It is therefore inadmissible to think of the walls of Jerusalem as still lying in ruins, as the majority of commentators have done, and to understand by the watchmen pious Israelites, who pray for their restoration, or (according to *b. Menachoth* 87*a*; cf. Zech. i. 12) angelic inter-cessors. The walls intended are those of the city, which, though once destroyed, is actually imperishable (ch. xlix. 16) and has now been raised up again. And who else could the watchmen stationed upon the walls really be, but prophets who are called *tsōphīm* (*e.g.* ch. lii. 8), and whose calling, according to Ezek. xxxiii., is that of watchmen? And if prophets are meant, who else can the person appointing them be but Jehovah Him-self? The idea that the author of these prophecies is speaking of himself, as having appointed the *shōm'rīm*, must therefore be rejected. Jehovah gives to the restored Jerusalem faithful prophets, whom He stations upon the walls of the city, that they may see far and wide, and be heard afar off. And from those walls does their warning cry on behalf of the holy city committed to their care ascend day and night to Jehovah, and their testimony go round about to the world. For after Jerusalem has been restored and re-peopled, the further end to be attained is this, that Jehovah should build up the newly founded city within (*cōnēn* the consequence of *bânâh*, Num. xxi. 27, and *'âsâh*, ch. xlv. 18, Deut. xxxii. 6; cf. ch. liv. 14, and Ps. lxxxvii. 5), and help it to attain the central post of honour in relation to those without, which He has destined for it. Such prophets of the times succeeding the captivity (*n^ebhî'îm 'achărōnîm*; cf. Zech. i. 4) were Haggai, Zechariah, and Malachi. Haggai stands upon the walls of Jerusalem, and proclaims the glory of the second temple as surpassing that of the first. Zechariah points from Joshua and Zerubbabel onwards to the sprout of Jehovah, who is priest and prince in one person, and builds the true temple of God. Malachi predicts the coming of the Lord to His temple, and the rising of the Sun of righteousness. Under the eyes of these prophets the city of God rose up again, and they stand upon its pinnacles, and look thence into the glorious future that awaits it, and hasten its approach through the word of their testimony. Such prophets, who carry the good of their people day and night upon their anxious praying hearts, does Jehovah give to the Jerusalem after the captivity, which is one in the prophet's view with the Jerusalem of the last days; and in so lively a manner does the prophet here call them up before his own mind, that he exclaims to them, "Ye who remind Jehovah, to finish gloriously the gracious work which He has begun," give yourselves no rest (*dŏmi* from *dâmâh* = *dâmam*, to grow dumb, *i.e.* to cease speaking or working, in distinction from *châshâh*, to be silent, *i.e.* not to speak or work), and allow Him no rest till He puts Jerusalem in the right state, and so glorifies it, that it shall be recognised and extolled as glorious over all the earth. Prophecy here sees the final glory of the church as one that gradually unfolds itself, and that not without human instrumentality. The prophets of the last times, with their zeal in prayer, and in the exercise of their calling as witnesses, form a striking contrast to the blind, dumb, indolent, sleepy hirelings of the prophet's own time (ch. lvi. 10).

The following strophe expresses one side of the divine promise, on which the hope of that lofty and universally acknowledged glory of Jerusalem, for whose completion the watchers upon its walls so ceaselessly exert themselves, is founded. Vers. 8, 9. "*Jehovah hath sworn by His right hand, and by His powerful arm, Surely I no more give thy corn for food to thine enemies; and foreigners will not drink thy must, for which thou hast laboured hard. No, they that gather it in shall eat it, and praise Jehovah; and they that store it, shall drink it in the courts of my sanctuary.*" The church will no more succumb to the tyranny of a worldly power. Peace undisturbed, and unrestricted freedom, reign there. With praise to Jehovah are the fruits of the land enjoyed by those who raised and reaped them. יָגְעוּ (with an auxiliary *pathach*, as in ch. xlvii. 12, 15) is applied to the cultivation of the soil, and includes the service of the heathen who are incorporated in Israel (ch. lxi. 5); whilst אָסַף (whence מְאַסְפָיו with ס *raphatum*) or אֹסֵף (*poel*, whence the reading מְאַסְּפָיו, cf. Ps. ci. 5, *m⁰loshnī*; cix. 10, *v⁰-dorshū*, for which in some codd. and editions we find מְאַסְפָיו, an intermediate form between *piel* and *poel*; see at Ps. lxii. 4) and קִבֵּץ stand in the same relation to one another as *condere* (*horreo*) and *colligere* (cf. ch. xi. 12). The expression *b⁰chats-rōth qodshī*, in the courts of my sanctuary, cannot imply that the produce of the harvest will never be consumed anywhere else than there (which is inconceivable), but only that their enjoyment of the harvest-produce will be consecrated by festal meals of worship, with an allusion to the legal regulation that two-tenths (*ma⁰ăsēr shēnī*) should be eaten in a holy place (*liphnē Jehovah*) by the original possessor and his family, with the addition of the Levites and the poor (Deut. xiv. 22–27: see Saalschütz, *Mosaisches Recht*, cap. 42). Such thoughts, as that all Israel will then be a priestly nation, or that all Jerusalem will be holy, are not implied in this promise. All that it affirms is, that the enjoyment of the harvest-blessing will continue henceforth undisturbed, and be accompanied with the grateful worship of the giver, and therefore, because sanctified by thanksgiving, will become an act of worship in itself. This is what Jehovah has sworn " by His right hand," which He only lifts up with truth, and " by His powerful arm," which carries out what it promises without the possibility of resistance. The Talmud (*b. Nazir 3b*) understands by זרוע עזו the left arm, after Dan. xii. 7; but the ו of ובזרוע is epexegetical.

The concluding strophe goes back to the standpoint of the captivity. Vers. 10–12. " *Go forth, go forth through the gates, clear the way of the people. Cast up, cast up the road, clean it of stones; lift up a banner above the nations! Behold, Jehovah hath caused tidings to sound to the end of the earth. Say to the daughter of Zion, Behold, thy salvation cometh; behold, His reward is with Him, and His recompense before Him. And men will call them the holy people, the redeemed of Jehovah; and men*

will call thee, Striven after, A city that will not be forsaken." We
cannot adopt the rendering proposed by Gesenius, " Go ye into
the gates," whether of Jerusalem or of the temple, since the
reading would then be בֹּאוּ שְׁעָרִים (Gen. xxiii. 10) or בִּשְׁעָרִים
(Jer. vii. 2). For although עֲבַר בְּ may under certain circumstances be applied to entrance into a city (Judg. ix. 26), yet it
generally denotes either passing through a land (ch. viii. 21,
xxxiv. 10; Gen. xli. 46; Lev. xxvi. 6, etc.), or through a
nation (2 Sam. xx. 14), or through a certain place (ch. x. 28);
so that the phrase עֲבַר בַּשַּׁעַר, which does not occur anywhere
else (for in Mic. ii. 13, which refers, however, to the exodus
of the people out of the gates of the cities of the captivity,
וַיַּעֲבֹרוּ שַׁעַר do not belong together), must refer to passing
through the gate; and the cry עִבְרוּ בִשְׁעָרִים means just the same
as צְאוּ מִבָּבֶל (" Go ye forth from Babylon") in ch. xlviii. 20, lii.
11. The call to go out of Babylon forms the conclusion of the
prophecy here, just as it does in ch. xlviii. 20, 21, lii. 11, 12.
It is addressed to the exiles; but who are they to whom the
command is given, " Throw up a way,"—a summons repeatedly found in all the three books of these prophecies (ch. xl. 3,
lvii. 14)? They cannot be the heathen, for this is contra-
dicted by the conclusion of the charge, "Lift ye up a banner
above the nations;" nor can we adopt what seems to us a useless fancy on the part of Stier, viz. that ver. 10 is addressed to
the watchmen on the walls of Zion. We have no hesitation,
therefore, in concluding that they are the very same persons
who are to march through the gates of Babylon. The van-
guard (or pioneers) of those who are coming out are here
summoned to open the way by which the people are to march,
to throw up the road (viz. by casting up an embankment,
hamsillâh, as in ch. xi. 16, xlix. 11 ; *maslûl,* ch. xxxv. 8), to
clear it of stones (*siqqēl,* as in ch. v. 2 ; cf. Hos. ix. 12, *shikkēl
mē'ādâm*), and lift up a banner above the nations (one rising
so high as to be visible far and wide), that the *diaspora* of all
places may join those who are returning home with the
friendly help of the nations (ch. xi. 12, xlix. 22). For Jehovah
hath caused tidings to be heard to the end of the earth, *i.e.* as
we may see from what follows, the tidings of their liberation ;
in other words, looking at the historical fulfilment, the proclamation of Cyrus, which he caused to be issued throughout his

empire at the instigation of Jehovah (Ezra i. 1). Hitzig
regards הִשְׁמִיעַ as expressing what had actually occurred at the
time when the prophet uttered his predictions; and in reality
the standpoint of the prophets was so far a variable one, that
the fulfilment of what was predicted did draw nearer and
nearer to it ἐν πνεύματι (p. 123). But as *hinnēh* throughout
the book of Isaiah (vol. i. 425), even when followed by a perfect
(p. 10), invariably points to something future, all that can be
said is, that the divine announcement of the time of redemption, as having now arrived, stands out before the soul of the
prophet with all the certainty of a historical fact. The conclusion which Knobel draws from the expression "to the end of
the earth," as to the Babylonian standpoint of the prophet, is a
false one. In his opinion, "the end of the earth" in such passages as Ps. lxxii. 8, Zech. ix. 10 (*'aphsē-'ârets*), and ch. xxiv.
16 (*kᵉnaph hâ'ârets*), signifies the western extremity of the *orbis
orientalis*, that is to say, the region of the Mediterranean, more
especially Palestine; whereas it was rather a term applied to
the remotest lands which bounded the geographical horizon
(compare ch. xlii. 10, xlviii. 20, with Ps. ii. 8, xxii. 28, and
other passages). The words that follow ("Say ye," etc.) might
be taken as a command issued on the ground of the divine
hishmīaʿ ("the Lord hath proclaimed"); but *hishmīaʿ* itself is
a word that needs to be supplemented, so that what follows is
the divine proclamation: Men everywhere, *i.e.* as far as the
earth or the dispersion of Israel extends, are to say to the
daughter of Zion—that is to say, to the church which has its
home in Zion, but is now in foreign lands—that "its salvation
cometh," *i.e.* that Jehovah, its Saviour, is coming to bestow a
rich reward upon His church, which has passed through severe
punishment, but has been so salutarily refined. Those to whom
the words "Say ye," etc., are addressed, are not only the prophets of Israel, but all the mourners of Zion, who become
mᵉbhassᵉrīm, just because they respond to this appeal (compare
the meaning of this "Say ye to the daughter of Zion" with
Zech. ix. 9 in Matt. xxi. 5). The whole of the next clause,
"Behold, His reward," etc., is a repetition of the prophet's own
words in ch. xl. 10. It is a question whether the words "and
they shall call thee," etc., contain the gospel which is to be
proclaimed according to the will of Jehovah to the end of the

earth (see ch. xlviii. 20), or whether they are a continuation of the prophecy which commences with "Behold, Jehovah hath proclaimed." The latter is the more probable, as the address here passes again into an objective promise. The realization of the gospel, which Jehovah causes to be preached, leads men to call those who are now still in exile "the holy people," "the redeemed" (lit. ransomed, ch. li. 10; like *p*ᵉ*dūyē* in ch. xxxv. 10). "*And thee*"—thus does the prophecy close by returning to a direct address to Zion-Jerusalem—"thee will men call *d*ᵉ*rūshâh*," sought assiduously, *i.e.* one whose welfare men, and still more Jehovah, are zealously concerned to promote (compare the opposite in Jer. xxx. 17),—"a city that will not be forsaken," *i.e.* in which men gladly settle, and which will never be without inhabitants again (the antithesis to '*ăzūbhâh* in ch. lx. 15), possibly also in the sense that the gracious presence of God will never be withdrawn from it again (the antithesis to '*ăzūbhâh* in ver. 4). נעזבה is the third pers. pr., like *nuchâmâh* in ch. liv. 11: the perfect as expressing the abstract present (Ges. § 126, 3).

The following prophecy anticipates the question, how Israel can possibly rejoice in the recovered possession of its inheritance, if it is still to be surrounded by such malicious neighbours as the Edomites.

SIXTH PROPHECY.—Chap. lxiii. 1–6.

JUDGMENT UPON EDOM, AND UPON THE WHOLE WORLD THAT IS HOSTILE TO THE CHURCH.

Just as the Ammonites had been characterized by a thirst for extending their territory as well as by cruelty, and the Moabites by boasting and a slanderous disposition, so were the Edomites, although the brother-nation to Israel, characterized from time immemorial by fierce, implacable, bloodthirsty hatred towards Israel, upon which they fell in the most ruthless and malicious manner, whenever it was surrounded by danger or had suffered defeat. The knavish way in which they acted in the time of Joram, when Jerusalem was surprised and plundered by Philistines and Arabians (2 Chron. xxi. 16, 17), has been depicted by Obadiah. A large part of the inhabitants

of Jerusalem were then taken prisoners, and sold by the
conquerors, some to the Phœnicians and some to the Greeks
(Obad. 20; Joel iv. 1–8); to the latter through the medium of
the Edomites, who were in possession of the port and commercial city of Elath on the Elanitic Gulf (Amos i. 6). Under
the rule of the very same Joram the Edomites had made themselves independent of the house of David (2 Kings viii. 20;
2 Chron. xxi. 10), and a great massacre took place among the
Judæans settled in Idumæa; an act of wickedness for which
Joel threatens them with the judgment of God (ch. iv. 19),
and which was regarded as not yet expiated even in the time of
Uzziah, notwithstanding the fact that Amaziah had chastised
them (2 Kings xiv. 7), and Uzziah had wrested Elath from
them (2 Kings xiv. 22). " *Thus saith Jehovah,*" was the prophecy of Amos (i. 11, 12) in the first half of Uzziah's reign,
"*for three transgressions of Edom, and for four, I will not take
it back, because he pursued his brother with the sword, and stifled
his compassion, so that his anger tears in pieces for ever, and he
keeps his fierce wrath eternally: And I let fire loose upon Teman,
and it devours the palaces of Bozrah.*" So also at the destruction
of Jerusalem by the Chaldeans, and the carrying away of the
people, Edom took the side of the Chaldeans, rejoiced over
Israel's defeat, and flattered itself that it should eventually
rule over the territory that had hitherto belonged to Israel.
They availed themselves of this opportunity to slake their
thirst for revenge upon Israel, placing themselves at the service
of its enemies, delivering up fugitive Judæans or else mas-
sacring them, and really obtaining possession of the southern
portion of Judæa, viz. Hebron (1 Macc. v. 65; cf. Josephus,
Wars of the Jews, iv. 9, 7). With a retrospective glance at
these, the latest manifestations of eternal enmity, Edom is
threatened with divine vengeance by Jeremiah in the prophecy
contained in Jer. xlix. 7–22, which is taken for the most part
from Obadiah; also in the Lamentations (iv. 21, 22), as well as
by Ezekiel (xxv. 12–14, and especially xxxv.), and by the author
of Ps. cxxxvii., which looks back upon the time of the captivity.
Edom is not always an emblematical name for the imperial
power of the world : this is evident enough from Ps. cxxxvii.,
from Isa. xxi., and also from Isa. xxxiv. in connection with
ch. xiii., where the judgment upon Edom is represented as a

different one from the judgment upon Babylon. Babylon and Edom are always to be taken literally, so far as the primary meaning of the prophecy is concerned; but they are also representative, Babylon standing for the violent and tyrannical world-power, and Edom for the world as cherishing hostility and manifesting hostility to Israel as Israel, *i.e.* as the people of God. Babylon had no other interest, so far as Israel was concerned, than to subjugate it like other kingdoms, and destroy every possibility of its ever rising again. But Edom, which dwelt in Israel's immediate neighbourhood, and sprang from the same ancestral house, hated Israel with hereditary mortal hatred, although it knew the God of Israel better than Babylon ever did, because it knew that Israel had deprived it of its birthright, viz. the chieftainship. If Israel should have such a people as this, and such neighbouring nations generally round about it, after it had been delivered from the tyranny of the mistress of the world, its peace would still be incessantly threatened. Not only must Babylon fall, but Edom also must be trodden down, before Israel could be redeemed, or be regarded as perfectly redeemed. The prophecy against Edom which follows here is therefore a well-chosen side-piece to the prophecy against Babel in ch. xlvii., at the point of time to which the prophet has been transported.

This is the smallest of all the twenty-seven prophecies. In its dramatic style it resembles Ps. xxiv.; in its visionary and emblematical character it resembles the tetralogy in ch. xxi.–xxii. 14. The attention of the seer is attracted by a strange and lofty form coming from Edom, or more strictly from Bozrah; not the place in Auranitis or Hauran (Jer. xlviii. 24) which is memorable in church history, but the place in Edomitis or Gebal, between Petra and the Dead Sea, which still exists as a village in ruins under the diminutive name of *el-Busaire.* Ver. 1. " *Who is this that cometh from Edom, in deep red clothes from Bozrah? This, glorious in his apparel, bending to and fro in the fulness of his strength?*" The verb *châmats* means to be sharp or bitter; but here, where it can only refer to colour, it means to be glaring, and as the Syriac shows, in which it is generally applied to blushing from shame or reverential awe, to be a staring red (ὀξέως). The question, what is it that makes the clothes of this new-comer so strik-

ingly red? is answered afterwards.   But apart from the colour,
they are splendid in their general arrangement and character.

The person seen approaching is הָדוּר בִּלְבוּשׁוֹ (cf. حدر and

هدر, to rush up, to shoot up luxuriantly, *ahdar* used for a
swollen body), and possibly through the medium of *hâdâr*
(which may signify primarily a swelling, or pad, ὄγκος, and
secondarily pomp or splendour), " to honour or adorn ;" so that
hâdûr signifies adorned, grand (as in Gen. xxiv. 65 ; Targ.
II. LXX. ὡραῖος), splendid.   The verb *tsâ'âh*, to bend or
stoop, we have already met with in ch. li. 14.   Here it is used
to denote a gesture of proud self-consciousness, partly with or
without the idea of the proud bending back of the head (or
bending forward to listen), and partly with that of swaying to
and fro, *i.e.* the walk of a proud man swinging to and fro upon
the hips.   The latter is the sense in which we understand *tsō'eh*
here, viz. as a syn. of the Arabic *mutamâil*, to bend proudly
from one side to the other (Vitringa : *se huc illuc motitans*).
The person seen here produces the impression of great and
abundant strength ; and his walk indicates the corresponding
pride of self-consciousness.

"Who is this ?" asks the seer of a third person.   But the
answer comes from the person himself, though only seen in the
distance, and therefore with a voice that could be heard afar off.
Ver. 1*b*. "*I am he that speaketh in righteousness, mighty to aid.*"
Hitzig, Knobel, and others, take righteousness as the object of
the speaking ; and this is grammatically possible (בְּ = περί,
e.g. Deut. vi. 7).   But our prophet uses בצדק in ch. xlii. 6, xlv.
13, and בצדקה in an adverbial sense : " strictly according to
the rule of truth (more especially that of the counsel of mercy
or plan of salvation) and right."   The person approaching says
that he is great in word and deed (Jer. xxxii. 19).   He speaks
in righteousness ; in the zeal of his holiness threatening judgment to the oppressors, and promising salvation to the oppressed ;
and what he threatens and promises, he carries out with mighty
power.   He is great (רַב, not רָב ; S. ὑπερμαχῶν, Jer. *pro-
pugnator*) to aid the oppressed against their oppressors.   This
alone might lead us to surmise, that it is God from whose
mouth of righteousness (ch. xlv. 23) the consolation of redemp-

tion proceeds, and whose holy omnipotent arm (ch. lii. 10, lix. 16) carries out the act of redemption.

The seer surmises this also, and now inquires still further, whence the strange red colour of his apparel, which does not look like the purple of a king's talar or the scarlet of a chlamys. Ver. 2. " *Whence the red on thine apparel, and thy clothes like those of a wine-presser?*" מַדּוּעַ inquires the reason and cause; לָמָּה, in its primary sense, the object or purpose. The seer asks, " Why is there red ('*âdōm*, neuter, like *rabh* in ver. 7) to thine apparel?" The *Lamed*, which might be omitted (wherefore is thy garment red?), implies that the red was not its original colour, but something added (cf. Jer. xxx. 12, and *lámō* in ch. xxvi. 16, liii. 8). This comes out still more distinctly in the second half of the question : " and (why are) thy clothes like those of one who treads (wine) in the wine-press " (*b^egath* with a pausal *á* not lengthened, like *baz* in ch. viii. 1), *i.e.* saturated and stained as if with the juice of purple grapes?

The person replies : Vers. 3–6. " *I have trodden the wine-trough alone, and of the nations no one was with me: and I trode them in my wrath, and trampled them down in my fury; and their life-sap spirted upon my clothes, and all my raiment was stained. For a day of vengeance was in my heart, and the year of my redemption was come. And I looked round, and there was no helper; and I wondered there was no supporter: then mine own arm helped me; and my fury, it became my support. And I trode down nations in my wrath, and made them drunk in my fury, and made their life-blood run down to the earth.*" He had indeed trodden the wine-press (*pūrâh* = *gath*, or, if distinct from this, the pressing-trough as distinguished from the pressing-house or pressing-place ; according to Fürst, something hollowed out ; but according to the traditional interpretation from *pūr* = *pârar*, to crush, press, both different from *yeqebh* : see at ch. v. 2), and he alone ; so that the juice of the grapes had saturated and coloured his clothes, and his only. When he adds, that of the nations no one was with him, it follows that the press which he trode was so great, that he might have needed the assistance of whole nations. And when he continues thus : And I trod them in my wrath, etc., the enigma is at once explained. It was to the nations themselves that the knife was applied. They were cut off like grapes and put into the wine-press (Joel iv. 13); and

this heroic figure, of which there was no longer any doubt that
it was Jehovah Himself, had trodden them down in the impulse
and strength of His wrath.   The red upon the clothes was the
life-blood of the nations, which had spirted upon them, and with
which, as He trode this wine-press, He had soiled all His garments. *Nētsach*, according to the more recently accepted derivation from *nâtsach*, signifies, according to the traditional idea,
which is favoured by Lam. iii. 18, *vigor*, the vital strength and
life-blood, regarded as the sap of life.   וַיֵּז (compare the historical tense וַיֵּז in 2 Kings ix. 33) is the future used as an imperfect, and it spirted, from *nâzâh* (see at ch. lii. 15).   אֶגְאָלְתִּי
(from גָּאַל = גָּעַל, ch. lix. 3) is the perfect *hiphil* with an Aramæan inflexion (compare the same Aramaism in Ps. lxxvi. 6,
2 Chron. xx. 35 ; and הֶלְאַנִי, which is half like it, in Job xvi. 7);
the Hebrew form would be הִגְאַלְתִּי.[1]   AE and A regard the form
as a mixture of the perfect and future, but this is a mistake.
This work of wrath had been executed by Jehovah, because
He had in His heart a day of vengeance, which could not
be delayed, and because the year (see at ch. lxi. 2) of His
promised redemption had arrived.   גְּאוּלַי (this is the proper reading, not גְּאוּלִי, as some codd. have it; and this was the reading
which Rashi had before him in his comm. on Lam. i. 6) is
the plural of the passive participle used as an abstract noun
(compare חַיִּים *vivi*, *vitales*, or rather *viva*, *vitalia = vita*).   And
He only had accomplished this work of wrath.   Ver. 5 is the
expansion of לְבַדִּי, and almost a verbal repetition of ch. lix. 16.
The meaning is, that no one joined Him with conscious free-
will, to render help to the God of judgment and salvation in
His purposes.   The church that was devoted to Him was itself
the object of the redemption, and the great mass of those who
were estranged from Him the object of the judgment.   Thus
He found Himself alone, neither human co-operation nor the
natural course of events helping the accomplishment of His
purposes.   And consequently He renounced all human help,
and broke through the steady course of development by a
marvellous act of His own.   He trode down nations in His
wrath, and intoxicated them in His fury, and caused their life-

---

[1] The Babylonian MSS. have אֶגְאָלְתִּי with *chirek*, since the Babylonian
(Assyrian) system of punctuation has no *seghol*.

blood to flow down to the ground. The Targum adopts the rendering " *et triturabo eos*," as if the reading were וַאֲשַׁבְּרֵם, which we find in Sonc. 1488, and certain other editions, as well as in some codd. Many agree with Cappellus in preferring this reading; and in itself it is not inadmissible (see Lam. i. 15). But the LXX. and all the other ancient versions, the Masora (which distinguishes ואשברם with כ, as only met with once, from ואשברם with ב in Deut. ix. 17), and the great majority of the MSS., support the traditional reading. There is nothing surprising in the transition to the figure of the cup of wrath, which is a very common one with Isaiah. Moreover, all that is intended is, that Jehovah caused the nations to feel the full force of this His fury, by trampling them down in His fury.

Even in this short and highly poetical passage we see a desire to emblematize, just as in the emblematic cycle of prophetical night-visions in ch. xxi.–xxii. 14. For not only is the name of Edom made covertly into an emblem of its future fate, אֱדֹם becoming אָדֹם upon the apparel of Jehovah the avenger, when the blood of the people, stained with blood-guiltiness towards the people of God, is spirted out, but the name of Bozrah also; for *bâtsar* means to cut off bunches of grapes (*vindemiare*), and *botsrâh* becomes *bâtsîr*, *i.e.* a vintage, which Jehovah treads in His wrath, when He punishes the Edomitish nation as well as all the rest of the nations, which in their hostility towards Him and His people have taken pleasure in the carrying away of Israel and the destruction of Jerusalem, and have lent their assistance in accomplishing them. Knobel supposes that the judgment referred to is the defeat which Cyrus inflicted upon the nations under Crœsus and their allies; but it can neither be shown that this defeat affected the Edomites, nor can we understand why Jehovah should appear as if coming from Edom-Bozrah, after inflicting this judgment, to which ch. xli. 2 sqq. refers. Knobel himself also observes, that Edom was still an independent kingdom, and hostile to the Persians (Diod. xv. 2) not only under the reign of Cambyses (Herod. iii. 5 sqq.), but even later than that (Diod. xiii. 46). But at the time of Malachi, who lived under Artaxerxes Longimanus, if not under his successor Darius Nothus, a judgment of devastation was inflicted upon Edom (Mal. i. 3–5),

from which it never recovered. The Chaldeans, as Caspari
has shown (*Obad.* p. 142), cannot have executed it, since the
Edomites appear throughout as their accomplices, and as still
maintaining their independence even under the first Persian
kings; nor can any historical support be found to the conjecture, that it occurred in the wars between the Persians and
the Egyptians (Hitzig and Köhler, *Mal.* p. 35). What the
prophet's eye really saw was fulfilled in the time of the
Maccabæans, when Judas inflicted a total defeat upon them,
John Hyrcanus compelled them to become Jews, and Alexander Jannai completed their subjection; and in the time of
the destruction of Jerusalem by the Romans, when Simon of
Gerasa avenged their cruel conduct in Jerusalem in combination with the Zelots, by ruthlessly turning their well-cultivated
land into a horrible desert, just as it would have been left by a
swarm of locusts (Jos. *Wars of the Jews*, iv. 9, 7).

The New Testament counterpart of this passage in Isaiah
is the destruction of Antichrist and his army (Rev. xix. 11
sqq.). He who effects this destruction is called the Faithful
and True, the Logos of God; and the seer beholds Him sitting
upon a white horse, with eyes of flaming fire, and many diadems
upon His head, wearing a blood-stained garment, like the person
seen by the prophet here. The vision of John is evidently
formed upon the basis of that of Isaiah; for when it is said of
the Logos that He rules the nations with a staff of iron, this
points to Ps. ii.; and when it is still further said that He treads
the wine-press of the wrath of Almighty God, this points back
to Isa. lxiii. The reference throughout is not to the first
coming of the Lord, when He laid the foundation of His kingdom by suffering and dying, but to His final coming, when He
will bring His regal sway to a victorious issue. Nevertheless
ch. lxiii. 1-6 has always been a favourite passage for reading
in Passion week. It is no doubt true that the Christian cannot
read this prophecy without thinking of the Saviour streaming
with blood, who trode the wine-press of wrath for us without
the help of angels and men, *i.e.* who conquered wrath for us.
But the prophecy does not relate to this. The blood upon the
garment of the divine Hero is not His own, but that of His
enemies; and His treading of the wine-press is not the conquest
of wrath, but the manifestation of wrath. This section can

only be properly used as a lesson for Passion week so far as this, that Jehovah, who here appears to the Old Testament seer, was certainly He who became man in His Christ, in the historical fulfilment of His purposes; and behind the first advent to bring salvation there stood with warning form the final coming to judgment, which will take vengeance upon that Edom, to whom the red lentil-judgment of worldly lust and power was dearer than the red life-blood of that loving Servant of Jehovah who offered Himself for the sin of the whole world.

There follows now in ch. lxiii. 7–lxiv. 11 a prayer commencing with thanksgiving as it looks back to the past, and closing with a prayer for help as it turns to the present. Hitzig and Knobel connect this closely with ch. lxiii. 1–6, assuming that through the great event which had occurred, viz. the overthrow of Edom, and of the nations hostile to the people of God as such, by which the exiles were brought one step nearer to freedom, the prophet was led to praise Jehovah for all His previous goodness to Israel. There is nothing, however, to indicate this connection, which is in itself a very loose one. The prayer which follows is chiefly an entreaty, and an entreaty appended to ch. lxiii. 1–6, but without any retrospective allusion to it: it is rather a prayer in general for the realization of the redemption already promised. Ewald is right in regarding ch. lxiii. 7–lxvi. as an appendix to this whole book of consolation, since the traces of the same prophet are unmistakeable; but the whole style of the description is obviously different, and the historical circumstances must have been still further developed in the meantime.

The three prophecies which follow are the *finale* of the whole. The announcement of the prophet, which has reached its highest point in the majestic vision in ch. lxiii. 1–6, is now drawing to an end. It is standing close upon the threshold of all that has been promised, and nothing remains but the fulfilment of the promise, which he has held up like a jewel on every side. And now, just as in the finale of a poetical composition, all the melodies and movements that have been struck before are gathered up into one effective close; and first of all, as in Hab. iii., into a prayer, which forms, as it were, the lyrical echo of the preaching that has gone before.

THE THREE CLOSING PROPHECIES.

FIRST CLOSING PROPHECY.—CHAP. LXIII. 7–LXIV.

THANKSGIVING, CONFESSION, AND SUPPLICATION OF THE CHURCH OF THE CAPTIVITY.

THE prophet, as the leader of the prayers of the church, here passes into the expanded style of the *tephillah*. Ver. 7. "*I will celebrate the mercies of Jehovah, the praises of Jehovah, as is seemly for all that Jehovah hath shown us, and the great goodness towards the house of Israel, which He hath shown them according to His pity, and the riches of His mercies.*" The speaker is the prophet, in the name of the church, or, what is the same thing, the church in which the prophet includes himself. The prayer commences with thanksgiving, according to the fundamental rule in Ps. l. 23. The church brings to its own remembrance, as the subject of praise in the presence of God, all the words and deeds by which Jehovah has displayed His mercy and secured glory to Himself. חַסְדֵי (this is the correct pointing, with ד protected by *gaya*; cf. בְּדְכֹר in ch. liv. 12) are the many thoughts of mercy and acts of mercy into which the grace of God, *i.e.* His one purpose of grace and His one work of grace, had been divided. They are just so many *t^ehillōth*, self-glorifications of God, and impulses to His glorification. On כְּעַל, as is seemly, see at ch. lix. 18. There is no reason for assuming that וְרַב־טוּב is equivalent to וּגְעַל רב־טוב, as Hitzig and Knobel do. רב־טוב commences the second object to אַזְכִּיר, in which what follows is unfolded as a parallel to the first. *Rabh*, the much, is a neuter formed into a substantive, as in Ps. cxlv. 7; *rōbh*, plurality or multiplicity, is an infinitive used as a substantive. *Tūbh* is God's benignant goodness; *rachămīm*, His deepest sympathizing tenderness; *chesed* (root חם, used of violent emotion; cf. Syr. *chăsad, chăsam, œmulari*; Arab. حَس, to be tender, full of compassion), grace which condescends to and comes to meet a sinful creature. After this introit, the prayer itself commences with a retrospective glance at the time of the giving of the law, when the relation of a child, in which Israel stood to Jehovah, was solemnly proclaimed and legally regulated. Ver. 8. "*He said, They are my people, children who will not lie; and He became their Saviour.*" אַךְ is used here in its primary affirmative sense. יְשַׁקֵּרוּ is the future of hope. When He made them His people, His children, He expected from them a grateful return of His covenant grace in covenant fidelity; and whenever they needed help from above, He became their Saviour (*mōshīă*). We can recognise the ring of Ex. xv. 2 here, just as in ch. xii. 2. *Mōshīă* is a favourite word in ch. xl.–lxvi. (compare, however, ch. xix. 20 also)

The next verse commemorates the way in which He proved Himself a Saviour in heart and action. Ver. 9. "*In all their affliction He was afflicted, and the Angel of His face brought them salvation. In His love and in His pity He redeemed them, and lifted them up, and bare them all the days of the olden time.*" This is one of the fifteen passages in which the *chethib* has לֹא, the *keri* לוֹ. It is only with difficulty that we can obtain any meaning from the *chethib*: "in all the affliction which He brought upon them He did not afflict, viz. according to their desert" (Targ., Jer., Rashi); or better still, as *tsăr* must in this case be derived from *tsūr*, and *tsăr* is only met with in an intransitive sense, "In all their distress there was no distress" (Saad.), with which J. D. Michaelis compares 2 Cor. iv. 8, "troubled on every side, yet not distressed." The oxymoron is perceptible enough, but the לָהֶם (לֹא צָר), which is indispensable to this expression, is wanting. Even with the explanation, "In all their affliction He was not an enemy, viz. Jehovah, to them" (Döderlein), or "No man persecuted them without the angel immediately," etc. (Cocceius and Rosenmüller), we miss לָהֶם or אֹתָם. There are other still more twisted and jejune attempts to explain the passage with לֹא, which are not worth the space they occupy. Even the older translators did not know how to deal with the לֹא in the text. The Sept. takes *tsăr* as equivalent to *tsīr*, a messenger, and renders the passage according to its own peculiar interpunctuation: οὐ πρέσβυς οὐδὲ ἄγγελος, ἀλλ' αὐτὸς ἔσωσεν αὐτούς (neither a messenger nor an angel, but His face, *i.e.* He

Himself helped them: Ex. xxxiii. 14, 15; 2 Sam. xvii. 11).
Everything forces to the conclusion that the *keri* לוֹ is to be
preferred. The Masora actually does reckon this as one of the
fifteen passages in which לוֹ is to be read for לֹא.[1] Jerome was
also acquainted with this explanation. He says: "Where we
have rendered it, 'In all their affliction He was not afflicted,'
which is expressed in Hebrew by LO, the adverb of negation,
we might read IPSE; so that the sense would be, 'In all their
affliction He, *i.e.* God, was afflicted.'" If we take the sentence
in this way, "In all oppression there was oppression to Him,"
it yields a forcible thought in perfect accordance with the Scripture (compare *e.g.* Judg. x. 16), an expression in harmony with
the usage of the language (compare *tsar-li*, 2 Sam. i. 26), and
a construction suited to the contents (לוֹ = *ipsi*). There is
nothing to surprise us in the fact that God should be said to
feel the sufferings of His people as His own sufferings; for
the question whether God can feel pain is answered by the
Scriptures in the affirmative. He can as surely as everything
originates in Him, with the exception of sin, which is a free
act and only originates in Him so far as the possibility is concerned, but not in its actuality. Just as a man can feel pain,
and yet in his personality keep himself superior to it, so God
feels pain without His own happiness being thereby destroyed.
And so did He suffer with His people; their affliction was
reflected in His own life in Himself, and shared Him inwardly. But because He, the all-knowing, all-feeling One,
is also the almighty will, He sent the angel of His face, and
brought them salvation. "The angel of His face," says
Knobel, "is the pillar of cloud and fire, in which Jehovah was
present with His people in the march through the desert, with
His protection, instruction, and guidance, the helpful presence
of God in the pillar of cloud and fire." But where do we ever
read of this, that it brought Israel salvation in the pressure of

---

[1] There are fifteen passages in which the *keri* substitutes לוֹ for לֹא.
See *Masora magna* on Lev. xi. 21 (*Psalter*, ii. 60). If we add Isa. xlix. 5,
1 Chron. xi. 20, 1 Sam. ii. 16, there are eighteen (*Job*, vol. i. p. 213). But
the first two of these are not reckoned, because they are doubtful; and in
the third, instead of לוֹ being substituted for לֹא, לֹא is substituted for לוֹ
(Ges. *Thes.* 735, *b*). 2 Sam. xix. 7 also is not a case in point, for there
the *keri* is לוֹ for לֹא.

great dangers? Only on one occasion (Ex. xiv. 19, 20) does it cover the Israelites from their pursuers; but in that very instance a distinction is expressly made between the angel of God and the pillar of cloud. Consequently the cloud and the angel were two distinct media of the manifestation of the presence of God. They differed in two respects. The cloud was a material medium—the veil, the sign, and the site of the revealed presence of God. The angel, on the other hand, was a personal medium, a ministering spirit (λειτουργικὸν πνεῦμα), in which the name of Jehovah was indwelling for the purpose of His own self-attestation in connection with the historical preparation for the coming of salvation (Ex. xxiii. 21). He was the mediator of the preparatory work of God in both word and deed under the Old Testament, and the manifestation of that redeeming might and grace which realized in Israel the covenant promises given to Abraham (Gen. xv.). A second distinction consisted in the fact that the cloud was a mode of divine manifestation which was always visible; whereas, although the angel of God did sometimes appear in human shape both in the time of the patriarchs and also in that of Joshua (Josh. v. 13 sqq.), it never appeared in such a form during the history of the exodus, and therefore is only to be regarded as a mode of divine revelation which was chiefly discernible in its effects, and belonged to the sphere of invisibility : so that in any case, if we search in the history of the people that was brought out of Egypt for the fulfilment of such promises as Ex. xxiii. 20–23, we are forced to the conclusion that the cloud was the medium of the settled presence of God in His angel in the midst of Israel, although it is never so expressed in the *thorah*. This mediatorial angel is called " the angel of His face," as being the representative of God, for " the face of God" is His self-revealing presence (even though only revealed to the mental eye); and consequently the presence of God, which led Israel to Canaan, is called directly " His face" in Deut. iv. 37, apart from the angelic mediation to be understood; and " my face " in Ex. xxxiii. 14, 15, by the side of " my angel" in Ex. xxxii. 34, and the angel in Ex. xxxiii. 2, appears as something incomparably higher than the presence of God through the mediation of that one angel, whose personality is completely hidden by his mediatorial instrumen-

tality. The genitive פָּנָיו, therefore, is not to be taken objectively in the sense of "the angel who sees His face," but as
explanatory, "the angel who is His face, or in whom His face
is manifested." The הוּא which follows does not point back to
the angel, but to Jehovah, who reveals Himself thus. But
although the angel is regarded as a distinct being from
Jehovah, it is also regarded as one that is completely hidden
before Him, whose name is in him. He redeemed them by
virtue of His love and of His *chemlâh*, *i.e.* of His forgiving
gentleness (Arabic, with the letters transposed, *chilm;* compare,
however, *chamûl*, gentle-hearted), and lifted them up, and
carried them (נִשָּׂא the consequence of נָטַל, which is similar in
sense, and more Aramæan ; cf. *tollere* root *tal,* and *ferre* root
bhar, perf. *tuli*) all the days of the olden time.

The prayer passes now quite into the tone of Ps. lxxviii.
and cvi., and begins to describe how, in spite of Jehovah's
grace, Israel fell again and again away from Jehovah, and yet
was always rescued again by virtue of His grace. For it is
impossible that it should leap at once in וַהֲפֵמָה to the people who
caused the captivity, and וַיִּזָּכֹר have for its subject the penitential church of the exiles which was longing for redemption
(Ewald). The train of thought is rather this: From the proofs
of grace which the Israel of the olden time had experienced,
the prophet passes to that disobedience to Jehovah into which
it fell, to that punishment of Jehovah which it thereby brought
upon itself, and to that longing for the renewal of the old
Mosaic period of redemption, which seized it in the midst of its
state of punishment. But instead of saying that Jehovah did
not leave this longing unsatisfied, and responded to the penitence of Israel with ever fresh help, the prophet passes at once
from the desire of the old Israel for redemption, to the prayer
of the existing Israel for redemption, suppressing the intermediate thought, that Israel was even now in such a state of
punishment and longing.

Israel's ingratitude. Ver. 10. "*But they resisted and vexed
His Holy Spirit: then He turned to be their enemy ; He made
war upon them.*" Not only has וְעִצְּבוּ (to cause cutting pain)
אֶת־רוּחַ קָדְשׁוֹ as its object, but מָרוּ has the same (on the primary
meaning, see at ch. iii. 8). In other cases, the object of *merôth*
(*hamrôth*) is Jehovah, or His word, His promise, His providence,

hence Jehovah himself in the revelations of His nature in word
and deed; here it is the spirit of holiness, which is distinguished
from Him as a personal existence. For just as the angel who
is His face, *i.e.* the representation of His nature, is designated
as a person both by His name and also by the redeeming
activity ascribed to Him; so also is the Spirit of holiness, by
the fact that He can be grieved, and therefore can feel grief
(compare Eph. iv. 30, "Grieve not the Holy Spirit of God").
Hence Jehovah, and the angel of His face, and the Spirit of
His holiness, are distinguished as three persons, but so that the
two latter derive their existence from the first, which is the
absolute ground of the Deity, and of everything that is divine.
Now, if we consider that the angel of Jehovah was indeed an
angel, but that he was the angelic anticipation of the appearance of God the Mediator "in the flesh," and served to fore-
shadow Him "who, as the image of the invisible God" (Col. i. 15),
as "the reflection of His glory and the stamp of His nature"
(Heb. i. 3), is not merely a temporary medium of self-manifestation, but the perfect personal self-manifestation of the divine
pânīm, we have here an unmistakeable indication of the mystery
of the triune nature of God the One, which was revealed in
history in the New Testament work of redemption. The subject
to וַיֵּהָפֵךְ is Jehovah, whose Holy Spirit they troubled. He who
proved Himself to be their Father (cf. Deut. xxxii. 6), became,
through the reaction of His holiness, the very reverse of what
He wished to be. He turned to be their enemy; הוּא, He, the most
fearful of all foes, made war against them. This is the way in
which we explain ver. 10*b*, although with this explanation it
would have to be accentuated differently, viz. וַיֵּהָפֵךְ *mahpach*,
לָהֶם *pashta*, לְאוֹיֵב *zakeph*, הוּא *tiphchah*, נִלְחַם־בָּם *silluk*. The
accentuation as we find it takes הוּא נִלְחַם־בָּם as an attributive
clause: "to an enemy, who made war against them."

Israel being brought to a right mind in the midst of this
state of punishment, longed for the better past to return.
Vers. 11–14. " *Then His people remembered the days of the olden
time, of Moses: Where is He who brought them up out of the sea
with the shepherd of his flock? where is He who put the spirit of
His holiness in the midst of them; who caused the arm of His
majesty to go at the right of Moses; who split the waters before
them, to make Himself an everlasting name: who caused them*

to pass through abysses of the deep, like the horse upon the plain,
without their stumbling?   Like the cattle which goeth down
into the valley, the Spirit of Jehovah brought them to rest: thus
hast Thou led Thy people, to make Thyself a majestic name."
According to the accentuation before us, ver. 11*a* should be
rendered thus: "Then He (viz. Jehovah) remembered the
days of the olden time, the Moses of His people" (LXX.,
Targ., Syr., Jerome).   But apart from the strange expression
"the Moses of His people," which might perhaps be regarded
as possible, because the proper name *mosheh* might suggest the
thought of its real meaning in Hebrew, viz. *extrahens=liberator*,
but which the Syriac rejects by introducing the reading '*abhdō*
(Moses, His servant), we have only to look at the questions of
evidently human longing which follow, to see that Jehovah
cannot be the subject to וַיִּזְכֹּר (remembered), by which these
reminiscences are introduced.   It is the people which begins its
inquiries with אַיֵּה, just as in Jer. ii. 6 (cf. ch. li. 9, 10), and
recals "the days of olden time," according to the admonition in
Deut. xxxii. 7.   Consequently, in spite of the accents, such
Jewish commentators as Saad. and Rashi regard "his people"
('*ammō*) as the subject; whereas others, such as AE, Kimchi,
and Abravanel, take account of the accents, and make the
people the suppressed subject of the verb "remembered," by
rendering it thus, "Then it remembered the days of olden time,
(the days) of Moses (and) His people," or in some similar way.
But with all modifications the rendering is forced and lame.
The best way of keeping to the accents is that suggested by
Stier, "Then men (indef. *man*, the French *on*) remembered the
days of old, the Moses of His people."   But why did the
prophet not say וַיִּזְכְּרוּ, as the proper sequel to ver. 10?   We
prefer to adopt the following rendering and accentuation: Then
remembered (*zakeph gadol*) the days-of-old (*mercha*) of Moses
(*tiphchah*) His people.   The object stands before the subject,
as for example in 2 Kings v. 13 (compare the inversions in
ch. viii. 22 *extr.*, xxii. 2 *init.*); and *mosheh* is a genitive govern-
ing the composite "days of old" (for this form of the construct
state, compare ch. xxviii. 1 and Ruth ii. 1).   The retrospect
commences with "Where is He who led them up?" etc.   The
suffix of הַמַּעֲלֵם (for הַמְעָלָם, like רֹדֵם in Ps. lxviii. 28, and therefore with the verbal force predominant) refers to the ancestors;

and although the word is determined by the suffix, it has the article as equivalent to a demonstrative pronoun (*ille qui sursum duxit, eduxit eos*). " The shepherd of his flock" is added as a more precise definition, not dependent upon *vayyizkōr*, as even the accents prove. אֵת is rendered emphatic by *yethib*, since here it signifies *unâ cum*. The Targum takes it in the sense of *instar pastoris gregis sui;* but though עִם is sometimes used in this way, אֵת never is. Both the LXX. and Targum read רֹעֵה; Jerome, on the other hand, adopts the reading רֹעִי, and this is the Masoretic reading, for the Masora in Gen. xlvii. 3 reckons four רֹעֵה, without including the present passage. Kimchi and Abravanel also support this reading, and Norzi very properly gives it the preference. The shepherds of the flock of Jehovah are Moses and Aaron, together with Miriam (Ps. lxxvii. 21; Mic. vi. 4). With these (*i.e.* in their company or under their guidance) Jehovah led His people up out of Egypt through the Red Sea. With the reading רֹעִי, the question whether *beqirbô* refers to Moses or Israel falls to the ground. Into the heart of His people (Neh. ix. 20) Jehovah put the spirit of His holiness: it was present in the midst of Israel, inasmuch as Moses, Aaron, Miriam, the Seventy, and the prophets in the camp possessed it, and inasmuch as Joshua inherited it as the successor of Moses, and all the people might become possessed of it. The majestic might of Jehovah, which manifested itself majestically, is called the "arm of His majesty ;" an anthropomorphism to which the expression " who caused it to march at the right hand of Moses" compels us to give an interpretation worthy of God. Stier will not allow that זְרֹעַ תִּפְאַרְתּוֹ is to be taken as the object, and exclaims, " What a marvellous figure of speech, an arm walking at a person's right hand !" But the arm which is visible in its deeds belongs to the God who is invisible in His own nature; and the meaning is, that the active power of Moses was not left to itself, but the overwhelming omnipotence of God went by its side, and endowed it with superhuman strength. It was by virtue of this that the elevated staff and extended hand of Moses divided the Red Sea (Ex. xiv. 16). בּוֹקֵעַ has *mahpach* attached to the ב, and therefore the tone drawn back upon the penultimate, and *metheg* with the *tsere*, that it may not be slipped over in the pronunciation. The clause לַעֲשׂוֹת וגו׳ affirms that the absolute purpose of God is in Himself. But He is holy love, and whilst willing for Himself, He wills at the same time the salvation of His creatures. He makes to Himself an "everlasting name," by glorifying Himself in such memorable miracles of redemption, as that performed in the deliverance of His people out of Egypt. According to the general order of the passage, ver. 13 apparently refers to the passage through the Jordan; but the psalmist, in Ps. cvi. 9 (cf. lxxvii. 17), understood it as referring to the passage through the Red Sea. The prayer dwells upon this chief miracle, of which the other was only an after-play. "As the horse gallops over the plain," so did they pass through the depths of the sea לֹא יִכָּשֵׁלוּ (a circumstantial minor clause), *i.e.* without stumbling. Then follows another beautiful figure: "like the beast that goeth down into the valley," not "as the beast goeth down into the valley," the Spirit of Jehovah brought it (Israel) to rest, viz. to the *m'nûchâh* of the Canaan flowing with milk and honey (Deut. xii. 9; Ps. xcv. 11), where it rested and was refreshed after the long and wearisome march through the sandy desert, like a flock that had descended from the bare mountains to the brooks and meadows of the valley. The Spirit of God is represented as the leader here (as in Ps. cxliii. 10), viz. through the medium of those who stood, enlightened and instigated by Him, at the head of the wandering people. The following כֵּן is no more a correlate of the foregoing particle of comparison than in ch. lii. 14. It is a recapitulation, and refers to the whole description as far back as ver. 9, passing with נִהַגְתָּ into the direct tone of prayer.

The way is prepared for the petitions for redemption which follow, outwardly by the change in ver. 14*b*, from a mere description to a direct address, and inwardly by the thought, that Israel is at the present time in such a condition, as to cause it to look back with longing eyes to the time of the Mosaic redemption. Ver. 15. "*Look from heaven and see, from the habitation of Thy holiness and majesty! Where is Thy zeal and Thy display of might? The pressure of Thy bowels and Thy compassions are restrained towards me.*" On the relation between הִבִּיט, to look up, to open the eyes, and רָאָה, to fix the eye upon a thing, see p. 185. It is very rarely that we meet with the words in the reverse order, ראה והביט (*vid.* Hab. i. 5; Lam. i. 11). In the second clause of ver. 15*a*, instead of *misshâmayim*

(from heaven), we have " from the dwelling-place (*mizz*ᵉ*bhul*)
of Thy holiness and majesty." The all-holy and all-glorious
One, who once revealed Himself so gloriously in the history of
Israel, has now withdrawn into His own heaven, where He is
only revealed to the spirits. The object of the looking and
seeing, as apparent from what follows, is the present helpless
condition of the people in their sufferings, to which there does
not seem likely to be any end. There are no traces now of the
kin'âh (zeal) with which Jehovah used to strive on behalf of
His people, and against their oppressors (ch. xxvi. 11), or of the
former displays of His *gᵉbhûrâh* (וּגְבוּרֹתֶךָ, as it is correctly written
in Ven. 1521, is a defective plural). In ver. 15*b* we have not
a continued question (" the sounding of Thy bowels and Thy
mercies, which are restrained towards me ?"), as Hitzig and
Knobel suppose. The words '*ēlai hith'appâqū* have not the
appearance of an attributive clause, either according to the new
strong thought expressed, or according to the order of the words
(with אֵלַי written first). On *strepitus viscerum*, as the effect
and sign of deep sympathy, see at ch. xvi. 11. רַחֲמִים and
מֵעַיִם, or rather מֵעִים (from מֵעֶה, of the form רֵעֶה), both signify
primarily σπλάγχνα, strictly speaking the soft inward parts
of the body; the latter from the root מַע, to be pulpy or soft,
the former from the root רח, to be slack, loose, or soft. הֲמוֹן, as
the plural of the predicate shows, does not govern רַחֲמֶיךָ also.
It is presupposed that the love of Jehovah urges Him towards
His people, to relieve their misery; but His compassion and
sympathy apparently put constraint upon themselves (*hith'appēq*
as in ch. xlii. 14, lit. *se superare*, from '*âphaq*, root פק), to abstain
from working on behalf of Israel.

The prayer for help, and the lamentation over its absence,
are now justified in ver. 16 : " *For Thou art our Father ; for
Abraham is ignorant of us, and Israel knoweth us not. Thou,
O Jehovah, art our Father ; our Redeemer is from olden time
Thy name.*" Jehovah is Israel's Father (Deut. xxxii. 6). His
creative might, and the gracious counsels of His love, have
called it into being : אָבִינוּ has not yet the deep and unrestricted
sense of the New Testament " Our Father." The second *kî*
introduces the reason for this confession that Jehovah was
Israel's Father, and could therefore look for paternal care and
help from Him alone. Even the dearest and most honourable

men, the forefathers of the nation, could not help it. Abraham
and Jacob-Israel had been taken away from this world, and
were unable to interfere on their own account in the history
of their people. יָדַע and הִכִּיר suggest the idea of participating
notice and regard, as in Deut. xxxiii. 9 and Ruth ii. 10, 19.
יַכִּירָנוּ has the vowel *â* (pausal for *a*, ch. lvi. 3) in the place of *ĕ*,
to rhyme with יְדָעָנוּ (see Ges. § 60, Anm. 2). In the concluding clause, according to the accents, גֹּאֲלֵנוּ מֵעוֹלָם are connected
together; but the more correct accentuation is גאלנו *tiphchah*,
מעולם *mercha*, and we have rendered it so. From the very
earliest time the acts of Jehovah towards Israel had been such
that Israel could call Him גאלנו.

But in the existing state of things there was a contrast
which put their faith to a severe test. Ver. 17. " *O Jehovah,
why leadest Thou us astray from Thy ways, hardenest our heart,
so as not to fear Thee? Return for Thy servants' sake, the tribes
of Thine inheritance.*" When men have scornfully and obstinately rejected the grace of God, God withdraws it from them
judicially, gives them up to their wanderings, and makes their
heart incapable of faith (*hiqshīăch*, which only occurs again in
Job xxxix. 16, is here equivalent to *hiqshâh* in Ps. xcv. 8,
Deut. ii. 30). The history of Israel from ch. vi. onwards has
been the history of such a gradual judgment of hardening, and
such a curse, eating deeper and deeper, and spreading its influence wider and wider round. The great mass are lost, but
not without the possibility of deliverance for the better part of
the nation, which now appeals to the mercy of God, and sighs
for deliverance from this ban. Two reasons are assigned for
this petition for the return of the gracious presence of God:
first, that there are still " servants of Jehovah" to be found,
as this prayer itself actually proves; and secondly, that the
divine election of grace cannot perish.

But the existing condition of Israel looks like a withdrawal
of this grace; and it is impossible that these contrasts should
cease, unless Jehovah comes down from heaven as the deliverer
of His people. Vers. 18, 19 (lxiv. 1). " *For a little time Thy
holy people was in possession. Our adversaries have trodden
down Thy sanctuary. We have become such as He who is from
everlasting has not ruled over, upon whom Thy name was not
called. O that Thou wouldst rend the heaven, come down, the*

mountains would shake before thy countenance." It is very natural
to try whether *yâr^eshū* may not have *tsârēnū* for its subject (cf.
Jer. xlix. 2) ; but all the attempts made to explain the words
on this supposition, show that *lammits^eâr* is at variance with the
idea that *yâr^eshū* refers to the foes. Compare, for example,
Jerome's rendering " *quasi nihilum* (*i.e. ad nihil et absque allo
labore) possederunt populum sanctum tuum ;* " that of Cocceius,
"*propemodum ad hæreditatem;*" and that of Stier, " for a little
they possess entirely Thy holy nation." *Mits^eâr* is the harsher
form for *miz^eâr*, which the prophet uses in ch. x. 25, xvi. 14,
xxix. 17 for a contemptibly small space of time; and as ל is commonly used to denote the time to which, towards which, within
which, and through which, anything occurs (cf. 2 Chron. xi.
17, xxix. 17 ; Ewald, § 217, *d*), *lammits^eâr* may signify for a
(lit. the well-known) short time (*per breve tempus ;* like εἰς, ἐπ',
κατ' ἐνιαυτόν, a year long). If *miqdâsh* could mean the holy
land, as Hitzig and others suppose, *miqdâshekhâ* might be the
common object of both sentences (Ewald, § 351, p. 838). But
miqdash Jehovah (the sanctuary of Jehovah) is the place of
His abode and worship ; and " taking possession of the temple "
is hardly an admissible expression. On the other hand, *yârash
hâ'ârets*, to take possession of the (holy) land, is so common a
phrase (*e.g.* ch. lx. 21, lxv. 9 ; Ps. xliv. 4), that with the words
"Thy holy people possessed for a little (time) " we naturally
supply the holy land as the object. The order of the words in
the two clauses is chiastic. The two strikingly different subjects touch one another as the two inner members. Of the
perfects, the first expresses the more remote past, the second
the nearer past, as in ch. lx. 10*b*. The two clauses of the verse
rhyme,—the holiest thing in the possession of the people, which
was holy according to the choice and calling of Jehovah, being
brought into the greatest prominence ; *bōsēs* = πατεῖν, Luke
xxi. 24, Rev. xi. 2. Hahn's objection, that the time between
the conquest of the land and the Chaldean catastrophe could
not be called *mits^eâr* (a little while), may be answered, from the
fact that a time which is long in itself shrinks up when looked
back upon or recalled, and that as an actual fact from the time
of David and Solomon, when Israel really rejoiced in the possession of the land, the coming catastrophe began to be fore-
boded by many significant preludes. The lamentation in ver.

19 proceeds from the same feeling which caused the better portion of the past to vanish before the long continuance of the mournful present (compare the reverse at p. 346). Hitzig renders הָיִינוּ "we were;" Hahn, "we shall be;" but here, where the speaker is not looking back, as in ch. xxvi. 17, at a state of things which has come to an end, but rather at one which is still going on, it signifies "we have become." The passage is rendered correctly in S.: ἐγενήθημεν (or better, γεγόναμεν) ὡς ἀπ᾽ αἰῶνος ὧν οὐκ ἐξουσίασας οὐδὲ ἐπικλήθη τὸ ὄνομά σου αὐτοῖς. The virtual predicate to *hâyînū* commences with *mē'ōlâm*: "we have become such (or like such persons) as," etc.; which would be fully expressed by כְּעַם אֲשֶׁר, or merely כַּאֲשֶׁר, or without אֲשֶׁר, and simply by transposing the words, כְּלֹא מָשַׁלְתָּ וגו׳ (cf. Obad. 16): compare the virtual subject יהוה אֲהֵבוֹ in ch. xlviii. 14, and the virtual object יִקְרָא בִשְׁמִי in ch. xli. 25 (Ewald, § 333, *b*). Every form of "as if" is intentionally omitted. The relation in which Jehovah placed Himself to Israel, viz. as its King, and as to His own people called by His name, appears not only as though it had been dissolved, but as though it had never existed at all. The existing state of Israel is a complete practical denial of any such relation. Deeper tones than these no lamentation could possibly utter, and hence the immediate utterance of the sigh which goes up to heaven: "O that Thou wouldst rend heaven!" It is extremely awkward to begin a fresh chapter with כִּקְדֹחַ (" as when the melting fire burneth"); at the same time, the Masoretic division of the verses is unassailable.[1] For ver. 19*b* (ch. lxiv. 1) could not be attached to ch. lxiv. 1, 2, since this verse would be immensely overladen; moreover, this sigh really belongs to ver. 19*a* (ch. lxiii. 19), and ascends out of the depth of the lamentation uttered there. On *utinam discideris = discinderes*, see at ch. xlviii. 18. The wish presupposes that the gracious presence of God had been withdrawn from Israel, and that Israel felt itself to be separated from the world beyond by a thick party-wall, resembling an impenetrable black cloud. The closing member of the optative clause is generally rendered (*utinam*) *a facie tua montes diffluerent* (*e.g.* Rosenmüller after

---

[1] In the Hebrew Bibles, chap. lxiv. commences at the second verse of our version; and the first verse is attached to ver. 19 of the previous chapter.—Tr.

the LXX. τακήσονται), or more correctly, *defluerent* (Jerome),
as *nâzal* means to flow down, not to melt. The meaning therefore would be, "O that they might flow down, as it were to
the ground melting in the fire" (Hitzig). The form *nâzollu*
cannot be directly derived from *nâzal*, if taken in this sense;
for it is a pure fancy that *nâzōllū* may be a modification of the
pausal נָזֵלּוּ with *ō* for *ā*, and the so-called *dagesh affectuosum*).
Stier invents a verb *med. o.* נֹזל. The more probable supposition is, that it is a *niphal* formed from *zâlāl* = *nâzal* (Ewald,
§ 193, *c*). But *zâlal* signifies to hang down slack, to sway to
and fro (hence *zōlēl*, lightly esteemed, and *zalzallīm*, ch. xviii. 5,
pliable branches), like *zūl* in ch. xlvi. 6, to shake, to pour down;[1]
and *nâzōllu*, if derived from this, yields the appropriate sense
concuterentur (compare the Arabic *zalzala*, which is commonly
applied to an earthquake). The nearest *niphal* form would be
נָזֹלּוּ (or resolved, נָזֹלוּ, Judg. v. 5); but instead of the *a* of the
second syllable, the *niphal* of the verbs ע"ע has sometimes *o*,
like the verb ע"ז (*e.g.* נָזֹלּוּ, ch. xxxiv. 4; Ges. § 67, Anm. 5).

The similes which follow cannot be attached to this *nâzōllū*,
however we may explain it. Yet ch. lxiv. 1 (2) does not form
a new and independent sentence; but we must in thought
repeat the word upon which the principal emphasis rests in ch.
lxiii. 19*b* (ch. lxiv. 1). Ch. lxiv. 1, 2 (2, 3). "(*Wouldst come
down) as fire kindles brushwood, fire causes water to boil; to make
known Thy name to Thine adversaries, that the heathen may tremble
before Thy face! When Thou doest terrible things which we hoped
not for; wouldst come down, (and) mountains shake before Thy
countenance!*" The older expositors gave themselves a great
deal of trouble in the attempt to trace *hămâsīm* to *mâsas*, to
melt. But since Louis de Dieu and Albert Schultens have
followed Saadia and Abulwâlid in citing the Arabic همس, to
crack, to mutter, to mumble, etc., and هشم, to break in pieces,
confringere, from which comes *hashim*, broken, dry wood, it is
generally admitted that *hămâsim* is from *hemes* (lit. crackling,
rattling, Arab. *hams*), and signifies "dry twigs," *arida sarmenta*.
The second simile might be rendered, "as water bubbles up

---

[1] Just as the Greek has in addition to σαλ-εύειν the much simpler and
more root-like σεί-ειν; so the Semitic has, besides זל, the roots זא, עו: compare the Arabic זלל, זאזע, עזעז, all three denoting restless motion.

in the fire;" and in that case *mayim* would be treated as a feminine (according to the rule in Ges. § 146, 3), in support of which Job xiv. 19 may be adduced as an unquestionable example (although in other cases it is masculine), and בְּאֵשׁ = אֵשׁ would be used in a local sense, like *lehâbhâh*, into flames, in ch. v. 24. But it is much more natural to take אֵשׁ, which is just as often a feminine as מִים is a masculine, as the subject of תִּבְעֶה, and to give to the verb בָּעָה, which is originally intransitive, judging from the Arabic بغى, to swell, the Chald. בּוּע, to spring up (compare אֲבַעְבֻּעוֹת, blisters, pustules), the Syr. בְּנָא, to bubble up, etc., the transitive meaning to *cause* to boil or bubble up, rather than the intransitive to boil (comp. ch. xxx. 13, נִבְעֶה, swollen = bent forwards, as it were *protumidus*). Jehovah is to come down with the same irresistible force which fire exerts upon brushwood or water, when it sets the former in flames and makes the latter boil; in order that by such a display of might He may make His name known (viz. the name thus judicially revealing itself, hence "in fire," ch. xxx. 27, lxvi. 15) to His adversaries, and that nations (viz. those that are idolaters) may tremble before Him (מִפָּנֶיךָ: cf. Ps. lxviii. 2, 3). The infinitive clause denoting the purpose, like that indicating the comparison, passes into the finite (cf. ch. x. 2, xiii. 9, xiv. 25). Modern commentators for the most part now regard the optative *lû'* (O that) as extending to ver. 2 also; and, in fact, although this continued influence of *lû'* appears to overstep the bounds of the possible, we are forced to resort to this extremity. Ver. 2 cannot contain a historical retrospect: the word "formerly" would be introduced if it did, and the order of the words would be a different one. Again, we cannot assume that יָרַדְתָּ מִפָּנֶיךָ הָרִים נָזֹלּוּ contains an expression of confidence, or that the perfects indicate certainty. Neither the context, the foregoing בַּעֲשׂוֹתְךָ נוֹרָאוֹת (why not עָשָׂה?), nor the parenthetical assertion לֹא נְקַוֶּה, permits of this. On the other hand, בעשותך וגו' connects itself very appropriately with the purposes indicated in ver. 1 (2): "may tremble when Thou doest terrible things, which we, *i.e.* such as we, do not look for," *i.e.* which surpass our expectations. And now nothing remains but to recognise the resumption of ch. lxiii. 19 (lxiv. 1) in the clause "The mountains shake at Thy presence," in which case ch.

lxiii. 19*b*–lxiv. 2 (lxiv. 1–3) forms a grand period rounded off palindromically after Isaiah's peculiar style.

The following clause gives the reason for this; וֹ being very frequently the logical equivalent for *kî* (*e.g.* ch. iii. 7 and xxxviii. 15). The justification of this wish, which is forced from them by the existing misery, is found in the incomparable acts of Jehovah for the good of His own people, which are to be seen in a long series of historical events. Ver. 3 (4). *" For from olden time men have not heard, nor perceived, nor hath an eye seen, a God beside Thee, who acted on behalf of him that waiteth for Him."* No ear, no eye has ever been able to perceive the existence of a God who acted like Jehovah, *i.e.* really interposed on behalf of those who set their hopes upon Him. This is the explanation adopted by Knobel; but he wrongly supplies נוֹרָאוֹת to יַעֲשֶׂה, whereas עָשָׂה is used here in the same pregnant sense as in Ps. xxii. 32, xxxvii. 5, lii. 11 (cf. *gâmar* in Ps. lvii. 3, cxxxviii. 8). It has been objected to this explanation, that הֶאֱזִין is never connected with the accusative of the person, and that God can neither be heard nor seen. But what is terrible in relation to שָׁמֵעַ in Job xlii. 5 cannot be untenable in relation to הַאֲזִין. Hearing and seeing God are here equivalent to recognising His existence through the perception of His works. The explanation favoured by Rosenmüller and Stier, viz., " And from olden time men have not heard it, nor perceived with ears, no eye has seen it, O God, beside Thee, what (this God) doth to him that waiteth for Him," is open to still graver objections. The thought is the same as in Ps. xxxi. 20, and when so explained it corresponds more exactly to the free quotation in 1 Cor. ii. 9, which with our explanation there is no necessity to trace back to either ch. lii. 15, 16, or a lost book, as Origen imagined (see Tischendorf's ed. vii. of the N. T. on this passage). This which no ear has heard, no eye seen, is not God Himself, but He who acts for His people, and justifies their waiting for Him (cf. Hofmann, *Die h. Schrift Neuen Testaments*, ii. 2, 51). Another proof that Paul had no other passage than this in his mind, is the fact that the same quotation is met with in Clement's *Epistle to the Corinthians* (ch. xxxiv.), where, instead of " those that love Him," we have " those that wait for Him," a literal rendering of לִמְחַכֵּה־לֹו. The quotation by Paul therefore by no means leads us to take

Elohim as a vocative or ישׂה וגו׳ as the object, although it must
not be concealed that this view of the passage and its reference
to the fulness of glory in the eternal life is an old rabbinical
one, as Rashi expressly affirms, when he appeals to R. Jose
(Joseph Kara) as bondsman for the other (see *b. Sanhedrin*
99*a*). Hahn has justly objected to this traditional explanation,
which regards Elohim as a vocative, that the thought, that
God alone has heard and perceived and seen with His eye
what He intends to do to His people, is unsuitable in itself,
and at variance with the context, and that if ישׂה וגו׳ was
intended as the object, אשׁר (את) would certainly be inserted.
And to this we may add, that we cannot find the words *Elohim
zûlâth^ekhâ* (God beside Thee) preceded by a negation anywhere
in ch. xl.–lxvi. without receiving at once the impression, that
they affirm the sole deity of Jehovah (comp. ch. xlv. 5, 21).
The meaning therefore is, " No other God beside Jehovah has
ever been heard or seen, who acted for (*ageret pro*) those who
waited for Him." *M^echakkēh* is the construct, according to Ges.
§ 116, 1 ; and *ya'ǎsēh* has *tsere* here, according to Kimchi
(*Michlol* 125*b*) and other testimonies, just as we meet with
תֵּעֲשֶׂה four times (in Gen. xxvi. 29; Josh. vii. 9; 2 Sam. xiii. 12;
Jer. xl. 16) and וַנַּעֲשֶׂה once (Josh. ix. 24), mostly with a disjunctive accent, and not without the influence of a whole or
half pause, the form with *tsere* being regarded as more emphatic
than that with *seghol*.[1]

After the long period governed by לוּא has thus been followed by the retrospect in ver. 3 (4), it is absolutely impossible
that ver. 4*a* (5*a*) should be intended as an optative, in the
sense of " O that thou wouldst receive him that," etc., as Stier
and others propose. The retrospect is still continued thus, ver.
4*a* (5*a*) : " *Thou didst meet him that rejoiceth to work righteousness, when they remembered Thee in Thy ways.*" שָׂשׂ וְעֹשֵׂה צֶדֶק is
one in whom joy and right action are paired, and is therefore

---

[1] In addition to the examples given above, we have the following forms
of the same kind in *kal* : יִמָּצֵה (with *tiphchah*) in Jer. xvii. 17 ; תֵּרָאֶה (with
tsakeph) in Dan. i. 13, compare תְּנַלֶּה (with *athnach*) in Lev. xviii. 7, 8,
and תְּנַלֶּה (with the smaller disjunctive *tiphchah*) in vers. 9–11 ; יִנָּקֶה (with
athnach) in Nah. i. 3 ; אֶזְרֶה (with *tsakeph*) in Ezek. v. 12. This influence
of the accentuation has escaped the notice of the more modern grammarians
(*e.g.* Ges. § 75, Anm. 17).

equivalent to שָׂשׂ לַעֲשׂוֹת. At the same time, it may possibly be
more correct to take צֶדֶק as the object of both verses, as Hofmann does in the sense of "those who let what is right be
their joy, and their action also;" for though שׂוּשׂ (שִׂישׂ) cannot
be directly construed with the accusative of the object, as we
have already observed at ch. viii. 6 and xxxv. 1, it may be
indirectly, as in this passage and ch. lxv. 18. On *pâga'*, "to
come to meet," in the sense of "coming to the help of," see at
ch. xlvii. 3 ; it is here significantly interchanged with בִּדְרָכֶיךָ of
the minor clause *bidrâkhekhâ yizkᵉrūkhâ*, "those who remember
Thee in Thy ways" (for the syntax, compare ch. i. 5 and xxvi.
16) : "When such as love and do right, walking in Thy ways,
remembered Thee (*i.e.* thanked Thee for grace received, and
longed for fresh grace), Thou camest again and again to meet
them as a friend."

But Israel appeared to have been given up without hope to
the wrath of this very God. Ver. 4*b* (5*b*). "*Behold, Thou, Thou
art enraged, and we stood as sinners there; already have we been
long in this state, and shall we be saved?*" Instead of *hēn 'attâh*
(the antithesis of now and formerly), the passage proceeds with
hēn 'attâh. There was no necessity for *'attâh* with *qâtsaphtâ;* so
that it is used with special emphasis: "Behold, Thou, a God who
so faithfully accepts His own people, hast broken out in wrath"
(see p. 345). The following word וַנֶּחֱטָא cannot mean "and
we have sinned," but is a *fut. consec.*, and therefore must mean
at least, "then we have sinned" (the sin inferred from the
punishment). It is more correct, however, to take it, as in
Gen. xliii. 9, in the sense of, "Then we stand as sinners, as
guilty persons :" the punishment has exhibited Israel before
the world, and before itself, as what it really is (consequently
the *fut. consec.* does not express the logical inference, but the
practical consequence). As ונחטא has *tsakeph*, and therefore the
accents at any rate preclude Schelling's rendering, "and we
have wandered in those ways from the very earliest times," we
must take the next two clauses as independent, if indeed בהם
is to be understood as referring to בדרכיך. Stier only goes half-
way towards this when he renders it, "And indeed in them (the
ways of God, we sinned) from of old, and should we be helped?"
This is forced, and yet not in accordance with the accents.
Rosenmüller and Hahn quite satisfy this demand when they

render it, "*Tamen in viis tuis æternitas ut salvemur ;*" but ʿ*ōlâm*,
αἰών, in this sense of αἰωνιότης, is not scriptural. The rendering adopted by Besser, Grotius, and Starck is a better one:
"(*Si vero*) *in illis* (*viis tuis*) *perpetuo* (*mansissemus*), *tunc servati
fuerimus*" (if we had continued in Thy ways, then we should
have been preserved). But there is no succession of tenses
here, which could warrant us in taking וְנִוָּשֵׁעַ as a *paulo-post
future ;* and Hofmann's view is syntactically more correct, "In
them (*i.e.* the ways of Jehovah) eternally, we shall find salvation, after the time is passed in which He has been angry and
we have sinned" (or rather, been shown to be guilty). But we
question the connection between בהם and דרכיך in any form. In
our view the prayer suddenly takes a new turn from *hēn* (behold) onwards, just as it did with *lū'* (O that) in ch. lxiv. 1 ;
and דרכיך in ver. 5*a* stands at the head of a subordinate clause.
Hence בהם must refer back to קצפת ונחטא ("in Thine anger
and in our sins," Schegg). There is no necessity, however,
to search for nouns to which to refer בָּהֶם. It is rather to be
taken as neuter, signifying "therein" (Ezek. xxxiii. 18, cf. Ps.
xc. 10), like עֲלֵיהֶם, thereupon = thereby (ch. xxxviii. 16), בָּהֵן
therein (xxxviii. 16), מֵהֶם thereout (ch. xxx. 6), therefrom (ch.
xliv. 15). The idea suggested by such expressions as these is
no doubt that of plurality (here a plurality of manifestations
of wrath and of sins), but one which vanishes into the neuter
idea of totality. Now we do justice both to the clause without
a verb, which, being a logical copula, admits simply of a present *sumus ;* and also to ʿ*ōlâm*, which is the accusative of
duration, when we explain the sentence as meaning, "In this
state we are and have been for a long time." ʿ*Olâm* is used in
other instances in these prophecies to denote the long continuance of the state of punishment (see ch. xlii. 14, lvii. 11), since
it appeared to the exiles as an eternity (a whole æon), and
what lay beyond it as but a little while (*mits῾âr*, ch. lxiii. 18).
The following word וְנִוָּשֵׁעַ needs no correction. There is no
necessity to change it into וַנֵּתַע, as Ewald proposes, after the
LXX. καὶ ἐπλανήθημεν ("and we fell into wandering"), or
what would correspond still more closely to the LXX. (cf. ch.
xlvi. 8, פֹּשְׁעִים, LXX. πεπλανήμενοι), but is less appropriate
here, into וַנִּפְשַׁע ("and we fell into apostasy"), the reading
supported by Lowth and others. If it were necessary to alter

the text at all, we might simply transpose the letters, and read וַנְשַׁוַּע, "and cried for help." But if we take it as a question, "And shall we experience salvation—find help?" there is nothing grammatically inadmissible in this (compare ch. xxviii. 28), and psychologically it is commended by the state of mind depicted in ch. xl. 27, lix. 10–12. Moreover, what follows attaches itself quite naturally to this.

The people who ask the question in ver. 5 do not regard themselves as worthy of redemption, as their self-righteousness has been so thoroughly put to shame. Ver. 5 (6). "*We all became like the unclean thing, and all our virtues like a garment soiled with blood; and we all faded away together like the leaves; and our iniquities, like the storm they carried us away.*" The whole nation is like one whom the law pronounces unclean, like a leper, who has to cry "*tâmē', tâmē'*" as he goes along, that men may get out of his way (Lev. xiii. 45). Doing right in all its manifold forms (*ts⁵dâqōth*, like ch. xxxiii. 15, used elsewhere of the manifestations of divine righteousness), which once made Israel well-pleasing to God (ch. i. 21), has disappeared and become like a garment stained with menstruous discharge (cf. Ezek. xxxvi. 17); (LXX. ὡς ῥάκος ἀποκαθημένης = *dâvâh*, ch. xxx. 22; *niddâh*, Lam. i. 17; *t⁵mē'âh*, Lev. xv. 33). '*Iddīm* (used thus in the plural in the Talmud also) signifies the monthly period (*menstrua*). In the third figure, that of fading falling foliage, the form *vannâbhel* is not *kal* (= *vannibbōl* or *vanibbal;* Ewald, § 232, *b*), which would be an impossibility according to the laws of inflexion; still less is it *niphal* = *vanninnâbhel* (which Kimchi suggests as an alternative); but certainly a *hiphil*. It is not, however, from *nâbhēl* = *vannabbel*, "with the reduplication dropped to express the idea of something gradual," as Böttcher proposes (a new and arbitrary explanation in the place of one founded upon the simple laws of inflexion), but either from *bâlal* (compare the remarks on *b⁵līl* in ch. xxx. 24, which hardly signifies "ripe barley" however), after the form וַיָּגֶל (from גָּלַל), וַיָּסֶךְ (from סָכַךְ), or from *būl*, after the form וַיָּקָם, etc. In any case, therefore, it is a metaplastic formation, whether from *bâlal* or *būl* = *nâbhēl*, like וַיָּשַׂר in 1 Chron. xx. 3, after the form וַיָּסַר, from שׁוּר = נָשַׂר, or after the form וַיִּרַע, from שָׂרַר = נָשַׂר (compare the rabbinical explanation of the name of the month *Bul* from the falling of the

leaves, in Buxtorf, *Lex. talm.* col. 271). The *hiphil* הֵבֵל or
הֵבִיל is to be compared to הֶאְדִים, to stream out red (= to be
red); הֶאֱרִיךְ, to make an extension (= to be long); הִשְׁרִישׁ, to
strike root (= to root), etc., and signifies literally to produce a
fading (= to fade away). In the fourth figure, עֲוֹנֵנוּ (as it is
also written in ver. 6 according to correct codices) is a defective plural (as in Jer. xiv. 7, Ezek. xxviii. 18, Dan. ix. 13)
for the more usual עֲוֹנֹתֵינוּ (ch. lix. 12). עָוֹן is the usual term
applied to sin regarded as guilt, which produces punishment of
itself. The people were robbed by their sins of all vital strength
and energy, like dry leaves, which the guilt and punishment
springing from sin carried off as a very easy prey.

Universal forgetfulness of God was the consequence of this
self-instigated departure from God. Ver. 6 (7). "*And there
was no one who called upon Thy name, who aroused himself to lay
firm hold of Thee: for Thou hadst hidden Thy face from us, and
didst melt us into the hand of our transgressions.*" There was
no one (see ch. lix. 16) who had risen up in prayer and intercession out of this deep fall, or had shaken himself out of the
sleep of security and lethargy of insensibility, to lay firm hold
of Jehovah, *i.e.* not to let Him go till He blessed him and his
people again. The curse of God pressed every one down; God
had withdrawn His grace from them, and given them up to the
consequences of their sins. The form וַתְּמוּגֵנוּ is not softened
from the *pilel* וַתְּמוֹגְגֵנוּ, but is a *kal* like וַיְכוֹנְנוּ in Job xxxi. 15
(which see), מוּג being used in a transitive sense, as *kūn* is there
(cf. *shūbh*, ch. lii. 8; *mūsh*, Zech. iii. 9). The LXX., Targ.,
and Syr. render it *et tradidisti nos;* but we cannot conclude
from this with any certainty that they read וַתְּמַגְּנֵנוּ, which
Knobel follows Ewald in correcting into the incorrect form
וַתְּמַגְּנֵנוּ. The prophet himself had the expression *miggēn b'yad*
(Gen. xiv. 20, cf. Job viii. 4) in his mind, in the sense of
liquefecisti nos in manum, equivalent to *liquefecisti et tradidisti*
(παρέδωκας, Rom. i. 28), from which it is evident that בְיַד is
not a mere διά (LXX.), but the "hand" of the transgressions
is their destructive and damning power.

This was the case when the measure of Israel's sins had
become full. They were carried into exile, where they sank
deeper and deeper. The great mass of the people proved themselves to be really *massa perdita*, and perished among the

heathen. But there were some, though a vanishingly small number, who humbled themselves under the mighty hand of God, and, when redemption could not be far off, wrestled in such prayers as these, that the nation might share it in its entirety, and if possible not one be left behind. With וְעַתָּה the existing state of sin and punishment is placed among the things of the past, and the petition presented that the present moment of prayer may have all the significance of a turning-point in their history. Vers. 7, 8 (8, 9). "*And now, O Jehovah, Thou art our Father: we are the clay, and Thou our Maker; and we are all the work of Thy hand. Be not extremely angry, O Jehovah, and remember not the transgression for ever! Behold, consider, we beseech Thee, we are all Thy people.*" The state of things must change at last; for Israel is an image made by Jehovah; yea, more than this, Jehovah is the begetter of Israel, and loves Israel not merely as a sculptor, but as a father (compare ch. xlv. 9, 10, and the unquestionable passage of Isaiah in ch. xxix. 16). Let Him then not be angry עַד־מְאֹד, " to the utmost measure" (cf. Ps. cxix. 8), or if we paraphrase it according to the radical meaning of מאד, " till the weight becomes intolerable." Let Him not keep in mind the guilt for ever, to punish it; but, in consideration of the fact that Israel is the nation of His choice, let mercy take the place of justice. הֵן strengthens the petition in its own way (see Gen. xxx. 34), just as נָא does; and הִבִּיט signifies here, as elsewhere, to fix the eye upon anything. The object, in this instance, is the existing fact expressed in " we are all Thy people." Hitzig is correct in regarding the repetition of " all of us" in this prayer as significant. The object throughout is to entreat that the whole nation may participate in the inheritance of the coming salvation, in order that the exodus from Babylonia may resemble the exodus from Egypt.

The re-erection of the ruins of the promised land requires the zeal of every one, and this state of ruin must not continue. It calls out the love and faithfulness of Jehovah. Vers. 9–11. " *The cities of Thy holiness have become a pasture-ground; Zion has become a pasture-ground, Jerusalem a desert. The house of our holiness and of our adorning, where our fathers praised Thee, is given up to the fire, and everything that was our delight given up to devastation. Wilt Thou restrain Thyself in spite of this,*

O Jehovah, be silent, and leave us to suffer the utmost ?" Jerusalem by itself could not possibly be called " *cities*" ('*ârê*), say
with reference to the upper and lower cities (Vitringa). It is
merely mentioned by name as the most prominent of the many
cities which were all " holy cities," inasmuch as the whole of
Canaan was the land of Jehovah (ch. xiv. 25), and His holy
territory (Ps. lxxviii. 54). The word *midbâr* (pasture-land,
heath, different from *tsiyyâh*, the pastureless desert, ch. xxxv.
1) is repeated, for the purpose of showing that the same
fate had fallen upon Zion-Jerusalem as upon the rest of the
cities of the land. The climax of the terrible calamity was
the fact, that the temple had also fallen a prey to the burning of the fire (compare for the fact, Jer. lii. 13). The people
call it " house of our holiness and of our glory." Jehovah's
qōdesh and *tiph'ereth* have, as it were, transplanted heaven
to earth in the temple (compare ch. lxiii. 15 with ch. lx. 7);
and this earthly dwelling-place of God is Israel's possession,
and therefore Israel's *qōdesh* and *tiph'ereth*. The relative
clause describes what sublime historical reminiscences are
attached to the temple: אֲשֶׁר is equivalent to אֲשֶׁר שָׁם, as in
Gen. xxxix. 20, Num. xx. 13 (compare Ps. lxxxiv. 4), Deut.
viii. 15, etc. הִלְלוּךְ has *chateph-pathach*, into which, as a
rule, the vocal *sheva* under the first of two similar letters is
changed. *Machămaddēnū* (our delights) may possibly include
favourite places, ornamental buildings, and pleasure grounds;
but the parallel leads us rather to think primarily of things
associated with the worship of God, in which the people found
a holy delight. כל, contrary to the usual custom, is here followed by the singular of the predicate, as in Prov. xvi. 2, Ezek.
xxxi. 15 (cf. Gen. ix. 29). Will Jehovah still put restraint
upon Himself, and cause His merciful love to keep silence,
עַל־זֹאת, with such a state of things as this, or notwithstanding
this state of things (Job x. 7) ? On הִתְאַפֵּק, see ch. lxiii. 15,
xlii. 14. The suffering would indeed increase עַד־מְאֹד (to the
utmost), if it caused the destruction of Israel, or should not be
followed at last by Israel's restoration. Jehovah's compassion
cannot any longer thus forcibly restrain itself ; it must break
forth, like Joseph's tears in the recognition scene (Gen. xlv. 1).

SECOND CLOSING PROPHECY.—Chap. lxv.

JEHOVAH'S ANSWER TO THE CHURCH'S PRAYER.

After the people have poured out their heart before Jehovah, He announces what they may expect from Him. But instead of commencing with a promise, as we might anticipate after the foregoing prayer, He begins with reproach and threatening; for although the penitential portion of the community had included the whole nation in their prayer, it was destruction, and not deliverance, which awaited one portion of the nation, and that portion was the greater one. The great mass were in that state of " sin unto death" which defies all intercession (1 John v. 16), because they had so scornfully and obstinately resisted the grace which had been so long and so incessantly offered to them. Vers. 1, 2. "*I was discernible to those who did not inquire, discoverable by those who did not seek me. I said, ' Here am I, here am I,' to a nation where my name was not called. I spread out my hands all the day to a refractory people, who walked in the way that was not good, after their own thoughts.*" The LXX. (A) render ver. 1*a*, " I was found by those who did not seek me, I became manifest to those who did not ask for me" (B reverses the order); and in Rom. x. 20, 21, Paul refers ver. 1 to the Gentiles, and ver. 2 to Israel. The former, to whom He has hitherto been strange, enter into fellowship with Him; whilst the latter, to whom He has constantly offered Himself, thrust Him away, and lose His fellowship. Luther accordingly adopts this rendering: " I shall be sought by those who did not ask for me, I shall be found by those who did not seek me. And to the heathen who did not call upon my name, I say, Here am I, here am I." Zwingli, again, observes on ver. 1, " This is an irresistible testimony to the adoption of the Gentiles." Calvin also follows the apostle's exposition, and observes, that " Paul argues boldly for the calling of the Gentiles on the ground of this passage, and says that Isaiah dared to proclaim and assert that the Gentiles had been called by God, because he announced a greater thing, and announced it more clearly than the reason of those times would bear." Of all the Jewish expositors, there is only one, viz. Gecatilia, who refers ver. 1 to the Gentiles; and of all the Christian expositors of modern times, there is only one, viz. Hendewerk, who interprets it in this way, without having been influenced by the quotation made by Paul. Hofmann, however, and Stier, feel obliged to follow the apostle's exposition, and endeavour to vindicate it. But we have no sympathy with any such untenable efforts to save the apostle's honour. In Rom. ix. 25, 26, he also quotes Hos. ii. 25 and ii. 1 in support of the calling of the Gentiles; whereas he could not have failed to know, that it is the restoration of Israel to favour which is alluded to there. He merely appeals to Hos. ii. in support of the New Testament fact of the calling of the Gentiles, so far as it is in these words of the Old Testament prophet that the fact is most adequately expressed. And according to 1 Pet. ii. 10, Peter received the same impression from Hosea's words. But with the passage before us it is very different. The apostle shows, by the way in which he applies the Scripture, how he depended in this instance upon the Septuagint translation, which was in his own hands and those of his readers also, and by which the allusion to the Gentiles is naturally suggested, even if not actually demanded. And we may also assume that the apostle himself understood the Hebrew text, with which he, the pupil of Rabban Gamaliel, was of course well acquainted, in the same sense, viz. as relating to the calling of the Gentiles, without being therefore legally bound to adopt the same interpretation. The interchange of גּוֹי (cf. ch. lv. 5) and עָם; the attribute לֹא קֹרָא בִשְׁמִי, which applies to heathen, and heathen only; the possibility of interpreting ch. lxv. 1, 2, in harmony with the context both before and after, if ver. 1 be taken as referring to the Gentiles, on the supposition that Jehovah is here contrasting His success with the Gentiles and His failure with Israel: all these certainly throw weight into the scale. Nevertheless they are not decisive, if we look at the Hebrew alone, apart altogether from the LXX. For *nidrashtī* does not mean " I have become manifest;" but, regarded as the so-called *niphal tolerativum* (according to Ezek. xiv. 3, xx. 3, 31, xxxvi. 37), " I permitted myself to be explored or found out ;" and consequently נִמְצֵאתִי, according to ch. lv. 6, " I let myself be found." And so explained, ver. 1 stands in a parallel relation to ch. lv. 6 : Jehovah was searchable, was discoverable (cf. Zeph. i. 6) to those who asked no questions, and did not seek Him (לְלוֹא = לַאֲשֶׁר לֹא, Ges. § 123, 3), *i.e.* He displayed to Israel the fulness of His nature and the possibility of His fellowship, although they did not bestir themselves or trouble themselves in the least about Him,—a view which is confirmed by the fact that ver. 1*b* merely refers to offers made to them, and not to results of any kind. Israel, however, is called גּוֹי לֹא־קֹרָא בִשְׁמִי, not as a nation that was not called by Jehovah's name (which would be expressed by נִקְרָא, ch. xliii. 7; cf. מִקְרָאִי, κλητός μου, ch. xlviii. 12), but as a nation where (supply *ǎsher*) Jehovah's name was not invoked (LXX. "who called not upon my name"), and therefore as a thoroughly heathenish nation; for which reason we have *gōi* (LXX. ἔθνος) here, and not *'am* (LXX. λαός). Israel was estranged from Him, just like the heathen; but He still turned towards them with infinite patience, and (as is added in ver. 2) with ever open arms of love. He spread out His hands (as a man does to draw another towards him to embrace him) all the day (*i.e.* continually, cf. ch. xxviii. 24) towards an obstinate people, who walked in the way that was not good (cf. Ps. xxxvi. 5, Prov. xvi. 29; here with the article, which could not be repeated with the adjective, because of the לֹא), behind their own thoughts. That which led them, and which they followed, was not the will of God, but selfish views and purposes, according to their own hearts' lusts; and yet Jehovah did not let them alone, but they were the constant thought and object of His love, which was ever seeking, alluring, and longing for their salvation.

But through this obstinate and unyielding rejection of His love they have excited wrath, which, though long and patiently suppressed, now bursts forth with irresistible violence. Vers. 3–5. "*The people that continually provoketh me by defying me to my face, sacrificing in the gardens, and burning incense upon the tiles; who sit in the graves, and spend the night in closed places; to eat the flesh of swine, and broken pieces of abominations is in their dishes; who say, Stop! come not too near me; for I am holy to thee: they are a smoke in my nose, a fire blazing continually.*" אֵלֶּה (these) in ver. 5*b* is retrospective, summing up the subject as described in vers. 3–5*a*, and what follows in ver. 5*b* contains the predicate. The heathenish practices of the exiles are here depicted, and in ver. 7 they are

expressly distinguished from those of their fathers. Hence
there is something so peculiar in the description, that we look
in vain for parallels among those connected with the idolatry
of the Israelites before the time of the captivity. There is
only one point of resemblance, viz. the allusion to gardens as
places of worship, which only occurs in the book of Isaiah, and
in which our passage, together with ch. lvii. 5 and lxvi. 17,
strikingly coincides with ch. i. 29. "Upon my face" ('al-
pânai) is equivalent to "freely and openly, without being
ashamed of me, or fearing me;" cf. Job i. 11, vi. 28,
xxi. 31. "Burning incense upon the bricks" carries us to
Babylonia, the true home of the *cocti lateres* (*laterculi*). The
thorah only mentions *l'bhēnīm* in connection with Babylonian
and Egyptian buildings. The only altars that it allows are
altars of earth thrown up, or of unhewn stones and wooden
beams with a brazen covering. "They who sit in the graves,"
according to Vitringa, are they who sacrifice to the dead. He
refers to the Greek and Roman *inferiæ* and *februationes*, or
expiations for the dead, as probably originating in the East.
Sacrifices for the dead were offered, in fact, not only in India
and Persia, but also in Hither Asia among the Ssabians, and
therefore probably in ancient Mesopotamia and Babylonia.
But were they offered in the graves themselves, as we must
assume from בַּקְּבָרִים (not עַל־קְברים)? Nothing at all is known
of this, and Böttcher (*de inferis*, § 234) is correct in rendering
it "among (*inter*) the graves," and supposing the object to be
to hold intercourse there with the dead and with demons. The
next point, viz. passing the night in closed places (*i.e.* places
not accessible to every one: *n^etsūrīm*, *custodita* = *clausa*, like
n^e'īmīm, *amœna*), may refer to the mysteries celebrated in
natural caves and artificial crypts (on the mysteries of the
Ssabians, see Chwolsohn, *Die Ssabier u. der Ssabismus*, ii. 332
sqq.). But the LXX. and Syriac render it ἐν τοῖς σπηλαίοις
κοιμῶνται δι' ἐνύπνια, evidently understanding it to refer to
the so-called *incubare*, ἐγκοιμᾶσθαι; and so Jerome explains it.
"In the temples of idols," he says, "where they were accustomed to lie upon the skins of the victims stretched upon the
ground, to gather future events from their dreams." The
expression *ubhann^etsūrīm* points not so much to open temples,
as to inaccessible caves or subterraneous places. G. Rawlinson

(*Monarchies*, ii. 269) mentions the discovery of "clay idols in holes below the pavement of palaces." From the next charge, "who eat there the flesh of the swine," we may infer that the Babylonians offered swine in sacrifice, if not as a common thing, yet like the Egyptians and other heathen, and ate their flesh ("the flesh taken from the sacrifice," 2 Macc. vi. 21); whereas among the later Ssabians (Harranians) the swine was not regarded as either edible or fit for sacrifice. On the synecdochical character of the sentence וּפְרַק פִּגֻּלִים כְּלֵיהֶם, see at ch. v. 12a, cf. Jer. xxiv. 2. Knobel's explanation, "pieces" (but it is not וּפִרְקֵי) "of abominations are their vessels, *i.e.* those of their ἱεροσκοπία," is a needless innovation. פִּגּוּל signifies a stench, putrefaction (Ezek. iv. 14, *b'sar piggŭl*), then in a concrete sense anything corrupt or inedible, a thing to be abhorred according to the laws of food or the law generally (syn. פָּסֻל, פָּסוּל); and when connected with פְּרַק (*chethib*), which bears the same relation to מְרַק as crumbs or pieces (from פְּרַק, to crumble) to broth (from מְרַק, to rub off or scald off), it means a decoction, or broth made either of such kinds of flesh or such parts of the body as were forbidden by the law. The context also points to such heathen sacrifices and sacrificial meals as were altogether at variance with the Mosaic law. For the five following words proceed from the mouths of persons who fancy that they have derived a high degree of sanctity either from the mysteries, or from their participation in rites of peculiar sacredness, so that to every one who abstains from such rites, or does not enter so deeply into them as they do themselves, they call out their "*odi profanum vulgus et arceo.*" קְרַב אֵלֶיךָ, keep near to thyself, *i.e.* stay where you are, like the Arabic *idhab ileika*, go away to thyself, for take thyself off. אַל־תִּגֶּשׁ־בִּי (according to some MSS. with *mercha tifchah*), do not push against me (equivalent to גֶּשׁ־הָלְאָה or גְּשָׁה־לָךְ, get away, make room; Gen. xix. 9, Isa. xlix. 20), for *q'dashtikhâ,* I am holy to thee, *i.e.* unapproachable. The verbal suffix is used for the dative, as in ch. xliv. 21 (Ges. § 121, 4), for it never occurred to any of the Jewish expositors (all of whom give *sanctus præ te* as a gloss) that the *Kal qâdash* was used in a transitive sense, like *châzaq* in Jer. xx. 7, as Luther, Calvin, and even Hitzig suppose. Nor is the exclamation the well-meant warning against the communication of a burdensome *q'dusshâh*, which

had to be removed by washing before a man could proceed to
the duties of every-day life (such, for example, as the qᵉdusshâh
of the man who had touched the flesh of a sin-offering, or been
sprinkled with the blood of a sin-offering; Lev. vi. 20, cf. Ezek.
xliv. 19, xlvi. 20). It is rather a proud demand to respect the
sacro-sanctus, and not to draw down the chastisement of the
gods by the want of reverential awe. After this elaborate
picture, the men who are so degenerate receive their fitting
predicate. They are fuel for the wrath of God, which manifests itself, as it were, in smoking breath. This does not now
need for the first time to seize upon them; but they are already
in the midst of the fire of wrath, and are burning there in
inextinguishable flame.

The justice of God will not rest till it has procured for
itself the fullest satisfaction. Vers. 6, 7. *"Behold, it is
written before me : I will not keep silence without having recom-
pensed, and I will recompense into their bosom. Your offences,
and the offences of your fathers together, saith Jehovah, that they
have burned incense upon the mountains, and insulted me upon
the hills, and I measure their reward first of all into their bosom."*
Vitringa has been misled by such passages as ch. x. 1, Job
xiii. 26, Jer. xxii. 30, in which *kâthabh* (*kittēbh*) is used to
signify a written decree, and understands by *khᵉthûbhâh* the sentence pronounced by God; but the reference really is to their
idolatrous conduct and contemptuous defiance of the laws of
God. This is ever before Him, written in indelible characters,
waiting for the day of vengeance; for, according to the figurative language of Scripture, there are heavenly books, in which
the good and evil works of men are entered. And this agrees
with what follows : "I will not be silent, without having first
repaid," etc. The accentuation very properly places the tone
upon the penultimate of the first *shillamtī* as being a pure
perfect, and upon the last syllable of the second as a *perf.
consec.* כִּי אִם preceded by a future and followed by a perfect
signifies, "but if (without having) first," etc. (ch. lv. 10; Gen.
xxxii. 27; Lev. xxii. 6; Ruth iii. 18; cf. Judg. xv. 7). The
original train of thought was, "I will not keep silence, for I
shall first of all keep silence when," etc. Instead of ῾al chēqâm,
"upon their bosom," we might have ᾽el chēqâm, into their
bosom, as in Jer. xxxii. 18, Ps. lxxix. 12. In ver. 7 the *keri*

really has *'el* instead of *'al*, whilst in ver. 6 the *chethib* is *'al*
without any *keri* (for the figure itself, compare Luke vi. 38,
"into your bosom"). The thing to be repaid follows in ver.
7*a*; it is not governed, however, by *shillamtī*, as the form of
the address clearly shows, but by *'ăshallēm* understood, which
may easily be supplied. Whether *'ăsher* is to be taken in the
sense of *qui* or *quod* (that), it is hardly possible to decide; but
the construction of the sentence favours the latter. Sacrificing
"upon mountains and hills" (and, what is omitted here, "under
every green tree") is the well-known standing phrase used to
describe the idolatry of the times preceding the captivity (cf.
ch. lvii. 7; Hos. iv. 13; Ezek. vi. 13). וּמַדֹּתִי points back to
vᵉshillamtī in ver. 6*b*, after the object has been more precisely
defined. Most of the modern expositors take פְּעֻלָּתָם רִאשֹׁנָה
together, in the sense of "their former wages," *i.e.* the recompense previously deserved by their fathers. But in this case
the concluding clause would only affirm, by the side of ver. 7*a*,
that the sins of the fathers would be visited upon them. Moreover, this explanation has not only the accents against it, but
also the parallel in Jer. xvi. 18 (see Hitzig), which evidently
stands in a reciprocal relation to the passage before us. Consequently *ri'shōnâh* must be an adverb, and the meaning evidently is, that the first thing which Jehovah had to do by virtue
of His holiness was to punish the sins of the apostate Israelites;
and He would so punish them, that inasmuch as the sins of the
children were merely the continuation of the fathers' sins, the
punishment would be measured out according to the desert of
both together.

As the word *ri'shōnâh* (first of all) has clearly intimated
that the work of the future will not all consist in the execution
of penal justice, there is no abruptness in the transition from
threatening to promises. Vers. 8, 9. "*Thus saith Jehovah, As
when the must is found in the cluster, men say, Do not destroy it,
for there is a blessing within it, so will I do for the sake of my
servants, that I may not destroy the whole. And I will bring
forth a seed out of Jacob, and an heir of my mountains out of
Judah, and my chosen ones shall inherit it, and my servants shall
dwell there.*" Of the two co-ordinate clauses of the protasis
(ver. 8*a*), the first contains the necessary condition of the
second. *Hattīrōsh* (must, or the juice of the grapes, from

yârash, possibly primarily nothing more than receipt, or the produce of labour) and *bâ'eshkōl* have both of them the article generally found in comparisons (Ges. § 109, Anm. 1); וְאָמַר signifies, as in ch. xlv. 24, "men say," with the most general and indefinite subject. As men do not destroy a juicy cluster of grapes, because they would thereby destroy the blessing of God which it contains; so will Jehovah for His servants' sake not utterly destroy Israel, but preserve those who are the clusters in the vineyard (ch. iii. 14, v. 1–7) or upon the vine (Ps. lxxx. 9 sqq.) of Israel. He will not destroy *hakkōl*, the whole without exception; that is to say, keeping to the figure, not "the juice with the skin and stalk," as Knobel and Hahn explain it, but "the particular clusters in which juice is contained, along with the degenerate neglected vineyard or vine, which bears for the most part only sour grapes (ch. v. 4) or tendrils without fruit (cf. ch. xviii. 5). The servants of Jehovah, who resemble these clusters, remain preserved. Jehovah brings out, causes to go forth, calls to the light of day (הוֹצִיא as in ch. liv. 16; here, however, it is by means of sifting : Ezek. xx. 34 sqq.), out of Jacob and Judah, *i.e.* the people of the two captivities (see ch. xlvi. 3), a seed, a family, that takes possession of His mountains, *i.e.* His holy mountain-land (ch. xiv. 25, cf. Ps. cxxi. 1, and *har qodshī*, which is used in the same sense in ch. xi. 9, lxv. 25). As "my mountain" is equivalent in sense to the "land of Israel," for which Ezekiel is fond of saying "the mountains of Israel" (*e.g.* ch. vi. 2, 3), the promise proceeds still further to say, "and my chosen ones will take possession thereof" (viz. of the land, ch. lx. 21, cf. viii. 21).

From west to east, *i.e.* in its whole extent, the land then presents the aspect of prosperous peace. Ver. 10. "*And the plain of Sharon becomes a meadow for flocks, and the valley of Achor a resting-place for oxen, for my people that asketh for me.*" *Hasshârōn* (Sharon) is the plain of rich pasture-land which stretches along the coast of the Mediterranean from Yafo to the neighbourhood of Carmel. *'Emeq 'Akhōr* is a valley which became renowned through the stoning of Achan, in a range of hills running through the plain of Jericho (see Keil on Josh. vii. 24 sqq.). From the one to the other will the wealth in flocks extend, and in the one as well as in the other will that peace prevail which is now enjoyed by the people of Jehovah,

who inquired for Him in the time of suffering, and therefore
bear this name in truth. The idyllic picture of peace is
thoroughly characteristic of Isaiah : see, for example, ch. xxxii.
20 ; and for *rēbhets* with *nāveh*, compare ch. xxxv. 7.

The prophecy now turns again to those already indicated
and threatened in vers. 1–7. Vers. 11, 12. "*And ye, who are
enemies to Jehovah, O ye that are unmindful of my holy mountain, who prepare a table for Gad, and fill up mixed drink for
the goddess of destiny,—I have destined you to the sword, and ye
will all bow down to the slaughter, because I have called and ye
have not replied, I have spoken and ye have not heard; and ye did
evil in mine eyes, and ye chose that which I did not like.*" It
may be taken for granted as a thing generally admitted, that
ver. 11*b* refers to two deities, and to the *lectisternia* (meals of
the gods, cf. Jer. vii. 18, li. 44) held in their honour. עֹרֵךְ
שֻׁלְחָן is the other side of the *lectum sternere*, *i.e.* the spreading of the cushions upon which the images of the gods were
placed during such meals of the gods as these. In the passage
before us, at any rate, the *lectus* answering to the *shulchán* (like
the *sella* used in the case of the goddesses) is to be taken as a
couch for eating, not for sleeping on. In the second clause,
therefore, וְהַמְמַלְאִים לַמְנִי מִמְסָךְ (which is falsely accentuated in
our editions with *tifchah mercha silluk*, instead of *mercha tifchah
silluk*), מִלֵּא מִמְסַךְ signifies to fill with mixed drink, *i.e.* with
wine mixed with spices, probably oil of spikenard. מִלֵּא may be
connected not only with the accusative of the vessel filled, but
also with that of the thing with which it is filled (*e.g.* Ex.
xxviii. 17). Both names have the article, like הַבַּעַל. הַגַּד is
perfectly clear; if used as an appellative, it would mean
"good fortune." The word has this meaning in all the three
leading Semitic dialects, and it also occurs in this sense in
Gen. xxx. 11, where the *chethib* is to be read בְּגָד (LXX. ἐν
τύχη). The Aramæan definitive is גַּדָּא (not גְּדָא), as the Arabic
'*gadd* evidently shows. The primary word is גָּדַד (Arab. '*gadda*),
to cut off, to apportion; so that جَدَّ, like the synonymous
حَظَّ, signifies that which is appointed, more especially the
good fortune appointed. There can be no doubt, therefore,
that *Gad*, the god of good fortune, more especially if the name

of the place *Baal-Gad* is to be explained in the same way as
Baal-hammân, is Baal (Bel) as the god of good fortune.
Gecatilia (Mose ha-Cohen) observes, that this is the deified
planet Jupiter. This star is called by the Arabs "the greater
luck" as being the star of good fortune; and in all probability it is also the *rabb-el-bacht* (lord of good fortune) worshipped by the Ssabians (Chwolsohn, ii. 30, 32). It is true
that it is only from the passage before us that we learn that
it was worshipped by the Babylonians; for although H.
Rawlinson once thought that he had found the names *Gad*
and *Menni* in certain Babylonian inscriptions (*Journal of the
Royal Asiatic Society*, xii. p. 478), the Babylonian Pantheon in
G. Rawlinson's *Monarchies* contains neither of these names.
With this want of corroborative testimony, the fact is worthy
of notice, that a Rabbi named '*Ulla*, who sprang from Babylon,
explains the דרגש of the *Mishna* by ערסא דגדא (a sofa dedicated
to the god of prosperity, and often left unused) (*b. Nedarim
56a*; cf. *Sanhedrin 20a*).[1] But if *Gad* is Jupiter, nothing is
more probable than that *Meni* is Venus; for the planet Venus is
also regarded as a star of prosperity, and is called by the Arabs
"the lesser luck." The name *Meni* in itself, indeed, does not
necessarily point to a female deity; for m^eni from *mânâh*, if taken
as a passive participial noun (like בְּרִי בְּרִיָה, a creature), signifies
"that which is apportioned;" or if taken as a modification
of the primary form *many*, like גְּדִי, טְלִי, צְבִי, and many others,
allotment, destination, fate. We have synonyms in the Arabic
mana-n and *meniye*, and the Persian *bacht* (adopted into the
Arabic), which signify the general fate, and from which *bago-
bacht* is distinguished as signifying that which is exceptionally
allotted by the gods. The existence of a deity of this name
m^eni is also probably confirmed by the occurrence of the per-

---

[1] The foreign formula of incantation given in *b. Sabbath 67a*, גד גדי
וסינוק לא אושכי ובושכי (according to the glosses, "O Fortune, give good
fortune, and be not tardy day and night"), also belongs here; whereas the
name of a place not far from Siloah, called *Gad-yavan* (Gad of Greece), contains some allusion to the mythology of Greece, which we are unable to
trace. In the later usage of the language *Gad* appears to have acquired
the general meaning of *numen* (e.g. *b. Chullin 40a*: גדא דהר, the mountain-
spirit); and this helps to explain the fact that in Pehlewi גדמן signifies
majesty in a royal, titular sense (see Vuller's *Lex.*; and Spiegel in the
Indische Studien, 3, 412).

sonal name עברדמני on certain Aramæo-Persian coins of the
Achæmenides,[1] with which Fürst associates the personal name
Achiman (see his *Lex.*), combining מן with *Mήν*, and מני with
Mήνη, as Movers (*Phönizier*, i. 650) and Knobel have also
done. מן and מני would then be Semitic forms of these Indo-
Germanic names of deities; for *Mήν* is *Deus Lunus*, the
worship of which in Carræ (*Charran*) is mentioned by Spartian
in ch. vi. of the Life of Caracalla, whilst Strabo (xii. 3, 31, 32)
speaks of it as being worshipped in Pontus, Phrygia, and other
places; and *Mήνη* is *Dea Luna* (cf. Γενείτη Μάνη in Plut.
quæst. rom. 52, *Genita Mana* in Plin. *h. n.* 29, 4, and *Dea
Mena* in Augustine, *Civ.* 4, 11), which was worshipped, according to Diodorus (iii. 56) and Nonnus (*Dionys.* v. 70 ss.), in
Phœnicia and Africa. The rendering of the LXX. may be
quoted in favour of the identity of the latter with מני (ἐτοιμά-
ζοντες τῷ δαιμονίῳ (another reading δαίμονι) τράπεζαν καὶ
πληροῦντες τῇ τύχῃ κέρασμα), especially if we compare with this
what Macrobius says in *Saturn.* i. 19, viz. that "according to
the Egyptians there are four of the gods which preside over the
birth of men, Δαίμων, Τύχη, Ἔρως, Ἀνάγκη. Of these *Daimōn*
is the sun, the author of spirit, of warmth, and of light. *Tychē*
is the moon, as the goddess through whom all bodies below the
moon grow and disappear, and whose ever changing course
accompanies the multiform changes of this mortal life."[2] In
perfect harmony with this is the following passage of Vettius
Valens, the astrologer of Antioch, which has been brought to
light by Selden in his *Syntagma de Diis Syris*: Κλῆροι τῆς
τύχης καὶ τοῦ δαίμονος σημαίνουσιν (viz. by the signs of
nativity) ἥλιον τε καὶ σελήνην. Rosenmüller very properly
traces back the Sept. rendering to this Egyptian view, according to which Gad is the sun-god, and *M^eni* the lunar goddess
as the power of fate. Now it is quite true that the passage
before us refers to Babylonian deities, and not to Egyptian;
at the same time there might be some relation between the two
views, just as in other instances ancient Babylonia and Egypt
coincide. But there are many objections that may be offered
to the combination of מְנִי (Meni) and *Mήνη*: (1) The Babylonian moon-deity was either called *Sīn*, as among the ancient

---

[1] See *Rödiger* in the concluding part of the *thes.* p. 97.

[2] See Ge. Zoega's *Abhandlungen*, edited by Welcker (1817), pp. 39, 40.

Shemites generally, or else by other names connected with יָרֵחַ (יֶרַח) and *chámar*. (2) The moon is called *más* in Sanscrit, Zendic *máo*, Neo-Pers. *máh* (*mah*); but in the Arian languages we meet with no such names as could be traced to a root *mán* as the expansion of *má* (to measure), like μήν (μήνη), Goth. *mena*; for the ancient proper names which Movers cites, viz. 'Αριαμένης, 'Αρταμένης, etc., are traceable rather to the Arian *manas* = μένος, *mens*, with which *Minerva* (*Menerva*, endowed with mind) is connected. (3) If *m͏ᵉni* were the Semitic form of the name for the moon, we should expect a closer reciprocal relation in the meanings of the words. We therefore subscribe to the view propounded by Gesenius, who adopts the pairing of Jupiter and Venus common among the Arabs, as the two heavenly bodies that preside over the fortunes of men; and understands by *M͏ᵉni* Venus, and by *Gad* Jupiter. There is nothing at variance with this in the fact that 'Ashtoreth (*Ishtar*, with 'Ashérâh) is the name of Venus (the morning star), as we have shown at ch. xiv. 12. *M͏ᵉni* is her special name as the bestower of good fortune and the distributor of fate generally; probably identical with *Manât*, one of the three leading deities of the præ-Islamitish Arabs.[1] The address proceeds with *umánīthī* (and I have measured), which forms an apodosis and contains a play upon the name of *Meni*, ver. 11 being as it were a protasis indicating the principal reason of their approaching fate. Because they sued for the favour of the two gods of fortune (the Arabs call them *es-saʿdáni*, "the two fortunes") and put Jehovah into the shade, Jehovah would assign them to the sword, and they would all have to bow down (כָּרַע as in ch. x. 4). Another reason is now assigned for this, the address thus completing the circle, viz., because when I called ye did not reply, when I spake ye did not hear (this is expressed in the same paratactic manner as in ch. v. 4, xii. 1, l. 2), and ye have done, etc.: an explanatory clause, consisting of four members, which is repeated almost word for word in ch. lxvi. 4 (cf. lvi. 4).

On the ground of the sin thus referred to again, the proclamation of punishment is renewed, and the different fates awaiting the servants of Jehovah and those by whom He is despised are here announced in five distinct *theses* and *anti-*

---

[1] See Krehl, *Religion der vorislamischen Araber*, p. 78. Sprenger in his *Life of Mohammad*, 1862, compares the Arabic *Manât* with מני.

theses. Vers. 13–16. " *Therefore thus saith the Lord, Jehovah:
Behold my servants will eat, but ye will hunger; behold my servants will drink, but ye will thirst; behold my servants will rejoice,
but ye will be put to shame; behold my servants will exult for
delight of heart, but ye will cry for anguish of heart, and ye will
lament for brokenness of spirit. And ye will leave your name
for a curse to my chosen ones, and the Lord, Jehovah, will slay
thee; but His servants He will call by another name, so that whoever blesseth himself in the land will bless himself by the God of
truthfulness, and whoever sweareth in the land will swear by the
God of truthfulness, because the former troubles are forgotten,
and because they have vanished from mine eyes.*" The name
Adonai is connected with the name *Jehovah* for the purpose of
affirming that the God of salvation and judgment has the
power to carry His promises and threats into execution.
Starving, confounded by the salvation they had rejected (תֵּבֹשׁוּ
as in ch. lxvi. 5), crying and wailing (תְּיֵלִילוּ, *fut. hiph.* as in ch.
xv. 2, with a double preformative; Ges. § 70, 2 Anm.) for
sorrow of heart and crushing of spirit (*shebher*, rendered very
well by the LXX. συντριβή, as in ch. lxi. 1, συντετριμμένους),
the rebellious ones are left behind in the land of captivity,
whilst the servants of Jehovah enjoy the richest blessings from
God in the land of promise (ch. lxii. 8, 9). The former, perishing in the land of captivity, leave their name to the latter as
*sh*eᵇhuʻâh*, *i.e.* to serve as a formula by which to swear, or rather
to execrate or curse (Num v. 21), so that men will say, "Jehovah
slay thee, as He slew them." This, at any rate, is the meaning
of the threat; but the words וְהֵמִיתְךָ וגו' cannot contain the
actual formula, not even if we drop the *Vav*, as Knobel proposes, and change לִבְחִירַי into לִבְחִירָיו; for, in the first place, although in the doxologies a Hebrew was in the habit of saying
" *b*eᵉrûkh sh*eᵉmô* " (bless his name) instead of *y*eᵉhî sh*eᵉmô bârukh*
(his name be blessed), he never went so far as the Arab with

his الله تبارك, but said rather יתברך. Still less could he make

use of the perfect (indicative) in such sentences as "may he
slay thee," instead of the future (voluntative) יְמִיתְךָ, unless the
perfect shared the optative force of the previous future by
virtue of the *consecutio temporum.* And secondly, the indispensable כָּהֵם or כָּאֵלֶּה would be wanting (see Jer. xxix. 22, cf. Gen.

xlviii. 20). We may therefore assume, that the prophet has
before his mind the words of this imprecatory formula, though
he does not really express them, and that he deduces from it
the continuation of the threat. And this explains his passing
from the plural to the singular. Their name will become an
execration; but Jehovah will call His servants by another
name (cf. ch. lxii. 2), so that henceforth it will be the God of
the faithfully fulfilled promise whose name men take into their
mouth when they either desire a blessing or wish to give assurance of the truth (*hithbârēkh b*, to bless one's self with any
one, or with the name of any one; Ewald, § 133, Anm. 1).
No other name of any god is now heard in the land, except
this gloriously attested name; for the former troubles, which
included the mixed condition of Israel in exile and the persecution of the worshippers of Jehovah by the despisers of
Jehovah, are now forgotten, so that they no longer disturb the
enjoyment of the present, and are even hidden from the eyes
of God, so that all thought of ever renewing them is utterly
remote from His mind. This is the connection between ver.
16 and vers. 13–15. אֲשֶׁר does not mean *eo quod* here, as in
Gen. xxxi. 49 for example, but *ita ut*, as in Gen. xiii. 16.
What follows is the result of the separation accomplished and
the promise fulfilled. For the same reason God is called
Elohē 'âmēn, "the God of Amen," *i.e.* the God who turns what
He promises into Yea and Amen (2 Cor. i. 20). The epithet
derived from the confirmatory Amen, which is thus applied to
Jehovah, is similar to the expression in Rev. iii. 14, where
Jesus is called "the Amen, the faithful and true witness."
The explanatory *kī* (for) is emphatically repeated in וְכִי, as in
Gen. xxxiii. 11 and 1 Sam. xix. 4 (compare Job xxxviii. 20).
The inhabitants of the land stand in a close and undisturbed
relation to the God who has proved Himself to be true to His
promises; for all the former evils that followed from the sin
have entirely passed away.

The fact that they have thus passed away is now still
further explained; the prophet heaping up one *kī* (for) upon
another, as in ch. ix. 3–5. Vers. 17–19. " *For behold I create
a new heaven and a new earth; and men will not remember the
first, nor do they come to any one's mind. No, be ye joyful
and exult for ever at that which I create: for behold I turn*

*Jerusalem into exulting, and her people into joy. And I shall
exult over Jerusalem, and be joyous over my people, and the voice
of weeping and screaming will be heard in her no more.*" The
promise here reaches its culminating point, which had already
been seen from afar in ch. li. 16. Jehovah creates a new
heaven and a new earth, which bind so fast with their glory,
and which so thoroughly satisfy all desires, that there is no
thought of the former ones, and no one wishes them back
again. Most of the commentators, from Jerome to Hahn,
suppose the *rĭshōnōth* in ver. 16 to refer to the former sorrowful times. Calvin says, "The statement of the prophet, that
there will be no remembrance of former things, is supposed
by some to refer to the heaven and the earth, as if he meant,
that henceforth neither the fame nor even the name of either
would any more be heard; but I prefer to refer them to the
former times." But the correctness of the former explanation
is shown by the parallel in Jer. iii. 16, which stands in by no
means an accidental relation to this passage, and where it is
stated that in the future there will be no ark of the covenant,
"neither shall it come to mind, neither shall they remember it,"
inasmuch as all Jerusalem will be the throne of Jehovah, and
not merely the capporeth with its symbolical cherubim. This
promise is also a glorious one ; but Jeremiah and all the other
prophets fall short of the eagle-flight of Isaiah, of whom the
same may be said as of John, "*volat avis sine meta.*" Luther
(like Zwingli and Stier) adopts the correct rendering, "that
men shall no more remember the former ones (*i.e.* the old
heaven and old earth), nor take it to heart." But *ʿâlâh ʿal-lēbh*
signifies to come into the mind, not "to take to heart," and is
applied to a thing, the thought of which "ascends" within us,
and with which we are inwardly occupied. There is no necessity to take the futures in ver. 17*b* as commands (Hitzig) ; for
כִּי אִם־שִׂישׂוּ (כי) with *munach*, as in Ven. 1521, after the Masora
to Num. xxxv. 33) fits on quite naturally, even if we take them
as simple predictions. Instead of such a possible, though not
actual, calling back and wishing back, those who survive the
new times are called upon rather to rejoice for ever in that
which Jehovah is actually creating, and will have created then.
אֲשֶׁר, if not regarded as the accusative-object, is certainly regarded as the object of causality, "in consideration of that

which" (cf. ch. xxxi. 6, Gen. iii. 17, Judg. viii. 15), equivalent to, "on account of that which" (see at ch. lxiv. 4, xxxv. 1).
The imperatives *sîsû v⁰gîlû* are not words of admonition so
much as words of command, and *kî* gives the reason in this
sense : Jehovah makes Jerusalem *gîláh* and her people *mâsôs*
(accusative of the predicate, or according to the terminology
adopted in Becker's syntax, the "factitive object," Ges. § 139,
2), by making joy its perpetual state, its appointed condition of
life both inwardly and outwardly. Nor is it joy on the part
of the church only, but on the part of its God as well (see the
primary passage in Deut. xxx. 9). When the church thus
rejoices in God, and God in the church, so that the light of
the two commingle, and each is reflected in the other; then
will no sobbing of weeping ones, no sound of lamentation, be
heard any more in Jerusalem (see the opposite side as expressed
in ch. li. 3*b*).

There will be a different measure then, and a much greater
one, for measuring the period of life and grace. Ver. 20.
" *And there shall no more come thence a suckling of a few days,
and an old man who has not lived out all his days ; for the youth
in it will die as one a hundred years old, and the sinner be
smitten with the curse as one a hundred years old.*" Our
editions of the text commence ver. 20 with לֹא־יִהְיֶה, but according to the Masora (see *Mas. finalis*, p. 23, col. 7), which
reckons five וְלֹא־יִהְיֶה at the commencement of verses, and
includes our verse among them, it must read וְלֹא־יִהְיֶה, as it is
also rendered by the LXX. and Targum. The meaning and
connection are not affected by this various reading. Henceforth there will not spring from Jerusalem (or, what *háyáh*
really means, "come into existence ;" "thence," *misshâm*, not
"from that time," but locally, as in Hos. ii. 17 and elsewhere,
cf. ch. lviii. 12) a suckling (see vol. i. p. 138) of days, *i.e.* one
who has only reached the age of a few days (*yámîm* as in Gen.
xxiv. 55, etc.), nor an old man who has not filled his days, *i.e.*
has not attained to what is regarded as a rule as the full
measure of human life. He who dies as a youth, or is regarded as having died young, will not die before the hundredth
year of his life ; and the sinner (וְהַחוֹטֶא with *seghol*, as in Eccl.
viii. 12, ix. 18 ; Ges. § 75, Anm. 21) upon whom the curse of
God falls, and who is overwhelmed by the punishment, will not

be swept away before the hundredth year of his life. We cannot maintain with Hofmann (*Schriftbeweis*, ii. 2, 567), that it is only in appearance that less is here affirmed than in ch. xxv. 8. The reference there is to the ultimate destruction of the power of death; here it is merely to the limitation of its power.

In the place of the threatened curses of the law in Lev. xxvi. 16 (cf. Deut. xxviii. 30), the very opposite will now receive their fullest realization. Vers. 21–23. "*And they will build houses and inhabit them, and plant vineyards and enjoy the fruit thereof. They will not build and another inhabit, nor plant and another enjoy; for like the days of trees are the days of my people, and my chosen ones will consume the work of their hands. They will not weary themselves in vain, nor bring forth for sudden disaster; for they are a family of the blessed of Jehovah, and their offspring are left to them.*" They themselves will enjoy what they have worked for, without some one else stepping in, whether a countryman by violence or inheritance, or a foreigner by plunder or conquest (ch. lxii. 8), to take possession of that which they have built and planted (read יְבַלּוּ without *dagesh*); for the duration of their life will be as great as that of *trees* (*i.e.* of oaks, terebinths, and cedars, which live for centuries), and thus they will be able thoroughly to enjoy in their own person what their hands have made. *Billâh* does net mean merely to use and enjoy, but to use up and consume. Work and generation will be blessed then, and there will be no more disappointed hopes. They will not weary themselves (יִיגָעוּ with a preformative ' without that of the root) for failure, nor get children *labbehâlâh*, *i.e.* for some calamity to fall suddenly upon them and carry them away (Lev. xxvi. 16, cf. Ps. lxxviii. 33). The primary idea of *bâhal* is either acting, permitting, or bearing, with the characteristic of being let loose, of suddenness, of overthrow, or of throwing into confusion. The LXX. renders it εἰς κατάραν, probably according to the Egypto-Jewish usage, in which *behâlâh* may have signified cursing, like *bahle, buhle* in the Arabic (see the Appendices). The two clauses of the explanation which follows stand in a reciprocal relation to the two clauses of the previous promise. They are a family of the blessed of God, upon whose labour the blessing of God rests, and their offspring are with them, without being lost to them by premature death. This is the true meaning, as in Job xxi. 8, and not "their offspring with them," *i.e.* in like manner, as Hitzig supposes.

All prayer will be heard then. Ver. 24. "*And it will come to pass: before they call, I will answer; they are still speaking, and I already hear.*" The will of the church of the new Jerusalem will be so perfectly the will of Jehovah also, that He will hear the slightest emotion of prayer in the heart, the half-uttered prayer, and will at once fulfil it (cf. ch. xxx. 19).

And all around will peace and harmony prevail, even in the animal world itself. Ver. 25. "*Wolf and lamb then feed together, and the lion eats chopped straw like the ox, and the serpent — dust is its bread. They will neither do harm nor destroy in all my holy mountain, saith Jehovah.*" We have frequently observed within ch. xl.–lxvi. (last of all at ch. lxv. 12, cf. lxvi. 4), how the prophet repeats entire passages from the earlier portion of his prophecies almost word for word. Here he repeats ch. xi. 6–9 with a compendious abridgment. Ver. 25*b* refers to the animals just as it does there. But whilst this custom of self-repetition favours the unity of authorship, כְּאֶחָד for יַחְדָּו = *unâ*, which only occurs elsewhere in Ezra and Ecclesiastes (answering to the Chaldee כַּחֲדָה), might be adduced as evidence of the opposite. The only thing that is new in the picture as here reproduced, is what is said of the serpent. This will no longer watch for human life, but will content itself with the food assigned it in Gen. iii. 14. It still continues to wriggle in the dust, but without doing injury to man. The words affirm nothing more than this, although Stier's method of exposition gets more out, or rather puts more in. The assertion of those who regard the prophet speaking here as one later than Isaiah, viz. that ver. 25 is only attached quite loosely to what precedes, is unjust and untrue. The description of the new age closes here, as in ch. xi., with the peace of the world of nature, which stands throughout ch. xl.–lxvi. in the closest reciprocal relation to man, just as it did in ch. i.–xxxix. If we follow Hahn, and change the animals into men by simply allegorizing, we just throw our exposition back to a standpoint that has been long passed by. But to what part of the history of salvation are we to look for a place for the fulfilment of such prophecies as these of the state of peace prevailing in nature around the church, except in the millennium? A prophet was certainly no fanatic, so that we could say, these are beautiful dreams. And if, what is certainly true, his prophecies are not intended to be interpreted according to the letter, but according to the spirit of the letter; the letter is the sheath of the spirit, as Luther calls it, and we must not give out as the spirit of the letter what is nothing more than a *quid-pro-quo* of the letter. The prophet here promises a new age, in which the patriarchal measure of human life will return, in which death will no more break off the life that is just beginning to bloom, and in which the war of man with the animal world will be exchanged for peace without danger. And when is all this to occur? Certainly not in the blessed life beyond the grave, to which it would be both absurd and impossible to refer these promises, since they presuppose a continued mixture of sinners with the righteous, and merely a limitation of the power of death, not its utter destruction. But when then? This question ought to be answered by the anti-millenarians. They throw back the interpretation of prophecy to a stage, in which commentators were in the habit of lowering the concrete substance of the prophecies into mere doctrinal *loci communes*. They take refuge behind the enigmatical character of the Apocalypse, without acknowledging that what the Apocalypse predicts under the definite form of the millennium is the substance of all prophecy, and that no interpretation of prophecy on sound principles is any longer possible from the standpoint of an orthodox antichiliasm, inasmuch as the antichiliasts twist the word in the mouths of the prophets, and through their perversion of Scripture shake the foundation of all doctrines, every one of which rests upon the simple interpretation of the words of revelation. But one objection may be made to the supposition, that the prophet is here depicting the state of things in the millennium; viz. that this description is preceded by an account of the creation of a new heaven and a new earth. The prophet appears, therefore, to refer to that Jerusalem, which is represented in the Apocalypse as coming down from heaven to earth after the transformation of the globe. But to this it may be replied, that the Old Testament prophet was not yet able to distinguish from one another the things which the author of the Apocalypse separates into distinct periods. From the Old Testament point of view generally, nothing was known of a state of blessedness beyond the grave. Hades lay beyond this present life; and nothing was known of a heaven in which men were blessed. Around the throne of God in heaven there were angels and not men. And, indeed, until the risen Saviour ascended to heaven, heaven itself was not open to men, and therefore there was no heavenly Jerusalem whose descent to earth could be anticipated then. Consequently in the prophecies of the Old Testament the eschatological idea of the new Cosmos does unquestionably coincide with the millennium. It is only in the New Testament that the new creation intervenes as a party-wall between this life and the life beyond; whereas the Old Testament prophecy brings down the new creation itself into the present life, and knows nothing of any Jerusalem of the blessed life to come, as distinct from the new Jerusalem of the millennium. We shall meet with a still further illustration in ch. lxvi. of this Old Testament custom of reducing the things of the life to come within the limits of this present world.

THIRD CLOSING PROPHECY.—Chap. LXVI.

EXCLUSION OF SCORNERS FROM THE COMING SALVATION.

Although the note on which this prophecy opens is a different one from any that has yet been struck, there are many points in which it coincides with the preceding prophecy. For not only is ch. lxv. 12 repeated here in ver. 4, but the sharp line of demarcation drawn in ch. lxv., between the servants of Jehovah and the worldly majority of the nation with reference to the approaching return to the Holy Land, is continued here. As the idea of their return is associated immediately with that of the erection of a new temple, there is nothing at all to surprise us, after what we have read in ch. lxv. 8 sqq., in the fact that Jehovah expresses His abhorrence at the thought of having a temple built by the Israel of the captivity, as the majority then were, and does so in such words as those which follow in vers. 1-4: " *Thus saith Jehovah: The heaven is my throne, and the earth my footstool. What kind of house is it that ye would build*

*me, and what kind of place for my rest? My hand hath made
all these things; then all these things arose, saith Jehovah; and
at such persons do I look, at the miserable and broken-hearted,
and him that trembleth at my word. He that slaughtereth the
ox is the slayer of a man; he that sacrificeth the sheep is a
strangler of dogs; he that offereth a meat-offering, it is swine's
blood; he that causeth incense to rise up in smoke, blesseth idols.
As they have chosen their ways, and their soul cherisheth pleasure
in their abominations; so will I choose their ill-treatments, and
bring their terrors upon them, because I called and no one replied,
I spake and they did not hear, and they did evil in mine eyes, and
chose that in which I took no pleasure."* Hitzig is of opinion
that the author has broken off here, and proceeds quite unexpectedly to denounce the intention to build a temple for Jehovah.
Those who wish to build he imagines to be those who have made
up their minds to stay behind in Chaldea, and who, whilst their
brethren who have returned to their native land are preparing
to build a temple there, want to have one of their own, just as
the Jews in Egypt built one for themselves in Leontopolis (see
vol. i. pp. 362–366). Without some such supposition as this,
Hitzig thinks it altogether impossible to discover the thread which
connects the different verses together. This view is at any rate
better than that of Umbreit, who imagines that the prophet
places us here " on the loftiest spiritual height of the Christian
development." " In the new Jerusalem," he says, " there will
be no temple seen, nor any sacrifice; Jehovah forbids these
in the strongest terms, regarding them as equivalent to mortal
sins." But the prophet, if this were his meaning, would involve
himself in self-contradiction, inasmuch as, according to ch. lvi.
and lx., there will be a temple in the new Jerusalem with
perpetual sacrifice, which this prophecy also presupposes in
vers. 20 sqq. (cf. ver. 6); and secondly, he would contradict
other prophets, such as Ezekiel and Zechariah, and the spirit
of the Old Testament generally, in which the statement, that
whoever slaughters a sacrificial animal in the new Jerusalem
will be as bad as a murderer, has no parallel, and is in fact
absolutely impossible. According to Hitzig's view, on the
other hand, ver. 3a affirms, that the worship which they would
be bound to perform in their projected temple would be an
abomination to Jehovah, however thoroughly it might be made

to conform to the Mosaic ritual. But there is nothing in the
text to sustain the idea, that there is any intention here to
condemn the building of a temple to Jehovah in Chaldæa,
nor is such an explanation by any means necessary to make the
text clear. The condemnation on the part of Jehovah has
reference to the temple, which the returning exiles intend to
build in Jerusalem. The prophecy is addressed to the entire
body now ready to return, and says to the whole without
exception, that Jehovah, the Creator of heaven and earth, does
not stand in need of any house erected by human hands, and
then proceeds to separate the penitent from those that are at
enmity against God, rejects in the most scornful manner all
offerings in the form of worship on the part of the latter, and
threatens them with divine retribution, having dropped in
vers. 3b-4 the form of address to the entire body. Just as in
the Psalm of Asaph (Ps. l.) Jehovah refuses animal and other
material offerings as such, because the whole of the animal
world, the earth and the fulness thereof, are His possession,
so here He addresses this question to the entire body of the
exiles: What kind of house is there that ye could build, that
would be worthy of me, and what kind of place that would
be worthy of being assigned to me as a resting-place? On
mâqōm mᵉnūchâthī, locus qui sit requies mea (apposition instead
of genitive connection), see p. 35. He needs no temple; for
heaven is His throne, and the earth His footstool. He is the
Being who filleth all, the Creator, and therefore the possessor,
of the universe; and if men think to do Him a service by building Him a temple, and forget His infinite majesty in their
concern for their own contemptible fabric, He wants no temple
at all. "All these" refer, as if pointing with the finger, to
the world of visible objects that surround us. וַיִּהְיוּ (from הָיָה,
existere, fieri) is used in the same sense as the וַיְהִי which
followed the creative יְהִי. In this His exaltation He is not concerned about a temple; but His gracious look is fixed upon
the man who is as follows (*zeh* pointing forwards as in ch.
lviii. 6), viz. upon the mourner, the man of broken heart, who
is filled with reverential awe at the word of His revelation.
We may see from Ps. li. 9 what the link of connection is
between vers. 2 and 3. So far as the mass of the exiles were
concerned, who had not been humbled by their sufferings, and

whom the preaching of the prophet could not bring to reflection, He did not want any temple or sacrifice from them. The
sacrificial acts, to which such detestable predicates are here
applied, are such as end with the merely external act, whilst
the inward feelings of the person presenting the sacrifice are
altogether opposed to the idea of both the animal sacrifice and
the meat-offering, more especially to that desire for salvation
which was symbolized in all the sacrifices; in other words, they
are sacrificial acts regarded as νεκρὰ ἔργα, the lifeless works of
men spiritually dead. The articles of *hasshōr* and *hasseh* are
used as generic with reference to sacrificial animals. The
slaughter of an ox was like the slaying (*makkēh* construct
with *tzere*) of a man (for the association of ideas, see Gen.
xlix. 6); the sacrifice (*zōbhĕăch* like *shâchat* is sometimes applied
to slaughtering for the purpose of eating; here, however, it
refers to an animal prepared for Jehovah) of a sheep like the
strangling of a dog, that unclean animal (for the association of
ideas, see Job xxx. 1); the offerer up (*mᵉʿōlēh*) of a meat-
offering (like one who offered up) swine's blood, *i.e.* as if he
was offering up the blood of this most unclean animal upon the
altar; he who offered incense as an *'azkârâh* (see at ch. i. 13*a*)
like one who blessed *'âven*, *i.e.* godlessness, used here as in
1 Sam. xv. 23, and also in Hosea in the change of the name of
Bethel into *Beth 'Aven*, for idolatry, or rather in a concrete
sense for the worthless idols themselves, all of which, according
to ch. xli. 29, are nothing but *'âven*. Rosenmüller, Gesenius,
Hitzig, Stier, and even Jerome, have all correctly rendered it
in this way, " as if he blessed an idol" (*quasi qui benedicat
idolo*); and Vitringa, " *cultum exhibens vano numini*" (offering
worship to a vain god). Such explanations as that of Luther,
on the other hand, viz. " as if he praised that which was wrong,"
are opposed to the antithesis, and also to the presumption of
a concrete object to מברך (blessing); whilst that of Knobel,
" praising vainly" (*'âven* being taken as an *acc. adv.*), yields too
tame an antithesis, and is at variance with the usage of the
language. In this condemnation of the ritual acts of worship,
the closing prophecy of the book of Isaiah coincides with the
first (ch. i. 11–15). But that it is not sacrifices in themselves
that are rejected, but the sacrifices of those whose hearts are
divided between Jehovah and idols, and who refuse to offer

to Him the sacrifice that is dearest to Him (Ps. li. 19, cf.
l. 23), is evident from the correlative double-sentence that
follows in vers. 3*b* and 4, which is divided into two masoretic
verses, as the only means of securing symmetry. *Gam* . . .
gam, which means in other cases, " both . . . and also," or in
negative sentences " neither . . . nor," means here, as in Jer. li. 12,
" as assuredly the one as the other," in other words, " as . . . so."
They have chosen their own ways, which are far away from
those of Jehovah, and their soul has taken pleasure, not in the
worship of Jehovah, but in all kinds of heathen abominations
(*shiqqūtsēhem*, as in many other places, after Deut. xxix. 16);
therefore Jehovah wants no temple built by them or with their
co-operation, nor any restoration of sacrificial worship at their
hands. But according to the law of retribution, He chooses
thaʻălūlēhem, vexationes eorum (LXX. τὰ ἐμπαίγματα αὐτῶν:
see at ch. iii. 4), with the suffix of the object: fates that
will use them ill, and brings their terrors upon them, *i.e.* such
a condition of life as will inspire them with terror (*mᵉgūrōth*, as
in Ps. xxxiv. 5).

From the heathenish majority, with their ungodly hearts,
the prophet now turns to the minority, consisting of those who
tremble with reverential awe when they hear the word of God.
They are called to hear how Jehovah will accept them in
defiance of their persecutors. Ver. 5. *" Hear ye the word of
Jehovah, ye that tremble at His word : your brethren that hate
you, that thrust you from them for my name's sake, say, ' Let
Jehovah get honour, that we may see your joy :' they will be put
to shame."* They that hate them are their own brethren, and
(what makes the sin still greater) the name of Jehovah is the
reason why they are hated by them. According to the accents,
indeed (מנדיכם *rebia*, שמי *pashta*), the meaning would be .
" your brethren say . . . ' for my name's sake (*i.e.* for me = out
of goodness and love to us) will Jehovah glorify Himself,'—then
we shall see your joy, but—they will be put to shame." Rashi
and other Jewish expositors interpret it in this or some similar
way ; but Rosenmüller, Stier, and Hahn are the only modern
Christian expositors who have done so, following the precedent
of earlier commentators, who regarded the accents as binding.
Luther, however, very properly disregarded them. If למען שמי
be taken in connection with יכבד, it gives only a forced sense,

which disturbs the relation of all the clauses; whereas this is preserved in all respects in the most natural and connected manner if we combine לְמַעַן שְׁמִי with שֹׂנְאֵיכֶם מְנַדֵּיכֶם, as we must do, according to such parallels as Matt. xxiv. 9. נד √ נָדָה, to scare away or thrust away (Amos vi. 3, with the object in the dative), corresponds to ἀφορίζειν in Luke vi. 22 (compare John xvi. 22, " to put out of the synagogue"). The practice of excommunication, or putting under the ban (*niddūi*), reaches beyond the period of the Herodians (see *Eduyoth* v. 6),[1] at any rate as far back as the times succeeding the captivity; but in the passage before us it is quite sufficient to understand *niddáh* in the sense of a defamatory renunciation of fellowship. To the accentuators this מְנַדֵּיכֶם לְמַעַן שְׁמִי appeared quite unintelligible. They never considered that it had a confessional sense here, which certainly does not occur anywhere else: viz. " for my name's sake, which ye confess in word and deed." With unbelieving scorn they say to those who confess Jehovah, and believe in the word of the true redemption: Let Jehovah glorify Himself (lit. let Him be, *i.e.* show Himself, glorious = *yikkábhēd*, cf. Job. xiv. 21), that we may thoroughly satisfy ourselves with looking at your joy. They regard their hope as deceptive, and the word of the prophet as fanaticism. These are they, who, when permission to return is suddenly given, will desire to accompany them, but will be disappointed, because they did not rejoice in faith before, and because, although they do now rejoice in that which is self-evident, they do this in a wrong way.

The city and temple, to which they desire to go, are nothing more, so far as they are concerned, than the places from which just judgment will issue. Ver. 6. " *Sound of tumult from the city! Sound from the temple! Sound of Jehovah, who repays His enemies with punishment.*" All three קוֹל, to the second of which שָׁאוֹן must be supplied in thought, are in the form of interjectional exclamations (as in ch. lii. 8). In the third, however, we have omitted the note of admiration, because here the interjectional clause approximates very nearly to a substantive clause (" it is the sound of Jehovah"), as the person shouting announces here who is the originator and cause of the noise

---

[1] Compare Wiesner: *Der Bann in seiner gesch. Entwickelung auf dem Boden des Judenthums*, 1864.

which was so enigmatical at first. The city and temple are indeed still lying in ruins as the prophet is speaking; but even in this state they both preserve the holiness conferred upon them. They are the places where Jehovah will take up His abode once more; and even now, at the point at which promise and fulfilment coincide, they are in the very process of rising again. A loud noise (like the tumult of war) proceeds from it. It is Jehovah, He who is enthroned in Zion and rules from thence (ch. xxxi. 9), who makes Himself heard in this loud noise (compare Joel iv. 16 with the derivative passage in Amos i. 2); it is He who awards punishment or reckons retribution to His foes. In other cases שִׁלֵּם (הֵשִׁיב) גְּמוּל generally means to repay that which has been worked out (what has been deserved; e.g. Ps. cxxxvii. 8, compare ch. iii. 11); but in ch. lix. 18 *gᵉmūl* was the parallel word to *chēmâh*, and therefore, as in ch. xxxv. 4, it did not apply to the works of men, but to the retribution of the judge, just as in Jer. li. 6, where it is used quite as absolutely. We have therefore rendered it " punishment;" " merited punishment" would express both sides of this double-sided word. By " His enemies," according to the context, we are to understand primarily the mass of the exiles, who were so estranged from God, and yet withal so full of demands and expectations.

All of these fall victims to the judgment; and yet Zion is not left either childless or without population. Vers. 7–9. " *Before she travailed she brought forth; before pains came upon her, she was delivered of a boy. Who hath heard such a thing? Who hath seen anything like it? Are men delivered of a land in one day? or is a nation begotten at once? For Zion hath travailed, yea, hath brought forth her children. Should I bring to the birth, and not cause to bring forth? saith Jehovah: or should I, who cause to bring forth, shut up? saith thy God.*" Before Zion travaileth, before any labour pains come upon her (*chēbhel* with *tzere*), she has already given birth, or brought with ease into the world a male child (*himlīt* like *millēt*, in ch. xxxiv. 15, to cause to glide out). This boy, of whom she is delivered with such marvellous rapidity, is a whole land full of men, an entire nation. The seer exclaims with amazement, like Zion herself in ch. xlix. 21, " who hath heard such a thing, or seen anything like it? is a land brought to the birth (*hăyūchal* followed by

'*erets* for *hăthăchal*, as in Gen. xiii. 6, Isa. ix. 18; Ges. § 147),
i.e. the population of a whole land (as in Judg. xviii. 30), and
that in one day, or a nation born all at once (*yivvâlēd*, with
munach attached to the *kametz*, and *metheg* to the *tzere*)?
This unheard-of event has taken place now, for Zion has
travailed, yea, has also brought forth her children,"—not one
child, but her children, a whole people that calls her mother.[1]
" For" (*kī*) presupposes the suppressed thought, that this unexampled event has now occurred: *yâl*e*dâh* follows *châlâh* with
gam, because *chīl* signifies strictly *parturire; yâlad, parere.*
Zion, the mother, is no other than the woman of the sun in
Rev. xii.; but the child born of her there is the shepherd of the
nations, who proceeds from her at the end of the days, whereas
here it is the new Israel of the last days; for the church,
which is saved through all her tribulations, is both the mother
of the Lord, by whom Babel is overthrown, and the mother of
that Israel which inherits the promises, that the unbelieving
mass have failed to obtain. Ver. 9 follows with an emphatic
confirmation of the things promised. Jehovah inquires: "Should
I create the delivery (cause the child to break through the
matrix) and not the birth (both *hiphil*, causative), so that
although the child makes an effort to pass the opening of the
womb, it never comes to the light of day? Or should I be one
to bring it to the birth, and then to have closed, viz. the womb,
so that the work of bringing forth should remain ineffectual,
when all that is required is the last effort to bring to the light
the fruit of the womb?" From the expression "thy God," we
see that the questions are addressed to Zion, whose faith they
are intended to strengthen. According to Hofmann (*Schriftbeweis*, ii. 1, 149, 150), the future יאמר affirms what Jehovah
will say, when the time for bringing forth arrives, and the
perfect אָמַר what He is saying now: " Should I who create
the bringing forth have shut up?" And He comforts the now
barren daughter Zion (ch. liv. 1) with the assurance, that her
barrenness is not meant to continue for ever. " The prediction,"

---

[1] There is a certain similarity in the saying, with which a talmudic
teacher roused up the sleepy scholars of the Beth ha-Midrash: " There
was once a woman, who was delivered of 600,000 children in one day,"
viz. Jochebed, who, when she gave birth to Moses, brought 600,000 to the
light of freedom (Ex. xii. 37).

says Hofmann, " which is contained in יאמר ה׳, of the ultimate
issue of the fate of Zion, is so far connected with the consolation administered for the time present, that she who is barren
now is exhorted to anticipate the time when the former promise
shall be fulfilled." But this change in the standpoint is artificial, and contrary to the general use of the expression יאמר ה׳
elsewhere (see at ch. xl. 1). Moreover, the meaning of the
two clauses, which constitute here as elsewhere a disjunctive
double question in form more than in sense, really runs into
one. The first member affirms that Jehovah will complete the
bringing to the birth ; the second, that He will not ultimately
frustrate what He has almost brought to completion : *an ego
sum is qui parere faciat et* (*uterum*) *occluserim* (*occludam*) ?
There is no other difference between יאמר and אמר, than that
the former signifies the word of God which is sounding at the
present moment, the latter the word that has been uttered and
is resounding still. The prophetic announcement of our prophet
has advanced so far, that the promised future is before the door.
The church of the future is already like the fruit of the body
ripe for the birth, and about to separate itself from the womb
of Zion, which has been barren until now. The God by whom
everything has been already so far prepared, will suddenly
cause Zion to become a mother ;—a boy, viz. a whole people
after Jehovah's own heart, will suddenly lie in her lap, and
this new-born Israel, not the corrupt mass, will build a temple
for Jehovah.

In the anticipation of such a future, those who inwardly
participate in the present sufferings of Zion are to rejoice
beforehand in the change of all their suffering into glory.
Vers. 10, 11. " *Rejoice ye with Jerusalem, and exult over her, all
ye that love her ; be ye delightfully glad with her, all ye that
mourn over her, that ye may suck and be satisfied with the breast
of her consolations, that ye may sip and delight yourselves in
the abundance of her glory.*" Those who love Jerusalem (the
abode of the church, and the church itself), who mourn over
her (*hith'abbēl*, inwardly mourn, 1 Sam. xv. 35, prove and show
themselves to be mourners and go into mourning, *b. Moëd
katan* 20*b*, the word generally used in prose, whereas אָבֵל, to be
thrown into mourning, to mourn, only occurs in the higher
style ; compare אֲבֵלֵי צִיּוֹן, ch. lvii. 18, lxi. 2, 3, lx. 20), these are

even now to rejoice in spirit with Jerusalem and exult on her account (*bâh*), and share her ecstatic delight with her (*'ittâh*), in order that when that in which they now rejoice in spirit shall be fulfilled, they may suck and be satisfied, etc. Jerusalem is regarded as a mother, and the rich actual consolation, which she receives (ch. li. 3), as the milk that enters her breasts (*shôd* as in ch. lx. 16), and from which she now supplies her children with plentiful nourishment. זִיז, which is parallel to שֹׁד (not זִיז, a reading which none of the ancients adopted), signifies a moving, shaking abundance, which oscillates to and fro like a great mass of water, from זָאָזָא, to move by fits and starts, for *pellere movere* is the radical meaning common in such combinations of letters as זא, זע, זר, Ps. xlii. 5, to which Bernstein and Knobel have correctly traced the word; whereas the meaning *emicans fluxus* (Schröder), or *radians copia* (Kocher), to pour out in the form of rays, has nothing to sustain it in the usage of the language.

The reason is now given, why the church of the future promises such abundant enjoyment to those who have suffered with her. Ver. 12. "*For thus saith Jehovah, Behold, I guide peace to her like a river, and the glory of the Gentiles like an overflowing stream, that ye may suck; ye shall be borne upon arms, and fondled upon knees.*" Jehovah guides or turns (Gen. xxxix. 21) peace to Jerusalem, the greatest of all inward blessings, and at the same time the most glorious of all the outward blessings, that are in the possession of the Gentile world (*kâbhôd* as in ch. lxi. 6), both of them in the richest superabundance ("like a river," as in ch. xlviii. 18), so that (*perf. cons.*) "ye may be able to suck yourselves full according to your heart's desire" (ch. lx. 16). The figure of the new maternity of Zion, and of her children as *quasimodogeniti*, is still preserved. The members of the church can then revel in peace and wealth, like a child at its mother's breasts. The world is now altogether in the possession of the church, because the church is altogether God's. The allusion to the heathen leads on to the thought, which was already expressed in a similar manner in ch. xlix. 22 and lx. 4: " on the side (arm or shoulder) will ye be carried, and fondled (שַׁעֲשָׁע, *pulpal* of the *pilpel* שִׁעֲשַׁע, ch. xi. 8) upon the knees," viz. by the heathen, who will vie with one another in the effort to show you tenderness and care (ch. xlix. 23).

The prophet now looks upon the members of the church as having grown up, as it were, from childhood to maturity : they suck like a child, and are comforted like a grown-up son. Ver. 13. *" Like a man whom his mother comforteth, so will I comfort you, and ye shall be comforted in Jerusalem."* Hitzig says that *'ĭsh* is not well chosen ; but how easily could the prophet have written *bēn* (son), as in ch. xlix. 15 ! He writes *'ĭsh*, however, not indeed in the unmeaning sense in which the LXX. has taken it, viz. ὡς εἴ τινα μήτηρ παρακαλέσει, but looking upon the people, whom he had previously thought of as children, as standing before him as one man. Israel is now like a man who has escaped from bondage and returned home from a foreign land, full of mournful recollections, the echoing sounds of which entirely disappear in the maternal arms of divine love there in Jerusalem, the beloved home, which was the home of its thoughts even in the strange land.

Wherever they look, joy now meets their eye. Ver. 14. *" And ye will see, and your heart will be joyful, and your bones will flourish like young herbage ; and thus does the hand of Jehovah make itself known in His servants, and fiercely does He treat His enemies."* They will see, and their heart will rejoice, *i.e.* (cf. ch. liii. 11, lx. 5) they will enjoy a heart-cheering prospect, and revive again with such smiling scenery all around. The body is like a tree. The bones are its branches. These will move and extend themselves in the fulness of rejuvenated strength (compare ch. lviii. 11, *et ossa tua expedita faciet*) ; and thus will the hand of Jehovah practically become known (*venōde'âh*, *perf. cons.*) in His servants,—that hand under whose gracious touch all vernal life awakens, whether in body or in mind. And thus is it with the surviving remnant of Israel, whereas Jehovah is fiercely angry with His foes. The first אֶת is used in a prepositional sense, as in Ps. lxvii. 2, viz. "in His servants, so that they come to be acquainted with it ;" the second in an accusative sense, for *zâ'am* is either connected with עַל, or as in Zech. i. 12, Mal. i. 4, with the accusative of the object. It is quite contrary to the usage of the language to take both אֶת according to the phrase (עָם) אֶת (רעה) עָשָׂה טוֹבָה.

The prophecy now takes a new turn with the thought expressed in the words, "and fiercely does He treat His

enemies." The judgment of wrath, which prepares the way
for the redemption and ensures its continuance, is described
more minutely in ver. 15 : "*For behold Jehovah, in the fire will
He come, and His chariots are like the whirlwind, to pay out His
wrath in burning heat, and His threatening passeth into flames of
fire.*" Jehovah comes *bâ'ēsh, in igne* (Jerome ; the LXX., on
the contrary, render it arbitrarily ὡς πῦρ, *kâ'ēsh*), since it
is the fiery side of His glory, in which He appears, and fire
pours from Him, which is primarily the intense excitement of
the powers of destruction within God Himself (ch. x. 17, xxx.
27 ; Ps. xviii. 9), and in these is transformed into cosmical
powers of destruction (ch. xxix. 6, xxx. 30 ; Ps. xviii. 13).
He is compared to a warrior, driving along upon war-chariots
resembling stormy wind, which force everything out of their
way, and crush to pieces whatever comes under their wheels.
The plural מַרְכְּבֹתָיו (His chariots) is probably not merely
amplifying, but a strict plural ; for Jehovah, the One, can
manifest Himself in love or wrath in different places at the
same time. The very same substantive clause וכסופה מרכבתיו
occurs in Jer. iv. 13, where it is not used of Jehovah, however, but of the Chaldeans. Observe also that Jeremiah there
proceeds immediately with a derivative passage from Hab. i. 8.
In the following clause denoting the object, לְהָשִׁיב בְּחֵמָה אַפּוֹ, we
must not adopt the rendering, "to breathe out His wrath in
burning heat" (Hitzig), for *hēshîbh* may mean *respirare*, but not
exspirare (if this were the meaning, it would be better to read
לְהַשִּׁיב from נָשַׁב, as Lowth does) ; nor "*ut iram suam furore sedet*"
(Meier), for even in Job ix. 13, Ps. lxxviii. 38, השיב אפו does not
mean to still or cool His wrath, but to turn it away or take it
back ; not even "to direct His wrath in burning heat" (Ges.,
Kn.), for in this sense *hēshîbh* would be connected with an object
with לְ, אֶל (Job xv. 13), עַל (i. 25). It has rather the meaning
reddere in the sense of *retribuere* (Arab. *athâba*, syn. *shillēm*),
and "to pay back, or pay out, His wrath" is equivalent to
hēshîbh nâqâm (Deut. xxxii. 41, 43). Hence בחמה אפו does not
stand in a permutative relation instead of a genitive one (viz.
in fervore, irâ suâ = irœ suœ), but is an adverbial definition,
just as in ch. xlii. 25. That the payment of the wrath deserved
takes place in burning heat, and His rebuke (*gᵉ'ârâh*) in flames
of fire, are thoughts that answer to one another.

Jehovah appears with these warlike terrors because He is coming for a great judgment. Ver. 16. "*For in the midst of fire Jehovah holds judgment, and in the midst of His sword with all flesh; and great will be the multitude of those pierced through by Jehovah.*" The fire, which is here introduced as the medium of judgment, points to destructive occurrences of nature, and the sword to destructive occurrences of history. At the same time all the emphasis is laid here, as in ch. xxxiv. 5, 6 (cf. ch. xxvii. 1), upon the direct action of Jehovah Himself. The parallelism in ver. 16a is progressive. *Nishpat 'ēth*, "to go into judgment with a person," as in Ezek. xxxviii. 22 (cf. עִם in ch. iii. 14, Joel iv. 2, 2 Chron. xxii. 8; μετά, Luke xi. 31, 32). We find a resemblance to ver. 16b in Zeph. ii. 12, and this is not the only resemblance to our prophecy in that strongly reproductive prophet.

The judgment predicted here is a judgment upon nations, and falls not only upon the heathen, but upon the great mass of Israel, who have fallen away from their election of grace and become like the heathen. Ver. 17. "*They that consecrate themselves and purify themselves for the gardens behind one in the midst, who eat swine's flesh and abomination and the field-mouse—they all come to an end together, saith Jehovah.*" The persons are first of all described; and then follows the judgment pronounced, as the predicate of the sentence. They subject themselves to the heathen rites of lustration, and that with truly bigoted thoroughness, as is clearly implied by the combination of the two synonyms *hammithqaddᵉshīm* and *hammittahărīm* (*hithpael* with an assimilated *tav*), which, like the Arabic *qadusa* and *tahura*, are both traceable to the radical idea ἀφορίζειν. The אֶל of אֶל־הַגַּנּוֹת is to be understood as relating to the object or behoof: their intention being directed to the gardens as places of worship (ch. i. 29, lxv. 3), *ad sacra in lucis obeunda*, as Schelling correctly explains. In the *chethib* אַחַר אחד בְּתָוֶךְ, the אֶחָד (for which we may also read אַחַר, the form of connection, although the two *pathachs* of the text belong to the *keri*) is in all probability the hierophant, who leads the people in the performance of the rites of religious worship; and as he is represented as standing in the midst (בְּתָוֶךְ) of the worshipping crowd that surrounds him, *'achar* (behind, after) cannot be understood locally, as if they formed his train or tail, but tempo-

rally or in the way of imitation. He who stands in their midst
performs the ceremonies before them, and they follow him,
i.e. perform them *after* him. This explanation leaves nothing
to be desired. The *keri, 'achath,* is based upon the assumption
that *'achad* must refer to the idol, and substitutes therefore the
feminine, no doubt with an allusion to *'ăshērâh,* so that *battâvekh*
(in the midst) is to be taken as referring not to the midst of
the worshipping congregation, but to the midst of the gardens.
This would be quite as suitable; for even if it were not expressly stated, we should have to assume that the sacred tree
of Astarte, or her statue, occupied the post of honour in the
midst of the garden, and *'achar* would correspond to the phrase
in the Pentateuch, זָנָה אַחֲרֵי אֱלֹהִים אֲחֵרִים. But the foregoing
expression, *sanctificantes et mundantes se* (consecrating and puri-
fying), does not favour this sense of the word *'achar* (why not
לְכָבוֹד = לְ?), nor do we see why the name of the goddess should
be suppressed, or why she should be simply hinted at in the
word אַחַת (one). אֶחָד (אַחַד) has its sufficient explanation in
the antithesis between the one choir-leader and the many
followers; but if we take *'achath* as referring to the goddess,
we can find no intelligible reason or object. Some again have
taken both *'achad* and *'achath* to be the proper name of the idol.
Ever since the time of Scaliger and Grotius, *'achad* has been
associated with the Phœnician Ἄδωδος βασιλεὺς θεῶν mentioned by Sanchuniathon in Euseb. *præp. ev.* 1, 10, 21, or with
the Assyrian sun-god *Adad,* of whom Macrobius says (*Saturn.*
1, 23), *Ejus nominis interpretatio significat unus;* but we should
expect the name of a Babylonian god here, and not of a
Phœnician or Assyrian (Syrian) deity. Moreover, Macrobius'
combination of the Syrian *Hadad* with *'achad* was a mere
fancy, arising from an imperfect knowledge of the language.
Clericus' combination of *'achath* with *Hecate,* who certainly
appears to have been worshipped by the Harranians as a
monster, though not under this name, and not in gardens
(which would not have suited her character), is also untenable.
Now as *'achath* cannot be explained as a proper name, and the
form of the statement does not favour the idea that *'achar
'achath* or *'achar 'achad* refers to an idol, we adopt the reading
'achad, and understand it to refer to the hierophant or mysta-
gogue. Jerome follows the *keri,* and renders it *post unam*

intrinsecus. The reading *post januam* is an ancient correction,
which is not worth tracing to the Aramæan interpretation of
'achar 'achad, "behind a closed door," and merely rests upon
some rectification of the unintelligible *post unam*. The Targum
renders it, "one division after another," and omits *battâvekh*.
The LXX., on the other hand, omits *'achar 'achad*, reads
ûbhattâvekh, and renders it καὶ ἐν τοῖς προθύροις (in the inner
court). Symmachus and Theodoret follow the Targum and
Syriac, and render it ὀπίσω ἀλλήλων, and then pointing the next
word בְּתֹוךְ (which Schelling and Böttcher approve), render the
rest ἐν μέσῳ ἐσθιόντων τὸ κρέας τὸ χοιρεῖον (in the midst of
those who eat, etc.). But אֹכְלֵי commences the further description of those who were indicated first of all by their zealous
adoption of heathen customs. Whilst, on the one hand, they
readily adopt the heathen ritual; they set themselves on the
other hand, in the most daring way, altogether above the law
of Jehovah, by eating swine's flesh (ch. lxv. 4) and reptiles
(*sheqets*, abomination, used for disgusting animals, such as
lizards, snails, etc., Lev. vii. 21, xi. 11[1]), and more especially
the mouse (Lev. xi. 29), or according to Jerome and Zwingli
the dormouse (*glis esculentus*), which the Talmud also mentions
under the name עכברא דברא (wild mouse) as a dainty bit with
epicures, and which was fattened, as is well known, by the
Romans in their *gliraria*.[2] However inward and spiritual may
be the interpretation given to the law in these prophecies, yet,
as we see here, the whole of it, even the laws of food, were
regarded as inviolable. So long as God Himself had not taken
away the hedges set about His church, every wilful attempt to
break through them was a sin, which brought down His wrath
and indignation.

The prophecy now marks out clearly the way which the
history of Israel will take. It is the same as that set forth by
Paul, the prophetic apostle, in Rom. ix.–xi. as the winding but
memorable path by which the compassion of God will reach its
all-embracing end. A universal judgment is the turning-point.
Ver. 18. "*And I, their works and their thoughts —— it comes to*

[1] See Levysohn, *Zoologie des Talmuds*, pp. 218–9.
[2] See Levysohn, *id.* pp. 108–9. A special delicacy was *glires isicio
porcino*, dormice with pork stuffing; see Brillat-Savarin's *Physiologie des
Geschmacks*, by C. Vogt, p. 253.

pass that all nations and tongues are gathered together, that they come and see my glory." This verse commences in any case with a harsh ellipsis. Hofmann, who regards ver. 17 as referring not to idolatrous Israelites, but to the idolatrous world outside Israel, tries to meet the difficulty by adopting this rendering: "And I, saith Jehovah, when their thoughts and actions succeed in bringing together all nations and tongues (to march against Jerusalem), they come and see my glory (*i.e.* the alarming manifestation of my power)." But what is the meaning of the opening וְאָנֹכִי (and I), which cannot possibly strengthen the distant כְּבוֹדִי, as we should be obliged to assume? Or what rule of syntax would warrant our taking מַעֲשֵׂיהֶם וּמַחְשְׁבֹתֵיהֶם בָּאָה as a participial clause in opposition to the accents? Again, it is impossible that ואנכי should mean "*et contra me;*" or מעשׂיהם ומחשבתיהם, "in spite of their works and thoughts," as Hahn supposes, which leaves ואנכי quite unexplained; not to mention other impossibilities which Ewald, Knobel, and others have persuaded themselves to adopt. If we wanted to get rid of the ellipsis, the explanation adopted by Hitzig would recommend itself the most strongly, viz. "and as for me, their works and thoughts have come, *i.e.* have become manifest (ἥκασιν, Susanna, ver. 52), so that I shall gather together." But this separation of בָּאָה לְקַבֵּץ (it is going to gather together) is improbable: moreover, according to the accents, the first clause reaches as far as ומחשבתיהם (with the twin-accent *zakeph-munach* instead of *zakeph* and *metheg*); whereupon the second clause commences with באה, which could not have any other disjunctive accent than *zakeph gadol* according to well-defined rules (see, for example, Num. xiii. 27). But if we admit the elliptical character of the expression, we have not to supply יָדַעְתִּי (I know), as the Targ., Syr., Saad., Ges., and others do, but, what answers much better to the strength of the emotion which explains the ellipsis, אֶפְקֹד (I will punish). The ellipsis is similar in character to that of the "*Quos ego*" of Virgil (Aen. i. 139), and comes under the rhetorical figure *aposiopesis:* "and I, their works and thoughts (I shall know how to punish)." The thoughts are placed after the works, because the reference is more especially to their plans against Jerusalem, that work of theirs, which has still to be carried out, and which Jehovah turns into a judgment upon them. The passage might have

been continued with *kī mishpâtī* (for my judgment), like the
derivative passage in Zeph. iii. 8 ; but the emotional hurry of
the address is still preserved : בָּאָה (properly accented as a participle) is equivalent to בָּאָה (בָּא) הָעֵת in Jer. li. 33, Ezek. vii.
7, 12 (cf. הַבָּאִים, ch. xxvii. 6). At the same time there is no
necessity to supply anything, since באה by itself may also be
taken in a neuter sense, and signify *venturum* (*futurum*) *est*
(Ezek. xxxix. 8). The expression " peoples and tongues " (as in
the genealogy of the nations in Gen. ch. x.) is not tautological,
since, although the distinctions of tongues and nationalities
coincided at first, yet in the course of history they diverged
from one another in many ways. All nations and all com-
munities of men speaking the same language does Jehovah
bring together (including the apostates of Israel, cf. Zech. xiv.
14) : these will come, viz. as Joel describes it in ch. iv. 9 sqq.,
impelled by enmity towards Jerusalem, but not without the
direction of Jehovah, who makes even what is evil subservient
to His plans, and will see His glory,—not the glory manifest in
grace (Ewald, Umbreit, Stier, Hahn), but His majestic manifestation of judgment, by which they, viz. those who have been
encoiled by sinful conduct, are completely overthrown.

But a remnant escapes ; and this remnant is employed by
Jehovah to promote the conversion of the Gentile world and
the restoration of Israel. Vers. 19, 20. " *And I set a sign upon
them, and send away those that have escaped from them to the
Gentiles to Tarshīsh, Phûl, and Lûd, to the stretchers of the bow,
Tûbal and Javan—the distant islands that have not heard my
fame and have not seen my glory, and they will proclaim my
glory among the Gentiles. And they will bring your brethren
out of all heathen nations, a sacrifice for Jehovah, upon horses and
upon chariots, and upon litters and upon mules and upon dromedaries, to my holy mountain, to Jerusalem, saith Jehovah, as the
children of Israel bring the meat-offering in a clear vessel to the
house of Jehovah.*" The majority of commentators understand
v'samtī bâhem 'ōth (and I set a sign upon them) as signifying, according to Ex. x. 2, that Jehovah will perform such a
miraculous sign upon the assembled nations as He formerly
performed upon Egypt (Hofmann), and one which will outweigh the ten Egyptian *'ōthōth* and complete the destruction
commenced by them. Hitzig supposes the *'ōth* to refer directly

to the horrible wonder connected with the battle, in which
Jehovah fights against them with fire and sword (compare the
parallels so far as the substance is concerned in Joel iv. 14–16,
Zeph. iii. 8, Ezek. xxxviii. 18 sqq., Zech. xiv. 12 sqq.). But
since, according to the foregoing threat, the expression "they
shall see my glory" signifies that they will be brought to experience the judicial revelation of the glory of Jehovah, if
v^esamtī bâhem 'ōth (and I set a sign upon them) were to be understood in this judicial sense, it would be more appropriate for
it to precede than to follow. Moreover, this *v^esamtī bâhem 'ōth*
would be a very colourless description of what takes place in
connection with the assembled army of nations. It is like a
frame without a picture; and consequently Ewald and Umbreit are right in maintaining that what follows directly after
is to be taken as the picture for this framework. The *'ōth*
(or sign) consists in the unexpected and, with this universal
slaughter, the surprising fact, that a remnant is still spared,
and survives this judicial revelation of glory. This marvellous
rescue of individuals out of the mass is made subservient in
the midst of judgment to the divine plan of salvation. Those
who have escaped are to bring to the far distant heathen world
the tidings of Jehovah, the God who has been manifested in
judgment and grace, tidings founded upon their own experience.
It is evident from this, that notwithstanding the expression
" all nations and tongues," the nations that crowd together
against Jerusalem and are overthrown in the attempt, are not
to be understood as embracing all nations without exception,
since the prophet is able to mention the names of many nations
which were beyond the circle of these great events, and had
been hitherto quite unaffected by the positive historical revelation, which was concentrated in Israel. By *Tarshish* Knobel
understands the nation of the Tyrsenes, Tuscans, or Etruscans;
but there is far greater propriety in looking for Tarshish, as
the opposite point to 'Ophir, in the extreme west, where the
name of the Spanish colony *Tartessus* resembles it in sound.
In the middle ages *Tunis* was combined with this. Instead
of פּוּל וְלוּד we should probably read with the LXX. פּוּט ולוד,
as in Ezek. xxvii. 10, xxx. 5. Stier decides in favour of
this, whilst Hitzig and Ewald regard פּוּל as another form of
פּוּט. The epithet מֹשְׁכֵי קֶשֶׁת (drawers of the bow) is ad-

mirably adapted to the inhabitants of *Pût*, since this people
of the early Egyptian *Phet* (*Phaiat*) is represented ideogra-
phically upon the monuments by nine bows.   According to
Josephus, *Ant.* i. 6, 2, a river of Mauritania was called *Phout*,
and the adjoining country *Phoute ;* and this is confirmed by
other testimonies.   As *Lud* is by no means to be understood as
referring to the Lydians of Asia Minor here, if only because
they could not well be included among the nations of the
farthest historico-geographical horizon in a book which traces
prophetically the victorious career of Cyrus, but signifies rather
the undoubtedly African tribe, the לוד which Ezekiel mentions
in ch. xxx. 5 among the nations under Egyptian rule, and in
ch. xxvii. 10 among the auxiliaries of the Tyrians, and which
Jeremiah notices in ch. xlvi. 9 along with *Put* as armed with
bows ; *Put* and *Lud* form a fitting pair in this relation also,
whereas *Pul* is never met with again.   The Targum renders it
by פּוּלָאֵי, *i.e.* (according to Bochart) inhabitants of *Φιλαί,* a
Nile island of Upper Egypt, which Strabo (xvii. 1, 49) calls
" a common abode of Ethiopians and Egyptians" (see Parthey's
work, *De Philis insula*) ; and this is at any rate better than
Knobel's supposition, that either Apulia (which was certainly
called *Pul* by the Jews of the middle ages) or Lower Italy is
intended here.   *Tubal* stands for the Tibarenes on the south-
east coast of the Black Sea, the neighbours of the Moschi
(מֶשֶׁךְ), with whom they are frequently associated by Ezekiel
(ch. xxvii. 13, xxxviii. 2, 3, xxxix. 1) ; according to Josephus
(*Ant.* i. 6, 1), the (Caucasian) Iberians.   *Javan* is a name
given to the Greeks, from the aboriginal tribe of the 'ΙάϜονες.
The eye is now directed towards the west : the "isles afar off"
are the islands standing out of the great western sea (the
Mediterranean), and the coastlands that project into it.   To
all these nations, which have hitherto known nothing of the
God of revelation, either through the hearing of the word or
through their own experience, Jehovah sends those who have
escaped ; and they make known His glory there, that glory the
judicial manifestation of which they have just seen for themselves. The prophet is speaking here of the ultimate *completion*
of the conversion of the Gentiles ; for elsewhere this appeared
to him as the work of the Servant of Jehovah, for which
Cyrus the oppressor of the nations prepared the soil.   His

standpoint here resembles that of the apostle in Rom. xi. 25,
who describes the conversion of the heathen world and the
rescue of all Israel as facts belonging to the future; although
at the time when he wrote this, the evangelization of the
heathen foretold by our prophet in ch. xlii. 1 sqq. was already
progressing most rapidly. A direct judicial act of God Himself will ultimately determine the entrance of the *Pleroma* of
the Gentiles into the kingdom of God, and this entrance of the
fulness of the Gentiles will then lead to the recovery of the
diaspora of Israel, since the heathen, when won by the testimony borne to Jehovah by those who have been saved, "bring
your brethren out of all nations." On the means employed to
carry this into effect, including *kirkârōth*, a species of camels
(female camels), which derives its name from its rapid swaying
motion, see the Lexicons.[1] The words are addressed, as in ver.
5, to the exiles of Babylonia. The prophet presupposes that
his countrymen are dispersed among all nations to the farthest
extremity of the geographical horizon. In fact, the commerce
of the Israelites, which had extended as far as India and Spain
ever since the time of Solomon, the sale of Jewish prisoners as
slaves to Phœnicians, Edomites, and Greeks in the time of
king Joram (Obad. 20; Joel iv. 6; Amos i. 6), the Assyrian
captivities, the free emigrations,—for example, of those who
stayed behind in the land after the destruction of Jerusalem
and then went down to Egypt,—had already scattered the Israelites over the whole of the known world (see at ch. xlix. 12).
Umbreit is of opinion that the prophet calls all the nations
who had turned to Jehovah "brethren of Israel," and represents them as marching in the most motley grouping to the
holy city. In that case those who were brought upon horses,
chariots, etc., would be proselytes; but who would bring them?
This explanation is opposed not only to numerous parallels in
Isaiah, such as ch. lx. 4, but also to the abridgment of the
passage in Zeph. iii. 10: "From the other side of the rivers of
Ethiopia (taken from Isa. xviii.) will they offer my worshippers,

---

[1] The LXX. render it σκιαδίων, *i.e.* probably palanquins. Jerome
observes on this, *quæ nos dormitoria interpretari possumus vel basternas.*
(On this word, with which the name of the Bastarnians as Ἀμαξόβιοι is
connected, see Hahnel's *Bedeutung der Bastarner für das german. Alter-
thum,* 1865, p. 34.)

the daughters of my dispersed ones, to me for a holy offering."
It is the *diaspora* of Israel to which the significant name " my
worshippers, the daughters of my dispersed ones," is there applied.   The figure hinted at in *minchâthî* (my holy offering) is
given more elaborately here in the book of Isaiah, viz. " as the
children of Israel are accustomed (*fut.* as in ch. vi. 2) to offer
the meat-offering" (*i.e.* that which was to be placed upon the
altar as such, viz. wheaten flour, incense, oil, the grains of the
first-fruits of wheat, etc.) " in a pure vessel to the house of
Jehovah," not in the house of Jehovah, for the point of comparison is not the presentation in the temple, but the bringing
to the temple.   The *minchah* is the *diaspora* of Israel, and the
heathen who have become vessels of honour correspond to the
clean vessels.

The latter, having been incorporated into the priestly congregation of Jehovah (ch. lxi. 6), are not even excluded from
the priestly and Levitical service of the sanctuary.   Ver. 21.
"*And I will also add some of them to the priests, to the Levites,*
saith Jehovah."   Hitzig and Knobel suppose *mēhem* to refer to
the Israelites thus brought home.   But in this case something
would be promised, which needed no promise at all, since the
right of the native *cohen* and Levites to take part in the priest-
hood and temple service was by no means neutralized by their
sojourn in a foreign land.   And even if the meaning were that
Jehovah would take those who were brought home for priests
and Levites, without regard to their Aaronic or priestly descent,
or (as Jewish commentators explain it) without regard to the
apostasy, of which through weakness they had made themselves
guilty among the heathen; this ought to be expressly stated.
But as there is nothing said about any such disregard of priestly
descent or apostasy, and what is here promised must be something extraordinary, and not self-evident, *mēhem* must refer to
the converted heathen, by whom the Israelites had been brought
home.   Many Jewish commentators even are unable to throw off
the impression thus made by the expression *mēhem* (of them);
but they attempt to get rid of the apparent discrepancy between this statement and the Mosaic law, by understanding
by the Gentiles those who had been originally Israelites of
Levitical and Aaronic descent, and whom Jehovah would
single out again.   David Friedländer and David Ottensosser

interpret it quite correctly thus : " *Mēhem, i.e.* of those heathen
who bring them home, will He take for priests and Levites,
for all will be saints of Jehovah ; and therefore He has just
compared them to a clean vessel, and the Israelites offered by
their hand to a *minchâh.*" The majority of commentators do
not even ask the question, in what sense the prophet uses
lakkōhănīm lal°viyyim (to the priests, to the Levites) with the
article. Joseph Kimchi, however, explains it thus : " לצורך
הכהנים, to the service of the priests, the Levites, so that they
(the converted heathen) take the place of the Gibeonites (cf.
Zech. xiv. 21*b*), and therefore of the former Cananæan *n°thīnīm*"
(see Köhler, *Nach-exil. Proph.* iii. p. 39). But so interpreted,
the substance of the promise falls behind the expectation
aroused by וגם מהם. Hofmann has adopted a more correct
explanation, viz. : " God rewards them for this offering, by
taking priests to Himself out of the number of the offering
priests, who are added as such to the Levitical priests." Apart,
however, from the fact that לבהנים ללוים cannot well signify " for
Levitical priests" according to the Deuteronomic הכהנים הלוים,
since this would require לבהנים הלוים (inasmuch as such permutative and more precisely defining expressions as Gen. xix. 9,
Josh. viii. 24 cannot be brought into comparison) ; the idea
" in addition to the priests, to the Levites," is really implied in
the expression (cf. ch. lvi. 8), as they would say לקח לְאִשָּׁה and
not לְאִשָּׁה, and would only use לקח לַנָּשִׁים in the sense of adding
to those already there. The article presupposes the existence of
priests, Levites (asyndeton, as in ch. xxxviii. 14, xli. 29, lxvi. 5),
to whom Jehovah adds some taken from the heathen. When
the heathen shall be converted, and Israel brought back, the
temple service will demand a more numerous priesthood and
Levitehood than ever before ; and Jehovah will then increase
the number of those already existing, not only from the מובאים,
but from the מביאים also. The very same spirit, which broke
through all the restraints of the law in ch. lvi., is to be seen at
work here as well. Those who suppose *mēhem* to refer to the
Israelites are wrong in saying that there is no other way, in
which the connection with ver. 22 can be made intelligible.
Friedländer had a certain feeling of what was right, when he
took ver. 21 to be a parenthesis and connected ver. 22 with
ver. 20. There is no necessity for any parenthesis, however.

The reason which follows, relates to the whole of the previous promise, including ver. 21; the election of Israel, as Hofmann observes, being equally confirmed by the fact that the heathen exert themselves to bring back the *diaspora* of Israel to their sacred home, and also by the fact that the highest reward granted to them is, that some of them are permitted to take part in the priestly and Levitical service of the sanctuary. Ver. 22. "*For as the new heaven and the new earth, which I am about to make, continue before me, saith Jehovah, so will your family and your name continue.*" The great mass of the world of nations and of Israel also perish; but the seed and name of Israel, *i.e.* Israel as a people with the same ancestors and an independent name, continues for ever, like the new heaven and the new earth; and because the calling of Israel towards the world of nations is now fulfilled and everything has become new, the former fencing off of Israel from other nations comes to an end, and the qualification for priest-hood and Levitical office in the temple of God is no longer merely natural descent, but inward nobility. The new heaven and the new earth, God's approaching creation (*quæ facturus sum*), continue eternally before Him (*l'phânai* as in ch. xlix. 16), for the old ones pass away because they do not please God; but these are pleasing to Him, and are eternally like His love, whose work and image they are. The prophet here thinks of the church of the future as being upon a new earth and under a new heaven. But he cannot conceive of the eternal in the form of eternity; all that he can do is to conceive of it as the endless continuance of the history of time. Ver. 23. "*And it will come to pass: from new moon to new moon, and from Sabbath to Sabbath, all flesh will come, to worship before me, saith Jehovah.*" New moons and Sabbaths will still be cele-brated therefore; and the difference is simply this, that just as all Israel once assembled in Jerusalem at the three great feasts, all flesh now journey to Jerusalem every new moon and every Sabbath. דַּי (construct דֵּי) signifies that which suffices, then that which is plentiful (see ch. xl. 16), that which is due or fitting, so that (שַׁבָּת) מִדֵּי חֹדֶשׁ (with a temporal, not an explana-tory *min*, as Gesenius supposes) signifies "from the time when, or as often as what is befitting to the new moon (or Sabbath) occurs" (cf. xxviii. 19). If (בשבת) בחדש be added, בְּ is that of

exchange: as often as new moon (Sabbath) for new moon
(Sabbath) is befitting, *i.e.* ought to occur: 1 Sam. vii. 16;
Zech. xiv. 16 (cf. 1 Sam. i. 7, 1 Kings v. 25, 1 Chron. xxvii.
1: "year by year," "month by month"). When we find
(בְּשַׁבַּתּוֹ) בְּחָדְשׁוֹ as we do here, the meaning is, "as often as it
has to occur on one new moon (or Sabbath) after the other,"
i.e. in the periodical succession of one after another. At the
same time it might be interpreted in accordance with 1 Kings
viii. 59, דְּבַר יוֹם בְּיוֹמוֹ, which does not mean the obligation of
one day after the other, but rather "of a day on the fitting
day" (cf. Num. xxviii. 10, 14), although the meaning of change
and not of a series might be sustained in the passage before
us by the suffixless mode of expression which occurs in connection with it.

They who go on pilgrimage to Jerusalem every new moon
and Sabbath, see there with their own eyes the terrible punishment of the rebellious. Ver. 24. "*And they go out and look at
the corpses of the men that have rebelled against me, for their
worm will not die and their fire will not be quenched, and they
become an abomination to all flesh.*" The perfects are *perf. cons.*
regulated by the foregoing יָבֹא. וְיָצְאוּ (accented with *pashta*
in our editions, but more correctly with *munach*) refers to their
going out of the holy city. The prophet had predicted in ver.
18, that in the last times the whole multitude of the enemies of
Jerusalem would be crowded together against it, in the hope
of getting possession of it. This accounts for the fact that the
neighbourhood of Jerusalem becomes such a scene of divine
judgment. רָאָה בְּ always denotes a fixed, lingering look directed
to any object; here it is connected with the grateful feeling of
satisfaction at the righteous acts of God and their own gracious
deliverance. דֵּרָאוֹן, which only occurs again in Dan. xii. 2, is
the strongest word for "abomination." It is very difficult to
imagine the picture which floated before the prophet's mind.
How is it possible that all flesh, *i.e.* all men of all nations,
should find room in Jerusalem and the temple? Even if the
city and temple should be enlarged, as Ezekiel and Zechariah
predict, the thing itself still remains inconceivable. And again,
how can corpses be eaten by worms at the same time as they
are being burned, or how can they be the endless prey of worms
and fire without disappearing altogether from the sight of man?

It is perfectly obvious, that the thing itself, as here described, must appear monstrous and inconceivable, however we may suppose it to be realized. The prophet, by the very mode of description adopted by him, precludes the possibility of our conceiving of the thing here set forth as realized in any material form in this present state. He is speaking of the future state, but in figures drawn from the present world. The object of his prediction is no other than the new Jerusalem of the world to come, and the eternal torment of the damned; but the way in which he pictures it, forces us to translate it out of the figures drawn from this life into the realities of the life to come; as has already been done in the apocryphal books of Judith (xvi. 17) and Wisdom (vii. 17), as well as in the New Testament, *e.g.* Mark ix. 43 sqq., with evident reference to this passage. This is just the distinction between the Old Testament and the New, that the Old Testament brings down the life to come to the level of this life, whilst the New Testament lifts up this life to the level of the life to come; that the Old Testament depicts both this life and the life to come as an endless extension of this life, whilst the New Testament depicts it as a continuous line in two halves, the last point in this finite state being the first point of the infinite state beyond; that the Old Testament preserves the continuity of this life and the life to come by transferring the outer side, the form, the appearance of this life to the life to come, the new Testament by making the inner side, the nature, the reality of the life to come, the δυνάμεις μέλλοντος αἰῶνος, immanent in this life. The new Jerusalem of our prophet has indeed a new heaven above it and a new earth under it, but it is only the old Jerusalem of earth lifted up to its highest glory and happiness; whereas the new Jerusalem of the Apocalypse comes down from heaven, and is therefore of heavenly nature. In the former dwells the Israel that has been brought back from captivity; in the latter, the risen church of those who are written in the book of life. And whilst our prophet transfers the place in which the rebellious are judged to the neighbourhood of Jerusalem itself; in the Apocalypse, the lake of fire in which the life of the ungodly is consumed, and the abode of God with men, are for ever separated. The Hinnom-valley outside Jerusalem has become *Gehenna,* and this is no longer within the precincts of the new

Jerusalem, because there is no need of any such example to the righteous who are for ever perfect.

In the lessons prepared for the synagogue ver. 23 is repeated after ver. 24, on account of the terrible character of the latter, "so as to close with words of consolation."[1] But the prophet, who has sealed the first two sections of these prophetic orations with the words, "there is no peace to the wicked," intentionally closes the third section with this terrible picture of their want of peace. The promises have gradually soared into the clear light of the eternal glory, to the new creation in eternity; and the threatenings have sunk down to the depth of eternal torment, which is the eternal foil of the eternal light. More than this we could not expect from our prophet. His threefold book is now concluded. It consists of twenty-seven orations. The central one of the whole, *i.e.* the fourteenth, is ch. lii. 13–liii.; so that the cross forms the centre of this prophetic trilogy. *Per crucem ad lucem* is its watch-word. The self-sacrifice of the Servant of Jehovah lays the foundation for a new Israel, a new human race, a new heaven and a new earth.

[1] Isaiah is therefore regarded as an exception to the rule, that the prophets close their orations בדברי שבח ותנחומים (*b. Berachoth* 31*a*), although, on the other hand, this exception is denied by some, on the ground that the words "they shall be an abhorring" apply to the Gentiles (*j. Berachoth* c. V. Anf. *Midras Tillim* on Ps. iv. 8).

APPENDIX.

———

Vol. I. page 66.—In the commentary on the second half of chap. xl.–lxvi., I have referred here and there to the expositions of J. Heinemann (Berlin 1842) and Isaiah Hochstädter (Carlsruhe 1827), both written in Hebrew,—the former well worthy of notice for criticism of the text, the latter provided with a German translation. For the psalm of Hezekiah (ch. xxxviii.) Professor Sam. David Luzzatto of Padua lent me his exposition in manuscript. Since then this great and noble-minded man has departed this life (on the 29th Sept. 1865). His commentary on Isaiah, so far as it has been printed, is full of information and of new and stirring explanations, written in plain, lucid, rabbinical language. It would be a great misfortune for the second half of this valuable work to remain unprinted. I well remember the assistance which the deceased afforded me in my earlier studies of the history of the post-biblical Jewish poetry (1836), and the affection which he displayed when I renewed my former acquaintance with him on the occasion of his publishing his Isaiah ; so that I lament his loss on my own account as well as in the interests of science. " Why have you allowed twenty-five years to pass," he wrote to me on the 22d Feb. 1863, "without telling me that you remembered me ? Is it because we form different opinions of the עלמה and the ילד ילד לנו of Isaiah ? Are you a sincere Christian ? Then you are a hundred times dearer to me than so many Israelitish scholars, the partizans of Spinoza, with whom our age swarms." These words indicate very clearly the standpoint taken in his writings.

Of the commentaries written in English, I am acquainted not only with *Lowth*, but with the thoroughly practical commen-

tary of *Henderson* (1857), and that of *Joseph Addison Alexander*,
Prof. in Princeton (1847, etc.), which is very much read as an
exegetical repertorium in England also. But I had neither of
them in my possession.

Vol. I. page 70.—What I have said here on ch. i. 1 as the
heading to the whole book, or at any rate to ch. i.-xxxix., has
been said in part by Photios also in his *Amphilochia,* which
Sophocles the M.D. has published complete from a MS. of
Mount Athos (Athens 1858, 4).

Vol. I. page 203, on Ch. vi. 13.—Hofmann in his
Schriftbeweis (ii. 2, 541) maintains with Knobel, that מַצֶּבֶת
cannot be shown to have any other meaning than "plant."
It is never met with in this sense, which it might have (after
נָטַע=נָצַב), though it is in the sense of *statua* and *cippus*, which,
when applied to a tree deprived of its crown, can only mean
stipes or *truncus.*—We take this opportunity of referring to a
few other passages of his work:—Ch. viii. 22. "And the deep
darkness is scared away : *m⁰nuddâch* with the accusative of the
object used with the passive." But this is only possible with the
finite verb, not with the passive participle. Ch. ix. 2. "By the fact
that Thou hast made the people many, Thou hast not made the
joy great; but now they rejoice before Thee (who hast appeared)."
It is impossible that הרבית and הגדלת, when thus surrounded
with perfects relating to the history of the future, should itself
relate to the historical past.—Ch. xviii. "It is Israel in its dispersion which is referred to here as a people carried away and
spoiled, but which from that time forward is an object of
reverential awe,—a people that men have cut in pieces and
trampled under foot, whose land streams have rent in pieces."
But does not this explanation founder on נורא מן־הוא והלאה? In
the midst of attributes which point to ill-treatment, can this
passage be meant to describe the position which Israel is henceforth to hold as one commanding respect (see our exposition)?
—Ch. xix. 28. "Egypt the land of cities will be reduced to five
cities by the judgment that falls upon it." But how can the
words affirm that there will be only five cities in all, when there is
nothing said about desolation in the judgment predicted before?
—Ch. xxi. 1-10. "What the watchman on the watch-tower sees

is not the hostile army marching against Babel, but the march
of the people of God returning home from Babel." Consequently *tsemed pârâshīm* does not mean pairs of horsemen, but
carriages full of men and drawn by horses. But we can see what
tsemed pârâshīm is from 2 Kings ix. 25 (*rōkh⁴bhīm ts⁴mâdīm*),
and from the combination of *rekhebh* and *pârâshīm* (chariots and
horsemen) in ch. xxii. 7, xxxi. 1. And the rendering "carriages" will never do for ch. xxi. 7, 9. Carriages with camels
harnessed to them would be something unparalleled; and
rekhebh gâmâl (cf. 1 Sam. xxx. 17) by the side of *tsemed
pârâshīm* has a warlike sound.

VOL. I. PAGE 279, ON CH. X. 28–32.—Professor Schegg
travelled by this very route to Jerusalem (cf. p. 560, Anm. 2):
From *Gifneh* he went direct to *Tayibeh* (which he imagined
to be the ancient *Ai*), and then southwards through *Muchmas*,
Geba, *Hizmeh*, *'Anata*, and *el-Isawiye* to Jerusalem.

VOL. II. PAGE 65.—*No* (*Nō' 'Amōn* in Nahum iii. 8) is
the Egyptian *nu-Amun* = Διόσπολις (*nu* the spelling of the
hieroglyphic of the plan of the city, with which the name of
the goddess *Nu. t* = *Rhea* is also written). The ordinary
spelling of the name of this city corresponds to the Greek
Ἀμμωνόπολις.

VOL. II. PAGE 66, ON CH. XXXIII. 23.—(Compare Grashof,
Ueber das Schiff bei Homer und Hesiod, Gymnasial-programm
1834, p. 23 sqq.). The μεσόδμη (= μεσοδόμη) is the cross
plank which connects the two sides of the ship. A piece is cut
out of this on the side towards the rudder, in which the mast
is supported, being also let into a hole in the boards of the keel
(ἱστοπέδη) and there held fast. The mast is also prevented
from falling backwards by ropes or stays carried forward to
the bows (πρότονοι). On landing, the mast is laid back into a
hollow place in the bottom of the ship (ἱστοδόκη). If the stays
are not drawn tight, the mast may easily fall backwards, and
so slip not only out of the μεσόδμη but out of the ἱστοπέδη
also. This is the meaning of the words בַּל־יְחַזְּקוּ כֵן־תָּרְנָם. It
would be better to understand *kēn* as referring to the ἱστοπέδη
than to the μεσόδμη. The latter has no "hole," but only a

notch, *i.e.* a semicircular piece cut out, and serves as a support
to the mast; the former, on the contrary, has the mast inserted
into it, and serves as a *kēn, i.e.* a *basis, theca, loculamentum.*
Vitringa observes (though without knowing the difference
between μεσόδμη and ἱστοπέδη): "*Oportet accedere funes, qui
thecam firment, h. e. qui malum sustinentes thecæ succurrant, qui
quod theca sola per se præstare nequit absque funibus cum ea
veluti concurrentes efficiant.*"

VOL. II. PAGE 75, ON CH. XXXIV. 16.—This transition
from words of Jehovah concerning Himself to words relating
to Him, may also be removed by adopting the following rendering: "For my mouth, it has commanded it, and its (my
mouth's) breath, it has brought it together" (*rūchō = rūăch pī*,
Ps. xxx. 6, Job xv. 30).

VOL. II. PAGE 104.—I am wrong in describing it here as
improbable that the land would have to be left uncultivated
during the year 713–12 in consequence of the invasion that
had taken place, even after the departure of the Assyrians.
Wetzstein has referred me to his Appendix on the Monastery
of Job (see *Comm. on Job,* vol. ii. 416), where he has shown
that the fallow-land (*wâgiha*) of a community, which is sown
in the autumn of 1865 and reaped in the summer of 1866,
must have been broken up, *i.e.* ploughed for the first time, in
the winter of 1864–65. "If this breaking up of the fallow
(*el-Bûr*) were obliged to be omitted in the winter of 1864–65,
because of the enemy being in the land, whether from the
necessity for hiding the oxen in some place of security, or from
the fact that they had been taken from the peasants and consumed by the foe, it would be impossible to sow in the autumn
of 1865 and reap a harvest in the summer of 1866. And if
the enemy did not withdraw till the harvest of 1865, only the
few who had had their ploughing oxen left by the war would find
it possible to break up the fallow. *But neither the one nor the
other could sow*, if the enemy's occupation of the land had prevented them from ploughing in the winter of 1864–65. If
men were to sow in the newly broken fallow, they would reap
no harvest, and the seed would only be lost. It is only in the
volcanic and therefore fertile region of *Haurân* (Bashan) that

the sowing of the newly broken fallow (*es-sikak*) yields a
harvest, and there it is only when the winter brings a large
amount of rain ; so that even in Haurân nothing but necessity
leads any one to sow upon the *sikak*. In western Palestine, even in
the most fruitful portions of it (round Samaria and Nazareth),
the farmer is obliged to plough three times before he can sow ;
and a really good farmer follows up the breaking up of the
fallow (*sikak*) in the winter, the second ploughing (*thânia*) in
the spring, and the third ploughing (*tethlith*) in the summer,
with a fourth (*terbîa*) in the latter part of the summer. Consequently no sowing could take place in the autumn of 713, if
the enemy had been in the land in the autumn of 714, in consequence of his having hindered the farmer from the *sikak* in
the winter of 714–3, and from the *thânia* and *tethlith* in the
spring and summer of 713. There is no necessity, therefore,
to assume that a second invasion took place, which prevented
the sowing in the autumn of 713."

VOL. II. PAGE 114, ON 2 KINGS XX. 9. — Even הָלַךְ is
syntactically admissible in the sense of *iveritne;* see Gen. xxi. 7,
Ps. xi. 3, Job xii. 9.

VOL. II. PAGE 244.—ἀλμενιχιακά in Plut., read Porph.,
viz. in the letter of Porphyrios to the Egyptian Anebo in
Euseb. *præp.* iii. 4, *init.*: τάς τε εἰς τοὺς δεκανοὺς τομὰς καὶ τοὺς
ὡροσκόπους καὶ τοὺς λεγομένους κραταιοὺς ἡγεμόνας, ὧν καὶ
ὀνόματα ἐν τοῖς ἀλμενιχιακοῖς φέρεται; compare Jamblichos,
de Mysteriis, viii. 4: τά τε ἐν τοῖς σαλμεσχινιακοῖς μέρος τι
βραχύτατον περιέχει τῶν Ἑρμαϊκῶν διατάξεων. This reading
σαλμεσχινιακοῖς has been adopted by Parthey after two
codices and the text in Salmasius, *de annis clim.* 605. But
ἀλμενιχιακοῖς is favoured by the form *Almanach* (Hebr. אלמנך,
see Steinschneider, *Catal. Codd. Lugduno-Batav.* p. 370), in
which the word was afterwards adopted as the name of an
astrological handbook or year-book. In Arabic the word appears to me to be equivalent to المَنَاخ, the *encampment* (of the
stars); but to all appearance it was originally an Egyptian
word, and possibly the Coptic *monk* (old Egyptian *mench*), a
form or thing formed, is hidden beneath it.

VOL. II. PAGE 376, ON CH. LVII. 10, נוֹאָשׁ.—*Fleischer* says:
"Just as in أمل and رجا, the meaning of hope springs out of
the idea of stretching and drawing out, so do أَيِسَ and يَئِسَ
(*spem deposuit, desperavit*) signify literally to draw in, to com-
press; hence the old Arabic يَأْس = سِلّ, consumption, *phthisis*.
And the other old Arabic word وَيْس, lit. squeezing, *res angustæ*
= *fakr wa-faka*, want, need, and penury, or in a concrete sense
the need, or thing needed, is also related to this."

VOL. II. PAGE 483-4, ON CH. LXV. 11.—*Μήνη* appears in
μηναγύρτης = *μητραγύρτης* as the name of Cybele, the mother
of the gods. In Egyptian, *Menhi* is a form of Isis in the city
of *Hat-uer*. The Ithyphallic *Min*, the cognomen of Amon,
which is often written in an abbreviated form with the spelling
men (Copt. *MHIN*, *signum*), is further removed.

VOL. II. PAGE 490, ON CH. LXV. 23.—לְבֶהָלָה. Fleischer says:
"בֶּהֶל and بَهَل are so far connected, that the stem בהל, like
בלה, signifies primarily to *let loose*, or *let go*. This passes over
partly into outward overtaking or overturning, and partly into
internal surprise and bewildering, and partly also (in Arabic)
into setting free on the one hand, and outlawing on the other
(compare the Azazel-goat of the day of atonement, which was
sent away into the wilderness); hence it is used as an equivalent for لَعَن (*execrare*)."